SPECIAL PUBLICATIONS

OF

THE NEW YORK ACADEMY OF SCIENCES

VOLUME VI

NEW YORK
PUBLISHED BY THE ACADEMY

March, 1965

Special Publications of The New York Academy of Sciences

VOLUME VI

HAROLD E. WHIPPLE, *Editor*
MARVIN I. SPITZER, *Managing Editor*

ABRAHAM LINCOLN'S
PHILOSOPHY
OF COMMON SENSE

An Analytical Biography of a Great Mind

PART II

EDWARD J. KEMPF

CONTENTS: PART II

Chapter XXII

PREPARATION FOR DESTINY

After Lincoln returned from Congress in 1848 to practise law in Springfield, "he despaired," his partner Herndon said, "of ever again rising in the political world and was very sad and terribly gloomy, unsocial and abstracted, but liked to study and improve his knowledge."

In his patient, analytic, thorough, persistent way, Lincoln continued to work at his method of self-education to improve his ability as a realistic, logical thinker and speaker, constantly imbued with the belief that somehow he was still destined to serve his country in the betterment of government of human relations. Much has been made of Lincoln's belief in his destiny, as if it were the sign of an occult faculty, or of unusual extra-sensory perception. Actually an intuitive sense of destiny, as self-direction of egoistic attitude in the course of its acquisitive and avoidance selections of social interactions, is natural to every normally functioning person. If he will listen to his own clear cut, conscientious egoistic intuition, and not to the prejudices of other people he will have the energy to work consistently to develop his strongest inborn aptitudes as his psychobiological destiny, and achieve maximal creative results with enjoyment of living in whatever conditions his environment provides.

What Interested Lincoln

The frank portrayals of Lincoln as a lawyer and student of political philosophy, by Herndon in private letters (Hertz, 1938), show the man doing his legal work daily with the purpose of achieving equitable results, always with a sense of the morality of justice in law and government of free people.

"Mr. Lincoln," he said, "was an extremely ambitious man and that ambition found its gratification only in the political field. Politics were his life and newspapers his food, . . . and it was in this field that he seemed to be happy."

"I was frequently on part of the circuit with Mr. Lincoln and found out there and especially in Sangamon County, that Mr. Lincoln was very deficient in the technical rules of the law. Mr. Lincoln, to my knowledge never thoroughly read any elementary law book. In fact I may truthfully say that I never knew him to read through and through any law book of any kind; he knew nothing of the laws of evidence, of pleading, or of practice, and did not care about them; he had a keen sense of justice and struck for that, throwing aside forms, methods, and rules of all law. . . . Mr. Lincoln was not a general reader in any field of knowledge; he was purely a practical man, and when he wished to know a fact . . . he thor-

413

oughly analyzed it, root and top, fiber and cell, and when all this was done, he used his information for practical ends."

The statement that Lincoln never read any book of law through is probably not entirely correct for his earlier history, although perhaps true in later years. He seems to have virtually memorized Blackstone in his storekeeping days, as he did much of the Bible and Shakespeare.

"The truth is," Herndon continued, "he never studied hard at any period of his life. He did not need to study hard. With him a single reading was sufficient to afford a clear insight into an ordinary subject."

Lincoln, the resolute advocate of equal rights to justice for all people under constitutional government, had such impressive potentialities for practical statesmanship that his enthusiastic, humanitarian young partner continuously urged him to take a more active interest in politics. This enthusiastic hero worship probably stimulated Lincoln, ever ambitious, to keep himself informed on the major trends of political policies. Although they made a good team of lawyers, they became a better team of students and, later, organizers of political sentiment as the national crisis over slavery developed.

In his politically dormant years Lincoln opposed abolitionism as unconstitutional, whereas Herndon became increasingly active as an abolitionist, corresponding with the leading advocates of social and political reform (Parker, Giddings, Phillips, Seward, Sumner, and others) and keeping copies of their speeches, books and articles on the table in the law office. He purchased numerous reports of anti-slavery and pro-slavery discussions along with other American and European sociological treatises and biographies, ever aspiring to write biography himself. An avid reader of serious sociological discussions, he would call Lincoln's attention to anything of merit or significance. Any minister or sociologist who defended slavery as a good institution aroused the ire of Lincoln, whereas he accepted its political defense as being constitutionally justified.

"Lincoln and I had many hot disputes in our office and yet those disputes were friendly— he was never insulting or dictatorial to me. He was too conservative for some of us . . . and yet I stuck to him in the hopes of his sense of justice and the eternal right."

They subscribed to the Chicago *Tribune,* New York *Tribune,* the *Anit-Slavery Standard,* Charleston *Mercury,* and the richmond *Enquirer.* Herndon, and not Lincoln, purchased numerous anti-slavery histories, reports of anti-slavery conventions, philosophical dissertations and other books on American politics up to 1861, including works by Emerson, Carlisle, Parker, McNaught, Strauss, Monel, Beecher, Feuerbach, Buckle, Froud, Darwin, Draper, Lecky, Lawes, Renan, Kant, Fichte, Hamilton, Mills, Corey, Spencer, McCullough, Wayland and others.

About 1855 Herndon purchased a copy of *The Annual of Science* and Lincoln immediately became interested in it. When he found that its purpose was to record and explain experiments of science he decided that he must buy the whole set. It was one of the few publications that he read with enthusiasm. His remarks (in Herndon's words) show a strong philosophical interest in natural science.

> "I have wanted such a book for years, because I sometimes make experiments and have thoughts about the physical world that I do not know to be true or false. I may, by this book, correct my errors and save time and expense. I can see where scientists and philosophers have failed and avoid the rock on which they split or see the means of their success and take advantage of their brains, toil and knowledge."

Lincoln bought very few books, and in his library at home the publications of the most progressive thinkers of his time were conspicuous by their absence. He preferred to read newspapers for information on current events and public opinion. However, all of Herndon's books were at his disposal and he browsed through most of them, but rarely consistently studied any subject except Mills, Carlisle, McCullough, and Wayland on political economy. He seemed to prefer this field for being more practical, and liked Wayland best except for his doctrines on *free trade*.

Lincoln constantly searched the *why-how* of the origins and interactions of things as far as he could get information,—reading without instruction, books on law, physics, economics, sociology, chemistry, astronomy, and other sciences, with confidence in his own common-sense ability to evaluate demonstration, proof, and theory. He had discovered for himself that whatever the field of science, as experimentally measured particular interactions of things, whatever its symbols for masses and forces, the same logical methods of qualitative and quantitative differentiation and mathematical and mechanical reasoning have to be applied in order to understand them intelligently, even as when building a house.

Herein Lincoln kept his mind constantly free to rely on the balanced reasoning of common sense and develop a practical philosophy of human relations and political organizations based on the vital needs and motivations of human nature. He kept his mind free of the bias of orthodox religious interpretations of meaning of statements in the Bible, in his analytical study of it as a history of the evolution of moral law. He maintained that Biblical prophets were not alone in receiving divine revelations of moral law, as their orthodox representatives claimed in order to give themselves superior moral authority and social prestige. He maintained consistently throughout his years as a lawyer and later as President, as he frequently declared, that man in his divine inheritance, today as in the biblical past, hears through his conscience the voice of God, if he will but listen and heed. He believed that when a man learns to know and serve the natural rights of the people to enjoy moral and legal equality he is serving the Divine Will and when he tries to induce God to give him special advantages over people he is indulging in wishful mythology.

These few, simple, basic, logical concepts of human nature, applied against its propensity for ganging up in self-advantageous political, economic, religious, and other social relations to gain unilateral privileges in exploiting the vital needs of the masses, gave Lincoln the carefully restrained freedom of a logically organized, lawfully obedient mind, able to expand its concepts consistently as he analyzed the essentials of his experiences and knowledge gained as a legislator, lawyer, politician, and statesman, and eventually as President.

Lincoln found that as a trial lawyer he had more ability to make sympathetic appeal and logical demonstration than most of his contemporaries for influencing the sentiments and judgments of a jury, as he had also for a political audience. His love of reasoning in argument by analysis of evidence and testimony, love of constructive legislation and inside politics, and of public speaking, increased with the realization that in understanding human nature and human relations, in simplicity, force and clarity of expression, in wit, humor, and pathos of presentation and in arresting style of delivery, he was a match for any man.

The observations of Lincoln's personality by his more intimate contemporaries in the practice of law have shown abundantly that all recognized in him the same unusual characteristics. They saw that he needed to believe, with more than normal reassurance and conviction that he interpreted the merits of a case correctly and that it had true cause of complaint and litigation, otherwise he would counsel compromise or refuse to represent it. He was alwyas more cautious and self-doubtful than most men until he had analyzed all of the conditions *for* and *against* a complaint, case, issue, person, proposition, situation, or policy. He needed more time than most lawyers for evaluating his considerations, which he did in a peculiarly slow, methodical way, until he could feel and believe consistently that his understanding and judgment of all factors involved was right. Upon forming a conviction he became unusually bold, firm, and audacious in presenting it to the court or people for judgment. He was for the same reason weak in ability to defend a case of doubtful claims, or even points of questionable validity in the case, and was unable to continue the defense of a person when he found him to be untruthful. Neither could he function efficiently in a new situation that involved irregular procedures. He avoided service as a prosecutor but was an unusually aroused and effective defender of two innocent men charged with murder. He functioned best as a compromiser of litigation and as a defensive, aggressive debater and politician.

His contemporaries also saw that he had a characteristic tendency to lapse into a gloomy state of listless mental detachment when not interested, and that he tended to worry unduly and develop headaches, insomnia, and indigestion whenever he became doubtful of the moral justness of his cause, or his execution of it, or when he felt that an opponent thought that he had unjustly volated his rights, or if he was accused, however falsely, of having violated a trust.

Lincoln was certainly far more sensitive and easily distressed than the normal man. In self-defense against his melancholic disposition he philosophically cultivated a friendly sense of humor and exercised it daily, particularly in story telling about human vanities ending in some amusing surprise that included a self-righting moral connotation. This endlessly repetitive mental mechanism had the pattern of unconscious compulsion.

Lincoln hated lying, cheating, misrepresentation, deception, obfuscation, cruelty, tyranny and injustice of any kind with obsessive force, and as intensely loved to explain, defend and uphold the principle of equality of moral and legal rights to justice for all oppressed people. These and other unusually strong personal characteristics, we have found, can now be accounted for as having been intelligent, self-preservative, volitional, egoistic self-righting, self-controlling compensations against mental confusion in childhood by family double talk about the secrets of illegitimate births among relatives, and an unusually sensitive and easily distressed nervous system as the result of the cerebral injury in his tenth year, augmented by sad memories of the tragic fates of his love attachments.

Through all his years as a man, including the time of being President, he continued to tell friends that he was never without "melancholy;" but the fundamental cause of it remained unknown to him and his physicians. No one related his repetitive tendency to lapse into a gloomy state of mental detachment of interest from his surroundings, and his tendency to develop diplopia, headaches, nervous indigestion, and anxiety upon frustration and fatigue, to an organic deficiency of his nervous system. His physicians continued to treat his melancholy as if caused by "indigestion," "constipation," and "inactive liver."

The basic need of Lincoln's mental organization, that he must understand things correctly and be able to express himself so clearly and concisely on all factors, both *for* and *against* an issue, that the common people would understand him, made him remarkably effective in legal argument and political debate. Conversely, the same compelling need punished him miserably when he found himself to be wrong or unjustly accused of doing anything dishonorable. He needed constantly, in order to feel self-respect, to be morally right, keep his promise, and uphold his client's and his client's opponent's legal rights to justice. Evidence of this disposition exists in numerous legal advices and letters to friends wherein he tried to influence their judgments on political issues.

Superstitious Intuition

From childhood throughout his life, Lincoln retained some of the superstitious sentimental beliefs characteristic of pioneering, backwoods people. His parents, relatives, and neighbors, like all ignorant and low literate people, believed themselves to be surrounded by a world of mysterious, spiritual, lawless, magical forces that act on natural forces and can be influenced by applying the right kinds of prayer or other sympathetic appeal. They were highly impressionable and naturally intuitive about the suggestive influences on each other's self-confidence, desires, volitions, emotions, abilities, and "good luck" of kindly eyes, encouraging words, exclamations of admiration and sympathetic wishing, versus the breaking down of self-confidence by jealous eyes, critical words and evil, hateful wishing for bad luck.

Lincoln had memorized and could cite most instances in the Bible of its numerous accounts of prophetic signs and revelations of good and bad protent. His interpretations of their meanings seem to have influenced him to continue to look for supernatural hints of favorable and unfavorable "signs" in his own personal and political crises. He believed himself, as boy and man, born with a destiny to be indicated to him at propitious times by signs which he could interpret. Although he was an extremely factual and logical thinker for the most part, he was never without interest in indicative meanings of omens of the fate of a course that he was doubtful about but wished to take, particularly when they seemed to have some suggestive connection by concomitant timing and placing, or some similarity of symbolical characteristics. He was inclined to believe that such associations were not merely disconnected, coincidental, accidental and meaningless natural actions, but they were supernatural indicators of the fate of his choice when perplexed over what he wished to do or not to do.

> "I always was superstitious;" Lincoln wrote to Speed (7, 4, 1842), "and as part of my superstitution, I believe God made me one of the instruments of bringing your Fanny and you together." When Speed urged him to quit courting Mary Todd or marry her, he could not decide one way or the other but said he would "stand still and see the salvation of the Lord."
>
> "I am superstitious," he wrote to J. W. Grimes (7, 12, 1856). "I have scarcely known a party, preceeding an election, to call in help from the neighboring states, but they lost the state. . . . It seems to stir up more enemies than friends."

Herein Lincoln has given hints for understanding how his superstitiousness worked when in an undecided state of mind in a pressing situation. By seeing a significant meaning in an unexpected or unusual happening he could feel that he had an indication that the time had come, or had not come, for him to act in accordance with his hunch and motive, not unlike a gambler playing his luck. Thereby he was inclined to play a wait-and-see game while he cultivated, intuitively, unusual sensitivity to the involvements of his own personal views and sentiments relative to the trends of conflicting public sentiment *for* or *against* each other in important moral, legal, political, or other social issues. When he then arrived at a decision to act it became a conviction. Thereby he reinforced his self-reliance in the rightwayness of his attitude, purpose, objective and reasoning, and reduced self-doubt to a cautious minimum.

Herndon (1889) commented on Lincoln's superstitiousness:

> "He repeatedly said, 'I am sure I shall meet with some terrible end.' He cited the case of Brutus and Caesar as an illustration of how the former was forced by laws and conditions over which he had no power to kill the latter and, vice versa, that the latter was especially created to be killed by the former." "This superstitious view of life," Herndon said, "ran through his being like a blue vein in whitest marble."
>
> Lincoln liked to quote from Hamlet "There's a divinity that shapes our ends, rough-hew them how we will."

Religious Implications of Lincoln's Philosophy of Common Sense

The most important records of Lincoln's expressions, as a lawyer, of philosophical beliefs having religious significance indicate that he interpreted his experience of life as being indicative of creation of the universe by an impersonal Supreme Intelligence. They exist in commentary phrases in political arguments, sentences in letters, notes and speeches, in personal reports by friends of conversations and conferences. His expressions of belief as President were entirely consistent, as will become evident in a later chapter, with the beliefs he held throughout his preceding years as a lawyer. He never changed his philosophical attitude or statements of belief after he became President. He was always sincere in what he had to say about his religious beliefs, and never expressed himself so as to gain political advantages of public approvals.

Many commentaries, papers, and several books have been written by wishful thinkers on Lincoln's philosophically religious statements to show that he adopted particular orthodox Christian dogmas and teachings, and by others equally ardent, to show that he rejected them. Arguments have been arranged by some reviewers to show that he was by their standards an "infidel," "an atheist," or not a believer in the divinity of Christ; and by others that he was a "theist" and a convert to a particular protestant version of Christianity.

No systematic presentation seems to have been made by Lincoln of his philosophical reasonings on religious beliefs after he wrote his paper on "infidelity," in New Salem in 1835.

In 1832, age twenty-three, in a handbill for election to the state legislature Lincoln said he believed that the welfare of the people and the state rested in "all [people] being able to read the scriptures and other works of both religious and moral nature for themselves."

In a letter to Mary Owens (5, 7, 1837) Lincoln said: "I've never been to church yet, nor probably shall not be soon. I stay away because I am conscious I should not know how to behave myself." A religious inclination of attitude is indicated in this worried letter, but the reasons for his feeling of not knowing what to do remain obscure. He had previously attended church services and was not ignorant of Baptist procedure.

In 1846, age 37, when Lincoln was subversively accused of being an infidel by a rival candidate for election, Reverend Peter Cartwright, a famous Methodist circuit preacher, he replied in his handbill: "That I am not a member of any Christian Church is true, but I have never denied the truth of the Scriptures; and I have never spoken with intentional disrespect of religion in general, or of any denomination of Christians in particular. It is true that in my early life I was inclined to believe in what I understand is the 'Doctrine of Necessity'—that is the human mind is impelled to action, or is held in rest by some power, over which the mind itself has no control."

He said "The Bible is a sacred legacy," and "the best cure for the blues." "The good old maxims of the Bible are truly applicable to human affairs and in this as in other things, we may say here that 'he who is not for us is against us, he who gathereth not with us scattereth.' " "The fear of the Lord is the beginning of wisdom." Throughout his record Lincoln's references to moral law are consistent in expression with Biblical sentiment. "The guarantee of the rights of conscience, as found in our Constitution, is most sacred and inviolable, and one that belongs no less to the Catholic, than to the Protestant" (1844). He accepted the Biblical account of creation and of genesis and recorded the births and deaths of his parents' family in his father's Bible, and of his own family in his Bible. In his self-education he was a careful but fearlessly consistent and earnest analyzer of Biblical accounts of human behavior, relative to his experiences in daily life. He read the Bible more studiously, and could quote from memory its "revelations" and morally significant passages more fully, and cite chapter and verse more appopriately, than many ministers. He interpreted its accounts of natural and unnatural events, and its maxims, morals, approvals, and prohibitions, with full reliance on his own common-sense estimation of their literal and symbolic meaning for mankind. (See Chapter XXIII for further evidence of Lincoln's interest in the Bible.)

None other than a naturally religious, practically religious mind could have been so thoroughly interested in learning to apply the humanitarian teachings of the Bible. Lincoln as a man continued to love its equalitarian morality and applied it so consistently in law, religion, politics, and government that probably he quoted from it to reinforce his arguments more often than any eminent statesman is history.

Baptist philosophy, like other Christian denominations, holds dogmatically that all of nature is the product of the creative will of an eternally existing, ever present, all knowing, supernaturally intelligent Divine Personal Being as the one and only God, who created man in his own image.

Lincoln often pondered over the incomprehensible involvements of scientific and religious views and seems to have preferred in principle the biblical version of special creation and its attribution to God of perfect power and wisdom. He seems to have believed that all creations and all later causes and effects are foreordained and predetermined in their interactions by natural laws from beginning to end. However, he believed consistently with Christian law that it is also God's will to have created man to be somewhat consciously free, to will to work as he chooses for self-preservation and greater mental and spiritual self-realization, amid the trials and temptations of social interactions and the benefits and vicissitudes of nature. He believed each person's social attitude and thinking to be largely, like his own, the product of his social environment. He believed that each man has a more or less limited degree of freedom of choice and action, and that the degree of his social, moral, and legal involvements in everyday life depends on how nearly normal he is physically and mentally and how well he has learned to know right from wrong. Judgment of human actions is to be determined by their volitional design and reasoning intention as well as by involitional impulse and unreasoning passion.

In his early years as a law student and lawyer Lincoln discussed freely the natural, moral, and religious implications of his views with Speed, Herndon, Gillespie, Lamon, Swett, Davis, and other close friends, as arrived at through common-sense analysis of observations of physical and mental experiences. Quotations in previous chapters have included some of Lincoln's indicative statements and some of the most definitive memories and interpretations of his meanings by friends. They are so generally consistent that a few additional comments from Herndon and from Lincoln's letters and private notes will be sufficient here to show how he arrived at a practical philosophy of predestination versus free will in cause and effect that was deeply religious and morally consistent, although as basically irreconcilable as science now finds these two sets of personal experiences.

Herndon said Lincoln borrowed and read thoroughly in 1846-47 *The Vestiges of Creation,* fifth or sixth edition, by a Mr. Chambers of Edinburgh, Scotland.

"Mr. Lincoln on reading the book became, and was for years, a firm believer in the theory of development (evolution) as presented in the *Vestiges of Creation.* Mr. Lincoln's speeches will show his unbounded faith in the theory of development. In after years there was taken by me the

Westminister Review and he read it. . . . I had up to sixty[,] all the works of Spencer, Darwin, Fauerback's Christianity and many of the like. Lincoln read some parts of these books and reviews. . . . he read none of them thoroughly at a setting; he would read by snatches, a little here and there now and then: He soon became a firm believer in evolution and of law. . . . believed in laws that imperiously ruled both matter and mind. With him there could be no miracles outside of law: he held that the universe was a grand mystery and a miracle. Nothing to him was lawless . . . there were no accidents in his philosophy. Every event had its cause. The past to him was the cause of the present and the present including the past will be the cause of the future and all are links in the endless chain stretching from the infinite to the finite. Everything to him was the result of the forces of Nature, playing on matter and mind . . . He said in his Cooper Institute speech this: 'Let us have faith that right makes might and in that faith let us to the end dare to do our duty as we understand it." . . .

"Mr. Lincoln firmly believed that conditions and circumstances make the man . . . he did not believe, only in a limited sense if any, in the freedom of the human will. He argued this question with me; he changed the expression and called it the freedom of the mind . . . he said to me that motives ruled the man always . . . I once contended that man could act without a motive; he smiled at my philosophy and it was not long before I saw as he saw. . . .

"Mr. Lincoln was a purely practical man, having great practical sagacities and did not as a general rule ever speculate on unknowable things; he never read anything on such subjects as first and final causes. . . . He discovered through experience that his mind, the mind of all men, had limitations attached or placed on it and hence he economized . . . by applying his powers and his time in the field of the practical. . . .

"He firmly believed in an overruling Providence, Maker, God, and the great moral of Him written in the human soul. His—late in life—conventional use of the word God must not by any means be interpreted that he believed in a personal God. I know that it is said that Mr. Lincoln changed his views. There is no evidence of this especially as to the extent of the change. nor which way. Did he go toward the force and matter theory of the universe, toward Spencer and Darwin? Mr. Lincoln was a thoroughly religious man, . . . a free religionist, an infidel, and so died. . . . "

Through courageous self-reliance in his self-education he had learned by experience that first of all he must make sure that he was right in his observations, and right in his practical interpretations of their relative meanings, and be ready to doubt, verify, and correct any judgments and beliefs in order to protect himself from making mistakes in reasoning. He learned the importance of discriminating observation and evidence from interpretation, and fact from wishful fancy and assumption, and proposition and theory from doctrine, dogma, and belief. He applied, whenever practical, the established rules of measuring values and proving right and disproving wrong. To improve his logic he applied Euclidian methods of forming and demonstrating propositions, but his basic premise was always the moral law of equal legal rights of justice for all people.

About 1854 Lincoln was placed in an untrue and embarrassing position by one Reverend James Smith of Scotland, who became the source of a persistent round of hearsays in religious circles that he was converting Lincoln to Christianity. Lawyer James H. Matheny, who had discussed religious views with Lincoln on many occasions, condemned Dr. Smith for placing him in the position of being a religious hypocrite playing a political game, for he never really changed his views. According to Herndon, Dr. Smith did present him with his book on Christianity and he took it to his office but never read it. Herndon later corresponded with Dr. Smith and asked certain questions of fact which were answered with glittering generalities but no definite commitments. He concluded that Smith was not honest and had taken advantage of Mrs. Lincoln's religious wishes.

Even as modern science has learned, by self-analysis in self-education, that its philosophy is based on the logic of common sense in the interpretation of the relative meanings of our sensory representations of internal and external bodily interactions with our environmental interactions, Lincoln learned in the same way to rely upon common sense in reasoning from demonstrable evidence of what he could see, hear, taste, smell, touch, and feel. Since common sense cannot conceive of something being created out of nothing, Lincoln believed, like science, that action and reaction and cause and effect obey natural laws of motion even though the laws are unknown. Wherein his thinking was free of uncritical acceptance of biblical versions of creation and miraculous intervention of Divine Will in natural law, his philosophy, as the consummation of realistic self-education, was as consistent and logical as that of modern science, although far less refined and accurate.

However, no faith in the interpretation of meaning of evidence, theory, or belief of science or religion, was for Lincoln beyond doubt of the possibility of involvements of error that might well be corrected. He learned early, from intensely conflicting sectarian interpretations of meanings of the Bible and justifications of opposite views by great judges and ministers, to realize that no man's opinion, whatever his religious, legal, or other education and whatever his authoritative office and title, can be accepted as infallible and beyond the possibility of error in making laws and interpreting their meanings in applying them to human behavior.

Lincoln used such terms as "God," "Father," and "Heavenly Father" in letters, speeches, conversations and proclamations with apparently the vague meaning in current usage of Supreme Being, and Creator. But he seems not to have believed in the orthodox teachings that God created man in his own bodily image and therefore God was an eternally existing supernatural man who lives somehow in a particular heavenly place.

Herndon has told us definitely, and the records of Lincoln's expressions of religious interests support the conclusion, that he did not believe in the divinity of Christ although he sometimes referred to him as "the Saviour." He did believe that Christ was a man of unusual understanding of human nature and a divinely inspired teacher of equalitarian morality, legal rights and justice. In his letter to console his elementary minded dying father he expressed sentiment that suggested belief in personal immortality, but according to Herndon this was meant to be comforting and not his real belief.

In a debate with Douglas (7, 10, 1858) involving the question of moral justification of slavery in law and religion he quoted one of Christ's admonitions of ethical behavior.

" 'As your Father in Heaven is perfect, be ye also perfect.' The Saviour, I suppose, did not expect that any human creature could be perfect as the Father in Heaven; . . . but he set up a standard, and he who did most towards reaching that standard, attained the highest degree of moral perfection. So I say in relation to the principle that all men are created free and equal, let it be as nearly reached as we can."

Philosophical Notes on Politics and Government

Nowhere do we feel so intimately close to Lincoln as when we read his meditations in notes that he wrote for himself to clarify his thinking on the greater political issues and philosophical questions of his time. Here we observe the pedestrian simplicity of his analytical method of self-education, that he worked out for himself as a boy, and continued to apply as a man with such extraordinary sincerity in arriving at consistent understanding of the logical interrelations of moral, legal, political and religious issues.

Since boyhood Lincoln made notes in books or on scraps of paper of anything that he wanted to remember from what he had read, or any idea that he had worked out in his studies. He often carried such material about with him inside of his high hat, to read again and again with endless contemplation for elaboration. This was indeed an intelligent method of cultivating practical associations of ideas. It was essentially like the correlative method of science in working out the comparative values of experimental and natural evidence.

Fortunately many of these notes have been preserved and published in *Collected Works.* They are painstaking records of his elementary analytical way of reasoning and give invaluable information on the steps in development of his political philosophy of human relations. A number of such notes will be presented in chronological order so that we may know his private contemplations on the political situations as they developed. The following were probably written about 1854.

On government: "The legitimate object of government, is to do for a community of people, whatever they need to have done, but cannot do, *at all,* or can not, *so well do,* for themselves—in their separate and in their individual capacities."

"In all that people can individually do as well for themselves, government ought not to interfere. [Herein are contemplations of the essentials of government of the people, by the people, and for the people, which he will so effectively proclaim later.]

"The desirable things which the individuals of a people can not do, or can not well do, for themselves, fall into two classes: those which have relation to *wrongs,* and those which have not. Each of these branch off into an infinite variety of subdivisions.

"The first—that in relation to wrongs—embraces all crimes, misdemeanors, and non-performance of contracts. The other embraces all which, in its nature, and without wrong, requires combined action, as public roads and highways, public schools, charities, pauperism, orphanage, estates of the deceased, and the machinery of government itself.

"From this it appears that if all men were just, there still would be *some,* though not *so much,* need of government."

Then he repeated, as if meditating on how better to express his thoughts:

"Government is a combination of the people of a country to effect certain objects by joint effort. The best framed and best administered governments are necessarily expensive; while by errors in frame and maladministration most of them are more onerous than they need be, and some of them very oppressive. Why, then, should we have government? Why not each individual take to himself the whole fruit of his labor, without having any of it taxed away, in services, corn, or money? Why not take just so much land as he can cultivate with his own hands, without buying it of anyone?

"The legitimate object of government is 'to do for the people what needs to be done but which they can not, by individual efforts do at all, or do so well, for themselves.' There are many such things—some of them exist independently of the injustice of the world. Making and maintaining roads, bridges, and the like; providing for the helpless young and afflicted; common schools; and disposing of deceased men's property, are instances.

"But a far larger class of objects springs from the injustice of men. If one people will make war upon another, it is a necessity with that other to unite and cooperate for defense. Hence the military department. If some men will kill, or beat, or constrain others, or despoil them of property, by force, fraud, or noncompliance with contracts, it is a common object with peaceful and just men to prevent it. Hence the criminal and civil department."

On slavery: [Evi] "dent truth. Made so plain by our good Father in Heaven, that all *feel* and *understand* it, even down to brutes and creeping insects. The ant, who has toiled and dragged a crumb to his nest, will furiously defend the fruit of his labor, against whatever robber assails him. So plain, that the most dumb and stupid slave that ever toiled for a master, does constantly *know* that he is wronged. So plain that no one, high or low, ever does mistake it, except in a plainly *selfish* way; for although volume upon volume is written to prove slavery is a very good thing, we never hear of the man who wishes to take the good of it, *by being a slave himself.*

"Most *governments* have been based, practically, on the denial of equal rights of men, as I have, in part, stated them; *ours* began, by *affirming* those rights. *They* said some men are too *ignorant,* and *vicious,* to share in government. Possibly so, said we; and, by your system, you would always keep them ignorant and vicious. We proposed to give *all* a chance; and we expected the weak to grow stronger, the ignorant, wiser; and all better, and happier together.

"We made the experiment; and the fruit is before us. Look at it—think of it. Look at it, in it's aggregate grandeur, of extent of country, and numbers of population—of ship, and steamboat, and rail—"

Again on slavery:

"If A. can prove, however conclusively, that he may, of right, enslave B. —why may not B. snatch the same argument, and prove equally, that he may enslave A?—

"You say A. is white, and B. is black. It is *color,* then; the lighter, having the right to enslave the darker? Take care. By this rule, you are to be slave to the first man you meet, with a fairer skin than you own."

"You do not mean *color* exactly?—You mean the whites are *intellectually* the superiors of the blacks, and, therefore have the right to enslave them? Take care again. By this rule, you are to be slave to the first men you meet, with an intellect superior to your own.

"But, say you, it is a question of *interest;* and, if you make it your *interest,* you have the right to enslave another. Very well. And if he can make it his interest, he has the right to enslave you."

Lincoln On Pro-Slavery Theology

In 1857 Reverend F. A. Ross published a book entitled *Slavery Ordained by God* and made numerous speeches morally justifying slavery. His arguments led Lincoln to write the following notes (10, 1, 1858):

"Suppose it is true, that the negro is inferior to the white, in the gifts of nature; is it not the exact reverse justice that the white should, for that reason, take from the negro, any part of the little which has been given him? *'Give* to him that is needy' is the christian rule of charity; but 'Take from him that is needy' is the rule of slavery.

"The sum of pro-slavery theology seems to be this: 'Slavery is not universally *right,* nor yet universally *wrong;* it is better for *some* people to be slaves; and, in such cases, it is the Will of God that they shall be such.'

"Certainly there is no contending against the Will of God; but still there is some difficulty in ascertaining, and applying it, to particular cases. [Italics inserted.] For instance we will suppose the Rev. Dr. Ross has a slave named Sambo, and the question is 'Is it the Will of God that Sambo shall remain a slave, or be set free?' The Almighty gives no audable answer to the question, and his revelation—the Bible—gives none—or, at most, none but such as admits of a squabble, as to it's meaning. No one thinks of asking Sambo's opinion on it. So, at last, it comes to this, that

Dr. Ross is to decide the question. And while he consider[s] it, he sits in the shade, with gloves on his hands, and subsists on the bread that Sambo is earning in the burning sun. If he decides that God wills Sambo to continue a slave, he thereby retains his own comfortable position; but if he decides that God wills Sambo to be free, he thereby has to walk out of the shade, throw off his gloves, and delve for his own bread. Will Dr. Ross be actuated by that perfect impartiality, which has ever been considered most favorable to correct decision?

"But, slavery is good for some people!!! As a *good* thing, slavery is strikingly peculiar, in this, that it is the only good thing which no man ever seeks the good of, *for himself.*

"Nonsense! Wolves devouring lambs, not because it is good for their own greedy maws, but because it [is] good for the lambs!!!"

The logical, equalitarian, bilateral application of Lincoln's double edged sense of justice, in these notes, indicates how deeply he felt disgust for the unilaterally privileged reasoning of the strong who pretend to justify themselves by claiming to express the Will of God in dominating the weak.

"But there is a larger issue," he wrote on the same day, "than the mere question of whether the spread of negro slavery shall or shall not be prohibited by Congress. That larger issue is stated by the Richmond 'Inquirer,' a Buchanan paper in the South, in the language I now read. It is also stated by the New York 'Day-book,' a Buchanan paper in the North, in this language.—And in relation to indigent white children, the same Northern paper says.—In support of the Nebraska bill, on its first discussion in the Senate, Senator Pettit of Indiana declared the equality of men, as asserted in our Declaration of Independence, to be a 'self-evident lie.' In his numerous speeches now being made in Illinois, Senator Douglas regularly argues against the doctrine of the equality of men; and while he does not draw the conclusion that the superiors ought to enslave the inferiors, he evidently wishes his hearers to draw that conclusion. He shirks the responsibility of pulling the house down, but he digs under it that it may fall of its own weight. Now, it is impossible to not see that these newspapers and senators are laboring at a common object, and in so doing are truly representing the controlling sentiment of their party.

"It is equally impossible to not see that the common object is to subvert, in the public mind, and in practical administration, our old and only standard of free government, that 'all men are created equal,' and to substitute for it some different standard. What that substitute is to be is not difficult to perceive. It is to deny the equality of men, and to assert the natural, moral, and religious right of one class to enslave another."

Quandary, Predetermination versus Free Will

Lincoln's uncritical acceptance of the belief in predetermination by Divine Will led him into a quandary over what were its blessings and curses for man. In a private note (9, 17, 1859) he outlined his thoughts on the moral relativity of free and slave labor.

"Advancement—improvement in condition—is the order of things in a free society of equals. As Labor is the common *burthen* of our race, so the effort of *some* to shift their share of the burthen on the shoulders of *others,* is the great, durable, curse of the race. Originally a curse for transgression upon the whole race, when, as by slavery, it is concentrated on a part only, it becomes the double-refined curse of God upon his creatures."

"Free labor has the inspiration of hope; pure slavery has not hope. The power of hope upon human exertion, and happiness, is wonderful."

Lincoln believed, as every socially fair minded, ethically disposed person must, but with far deeper compulsion to uphold the morality of law, that the foundation of constitutional democracy rests in the elementary moral rule of equal rights. He believed that this moral principle should be practised in religion, in the family, in play, in love, in business, in law, in politics, and in government. He was entirely consistent and boldly aggressive in asserting his principles, as will become more evident later. So great was his confidence in his own estimation of relative moral values of political policies that, while he submitted his propositions to friends for advice, he finally exercised his own judgment of application, come what may as a result. Eventually he became one of the most morally practical, socially understanding and influential philosophers of human nature, human relations and equalitarian political organization, of history.

In order to understand the moral philosophy and social behavior of Lincoln as deeply and naturally as science now permits, we must correlate it with the evidence of basic principles of modern psychobiodynamics.

Psychobiodynamics of Morality and Man's Personal and Social Neuroses

I have shown (Kempf, 1918, 1935, 1941, 1945, 1949, 1953, 1958) how appropriate correlations of experimental evidence of the biological sciences demonstrate the basic laws of life and the organization of mind. In brief, each living thing (virus, bacterium, and unicellular and multicellular plant and animal organism, including man) inherits from its parents a highly specialized chromosomal organization of highly specialized genes that determine the production by each cell and organism of highly specialized qualities of proteins, carbohydrates, fats, and other essential energic materials for viability, growth and reproduction, and its continuous need to equilibrate itself with its environmental energies makes its environment determine the quantitative ratios and proportions, timing and spacing of distributions and uses of these energic materials. This is the basic universal law of life. Stated in more general terms, all living things grow and reproduce as determined by their inherited genotypes, interacting in adaptive equilibration against disequilibration with their environmental energic conditions, as they vary endlessly quantitatively and qualitatively.

Each living organism is a highly specialized self-constructive and self-consuming metabolic mechanism. It must work continuously repetitively, to acquire and assimilate such specific qualities and quantities of energic substances, from its ever-changing environment, as it can utilize to maintain the organization as a whole of its internal with external equilibrating interactions. Concomitantly it must avoid and eliminate causes of internal and external disequilibrating interactions. Thereby the quantitatively qualitatively specialized physicochemical organization of each form of life naturally, automatically, differentiates its environment into a very narrowly limited range of qualitative and quantitative materials (nutritional substances) and other energic conditions (heat, light, moisture, atmospheric gases and pressure, gravity) that must economically support and ease its work to live and reproduce. These constructive energic ranges are surrounded and intermingled with quantitatively unfitting, excessive or deficient, conditions that imbalance and increase its work to live and tend to destroy its integrity.

It is a secondary universal law of life that whenever any living thing, including man, is forced to acquire, accept and assimilate whatever it metabolically needs to avoid or eliminate, or is forced to avoid what it needs to acquire, a state of nervous and metabolic confusion of internal and external functioning follows immediately which, if too long continued and not relieved, eventually produces degenerative cellular changes, first in the most stressed organs, followed eventually by the disintegration and death of the organism.

Since environmental situations for each form of life generally include *at the same time* more or less favorable, supporting, work-easing, potentially constructive conditions, and opposing, frustrating, work-increasing, potentially destructive conditions, in more or less complex mixtures, all forms of life must work repetitively with sensory-motor discrimination of what to acquire and assimilate and what to avoid and eliminate. Man and other higher animals must also work volitionally, consciously, reciprocally, in acquisitive and avoidance selective directions *at the same time,* and keep endlessly deciding *what to do* and *what not to do* in order to live. Successful work in acquiring whatever is needed to maintain, economically, holistic mental and bodily equilibration and, concomitantly, reciprocally avoiding what is less fit or unfit, produces pleasurable feelings of well balanced neuromuscular tensions in the vital, autonomic, energy-circulating, involitionally motivating organs and in the somatic-kinesthetizing, energy-projecting and volitionally working organs of the body. This pleasurably efficient state is felt as love of living, and the mental, bodily, and environmental conditions that produce it are conditionally also loved. Frustration of acquiring whatever is needed to continue love of living tends to cause painful and fearful increases of neuromuscular tensions, and excites counterbalancing action. When the opposing forces of the environment are stronger than the organism, they excite avoidance fear reactions to escape; and when they are weaker, the organism tends to become enraged and impelled to attack and overcome or destroy the opposing force.

In man, successful discriminations between environmental conditions that are favorable, versus the unfavorable, for the needs of love of living, depend entirely upon the degree of integrity of the particular form of consciousness-producing egoistic attitude that is being holistically integrated in the brain, by the organization of internally and externally equilibrating interactions of the body as a whole at that time. The orderly, consciously discriminating integrative organization of the cerebral cortex in man, as in other higher animals, tends to become involved in conflicting involitional and volitional interactions when he gets into an unavoidable or otherwise binding, closed situation that imposes increasing excitation of emotional compulsion to discriminate what he needs to acquire from what he needs to avoid, under increasing danger of frustration and/or punishment with decreasing limitation of time.

As constructive supporting conditions and destructive opposing conditions of the environment become too nearly alike, and too closely and complexly involved, for the egoistic attitude's wilful capacity to perceive the sensory differences of what it needs to acquire from what it needs to avoid, it becomes unable to decide *what to do* from *what not to do*. It then develops distressing anxiety tensions and tremors in the heart, lungs and gut, from conflicting, unreciprocal, involitional nervous interactions.

Furthermore, when a person cannot maintain a consistent egoistic attitude because of conflicting previous experience-conditioned emotions of love, fear, and hate, in reaction to similar situations or the same person, he cannot discriminate moral, legal, or economic right from wrong, fact from fancy, or good from bad; and he cannot maintain a self-justifiable, self-respectful egoistic attitude that is sufficient to continue making consistent decisions. As he tends to develop increasing neurotic anxiety he becomes disposed impulsively to adopt helpful suggestions offering wishful, hopeful solutions even though unreasonable and fictitious. If he cannot be relieved by friendly counsel, he tends to slump into a defeated, frustrated egoistic attitude and depressed state of mind, to avoid getting into more binding responsibilities and difficult decisions, leading to unambitious mediocrity and eventually to apathetic indifference of character.

Each person, in his natural social dependence and egoistic drive to be first and get best and most in the quickest and easiest way, and avoid being last and least, is endlessly, potentially, more or less of a competitor and antipathic opponent, and a cooperator and sympathetic supporter, with every other person in immediate and distant spatial and temporal social relations. Each successful advance of oneself or of a supporter, or failure of a competitor, in the struggle for relative superiority and security of self-determination, feels pleasurable as it tends to ease the work to live; and conversely, each failure of oneself or of a supporter, or success of a competitor, feels painful as it reduces security and self-determination and increases relative inferiority and work to live. Hence each man's welfare is dependent upon the part he plays in the social organization of personal interactions. His culture of conscience as morally equalitarian feeling of what is clean versus unclean, right or wrong, good or bad, and just or unjust, is based naturally on the conditioning approvals versus disapprovals of his social group. They are generally more or less concomitant and intermingled, and often so closely similar in qualities that their harmonizing and conflicting values for individuals and for social organization cannot be easily correctly discriminated or even practically estimated. The stronger are naturally inclined to dominate and exploit the weaker and, wherein they do not compete among themselves, they tend to gang up and organize cooperative interests toward establishing legal and religious justifications for exercising graded superiorities, rights and privileges which force the weaker to remain confused, degraded, disorganized, and underprivileged.

Social neuroses tend to develop en masse when people are bound to work or live together in family, religious, business or other unavoidable groups and have conflicting needs and motivations which they refuse to compromise. Such was the conflict over Federal versus states' rights on the regulation of slavery. Equalitarian morals and laws are social compensations adopted to reduce such causes of neuroses.

Lincoln's Psychosocio Dynamics

Lincoln's numerous sage comments and humorous stories on the legal, religious, political, and other social involvements of people reveal his profound insight into the egocentric motivations of human individual and group behavior. As will become more evident, he saw the natural need for evolution in the application of religious and moral as well as legal regulations, to relieve the complexities of social interactions attending improvements in mechanics and economics. Lincoln realized that mechanical and economical determinants of man's self-preservative thinking are generally stronger than his culture of moral thinking; and his propensity to gang up for economic advantages and egoistic security is generally stronger than his love of independence and equalitarian justice in the struggle for life. However, such selfish tendencies eventually reinforce rather than weaken mandkind's need of understanding and cultivating equalitarian moral standards and legal rights for both sexes and all races, regardless of personal ability. Government, he maintained, should improve human welfare and not degrade it. The philosophy of Christianity tends to reduce conflicts of mind throught culture of sympathetic cooperation.

We have seen how Lincoln developed anxiety neurosis when he broke his promise to marry Mary Todd and lost faith in his ability to keep his promise—'the gem of his character.' We have seen how he developed, a hundred years before modern psychiatry, the common-sense realization that the healtful mental integrity and happiness of each person depends upon the continuity of egoistic self-justification of his wilful actions, through obtaining from other persons freely given sympathetic approvals of rightwayness of acting, and sympathetic, and not antipathetic, disapprovals of wrongwayness. Unjust, critical, antipathic disapprovals tend to injure egoistic self-respect, and excite resentment and repetitive mental preoccupations of self-doubt and gloomy brooding frustration.

We have seen how Lincoln's philosophy of common sense anticipated the salutary principles since adopted by modern science in treating personal and social neuroses, by virtue of being psychobiologically natural and sound in understanding and treating his own neurosis. His philosophy of democracy was based on majority rule, with reciprocal inhibition of minority powers but not suppression of their rights to oppose. He had developed with cumulative experience by the age of forty a deeply practical understanding of the basic egoistic motivations of human individual and group behavior, and the indispensable need for human welfare of freedom of self-expression and equal rights for all people under a constitutional system of government, established and maintained by the people for the people. With increasing clarity of reasoning and force of moral conviction, he was realizing that his interest lay in (1) extending equal moral and legal rights of all people, (2) defending the inviolability of the Constitution, (3) preserving the Union, and (4) legally limiting the spread of slavery. Lincoln was eager and ready, in the confidence of his powers to appeal to reason of the people, to step into the bitter social conflict over these involved issues if ever they threatened the integrity of the nation. He was indeed preparing his mind for destiny.

Chapter XXIII

FAILURE AS A PUBLIC LECTURER

Lincoln would rather have been a successful orator and statesman working for human progress than the king of a hereditary ruling class. Without sufficient call to make campaign speeches, and his law practice inadequate to engage his entire time, he experimented in theoretical invention and essayed public lecturing.

Inventive Mechanic

Some of Lincoln's biographers have said that he lacked inventive imagination. In his youth and New Salem days, as a leader of the Whigs in the state legislature, he was always mechanistically minded, with an unusual capacity for methodically correlating evidence so as to discriminate essentials from inconsequentials. He liked to analyze for basic causes in situations, upon which to build logically a dual system of reasons *for* and *against* a conclusion, which he held tentatively, in the scientific manner, until discredited, and not with dogmatic obstinacy as in the political and religious manner.

We have cited a number of instances in which he solved difficult mechanical situations and political and legal situations, with ingenious innovations that gave evidence of superior inventive mindedness. It is impossible to understand his mind when President without recognizing his genius for estimating mechanistic resultants produced by multiple forces of various kinds, working in alliance and opposition.

Lincoln, the lawyer, once a riverman, applied (3, 10, 1849) for a patent on an improved method of lifting river vessels over shoals (Patent Office No. 6469).

> "Be it known that I, Abraham Lincoln, . . . have invented a new and improved manner of combining adjustable buoyant air chambers with a steam boat or other vessel for the purpose of enabling their draught of water to be readily lessened to enable them to pass over bars, or through shallow water, without discharging their cargoes."

The application was accompanied by a well-drawn diagram of how the mechanism would work when installed on a large boat. On each side of the boat a parallel series of vertical shafts were connected with a central, horizontal shaft that extended through its length.

> The vertical shafts were fitted into apertures and connected at the water level with a series of "buoyant chambers" constructed in such a manner that they could "be expanded so as to hold a large volume of air when required for use," and "be contracted, into a very small space and safely secured as soon as their services can be dispensed

433

with." "The top and bottom of each buoyant chamber is composed of plank or metal, of suitable strength and stiffness, and the flexible sides and ends of the chambers, are composed of india-rubber cloth, or other suitable water proof fabric, securely united to the edges and ends of the top and bottom of the chamber." . . .

"What I claim as my invention and desire to secure by letters patent, is the combination of expansible, buoyant chambers placed at the sides of a vessel, with the main shaft or shafts, by means of the sliding spars, . . . which pass down through the buoyant chambers and are made fast to their bottoms, and the series of ropes and pullies, or their equivalents, in such a manner that by turning the main shaft or shafts in one direction, the buoyant chambers will be forced downwards into the water and at the same time expanded and filled with air for buoying up the vessel by displacement of water, and by turning the shaft in an opposite direction, the buoyant chambers will be contracted into a small space and secured against injury."

Although this cumbersome mechanism was not put into practical use, it is indicative of the inventive imagination that Lincoln was able to apply to any problem of interacting allied and conflicting forces—political, legal, military or economic as well as mechanical.

Lectures on Discoveries and Inventions

Before the Young Men's Association in Bloomington he delivered his first lecture on Discoveries and Inventions (4, 6, 1858). After some revision he delivered it again before the Phi Alpha Society of Illinois College, at Jacksonville (2, 14, 1859) and at Springfield. The lectures were far from impressive in information and comprehension of his subject but they present a side of Lincoln's mind that must not be ignored if we are to understand him. We repeat here from *Collected Works* such of his statements as have significant indications. The lectures, more than his legal and political papers, reveal the limited extent of his self-education outside of his profession. The first one shows, despite contradictory statements by numerous biographers, that he was a thorough student of the Bible and accepted its account of the creation and the origin and early history of man. The second gives, by examples, some of his methods of psychological analysis. The lectures are to be judged by the knowledge and beliefs of that time. The first one starts:

"All creation is a mine, and every man, a miner.

"The whole earth, and all *within* it, *upon* it, and *round about it,* including *himself,* in his physical, moral, and intellectual nature, and his susceptibilities, are the infinitely various 'leads' of which, man, from the first, was to dig out his destiny.

"In the beginning, the mine was unopened, and the miner stood *naked* and *knowledgeless,* upon it.

"Fishes, birds, beasts, and creeping things, are not miners, but *feeders* and *lodgers,* merely. Beavers build houses; but they build them in nowise differently, or better now, than they did, five thousand years ago. Ants, and honey-bees, provide food for winter; but just in the *same way* they did, when Solomon referred the sluggard to them as patterns of prudence.

"Man is not the only animal who labors; but he is the only one who *improves* his workmanship. This improvement, he effects by *Discoveries,* and *Inventions.* His first important discovery was the fact that he was naked; and his first invention was the fig-leaf-apron. This simple article—the apron—made of leaves, seems to have been the origin of *clothing*—the one thing for which nearly half of the toil and care of the human race has ever since been expended. The most important improvement ever made in connection with clothing, was the invention of *spinning* and *weaving.* . . . Exactly *when,* or *where* spinning and weaving originated is now known. At the first interview of the Almighty with Adam and Eve, after the fall, He made 'coats of skins, and clothed them' Gen: 3-21.

"The Bible makes no other alusion to clothing *before* the flood. Soon *after* the deluge Noah's two sons covered him with a *garment;* but of what *material* the garment was made is not mentioned. Gen. 9-23.

"Abraham mentions *'thread'* in such connection as to indicate that spinning and weaving were in use in his day—Gen. 14-23—and soon after, reference to the art is frequently made. 'Linen breeches' are mentioned—Exod. 28.42—and it is said 'all the women that were wise hearted, did *spin* with their hands' (35-25) and, 'all the women whose hearts stirred them up in widom, *spun* goat's hair' (35-26). . . . In the book of Job, a very old book,—the 'weaver's shuttle' is mentioned.

"The above mention of 'thread' by Abraham is the oldest recorded alusion to spinning and weaving; and it was made about two thousand years after the creation of man, and now, near four thousand years ago. Profane authors think these arts originated in Egypt; and this is not contradicted, or made improbable, by any thing in the Bible; for the alusion of Abraham, mentioned, was not made until after he had sojourned in Egypt.

"The discovery of the properties of *iron,* and the making of *iron tools,* must have been among the earliest of important discoveries and inventions. . . . How could *'gopher-wood'* of the Ark, have been gotten out without an axe? It seems to me an axe, or a miracle, was indispensable. Corresponding with the prime necessity for iron, we find at least one very early notice of it. Tubal-cain was 'an instructor of every artificer in *brass* and *iron'*—Gen: 4-22. Tubal-cain was the seventh in descent from Adam; and his birth was about one thousand years before the flood. *After* the flood, frequent mention is made of *iron,* and *instruments* made of iron. Thus 'instrument of iron' at Num: 35-16; 'bed-stead of iron' at Deut. 3-11—; 'the iron furnace' at 4-20— and 'iron tool' at 27-5. At 19-5—very distinct mention of 'the axe to cut down the tree' is made; and also at 8-9, the promised land is described as 'a land whose stones are iron, and out of whose hills thou mayest dig brass.' . . .

"Transportation—the removal of person, and goods—from place to place—would be an early *object,* if not a *necessity* with man. . . .

"The oldest recorded alusion to the wheel and axle is the mention of a 'chariot' Gen: 41-43. This was in Egypt, upon the occasion of Joseph being made Governor by Pharaoh. It was about twentyfive hundred years after the creation of Adam. . . . [There is] the mention of chariot-*wheels,* at Exod. 14-25, and the mention of chariots in connection with *horses,* in the same chapter, verses 9 & 23.

"Now as to transportation by *water,* I have concluded, without sufficient authority perhaps, to use the term 'boat' as a general name for all water craft. . . . It is not probable that the philosophical principle upon which the use of the boat primarily depends—towit, the *principle,* that anything will float, which can not sink without displacing more that it's own *weight* of water—was known or even thought of, before the first boats were made. . . .

"If we pass by the Ark, which may be regarded as belonging rather to the *miracalous,* then to *human* invention, the first notice we have of water-craft, is the mention of 'ships' by Jacob—Gen. 49-13. It is not till we reach the book of Isaiah that we meet with the mention of 'oars' and 'sails.'

"As mans *food*—his first necessity—was to be derived from the vegitation of the earth, it was natural that his first care should be directed to the assistance of that vegitation. And accordingly we find that, even before the fall, the man was put into the garden of Eden 'to dress it, and to keep it.' And when afterwards, in consequence of the first transgression, *labor* was imposed on the race, as a *penalty* —a *curse*—we find the first born man—the first heir of the curse—was 'a tiller of the ground.' This was the beginning of agriculture; and although, both in point of time, and of importance, it stands at the head of all branches of human industry, it has derived less direct advantage from Discovery and Invention, than almost any other. . . . the plow, could not have been conceived of, until a precedent conception had been caught and put into practice. . . .

"Climbing upon the back of an animal, and making it carry us, might not, occur very readily. I think the back of the camel would never have suggested it. . . .

"The earliest instance of it mentioned, is when 'Abraham rose up early in the morning, and saddled his ass,' Gen. 2ˀ-3 preparatory to sacrificing Isaac as a burnt-offering; but the alusion to the *saddle* indicates that riding had been in use some time; for it is probable they rode bare-backed awhile, at least, before they invented saddles.

"The *idea,* being once conceived, of riding *one* species of animals, would soon be extended to others. Accordingly we find that when the servant of Abraham went in search of a wife for Isaac, he took ten *camels* with him; and on his return trip Rebekah arose, and her damsels, and they rode upon the camels, and followed the man' Gen. 24-61.

"The *horse,* too, as a riding animal, is mentioned early. The Red-sea being safely passed, Moses and the children of Israel sang to the Lord 'the *horse,* and his *rider* hath he thrown into the sea Exo.' 15-1.

"Seeing that animals could bear *man* upon their backs, it would soon occur that they could also bear other burthens. Accordingly we find that Joseph's bretheren, on their first visit to Egypt, 'loaded their asses with the corn, and departed thence' Gen. 42-26.

"Also it would occur that animals could be made to *draw* burthens *after* them, . . . and hence plows and chariots came into use early enough to be often mentioned in the book of Moses—Deut. 22-10. Gen. 41-43. Gen. 46-29. Exo. 14-25.

"Of all the forces of nature, I should think the wind contains the largest amount of *motive power,* that is, power to move things. . . . and quite possibly one of the greatest discoveries hereafter to be made, will be the taming, and harnessing of the wind. . . . that power was applied to sail-vessels, at least as early as the time of the prophet Isaiah.

"In speaking of *running streams,* as a motive power, I mean its application to mills and other machinery by means of the '*water wheel*'—no mention is made in the bible. . . . The language of the Saviour 'Two women shall be grinding at the mill &c' indicates that in the populous city of Jerusalem, at that day, mills were operated by hand. . . .

"The advantageous use of *Steam-power* is, unquestionably, a modern discovery.

"And yet, as much as two thousand years ago the power of steam was not observed, but an ingenious toy was actually made and put in motion by it, at Alexandria in Egypt.

"What appears strange is, that neither the inventor of the toy, nor anyone else, for so long a time afterwards, should perceive that steam would move *useful* machinery as well as a toy."

Herndon heard this lecture and described it many years later to Weik (2, 21, 1891) as dealing mostly with the discoveries mentioned in the Bible.

"Knowing Mr. L. as well as I did, I was anxious to hear him, and did listen to him well, thoroughly, attentively, and curiously too. I know that Mr. L. was not fitted, qualified, in any way to deliver a lecture to our people, who were intelligent, and well read and well educated. . . . it was a lifeless thing, a dead thing, 'died aborning.' It fell on the ears of the audience a cold flat thing. There was no life, imagination, or fancy in it, no spirit and no life. The whole thing was a kind of farce and injured Mr. L's reputation as a man of sense among his friends and enemies."

"He had not the fire, taste, reading and eloquence which would make him a lecturer, had no imagination, no fancy, no taste, no emotion, no readings in that peculiar line." . . . "He would, in the absence of a friend's opinion, as soon take up the Beautiful as any

other subject for a lecture when he had no sense of it. Lincoln had
poor judgment of the fitness and appropriateness of things. . . .
Mr. Lincoln was a curious being; he had an idea that he was equal to,
if not superior to, all things; thought he was fit and skilled in all
things, master of all things, and graceful in all things."

As a lyceum lecturer, Nicolay and Hay (1890) described him as
dull, uninteresting and monotonous. He only became interesting when
he talked on a subject that aroused him emotionally, but he generally
avoided the temptation to please his audience by flaring into oratorical
eloquence.

Some biographers have held that Lincoln's interest in the Bible
later, as President, was only casual. As will be seen, it continued then
as it had all of his life, to be a major source of solace in defeat as well
as practical understanding of human nature in everyday life. His
lecture on Discoveries and Inventions contains so many references to
first mentions in the Bible of the use of certain mechanical devices
for labor, and various domestic animals for transportation, that evidently he continued to have an historical as well as philosophical
interest in this book. He seems to have accepted its story of the
creation of the universe and of man and the Ark as evidence of the
miraculous powers of "the Almighty." Darwin's theory of evolution
was not published until 1859, and a new generation of scientists had
to replace the old before it was generally adopted. Anthropology
was still unborn and the Bible contained by far the best history of
ancient man.

Invention of Language

In the second lecture, delivered to college students (2, 11, 1859),
Lincoln dropped biblical citations of mechanical devices and devoted
himself humorously to random discussion of youth's passion for the
new and impatience with the old. We can see in it Lincoln retrospec-
tively contemplating his own mental transition from youth to manhood.

"We have all heard of Young America. He is the most *current*
youth of the age. Some think him conceited, and arrogant; but has
he not reason to entertain a rather extensive opinion of himself? Is
he not the inventor and owner of the *present*, and sole hope of the
future? Men, and things, everywhere, are ministering unto him."
Following this introduction with an account of numerous things used
by man and the foreign origins of their raw materials he said: "Young
America . . . has a great passion . . . for the *'new;'* particularly
new men for office, and the new earth mentioned in the revelations,
. . . He is a great friend of humanity; and his desire for land is not
selfish, but merely an impulse to extend the area of freedom. He is
very anxious to fight for the liberation of enslaved nations and colonies,
provided, always, they *have* land, and have *not* any liking for
his interference. As to those who have no land, and would be glad

of help from any quarter, he considers *they* can afford to wait a few hundred years longer. In knowledge he is particularly rich. He knows all that can possibly be known; inclines to believe in spiritual rappings, and is the unquestioned inventor of *'Manifest Destiny.'* His horror is for all that is old, particularly 'Old Fogy;' and if there be any thing old which he can endure, it is only old whiskey and old tobacco. . . .

"The great difference between Young America and Old Fogy, is the result of *Discoveries, Inventions* and *Improvemtns*. These, in turn are the result of *observation, reflection* and *experiment*. For instance, it is quite certain that ever since water has been heated in covered vessels, men have seen the lids of the vessels rise and fall a little, with a sort of fluttering motion, by force of the steam; but so long as this was not specially observed, and reflected and experimented upon, it came to nothing." After sketching "the general principle" of the invention of control of steam-power he continued:

"But was this first inventor of the application of steam, wiser or more ingenious than those who had gone before him? Not at all. Had he not learned much of them, he never would have succeeded—probably never would have thought of making the attempt. To be fruitful in invention, it is necessary to have a *habit* of observation and reflection; and this *habit,* our steam friend acquired, no doubt, from those who, to him, were old fogies. . . .

"The inclination to exchange thoughts with one another is probably an original impulse of our nature. If I be in pain I wish to let you know it, and to ask your sympathy and assistance; and my pleasurable emotions also, I wish to communicate to, and share with you." . . .

Such reactions to pain and pleasure we have found characteristic of Lincoln to an unusual degree and have correlated the lack of stoic virtues with the hypersensitivity of his nervous system.

"Accordingly *speech*—articulate sounds rattled off from the tongue —was used by our first parents, and even by Adam, before the creation of Eve. He gave names to animals while she was still a bone in his side; and he broke out quite volubly when she first stood before him, the best present of his maker. From this it would appear that speech was not an invention of man, but rather the direct gift of his Creator. . . . speech must have been the first, from the superior adaptation to the end, of the organs of speech, over every other means within the whole range of nature. Of the organs of speech the tongue is the principal; and if we shall test it, we shall find the capacities of the tongue, in the utterance of articulate sounds, absolutely wonderful. You can count from one to one hundred, quite distinctly in about forty seconds. In doing this two hundred and eighty three distinct sounds or syllables are uttered, being seven to each second; and yet there shall be enough difference between every two, to be easily recognized by the ear of the hearer."

Lincoln was interested in the experimental evidence of modern science wherever it had practical application, and his psychological approach was analytically sound though crude.

"What other *signs* to represent *things* could possibly be produced so rapidly? or, even, if ready made, could be *arranged* so rapidly to express sense? *Motions* with the hands, are no adequate substitute. *Marks* for the recognition of the eye—writing—although a wonderful auxiliary for speech, is no worthy substitute for it. . . . Speech, then, by enabling different individuals to interchange thoughts, and thereby to combine their powers of observation and reflection, greatly facilitates useful discoveries and inventions. What one observes, and would himself infer nothing from, he tells to another, and that other at once sees a valuable hint in it. A result is reached which neither *alone* would have arrived at. . . .

"But speech alone, valuable as it ever has been, and is, has not advanced the condition of the world much. This is abundantly evident when we look at the degraded condition of all those tribes of human creatures who have no considerable additional means of communicating thoughts. *Writing*—the art of communicating thoughts to the mind, through the eye—is the great invention of the world. Great in the astonishing range of analysis and combination which necessarily underlies the most crude and general conception of it—great, very great in enabling us to converse with the dead, the absent, and the unborn, at all distances of time and space; and great, not only in its direct benefits, but greatest help, to all other inventions."

Lincoln probably had here in mind wills and other legal documents, public and other historical records, as well as personal communications.

. . . "The precise period at which writing was invented, is not known; but it certainly was as early as the time of Moses; from which we may safely infer that it's inventors were very old fogies.

"Webster, at the time of writing his Dictionary, speaks of the English Language as then consisting of seventy or eighty thousand words. If so, the language in which the five books of Moses were written must, at that time, now thirtythree or four hundred years ago, have consisted of at least one quarter as many, or, twenty thousand. When we remember that words are *sounds* merely, we shall conclude that the idea of representing those sounds by *marks,* so that whoever should at any time after see the marks, would understand what sounds they meant, was a bold and ingenious conception, not likely to occur to one man of a million, in a run of a thousand years. And, when it did occur, a distinct mark for each word, giving twenty thousand different marks first to be learned, and afterwards remembered, would follow as the second thought, and would present such a difficulty as would lead to the conclusion that the whole thing was impracticable. But the *necessity* still would exist; and we may readily suppose that the idea was conceived, and lost, and reproduced, and dropped, and taken up again and again, until at last, the thought of dividing sounds into parts, and making a mark, not to represent a whole sound, but only a part of one, and then combining these marks, not very many in number, upon the principles of permutation, so as to represent any and all of the whole twenty thousand words, and even an additonal number was somehow conceived and pushed into

practise. This was the invention of *phoenetic* writing, as distinguished
from the clumsy picture writing of some of the nations. That it was
difficult of conception and execution, is apparent, as well by the
foregoing reflections, as by the fact that so many tribes of men have
come down from Adam's time to ours without ever having possessed
it. It's utility may be conceived, by the reflection that, to *it* we owe
everything that distinguishes us from savages. Take it from us, and
the Bible, all history, all science, all government, all commerce, and
nearly all social intercourse go with it."

Lincoln's speculations on the creative origin of speech and the
conceptual development of writing are characteristic of the notions
held under the biblical ideology that each part of a thing was the
product of a special act of creation and each invention was the product
of some person's conception. Application later of the theory of
evolution to these problems has shown that man's speech was not
the product of sudden creative design but the adaptive accumulation
of means of communication through vocal imitation and manual
production. Writing evolved gradually to its present economical system
of alphabetical construction of words through economical reduction,
into least signs, upon endless repetition, of various methods of
pictographic representation, among many peoples having commercial
trade relations with each other. It is clear that Lincoln believed that
the human mind could develop and civilization could only progress
as far as the education of the people provided means. Hence the
peaceful solution of the slavery problem depended upon the education
of slaves as well as masters.

Emancipate the Mind

   . . . "in the world's history, certain inventions and discoveries occurred, of peculiar value, on account of their great efficiency in facili-
tating all other inventions and discoveries. Of these were the arts of
writing and of printing—the discovery of America, and the introduction
of Patent-laws. The date of the first, . . . is unknown; but it certainly
was as much as fifteen hundred years before the Christian era; the
second—printing—came in 1436, or nearly three thousand years after the
first. The others followed more rapidly—the discovery of America in
1492, and the first patent laws in 1624. . . . it is but justice . . . to
mention two other important events—the Lutheran Reformation in 1517,
and, still earlier, the invention of negroes, or, or the present mode of
using them, in 1434."
   On printing he said: "it is . . . in real utility . . . the *better*
half of writing. . . . When man was possessed of speech alone, the
chances of invention . . . were very limited; but by the introduction of
each of these they were greatly multiplied. . . . by means of writing,
the seeds of invention were more permanently preserved, and more
widely sown. And yet, for three thousand years . . . only a small
portion of the people . . . could write, or read writing; and consequently the field of invention . . . continued very limited. At length

printing came. It gave ten thousand copies of any written matter, quite as cheaply as ten were given before; and consequently a thousand minds were brought into the field where there was but one before. . . .

"I will venture to consider *it,* the true termination of that period called 'the dark ages.' Discoveries, inventions and improvements followed rapidly. . . . The effects could not come, all at once. It required time. . . . The *capacity* to read, could not be multiplied as fast as the *means* of reading. Spelling-books just began to go into the hands of the children; but the teachers were not very numerous, or very competent; so that it is safe to infer that they did not advance so speedily as they do now-a-days. It is very probable—almost certain—that the great mass of men, at that time, were utterly unconscious, that their *conditions,* or their *minds* were capable of improvement. They not only looked upon the educated few as superior beings; but they supposed themselves to be naturally incapable of rising to equality. To imancipate the mind from this false and under estimate of itself, is the great task which printing came into the world to perform. It is difficult for us, *now* and *here,* to conceive how strong this slavery of the mind was; and how long it did, of necessity, take, to break it's shackles, and to get a habit of freedom of thought, established."

Lincoln's argument on the importance for civilization of emancipation of the mind is remarkably sound and has since been amply verified by the experience of education, psychology and anthropology. He continued:

"It is, in this connection, a curious fact that a new country is most favorable—is almost necessary—to the immancipation of thought, and the consequent advancement of civilization and the arts. The human family originated, as is thought, somewhere in Asia, and have worked their way principally Westward. Just now, in civilization, and in the arts, the people of Asia are entirely behind those of Europe; those of the East of Europe behind those of the West of it; while we, here in America, *think* we discover, and invent, and improve, faster than any of them. *They* may think this is arrogance; but they can not deny that Russia has called on us to show her how to build steam-boats and railroads. . . . In anciently inhabited countries, the dust of ages—a real downright old-fogyism—seems to settle upon and smother the intellects and energies of man."

On the patent laws he said: "These began in England in 1624; and, in this country, with the adoption of our constitution. Before then, any man might instantly use what another had invented; so that the inventor had no special advantage from his own invention. The patent system changed this; secured to the inventor, for a limited time, the exclusive use of his invention; and thereby added the fuel of *interest* to the *fire* of genius, in the discovery and production of new and useful things."

Lincoln did not regard himself successful as a popular lecturer as this comment (4, 7, 1860) to F. C. Herbruger shows:

"Yours of March 14th. addressed to me at Chicago, and seeking to arrange with me to Lecture for the Harrison Literary Institute, has been received. I regret to say I can not make such arrangement. I am not a professional lecturer—have never got up but one lecture; and that, I think a rather poor one."

Chapter XXIV

WHEELS OF DESTINY

In 1850 Lincoln complained to Herndon that "the political world is dead." The enactment of the Missouri Compromise in 1820, forever prohibiting the extension of slavery north of the line of 36° 30′, seemed to have settled the issue of slavery between the slave states versus the free states. Politics seemed. to have grown stagnant and there was no issue to arouse action for moral progress.

Revival of Urge to Refute Douglas

However, as Lincoln wrote in his letter to Scripps (1860):

"In 1851 he was upon the Scott electoral ticket, and did something in the way of canvassing, but owing to the hopelessness of the cause in Illinois he did less than in previous presidential canvasses."

The deteriorating Whig party had nominated General Winfield Scott, Mexican War hero next in importance to General Zachary Taylor, as its candidate for president. Twice the tottering Whigs had won the national election through nominating popular military heroes (Harrison and Taylor) and they now tried to repeat the trick with Scott.

Stephen A. Douglas, age 39, had within five years as a United States Senator, worked up such national political influence that he was able to rally strong support to himself for nomination by his party as its presidential candidate. Although defeated in the national Democratic convention of 1852 by General Franklin Pierce, a man of recognized inferior ability and prestige, he supported his party's choice with vigorous loyalty. He attacked the conservative Whig policies and the fitness of General Scott for the administrative duties of president.

Lincoln, ever envious opponent of Douglas, and burning with indignation over the ruthlessness of his defamation of General Scott, obtained permission of the Springfield Scott Club to refute his charges:

"I do not appear before you on a flattering invitation, or on any invitation at all; but, on the contrary I am about to address you, by your permission, given me at my own special request. Soon after the Democratic nomination for President and vice-President in June last at Baltimore, it was announced somewhat ostentatiously, as it seemed to me, that Judge Douglas would, previous to the election, make speeches in favor of the nominations, in twenty-eight of the thirty-one States. Since then, and as I suppose, in part performance of this undertaking, he has actually made one speech at Richmond, Virginia. . . . When I first saw it, and read it, I was reminded of old times—of the times when Judge Douglas was not so much greater man than all the rest of us, as he now is—of the Harrison campaign, twelve years ago, when I used to hear, and *try* to answer many of his speeches; and believing that the Richmond speech though marked with the same species of 'shirks and quirks' as the old ones, was not marked with any greater ability, I was seized with a strong inclination to attempt an answer to it; and this inclination it was that prompted me to seek the privilege of addressing you on this occasion."

This speech is now important as a basis for comparing the opposing trends in development of the rival political philosophies of Lincoln and Douglas. The bold statements of Douglas, made to arouse uninformed, popular prejudice, offended Lincoln as being falsely exaggerated, intentionally misleading and inexcusably unjust and therefore immoral. He resented such opportunistic political agitation with cool, logical expositions of facts and ironical metaphor designed to disprove "the little giant."

With characteristic method he took each broad generalization in Douglas' speech and reduced it to crass absurdity by critically analyzing its arguments. He compared the brilliant military career of Major-General Scott to the weak record of Brigadier-General Pierce, and the administrative achievements as a commander of the former with the supine obedience to political bosses of the latter when in Congress. Douglas had charged that the Whig administration under President Fillmore had spent 60 million of the taxpayers' money, more in a time of peace than the Democrats had ever spent, even in time of war. Lincoln showed this to be a reckless exaggeration far exceeding the facts. The *payment* (net expenses) of the government for the fiscal year 1850 and 1851 was a little over 48 million. From this he deducted $5,759,091 for payment on Mexican debts, and expenses for collecting revenues, refunds of excess duties collected, and for charges on the sale of lands, pensions for soldiers, expanding the mail service, and financing the Smithsonian Institution. According to Lincoln:

"A just computation of the 'ordinary' expeditures of the Government for the year 1851 is, therefore, by this analysis, reduced to little more than thirty five millions of dollars, being a less annual amount, as before stated, than the Government expenditure had risen to before the Whigs had ever had any effective share in the administration of the General Government.

"By this it appears that in this twice made assault upon the Administration, Judge Douglas is only mistaken about twenty five millions of dollars—a mere trifle for a giant."

Lincoln's speeches in Illinois in 1852 against Douglas' arguments made little impression. Pierce was elected President, and Douglas was reelected to the Senate, each by a large majority, and Illinois became a Democratic stronghold.

Lincoln still had an attitude of egoistic inferiority toward Douglas, as he had "twelve years ago" when they argued in Speed's store and the Springfield debating societies and both courted Mary Todd. He never forgot the deep humiliation he felt when engaged to her and she flirted gaily with Douglas in public in a way that expressed admiration for his superior abilities, and how he broke the engagement and slumped into a frustrated state of mental depression. Even though Douglas withdrew his interest in Mary and Lincoln later married her, he never forgot, as no man could, that his rival in politics and law had humiliated him in love, the only experience in life that he had ever really dreaded. This unforgetable personal experience naturally obsessed him to desire to defeat Douglas wherein he was most ambitious to succeed; namely to become President of the United States. In order to appreciate how deeply and constantly Lincoln was motivated from 1852 on to refute Douglas, we must bear in mind that the two men were, in physical and mental constitution and philosophy of living, naturally polar opposites. Furthermore, we must remember that Lincoln, in his egoistic compensatory development to control his nervous disposition, was so highly conscientious and morally sensitive about self-respecting personal rights and justice that he was being constantly offended by the broad and loose exaggerations, prejudiced arguments and unmoral proslavery political opportunism of Douglas. As we understand how Lincoln's mind worked we can better understand how he became "aroused" to follow Douglas, from city to city and speech after speech, for eight years, to refute him.

Lincoln might have finished his career as a lawyer, letting Illinois politics and the Federal compromise on slavery take their courses, for such was his philosophy of acceptance of the constitutional right of slavery as a national condition, if Douglas, now the most powerful leader in the United States Senate and the Democratic party, had not succeeded in getting the Kansas-Nebraska Bill passed by Congress in 1854. It repealed the old Missouri Compromise and permitted the extension of slavery wherever the settlers of Kansas, Nebraska, or any other territorial section would take slaves, as property, before it was voted whether or not to permit it in their constitutions, later called by Douglas "the right of popular sovereignty."

Senator Douglas, as chairman of the Committee on Territories, had introduced a bill every year from 1844 to 1854 for the organization of new states in the vast territories west of the Mississippi. In 1850 he had drafted bills that instituted governments in the territories of New Mexico and Utah under domestic laws established by their people. The former permitted slavery, and its Southern popularity led him to extend the principle in 1854 to two new border Northwest territories, Kansas and Nebraska. Unforeseen, bitter, violent physical and political conflict followed between pro- and anti-slavery interests in these territories that spread to the adjacent states and soon involved national participation.

The Kansas-Nebraska Act aroused in the Northern free states uncompromising opposition to the extension of slavery and demand for its eventual national abolition. In the Southern slave states it aroused enthusiastic preparation for the extension and exploitation of slavery. Lincoln's moral indignation and determination to obtain repeal of the Act, as a violation of the intent and law of the Constitution, and restoration of the Missouri Compromise, grew in vigor of conviction, force of argument and popular appeal as he attacked over and over again the principles advanced by Douglas in justification of his philosophy of popular sovereignty.

Lincoln's Argument Against Extension of Slavery

The Democrats of Illinois surprised Senator Douglas when they became aroused to a high pitch of indignation over his instigation of the annulment of the Missouri Compromise. A serious revolt spread rapidly in the ranks of his party and, taking definite form under the merciless logic of Lincoln's denunciation, compelled him to return to Illinois and justify his actions to the people in order to preserve his political influence.

Lincoln made his first speech against the Kansas-Nebraska Act on August 26, 1854, at a Whig meeting in the old courthouse of the little town of Winchester in Scott County. No one saw in this speech indications of the rise of a political personage whose argument would expand in influence with irrepressible social as well as political force. The speech was not published, so its record is based on hearsay. He spoke of the aggressiveness of the slave-holding party and their eagerness to expand into new territory and he condemned the arguments of Douglas, in favor of the Kansas-Nebraska Act, as a violation of the sacred agreement established by the Missouri Compromise. James Miner, who heard the speech, said he was impressed by Lincoln's solemn earnestness and the logic of his argument that the country was facing a great danger of disunion because of its sectionally opposed social systems. Lincoln, still politically unimportant, repeated his arguments in a series of speeches (Carrollton, Bloomington, Springfield, Quincy, Peoria and many other towns) with such definitive clarity and logical force, stirring wit and vigorous emotional appeal, that he soon found himself becoming a powerful personal influence in the political cauldron of the state, as more and more people demanded to hear him.

Makes Personal Appeal to Reject the Nebraska Act

Democrats opposed to the Kansas-Nebraska Act were rebuking their party leaders for urging acceptance of Douglas' new principles; and Lincoln made the most of the opportunity to encourage their opposition and promote acceptance of his own principles.

To J. M. Palmer he wrote (9, 7, 1854):

"You know how anxious I am that the Nebraska measure shall be rebuked and condemned every where. Of course I hope something from your position; yet I do not expect you to do any thing which may be wrong in your own judgment; nor would I have you do anything personally injurious to yourself. You are, and always have been, *honestly,* and *sincerely* a democrat; and I know how painful it must be to an honest sincere man, to be urged by his party to the support of a measure, which on his conscience he believes to be wrong. You have had a severe struggle with yourself, and you have determined *not* to swallow the *wrong.* Is it not just to yourself that you should, in a few public speeches, state your reasons, and thus justify yourself? I wish you would; and yet I say 'don't do it, if you think it will injure you.' You may have given your word to vote for Major Harris, and if so, of course you will stick to it. But allow me to suggest that you should avoid speaking of this; for it will probably induce some of your friends, in like manner, to cast their votes. You understand. And now let me beg your pardon for obtruding this letter upon you, to whom I have ever been opposed in politics. Had your party omitted to make Nebraska a test of party fidelity; you probably would have been the Democratic candidate for congress in the district. You deserved it, and I believe it would have been given to you. In that case I should have been quit, happy that Nebraska was to be rebuked at all events. I still should have voted for the Whig candidate; but I should have made no speeches, written no letters; and you would have been elected by at least a thousand majority."

Here was indeed a moral appeal to an old political opponent to unite with him against the Douglas policy towards slavery. Some professional politicians have condemned this letter as a deliberate expression of indifference to his own party's candidate.

Beginning of Lincoln-Douglas Debates of 1854

It was an expedient custom of that time in Illinois for an audience to call upon additional speakers of different parties to address them after the main speech. Lincoln went to hear Douglas speak at Bloomington (9, 26, 1854), and at the close of the speech he was called to the platform. In high good humor he delighted the crowd with a few impromptu sallies, one of which is given here to show how he reduced the broad and loose arguments of Douglas to ridiculous absurdities.

Senator Douglas had been known in Illinois as "Judge Douglas" ever since he had served a term as judge in the state supreme court, and Lincoln habitually, and perhaps cunningly, continued to address him as "Judge' and not more honorably as 'Senator." The main purpose of Douglas, Lincoln pointed out, was to convince the people of the wisdom of passing the Kansas-Nebraska Act and repealing the Missouri Compromise. He briefly reviewed the history of the latter and showed how Douglas contradicted himself. "After the Compromise had stood a good long time," Lincoln said graciously, "a gentleman, in language much finer and more eloquent than I am capable of constructing, expressed himself in reference to it as follows:"

" 'All the evidence of public opinion at that day seemed to indicate that this Compromise had become canonized in the hearts of the American people as a sacred thing, which no ruthless hand should attempt to disturb.'

"This was certainly very strong, and it was spoken after the Missouri Compromise had been in existence twenty-nine years. Who was it that uttered this statement? What 'Black Republican?' [Immense laughter. A voice "Douglas."] No other than Judge Douglas himself. A more beautiful or more forceful expression was not to be found in the English language."

The turns, in 1854, of the wheels of destiny in human relations excited public demand for debates between Lincoln and Douglas that eventually grew so spirited that they aroused national slavery and antislavery forces among the American people into intensely uncompromising antagonism. We will present in this and the following chapters the decisive steps in development of Lincoln's political philosophy under the proslavery ambitions and relentless criticisms of Douglas.

Aroused as Never Before

"In 1854," Lincoln wrote for Scripps in June, 1860, "His profession had almost superseded the thought of politics in his mind, when the repeal of the Missouri Compromise aroused him as he had never been before.

"In the autumn of that year he took the stump with no broader practical aim or object that [than?] to secure, if possible, the reelection of Hon. Richard Yates to congress. His speeches at once attracted a more marked attention than they had ever before done. As the canvass proceeded, he was drawn to different parts of the State, outside of Mr. Yates' district. He did not abandon the law, but gave his attention, by turns, to that and politics. The State agricultural fair was at Springfield that year, and Douglas was announced to speak there."

Lincoln's curiously unqualified reference to the announcement that Douglas was to speak at the Springfield State Agricultural Fair, obviously in justification of his political principles, expressed a contributing factor in arousing him as he had never been before. He felt himself compelled again, as if by destiny, to refute the political arguments of his old rival. Its due significance is revealed when correlated with the past personal antagonisms that had accumulated in his mind against Douglas and summated with the stirring events of the time. Senator Douglas, now one of the nation's most famous orators and a most influential statesman and politician, enjoyed having his speeches published nationally, whereas Lincoln, politically rejected, and unimportant in Illinois outside of his district, felt unhappily the inferiority given him by local newspapers in rarely publishing more than a passing notice about his speeches.

Lincoln realized that Senator Douglas, following his defeat for the Democratic presidential nomination in 1852, had fathered the Kansas-Nebraska bill with foresight that he would probably obtain

thereby Southern support for the nomination in 1856. This opportunistic exploitation of human rights and the intent of the Constitution and the dogmatic justifications made by Douglas, toward
gaining political dominance in the nation, constituted major sum-
mating excitements for Lincoln.

Joshua Speed (1896) understood best of their contemporaries the
intense personal rivalry inherent in the inborn natures of Lincoln and
Douglas from its beginning when they argued night after night in his
store and courted the same girl. He has compared the tyrannical intolerance of Douglas as a political leader with the kindly patience and
reasonable tolerance of Lincoln, and commented on how Lincoln,
politically unimportant, suffered in humiliation under Senator
Douglas' assumptions of intellectual superiority. Herein we now point
out that Lincoln's lifelong accumulation of resentment against tyrannical injustice of any kind had found at last a real opportunity to assert
itself logically to the limit of his ability in getting satisfaction. Never
again did he relax his critical challenge of his ambitious rival's ambivalent
demagoguery.

In the speech at the Springfield State Fair (10, 3, 1854), mentioned
by Lincoln in his Scripps letter as the turning point in his political
career, Douglas gave a vigorous oration in which he defended the
Kansas-Nebraska Act at great length. Lincoln heard the argument
and announced to the audience that he would answer it the next day.
Whereupon Douglas promptly countered with a declaration that he
would hear Lincoln and reply after his speech. This spontaneous debate
caused a great furor among Illinois people for it meant that mighty
Senator Stephen A. Douglas now thought enough of lowly Mr. Abraham
Lincoln's ideas to answer them. Overnight Lincoln found that he was
becoming a vile anathema on some editorial pages and on others an
ascending star. He spoke for three hours, repeating with elaboration
largely what he had said previously in Bloomington, and Senator
Douglas replied for two hours, "pounding him to a pumice with his
terrible war club of retort and argument," as one Democratic newspaper reported.

Two weeks later Douglas and Lincoln repeated practically the same
speeches at Peoria. Since Lincoln's speech was reported more completely
than any other of his in this period we present it here in full, in order
to follow the development of his personal attitude and political views
through this time. In his speeches in 1854, probably, he repeated the
same points of argument in very much the same manner, although no
complete records exist for this general estimation. It would be only natural under the same political conditions to repeat the same facts and
interpretations although in somewhat different ways to different audiences. The Peoria speech has been held by many to have been the most
spontaneously eloquent of Lincoln's career up to this time. It certainly
was one of the most decisive in its political consequences. He took great

care to present the important historical steps in the origin and progress of slavery in the United States and his interpretations of their political meaning. He also made critical rebuttals against the reasons given by Douglas in justification of his new policies. It is necessary in order to understand the development of Lincoln's political philosophy and the national conditions leading up to the crisis of 1854, and eventually to the Civil War, to read this speech entirely. It is quoted as presented in the *Collected Works,* but I have divided it into sections and inserted captions and brief remarks in order to direct attention to the points that eventually assumed most public importance in their later debates.

Peoria Debate of 1854

Douglas addressed a large and enthusiastic audience at Peoria on October 16, 1854. When he closed he announced that Lincoln was by agreement to speak after him. The crowd gave Douglas mighty cheers and the band played a stirring air. When the crowd called for Lincoln he took the stand and, as reported in the *Illinois Journal,* he said:

"I do not arise to speak now, if I can stipulate with the audience to meet me here at half past 6 or 7 o'clock. It is now several minutes past five, and Judge Douglas has spoken over three hours. If you will hear me at all, I wish you would hear me thro'. It will take me as long as it has taken him. That will carry us beyond eight o'clock tonight. Now every one of you who can remain that long, can just as well get his supper, meet me at seven, and remain one hour or two later. The Judge has already informed you that he is to have an hour to reply to me. I doubt not you have been a little surprised to learn that I have consented to give one of his high reputation and known ability, this advantage of me. Indeed, my consenting to it, though reluctant, was not wholly unselfish, for I suspected if it were understood, that the Judge was entirely done, you democrats would leave, and not hear me; but by giving him the close, I felt confident you would stay for the fun of hearing him skin me."

At seven o'clock, P.M., the audience reassembled and Mr. Lincoln spoke substantially as follows.

"The repeal of the Missouri Compromise, and the propriety of its restoration, constitute the subject of what I am about to say.

"As I desire to present my own connected view of this subject, my remarks will not be, specifically, an answer to Judge Douglas; yet, as I proceed, the main points he has presented will arise, and will receive such respectful attention as I may be able to give them.

"I wish further to say that I do not propose to question the patriotism, or to assail the motives of any man, or class of men; but rather to strictly confine myself to the naked merits of the question.

"I also wish to be no less than National in all the positions I may take; and wherever I take ground which others have thought, or may think, narrow, sectional and dangerous to the Union, I hope to give a reason, which will appear sufficient, at least to some, why I think differently.

"And, as this subject is no other, than part and parcel of the larger general question of domestic-slavery, I wish to MAKE and to KEEP the distinction between the EXISTING institution, and the EXTENSION of it, so broad, and so clear, that no honest man can misunderstand me, and no dishonest one, successfully misrepresent me."

The impartiality of Lincoln's review of the history of congressional legislation on slavery shows how conscientiously he analyzed each point of issue and depended entirely on the moral force of equal legal rights of free people, as the foundation of our constitutional government, to overcome the injustice of slavery. It is remarkable that in the long series of critical speeches and debates on the policies of Douglas, every major point that Lincoln made eventually became a critical factor in the national issue over slavery.

Missouri Compromise

"In order to [get] a clear understanding of what the Missouri Compromise is, a short history of the preceding kindred subjects will perhaps be proper. When we established our independence we did not own, or claim, the country to which this compromise applies. Indeed, strictly speaking, the confederacy then owned no country at all; the States respectively owned the country within their limits; and some of them owned territory beyond their strict State limits. Virginia thus owned the North-Western territory—the country out of which the principal part of Ohio, all Indiana, all Illinois, all Michigan and all Wisconsin, have since been formed. She also owned (perhaps within her limits) what has since been formed into the State of Kentucky. North Carolina thus owned what is now the State of Tennessee; and South Carolina and Georgia, in separate parts, owned what are now Mississippi and Alabama. Connecticut, I think, owned the little remaining part of Ohio—being the same where they now send Giddings to Congress, and beat all creation at making cheese. These territories, together with the States themselves, constituted all the country over which the confederacy then claimed any sort of jurisdiction. We were then living under the Articles of Confederation, which were superseded by the Constitution several years afterwards. The question of ceding these territories to the general government was set on foot. Mr. Jefferson, the author of the Declaration of Independence, and otherwise a chief actor in the revolution; then a delegate in Congress; afterwards twice President; who was, is, and perhaps will continue to be, the most distinguished politician in our history; a Virginian by birth and continued residence, and withal, a slave-holder; conceived the idea of taking that occasion, to prevent slavery ever going into the north-western territory. He prevailed on the Virginia Legislature to adopt his views, and to cede the territory, making the prohibition of slavery therein, a condition of the deed. Congress accepted the cession, with the condition; and the first Ordinance (which acts of Congress were then called) for the government of the territory, provided that slavery should never be permitted therein. This is the famed ordinance of '87 so often spoken of. Thenceforward for sixty-one years, and until in 1848, the last scrap of this territory came into the Union as the State of Wisconsin, all parties acted in quiet obedience to this ordinance. It is now what Jefferson foresaw and intended—the happy home of teeming millions of free, white, prosperous people, and no slave amongst them.

"Thus, with the author of the declaration of Independence, the policy of prohibiting slavery in new territory originated. Thus, away back of the constitution, in the pure fresh, free breath of the revolution, the State of Virginia, and the National congress put that policy in practise. Thus, through sixty odd of the best years of the republic did that policy steadily work to its great and beneficient end. And thus, in those five states, and five millions of free, enterprising people, we have before us the rich fruits of this policy. But *now* new light breaks upon us. Now congress declares this ought never have been; and the like of it, must never be again. The sacred right of self-government is grossly violated by it! We even find some men, who drew their first breath, and every breath of their lives, under this very restriction, now live in dread of absolute suffocation, if they should be restricted in the 'sacred right' of taking slaves to Nebraska. That *perfect* liberty they sigh for—the liberty of making slaves of other people—Jefferson never thought of; their own father never thought of; they never thought of themselves a year ago. How fortunate for them, they did not sooner become sensible of their great misery! Oh, how difficult it is to treat with respect, such assaults upon all we have ever really held sacred.

"But to return to history. In 1803 we purchased what was then called Louisiana, of France. It included the now states of Louisiana, Arkansas, Missouri, and Iowa; also the territory of Minnesota, and the present bone of contention, Kansas and Nebraska. Slavery already existed among the French at New Orleans; and, to some extent, at St. Louis. In 1812 Louisiana came into the Union as a slave state, without controversy. In 1818, or '19, Missouri showed signs of a wish to come in with slavery. This was resisted by northern members of Congress; and thus began the first great slavery agitation in the Nation. This controversy lasted several months; and became very angry and exciting; the House of Representatives voting steadily for the prohibition of slavery in Missouri, and the Senate voting as steadily against it. Threats of breaking up the Union were freely made; and the ablest public men of the day became seriously alarmed. At length a compromise was made, in which, like in all compromises, both sides yielded something. It was a law passed on the 6th day of March, 1820, providing that Missouri might come into the Union *with* slavery, but that in all the remaining part of the territory purchased of France, which lies north of 36 degrees and 30 minutes north latitude, slavery should never be permitted. This provision of law, *is the Missouri Compromise.* In excluding slavery North of the line, the same language is employed as in the Ordinance of '87. It directly applied to Iowa, Minnesota and to the present bone of contention, Kansas and Nebraska. Whether there should or should not, be slavery south of that line, nothing was said in the law; but Arkansas constituted the principle remaining part, south of the line; and it has since been admitted as a slave state without serious controversy. More recently, Iowa, north of the line, came in as a free state without controversy. Still later, Minnesota, north of the line, had a territorial organization without controversy. Texas principally south of the line, and West of Arkansas; though originally within the purchase of France, had, in 1819, been traded off to Spain, in our treaty for the acquisition of Florida. It had thus become a part of Mexico. Mexico revolutionized and became independent of Spain. American citizens began settling rapidly, with their slaves in the southern part of Texas. Soon they revolutionized against Mexico, and established an independent government of their own, adopting a constitution, with slavery, strongly resembling the constitutions of our slave states. By still another rapid move, Texas, claiming a boundary much farther West, than when we parted with her in 1819, was brought back to the United States, and admitted into the Union as a slave state. There then was little or no settlement in the northern part of Texas, a considerable portion of which lay north of the Missouri line; and in the resolution admitting her into the Union, the Missouri restriction was expressly extended westward across her territory. This was in 1845 only nine years ago."

Quotes Douglas

"Thus originated the Missouri Compromise; and thus has it been respected down to 1845. And even four years later, in 1849, our distinguished Senator, in a public address, held the following language in relation to it:

" 'The Missouri Compromise had been in practical operation for about a quarter of a century, and had received the sanction and approbation of men of all parties in every section of the Union. It had allayed all sectional jealousies and irritations growing out of this vexed question, and harmonized and tranquilized the whole country. It had given to Henry Clay, as its prominent champion, the proud sobriquet of the *'Great Pacificator'* and by that title and for that service, his political friends had repeatedly appealed to the people to rally under his standard, as a presidential candidate, as the man who had exhibited the patriotism and the power to suppress, an unholy and treasonable agitation, and preserve the Union. He was not aware that any man or any party from any section of the Union, had urged as an objection to Mr. Clay, that he was the great champion of the Missouri Compromise. On the contrary, the effort was made by the opponents of Mr. Clay, to prove that he was not entitled to the exclusive merit of that great patriotic measure, and that the honor was equally due to others as well as to him, for securing its adoption—that it had its origin in the hearts of all patriotic men, who desired to preserve and perpetuate the blessings of our glorious Union—an origin akin that of the constitution of the United States, conceived in the same spirit of fraternal affection, and calculated to remove forever, the only danger, which seemed to threaten, at some distant day, to sever the social bond of union. All the evidences of public opinion at that day, seemed to indicate that this Compromise had been canonized in the hearts of the American people, as a sacred thing which no ruthless hand would ever be reckless enough to disturb.'

"I do not read this extract to involve Judge Douglas in an inconsistency. If he afterwards thought he had been wrong, it was right for him to change. I bring this forward merely to show the high estimate placed on the Missouri Compromise by all parties up to so late as the year 1849."

Wilmot Proviso

"But, going back a little, in point of time, our war with Mexico broke out in 1846. When Congress was adjourning that session, President Polk asked them to place two millions of dollars under his control to be used by him in the recess, if found practicable and expedient in negotiating a treaty of peace with Mexico, and acquiring some part of her territory. A bill was duly got up, for the purpose, and was progressing swimmingly, in the House of Representatives, when a member by the name of David Wilmot, a democrat from Pennsylvania, moved as an amendment 'Provided that in any territory thus acquired there shall never be slavery.'

"This is the origin of the far-famed 'Wilmot Proviso.' It created a great flutter; but it stuck like wax, was voted into the bill, and the bill passed with it through the House. The Senate, however, adjourned without final action on it and so both appropriation and proviso were lost, for the time. The war continued, and at the next session, the president renewed his request for the appropriation, enlarging the amount, I think, to three million. Again came the proviso; and defeated the measure. Congress adjourned again, and the war went on. In Dec., 1847, the new congress assembled. I was in the lower House that term. The 'Wilmot Proviso' or the principle of it, was constantly coming up in some shape or other, and I think I may venture to say I voted for it at least forty times; during the short term I was there. The Senate, however, held it in check, and it never became law. In the spring of 1848 a treaty of peace was made with Mexico; by which we obtained that portion of her country which now constitutes the territories of New Mexico and Utah, and the now state of California. By this treaty the Wilmot Proviso was defeated, as so far as it was intended to be, a condition of the acquisition of territory. Its friends, however, were still determined to find some way to restrain slavery from getting into the new country."

Compromise of 1850

"This new acquisition lay directly West of our old purchase from France, and extended west to the Pacific Ocean—and was so situated that if the Missouri line should be extended straight West, the new country would be divided by such extended line, leaving some North and some South of it. On Judge Douglas' motion a bill, or provision of a bill, passed the Senate to so extend the Missouri line. The Proviso men in the House, including myself, voted it down, because by implication, it gave up the Southern part to slavery, while we were bent on having it *all* free.

"In the fall of 1848, the gold mines were discovered in California. This attracted people to it with unprecedented rapidity, so that on, or soon after, the meeting of the new Congress in Dec., 1849, she already had a population of nearly a hundred thousand, had called a convention, formed a state constitution, excluding slavery, and was knocking for admission into the Union. The Proviso men, of course were for letting her in, but the Senate, always true to the other side would not consent to her admission. And there California stood, kept *out* of the Union, because she would not let slavery *into* her borders. Under all the circumstances perhaps this was not wrong. There were other points of dispute, connected with the general question of slavery, which equally needed adjustment. The South clamored for a more efficient fugitive slave law. The North clamored for the abolition of a peculiar species of slave trade in the District of Columbia, in connection with which, in view from the windows of the capitol, a sort of negro-livery stable, where droves of negroes were collected, temporarily kept, and finally taken to the Southern markets, precisely like droves of horses, had been openly maintained for fifty years. Utah and New Mexico needed territorial governments; and whether slavery should or should not be prohibited within them, was another question. The indefinite Western boundary of Texas was to be settled. She was received a slave state; and consequently the farther West the slavery men could push her boundary, the more slave country they secured. And the farther East the slavery opponents could thrust the boundary back, the less slave ground was secured. Thus this was just as clearly a slavery question as any of the others.

"These points all needed adjustment; and they were all held up, perhaps wisely to make them help to adjust one another. The Union, now, as in 1820, was thought to be in danger; and devotion to the Union rightfully inclined men to yield somewhat, in points where nothing else could have so inclined them. A compromise was finally effected. The South got their new fugitive-slave law; and the North got California (the far best part of our acquisition from Mexico) as a free State. The South got a provision that New Mexico and Utah, *when admitted as States,* may come in *with* or *without* slavery as they may then choose; and the North got slave-trade abolished in the District of Columbia. The North got the western boundary of Texas, thence farther back eastward than the south desired; but, in turn, they gave Texas ten millions of dollars, with which to pay her old debts. This is the Compromise of 1850."

Repeal of the Missouri Compromise

"Preceding the Presidential election of 1852, each of the great political parties, democrats and whigs, met in convention, and adopted resolutions endorsing the compromise of '50; as a 'finality,' a final settlement, so far as these parties could make it so, of all slavery agitation. Previous to this, in 1851, the Illinois Legislature had indorsed it.

"During this long period of time Nebraska had remained, substantially an uninhabited country, but now emigration to, and settlement within it began to take place. It is about one third as large as the present United States, and its importance so long overlooked, begins to come into view. The restriction of slavery by the Missouri Compromise directly applies to it; in fact, was first made, and has since been maintained expressly for it. In 1853, a bill to give it a territorial government passed the House of Representatives, and, in the hands of Judge Douglas, failed of passing the Senate only for want of time. This bill contained no repeal of the Missouri Compromise. Indeed, when it was assailed because it did not contain such repeal, Judge Douglas defended it in its existing form. On

January 4th, 1854, Judge Douglas introduces a new bill to give Nebraska territorial government. He accompanies this bill with a report, in which last, he expressly recommends that the Missouri Compromise shall neither be affirmed nor repealed.

"Before long the bill is so modified as to make two territories instead of one; calling the Southern one Kansas.

"Also, about a month after the introduction of the bill, on the judge's own motion, it is so amended as to declare the Missouri Compromise inoperative and void; and, substantially, that the People who may go and settle there may establish slavery, or exclude it, as they may see fit. In this shape the bill passed both branches of congress, and became a law.

"This is the *repeal* of the Missouri Compromise. The foregoing history may not be precisely accurate in every particular; but I am sure it is sufficiently so, for all the uses I shall attempt to make of it, and in it, we have before us, the chief material enabling us to correctly judge whether the repeal of the Missouri Compromise is right or wrong."

"Douglas' Covert Real Zeal for Slavery I Cannot but Hate"

"I think, and shall try to show, that it is wrong; wrong in its direct effect, letting slavery into Kansas and Nebraska—and wrong in its prospective principle, allowing it to spread to every other part of the wide world, where men can be found inclined to take it.

"This *declared* indifference, but as I must think, covert *real* zeal for the spread of slavery, I can not but hate. I hate it because of the monstrous injustice of slavery itself. I hate it because it deprives our republican example of its just influence in the world—enables the enemies of free institutions, with plausibility, to taunt us as hypocrites—causes the real friends of freedom to doubt our sincerity, and especially because it forces so many really good men amongst ourselves into an open war with the very fundamental principles of civil liberty—criticising the Declaration of Independence, and insisting that there is no right principle of action but *self-interest*."

"I Have No Prejudice Against Southern People"

. . . "They are just what we would be in their situation. If slavery did not now exist amongst them, they would not introduce it. If it did now exist amongst us, we should not instantly give it up. This I believe of the masses of the north and south. Doubtless there are individuals, on both sides, who would not hold slaves under any circumstances; and others who would gladly introduce slavery anew, if it were out of existence. We know that some southern men do free their slaves, go north, and become tip-top abolitionists, while some northern ones go south and become most cruel slave-masters.

"When southern people tell us they are no more responsible for the origin of slavery, than we; I acknowledge the fact. When it is said that the institution exists; and that it is very difficult to get rid of it, in any satisfactory way, I can understand and appreciate the saying. I surely will not blame them for not doing what I should not know how to do myself. If all earthly power were given me, I should not know what to do, as to the existing institution. My first impulse would be to free all the slaves, and send them to Liberia,—to their native land. But a moment's reflection would convince me, that whatever of high hope, (as I think there is) there may be in this, in the long run, its sudden execution is impossible. If they were all landed there in a day, they would all perish in the next ten days; and there are not surplus shipping and surplus money enough in the world to carry them there in many times ten days. What then? Free them all, and keep them among us as underlings? Is it quite certain that this betters their condition? I think I would not hold one in slavery, at any rate; yet the point is not clear enough for me to denounce people upon. What next? Free them, and make them politically and socially, our equals? My own feelings will not admit of this; and if mine would, we well know that those of the great mass of white people will not. Whether this feeling accords with justice and sound judgment, is not the sole question, if indeed, it is any part of it. A universal feeling, whether well or ill-founded, cannot be safely disregarded. We can not, then, make them equals. It does seem to me that systems of gradual emancipation might be adopted; but for their tardiness in this, I will not undertake to judge our brethren of the south.

"When they remind us of their constitutional rights, I acknowledge them, not grudgingly, but fully, and fairly; and I would give them any legislation for the reclaiming of their fugitives, which should not, in its stringency, be more likely to carry a free man into slavery, than our ordinary criminal laws are to hang an innocent one.

"But all this; to my judgment, furnishes no more excuse for permitting slavery to go into our own free territory, than it would for reviving the African slave trade by law. The law which forbids the bringing of slaves *from* Africa, and that which has so long forbid the taking of them *to* Nebraska, can hardly be distinguished on any moral principle; and the repeal of the former could find quite as plausible excuses as that of the latter."

Argument Against Repeal of the Missouri Comprise

Lincoln had presented his own view of the course of slavery in the United States so that 'no honest man could misunderstand him and no dishonest one successfully misrepresent him.' He then proceeded methodically to present "the arguments by which the repeal of the Missouri Compromise is sought to be justified." The modesty and reasonableness of his method stands in striking contrast to the recklessly bold, dogmatic assertions of Douglas. Lincoln believed that if the Missouri Compromise was restored the Union would be safe from factional dissension, but if it was not restored the moral and economic division of the nation into two sections of pro- and antislavery states, extending from the Atlantic to the Pacific, threatened disunion. As we follow his arguments, we become impressed with the potentiality of his views for winning converts to his philosophy of equal constitutional rights for all men, to be worked out gradually upon changes in public sentiment and not by congressional action.

In reply to the claim of Douglas that the public had demanded a repeal of the Missouri Compromise Lincoln pointed out that the State of Iowa and territory of Minnesota had been organized out of the Nebraska area without repeal "and this in the hands of the same men who are now champions of repeal."

"The arguments by which the repeal of the Missouri Compromise is sought to be justified, are these:

"First, that the Nebraska country needed a territorial government.

"Second, that in various ways, the public had repudiated it, and demanded the repeal; and therefore should not complain of it.

"And lastly, that the repeal establishes a principle, which is intrinsically right.

"I will attempt an answer to each of them in turn.

"First, then, if that country was in need of a territorial organization, could it not have had it as well without as with the repeal?" . . .

"Now I deny that the public ever demanded any such thing—ever repudiated the Missouri Compromise—ever commanded its repeal. I deny it, and I call for the proof. It is not contended, I believe, that any such command has ever been given in express terms. It is only said that it was done *in principle.* The support of the Wilmot Proviso, is the first fact mentioned, to prove that the Missouri restriction was repudiated in *principle,* and the second is, the refusal to extend the Missouri line over the country as acquired from Mexico. These are enough alike to be treated together. The one was to exclude the chances of slavery from the *whole* new acquisition by the lump; and the other was to reject a division of it, by which one *half* was to be given up to those chances. Now whether this was a repudiation of the Missouri line in *principle,* depends upon whether the Missouri law contained any *principle* requiring the line to be extended over the country acquired from Mexico. I contend it did not. I insist that it contained no general principle, but that it was, in every sense, specific. That its terms limit it to the country purchased from France, is undenied and undeniable. It could have no principle beyond the intention of those who made it. They did not intend to extend the line to the country which they did not own. If they intended to extend it, in the event of acquiring additional territory, why did they not say so? It was just as easy to say, that 'in all the country west of the Mississippi, which we now own, *or may hereafter acquire* there shall never be slavery,' as to say, what they did say; and they would have said it if they had meant it. An intention to extend the law is not only not mentioned in the law, but is not mentioned in any contemporaneous history. Both the law itself, and the history of the times are a blank as to any *principle* of extension; and by neither the known rules for constructing statutes and contracts, nor by common sense, can any such *principle* be inferred.

"Another fact showing the *specific* character of the Missouri law—showing that it intended no more than it expressed—showing that the line was not intended as a universal dividing line between free and slave territory, present and prospective—north of which slavery could never go—is the fact that by that very law, Missouri came in as a slave state, *north* of that line. If that law contained any other prospective *principle,* the whole law must be looked to in order to ascertain what the *principle* was. And by this rule, the south could fairly contend that inasmuch as they got one slave state north of the line at the inception of the law, they have the right to have another given them *north* of it occasionally—now and then in the indefinite westward extension of the line. This demonstrates the absurdity of attempting to deduce a prospective *principle* from the Missouri Compromise line.

"When we voted for the Wilmot Proviso we voted to keep slavery *out* of the whole Missouri [Mexican?] acquisition; and little did we think we were thereby voting, to let it *into* Nebraska, laying several hundred miles distant. When we voted against extending the Missouri line, little did we think we were voting to destroy the old line, then of near thirty years standing. To argue that we thus repudiated the Missouri Compromise is no less absurd than it would be to argue that because we have, so far, forborne to acquire Cuba, we have thereby, *in principle,* repudiated our former acquisitions, and determined to throw them out of the Union! No less absurd than it would be to say that because I have refused to build an addition to my house, I thereby have decided to destroy the existing house! . . . The most conclusive argument, however, that, while voting for the Wilmot proviso, and while voting against the EXTENSION of the Missouri line, we never thought of disturbing the original Missouri Compromise, is found in the facts, that there was, then, and still is, an unorganized tract of fine territory, nearly as large as the state of Missouri, lying immediately west of Arkansas, and south of the Missouri Compromise line; and that we never attempted to prohibit slavery as to it. I wish particular attention to this. It adjoins the original Missouri Compromise line, by its northern boundary; and consequently is part of the country, into which, by implication, slavery was permitted to go, by that compromise. There it has lain open ever since, and there it still lies. And yet no effort has been made at any time to wrest it from the south. In all our struggles to prohibit slavery within our Mexican acquisitions, we never so much as lifted a finger to prohibit it, as to this tract. Is not this entirely conclusive that at all times, we have held the Missouri Compromise a sacred thing; even when against ourselves as well as when for us?

"Senator Douglas sometimes says the Missouri line itself was, *in principle,* only an extension of the line of the ordinance of '87—that is to say, an extension of the Ohio river. I think this is weak enough on its face. I will remark, however that, as a glance at the map will show, the Missouri line is a long way farther South than the Ohio; and that if our Senator, in proposing his extension has stuck to the *principle* of jogging southward, perhaps it might not have been voted down so readily.

"But next it is said that the compromises of '50 and the ratification of them by both political parties, in '52, established a *new principle,* which required the repeal of the Missouri Compromise. This again I deny. I deny it, and demand the proof. I have already stated fully what the compromises of '50 are. That particular part of those measures, for which the virtual repeal of the Missouri compromise is sought to be inferred (for it is admitted they contain nothing about it, in express terms) is the provision in the Utah and New Mexico laws, which permits them when they seek admission into the Union as States, to come in with or without slavery as they shall then see fit. Now I insist this provision was made for Utah and

New Mexico, and for no other place whatever. It had no more direct reference to Nebraska than it had to the territories of the moon. But, say they, it had reference to Nebraska, *in principle.* Let us see. The North consented to this provision, not because they considered it right in itself; but because they were compensated—paid for it. They, at the same time, got California into the Union as a free State. This was far the best part of all they had struggled for by the Wilmot Proviso. They also got the area of slavery somewhat narrowed in the settlement of the boundary of Texas. Also, they got the slave trade abolished in the District of Columbia. For all these desirable objects the North could ' afford to yield something; and they did yield to the South the Utah and New Mexico provision. I do not mean that the whole North, or even a majority yielded, when the law passed; but enough yielded, when added to the vote of the South, to carry the measure. Now can it be pretended that the *principle* of this arrangement requires us to permit the same provision to be applied to Nebraska, *without any equivalent at all?* Give us another free State; press the boundary of Texas still further back, give us another step toward the destruction of slavery in the District, and you present us a similar case. But ask us not to repeat, for nothing, what you paid for in the first instance. If you wish the thing again, pay again. That is the *principle* of the compromises of '50, if indeed they had any principles beyond their specific terms—it was the system of equivalents.

"Again, if Congress, at that time, intended that all future territories should, when admitted as States, come in with or without slavery, at their own option, why did it not say so? With such an universal provision, all know the bills could not have passed. Did they then—could they—establish a *principle* contrary to their own intention? Still further, if they intended to establish the principle that wherever Congress had control, it should be left to the people to do as they thought fit with slavery why did they not authorize the people of the District of Columbia at their adoption to abolish slavery within these limits? I personally know that this has not been left undone, because it was unthought of. It was frequently spoken of by members of Congress and by citizens of Washington six years ago; and I heard no one express a doubt that a system of gradual emancipation, with compensation to owners, would meet the approbation of a large majority of the white people of the District. But without the action of Congress they could say nothing; and Congress said "no." In the measures of 1850 Congress had the subject of slavery in the District expressly in hand. If they were then establishing the *principle* of allowing the people to do as they please with slavery, why did they not apply the *principle* to that people?

"Again, it is claimed that by the Resolutions of the Illinois Legislature, passed in 1851, the repeal of the Missouri Compromise was demanded. This I deny also. Whatever may be worked out by a criticism of the language of those resolutions, the people have never understood them· as being any more than an endorsement of the compromises of 1850; and a release of our Senators from voting for the Wilmot Proviso. The whole people are living witnesses, that this only, was their view. Finally, it is asked 'If we did not mean to apply the Utah and New Mexico provision, to all future territories, what did we mean, when we, in 1852, endorsed the compromises of '50?' "

Accepts Fugitive Slave Law

"For myself, I can answer this question most easily. I meant not to ask a repeal, or modification of the fugitive slave law. I meant not to ask for the abolition of slavery in the District of Columbia. I meant not to resist the admission of Utah and New Mexico, even should they ask to come in as slave States. I meant nothing about additional territories, because, as I understood, we then had no territory whose character as to slavery was not already settled. As to Nebraska, I regarded its character as being fixed, by the Missouri compromise, for thirty years—as unalterably fixed as that of my own home in Illinois. As to new acquisitions I said 'sufficient unto the day is the evil thereof.' When we make new acquaintances, [acquisitions?] we will, as heretofore, try to manage them somehow. That is my answer. That is what I meant and said; and I appeal to the people to say, each to himself, whether that was not also the universal meaning of the free States.

"And now, in turn, let me ask a few questions. If by any, or all these matters, the repeal of the Missouri Compromise was commanded, why was not the command sooner obeyed? Why was the repeal omitted in the Nebraska bill of 1853? Why was it omitted in the original bill of 1854? Why, in the accompanying report, was such a repeal characterized as a *departure* from the course pursued in 1850? and its continued omission recommended?

"I am aware Judge Douglas now argues that the subsequent express repeal is no substantial alteration of the bill. This argument seems wonderful to me. It is as if one should argue that white and black are not different. He admits, however, that there is a literal change in the bill; and that he made the change in deference to other Senators, who would not support the bill without. This proves that those other Senators thought the change a substantial one; and that the Judge thought their opinions worth deferring to. His own opinions, therefore, seem not to rest on a very firm basis even in his own mind—and I suppose the world believes, and will continue to believe, that precisely on the substance of that change this whole agitation has arisen.

"I conclude then, that the public never demanded the repeal of the Missouri Compromise."

Questions Intrinsic Right of Repeal of Missouri Compromise

"I now come to consider whether the repeal, with its avowed principle, is intrinsically right. I insist that it is not. Take the particular case. A controversy had arisen between the advocates and opponents of slavery, in relation to its establishment within the country we had purchased of France. The southern, and then best part of the purchase, was already in as a slave State. The controversy was settled by also letting Missouri in as a slave State; but with the agreement that within all the remaining part of the purchase, North of a certain line, there should never be slavery. As to what was to be done with the remaining part south of the line, nothing was said; but perhaps the fair implication was, that it should come in with slavery if it should so choose. The southern part, except a portion heretofore mentioned, afterwards did come in with slavery, as the State of Arkansas.

All these many years since 1820, the Northern part had remained a wilderness. At length settlements began in it also. In due course, Iowa, came in as a free State, and Minnesota was given territorial government, without removing the slavery restriction. Finally the sole remaining part, North of the line, Kansas and Nebraska, was to be organized; and it is proposed, and carried, to blot out the old dividing line of thirty-four years standing, and to open the whole of that country to the introduction of slavery. Now, this, to my mind, is manifestly unjust. After an angry and dangerous controversy, the parties made friends by dividing the bone of contention. The one party first appropriates her own share, beyond all power to be disturbed in the possession of it; and then seizes the share of the other party. It is as if two starving men had divided their only loaf; the one had hastily swallowed his half; and then grabbed the other half just as he was putting it to his mouth!"

Palliative Lullabies

"Let me here drop the main argument, to notice what I consider rather an inferior matter. It is argued that slavery will not go to Kansas and Nebraska, *in any event*. This is *palliation*—a *lullaby*. I have some hope that it will not; but let us not be too confident. As to climate, a glance at the map shows that there are five slave States——Delaware, Maryland, Virginia, Kentucky, and Missouri—and also the District of Columbia, all north of the Missouri compromise line. The census returns of 1850 show that, within these, there are 867,276 slaves—being more than one-fourth of all the slaves in the nation.

"It is not climate, then that will keep slavery out of these territories. Is there any thing in the peculiar nature of the country? Missouri adjoins these territories, by her entire western boundary, and slavery is already within every one of her western counties. I have even heard it said that there are more slaves, in proportion to whites, in the north western county of Missouri, than within any county of the State. Slavery pressed entirely up to the old western boundary of the State, and when, rather recently, a part of that boundary, at the north-west was moved out a little farther west, slavery followed on quite up to the new line. Now, when the restriction is removed, what is to prevent it from going still further? Climate will not. No peculiarity of the country will—nothing in *nature* will. Will the disposition of the people prevent it? Those nearest the scene, are all in favor of the extension. The yankees, who are opposed to it may be more numerous; but in military phrase, the battle-field is too far from *their* base of operations.

"But it is said, there now is *no* law in Nebraska on the subject of slavery; and that, in such case, taking a slave there, operates his freedom. This *is* good book-law; but it is not the rule of actual practice. Wherever slavery is, it has been first introduced without law. The oldest laws we find concerning it, are not laws introducing it; but *regulating* it, as an already existing thing. A white man takes his slave to Nebraska now; who will inform the negro that he is free? Who will take him before court to test the question of his fredom? In ignorance of his legal emancipation, he is kept chopping, splitting and plowing. Others are brought, and move on in the same track. At last, if ever the time for voting comes, on the question of slavery, the institution already in fact exists in the country, and cannot well be removed. The fact of its presence, and the difficulty of its removal will carry the vote in its favor. Keep it out until a vote is taken, and a vote in favor of it, can not be got in any population of forty thousand, on earth, who have been drawn together by the ordinary motives of emigration and settlement. To get slaves into the country simultaneously with the whites, in the incipient stages of settlement, is the precise stake played for, and won in this Nebraska measure.

"The question is asked us, 'If the slaves will go in, notwithstanding the general principle of law liberates them, why would they not equally go in against positive statute law?—go in, even if the Missouri restriction were maintained?' I answer, because it takes a much bolder man to venture in, with his property, in the latter case, than in the former—because the positive congressional enactment is known to, and respected by all, or nearly all; whereas the negative principle that *no* law is free law, is not much known except among lawyers. We have some experience of this practical difference. In spite of the Ordinance of '87, a few negroes were brought into Illinois, and held in a state of quasi slavery; not enough, however to carry a vote of the people in favor of the institution when they came to form a constitution. But in the adjoining Missouri country, where there was no ordinance of '87—was no restriction—they were carried ten times, nay a hundred times, as fast, and actually made a slave State. This is fact—naked fact.

"Another LULLABY argument is, that taking slaves to new countries does not increase their number—does not make any one slave who otherwise would be free. There is some truth in this, and I am glad of it, but it [is] not WHOLLY true. The African slave trade is not yet effectually suppressed; and if we make a reasonable deduction for the white people amongst us, who are foreigners, and the descendants of foreigners, arriving here since 1808, we shall find the increase of the black population out-running that of the white, to an extent unaccountable, except by supposing that some of them too, have been coming from Africa. If this be so, the opening of new countries to the institution, increases the demand for, and augments the price of slaves, and so does, in fact, makes slaves of freemen by causing them to be brought from Africa, and sold into bondage.

"But, however this may be, we know the opening of new countries to slavery, tends to the perpetuation of the institution, and so does KEEP men in slavery who otherwise would be free. This result we do not FEEL like favoring, and we are under no legal obligation to suppress our feelings in this respect.

"Equal justice to the south, it is said, requires us to consent to the extending of slavery to new countries. That is to say, inasmuch as you do not object to my taking my hog to Nebraska, therefore I must not object to you taking your slave. Now, I admit this is perfectly logical, if there is no difference between hogs and negroes. But while you thus require me to deny the humanity of the negro, I wish to ask whether you of the south yourselves, have ever been willing to do so much? It is kindly provided that of all those who come into the world, only a small percentage are natural tyrants. That percentage is no larger in the slave South than in the free. The great majority, south as well as north, have human sympathies, of which they can no more divest themselves than they can of their sensibility to physical pain. These sympathies in the bosoms of the southern people manifest in many ways, their sense of the wrong of slavery, and their consciousness that, after all, there is humanity in the negro. If they deny this, let me address them a few plain questions. In 1820 you joined the north, almost unanimously, in declaring the African slave trade piracy, and in annexing to it the punishment of death. Why did you do this? If you did not feel that it was wrong, why did you join in providing that men should be hung for it? The practice was no more than bringing wild negroes from Africa, to sell to such as would buy them. But you never thought of hanging men for catching and selling wild horses, wild buffaloes or wild bears."

Abhorrent Slave-Traders

Lincoln's scathing denunciation of the slave-trader provoked, no doubt, bitter personal resentment against himself among the most radical, selfish, violent-tempered people in the South, regardless later of his appeal to reason. They formed the nucleus of an uncompromising anti-Lincoln sentiment that was to inflame the disunion movement six years later upon his election as President.

"Again, you have amongst you, a sneaking individual, of the class of native tyrants, known as the 'SLAVE-DEALER.' He watches your necessities, and crawls up to buy your slave, at a speculating price. If you cannot help it, you sell to him; but if you can help it, you drive him from your door. You despise him utterly. You do not recognize him as a friend, or even as an honest man. Your children must not play with his; they may rollick freely with the little negroes, but not with the 'slave-dealers' children. If you are obliged to deal with him, you try to get through the job without so much as touching him. It is common with you to join hands with the men you meet; but with the slave dealer you avoid the ceremony—instinctively shrinking from the snaky contact. If he grows rich and retires from business, you still remember him, and still keep up the ban of non-intercourse upon him and his family. Now why is this? You do not treat the man who deals in corn, cattle or tobacco.

"And yet again; there are in the United States and territories, including the District of Columbia, 433,643 free blacks. At $500 per head they are worth over two hundred millions of dollars. How comes this vast amount of property to be running about without owners? We do not see free horses or free cattle running at large. How is this? All these free blacks are the descendants of slaves, or have been slaves themselves, and they would be slaves now, but for SOMETHING which has operated on their white owners, inducing them, at vast pecuniary sacrifice, to liberate them. What is that SOMETHING? Is there any mistaking it? In all these cases it is your sense of justice, and human sympathy, continually telling you, that the poor negro has some natural right to himself—that those who deny it, and make mere merchandise of him, deserve kickings, contempt and death.

"And now, why will you ask us to deny the humanity of the slave? and estimate him only as the equal of the hog? Why ask us to do what you will not do yourselves? Why ask us to do for *nothing,* what two hundred millions of dollars could not induce you to do?"

"I Take the Bull by the Horns"

"But one great argument in the support of the repeal of the Missouri Compromise, is still to come. That argument is 'the sacred right of self-government.' It seems our distinguished Senator has found great difficulty in getting his antagonists, even in the Senate to meet him fairly on this argument—some poet has said
" 'Fools rush in where angels fear to tread.'
"At the hazard of being thought one of the fools of this quotation, I meet that argument—I rush in, I take the bull by the horns.
"I trust I understand, and truly estimate the right of self-government. My faith in the proposition that each man should do precisely as he pleases with all which is exclusively his own, lies at the foundation of the sense of justice there is in me. I extend the principles to communities of men, as well as to individuals. I so extend it, because it is politically wise, as well as naturally just; politically wise, in saving us from broils about matters which do not concern us. Here, or at Washington, I would not trouble myself with the oyster laws of Virginia, or the cranberry laws of Indiana.
"The doctrine of self government is right—absolutely and eternally right—but it has no just application, as here attempted. Or perhaps I should rather say that whether it has such just application depends upon whether a nego is *not* or *is* a man. If he is *not* a man, why in that case, he who *is* a man may, as a matter of self-government, do just as he pleases with him. But if the negro *is* a man, is it not to that extent, a total destruction of self-government, to say that he too shall not govern *himself?* When the white man governs himself that is self-government; but when he governs himself, and also governs *another* man, that is *more* than self-government—that is despotism. If the negro is a *man,* why then my ancient faith teaches me that 'all men are created equal;' and that there can be no moral right in connection with one man's making a slave of another."

No Man Is Good Enough to Govern Another Man

"Judge Douglas frequently, with bitter irony and sarcasm, paraphrases our argument by saying 'The white people of Nebraska are good enough to govern themselves, *but they are not good enough* to govern a few miserable negroes.'
"Well I doubt not that the people of Nebraska are, and will continue to be as good as the average of people elsewhere. I do not say the contrary. What I do say is, that no man is good enough to govern another man, *without that other's consent.* I say this is the leading principle—the sheet anchor of American republicanism. Our Declaration of Independence says:
" 'We hold these truths to be self evident: that all men are created equal; that they are endowed by their Creator with certain inalienable rights; that amongst these are life, liberty and the pursuit of happiness. That to secure these rights, governments are instituted among men, DERIV-

ING THEIR JUST POWERS FROM THE CONSENT OF THE GOVERNED.'

"I have quoted so much at this time merely to show that according to our ancient faith, the just powers of government are derived from the consent of the governed. Now the relation of masters and slaves is, PRO TANTO, a total violation of this principle. The master not only governs the slave without his consent; but he governs him by a set of rules altogether different from those which he prescribes for himself. Allow ALL the governed an equal voice in the government, and that, and that only is self-government.

"Let it not be said I am contending for the establishment of political and social equality between the whites and blacks. I have already said the contrary. I am not now combating the argument of NECESSITY, arising from the fact that the blacks are already amongst us; but I am combating what is set up as MORAL argument for allowing them to be taken where they have never yet been—arguing against the EXTENSION of a bad thing, which where it already exists, we must of necessity, manage as we best can.

"In support of his application of the doctrine of self-government, Senator Douglas has sought to bring to his aid the opinions and examples of our revolutionary fathers. I am glad he has done this. I love the sentiments of those old-time men; and shall be most happy to abide by their opinions. He shows us that when it was in contemplation for the colonies to break off from Great Britan, and set up a new government for themselves, several states instructed their delegates to go for the measure PROVIDED EACH STATE SHOULD BE ALLOWED TO REGULATE ITS DOMESTIC CONCERNS IN ITS OWN WAY. I do not quote; but this in substance. This was right. I see nothing objectionable in it. I also think it probable that it had some reference to the existence of slavery amongst them. I will not deny that it had. But had it, in any reference to the carrying of slavery into NEW COUNTRIES? That is the question; and we will let the fathers themselves answer it.

"This same generation of men, and mostly the same individuals of the generation, who declared this principle—who declared independence —who fought the war of the revolution through—who afterwards made the constitution under which we still live—these same men passed the ordinance of '87, declaring that slavery should never go to the north-west territory. I have no doubt Judge Douglas thinks they were very inconsistent in this. It is a question of discrimination between them and him. But there is not an inch of ground left for his claiming that their opinions— their example—their authority—are on his side in this controversy.

"Again, is not Nebraska, while a territory, a part of us? Do we not own the country? And if we surrender the control of it, do we not surrender the right of self-government? It is part of ourselves. If you say we shall not control it because it is ONLY part, the same is true of every other part; and when all the parts are gone, what has become of the whole? What is then left of us? What use for the general government, where there is nothing left for it [to] govern?

"But you say this question should be left to the people of Nebraska, because they are more particularly interested. If this be the rule, you must leave it to each individual to say for himself whether he will have slaves. What better moral right have thirty-one citizens of Nebraska to say, that the thirty-second shall not hold slaves, than the people of the thirty-one States have to say that slavery shall not go into the thirty-second State at all?

"But if it is a sacred right for the people of Nebraska to take and hold slaves there, it is equally their sacred right to buy them where they can buy them cheapest; and that undoubtedly will be on the coast of Africa; provided you will consent to not hang them for going there to buy them. You must remove this restriction too, from the sacred right of self-government. I am aware you say that taking slaves from the States to Nebraska, does not make slaves of freemen; but the African slave-trader can say just as much. He does not catch free negroes and bring them here. He finds them already slaves in the hands of their black captors, and he honestly buys them at the rate of about a red cotton handkerchief a head. This is very cheap, and it is a great abridgement of the sacred right of self-government to hang men for engaging in this profitable trade!"

Few Deprive Many

"Another important objection to this application of the right of self-government, is that it enables the first FEW, to deprive the succeeding MANY, of a free exercise of the right of self-government. The first few may get slavery IN, and the subsequent many cannot easily get it OUT. How common is the remark now in the slave states—'If we were only clear of our slaves, how much better it would be for us.' They are actually deprived of the privilege of governing themselves as they would, by the action of a very few, in the beginning. The same thing was true of the whole nation at the time our constitution was formed.

"Whether slavery shall go into Nebraska, or other new territories, is not a matter of exclusive concern to the people who may go there. The whole nation is interested that the best use shall be made of these territories. We want them for the homes of free white people. This they cannot be, to any considerable extent, if slavery shall be planted within them. Slave States are places for poor white people to remove FROM; not to remove TO. New free States are the places for poor people to go to and better their condition. For this use, the nation needs these territories.

Degradation of Free State Vote

"Still further; there are constitutional relations between the slave and free States, which are degrading to the latter. We are under legal obligations to catch and return their runaway slaves to them—a sort of dirty, disagreeable job, which I believe, as a general rule the slave-holders will not perform for one another. Then again, in the control of the government —the management of the partnership affairs—they have greatly the advantage of us. By the constitution, each State has two Senators—each has a number of Representatives; in proportion to the number of its people— and each has a number of presidential electors, equal to the whole number of its Senators and Representatives together. But in ascertaining the number of the people, for this purpose, five slaves are counted as being equal to three whites. The slaves do not vote; they are only counted and so used, as to swell the influence of the white people's votes. The practical effect of this is more aptly shown by a comparison of the States of South Carolina and Maine.

"South Carolina has six representatives, and so has Maine: South Carolina has eight presidential electors, and so has Maine. This is precise equality so far; and, of course they are equal in Senators, each having two. Thus in the control of the government, the two States are equals precisely. But how are they in the number of their white people? Maine has 581,813—while South Carolina has 274,567. Maine has twice as many as South Carolina, and 32,679 over. Thus each white man in South Carolina is more than the double of any man in Maine. This is all because South Carolina, besides her free people, has 384,984 slaves. The South Carolinian has precisely the same advantage over the white man in every other free State, as well as in Maine. He is more than the double of any one of us in this crowd. The same advantage, but not to the same extent, is held by all the citizens of the slave States, over those of the free; and it is an absolute truth, without an exception, that there is no voter in any slave State, but who has more legal power in the government, than any voter in any free State. There is no instance of exact equality; and the disadvantage is against us the whole chapter through. This principle, in the aggregate, gives the slave States, in the present Congress, twenty additional representatives—being seven more than the whole majority by which they passed the Nebraska bill.

The Constitution—I Stand To It

"Now all this is manifestly unfair; yet I do not mention it to complain of it, in so far as it is already settled. It is in the constitution; and I do not, for that cause, or any other cause, propose to destroy, or alter, or disregard the constitution. I stand to it, fairly, fully, and firmly.

"But when I am told I must leave it altogether to OTHER PEOPLE to say whether new partners are to be bred up and brought into the firm, on the same degrading terms against me, I respectfully demur. I insist, that whether I shall be a whole man, or only, the half of one, in comparison with others, is a question in which I am somewhat concerned; and one which no other man can have a sacred right of deciding for me. If I am wrong in this—if it really be a sacred right of self-government, in the man who shall go to Nebraska, to decide whether he will be the EQUAL of me or the DOUBLE of me, then after he shall have exercised the right, and thereby shall have reduced me to a still smaller fraction of a man than I already am, I should like for some gentleman deeply skilled in the mysteries of sacred rights, to provide himself with a microscope, and peep about, and find out, if he can, what has become of my sacred rights! They will surely be too small for detection with the naked eye.

"Finally, I insist, that if there is ANY THING which it is the duty of the WHOLE PEOPLE to never entrust to any hands but their own, that thing is the preservation and perpetuity, of their own liberties, and institutions. And if they shall think, as I do, that the extension of slavery endangers them, more than any, or all other causes, how recreant to themselves, if they submit the question, and with it, the fate of their country, to a mere hand-full of men, bent only on temporary self-interest. If this question of slavery extension were an insignificant one—one having no power to do harm—it might be shuffled aside in this way. But being, as it is, the great Behemoth of danger, shall the strong gripe of the nation be loosened upon him, to entrust him to the hands of such feeble keepers?"

I Go For Saving the Nation

"I have done with this mighty argument, of self-government. Go, sacred thing! Go in peace.

"But Nebraska is urged as a great Union-saving measure. Well I too, go for saving the Union. Much as I hate slavery, I would consent to the extension of it rather than see the Union dissolved, just as I would consent to any GREAT evil, to avoid a GREATER one. But when I go to Union saving, I must believe, at least, that the means I employ has some adaptation to the end. To my mind, Nebraska, has no such adaptation.

'It hath no relish of salvation in it.'

It is an aggravation, rather, of the only one thing which ever endangers the Union. When it came upon us, all was peace and quiet. The nation was looking to the forming of new bonds of Union; and a long course of peace and prosperity seemed to lie before us. In the whole range of possibility, there scarcely appears to me to have been any thing, out of which the slavery agitation could have been revived, except the very project of repealing the Missouri compromise. Every inch of territory we owned, already had a definite settlement of the slavery question, and by which, all parties were pledged to abide. Indeed, there was no uninhabited country on the continent, which we could acquire; if we except some extreme northern regions, which are wholly out of the question. In this state of case, the genius of Discord himself, could scarcely have invented a way of again getting us by the ears, but by turning back and destroying the peace measures of the past. The councils of that genius seem to have prevailed, the Missouri compromise was repealed; and here we are, in the midst of a new slavery agitation, such, I think, as we have never seen before. Who is responsible for this? Is it those who resist the measure; or those who, causelessly, brought it forward, and pressed it through, having reason to know, and, in fact, knowing it must and would be so resisted? It could not but be expected by its author, that it would be looked upon as a measure for the extension of slavery, aggravated by a gross breach of faith. Argue as you will, and long as you will, this is the naked FRONT and ASPECT, of the measure. And in this aspect, it could not but produce agitation. Slavery is founded in the selfishness of man's nature—opposition to it, is [in?] his love of justice. These principles are an eternal antagonism; and when brought into collision so fiercely, as slavery extension brings them, shocks, and throes, and convulsions must ceaselessly follow. Repeal the Missouri compromise—repeal all compromises—repeal the declaration of independence—repeal all past history, you still can not repeal human nature. It still will be the abundance of man's heart, that slavery extension is wrong; and out of the abundance of his heart, his mouth will continue to speak.

How Decide For or Against Slavery

"The structure, too, of the Nebraska bill is very peculiar. The people are to decide the question of slavery for themselves; but WHEN they are to decide; or HOW they are to decide; or whether, when the question is once decided, it is to remain so, or is it to be subject to an indefinite succession of new trials, the law does not say. Is it to be decided by the first dozen settlers who arrive there or is it to await the arrival of a hundred? Is it to be decided by a vote of the people? or a vote of the legislature? or, indeed by a vote of any sort? To these questions, the law gives no answer. There is a mystery about this; for when a member proposed to give the legislature express authority to exclude slavery, it was hooted down by the friends of the bill. The fact is worth remembering. Some yankees, in the east, are sending emigrants to Nebraska, to exclude slavery from it; and, so far as I can judge, they expect the question to be decided by voting, in some way or other. But the Missourians are awake too. They are within a stone's throw of the contested ground. They hold meetings, and pass resolutions, in which not the slightest allusion to voting is made. They resolve that slavery already exists in the territory; that more shall go there; that they, remaining in Missouri will protect it; and that abolitionists shall be hung, or driven away. Through all this, bowie-knives and six-shooters are seen plainly enough; but never a glimpse of the ballot box. And, really, what is to be the result of this? Each party WITHIN, having numerous and determined backers WITHOUT, is it not probable that the contest will come to blows, and bloodshed? Could there be a more apt invention to bring about collision and violence, on the slavery question, than this Nebraska project is? I do not charge, or believe, that such was intended by Congress; but it they had literally formed a ring, and placed champions within it to fight out the controversy, the fight could be no more likely to come off, than it is. And if this fight should begin, is it likely to take a very peaceful, Union-saving turn? Will not the first drop of blood so shed, be the real knell of the Union?"

Argument For Restoring the Missouri Compromise

"The Missouri Compromise ought to be restored. For the sake of the Union, it ought to be restored. We ought to elect a House of Representatives which will vote its restoration. If by any means, we omit to do this, what follows? Slavery may or may not be established in Nebraska. But whether it be or not, we shall have repudiated—discarded from the councils of the Nation—the SPIRIT of COMPROMISE; for who after this will ever trust in a national compromise? The spirit of mutual concession—that spirit which first gave us the constitution, and which has thrice saved the Union—we shall have strangled and cast from us forever. And what shall we have in lieu of it? The South flushed with triumph and tempted to excesses; the North, betrayed, as they believe, brooding on wrong and burning for revenge. One side will provoke; the other resent. The one will taunt, the other defy; one agrees [agresses?], the other retaliates. Already a few in the North, defy all constitutional restraints, resist the execution of the fugitive slave law, and even menace the institution of slavery in the states where it exists.

"Already a few in the South, claim the constitutional right to take to and hold slaves in the free states—demand the revival of the slave trade; and demand a treaty with Great Britain by which fugitive slaves may be reclaimed from Canada. As yet they are but few on either side. It is a grave question for the lovers of the Union, whether the final destruction of the Missouri Compromise, and with it the spirit of all compromise will or will not embolden and embitter each of these, and fatally increase the numbers of both.

"But restore the compromise, and what then? We thereby restore the national faith, the national confidence, the national feeling of brother-hood. We thereby reinstate the spirit of concession and compromise—that spirit which has never failed us in past perils, and which may be safely trusted for all the future. The south ought to join in doing this. The peace of the nation is as dear to them as to us. In memories of the past and hopes of the future, they share as largely as we. It would be on their part, a great act—great in its spirit, and great in its effect. It would be worth to the nation a hundred years' purchase of peace and prosperity. And what of sacrifice would they make? They only surrender to us, what they gave us for a consideration long, long ago; what they have not now, asked for, struggled or cared for; what has been thrust upon them, not less to their own astonishment than to ours.

"But it is said we cannot restore it; that though we elect every member of the lower house, the Senate is still against us. It is quite true, that of the Senators who passed the Nebraska bill, a majority of the whole Senate will retain their seats in spite of the elections of this and next year. But if at these elections, their several constituencies shall clearly express their will against Nebraska, will these senators disregard their will? Will they neither obey, nor make room for those who will?

"But even if we fail to technically restore the compromise, it is still a great point to carry a popular vote in favor of the restoration. The moral weight of such a vote can not be estimated too highly. The authors of Nebraska are not at all satisfied with the destruction of the compromise—an endorsement of this PRINCIPLE, they proclaim to be the great object. With them, Nebraska alone is a small matter—to establish a principle, for FUTURE USE, is what they particularly desire.

"That future use is to be the planting of slavery wherever in the wide world, local and unorganized opposition can not prevent it. Now if you wish to give them this endorsement—if you wish to establish this principle —do so. I shall regret it; but it is your right. On the contrary if you are opposed to the principle—intend to give it no such endorsement—let no wheedling, no sophistry, divert you from throwing a direct vote against it."

Stand With the Moral Right

"Some men, mostly whigs, who condemn the repeal of the Missouri Compromise, nevertheless hesitate to go for its restoration, lest they be thrown in company with the abolitionist. Will they allow me as an old whig to tell them good humoredly, that I think this is very silly? Stand with anybody that stands RIGHT. Stand with him while he is right and PART with him when he goes wrong. Stand WITH the abolitionist in restoring the Missouri compromise; and stand AGAINST him when he attempts to repeal the fugitive slave law. In the latter case you stand with the southern disunionist. What of that? you are still right. In both cases you are right. In both cases you oppose the dangerous extremes. In both you stand on middle ground and hold the ship level and steady: In both you are national and nothing less than national. This is good old whig ground. To desert such ground, because of any company, is to be less than a whig—less than a man—less than an American.

"I particularly object to the NEW position which the avowed principle of this Nebraska law gives to slavery in the body politic. I object to it because it assumes that there CAN be MORAL RIGHT in the enslaving of one man by another. I object to it as a dangerous dalliance for a few [free?] people—a sad evidence that, feeling prosperity we forget right—that liberty, as a principle, we have ceased to revere. I object to it because the fathers of the republic eschewed, and rejected it. The argument of 'Necessity' was the only argument they ever admitted in favor of slavery; and so far, and only as it carried them, did they ever go. They found the institution existing among us, which they could not help; and they cast blame upon the British King for having permitted its introduction. BEFORE the constitution, they prohibited its introduction into the north-western Territory—the only country we owned, then free from it. At the framing and adoption of the constitution, they forbore to so much as mention the word 'slave' or 'slavery' in the whole instrument. In the provision for the recovery of fugitives, the slave is spoken of as a 'PERSON HELD TO SERVICE OR LABOR.' In that prohibiting the abolition of the African slave trade for twenty years, that trade is spoken of as 'The migration or importation of such persons as any of the States NOW EXISTING, shall think proper to admit,' etc. These are the only provisions alluding to slavery. Thus, the thing is hid away, in the constitution, just as an afflicted man hides away a wen or a cancer which he dares not cut out at once, lest he bleed to death; with the promise, nevertheless, that the cutting may begin at the end of a given time. Less than this our fathers COULD not do; and NOW [MORE?] they WOULD not do. Necessity drove them so far, and farther, they would not go. But this is not all. The earliest Congress, under the constitution, took the same view of slavery. They hedged and hemmed it in to the narrowest limits of necessity."

Acceptance and Prohibition of Slave Trade   ·

"In 1794, they prohibited the bringing of slaves from Africa, INTO the Mississippi Territory—this territory then comprising what are now the States of Mississippi and Alabama. This was TEN YEARS before they had the authority to do the same thing as to the States existing at the adoption of the constitution.

"In 1800 they prohibited AMERICAN CITIZENS from trading in slaves between foreign countries—as, for instance, from Africa to Brazil.

"In 1803 they passed a law in aid of one or two State laws, in restraint of the internal slave trade.

"In 1807, in apparent hot haste, they passed the law, nearly a year in advance, to take effect the first day of 1808—the very first day the constitution would permit—prohibiting the African slave trade by heavy pecuniary and corporal penalties.

"In 1820, finding these provisions ineffectual, they declared the trade piracy, and annexed to it, the extreme penalty of death. While all this was passing in the general government, five or six of the original slave States had adopted systems of gradual emancipation; and by which the institution was rapidly becoming extinct within these limits.

"Thus we see, the plain unmistakable spirit of that age, towards slavery, was hostility to the PRINCIPLE, and toleration, ONLY BY NECESSITY.

"But NOW it is to be transformed into a 'sacred right.' Nebraska brings it forth, places it on the high road to extension and perpetuity; and, with a pat on its back, says to it, 'Go, and God speed you.' Henceforth it is to be the chief jewel of the nation—the very figure-head of the ship of State. Little by little, but steadily as man's march to the grave, we have been giving up the OLD for the NEW faith. Near eighty years ago we began by declaring that all men are created equal; but now from that beginning we have run down to the other declaration, that for SOME men to enslave OTHERS is a 'sacred right of self-government.' These principles can not stand together. They are as opposite as God and mammon; and whoever holds to the one, must despise the other. When Pettit, in connection with his support of the Nebraska bill, called the Declaration of Independence 'a self-evident lie' he only did what consistency and candor require all other Nebraska men to do. Of the forty odd Nebraska Senators who sat present and heard him, no one rebuked him. Nor am I apprized that any Nebraska newspaper, or any Nebraska orator, in the whole nation, has ever yet rebuked him. If this had been said among Marion's men, Southerners though they were, what would have become of the man who said it? If this had been said in old Independence Hall, seventy-eight years ago, the very door-keeper would have throttled the man, and thrust him into the street."

"Fellow Countrymen, Arrest This"

"Let no one be deceived. The spirit of seventy-six and the spirit of Nebraska, are utter antagonisms; and the former is being rapidly displaced by the latter.

"Fellow countrymen—Americans south, as well as north, shall we make no effort to arrest this? Already the liberal party throughout the world, express the apprehension 'that the one retrograde institution in America, is undermining the principles of progress, and fatally violating the noblest political system the world ever saw.' This is not the taunt of enemies, but the warning of friends. Is it quite safe to disregard it—to despise it? Is there no danger to liberty itself, in discarding the earliest practice, and first precept of our ancient faith? In our greedy chase to make profit of the negro, let us beware, lest we 'cancel and tear to pieces' even the white man's charter of freedom.

"Our republican robe is soiled, and trailed in the dust. Let us repurify it. Let us turn and wash it white, in the spirit, if not the blood, of the Revolution. Let us turn slavery from its claims of 'moral right' back upon its existing legal rights, and its arguments of 'necessity.' Let us return it to the position our fathers gave it; and there let it rest in peace. Let us re-adopt the Declaration of Independence, and with it, the practices, and policy, which harmonize with it. Let north and south—let all Americans—let all lovers of liberty everywhere—join in the great and good work. If we do this, we shall not only have saved the Union; but we shall have so saved it, as to make, and to keep it, forever worthy of the saving. We shall have so saved it, that the succeeding millions of free happy people, the world over, shall rise up, and call us blessed, to the latest generations.

I Shall Anticipate Him

"At Springfield, twelve days ago, where I had spoken substantially as I have here, Judge Douglas replied to me—and as he is to reply to me here, I shall attempt to anticipate him, by noticing some of the points made there.

"He commenced by stating I had assumed all the way through, that the principle of the Nebraska bill, would have the effect of extending slavery. He denied that this was INTENDED, or that this EFFECT would follow.

"I will not re-open the argument upon this point. That such was the intention, the world believed at the start, and will continue to believe. This was the COUNTENANCE of the thing; and, both friends and enemies, instantly recognized it as such. That countenance can not now be changed by argument. You can as easily argue the color out of the negroes' skin. Like the 'bloody hand' you may wash it, and wash it, the red witness of guilt still sticks, and stares horribly at you.

"Next, he says, congressional intervention never prevented slavery, any where—that it did not prevent it in the north west territory, now [nor?] in Illinois—that in fact, Illinois came into the Union as a slave state—that the principle of the Nebraska bill expelled it from Illinois, from several old States, from every where.

"Now this is mere quibbling all the way through. If the ordinance of '87 did not keep slavery out of the north west territory, how happens it that the north west shore of the Ohio river is entirely free from it; while the south east shore, less than a mile distant, along nearly the whole length of the river, is entirely covered with it?

"If that ordinance did not keep it out of Illinois, what is it that made the difference between Illinois and Missouri? They lie side by side, the Mississippi river only dividing them; while their early settlements were within the same latitude. Between 1810 and 1820 the number of slaves in Missouri INCREASED 7,211; while in Illinois; in the same ten years, they DECREASED 51. This appears by the census returns. During nearly all of that ten years, both were territories—not States. During this time, the ordinance forbid slavery to go into Illinois; and NOTHING forbid it to go into Missouri. It DID go into Missouri, and did NOT go into Illinois. That is the fact. Can any one doubt as to the reason of it?

Contradicts Douglas' Bold Assertion

"But, he says, Illinois came into the Union as a slave State. Silence, perhaps, would be the best answer to this flat contradiction of the known history of the country. What are the facts upon which this bold assertion is based? When we first acquired the country, as far back as 1787, there were some slaves within it, held by the French inhabitants at Kaskaskia. The territorial legislation, admitted a few negroes, from the slave States, as indentured servants. One year after the adoption of the first State constitution the whole number of them was—what do you think? just 117—while the aggregate free population was 55,094—about 470 to one. Upon this state of facts, the people framed their constitution prohibiting the further introduction of slavery, with a sort of guaranty to the owners of the few indentured servants, giving freedom to their children to be born thereafter, and making no mention whatever, of any supposed slave for life. Out of this small matter, the Judge manufactures his argument that Illinois came into the Union as a slave State. Let the facts be the answer to the argument.

"The principles of the Nebraska bill, he says, expelled slavery from Illinois? The principle of that bill first planted it here—that is, it first came, because there was no law to prevent it—first came before we owned the country; and finding it here, and having the ordinance of '87 to prevent its increasing, our people struggled along, and finally got rid of it as best they could.

"But the principle of the Nebraska bill abolished slavery in several of the old States. Well, it is true that several of the old States, in the last quarter of the last century, did adopt systems of gradual emancipation, by which the institution has finally become extinct within their limits; but it MAY OR MAY NOT be true that the principle of the Nebraska bill was the cause that led to the adoption of these measures. It is not more than fifty years, since the last of these States adopted its system of emancipation. If Nebraska bill is the real author of these benevolent works, it is rather deplorable, that he has, for so long a time, ceased working all together. Is there not some reason to suspect that it was the principle of the REVOLUTION, and not the principle of the Nebraska bill, that led to emancipation in these old States? Leave it to the people of those old emancipating States, and I am quite sure they will decide, that neither that, nor any other good thing, ever did, or ever will come of Nebraska bill.

Challenges Divine Right to Enslave

"In the course of my main argument, Judge Douglas interrupted me to say, that the principle [of] the Nebraska bill was very old; that it originated when God made man and placed good and evil before him, allowing him to choose for himself, being responsible for the choice he should make. At the time I thought this was merely playful; and I answered it accordingly. But in his reply to me he renewed it, as a serious argument. In seriousness then, the facts of this proposition are not true as stated. God did not place good and evil before man, telling him to make his choice. On the contrary, he did tell him there was one tree, of the fruit of which, he should not eat, upon pain of certain death. I should scarcely wish so strong a prohibition against slavery in Nebraska.

"But this argument strikes me as not a little remarkable in another particular—in its strong resemblance to the old argument for the 'Divine right of Kings.' By the latter, the King is to do just as he pleases with his white subjects, being responsible to God alone. By the former the white man is to do just as he pleases with his black slaves, being responsible to

God alone. The two things are precisely alike; and it is but natural that they should find similar arguments to sustain them.

"I had argued, that the application of the principle of self-government, as contended for, would require the revival of the African slave trade—that no argument could be made in favor of a man's right to take slaves to Nebraska, which could not be equally well made in favor of his right to bring them from the coast of Africa. The Judge replied, that the constitution requires the suppression of the foreign slave trade; but does not require the prohibition of slavery in the territories. That is a mistake, in point of fact. The constitution does NOT require the action of Congress in either case; and it does AUTHORIZE it in both. And so, there is still no difference between the cases.

"In regard to what I had said, the advantage the slave States have over the free in the matter of representation, the Judge replied that we, in the free States, count five free negroes as five white people, while in the slave States, they count five slaves as three whites only; and that the advantage, at last, was on the side of the free States.

"Now, in the slave States, they count free negroes just as we do; and it so happens that besides their slaves, they have as many free negroes as we have, and thirty-three thousand over. Thus their free negroes more than balance ours; and their advantage over us, in consequence of their slaves, still remains as I stated it.

Compromise by Equivalents

"In reply to my argument, that the compromise measures of 1850, were a system of equivalents; and that the provisions of no one of them could fairly be carried to other subjects, without its corresponding equivalent being carried with it, the Judge denied out-right, that these measures had any connection with, or dependence upon, each other. This is mere desperation. If they have no connection, why are they always spoken of in connection? Why has he so spoken of them, a thousand times? Why has he constantly called them a SERIES of measures? Why does everybody call them a compromise? Why was California kept out of the Union, six or seven months, if it was not because of its connection with the other measures? Webster's leading definition of the verb 'to compromise' is 'to adjust and settle a difference, by mutual agreement with concessions of claims by the parties.' This conveys precisely the popular understanding of the word compromise. We knew, before the Judge told us, that these measures passed separately, and in distinct bills; and that no two of them were passed by the votes of precisely the same members. But we also know, and so does he know, that no one of them could have passed both branches of Congress but for the understanding that the others were to pass also. Upon this understanding each got votes, which it could have got in no other way. It is this fact, that gives to the measures their true character; and it is the universal knowledge of this fact, that has given them the name of compromise so expressive of that true character.

"I had asked 'If in carrying the provisions of the Utah and New Mexico laws to Nebraska, you could clear away other objection, how can you leave Nebraska 'perfectly free' to introduce slavery BEFORE she forms a constitution—during her territorial government?—while the Utah and New Mexico laws only authorize it WHEN they form constitutions and are admitted into the Union?' To this Judge Douglas answered that the Utah and New Mexico laws, also authorize it BEFORE; and to prove this, he read from one of their laws, as follows: 'That the legislative power of said territory shall extend to all rightful subjects of legislation consistent with the constitution of the United States and the provisions of this act.'

"Now it is perceived from the reading of this, that there is nothing express upon the subject; but that the authority is sought to be implied merely, for the general provision of 'all rightful subjects of legislation.' In reply to this, I insist, as a legal rule of construction, as well as the plain popular view of the matter, that the EXPRESS provision for Utah and New Mexico coming in with slavery if they choose, when they shall form constitutions, is an EXCLUSION of all implied authority on the same subject—that Congress, having the subject distinctly in their minds, when they made the express provision, they therein expressed their WHOLE meaning on that subject."

Washington Territorial Law

"The Judge rather insinuated that I had found it convenient to forget the Washington territorial law passed in 1853. This was a division of Oregon, organizing the northern part, as the territory of Washington. He asserted that, by this act, the ordinance of '87 theretofore existing in Oregon, was repealed; that nearly all the members of Congress voted for it, beginning in the H.R., with Charles Allen of Massachusetts, and ending with Richard Yates, of Illinois; and that he could not understand how those who now oppose the Nebraska bill, so voted then, unless it was because it was then too soon after both the great political parties had ratified the compromises of 1850, and the ratification therefore too fresh, to be then repudiated.

"Now I had seen the Washington act before; and I have carefully examined it since; and I aver that there is no repeal of the ordinance of '87, or of any prohibition of slavery, in it. In express terms, there is absolutely nothing in the whole law upon the subject—in fact, nothing to lead a reader to THINK of the subject. To my judgment, it is equally free from every thing from which such repeal can be legally implied; but however this may be, are men now to be entrapped by the legal implication, extracted from covert language, introduced perhaps, for the very purpose of entrapping them? I sincerely wish every man could read this law quite through, carefully watching every sentence, and every line, for a repeal of the ordinance of '87 or any thing equivalent to it.

"Another point on the Washington act. If it was intended to be modelled after the Utah and New Mexico acts, as Judge Douglas, insists, why was it not inserted in it, as in them, that Washington was to come in with or without slavery as she may choose at the adoption of her constitution? It has no such provision in it; and I defy the ingenuity of many to give a reason for the omission, other than that it was not intended to follow Utah and New Mexico laws in regard to the question of slavery.

"The Washington act not only differs vitally from the Utah and New Mexico acts; but the Nebraska act differs vitally from both. By the latter act the people are left 'perfectly free' to regulate their own domestic concerns, etc.; but in all the former, all their laws are to be submitted to Congress, and if disapproved are to be null. The Washington act goes even further; it absolutely prohibits the territorial legislation [legislature?], by very strong and guarded language, from establishing banks, or borrowing money on the faith of the territory. Is this the sacred right of self-government we hear vaunted so much? No sir, the Nebraska bill finds no model in the acts of '50 or the Washington act. It finds no model in any law from Adam till today. As Phillips says of Napoleon, the Nebraska act is grand, gloomy, and peculiar; wrapped in the solitude of his own originality; without a model, and without a shadow upon the earth."

The Negro Is Human

"In the course of his reply, Senator Douglas remarked, in substance that he had always considered this government was made for the white people and not for the negroes. Why, in point of mere fact, I think so too. But in this remark of the Judge, there is a significance, which I think is the key to the great mistake (if there is any such mistake) which he has made in this Nebraska measure. It shows that the Judge has no very vivid impression that the negro is a human; and consequently has no idea that there can be any moral question in legislating about him. In his view, the question of whether a new country shall be slave or free, is a matter of as utter indifference, as it is whether his neighbor shall plant his farm with tobacco, or stock it with horned cattle. Now, whether this view is right or wrong, it is very certain that the great mass of mankind take a totally different view. They consider slavery a great moral wrong; and their feelings against it, is not evanescent, but eternal. It lies at the very foundation of their sense of justice; and it cannot be trifled with. It is a great and durable element of popular action, and, I think, no statesman can safely disregard it.

"Our Senator also objects that those who oppose him in this measure do not entirely agree with one another. He reminds me that in my firm adherence to the constitutional rights of the slave States, I differ widely from others who are co-operating with me in opposing the Nebraska bill; and he says it is not quite fair to oppose him in this variety of ways. He should remember that he took us by surprise—astounded us—by this measure. We were thunderstruck and stunned; and we reeled and fell in utter confusion. But we rose each fighting, grasping whatever he could first reach—a scythe—a pitchfork—a chopping axe, or a butcher's cleaver. We struck in the direction of the sound; and we are rapidly closing in upon him. He must not think to divert us from our purpose, by showing us that our drill, our dress, and our weapons, are not entirely perfect and uniform. When the storm shall be past, he shall find us still Americans; no less devoted to the continued Union and prosperity of the country than heretofore.

"Finally, the Judge invokes against me, the memory of Clay and of Webster. They were great men; and men of great deeds. But where have

I assailed them? For what is it, that their life-long enemy, shall now make profit, by assuming to defend them against me, their life-long friend? I go against the ,repeal of the Missouri compromise; did they ever go for it? They were greatly devoted to the Union; to the small measure of my ability, was I ever less so? Clay and Webster were dead before this question arose; by what authority shall our Senator say they would espouse his side of it, if alive? Mr. Clay was the leading spirit in making the Missouri compromise; is it very credible that if now alive, he would take the lead in the breaking of it? The truth is that some support from the whigs is now a necessity with the Judge, and for thus it is that the names of Clay and Webster are now invoked. His old friends have deserted him in such numbers as to leave too few to live by. He came to his own, and his own received him not, and Lo! he turns unto the Gentiles."

The Judge's Desperate Assumption

"A word now as to the Judge's desperate assumption that the compromises of '50 had no connection with one another; that Illinois came into the Union as a slave state, and some other similar ones. This is no other than a bold denial of the history of the country. If we do not know that the Compromises of '50 were dependent on each other; if we do not know that Illinois came into the Union as a free state—we do not know any thing. If we do not know these things, we do not know that we ever had a revolutionary war, or such a chief as Washington. To deny these things is to deny our national axioms, or dogmas, at least; and it puts an end to all argument. If a man will stand up and assert, and repeat, and re-assert, that two and two do not make four, I know nothing in the power of argument that can stop him. I think I can answer the Judge so long as he sticks to his premises; but when he flies from them, I can not work an argument into the consistency of a maternal gag, and actually close his mouth with it. In such a case I can only commend him to the seventy thousand answers just in from Pennsylvania, Ohio and Indiana."

Unfortunately the limitations of space prevent the inclusion here of the arguments of Douglas on the involvements of the Kansas-Nebraska Act. Lincoln's constant attention to making factually pointed rebuttals of the "Judge's desperate assumptions" is indicative of the differences in political thinking of the two men. Douglas had not changed his natural egoistic disposition to let his emotional prejudices influence his argument and thereby excite the passions and prejudices of people, whereas Lincoln had at 45 years wisely cultivated an egoistic attitude of cool self-control in order to dominate passion with logically incisive but kindly reasoning.

Lincoln's Peoria speech of October 16, 1954 was so thoroughly studied and carefully prepared in arrangement of arguments that he covered most of the important political issues of that time. The speeches he will make in the next six years will largely repeat these arguments, although in somewhat different ways with the additions of secondary delineations. The historical biographer finds it sufficient to his purpose to present summaries of the repetitions in the later speeches, whereas the analytical biographer finds it necessary to repeat them for each important presentation, in order to keep pace with the steps in development of Lincoln's thinking as it grows in influence on the people.

Without intent of reestablishing himself politically, after 10 years of scorn by the people for his previous Mexican War policy, Lincoln expressed his moral political philosophy in 1854 consistently with the principles he upheld as a young lawyer and congressman. From 1854 through 1860 and his presidency he never changed them to gain political favor. He was always opposed to slavery, as an immoral violation of human rights, but he recognized its established constitutional rights, including the fugitive slave law, and was not in favor of its radical total abolition—although uncompromisingly opposed to its extension. He believed that slavery would naturally die out as an economic system if restricted by the Missouri Compromise to the Southern states. Now, however, since this restriction was annulled by the Kansas-Nebraska Act, he foresaw that it could spread into the new territories, and might even be extended to Central and South America and other nations if its ideology was not rejected by the people.

Chapter XXV

THE RISE OF LINCOLN IN ILLINOIS

Lincoln, having thoroughly informed himself on the history of slavery in relation to equal rights of all people under the Constitution, took "the bull by the horns," to use his metaphor, and by moral argument forced Douglas, ever extroverted and aggressive, wealthy, and powerfully intrenched in Illinois and national Democratic political organization, into a self-justifying, defensive position. With logical analysis of the issue between pro- and antislavery factions he persisted for the next six years in arousing the people to demand the restoration of the Missouri Compromise. "That being done," he said, "the Union would again be safe and the people happy."

Cautious Candidate for Senate

The political influence of Lincoln grew daily more important, as Whigs, Democrats, Abolitionists, and Free-Thinkers, becoming converted to the plan of stopping the extension of slavery by having Congress restore the Missouri Compromise, rallied to his leadership.

The coming vacancy for Illinois in the United States Senate now tempted him to become a candidate against James Shields, his old duelling opponent who was supported by Douglas, and Lyman Trumbull.

To T. J. Henderson he wrote (11, 27, 1854): "It has come round that a whig may, by possibility, be elected to the U. S. Senate; and I want a chance of being that man. You are a member of the Legislature, and have a vote to give.* Think it over, and see whether you can do better than to go for me.

"Write me, at all events; and let this be confidential."

To Hugh Lemaster (11, 29, 1854): "I have got it into my head to try to be U. S. Senator, and I wish somehow to get at your Whig member, Mr. Babcock."

To Joseph Gillespie (12, 1, 1854): "I have really got it into my head to try to be United States Senator; and if I could have your support my chances would be reasonably good. But I know, and acknowledge, that you have as just claims to the place as I have; and therefore I do not ask you to yield to me, if you are thinking of becoming a candidate yourself. If, however, you are not, then I should like to be remembered affectionately by you; and also to have you make a mark for me with the Anti-Nebraska members, down your way."

*Prior to the 17th amendment of the Constitution in 1913, Senators were chosen by the legislatures of the states. As the legislators were elected by popular vote, the candidates for the United States Senate appealed to people and their legislators for support.

To H. W. Fay (12, 11, 1854): "When you were in the legislature you helped to pass some bills of mutual interest, at that time either in jest or earnest you suggested me for Senator. My friends are now asking me to make the race. See the representatives and senator of your district and let me know what indorsement I may expect in that locality."

To E. B. Washburne (12, 11, 1854): "Today I had a letter from Turner [T. G.]. He says he is not committed, & will not be until he sees how most effectively to oppose slavery extension.

"I have not ventured to write all the members of your district lest some of them shall be offended by the indelicacy of the thing—that is, coming from a total stranger."

To T. J. Henderson (12, 15, 1854): "Of course I prefer myself to all others; yet it is neither in my heart nor my conscience to say I am any better man than Mr. Williams. We shall have a terrible struggle with our adversaries. They are desperate, and bent on desperate deeds. I accidentally learned of one of the leaders here writing to a member South of here, in about the following language. 'We are beaten. They have a clear majority of at least nine, on joint ballot. They *outnumber* us, but we must *outmanage* them. Douglas must be sustained.' . . .

"I send you by this mail, a copy of my Peoria speech. You may have seen it before; or you may think it not worth seeing now."

To E. B. Washburne (12, 19, 1854): "The objection of your friend at Winnebago rather astonishes me. For a Senator to be the impartial representative of his whole State, is so plain a duty, that I pledge myself to the observance of it without hesitation; but not without some mortification that any one should suspect me of an inclination to the contrary."

To E. B. Washburne (1, 6, 1855), Lincoln gave his estimation of the way the different members of the Legislature would vote in the election of a Senator: "I do not know that it is much advantage to have the largest number of votes at the start. If I did know this to be an advantage I should feel better; for I can not doubt but I have more committals than any other one man."

Defeated—Not Nervous About It

Lincoln was defeated by Trumbull for the Senate. His comments to E. B. Washburne (2, 9, 1855) best express his feelings and thoughts (italics inserted):

"The agony is over at last; and the result you doubtless know. I write this only to give you some particulars to explain what might be difficult of understanding. I began with 33 votes, Shields 41 and Trumbull 5—yet Trumbull was elected. In fact 47 different members voted for me—getting three new ones on the second ballot and losing four old ones. How came my 47 to yield to T's 5? It was Govr. Matteson's work. He has been secretly a candidate ever since (before even) the fall election. All the members round about the canal were Anti-Nebraska; but were, nevertheless nearly all democrats, and old personal friends of his. His plan was to privately impress them with the belief that he was as good Anti-Nebraska as anyone else—at least could be secured to be so by instructions, which could be easily passed. . . ."

"The Nebraska men, of course, were not for Matteson; but when they found they could elect no avowed Nebraska man they tardily determined, to let him get whomever of our men he could by whatever means he could and ask him no questions. . . . With the united Nebraska force, and their recruits, . . . it gave Matteson more than enough to elect him. We saw into it plainly ten days ago; but with every possible effort, could not head it off. . . . and so we went into the fight yesterday; the Nebraska men very confident of the election of Matteson, though denying that he was a candidate, and we very much believing also, that they would elect him. But they wanted first to make a good show of faith to Shields by voting for him a few times, and our secret Matteson men also wanted to make a good show of faith by voting with us a few times. So we led off. On the second ballot, I think, the signal was given to the Neb. men, to turn on to Matteson, which they acted on to a man, with one exception . . . giving him 44 votes. Next ballot the remaining Neb. man, & one pretended Anti- went on to him, giving him 46. The next still another giving him 47, wanting only three of an election. In the mean time, our friends with a view of detaining our expected bolters have been turning from me to Trumbull till he he [*sic*] had risen to 35 & I had been reduced to 15. These would never desert me except by my direction; but I was satisfied that if we could prevent Matteson's election one or two ballots more, we could not possibly do so a single ballot after my friends should return to me from Trumbull. So I determined to strike at once; and accordingly advised my friends to go for him which they did & elected him on the 10th. ballot.

"Such is the way the thing was done. I think you would have done the same under the circumstances; though Judge Davis, who came down this morning, declared he never would have consented to the 47 men being controlled by the 5. *I regret my defeat moderately, but I am not nervous about it.* I could have headed off every combination and been elected, had it not been for *Matteson's double game—and his defeat now gives me more pleasure than my own gives me pain.* On the whole, it is perhaps as well for our general cause that Trumbull is elected. The Neb. men confess that they hate it worse than any thing that could have happened. It is a great consolation to see them worse whipped than I am. I tell them it is their own fault—that they had abundant oppertunity [*sic*] to choose between him & me, which they declined, and instead forced it on me to decide between him & Matteston."

To W. H. Henderson (2, 21, 1855): "The election is over, the Session is ended, and I am *not* Senator. I have to content myself with the honor of having been the first choice of a large majority of the fiftyone members who finally made the election. My larger number of friends had to surrender to Trumball's smaller number, in order to prevent the election of Matteson, which would have been a Douglas victory."

"I started with 44 votes and T. with 5. It was rather hard for the 44 to have to surrender to the 5—and a less good humored man that I perhaps would not have consented to it—and it would not have been done without my consent. I could not, however, let the whole political result go to ruin, on a point merely personal to myself.'

These letters show that Lincoln's personality, with all its honesty, humility, humor, and tolerance, was balanced by a practical degree of egoistic pride and cunning aggressiveness that could resent the political machinations of his opponents and defeat them instantly by decisive countermeasures and then enjoy their chagrin and confusion. They also show that he placed party welfare above personal interests and bore no grudges or malice against opponents after his defeat.

Appeal to Each Person's Conscience

We get some idea of how persistently and thoroughly he continued to prepare himself for his political mission, from notes for a speech to the Colonization Society (1, 4, 1855). Appeal to each person's conscience became his principle.

1434— A portaguse [Portuguese] captain, on the coast of Guinea, seizes a few African lads, and sells them in the South of Spain.

1501-2-3 Slaves are carried from Africa to the Spanish colonies in America.

1516-17 Charles 5th. of Spain gives encouragement to the African slave trade.

1562— John Hawkins carries slaves to the British West Indies.

1620— A dut[c]h ship carries a cargo of African slaves to Virginia.

1626— Slaves introduced into New-York.

1630 to 41 Slaves introduced into Massachusetts.

1776— The period of our revolution, there were about 600,000 slaves in the colonies; and there are now in the U.S. about 3-1/4 million. Soto, the Catholic confessor of Charles 5. opposed Slavery and the slave trade from the beginning; and in 1543, procured from the King some amelioration of its rigors.

The American colonies, from the beginning, appealed to the British crown, against the Slave trade, but without success.

1727— Quakers begin to agitate for the abolition of slavery within their own denomination.

1751— Quakers succeed in abolishing slavery within their own denomination.

1787— Congress, under the confederation, passes an Ordinance forbidding Slavery to go to the North Western Territory.

1808— Congress, under the constitution, abolishes the Slave trade, and declares it piracy.

1776- to 1800— Slavery abolished in all the States North of Maryland and Virginia.*

All the while—Individual conscience at work.

1816— Colonization Society is organized—its direct object—history—and present prospects of success.

Its colateral objects—suppression of Slave trade—commerce—civilization and religion.

---

*Lincoln made a mistake in this item. He overlooked Delaware which remained a slave state during the Civil War until slavery was abolished by the Emancipation Proclamation.

Calculated Generosity

To Jacob Harding (publisher of a little country newspaper, the *Prairie Beacon*) he wrote (5, 25, 1855):

> "I have been reading your paper three or four years, and have paid you nothing for it. Herewith is a receipt of Sylvanus Sandford for two claims amounting to ten dollars. If he has collected the money, get it from him, and put it into your pocket, saying nothing further about it."

This offer, Herndon said (1889) was not as generous as it seems. A few weeks later Lincoln asked Harding to publish a political article on his editorial page but it was refused. Herndon commented: "Although the laugh was on Lincoln he joked heartily about the editor's lofty but proper conception of true journalism."

Would Fuse With Anybody Who Is Right

To O. Lovejoy (8, 11, 1855):

> "Not even *you* are more anxious to prevent the extension of slavery than I; and yet the political atmosphere is such, just now, that I fear to do anything, lest I do wrong. Know-nothingism has not yet entirely tumbled to pieces . . . . Of their principles I think little better than I do of those of the slavery extensionists. Indeed I do not perceive how any one professing to be sensitive to the wrongs of the negroes, can join in a league to degrade a class of white men.
>
> "I have no objection to 'fuse' with anybody provided I can fuse on ground which I think is right; and I believe the opponents of slavery extension could now do this, if it were not for this K.N. ism [Know-Nothingism]. In many speeches last summer I advised those who did me the honor of a hearing to 'stand with any body who stands right'—and I am still quite willing to follow my own advice."

Can the Nation Continue Half Slave—Half Free?

The earliest application of the allegory that was later to give Lincoln national prominence appears in a letter to G. Robertson, a lawyer of Lexington, Kentucky (8, 15, 1855):

> "You are not a friend of slavery in the abstract. In that speech you spoke of '*the peaceful extinction of slavery*' and used other expressions indicating your belief that the thing was, at some time, to have an end. Since then we have had thirty six years of experience; and this experience has demonstrated, I think, that there is no peaceful extinction of slavery in prospect for us. The signal failure of Henry Clay and other good and great men, in 1849, to effect anything in favor of gradual emancipation in Kentucky, together with a thousand other signs, extinguishes that hope utterly. On the question of liberty, as a principle, we are not what we have been. When we were the political slaves of King George, and wanted to be free, we called the maxim that 'all men are created equal' a self evident truth; but now when we have grown fat, and have lost the dread of being

slaves ourselves, we have become so greedy to be *masters* that we call the same maxim 'a self-evident lie.' The fourth of July has not quite dwindled away; it is still a great day—*for burning fire-crackers!!!* . . .

"Our political problem now is 'Can we, as a nation, continue together *permanently—forever*—half slave, and half free?' The problem is too mighty for me. May God, in his mercy, superintend the solution."

Cheerful Optimism Changed to Gloomy Pessimism

Lincoln's optimistic belief that popular sentiment when aroused would restore the Missouri Compromise and all would be peaceful and happy again in the nation seems to have been changed to gloomy pessimism by a letter from his old friend Joshua Speed in May. A member of an old Kentucky slave-holding family, Speed misinterpreted Lincoln's attitude toward slavery and expressed himself in uncompromising terms about it. Three months later Lincoln replied (8, 24, 1855) with respectful consideration of each objection. Since the letter is important for having given the most frankly intimate, unpolitical expression of Lincoln's feelings on the slavery situation we quote it in full.

"You know what a poor correspondant I am. Ever since I received your very agreeable letter of the 22nd. of May I have been intending to write you in answer to it. You suggest that in political action now, you and I would differ. I suppose we would; not quite as much, however, as you may think. You know I dislike slavery; and you fully admit the abstract wrong of it. So far there is no cause of difference. But you say that sooner than yield your legal right to the slave—especially at the bidding of those who are not themselves interested, you would see the Union dissolved. I am not aware that *any one* is bidding you to yield that right; very certainly I am not. I leave the matter entirely to yourself. I also acknowledge *your* rights and *my* obligations, under the constitution, in regard to your slaves. I confess I hate to see the poor creatures hunted down, and caught, and carried back to their stripes, and unrewarded toils; but I bite my lip and keep quiet. In 1841 you and I had together a tedious low-water trip, on a Steam Boat from Louisville to St. Louis. You may remember, as I well do, that from Louisville to the mouth of the Ohio there were, on board, ten or a dozen slaves, shackled together with irons. That sight was a continual torment to me; and I see something like it every time I touch the Ohio, or any other slave-border. It is hardly fair for you to assume, that I have no interest in a thing which has, and continually exercises, the power of making me miserable. You ought rather to appreciate how the great body of Northern people do crucify their feelings; in order to maintain their loyalty to the constitution and the Union.

"I do oppose the extension of slavery, because my judgment and feelings so prompt me; and I am under no obligation to the contrary. If for this you and I must differ, differ we must. You say if you were President, you would send an army and hang the leaders of the Missouri outrages upon the Kansas elections; still, if Kansas fairly votes herself a slave state, she must be admitted, or the Union must be dissolved. But how if she votes herself a slave state *unfairly*—that is, by the very means for which you say you would hang men? Must she still be admitted, or the Union be dissolved? That will be the phase of the question when first it becomes a practical one. In your assumption that there may be a *fair* decision of the slavery question in Kansas, I plainly see you and I would differ about the Nebraska-law. I look upon that enactment not as a *law,* but as *violence* from the beginning. It was conceived in violence, passed in violence, is maintained in violence, and is being executed in violence. I say it was *conceived* in violence, because the destruction of the Missouri Compromise, under the circumstances, was nothing less than violence. It was *passed* in violence, because it could not have passed at all but for the votes of many members, in violent disregard of the known will of their constituents. It is *maintained* in violence because the elections since, clearly demand its repeal, and this demand is openly disregarded. *You* say men ought to be hung for the way they are executing that law; and *I* say the way it is being executed is quite as good as any of its antecedents. It is being executed in the precise way which was intended from the first; else why does no Nebraska man express astonishment or condemnation? Poor Reeder [A. H.]* is the only public man who is silly enough to believe that any thing like fairness was ever intended; and he has been bravely undeceived.

"That Kansas will form a Slave constitution, and, with it, will ask to be admitted into the Union, I take to be an already settled question; and so settled by the very means you so pointedly condemn. By every principle of law, ever held by any court, North or South, every negro taken to Kansas is free; yet in utter disregard of this—in the spirit of violence merely—that beautiful Legislature gravely passes a law to hang men who shall venture to inform a negro of his legal rights. This is the substance, and the real object of the law. If, like Haman, they should hang upon the gallows of their own building, I shall not be among the mourners for their fate.

"In my humble sphere, I shall advocate the restoration of the Missouri Compromise, so long as Kansas remains a territory; and when, by all these foul means, it seeks to come into the Union as a Slave-state, I shall oppose it. I am very loth, in any case, to with-hold my assent to the enjoyment of property *acquired,* or *located,* in good faith; but I do not admit that *good faith,* in taking a negro into Kansas, to be held in slavery, is a *possibility* with any man. Any man who has sense enough to be the controller of his own property, has too much sense to misunderstand the outrageous character of this whole Nebraska business. But I digress. In my opposition to the admission of Kansas I shall have some company; but we may be beaten. If we are, I shall not, on that account attempt to dissolve the Union. On the contrary, if we succeed, there will be enough of us to take care of the Union. I think it probable, however, we shall be beaten. Standing as a unit among yourselves, you can, directly, and indirectly, bribe enough of our men to carry the day—as you could on an open proposition to establish monarchy. Get hold of some man in the North, whose position and ability is such, that he can make the support of your measure—whatever it may be—*a democratic party necessity,* and the thing is done. . . . Douglas introduced the Nebraska bill in January. In February, afterwards, there was a call session of the Illinois Legislature.

*Appointed governor of Kansas Territory by President Pierce.

Of the one hundred members compassing the two branches of that body, about seventy were democrats. These latter held a caucus, in which the Nebraska bill was talked of, if not formally discussed. It was thereby discovered that just three, and no more, were in favor of the measure. In a day or two Douglas' orders came on to have resolutions passed approving the bill; and they were passed by large majorities!!! The truth of this is vouched for by a bolting democratic member. The masses too, democratic as well as whig, were even, nearer unanamous against it; but as soon as the party necessity of supporting it, became apparent, the way the democracy began to see the *wisdom* and *justice* of it, was perfectly astounding.

"You say if Kansas fairly votes herself a free state, as a christian you will rather rejoice at it. All decent slave-holders *talk* that way; and I do not doubt their candor. But they never *vote* that way. Although in a private letter, or conversation, you will express your preference that Kansas shall be free, you would vote for no man for Congress who would say the same thing publicly. No such man could be elected from any district in any slave-state. You think Stringfellow* & Co ought to be hung; and yet, at the next presidential election you will vote for the exact type and representative of Stringfellow. The slave-breeders and the slave-traders, are a small, odious and detested class, among you; and yet in politics, they dictate the course of all of you, and are as completely your masters, as you are the masters of your own negroes.

"You enquire now where I stand. That is a disputed point. I think I am a Whig; but others say there are no whigs; and that I am an abolitionist. When I was at Washington I voted for the Wilmot Proviso at least forty times, and I never heard of anyone attempting to unwhig me for that. I now do no more than oppose the *extension* of slavery.

"I am not a Know-Nothing. That is certain. How could I be? How can any one who abhors the oppression of negroes, be in favor of degrading classes of white people? Our progress in degeneracy appears to me to be pretty rapid. As a nation, we began, by declaring that '*all men are created equal.*' We now practically read it 'all men are created equal, *except negroes.*' When the Know-Nothings get control, it will read 'all men are created equal, except negroes, *and foreigners, and catholics.*' When it comes to this I should prefer emigrating to some country where they make no pretense of loving liberty—to Russia, for instance, where despotism can be taken pure, and without the base alloy of hypocracy.

"Mary will probably pass a day or two in Louisville in October. My kindest regards to Mrs. Speed. On the leading subject of this letter, I have more of her sympathy than I have of yours.

"And yet let [me] say I am

Your friend forever."

Speed's uncompromising statement that "sooner than yield his legal right to the slave—he would see the Union dissolved" expressed the proud, defiant attitude of the large majority of southern slaveholders. It was probably the narrow selfishness and unpatriotic inhumanity of his best friend that turned Lincoln's view of the future of the Union and

*A leader of pro-slavery armed forces in Kansas.

slavery from cheerful optimism to gloomy pessimism. He saw, because of this proud sentiment, that slave-breeders and slave-dealers, as violent minded and unprincipled radicals, were the masters of the slave holders and the slave states. In his humble way he would continue, however, to advocate the peaceful restoration of the Missouri Compromise and oppose the admission of Kansas into the Union as a slave state under an unjustly begotten slave constitution.

Man's Natural Right to Acquire Freedom and Avoid Suffering and Degradation

Jefferson's positive assertion of man's inherent right by the grace of God, to life, liberty, and the pursuit of happiness expressed the basic self-evident acquisitive need of the people in framing the Constitution of the United States for the establishment of its government of, by, and for the people as a republic. This equalitarian principle of human rights contradicted government based on the old assumption of Divine rights by a privileged ruling class. In his reply to Speed, Lincoln argued from the negative or avoidance side of this axiom, based on his naturally inherent need and right to prevent that which made him miserable, arousing feelings of compulsion to oppose the extension of the injustice of slavery.

His emphasis of a person's right to prevent the degrading miseries of injustice functioned reciprocally with Jefferson's assertion of the right of acquiring the happiness of freedom of self-determination and legal equality. Having accepted Jefferson's axioms, the harmonizing of avoidance and acquisitive claims completed the natural basis of Lincoln's moral philosophy for the legal organization of human relations. More than normally sensitive to the suffering and degradation of loss of self-determination as engendered by authoritative tyranny and intolerance, he felt himself compelled to prevent any person from tyranically governing another person or misusing him against his will. This deeply obsessive feeling did more than reinforce his belief in the moral justice of equalitarian rights; it made him become aggressively authoritative as an inspired, predestined moral teacher of the people to assume a more vigorous ethical attitude in their personal relations by which the strong would learn to acknowledge the rights of the weak and the weak would learn to claim recognition from the strong. His argument was now becoming thoroughly integrated by the logical reinforcement of acquisitive and avoidance interests becoming allied in gaining the same objectives. He grew increasingly disposed to challenge, with self-assured dignity, the authoritative interpretations and judgments of any man on the morality of any law, no matter what his legal investment or official pretension in claiming guidance of conscience by divine will.

Lincoln's letters to Lovejoy and Speed, and his speeches show that he had not yet made up his mind on what was best to do about slavery other than to keep it restricted.

Death of Whigism, Birth of Republicanism

"In the canvass of 1856," Lincoln said in his Scripps letter of 1860, "Mr. L. made over fifty speeches, no one of which, so far as he remembers, was put in print. One of them was at Galena, but Mr. L. has no recollection of any part of it being printed, nor does he remember whether in that speech he said anything about a Supreme Court decision. He may have spoken upon that subject; and some newspapers may have reported him as saying what is now ascribed to him; but he thinks he could not have expressed himself as represented."

At a political rally of Anti-Nebraska editors in Decatur, Illinois (2, 22, 1856), Lincoln was toasted by his friends as their next candidate for the United States Senate.

He replied "in his happiest vein," the *Decatur State Chronicle* reported. He accepted the resolutions of the convention to secure for "Kansas and Nebraska the legal guaranty against slavery of which they were deprived at the cost of the violation of the plighted faith of the nation."

The Whig party had broken down nationally into many small cliques managed by local bosses without grasp of national issues or principles of government. In New York and Massachusetts and other eastern states a realignment of advocates of anti-slavery and anti-Democratic sentiments was forming as the new Republican party. Cooperative interest was now being aroused in Illinois by the younger, more radical Whigs, Free-Soilers and Abolitionists, including Herndon and his associates. The citizens of Sangamon County held a Republican convention in Springfield on May 24, 1856, to appoint delegates to the Bloomington State Convention. The names of Herndon and Lincoln head the membership list of one hundred and twenty nine signers of the call.

The "Lost Speech"

Five days later at Bloomington (5, 29, 1856) Lincoln addressed the Republican convention "amid deafening applause." The new Republican party was in the hands of patriotic, zealous progressives, with Herndon one of the most active. The convention had adopted strong anti-Kansas-Nebraska Act resolutions and called wildly on Lincoln for a speech. His famous response was made extemporaneously and lost because unreported except for editorial comments in the Alton *Weekly Courier*. Many who heard it and other of Lincoln's speeches have claimed that it was his greatest. In it he said that he was ready to fuse with anyone who would unite with him to oppose slave power; and, against the bugbear of disunion which was so vaguely threatened, he urged "Liberty and Union, now and forever, one and inseparable." The lengthy reconstruction of the speech by his contemporary H. C. Whitney in 1896, 40 years later, is held by the editors of *Collected Works* as "not worthy of serious consideration."

Herndon (1889) said:

"I have heard or read all of Mr. Lincoln's great speeches, and I give it as my opinion that the Bloomington speech was the grand effort of his life. Heretofore he had simply argued the slavery question on grounds of policy—the statesman's grounds,—never reaching the question of the radical and the eternal right. Now he was newly baptized and freshly born; he had the fervor of a new convert; the smothered flame broke out; enthusiasm unusual to him blazed up; his eyes were aglow with an inspiration; he felt justice; his heart was alive to the right; his sympathies, remarkably deep for him, burst forth, and he stood before the throne of the eternal Right. His speech was full of fire and energy and force; it was logic; it was pathos; it was enthusiasm; it was justice, equity, truth, and right set ablaze by the divine fires of a soul maddened by the wrong; it was hard, heavy, knotty, gnarly, backed with wrath. I attempted for about fifteen minutes . . . to take notes, but at the end of that time I threw pen and paper away and lived only in the inspiration of the hour."

Proposed for Vice-President

The effect of Lincoln's impromptu speech on his audience was terrific. The Illinois Republicans adopted him at once as their leader and some even then saw him as a potential candidate for President. Seventeen days later in their national convention at Philadelphia the Republicans nominated Fremont for President and Dayton for Vice-President. Much to the surprise of Lincoln and his close friends he received 110 votes for Vice-President on the first ballot. He had now become a person of national political importance.

He campaigned hard for Fremont and Dayton although it was generally conceded they could not win. Lincoln, however, profited in numerous stump speeches by learning how to present more and more clearly and consistently his facts and arguments. One choleric old Democrat exlaimed after listening to him, "He is a dangerous man for he convinces you against your will."

Implication of Sectionalism

Douglas was compelled in 1856 to withdraw as a candidate for nomination for President by the Democratic National Convention in Cincinnati, in favor of James Buchanan of Pennsylvania. Ex-President Millard Fillmore was nominated by the Know Nothings.

Lincoln's notes (about 7, 23, 1856) for his campaign speeches to be delivered at Galena and other cities contain his estimation of the political policies and probabilities then involved in the claims of the three parties and their candidates. They were intended for his private study and not for public presentation, hence they reveal how he then analyzed the political situation. "Keep calm," "keep cool" seems to have been his endlessly reiterated self-advice.

"It is constantly objected to Fremont & Dayton, that they are supported by a *sectional* party, who, by their *sectionalism,* endanger the National Union. This objection, more than all the others, causes men, really opposed to slavery extension, to hesitate. Practically, it is the most difficult objection we have to meet.

"For this reason, I now propose to examine it, a little more carefully than I have heretofore done, or seen it done by others.

"First, then, what is the question between the parties, respectively represented by Buchanan and Fremont?

"Simply this: *Shall slavery be allowed to extend into U.S. territories now legally free:* Buchanan says it *shall* and Fremont says it shall *not.*

"That is the *naked* issue, and the *whole* of it. Lay the respective platforms side by side; and the difference between them, will be found to amount to precisely that.

"True, each party charges upon the other, *designs* much beyond what is involved in the issue, as stated; but as these charges cannot be freely proved either way, it is probably better to reject them on both sides, and stick to the naked issue, as it is clearly made upon on the record.

"And now, to restate the question *"Shall slavery be allowed to extend into U.S. territories, now legally free?'* I beg to know *how one* side of that question is more sectional than the other? Of course I expect to affect nothing with the man who makes this charge of sectionalism without caring whether it is just or not. But of the *candid, fair,* man, who has been puzzled with this charge, I do ask how is one side of the question more *sectional,* than the other? I beg of him to consider well, and answer calmly.

"If one side be as sectional as the other, nothing is gained, as to sectionalism, by changing sides; so that each must choose sides of the question on some other ground—as I should think, according, as the one side or the other, shall appear nearest right.

"If he shall think slavery *ought* to be extended, let him go to Buchanan, if he think it ought *not* let [him] go to Fremont.

"But, Fremont and Dayton, are both residents of free-states; and this fact can be vaunted, in high places, as excessive *sectionalism.*

"While interested individuals become *indignant* and *excited,* against this manifestation of *sectionalism,* I am very happy to know, that the Constitution remains calm—keeps cool—upon the subject. It does say that President and Vice-President shall be residents of different states; but it does not say one must live in a *slave,* and the other in a *free* state.

"It has been a *custom* to take one from a *slave,* and the other from a *free* state; but the custom has not, at all been uniform. In 1828 Gen. Jackson and Mr. Calhoun, both from slave-states, were placed on the same ticket, and Mr. Adams and Dr. Rush both from the free-states, were pitted against them. Gen: Jackson and Mr. Calhoun were elected; and qualified and served under the election; yet the whole thing never suggested the idea of sectionalism.

"In 1841, the president, Gen. Harrison, died, by which Mr. Tyler, the Vice-President & a slave state man, became president. Mr. [W. P.] Mangum, another slave-state man, was placed in the Vice Presidential chair, served out the term and no fuss about it—no sectionalism thought of.

"In 1853 the present president came into office. He is a free-state man. Mr. King, the New Vice President elect, was a slave-state man; but he died without entering on the duties of his office. At first his vacancy was filled by [D. R.] Atchison, another slave-state man, but he soon resigned, and the place was supplied by [J. D.] Bright, a free-state man. So that right now, and for the year and a half last past, our president and vice-president are actually free-state men.

"But, it is said, the friends of Fremont avow the purpose of electing him exclusively by free-state votes, and that this is unendurable *sectionalism.*

"This statement of fact, is not exactly true. With the friends of Fremont, it is an *expected necessity,* but it is not an *'avowed purpose'* to elect him, if at all, principally, by free-state votes; but it is, with equal intensity, true that Buchanan's friends, expect to elect him, if at all, chiefly by slave-state votes.

"Here, again, the sectionalism, is just as much on one side as the other.

"The thing which gives most color to the charge of Sectionalism, made against those who oppose the spread of slavery into free territory, is the fact *they* can get no votes in the slave-states, while their opponents get all, or nearly so, in the slave-states, and also, a large number in the free States. To state it in another way, the Extensionists, can get votes all over the Nation, while the Restrictionists can get votes only in the free states.*

"This being the fact, *why* is it so? It is not because one *side* of the question dividing them, is more sectional than the other; nor because of any differences in the mental or moral structure of the people in the North and South. It is because, in that question, the people of the South have an immediate palpable and immensely great pecuniary interest, while, with the people of the North, it is merely an abstract question of moral right, with only *slight* and remote pecuniary interest added.

"The slaves of the South, at a moderate estimate, are worth a thousand million dollars. Let it be permanently settled that this property may extend to new territory, without restraint, and it greatly *enhances,* perhaps quite *doubles,* its value at once. This immense, palpable pecuniary interest, on the question of extending slavery, unites the Southern people, as one man. But it can not be demonstrated that the North will gain a dollar by restricting it."

Moral Bonds are Weaker than Economic Bonds

Lincoln continued his notes on sectionalism:

"Moral principle is all, or nearly all that unites us of the North. Pity 'tis, it is so, but this is a looser bond, than pecuniary interest. Right here

*This solidarity of pro-slavery sentiment in the South and division of anti- and pro-slavery sentiment in the North, probably more than any other factor, led from sectionalism to secessionism as a political scheme, for it encouraged the organized Southern minority to feel strong enough to dominate the divided Northern majority. Later this political chaos continued and influenced the war policies of President Lincoln and General G. B. McClellan for the North, and General R. E. Lee for the South.

is the plain cause of *their perfect* union and *our want* of it. And see how it works. If a Southern man aspires to be president, they choke him down instantly, in order that the glittering prize of the presidency, may be held up, on Southern terms, to the greedy eyes of Northern ambition. With this they tempt us, and break in upon us.

"The democratic party, in 1844, elected a Southern president. Since then, they have neither had a Southern candidate for *election,* or *nomination.* Their Conventions of 1848—1852 and 1856, have been struggles excessively among *Northern* men, each vieing to outbid the other for the Southern vote—the South standing calmly by to finally cry going, going, gone, to the highest bidder; and, at the same time, to make its power more distinctly seen, and thereby to secure a still higher bid at the next succeeding struggle.

" 'Actions speak louder than words,' is the maxim; and if true, the South now distinctly says to the North 'Give us the *measures,* and you take the men.'

"The total withdrawal of Southern aspirants, for the presidency, multiplies the number of the Northern ones. These last, in competing with each other, commit themselves to the utmost verge that, through their own greediness, they have the least hope their Northern supporters will bear. Having got committed, in a race of competition, necessity drives them into union to sustain themselves. Each, at first secures all he can, on personal attachments to him, and through hopes resting on him personally. Next, they unite with one another, and with the perfectly banded South, to make the offensive position they have got into, 'a party measure.' This done, large additional numbers are secured.

"When the repeal of the Missouri Compromise was first proposed, at the North there was literally *'nobody'* in favor of it. In February 1854 our Legislature met in call, in extra, session. From them Douglas sought an indorsement of his then pending measure of Repeal. In our Legislature were about 70 democrats to 30 whigs. The former held a caucus, in which it was resolved to give Douglas the desired indorsement. Some of the members of that caucus bolted—would not stand it— and they now divulge the secrets. They say that the caucus fairly confessed that the Repeal was wrong; and they placed their determination to indorse it, solely on the ground that it was *necessary* to sustain Douglas. Here we have the direct evidence of how the Nebraska-bill obtained its strength in Illinois. It was given, not in a sense of right, but in the teeth of a sense of wrong, *to sustain Douglas.* So Illinois was divided. So New England for Pierce; Michigan for Cass; Pennsylvania for Buchan[an], and all for the Democratic party.

"And when, by such means, they have got a large portion of the Northern people into a position contrary to their own honest impulses, and sense of right; they have the impudence to turn upon those who do stand firm and call them sectional.

"Were it not too serious a matter, this cool impudence would be laughable, to say the least.

"Recurring to the question *'Shall slavery be allowed to extend into U. S. Territory now legally free?'*

"This *is* a sectional question—that is to say, it is a question, in its nature calculated to divide the American people geographically. Who is to *blame* for that? *Who* can help it? Either side *can* help it; but how? Simply by *yielding* to the other side. There is no other way. In the whole range of *possibility,* there is no other way. Then, which side shall yield? To this again, there can be but one answer—the side which is in the *wrong.* True, we differ, as to which side *is* wrong; and we boldly say, let all who think slavery ought to spread into free territory, openly go over against us. There is where they rightfully belong.

"But why should any go, who really think slavery ought not to spread? Do they really think the *right* ought to yield to the *wrong?* Are they afraid to stand by the *right?* Do they fear that the Constitution is too weak to sustain them in the right? Do they really think that by right surrendering to wrong, the hopes of our constitution, our Union, and our liberties, can possibly be bettered?"

Counterbalancing Thinker

Lincoln's wise habit at 47, of considering both the acquisitive *do* and avoidant *don't* sides of any issue, we have found, developed naturally since boyhood as his method of proving the solution of problems in self-education. Later, he continued to use this method when President, even though at times it involved his mind in dangerous periods of indecision and anxiety until he had obtained sufficient reliable evidence *for* and *against* a plan or proposition to make an irrevocable decision. By this mental method Lincoln was able to hold himself fully conscious of all information obtainable on both sides of issues and consider it for its true values without prejudice or preference either way. Thus he let facts speak for themselves and, through abiding by their relative weights, his reasoning and judgment were carried along with the changes in the evolution of human destiny towards establishing equal rights with preservation of the Union and reduction of want and suffering in underprivileged people.

Lincoln's mind, in working concomitantly on both sides (acquisitively and avoidantly) of the *pros* and *cons* of issues, was the prototype of the modern, scientific, philosophical mind. The unscientific type of mind, educated or illiterate, gives wishful prejudicial conscious consideration to mostly one side of an issue and keeps itself obstinately unconscious of the opposite in order not to be anxiously confused by having to make too difficult discriminations and judgments. The acquisitive-avoidance bilateral reasoning of scientific minds clashes inevitably with the acquisitive *or* avoidance unilateral prejudice of unscientific minds. The latter have far outnumbered the former in the evolution of social organization and intelligence, and hatefully resented any correcting influence until adopted. Hence the transition from the assumption of unilateral privilege to recognizing the value of equilateral needs and rights in the organization of human societies constitutes a bitter cross to bear for egocentric jealousy.

Press Comments on Speeches of 1856

Lincoln's speeches of 1856 were not published by newspapers with the exception of the one delivered at Kalamazoo, Michigan. Reporters gave their versions of what he said according to their political prejudices.

"Hon. Abraham Lincoln hit the nail on the head every time . . . in his artument in relation to Disunion." Gaelena *Weekly Northwestern Gazette,* 7, 29, 1856.

"His arguments on the leading issue [extension of slavery] between the parties were unanswerable." Paris *Prairie Beacon,* 8, 8, 1856.

"Lincoln . . . made a three hours speech. It was prosy and dull in the extreme—all about 'freedom,' 'liberty' and niggers. . . . He ridiculed the idea of disunion, and used a great many sophisms to direct the public mind from the true issue of the day." Petersburg *Illinois State Register,* 8, 9, 1856.

"The speech at Kalamazoo, Michigan (8, 27, 1856), reported at length in the Detroit *Daily Advertiser,* shows that Lincoln was having difficulty in creating public interest in his principles. "The question of slavery," he said, "at the present day, should be not only the greatest question, but very nearly the sole question. Our opponents, however, prefer that this should not be the case." . . . "We believe that it is right that slavery should not be tolerated in the territories, yet we cannot get support for this doctrine."

"At Petersburg," said the *Illinois State Register* (8, 30, 1856), "on saturday last our town was honored by the great high-priest of abolitionism, Abram Lincoln . . . I heard him pronouncing with thundering emphasis, a beautiful passage from Webster's compromise speech, and that, too, *without the quotations* . . . but it was soon evident that he had read Webster for the *letter* rather than the *spirit.*"

The report of the *Illinois Sentinel* of Lincoln's speech at Jacksonville (9, 6, 1856) condemns it for upholding Black Republicanism and sectionalism:

"The meeting was addressed during the afternoon by Hon. Abe Lincoln, in a speech which occupied some two hours. . . . He referred to the principle of the Kansas law; it permitted the people to settle the question of slavery for themselves, yet the territorial legislature, elected by a Missouri constituency, had passed, together with good wholesome laws, a law in direct conflict with this principle, making it a penal offense to declare that slavery was not legal in Kansas, or that Kansas should become a free State, and punishing the individual so offending by attaching to his leg a chain and ball. He omitted, however, to inform the audience that this very law was annulled by the Kansas bill which recently passed the democratic U. S. Senate; that every black republican in the Senate voted against thus annulling the obnoxious law; that the black republicans in the House also refused to pass the bill which annulled the law; and that, therefore, the black republicans are alone responsible for the present existence of such a law in Kansas. . . . He denied that the black repub-

licans were a sectional party, although he admitted they expected˙to elect
their ticket by the exclusive vote of the free states; and charged, as an offset,
that the democrats rested their hopes for the success of Buchanan on the
southern states alone.

"The attempt of Mr. Lincoln to evade the conclusion that the black
republicans are a sectional party by referring to the fact that Mr. Pierce
is also a northern man, is a dodge we have seen attempted by some of the
country fusion papers, but were surprised to see such a weak and silly
subterfuge advanced to an intelligent audience by a gentleman of ability
and standing like Mr. Lincoln.

"We must say that we regard Mr. Lincoln as a fine speaker. He is certainly
the ablest black republican that has taken the stump at this place during
the canvass; yet he utterly failed to sustain by satisfactory arguments the
black republican issue of intervention."

At Bloomington (9, 12, 1856) the *Weekly Pantagraph* said: "Hon.
A. Lincoln addressed the audience in a speech of great eloquence and
power."

At Olney (9, 20, 1856) the St. Louis *Missouri Republican:* "Abe
Lincoln tried his best to get up steam, but with all his tact in that line, it was
a dead failure. But about thirty listened. Said he, 'I am an old one; if twelve
of you will sit down and look at me, I will talk to you, if not, I will desist.'
The twelve sat down, he spoke a few minutes, and throwing up his hands
in disgust and dispair, said—'Oh, I can't interest this crowd,' and left the
stand."

Holds Party Welfare Above Personal Advantages

Lincoln's sense of honor, as a public man of moral principles to uphold the common welfare and the nation above personal advantages,
was offended by the alluring suggestions of Reverend J. M. Sturtevant,
President of Illinois College, who had pointed out certain compensations to be gained by accepting the Republican nomination for Congress.
Lincoln refused to be interested for reasons stated in his reply to Sturtevant (9, 27, 56):

"I want to thank you for your good opinion of me personally, and still
more for the deep interest you take in the cause of our common country.
It pains me a little that you have deemed it necessary to point out to me
how I may be compensated by throwing myself in the breach now. This
assumes that I am merely calculating the chances of my personal advancement. Let me assure you that I decline to be a candidate for congress, on
my clear conviction, that my running would *hurt,* & not *help* the
cause. I am willing to make any personal sacrifice, but I am not willing to
do, what in my own judgment, is, a sacrifice of the cause itself."

Election of Buchanan

The Northern antislavery Republican and Democratic vote was divided between Fremont and Fillmore so that Buchanan was elected by

the pro-slavery Northern and Southern vote, with over 400,000 votes less than a majority of the total.

Proslavery Northern and Southern politicians had made successful propaganda against Fremont as a sectional candidate, boldly stating that his election would cause disunion, through his opposition to admitting Kansas as a slave state into the Union. Antislavery politicians had urged that a vote for Fillmore was a vote against Fremont and for Buchanan and the admission of Kansas as a slave state.

We will find that in 1860 similar propaganda was repeated by four opposing political factions, with the difference that the proslavery Democrats were split between Douglas and Breckenridge. The old Democratic condemnation of the election of a Republican as sectionalism, and a cause of disunion, was effectively contradicted by its own sectionalism.

States' Rights and Union or Disunion

The first important speech by Lincoln after the election of President Buchanan was delivered at a Republican banquet in Chicago, Illinois (12, 10, 1856). He replied to the President's toast—"1st *the Union*—the North will maintain it—the South will not depart therefrom."

He gave transcripts of his speech to the Chicago *Democratic Press* and the *Illinois State Journal,* and summaries were published in both papers. The great political controversy was rapidly shifting in the minds of the Northern and Southern people around questions of the constitutional rights of states to adopt or abolish slavery and the rights of states for admission to the Union and secession from it. The following abstractions give the main points of his argument.

"Hon. Abram Lincoln of Springfield, [the Chicago *Democratic Press* reported,] amid most deafening cheers, arose to reply to the toast. He said he could most heartily indorse the sentiment expressed in the toast. During the whole canvass we had been assailed as the enemies of the Union, and he often had occasion to repudiate the sentiments attributed to us. He said that the Republican party was the friend of the Union. . . . He quoted Webster: 'Not Union without liberty, nor liberty without Union; but Union and liberty, now and forever, one and inseparable.' [He said] we had selected and elected a Republican State ticket . . . [and] it is now the duty of those elected to give us a good Republican Administration. . . . Our government rests in public opinion. Whoever can change public opinion, can change the government, practically just so much. Public opinion on any subject, always has a *'central idea,'* from which all its minor thoughts radiate. That 'central idea' in our political public opinion, at the beginning was, and until recently has continued to be, 'the equality of men.' And although it was always submitted patiently to whatever of inequality there seemed to be as a matter of actual necessity, its constant working has been a steady progress towards the practical equality of all men. The late Presidential election was a struggle, by one party, to discard that central idea, and to substitute for it the opposite idea that slavery is right, in the abstract, the workings of which, as a central idea, may be the perpetuity of human slavery, and its extension to all countries and colors.

Less than a year ago, the Richmond *Enquirer,* an avowed advocate of slavery, regardless of color, in order to favor his views, invented the phrase, 'State equality,' and now the President [Pierce], in his Message, adopts the *Enquirer's* catch-phrase, telling us the people 'have asserted the constitutional equality of each and all of the States of the Union as States.' The President flatters himself that the new central idea is completely inaugurated; and so, indeed, it is, so far as the mere fact of a Presidential election can inaugurate it. To us it is left to know that the majority of the people have not yet declared for it, and to hope that they never will.

"All of us who did not vote for Mr. Buchanan, taken together, are a majority of four hundred thousand. But, in the late contest we were divided between Fremont and Fillmore. Can we not come together, for the future. Let every one who really believes, and is resolved, that free society is not, *and shall not be,* a failure, and who can conscientiously declare that in the past contest he has done only what he thought best—let every such one have charity to believe that every other one can say as much. Thus let bygones be bygones. Let past differences, as nothing be; and with steady eye on the real issue, let us reinaugurate the good old 'central ideas' of the Republic. We *can* do it. The human heart *is* with us—God is with us. We shall again be able not to declare, that 'all States as States, are equal,' nor yet that 'all citizens as citizens are equal,' but to renew the broader, better declaration, including both these and much more, that 'all *men* are created equal.' "

Lincoln's political philosophy was now becoming more definitively practical. "Our government rests on public opinion and whoever can change public opinion can change the government practically just so much." He challenged the new political proslavery dogma that asserted the constitutional right of extension of slavery and the constitutional rights of the individual states, by claiming that they were not founded on the opinion of the majority of the people. Urging the good old "central idea of the Republic" that "all men are created equal" is founded in the "heart" and conscience of man and "the will of God," he called upon every person so believing to resolve that a "free society is not and shall not be a failure." This stirring moral appeal to public sentiments of patriotic Americans, urging them to preserve liberty and Union, began to produce results. Chicago became the stronghold of Lincoln Republicans.

Chapter XXVI

MR. REPUBLICAN OF ILLINOIS

"Upon those men who are, in sentiment, opposed to the spread, and nationalization of slavery, rests the task of preventing it," wrote Lincoln in his analytical notes (2, 28, 1857). "The Republican organization is the embodiment of that sentiment," he continued, "though as yet, it by no means embraces all the individuals holding that sentiment. The party is newly formed; and in forming, old party ties had to be broken and the attractions of party pride, and influential leaders were wholly wanting. In spite of old differences, prejudices, and animosities, it's members were drawn together by a paramount danger. They formed and maneuvered in the face of a disciplined enemy, and in the teeth of all his persistent mis-representations. Of course, they fell far short of gathering in all of their own. And yet, a year ago, they stood up, an army over thirteen hundred thousand strong. That army is, to-day, the best hope of the nation, and of the world. Their work is before them; and from which they may not guiltlessly turn away."

In notes for a speech in Chicago he wrote the same day:

"We were without party history, party pride, or party idols.

"We were a collection of individuals, but recently in political hostility, one to another; and thus subject to all that distrust, and suspicion, and jealousy could do.

"Every where in the ranks of the common enemy, were old party and personal friends, jibing, and jeering, and framing deceitful arguments against us.

"We were scarcely met at all on the real issue.

"Thousands avowed our principles, but turned from us, professing to believe we *meant* more than we *said.*

"No argument which was true in fact, made any head-way against us. This we know.

"We were constantly charged with seeking an amalgamation of the white and black races; and thousands turned from us, not believing the charge (no one believed it) but *fearing* to face it themselves."

"Too Poor to Lose Two Years"

In reply to an invitation from C. D. Gilfillan to assist in organizing the new Republican party in his Territory of Minnesota, Lincoln, with characteristic diffidence wrote (5, 9, 1857):

"I have no great faith in the success of my efforts; still it is with some regret I have to say I can not visit you before the June election; and I can not as yet, say I will be able to do so in the summer or fall. Having devoted the most of last year to politics, it is a *necessity* with me to devote this, to my private affairs."

To J. W. Grimes (8, 17, 1857): "I lost nearly all the working part of last year, giving my time to the canvass; and I am altogether too poor to lose two years together."

The Dred Scott Case

Dred Scott was a Negro slave and body servant of Dr. John Emerson, a surgeon in the United States Army. Dr. Emerson was stationed in 1834 in St. Louis, Missouri, and then ordered to Rock Island, Illinois for two years and then to Fort Snelling, Minnesota, a part of then North-west Territory, accompanied always by his slave. In Minnesota Dred Scott married another slave with the consent of their owners, and his wife gave birth to two girls, who also became lawfully the property of Dr. Emerson. Later the Emersons returned to Missouri, accompanied by the Scotts. Here the doctor died in 1844 and the slaves were inherited by Mrs. Emerson who was administrator of the estate.

In 1846 Dred Scott brought suit for freedom against Mrs. Emerson in one of the Missouri state courts at St. Louis. Scott claimed that while living in Illinois he had been made free by the State Constitution which forbade slavery; and he had been emancipated when living in Minnesota by virtue of the Missouri Compromise. The trial court of Missouri, a slave state, awarded Dred Scott his freedom, whereupon Mrs. Emerson appealed to the State Supreme Court, which decided in March 1852 that as Scott had returned to Missouri with Dr. Emerson his status as a slave was resumed.

In 1850, while the Supreme Court of Missouri had the Dred Scott case under advisement, Mrs. Emerson married Dr. Clifford Chaffee, of Springfield, Massachusetts. He was a member of Congress, elected as a Know-Nothing, and abolitionist. As the husband of Mrs. Emerson he held property rights in her slaves. The Chaffees decided, apparently with the approval of Dred Scott and the support of abolitionist friends, to make an interstate test of the case and bring a suit under the juris-diction of a Federal Court. To effect this purpose Mrs. Emerson Chaffee sold Dred Scott to her brother John Sanford, then a resident of New York, and Dred Scott brought suit again, repeating the claims made in the previous suit. The Court held that the claims of Scott were valid and that he was free. Whereupon the lawyers representing the Chaffee-Sanford interests and the Scott interests made up an agreed case of facts and submitted it to a trial by jury in the same Federal Court under the same Federal judge. The judge then reversed his ruling and instructed the jury that Scott was still a slave of Sanford. Dred Scott's attorneys then filed an appeal (December, 1854) in the United States Supreme Court, so worded as to call for a decision that would include judgment on Scott's right to freedom, the legal rights of slaves, and the validity of the Missouri Compromise and the powers of Congress to regulate slavery.

After two years of waiting in due course on the docket, the case finally came up for argument in February, 1856. Definitive statements of the powers of Congress, and of Territories and states to legislate on slavery became the critical issue.

Lincoln's Notes On The Dred Scott Case

The nation was in a turmoil of political excitement over the prospective Court's decision and the murderous conflict then waging between pro- and antislavery interests in Kansas, when Lincoln wrote contemplatively in his notes (January, 1857?):

> "What would be the effect of this, if it should ever become the creed of a dominant party in the nation? Let us analyze, and consider it.
> "It affirms that, whatever the Supreme Court may decide as to the constitutional restriction on the power of a territorial Legislature, in regard to slavery in the territory, must be obeyed, and enforced by all the departments of the federal government.
> "Now, if this is sound, as to this particular constitutional question, it is equally sound of *all* constitutional questions; so that the proposition substantially, is "Whatever decision the Supreme court makes on *any* constitutional question, must be obeyed, and enforced by all the departments of the federal government.'
> "Again, it is not the full scope of this creed, that if the Supreme court, having the particular question before them, shall decide that Dred Scott is a slave, the executive department must enforce the decision against Dred Scott. If this were its full scope, it is presumed, no one would controvert it's correctness. But in this narrow scope, there is no room for the Legislative department to enforce the decision; while the creed affirms that *all* the departments must enforce it. The creed, then, has a broader scope; and what is it? It is this; that as soon as the Supreme court decides that Dred Scott is a slave, the whole community must decide that not only Dred Scott, but that *all* persons in like condition, are rightfully slave."

Lincoln, at this time, seems to have had no inclination to think that the political conspiracy to extend the rights of slavery, that had passed the Kansas-Nebraska Bill and annulled the Missouri Compromise, involved members of the Supreme Court.

The Supreme Court Decision

The United States Supreme Court had at this time five judges of Southern or slave state origin and four of Northern or free state origin. Before his inauguration (3, 4, 1857) President Buchanan was prematurely informed, a gross irregularity, that the Court would soon give its decision and would uphold the Missouri Supreme Court and further it would affirm the unconstitutionality of the Missouri Compromise and state the limitations of the powers of Congress and states and Territories on the regulation of slavery. President Buchanan took the opportunity to try to placate the public dissension over slavery and prepare it for acceptance of the Court's decision by remarking, in his inaugural address, that the national conflict over slavery would soon be "finally" and "happily" settled and that he "in common with all good citizens" would cheerfully submit to the decision "whatever it may be."*

Two days later, 81-year-old Chief Justice Roger B. Taney (a highly respected lawyer and judge, a devout Catholic from Maryland who had liberated the slaves he had inherited) gave the majority opinion in a lengthy five to four decision, Justices Curtis and McLean expressing dissent.

Limitations of space permit giving here abstractions only of the principles that aroused the great conflict of public opinion that followed and became the points of political action by freedom-loving people, including Lincoln. Justice Taney reviewed, according to his conception of the history, the pertinent facts in the origin of the Constitution and its empowerment of Federal, state, and territorial government as evidence of the intent of the Founders. He held that although Negroes had improved under civilization they were regarded by the Founders as being too inferior "to have any rights that the white man was bound to respect." The statement in the Declaration of Independence that "all men are created free and equal" was not meant to apply to them. Negroes were not "people" and slaves and their free descendants were not entitled to be citizens of any state, hence not of the United States. Therefore Scott had no right to sue in a Federal court and the case must be dismissed.

The decision held further that the Missouri Compromise was void, for a strict interpretation of the Constitution did not confer such powers on Congress in preparing the government of territories. Citizens had the right to property, slaves were property and Congress had no power to exclude them from a territory. Therefore Congress in creating a territorial legislature could not confer upon it a power that it did not have, namely, the prohibition of slavery. Only upon the adoption of a state Constitution for admission into the Union could the citizens of a territory exclude slavery.

The decision implied that states' rights superceded Federal rights in the regulation of slavery. It also implied that its assumption of what constituted significant historical facts and its interpretations of their relative values and meanings were true and therefore the rightful basis of interpretation of the meaning of the Constitution and judgment on the validity of the laws of the nation.

Secession Meetings in New England

Could free-minded people accept any Court's interpretation of history as pontifically infallible? Although it would be accepted, until

*President Pierce had made a statement of similar meaning in his last annual message to Congress.

changed, as the law to be executed, it would not be accepted as being beyond the pale of public criticism and political action. Obviously the people's right to take due legal steps to obtain a change of decision by the Court is the indispensable orderly means in a democracy by which the interpretation of the meaning of the Constitution can be maintained in harmony with the inevitable evolution in social culture consequent upon increase of territory, population, and interpersonal dependency as the result of the economies in the advances of science, mechanics, the arts, and agriculture.

Justice Taney's statement of the historical intent of the Constitution, as a basis for his intensely proslavery opinion, was challenged by the minority opinion of Associate Justices Curtis and McLean, and their critical argument was supported by numerous apostles of freedom, including Lincoln. Douglas, on the other hand, accepted the Court's decision entirely, as a confirmation of his principle that the people of a territory should have the right to hold slaves and then decide for the adoption or rejection of slavery upon forming their state Constitution.

The decision opened all of the nation's territories to slavery, and the antislavery reaction in the North grew extremely excited and radical. Meetings were held in New England demanding secession of the free states, and the eminent preacher Wendell Phillips declared publicly that the Union was "accursed of God" and should be dissolved. Horace Greeley, editor of the New York *Tribune,* denounced the decision as a step in a plot with the Kansas-Nebraska Act to nationalize slavery. Similar charges were reiterated in the Northern press with highly inflamatory, uncompromising arguments. In opposition, the Southern press applauded the Court's recognition that only States hold the right under the Constitution to decide on slavery. President Buchanan was accused on the floor of Congress with having influenced the decision of the Supreme Court.

Challenges Dred Scott Decision and Douglas' Approval

In Springfield (6, 26, 1857) Lincoln defended his opinions against the claims of Douglas, made in a speech in that city two weeks previously. He assumed that Douglas would again be the Democratic candidate for reelection to the United States Senate the next year, and expecting himself to be the Republican candidate, he made the most of the opportunity. This speech covers all of the major political changes that had transpired since his Peoria speech in 1856. Careful study of it will inform the reader of the issues of 1857 up to June. Lincoln gives us his view of the moral principles of both great political parties, and applies analytically his philosophy of common sense with magnificent fairness and justice to both sides. (Captions inserted.)

"I am here to-night, partly by the invitation of some of you, and partly by my own inclination. Two weeks ago Judge Douglas spoke here

on the several subjects of Kansas, the Dred Scott decision, and Utah. I
listened to the speech at the time, and have read the report of it since.
It was intended to controvert opinions which I think just, and to assail
(politically, and not personally,) those men, who in common with me,
entertain those opinions. For this reason I wished then, and still wish, to
make some answer to it, which I now take the opportunity of doing."

Coerce Rebellious Utah into Obedience

"I begin with Utah. If it prove to be true, as is probable, that the
people of Utah are in open rebellion to the United States, then Judge
Douglas is in favor of repealing their territorial organization, and attaching
them to the adjoining States for judicial purposes. I say, too, if they are
in rebellion, they ought to be somehow coerced into obedience; and I
am not now prepared to admit or deny that the Judge's mode of coercing
them is not as good as any. The Republicans can fall in with it without
taking back anything they have ever said. To be sure, it would be a
considerable backing down by Judge Douglas from his much vaunted
doctrine of self-government for the territories; but this is only additional
proof of what was very plain from the beginning, that the doctrine was
a mere deceitful pretense for the benefit of slavery. Those who could not
see that much in the Nebraska act itself, which forced Governors and
Secretaries, and Judges on the people of the territories, without their
choice or consent, could not be made to see, though one should rise from
the dead to testify."

Utah's Right to Polygamy

"But in all this, it is very plain the Judge evades the only question
the Republicans have ever pressed upon the Democracy in regard to Utah.
That question the Judge well knows to be this: 'If the people of Utah
shall peacefully form a State Constitution tolerating polygamy, will the
Democracy admit them into the Union?' There is nothing in the United
States Constitution or law against polygamy; and why is it not a part of
the Judge's 'sacred right of self-government' for that people to have it,
or rather to *keep* it, if they choose? These questions, so far as I know,
the Judge never answers. It might involve the Democracy to answer
them either way, and they go unanswered.

Kansas' "Farce" Vote

"As to Kansas. The substance of the Judge's speech on Kansas is an
effort to put the free State men in the wrong for not voting at the election of delegates to the Constitutional Convention. He says *'There is
every reason to hope and believe that the law will be fairly interpreted
and impartially executed, so as to insure to every bone fide inhabitant the
free and quiet exercise of the elective franchise.'*
"It appears extraodinary that Judge Douglas should make such a statement. He knows that, by the law, no man can vote who has not been
registered; and he knows that the free State men place their refusal to
vote on the ground that but few of them have been registered. . . . He

knows it is boldly declared that the people of many whole counties, and many whole neighborhoods in others, are left unregistered; yet, he does not venture to contradict the declaration, nor to point out how they *can* vote without being registered; but he just slips along, not seeming to know there is any such question of fact and complacently declares: 'There is every reason to hope and believe that the law will be fairly and impartially executed, so as to insure to every bona fide inhabitant the free and quiet exercise of the elective franchise.'

"I readily agree that if all had a chance to vote, they ought to have voted. If, on the contrary, as they allege and Judge Douglas ventures not to particularly contradict, few only of the free State ever had a chance to vote, they were perfectly right in staying from the polls in a body.

"By the way since the Judge spoke, the Kansas election has come off. The Judge expressed his confidence that all the Democrats in Kansas would do their duty—including 'free state Democrats' of course. The returns received here as yet are very incomplete; but so far as they go, they indicate that only about one sixth of the registered voters, have really voted; and this too, when not more, perhaps, than one half of the rightful voters have been registered, thus showing the thing to have been the most exquisite farce ever enacted. . . .

"Allow me to barely whisper my suspicion that there were no such things in Kansas 'as free state Democrats'—that they were altogether mythical, good only to figure in newspapers and speeches in free states. If there should prove to be one real living free state Democrat in Kansas, I suggest that it might be well to catch him, and stuff and preserve his skin, as an interesting specimen of that soon to be extinct variety of the genus, Democrat."

Would Have Supreme Court Reverse Itself

"And now as to the Dred Scott decision. That decision declares two propositions—first, that a negro cannot sue in the U. S. Courts, and secondly, that Congress cannot prohibit slavery in the Territories. It was made by a divided court—dividing differently on the different points. Judge Douglas does not discuss the merits of the decision; and, in that respect, I shall follow his example, believing I could no more improve on McLean and Curtis, than he could on Taney.

"He denounces all who question the correctness of that decision, as offering violent resistance to it. But who resists it? Who has, in spite of that decision, declared Dred Scott free, and resisted the authority of his master over him?

"Judicial decisions have two uses—first, to absolutely determine the case decided, and secondly, to indicate to the public how other similar cases will be decided when they arise. For the latter use they are called 'precedents' and 'authorities.'

"We believe, as much as Judge Douglas, (perhaps more) in obedience to, and respect for the judicial department of the government. We think its decisions on constitutional questions, when fully settled, should control, not only the particular cases decided, but the general policy of the country, subject to be disturbed only by amendments of the Constitution as provided in that instrument itself. More than this would be revolution.

But we think the Dred Scott decision is erroneous. We know the court that made it, has often over-ruled its own decisions, and we shall do what we can to have it over-rule this. We offer no *resistance* to it."

Philosophy of Common Sense

"Judicial decisions are of greater or lesser authority as precedents, according to circumstances. That this should be so, accords both with common sense, and the customary understanding of the legal profession.

"If this important decision had been made by the unanimous concurrence of the judges, and without any apparent partisan bias, and in accord with legal public expectation, and with the steady practice of the departments throughout our history, and had been in no part, based on assumed historical facts which are not really true; or, if wanting in some of these, it had been before the court more than once, and had there been affirmed and re-affirmed through a course of years, it then might be, perhaps would be, factious, nay, even revolutionary, to not acquiesce in it as a precedent.

"But when, as it is true we find it wanting in all these claims to the public confidence, it is not resistance, it is not factious, it is not even disrespectful, to treat it as not having yet quite established a settled doctrine for the country—But Judge Douglas considers this view awful. Hear him:

> " 'The courts are the tribunals prescribed by the Constitution and created by the authority of the people to determine, expound and enforce the law. Hence, whoever resists the final decision of the highest judicial tribunal, aims a deadly blow at our whole Republican system of government—a blow, which if successful would place all our rights and liberties at the mercy of passion, anarchy and violence. I repeat, therefore, that if resistance to the decisions of the Supreme Court of the United States, in a matter like the points decided in the Dred Scott case, clearly within their jurisdiction as defined by the Constitution, shall be forced upon the country as a political issue, it will become a distinct and naked issue between the friends and enemies of the Constitution—the friends and the enemies of the supremacy of the laws.' "

The political position of Douglas would have been greatly strengthened if he could have prevented the Supreme Court's decision from being made a political issue. Lincoln has been blamed (Masters, 1939), in taking this step, for contributing to the confusion and conflict that followed.

Jackson's Disregard of Supreme Court Decision

"Why this same Supreme court once decided a national bank to be constitutional; but Gen. Jackson, as President of the United States, disregarded the decision, and vetoed a bill for a re-charter, partly on constitutional ground, declaring that each public functionary must support the Constitution, *'as he understands it.'* But hear the General's own words. Here they are taken from his veto message:

> " 'It is maintained by the advocates of the bank, that its constitutionality, in all its features, ought to be considered as settled by precedent, and by the decision of the Supreme Court. To this conclusion, I cannot assent. Mere precedence is a dangerous source of authority, and should not be regarded as deciding questions of constitutional power, except where the acquiescence of the people and the States can be considered as well settled. So far from this being the case on this subject,

an argument against the bank might be based on precedent. One Congress in 1791, decided in favor of a bank, another in 1811, decided against it. One Congress in 1815 decided against a bank; another in 1816 decided in its favor. Prior to the present Congress, therefore the precedents drawn from that source were equal. If we resort to the States, the expressions of legislative, judicial and executive opinions against the bank have been probably to those in its favor as four to one. There is nothing in precedent, therefore, which if its authority were admitted, ought to weigh in favor of the act before it.'

"I drop the quotations merely to remark that all there ever was, in the way of precedent up to the Dred Scott decision on the points therein decided, had been against that decision. But here Gen. Jackson further—

" 'If the opinion of the Supreme Court covered the whole ground of this act, it ought not to control the co-ordinate authorities of this Government. The Congress, the executive and the court, must each for itself be guided by its own opinion of the Constitution. Each public officer, who takes an oath to support the Constitution, swears that he will support it as he understands it, and not as it is understood by others.' "

Lincoln's use of Jackson's argument to support his own political position raised a controversy in political philosophy. Jackson was within his constitutional rights as President in disregarding the Court's previous decision on the national bank. However his statement that "each public officer, who takes an oath to support the Constitution swears that he will support it as he understands it, and not as understood by others" implies that each person has the right to interpret the Constitution as he understands it, regardless of the meaning given to it by the Supreme Court. This principle is potentially anarchical, for without the Supreme Court to serve as the final authority of the people on the meaning and application of the Constitution to congressional and state laws and the manner of execution by officials of the government, pandemonium and rebellion, gangster tyranny and anarchy would follow and destroy the Union. Lincoln did not adopt Jackson's wilful advice to government officials. He held that so long as an interpretation of the Constitution was given by a majority opinion of the Supreme Court it must be accepted as the law, but since most of its decisions have a dissenting minority and are subject to reconsideration and change by the Court itself, each decision is logically subject to question and criticism by the people.

"Again and again," Lincoln asserted, "have I heard Judge Douglas denounce that bank decision, and applaud Gen. Jackson for disregarding it. It would be interesting for him to look over his recent speech, and see how exactly his fierce philippics against us for resisting the Supreme Court decisions, fall upon his own head. It will call to his mind a long and fierce political war in this country, upon an issue which, in his own language, and, of course, in his own changeless estimation, was 'a distinct and naked issue between the friends and the enemies of the Constitution,' and in which war he fought in the ranks of the enemies of the Constitution."

Challenges Taney's 'Historical Facts'

"I have said, in substance, that the Dred Scott decision was, in part; based on assumed historical facts which were not really true; and I ought not to leave the subject without giving some reasons for saying this; I therefore give an instance or two, which I think fully sustain me. Chief Justice Raney, in delivering the majority opinion of the Court, insists at great length that negroes were no part of the people who made, and for whom was made, the Declaration of Independence, or the Constitution of the United States.

"On the contrary, Judge Curtis, in his dissenting opinion, shows that in five of the then thirteen states, to wit, New Hampshire, Massachusetts, New York, New Jersey and North Carolina, free negroes were voters, and, in proportion to their numbers, had the same part in making the Constitution that the white people had. He shows this with so much particularity as to leave no doubt of its truth; and, as a sort of conclusion on that point, holds the following language.

" 'The Constitution was ordained and established by the people of the United States, through the action, in each State, of those persons who were qualified by its laws to act thereon in behalf of themselves and all other citizens of the State. In some of the States, we have seen, colored persons were among those qualified by law to act on the subject. These colored persons were not only included in the body of 'the people of the United States,' by whom the Constitution was ordained and established; but in at least five of the States they had the power to act, and, doubtless, did act, by their suffrages, upon the question of its adoption.'

"Again, Chief Justice Taney says: 'It is difficult, at this day to realize the state of public opinion in relation to that unfortunate race, which prevailed in the civilized and enlightened portions of the world at the time of the Declaration of Independence, and when the Constitution of the United States was framed and adopted.' And again after quoting from the Declaration, he says: 'The general words above quoted would seem to include the whole human family, and if they were used in a similar instrument at this day, would be so understood.' "

"In these the Chief Justice does not directly assert, but plainly assumes, as a fact, that the public estimate of the black man is more favorable *now* than it was in the days of the Revolution. This assumption is a mistake. In some trifling particulars the condition of the race has been ameliorated; but, as a whole, in this country, the change between then and now is decidedly the other way; and their ultimate destiny has never appeared so hopeless as in the last three or four years. In two of the five states—New Jersey and North Carolina—that then gave the free negro the right of voting, the right has since been taken away; and in a third—New York—it has been greatly abridged; while it has not been extended, so far as I know, to a single additional State, though the number of the States has more than doubled. In those days, as I understand, masters could, at their own pleasure, emancipate their slaves; but since then, such legal restraints have been made upon emancipation, as to amount almost to prohibition. In those days, Legislatures held the unquestioned power to abolish slavery in their respective States; but now it is becoming quite fashionable for State Constitutions to withhold that power from the Legislatures. In those days, by common consent, the spread of the black man's bondage to new countries was prohibited; but now Congress decides that it *will* not continue the prohibition, and the Supreme Court decided that it *could* not if it would. In those days, our

Declaration of Independence was held sacred by all, and thought to include all; but now to aid in making the bondage of the negro universal and eternal, it is assailed, and sneered at, and construed, and hawked at, and torn, till, if its framers could rise from their graves, they could not at all recognize it. All the powers of earth seem rapidly combining against him. Mammon is after him; ambition follows, and philosophy follows, and the Theology of the day is fast joining the cry. . . .

"It is grossly incorrect to say or assume, that the public estimate of the negro is more favorable now than it was at the origin of the government."

Douglas' "Counterfeit Logic"

"Three years and a half ago, Judge Douglas brought forward his famous Nebraska bill. The country was at once in a blaze. He scorned all opposition and carried it through Congress. Since then he has seen himself superseded in a Presidential nomination, by one endorsing the general doctrine of his measure, but at the same time standing clear of the odium of its untimely agitation, and its gross breach of national faith; and he has seen that successful rival Constitutionally elected, not by the strength of friends, but by the division of adversaries, being in a popular minority of nearly four hundred thousand votes. He has seen his chief aids in his own State, Shields and Richardson, politically speaking, successively tried, convicted, and executed, for an offense not their own, but his. And now he sees his own case, standing next on the docket for trial.

"There is a natural disgust in the minds of nearly all the white people, to the idea of an indiscriminate amalgamation of the white and black races; and Judge Douglas is evidently basing his chief hope, upon the chances of being able to appropriate the benefit of this disgust to himself. If he can, by much drumming and repeating, fasten the odium of that idea upon his adversaries, he thinks he can struggle through the storm. He therefore clings to this hope, as a drowning man to the last plank. He makes an occasion for lugging it in from the opposition to the Dred Scott decision. He finds the Republicans insisting that the Declaration of Independence includes ALL men, black as well as white; and forthwith he boldly denies that it includes negroes at all, and proceeds to argue gravely that all who contend it does, do so only because they want to vote, and eat, and sleep, and marry with negroes! He will have it that they cannot be consistent else. Now I protest against that counterfeit logic which concludes that, because I do not want a black woman for a *slave* I must necessarily want her for a wife. I need not have her for either, I can just leave her alone. In some respects she certainly is not my equal; but in her natural right to eat the bread she earns with her own hands without asking leave of anyone else, she is my equal, and the equal of all others."

Inalienable Rights of All Men Equal

"Chief Justice Taney, in his opinion on the Dred Scott case, admits that the language of the Declaration is broad enough to include the whole human family, but he and Judge Douglas argue that the authors of the instrument did not intend to include negroes, by the fact that they did not at once, actually place them on an equality with the whites. Now this grave argument comes to just nothing at all, by the other fact, that they did not at once, *or ever afterwards,* actually place all white people on an equality with one or another. And this is the staple argument of both the Chief Justice and the Senator, for doing this obvious violence to the plain unmistakable language of the Declaration. I think the authors of that notable instrument intended to include *all* men, but they did not intend to declare all equal *in all respects.* They did not mean to say all men were equal in color, size, intellect, moral developments, or social capacity. They defined with tolerable distinctness, in what respects they did consider all men created equal—equal in 'certain inalienable rights, among which are life, liberty and the pursuit of happiness.' This they said, and this they meant. They did not mean to assert the obvious untruth, that all were then actually enjoying that equality, nor yet, that they were about to confer it immediately upon them. In fact they had no power to confer such a boon. They meant simply to declare the *right,* so that the *enforcement* of it might follow as fast as circumstances should permit. They meant to set up a standard maxim for free society, which should be familiar to all, and revered by all; constantly looked to, constantly labored for, and even though never perfectly attained, constantly approximated, and thereby constantly spreading and deepening its influence, and augmenting the happiness and value of life to all people of all colors everywhere. The assertion that 'all men are created equal' was of no practical use in effecting our separation from Great Britain; and it was placed in the Declaration, not for that, but for future use. Its authors meant it to be, thank God, it is now proving itself, a stumbling block to those who in after times might seek to turn a free people back into the hateful paths of despotism. They knew the proneness of prosperity to breed tyrants, and they meant when such should re-appear in this fair land and commence their vocation they should find left for them at least one hard nut to crack."

"I have now briefly expressed my view of the *meaning* and *objects* of that part of the Declaration of Independence which declared 'all men are created equal.'

"Now let us hear Judge Douglas' view on the same subject, as I find it in the printed report of his late speech. Here it is:

 " 'No man can vindicate the character, motives and conduct of the signers of the Declaration of Independence, except upon the hypothesis that they referred to the white race alone, and not to the African, and when they declared all men to have been created equal—that they were speaking of British subjects on this continent being equal to British subjects born and residing in Great Britain—that they were entitled to the same inalienable rights, and among them were enumerated life, liberty and the pursuit of happiness. The Declaration was adopted for the purpose of justifying the colonists in the eyes of the world in withdrawing their allegiance to the British crown, and dissolving their connection with the mother country.'*

"My good friends, read that carefully over some leisure hour, and ponder well upon it—see what a mere wreck—mangled ruin—it makes of our once glorious Declaration.

 " 'They were speaking of British subjects on this continent being equal to British subjects born and residing in Great Britain!' Why, according to

*It was also a declaration by the colonies of rights to equal representation in government as a protest against the crown for taxation without representation. We will see later in the debates how Lincoln's satirical criticism of Douglas' demogoguery forced him to include white Europeans with British subjects.

this, not only negroes but white people outside of Great Britain and America are not spoken of in that instrument. The English, Irish and Scotch, along with the Americans, were included to be sure, but the French and Germans and other white people of the world are all gone to pot along with the Judge's inferior races.

"I had thought the Declaration promised something better than the condition of British subjects; but no, it only meant that we should be *equal* to them in their own oppressed and *unequal* condition. According to that, it gave no promise that having kicked off the King and the Lords of Great Britain, we should not at once be saddled with a King and Lords of our own.

"I had thought the Declaration contemplated the progressive improvement in the condition of all men everywhere; but no, it merely 'was adopted for the purpose of justifying the colonists in the eyes of the civilized world in withdrawing their allegiance from the British crown, and dissolving their connection with the mother country.' Why, that object having been effected some eighty years ago, the Declaration is of no practical use now—mere rubbish—old wadding left to rot on the battlefield after the victory is won."

Glorious or Sham Fourth

"I understand you are preparing to celebrate the 'Fourth,' to-morrow week. What for? The doings of that day had no reference to the present; and quite half of you are not even descendents of those who were referred to at that day. But I suppose you will celebrate; and will even go so far as to read the Declaration. Suppose after you read it once in the old fashioned way, you read it once more with Judge Douglas' version. It will then run thus 'We . . . who were on this continent eighty-one years ago, were created equal to all British subjects born and *then* residing in Great Britain.'

"And now I appeal to all—to Democrats as well as others,—are you really willing that the Declaration shall be thus frittered away?—thus left no more at most, than an interesting memorial of the dead past? thus shorn of its vitality, and practical value; and left without the *germ* or even the *suggestion* of the individual rights of man in it?"

Racial Amalgamation Under Slavery

"But Judge Douglas is especially horrified at the thought of the mixing blood by the white and black races; agreed at once—a thousand times agreed. There are white men enough to marry all the white women, and black men enough to marry all the black women; and so let them be married. On this point we fully agree with the Judge; and when he shall show that his policy is better adapted to prevent amalgamation than ours we shall drop ours, and adopt his. Let us see. In 1850 there were in the United Stateees, 405,751 mulattoes. Very few of these were the offspring of whites and *free* blacks; nearly all have sprung from black *slaves* and white masters. A separation of the races is the only perfect preventive of amalgamation but as an immediate separation is impossible the next best thing is to *keep* them apart *where* they are not already together. If white and black people never get together in Kansas, they will never mix blood in Kansas. This is at least one self-evident truth. A few free colored people may get into the free

States, in any event; but their number is too insignificant to amount to much in the way of mixing blood. In 1850 there were in the free states, 56,649 mulattoes; but for the most part they were not born there—they came from the slave States, ready made up. In the same year the slave States had 348,874 mulattoes all of home production. The proportion of free mulattoes to free blacks—the only colored classes in the free states—is much greater in the slave than in the free states. It is worthy of note too, that among the free states those which make the colored man the nearest to equal the white, have, proportionately the fewest mulattoes the least of amalgamation. In New Hampshire, the state which goes farthest towards equality between the races, there are just 184 Mulattoes while there are in Virginia—how many do you think? 79,775, being more than 23,126 more than in all the free States together.

"These statistics show that slavery is the greatest source of amalgamation; and next to it, not the elevation, but the degeneration of the free blacks. Yet Judge Douglas dreads the slightest restraints on the spread of slavery, and the slightest human recognition of the negro, as tending horribly to amalgamation.

"This very Dred Scott case affords a strong test as to which party most favors amalgamation, the Republican or the dear Union-saving Democracy. Dred Scott, his wife and two daughters were all involved in the suit. We desired the court to have held that they were citizens so far at least as to entitle them to a hearing as to whether they were free or not; and then, also, that they were in fact and in law really free. Could we have had our way, the chances of these black girls, ever mixing their blood with that of the white people, would have been diminished at least to the extent that it could not have been without their consent. But Judge Douglas is delighted to have them decided to be slaves, and not human enough to have a hearing, even if they were free, and thus left subject to the forced concubinage of their masters, and liable to become mothers of mulattoes in spite of themselves—the very state of case that produces nine tenths of all mulattoes—all the mixing of blood in the nation.

"Of course, I state this as an illustration only, not meaning to say that the master of Dred Scott and his family, or any more than a per centage of masters generally, are inclined to exercise this particular power which they hold over their female slaves."

African Colonization

"I have said that the separation of the races is the only perfect prevention of amalgamation. I have no right to say all the members of the Republican party are in favor of this, nor to say that as a party they are in favor of it. There is nothing in their platform directly on the subject. But I can say a very large proportion of its members are for it, and that the chief plank in their platform—opposition to the spread of slavery—is most favorable to that separation.

"Such separation, if ever effected at all, must be effected by colonization; and no political party, as such, is now doing anything directly for colonization. Party operations at present only favor or retard colonization incidentally. The enterprise is a difficult one; but, 'when there is a will there is a way,' and what colonization needs most is a hearty will. Will springs from the two elements of moral sense and self-interest. Let us be brought to believe it is morally right, and, at the same time, favorable to, or, at least, not against, our interest, to transfer the African to his native clime, and we shall find a way to do it, however great the task may be. The children of Israel, to such numbers as to include four hundred thousand fighting men, went out of Egyptian bondage in a body.

"How differently the respective courses of the Democratic and Republican parties incidentally bear on the question of forming a will—a public sentiment—for colonization, is easy to see. The Republicans inculcate, with whatever of ability they can, that the negro is a man; that his bondage is cruelly wrong, and that the field of his oppression ought not to be enlarged. The Democrats deny his manhood; deny, or dwarf into insignificance, the wrong of his bondage; so far as possible, crush all sympathy for him, and cultivate and excite hatred and disgust against him; compliment themselves as Union-savers for doing so; and call the indefinite outspreading of his bondage 'a sacred right of self-government.'

"The plainest print cannot be read through a gold eagle; and it will be ever hard to find many men who will send a slave to Liberia, and pay his passage while they can send him to a new country, Kansas for instance, and sell him for fifteen hundred dollars, and the rise."

Lincoln's political argument had grown so vigorously pointed in 1857 that it aroused intense western interest and became the means of exciting national interest through 1858 to 1861.

Buchanan and Douglas Fight over Kansas Constitution

The territory of Kansas, inhabited by small centers of intensely determined, uncompromising pro-slavery and anti-slavery factions, reinforced by Southern and Northern money and radical agitation, had become inevitably a bloody battle ground, despite the free legal rights to vote and legislate assured by the Constitution of the United States. The pro-slavery party chose Lecompton in 1855 for its capital and, with a territorial Legislature elected by fradulent and violent exclusion of the anti-slavery vote through the help of Missouri gangsters, presented a constitution, with a pro-slavery clause, for admission into the Union as a state. The anti-slavery free-soilers retaliated by organizing a rival government at Topeka, and the contest for control of the territory promptly assumed the violence of guerilla warfare. "Bleeding Kansas" thus became the political prototype of the nation-to-be within three years. The violent tempered extremists of both sides were acting without equitable consideration of the rights of the opposition.

President Buchanan, desirous of ending the strife in Kansas and intimidated by the uncompromising Southern pressure that had increased greatly upon the Supreme Court's Dred Scott decision, urged Congress to admit Kansas under the Lecompton constitution. He demanded of Senator Douglas, chairman of the Committee on Territories, that, as a matter of national expediency and party discipline, he support the scheme. But Douglas instead courageously defied Buchanan and attacked the fraud as a misuse of popular sovereignty. "I will stand," he declared in a speech to the Senate, "on the great principle of popular sovereignty, which declares the rights of all people to be perfectly free to form and regulate their domestic institutions in their own way."

Buchanan then tried to destroy Douglas politically in Illinois, even though the latter had supported him after the demoncratic nomination for President, by transferring all political patronage in favor of his enemies. Valiant Douglas fought it out and, with the aid of the Republican advocates of the rights of free men as much as that of anti-slavery Democrats, he broke Buchanan's power in the west and effectively rejected the Lecompton constitution.

Lincoln Worries over the New Popularity of Douglas

So vigorously did Douglas seize the new opportunity and make the most of his Northern popularity that many Eastern Republicans proposed him for leadership of the new party, hoping thereby to form an alliance of all northern and southern anti-slavery sentiments.

"What think you of the probable *"rumpus"* among the democracy over the Kansas Constitution?" Lincoln wrote to Senator Trumbull (11, 30, 1857). "I think the Republicans should stand clear of it. In their view both the President and Douglas are wrong; and they should not espouse the cause of either, because they may consider the other a little farther wrong of the two."

"From what I am told here, Douglas tried, before leaving, to draw off some Republicans on this dodge and even succeeded in making some impression on one or two."

"What does the New-York Tribune mean," he wrote again to Senator Trumbull (12, 28, 1857), "by it's constant eulogizing, and admiring, and magnifying Douglas? Does it, in this, speak the sentiments of the republicans of Washington? Have they concluded that the republican cause, generally, can be best promoted by sacrificing us here in Illinois? If so we would like to know it soon; it will save us a great deal of labor to surrender at once.

"As yet I have heared of no republican here going over to Douglas; but if the Tribune continues to din his praises into the ear of it's five or ten thousand republican readers in Illinois, it is more than can be hoped that all will stand firm."

Chapter XXVII

A HOUSE DIVIDED AGAINST
ITSELF CANNOT STAND

In 1858 Illinois would elect a United States Senator and a number of congressmen. Lincoln expected to be nominated as the Republican candidate for the Senate in opposition to Douglas who would seek re-election as a Democrat. It was a critical election year for the Democratic and young Republican parties throughout the nation.

Herndon Goes East

Herndon had been, since a young lawyer, in active correspondance with many of the progressive writers of America on social and political issues, and seems to have been held in high esteem by them for the pertinence and progressiveness of his views. Lincoln was dejected over the popularity of Douglas in the East and the way Horace Greeley of the New York *Tribune* and other editors were recommending his reelection and support by members of the young Republican party. He complained to Herndon (1889) that Greeley's attitude would damage him with Sumner, Seward, Wilson, Phillips, and other friends in the East who were leaders of the new Republican movement so that, at least, they would quit pulling for him, a tried and true member, in order to elevate a Democrat.

Herndon decided, upon his own initiative and expense, to go East and confer with Democratic and Republican antislavery editors and social leaders on the existing political problems of slavery. It was his first trip (March, 1858) beyond the Alleghenies and he was well received and given opportunity to exchange views with many prominent men. In Washington he saw Trumbull, Douglas, Seward, Sumner, and Wilson; Phillips and Greeley in New York; and Governor Banks, Theodore Parker, and Garrison in Boston. He found that Greeley was greatly impressed by the arguments and courage of Douglas and wanted to see him reelected, as did also Governor Banks of Massachusetts. Women, he found, liked Abe Lincoln's antislavery speeches and were surprisingly active and influential with their men. Estimations of the influence of Herndon's interviews with these men vary among historians but we know that out of it came a number of important invitations to Lincoln in the next two years to speak in Eastern cities, giving him opportunities to meet Eastern political leaders and express his views on Western slavery and other current issues.

517

Herndon was amazed at the size, development, wealth, and mechanical efficiencies of the great Eastern cities, and was greatly impressed by the cordiality, information, and views of Eastern men. He brought back with him numerous books, lectures, and papers on social and political issues, one of which impressed him so greatly that he gave it to Lincoln to read. The lecture was by Theodore Parker on "The Effects of Slavery on the American People." After Lincoln's death he found the following lines had been marked by him: "Democracy is direct self-government, over all of the people, for all of the people, by all of the people." Later Lincoln restated this idea in his Gettysburg Address.

Democrats Split

The split in the Democratic ranks included pro-Buchanan versus pro-Douglas groups, who held conventions in Springfield on the same day (4, 22, 1858) to form a definite policy on the Kansas situation. Proslavery extension versus antislavery restriction and pro-Missouri Compromise versus popular sovereignty contributed to the dissention. Douglas' frustration of Buchanan's scheme to make Congress accept the Lecompton constitution had greatly increased his popularity in Northern Democratic and Republican ranks but seriously discredited him in the South.

> "I was in Springfield during the sittings of the two democratic conventions day-before-yesterday. Say what they will, they are having an abundance of trouble," Lincoln wrote to T. A. Marshall (4, 23, 1858).

Three days later (4, 26) he wrote to E. B. Washburne.

> "The day before the conventions I received a letter from Chicago having, among other things, on other subjects, the following in it: 'A reliable republican, but an old line whig lawyer, in this city told me today that *he himself had seen* a letter from one of our republican congressmen, advising us all to go for the reelection of Judge Douglas.'
> "Several of our friends were down from Chicago, and they had something of the same story amongst them, . . .
> "A word about the conventions. The democracy parted in not a very encouraged state of mind.
> "On the contrary, our friends, a good many of whom were present, parted in high spirits. They think if we do not triumph the fault will be our own, and so I really think."

Lincoln took every opportunity in his personal communications to keep the Kansas question agitated in order to win over antislavery Democratic friends and Republicans to his political philosophy.

Again to Washburne (5, 15, 1858):

> "The [Illinois] State Register, here [Springfield], is evidently laboring to bring it's old friends into what the doctors call the '*comatose*

state'—that is, a sort of drowsy, dreamy condition, in which they may not perceive or remember that there has ever been, or is, any difference between Douglas & the President. This could be done, *if* the Buchanan men would allow it—which, however, the latter seem determined not to do."

Lincoln Continues to Worry About Douglas

Lincoln continued to worry lest Douglas might win the support of Republicans because of the parallel nature of certain of their principles, as defined in his letter to J. F. Alexander (5, 15, 1858).

"I will only say now that, as I understand, there remains all the difference there ever was between Judge Douglas & the Republicans—*they* insisting that Congress *shall,* and *he* insisting that congress *shall not,* keep slavery out of the Territories *before & up to the time* they form State constitutions. No republican has ever contended that, when a constitution is formed, any but the *people* of the territory shall form it. Republican's have never contended that congress should *dictate* a constitution to any state or territory; but they have contended that the people should be *perfectly* free to form their constitution in their own way—as *perfectly* free from the presence of slavery amongst them, as from every other improper influence.

"In voting together in opposition to a constitution being forced upon the people of Kansas, neither Judge Douglas nor the Republicans, has conceded anything which was ever in dispute between them."

This letter draws precisely the line of differentiation between the political principles of Lincoln and Douglas. Both held that Congress had no power under the Constitution to impose a constitution upon a territory, and that the citizens of the territory must be free to form their own constitution, but they differed on the power of Congress to regulate the admission of slaves into a territory before the constitution was formed. Lincoln continued to hold that Congress had this power under the Constitution and the Missouri Compromise was legal, hence slavery was illegal in Kansas and Nebraska Territories before its annulment and should continue to be so. Douglas held that the Kansas-Nebraska Act had annulled the Missouri Compromise and the Supreme Court had decided that slaves, as property, could be taken anywhere by their owners unless prohibited by the constitution of a state. Herein Douglas now stood on lawfully established ground whereas Lincoln had only a morally conscientious attitude supported by the "intent" of the Constitution, but his influence was spreading rapidly throughout the North and increasing public determination to prevent the extension of slavery.

Notes for Campaign Speeches

Lincoln, anticipating nomination in 1858 as the Republican candidate for the United States Senate, saw himself confronted with a double political problem: the preservation of his party against appeal within to adopt Douglas and his policies, and the defeat of Douglas through splitting the Democratic party. In notes prepared in May 1858 for the speeches he expected to deliver during the campaign, he drew the lines of issue clearly and logically in his mind. Since most of his ideas were presented later in his nomination acceptance and other speeches, we give the notes that reveal how he worried over the possibility that Douglas might get control of the young Republican party. He raised questions as if asked by another person and then answered them. This method indicates the action of a subconscious alter-ego that was skeptical of his conscious reasoning as well as that of Douglas and everyone else. In this way he was able to keep his thoughts under severe criticism and thoroughly objective and unwishfully balanced (captions inserted).

"From time to time, ever since the Chicago "Times" and the "Illinois State Register" declared their opposition to the Lecompton constitution, and it began to be understod that Judge Douglas was also opposed to it, I have been accosted by friends of his with the question, 'What do you think now?' Since the delivery of his speech in the Senate, the question has been varied a little. 'Have you read Douglas's speech?' 'Yes.' 'Well, what do you think of it?' In every instance the question is accompanied with an anxious inquiring stare, which asks, quite as plainly as words could, 'Can't you go for Douglas now?' Like boys who have set a bird-trap, they are watching to see if the birds are picking at the bait and likely to go under."

Foresees Douglas' Strategy

"I think, then, Judge Douglas knows that the Republicans wish Kansas to be a free State. He knows that they know, if the question be fairly submitted to a vote of the people of Kansas, it will be a free State; and he would not object at all if, by drawing their attention to this particular fact, and himself becoming vociferous for such a fair vote, they should be induced to drop their own organization, fall into rank behind him, and form a great free-State Democratic party.

"But before Republicans do this, I think they ought to require a few questions to be answered on the other side. If they do fall in with Judge Douglas, and Kansas shall be secured as a free State, there then remaining no cause of difference between them and the regular Democracy, will not the Republicans stand ready, haltered and harnessed, to be handed over by him to the regular Democracy, to filibuster indefinitely for additional slave territory,—to carry slavery into all the States, as well as Territories, under the Dred Scott decision, construed and enlarged from time to time, according to the demands of the regular slave Democracy,—and to assist in reviving the African slave-trade in order that all may buy negroes where they can be bought cheapest, as a clear incident of that 'sacred right of property,' now held in some quarters to be above all constitutions?

"By so falling in, will we not be committed to or at least compromitted with the Nebraska policy?

"If so, we should remember that Kansas is saved, not by that policy or its authors, but in spite of both—by an effort that cannot be kept in future cases.

"Did Judge Douglas help any to get a free-State majority into Kansas? Not a bit of it—the exact contrary. Does he now express a wish that Kansas, or any other place, shall be free? Nothing like it. He tells us, in this very speech [12, 9, 1857], expected to be so palatable to Republicans, that he cares not whether slavery is voted down or voted up. His whole effort is devoted to clearing the ring, and giving slavery and freedom a fair fight. With one who considers slavery just as good as freedom, this is perfectly natural and consistent.

"But have Republicans any sympathy with such a view? They think slavery is wrong; and that, like every other wrong which some men will commit if left alone, it ought to be prohibited by law. They consider it not only morally wrong, but a 'deadly poison' in a government like ours, professedly based on the equality of man. Upon this radical difference of opinion with Judge Douglas, the Republican party was organized. There is all the difference between him and them that there ever was. He will not say that he has changed; Have you?"

"Again, we ought to be informed as to Judge Douglas's present opinion as to the inclination of Republicans to marry with negroes. By his Springfield speech we know what it was last June; and by his resolution dropped at Jacksonville in September we know what it was then. Perhaps we have something even later in a Chicago speech, in which the danger of being 'stunk out of church' [quotation from Douglas] was descanted upon. But what is his opinion on the point now? There is, or will be, a sure sign to judge by. If this charge shall be silently dropped by the Judge and his friends, if no more resolutions on the subject shall be passed in the Douglas Democratic meetings and conventions, it will be safe to swear that he is courting. Our 'witching smile' has 'caught his youthful fancy'; and henceforth Cuffy and he are rival beaux for our gushing affections"*

What Republicans Ought to Support

"In the present aspect of affairs what ought Republicans to do? I think they ought not to oppose any measure merely because Judge Douglas proposes it. . . . If . . . Judge Douglas's bill secures a fair vote to the people of Kansas, without contrivance to commit any one farther, I think Republican members of Congress ought to support it. They can do so without inconsistency."

---

*Lincoln's literary style of meditative self-expression on how to foresee the intentions of Douglas is remindful of Hamlet's meditations on how to foresee the intentions of his rival, the King.

"I Am Glad"

"I am glad Judge Douglas has, at last, distinctly told us that he cares not whether slavery be voted down or voted up. Not so much that this is any news to me; nor yet that it may be slightly new to some of that class of his friends who delight to say that they 'are as much opposed to slavery as anybody.'

"I am glad because it affords such a true and excellent definition of the Nebraska policy itself. That policy, honestly administered, is exactly that. It seeks to bring the people of the nation to not care anything about slavery. This is Nebraskaism in its abstract purity—in its very best dress.

"Now, I take it, nearly everybody does care something about slavery—is either for it or against it; and that the statesmanship of a measure which conforms to the sentiments of nobody might well be doubted in advance.

"But Nebraskaism did not originate as a piece of statesmanship. General Cass, in 1848, invented it, as a political manoeuver, to secure himself the Democratic nomination for the presidency. It served its purpose then, and sunk out of sight. Six years later Judge Douglas fished it up and glozed it over with what he called, and still persists in calling, 'sacred rights of self-government.'"

"I, Too, Believe in Self-Government"

"Well, I, too, believe in self-government as I understand it; but I do not understand that the privilege one man takes of making a slave of another, or holding him as such is any part of 'self-government.' To call it so is, to my mind, simply absurd and ridiculous. I am for the people of the whole nation doing just as they please in matters which concern the whole nation; for those of each part doing just as they choose in all matters which concern no other part; and for each individual doing just as he chooses in all matters which concern nobody else. This is the principle. Of course I am content with any exception which the Constitution, or the actually existing state of things, makes a necessity. But neither the principle nor the exception will admit the indefinite spread and perpetuity of slavery."

A House Divided Against Itself Cannot Stand

"I believe the government cannot endure permanently half slave and half free. I expressed this belief a year ago; and subsequent developments have confirmed me. I do not expect the Union to be dissolved. I do not expect the house to fall, but I do expect it will cease to be divided. It will become all one thing or all the other. Either the opponents of slavery will arrest the further spread of it, and put it in course of ultimate extinction; or its advocates will push it forward till it shall become alike lawful in all the States, old as well as new. Do you doubt it? Study the Dred Scott decision, and then see how little even now remains to be done. That decision may be reduced to three points.

"The first is that a negro cannot be a citizen. That point is made in order to deprive the negro, in every possible event, of the benefit of that provision of the United States Constitution which declares that 'the citizens of each State shall be entitled to all privileges and immunities of citizens in the several States.'

"The second point is that the United States Constitution protects slavery, as property, in all the United States Territories, and that neither Congress, nor the people of the Territories, nor any other power, can prohibit it at any time prior to the formation of State constitutions.

"This point is made in order that the Territories may safely be filled up with slaves, before the formation of State constitutions, thereby to embarrass the free-State sentiment, and enhance the chances of slave constitutions being adopted.

"The third point decided is that the voluntary bringing of Dred Scott into Illinois by his master, and holding him here a long time as a slave, did not operate his emancipation, did not make him free.

"This point is made, not to be pressed immediately; but if acquiesced in for a while, then to sustain the logical conclusion that what Dred Scott's master might lawfully do with Dred in the free State of Illinois, every other master may lawfully do with any other one or one hundred slaves in Illinois, or in any other free State. Auxiliary to all this, and working hand in hand with it, the Nebraska doctrine is to educate and mold public opinion to 'not care whether slavery is voted up or voted down.' At least Northern public opinion must cease to care anything about it. Southern public opinion may, without offense, continue to care as much as it pleases.

"Welcome, or unwelcome, agreeable, or disagreeable, whether this shall be an entire slave nation, *is* the issue before us. Every incident—every little shifting of scenes or of actors—only clears away the intervening trash, compacts and consolidates the opposing hosts, and brings them more and more distinctly face to face. The conflict will be a severe one; and it will be fought through by those who *do* care for the result, and not by those who do not care—by those who are *for,* and those who are against a legalized national slavery. The combined charge of Nebraskaism and Dred Scottism must be repulsed, and rolled back. The deceitful cloak of 'self-government' wherewith the 'sum of all villanies' seeks to protect and adorn itself, must be torn from it's hateful carcass. That burlesque upon judicial decisions, and slander and profanation upon honored names, and sacred history of republican America, must be over-ruled, and expunged from the books of authority.

"To give victory to the right, not *bloody bullets,* but *peaceful ballots* only, are necessary. Thanks to our good old Constitution, and organization under it, these alone are necessary. It only needs that every right thinking man, shall go to the polls, and without fear or prejudice *vote* as he *thinks.*"

Douglas' Double Game

Within a few weeks after the Democratic schism the Buchanan and Douglas factions had reconciled their differences, with Douglas emerging as the real leader of the party.

"Political matters just now," Lincoln wrote to his now confidential friend and adviser, Washburne (5, 27, 1858), "bear a very *mixed* and *incongruous* aspect. For several days the signs have been that Douglas and the

President had probably burned [sic] the hatchet, Doug's friends at Washington going over to the President's side, and his friends here & South of here, talking as if there never had been any serious difficulty, while the President himself does nothing for his own peculiar friends here. But this morning my partner, Mr. Herndon, receives a letter from Mr. Medill of the Chicago Tribune, showing the writer to be in great alarm at the prospect North of Republicans going over to Douglas, on the idea that Douglas is going to assume steep free-soil ground, and furiously assail the administration on the stump when he comes home. There certainly is a double game being played some how. Possibly even *probably*—Douglas is temporarily deceiving the President in order to crush out the 8th. of June convention here. Unless he plays his double game more successfully than we have often seen done, he can not carry many republicans North, without at the same time losing a large number of his old friends South."

Lincoln's estimation of Douglas' issue-straddling position to catch both Northern antislavery and Southern proslavery votes shows that he had, by this time, determined to attack the dangerous contradiction in his rival's political philosophy if he could somehow find a way to expose it. We will see how a few months later he trapped Douglas and nailed him to his own double cross. He had become a master of political strategy and was determined to force Douglas to declare himself so that either he must lose on the Southern side in order to win on the Northern side and retain his seat in the Senate, or possibly lose both. Lincoln felt quite sure that he would, above all, act to save himself. But Douglas was still the most powerful Democrat in the state and in the nation, and so redoubtable and resourceful in politics that he continued to worry Lincoln lest he might again lose what he loved to the wooing abilities of his rival.

"*I* do not find republicans," he wrote to S. A. Hurlbut (6, 1, 1858), "from the old *democratic* ranks more inclined to Douglas than those from the old whig ranks—indeed I find very little of such inclination in either class; but of that little, the larger portion, falling under my observation, has been among the old whigs."

Greeley Worries Lincoln

Horace Greeley, editor of the *New York Tribune* (Republican) cast a bomb into Lincoln's camp by advocating the support of Douglas by the Republican party. Lincoln's comments (6, 1, 1858) to C. L. Wilson on Greeley's attitude show how astutely and fairly he measured men:

"I have never said, or thought more, as to the inclination of some of our Eastern republican friends to favor Douglas, than I expressed in your hearing on the evening of the 21st. April, at the State Library in this place [Springfield]. I have believed—do believe—that Greely, for instance, would be rather pleased to see Douglas

reelected over me or any other republican; and yet I do not believe
it is so, because of any secret arrangement with Douglas. It is because
he thinks Douglas' superior position, reputation, experience and
ability, if you please, would more than compensate for his lack of
a pure republican position, and therefore, his reelection do the general
cause of republicanism, more good, than would the election of any one
of our better undistinguished pure republicans. I do not know how *you*
estimate Greely, but *I* consider him incapable of corruption, or
falsehood. . . . I have also thought that Govr. [W. H.] Seward [formerly
governor of New York, now United States Senator] too, feels about as
Greely does; but not being a newspaper editor, his feeling, in this respect,
is not much manifested. I have no idea that he is, by conversation or by
letters, urging Illinois republicans to vote for Douglas.

"As to myself, let me pledge you my word that neither I, nor
any friend of mine so far as I know, has been setting stake against
Gov. Seward. No combination has been made *with* me, or *proposed*
to me, in relation to the next Presidential candidate. The same thing
is true in regard to [the] next Governor of our State. I am not
directly or indirectly committed to any one; nor has any one made
any advance to me upon the subject."

Lincoln seems at this time to have had sufficient reason to think
that Senator Seward of New York would probably be a candidate for
the Republican nomination for President in 1860; but he had not
the remotest idea that he, himself, then nationally unimportant, might
be a contender for the same position, even though he had been proposed in the Republican national convention in 1856 as a candidate
for the nomination of vice-president.

The new Republican cauldron was boiling with a welter of contradictory ideas on the "principles" involved as opposing factions
shouted them at each other. Lincoln's impression of their relative
values, as expressed in his letter to Samuel Wilkinson (6, 10, 1858),
shows how confidently he believed that he could resolve them. Public
opinion, he realized, cannot readily reverse itself or contradict itself
after its attitude is set *acquisiticely for* a certain line of action and
avoidantly against its logical antithesis:

"I *know* of no effort to unite the Reps. & Buc. men, and
believe there is none. Of course the Republicans do not try to
keep the common enemy from dividing; but, so far as I *know* or
believe, they will not unite with either branch of the division.
Indeed it is difficult for me to see, on what ground they could unite;
but it is useless to spend words, there is simply nothing of it. It is a
trick of our enemies to try to excite all sorts of suspicions and jealousies amongst us. We hope that our convention on the 16th.
bringing us together, and letting us hear each other talk will put an
end to most of this."

Senatorial Nomination Speech

On June 16, 1858, upon accepting the nomination for the United States Senate by the Republican convention at Springfield, Ill. Abraham Lincoln made one of the most important speeches of his life. He had written on scraps of paper ideas that occurred to him in preparation for his speech, and carried them in his hat for several days. He finished writing it midst the turmoil of the convention, and then read it privately to a few chosen friends for their opinions. According to Herndon (1889), he sought in particular, approval for application of the allegory "a house divided against itself cannot stand." They all urged against the introduction into politics of biblical Christian truisms. He replied:

> "That expression is a truth of all human experience. . . . I want to use some universally known figure expressed in simple language . . . that may strike home to the minds of men in order to raise them up to the peril of the time."

All present except one persisted strongly in objecting to the radical innovation. Herndon enthusiastically endorsed it and predicted that the speech "will make you president." Lincoln concluded the conference with saying:

> "Friends, this thing has been retarded long enough. The time has come when these sentiments should be uttered, and if it is desired that I should go down because of this speech, then let me go down in defeat with the truth—let me die in the advocacy of what is just and right."

The following presentation of this speech is taken from the newspaper clippings, as published in *Collected Works*, contained in the scrapbook which Lincoln sent (12, 19, 1859) to G. M. Parsons of the Republican Central Executive Committee, for publication with other speeches by himself and Douglas in *The Debates*. A complete transcript of the speech, which was largely extemporaneous, was not made. Captions are inserted.

> "Mr. President and Gentlemen of the Convention: If we could first know *where* we are and *whither* we are tending we could then better judge *what* to do and *how* to do it.
> "We are now far in the *fifth* year, since a policy was initiated with the *avowed* object and *confident* promise of putting an end to slavery agitation.
> "Under the operation of that policy, that agitation has not only *not ceased,* but has *constantly augmented.*
> "In *my* opinion, it *will* not cease, until a *crisis* shall have been reached, and passed.
> " 'A house divided against itself cannot stand.'
> "I believe this government cannot endure, permanently half *slave* and half *free*.

"I do not expect the Union to be *dissolved*—I do not expect the house to *fall*—but I *do* expect it will cease to be divided.

"It will become *all* one thing or *all* the other.

"Either the *opponents* of slavery, will arrest the further spread of it, and place it where the public mind shall rest in the belief that it is in course of ultimate extinction; or its *advocates* will push it forward, till it shall become alike lawful in *all* the States, *old* as well as *new—North* as well as *South*. Have we no *tendency* to the latter condition?"

Turns the South Against Himself

Lincoln answered this question with a long arrangement of inferences from recent events that, he held, indicated a cultural trend toward popularizing slavery and also indicated political scheming in high official circles to bring about its general legal adoption. We give this argument in full, for it soon proved a double-edged sword that turned the South against him, convinced that he intended to abolish slavery eventually.

"Let any one who doubts, carefully contemplate that now almost complete legal combination—piece of *machinery* so to speak—compounded of the Nebraska doctrine, and the Dred Scott decision. Let him consider not only what work the machinery is adapted to do, and *how well* adapted; but also, let him study the *history* of its construction, and trace, if he can, or rather fail, if he can, to trace the evidences of design, and concert of action, among its chief bosses, from the beginning.

"But, so far, *Congress* only, had acted; and an *indorsement* by the people, *real* or apparent, was indispensable, to *save* the point already gained, and give chance for more.

"The new year of 1854, found slavery excluded from more than half the States by State Constitutions, and from most of the national territory by Congressional prohibition.

"Four days later, commenced the struggle, which ended in repealing that Congressional prohibition.

"This opened all the national territory to slavery; and was the first point gained.

"This necessity had not been overlooked; but had been provided for, as well as might be, in the notable argument of *'squatter sovereignty,'* otherwise called *'sacred right of self-government,'* which latter phrase, though expressive of the only rightful basis of any government, was so perverted in this attempted use of it as to amount to just this: That if any *one* man, choose to enslave *another,* no *third* man shall be allowed to object.

"That argument was incorporated in the Nebraska bill itself, in the language which follows: *'It being the true intent and meaning of this act not to legislate slavery into any Territory or state, not exclude it therefrom; but to leave the people thereof perfectly free to form and regulate their domestic institutions in their own way, subject only to the Constitution of the United States.'*

"Then opened the roar of loose declamation in favor of 'Squatter Sovereignty,' and 'Sacred right of self-government.'

" 'But,' said opposition members, 'let us be more *specific*—let us *amend* the bill so as to expressly declare that the people of the territory *may* exclude slavery.' 'Not we,' said the friends of the measure and down they voted the amendment.

"While the Nebraska bill was passing through congress, a *law case,* involving the question of a negroe's freedom, by reason of his owner having voluntarily taken him first into a free state and then a territory covered by the congressional prohibition, and held him as a slave, for a long time in each, was passing through the U. S. Circuit Court for the District of Missouri; and both Nebraska bill and law suit were brought to a decision in the same month of May, 1854. The negroe's name was 'Dred Scott,' which name now designates the decision finally made in the case."

Correlates Indications of Political Conspiracy

"*Before* the *then* next Presidential election, the law case came *to,* and was argued *in* the Supreme Court of the United States; but the *decision* of it was deferred until *after* the election. Still, *before* the election, Senator Trumbull, on the floor of the Senate, requests the leading advocate of the Nebraska bill to state *his opinion* whether the people of a territory can constitutionally exclude slavery from their limits; and the latter answers, 'That is a question for the Supreme Court.'

"The election came. Mr. Buchanan was elected, and the *indorsement,* such as it was, secured. That was the *second* point gained. The indorsement, however, fell short of a clear popular majority by nearly four hundred thousand votes, and so, perhaps, was not overwhelmingly reliable and satisfactory.

"The *outgoing* President, in his last annual message, as impressively as possible *echoed back* upon the people the *weight* and *authority* of the indorsement.

"The Supreme Court met again; *did not* announce their decision, but ordered a re-argument.

"The Presidential inauguration came, and still no decision of the court; but the *incoming* President, in his inaugural address, fervently exhorted the people to abide by the forthcoming decision, *whatever it might be.*

"Then, in a few days, came the decision.

"The reputed author of the Nebraska bill finds an early occasion to make a speech at this capitol indorsing the Dred Scott Decision, and vehemently denouncing all opposition to it.

"The new President, too, siezes the early occasion of the Silliman letter to *indorse* and strongly *construe* that decision, and to express his *astonishment* that any different view had ever been entertained.

"At length a squabble springs up between the President and the author of the Nebraska bill, on the *mere* question of *fact,* whether the Lecompton constitution was or was not, in any just sense, made

PLATE 12. "Morally Aroused." August 26, 1858. Ambrotype by W. P. Pierson. Courtesy of the Illinois State Historical Library.

PLATE 13. Mr. Republican of Illinois. October 4, 1859. Photograph by S. M. Fassett. Courtesy of the Illinois State Historical Library.

by the people of Kansas; and in that squabble the latter declares that all he wants is a fair vote for the people, and that he *cares* not whether slavery be voted *down* or voted *up.* I do not understand his declaration that he cares not whether slavery be voted down or up to be intended by him other than as an *apt definition* of the *policy* he would impress upon the public mind—the *principle* for which he declares he has suffered much, and is ready to suffer to the end.

"And well may he cling to that principle. If he has any parental feeling, well may he cling to it. That principle, is the only *shred* left of his original Nebraska doctrine. Under the Dred Scott decision, 'squatter sovereignty' squatted out of existence, tumbled down like temporary scaffolding—like the mould at the foundry served through one blast and fell back into loose sand—helped to carry an election, and then was kicked to the winds. His late *joint* struggle with the Republicans, against the Lecompton Constitution, involves nothing of the original Nebraska doctrine. That struggle was made on a point, the right of a people to make their own constitution, upon which he and the Republicans have never differed.

"The several points of the Dred Scott decision, in connection with Senator Douglas' 'care not' policy, constitute the piece of machinery, in its present state of advancement. This was the third point gained."

How the Machine Works

"The *working* points of that machinery are:

"First, that no negro slave, imported as such from Africa, and no descendent of such a slave can ever be a *citizen* of any State in the sense of that term as used in the Constitution of the United States.

"This point is made in order to deprive the negro, in every possible event, of the benefit of this provision of the United States Constitution, which declares that—

" 'The citizens of each State shall be entitled to all privileges and immunities of citizens in the several States.'

"Secondly, that 'subject to the Constitution of the United States,' neither *Congress* nor a *Territorial Legislature* can exclude slavery from any United States territory.'

"This point is made in order that individual men may *fill up* the territories with slaves, without danger of losing them as property, and thus to enhance the chances of *permanency* to the institution through all the future.

"Thirdly, that whether the holding a negro in actual slavery in a free State, makes him free, as against the holder, the United States courts will not decide, but will leave to be decided by the courts of any slave State the negro may be forced into by the master.

"This point is made, not to be pressed *immediately;* but, if acquiesced in for a while, and apparently *indorsed* by the people at an election, *then* to sustain the logical conclusion that what Dred Scott's master might lawfully do with Dred Scott, in the free State of Illinois, every other master may lawfully do with any other *one,* or one *thousand* slaves, in Illinois, or in any free State.

"Auxiliary to all this, and working hand in hand with it, the Nebraska doctrine, or what is left of it, is to *educate* and *mould* public opinion, at least *Northern* public opinion, to not *care* whether slavery is voted *down* or voted *up.*"

Whither Tending

"This shows exactly where we now *are;* and *partially* also, whither we are tending.

"It will throw additional light on the latter, to go back, and run the mind over the string of historical facts already stated. Several things will *now* appear less *dark* and *mysterious* than they did *when* they were transpiring. The people were to be left 'perfectly free' 'subject only to the Constitution.' What the *Constitution* had to do with it outsiders could not *then* see. Plainly enough *now,* it was an exactly fitted *niche,* for the Dred Scott decision to afterwards come in, and declare the *perfect freedom* of the people, to be just no freedom at all.

"Why was the amendment, expressly declaring the right of the people to exclude slavery, voted down? Plainly enough *now,* the adoption of it, would have spoiled the niche for the Dred Scott decision.

"Why was the court decision held up? Why, even a Senator's individual opinion withheld, till *after* the Presidential election? Plainly enough *now,* the speaking out *then* would have damaged the *'perfectly free'* argument upon which the election was to be carried.

"Why the *outgoing* President's felicitation on the indorsement? Why the delay of a reargument? Why the incoming President's *advance* exhortation in favor of the decision?

"These things *look* like the cautious *patting* and *petting* a spirited horse, preparatory to mounting him, when it is dreaded that he may give the rider a fall.

"And why the hasty after indorsements of the decision by the President and others?"

Suspicion of Preconcert

"We can not absolutely *know* that all these exact adaptations are the result of preconcert. But when we see a lot of framed timbers, different potions of which we know have been gotten out at different times and places by different workmen-Stephen [Douglas], Franklin [Pierce], Roger [Taney] and James [Buchanan], for instance—and when we see these timbers joined together, and see they exactly make the frame of a house or a mill, all the tenons and mortices exactly fitting, and all the lengths and proportions of the different pieces exactly adapted to their respective places, and not a piece too many or too few—not omitting even scaffolding—or, if a single piece be lacking, we can see the place in the frame exactly fitted and prepared to yet bring such a piece in—in *such* a case, we find it impossible not to *believe* that Stephen and Franklin and Roger and James all understood one another from the beginning, and all worked upon a common *plan* or *draft* drawn up before the first lick was struck.

"It should not be overlooked that, by the Nebraska bill, the people of a *State,* as well as *Territory,* were to be left *'perfectly free' 'subject only to the Constitution.'*

"Why mention a *State?* They were legislating for *territories,* and not *for* and *about* States; Certainly the people of a State *are* and *ought to be* subject to the Constitution of the United States; but why is mention of this *lugged* into this merely *territorial* law? Why are the people of a *territory* and the people of a *state* therein *lumped* together, and their relation to the Constitution therein treated as being *precisely* the same?

"While the opinion of *the Court,* by Chief Justice Taney, in the Dred Scott case, and the separate opinions of all the concurring Judges, expressly declare that the Constitution of the United States neither permits Congress nor a Territorial legislature to exclude slavery from any United States territory, they all *omit* to declare whether or not the same Constitution permits a *state,* or the people of a State, to exclude it.

"Possibly, this was a mere *omission;* but who can be *quite* sure, if McLean or Curtis had sought to get into the opinion a declaration of unlimited power in the people of a *state* to exclude slavery from their limits, just as [Senator S. P.] Chase [of Ohio] and [Representative D.] Macy [of Indiana] sought to get such declaration, in behalf of the people of a territory, into the Nebraska bill—I ask, who can be quite *sure* that it would not have been voted down, in the one case, as it had been in the other."

Weakening of States' Rights

"The nearest approach to the point of declaring the power of a State over slavery, is made by Judge [Justice Samuel] Nelson. He approaches it more than once, using the precise idea, and *almost* the language too, of the Nebraska act. On one occasion his exact language is, 'except in cases where the power is restrained by the Constitution of the United States, the law of the State is Supreme over the subject of slavery within its jurisdiction.'

"In what *cases* the power of the *states is* so restrained by the U. S. Constitution, is left an *open* question, precisely as the same question, as to the restraint on the power of the *territories* was left open in the Nebraska act. Put *that* and *that* together, and we have another nice little niche, which we may, ere long, see filled with another Supreme Court decision, declaring that the Constitution of the United States does not permit a *state* to exclude slavery from its limits.

"And this especially be expected if the doctrine of 'care not whether slavery be voted *down* or voted *up,'* shall gain upon the public mind sufficiently to give promise that such a decision can be maintained when made.

"Such a decision is all that slavery now lacks of being alike lawful in all the States.

"Welcome or unwelcome, such a decision *is* probably coming, and will soon be upon us, unless the power of the present political dynasty shall be met and overthrown.

"We shall *lie down* pleasantly dreaming that the people of *Missouri* are on the *verge* of making their State *free;* and we shall *awake* to the *reality,* instead, that the *Supreme* Court has made *Illinois* a *slave* State."

To Overthrow Democratic Dynasty

"To meet and overthrow the power of that dynasty, is the work now before all those who would prevent that consummation.

"That is *what* we have to do.

"But *how* can we best do it?

"There are those who denounce us *openly* to their *own* friends, and yet whisper *us softly,* that *Senator Douglas* is the *aptest* instrument there is, in which to effect that object. *They* do *not* tell us, nor has *he* told us, that he *wishes* any such object to be effected. They wish us to *infer* all; from the facts, that he now has a little quarrel with the present head of the dynasty; and that he has regularly voted with us, on a single point, upon which, he and we, have never differed."

Douglas a Caged, Toothless Lion

"They remind us that *he* is a very *great man,* and that the largest of *us* are very small ones. Let this be granted. But *'a living dog is* better than a *dead lion.'* Judge Douglas, if not a *dead* lion *for this work,* is at least a *caged* and *toothless* one. How can we oppose the advances of slavery? He don't *care* anything about it. His avowed *mission is impressing* the 'public heart' to *care* nothing about it.

"A leading Douglas Democratic newspaper thinks Douglas' superior talent will be needed to resist the revival of the African slave trade.

"Does Douglas believe an effort to revive that trade is approaching? He has not said so. Does he really thing so? But if it is, how can he resist it? For years he has labored to prove it a *sacred right* of white men to take negro slaves into new territories. Can he possibly show that it is a *less* sacred right to *buy* them where they can be bought cheapest? And, unquestionably they can be bought *cheaper in Africa* than in *Virginia.*

"He has done all in his power to reduce the whole question of slavery to one of a mere *right of property;* and as such, how can *he* oppose the foreign trade—how can he refuse that trade in that 'property' shall be 'perfectly free'— unless he does it as a *protection* to the home production? And as the home *producers* will probably not *ask* the protection, he will be wholly without a ground of opposition.

"Senator Douglas holds, we know, that a man may rightfully be *wiser today* than he was yesterday—that he may rightfully *change* when he finds himself wrong.

"But, can we, for that reason, run ahead, and *infer* that he *will* make any particular change, of which he, himself, has given no intimation? Can we *safely* base *our* action upon any such vague inference?"

Wish Not to Misrepresent Douglas

"Now, as ever, I wish not to *misrepresent* Judge Douglas' *position*, question his *motives*, or do ought that can be personally offensive to him.

"Whenever, *if ever*, he and we can come together on *principle* so that *our great cause* may have assistance from *his great ability*, I hope to have interposed no adventitious obstacle.

"But clearly, he is not *now* with us—he does not *pretend* to be—he does not *promise to ever* be."

Our Cause Shall Not Fail

"Our cause, then, must be intrusted to, and conducted by its own un-doubted friends—those whose hands are free, whose hearts are in the work—who *do care* for the result.

"Two years ago the Republicans of the nation mustered over thirteen hundred thousand strong.

"We did this under the single impulse of resistance to a common danger, with every external circumstance against us.

"Of *strange, discordant,* and even, *hostile* elements, we gathered from the four winds, and *formed* and fought the battle through, under the constant hot fire of a disciplined, proud, and pampered enemy.

"Did we brave all *then* to *falter* now?—*now*—when that same enemy is *wavering,* dissevered and belligerent?

"The result is not doubtful. We shall not fail—if we stand firm, we shall not fail.

"*Wise councils* may *accelerate* or *mistakes delay* it, but, sooner or later the victory is *sure* to come."

Public Reaction

Lincoln had indeed seized the bull of opportunity by the horns in his acceptance speech. He boldly applied the moral teaching of Christ that "a house divided against itself cannot stand," to the nationally dangerous cultural trend of conflicting philosophies of freedom versus slavery and the political crisis engendered by it, with such aptness that it aroused national as well as state enthusiasm in his favor. Although he had expressed the same idea in the same words in speeches of the past year, they had excited little comment. Now, however, as a senatorial candidate challenging the great Senator Douglas for office in this election year, and boldly connecting him by inferential indications, with the President of the United States, and the Chief Justice of the Supreme Court, in machinations to obtain for slave holders the right to take slaves into the free states as well as the free territories, Lincoln sowed dragons' teeth of suspicion in the North about a vast Southern political plot to extend slavery, and in the South, of a Northern counterplot to abolish it. His was not an original or new idea. Extremists on both sides, newspapers, editors, politicians, and preachers, had been hurling such charges and counter-charges at each other since the organization of the Union. Lincoln added fuel to the fire by naming President Buchanan, Chief-Justice Taney, and Senator Douglas as leaders of the new slavery extension policy.

Intense national reactions for and against it echoed and reechoed through press and pulpit. Many of his staunchest friends condemned it and predicted his defeat. The Democrats rejoiced, for the statement that the government cannot endure half slave and half free seemed to clarify the issue in their favor. Before the summer was over Lincoln found that it had made him the leader of most of the radical opponents of slavery, regardless of politics. Popular sentiment among the younger men of the Republican party started to shift from the leadership of Seward, who had followed Lincoln's lead by vaguely espousing the idealization of "higher sentiments" as the best defense against slavery, to the man who pointed out the peril to the Union in being divided against itself.

Lincoln's decision to apply from now on, in his speeches, the universally known homely truths of human relations to political situations was a stroke of genius that led on to fortune and misfortune. He had habitually thought of all the people of a state or nation, regardless of race or creed, as one great family of interdependent souls in which the welfare and fate of each one more or less involved the welfare and fate of all the others. Such was the philosophy engendered by his childhood family experience. The practical application of this ancient biblical learning to national political and other social conditions caught on like wildfire. It was fundamentally sound, and based on the first principle of equalitarian rights in human relations. It taught people that, so long as they apply to complexly involved social and political situations the common sense of everyday, familial interpersonal relations, they are on sound grounds and will not be carried away and befuddled by high sounding authoritarian applications of abstract, ambivalent ideologies based on prejudiced, privileged, wishful premises for the solution of state, national or international political problems, today and tomorrow.

The common man felt and believed that he understood Lincoln and now also understood his own constitutional rights and political relations with every other person and what constituted just government. Most American people felt profoundly then, as they do now, that the Constitution should not provide special freedoms and rights for people of certain race, color, creed, wealth, education or family, and less or no rights for others. Such privileges violated the golden rule of Christianity and Divine Justice, principles upon which the Constitution was founded. Lincoln, probably more than anyone, appreciated the potential influence on public opinion of his political philosophy, and he advanced it with cautious but consummate skill as fast as the people could assimilate and apply it. This inspiration developed into his supreme determination to preserve the Union and restrict slavery, repeated over and over again in every critical test of policy.

Sage Advice

Enthusiastic Republican leaders were in favor of a "whooping it up" campaign but Lincoln discouraged it. To A. McCallen, publisher of the *Southern Illinoisian* he wrote (6, 19, 1858):

> "I think too much reliance is placed in noisy demonstrations—importing speakers from a distance and the like. They excite prejudice and close the avenues of sober reason. The 'home production' principle in my judgment is the best. You and [O.] Sexton and [J.] Olney [delegates to the Republican convention] and others whose hearts are in the work should quietly form your plans and carry them out energetically among your own neighbors. You perceive my idea; and I really think it the best."

When we compare this sage advice to Editor McCallen with the advice he gave when a congressman in 1848 to his young partner Herndon, to get "the young men together and form a Rough and Ready club" and "gather up all the shrewd, wild boys in town" and "let every one play the part he can play best—some speak, some sing, and all hollow," we sense the serenity and gravity of Lincoln's mental maturation in 10 years from 39 to 49 years of age.

Within a week after his acceptance speech Lincoln began to reap the harvest of dragons' teeth in the form of misunderstanding, distrust, denunciation, and recrimination from one side, with praise and push toward conflict from the other. It was to continue for the rest of his life despite all of his efforts to explain it away.

To John L. Scripps, editor of the politically influential Chicago *Daily Democratic Press,* he wrote (6, 23, 1858):

> "I am much flattered by the estimate you place on my late speech; and yet I am much mortified that any part of it should be construed so differently from any thing intended by me. The language, 'place it where the public mind shall rest in the belief that it is in course of ultimate extinction,' I used deliberately, not dreaming then, nor believing now, that it asserts, or intimates, any power or purpose, to interfere with slavery in the States where it exists. But, to not cavil about language, I declare that whether the clause used by me, will bear such construction, or not, I never intended it. I have declared a thousand times, and now repeat that, in my opinion, neither the General Government, nor any other power outside of the slave states, can constitutionally or rightfully interfere with slaves or slavery where it already exists. I believe that whenever the effort to spread slavery into the new territories, by whatever means, and into the free states themselves, by Supreme court decisions, shall be fairly headed off, the institution will then be in course of ultimate extinction; and by the language used I meant only this. . . . I think I shall, as you suggest,

take some early occasion to publicly repeat the declaration I have already so often made as before stated."

Uneasy Protest to Crittenden

United States Senator J. J. Crittenden of Kentucky had openly expressed in conversation and letters the belief that the election of Douglas and Harris in Illinois was a necessity. One such letter was published by a Douglas paper in Missouri.

Lincoln wrote Crittenden the following diplomatic letter of protest (7, 7, 1858). It shows characteristically how carefully, yet firmly, he treated his personal relations, always for the best and never for the easiest way.

"I beg you will pardon me for the liberty in addressing you upon only so limited an acquaintance, and that acquaintance so long past. I am prompted to do so by a story being whispered about here that you are anxious for the reelection of Mr. Douglas to the United States Senate, and also of Harris, of our district, to the House of Representatives, and that you are pledged to write letters to that effect to your friends here in Illinois, if requested. I do not believe the story, but still it gives me some uneasiness. If such was your inclination, I do not believe you would so express yourself. It is not in character with you as I have always estimated you.

"You have no warmer friends than here in Illinois, and I assure you nine tenths—I believe ninety-nine hundredths—of them would be mortified exceedingly by anything of the sort from you. When I tell you this, make such allowance as you think just for my position, which, I doubt not, you understand. Nor am I fishing for a letter on the other side. Even if such could be had, my judgment is that you would better be hands off!

"Please drop me a line; and if your purposes are as I hope they are not, please let me know. The confirmation would pain me much, but I should still continue your friend and admirer."

Crittenden replied to Lincoln that he had "openly, ardently and frequently expressed" his belief that the election of Douglas was a necessity but denied having written letters to Illinoisians. (See in Chapter XXXIII, Lincoln's letter (11, 4, 1858) upon his defeat, to Crittenden.)

Meditations on a Higher Aim than Mere Office

After his nomination as Republican candidate for the United States Senate, Lincoln spent days in contemplation of the factors and chances involved in the race. He tabulated the probable vote of each district in the previous national election and deduced from this which districts "would be lost" to the Democrats with 22 representatives, and which "would be gained" by the Republicans "without question" with 27 representatives, leaving those "as doubtful and to be struggled for" with 26 representatives.

On a scrap of paper he wrote the following meditations on his purpose:

"I have never professed an indifference to the honors of official station; and were I to do so now, I should only make myself ridiculous. Yet I have never failed—do not now fail—to remember that in the republican cause there is a higher aim than that of mere office. I have not allowed myself to forget that the abolition of the Slave-trade by Great Britain, was agitated a hundred years before it was a final success; that the measure had it's open fire-eating opponents; it's stealthy 'don't care' opponents; its dollar and cent opponents; it's inferior race opponents; its negro equality opponents; its religion and good order opponents; that all these opponents got offices, and their adversaries got none. But I have also remembered that though they blazed like tallow-candles for a century, at last they flickered in the socket, died out, stank in the dark for a brief season, and were remembered no more, even by the smell. School-boys know that Wilbe[r]force, and Granville Sharpe, helped that cause forward; but who can now name a single man who labored to retard it? Remembering these things I can not but regard it as possible that the higher object of this contest may not be completely attained within the term of my natural life. But I can not doubt either that it will come in due time. Even in this view, I am proud, in my passing speck of time, to contribute an humble mite to that glorious consummation, which my own poor eyes may not last to see."

Herein Lincoln admitted to himself that he was ambitious to do something toward improving freedom in human relations that would make his name honored by the people. He would do it in the way of peacefully, legally abolishing slavery in the United States through education and economic measures proven so effective by Wilberforce and Sharpe in Great Britain and her colonies in 1834, when he began the study of law.

Chapter XXVIII

LINCOLN ENVIES DOUGLAS

"Twenty-two years ago," Lincoln wrote in his notes (12, 1856 ?), "Judge Douglas and I first became acquainted. We were both young then; he a trifle younger than I. Even then, we were both ambitious; I, perhaps quite as much as he. With *me,* the race of ambition has been a failure—a flat failure; with *him* it has been one of splendid success. His name fills the nation; and is not unknown, even, in foreign lands. I affect no contempt for the high eminence he has reached. So reached, that the oppressed of my species, might have shared with me in the elevation, I would rather stand on that eminence, than wear the richest crown that ever pressed a monarch's brow."

Lincoln persisted in following Douglas closely in time and place as well as argument, at every opportunity, in making speeches. It had been his practice in previous campaigns to read or hear what Douglas had to say and then follow on the same day or as soon thereafter as possible with a critical speech in reply. This assured him of an interested audience of Democrats and Republicans that otherwise would not have gathered to hear him speak. Douglas rarely honored Lincoln by attending his speeches. Feeling sure, after his defeat of the Lecompton Constitution, that the people would approve of his fair play, popular sovereignty policy for the territories, he deemed it unnecessary to answer his opponent's arguments. However, when Lincoln attended his great Democratic rally in Chicago and answered his speech before an impromptu Republican rally the next night (7, 10, 1858) with such rousing approval from an enthusiastic audience that the Chicago papers published his speech, and he repeated this success a few days later in Springfield, Douglas heeded his advisors and became interested in what Lincoln had to say about the political situation.

Impromptu Chicago Speech*

In his impromptu reply to Douglas Lincoln caught the spirit of liberty of the time. Since the arguments in this speech are largely repeated in prepared statements of the next Springfield speech and in the debates, we present only its more important comments as evidence of impromptu oratorical ability and progress in applying a more active political philosophy in reaction to new issues as they drove to-

*This speech was reported in the Chicago *Daily Democrat* (7, 13, 1858) and Chicago *Daily Press* and *Tribune* (7, 12, 1858) and later used by Lincoln for his Scrap Book.

ward winning favorable public sentiment. Douglas' penchant for bombastic exhibitionism and demagoguery was becoming meat and nuts for Lincoln's wit. He began:

> "My Fellow Citizens, on yesterday evening, upon the occasion of the reception given to Senator Douglas, I was furnished with a seat very convenient for hearing him, and was otherwise very courteously treated by him and his friends, and for which I thank him and them. During the course of his remarks my name was mentioned in such a way, as I suppose renders it at least not improper that I should make some sort of reply to him. I shall not attempt to follow in the precise order in which he addressed the assembled multitude upon that occasion, though I shall perhaps do so in the main."

Douglas, in his speech the night before, had referred patronizingly to Lincoln as a "kind, amiable, intelligent gentleman" and then charged him with leading the Republicans to form an alliance with Buchanan Democrats to defeat him in the coming election. Lincoln read Douglas' statement before answering it. In part, it said:

> " 'I have made up my mind to appeal to the people against the combination that has been formed against me! The Republican leaders have formed an alliance, an unholy and unnatural alliance, with a portion of unscrupulous federal office-holders. I intend to fight that allied army wherever I meet them . . . just as the Russians dealt with the allies at Sebastopol—that is, the Russians did not stop in inquire, when they fired a broadside, whether it hit an Englishman, a Frenchman or a Turk. Nor will I stop to inquire, nor shall I hesitate, whether my blows will hit these Republican leaders or their allies who are holding the federal offices and yet acting in concert with them.' "

Bombastic demagoguery was always meat for Lincoln. With consummate wit he seized the advantage:

> "Well now, gentlemen, is not that very alarming? [Laughter.] Just to think of it! right at the outset of his canvass, I, a poor, kind, amiable, intelligent, [laughter] gentlemen, [laughter and renewed cheers] I am to be slain in this way. Why, my friend, the Judge, is not only, as it turns out, not a dead lion, not even a living one—he is a rugged Russian Bear! [Roars of laughter and loud applause.]
>
> "But if they will have it—for he says that we deny it—that there is any such alliance, as he says there is—and I don't propose hanging very much on this question of veracity—but if he will have it that there is such an alliance—that the Administration men and we are allied, and we stand in the attitude of English, French and Turk, he occupying the position of the Russians, in that case, I beg that he will indulge us while we barely suggest to him, that the allies took Sebastopol. [Long and tremendous applause.]"
>
> As to the alleged alliance Lincoln said: "If there be any such thing, I protest that I neither know anything of it, nor do I believe it." . . .

Popular Sovereignty—Squatter Sovereignty

Douglas was gaining vigorous public approval in Illinois and the nation by his exposition of popular sovereignty as the practical way of solving the conflict over slavery in the territories. Lincoln identified popular sovereignty with squatter sovereignty and the right of the people to self-government as asserted in the Preamble to the Constitution.

"What is popular sovereignty? We recollect that at an early period of this struggle there was another name for the same thing—Squatter Sovereignty. . . . It was the right of the people to govern themselves. . . . What has become of it? . . . Today it has been decided . . . by the Supreme Court [Dred Scott Decision] that if any man chooses to take slaves into a territory, all the rest of the people have no right to keep him out. . . .

"All that space of time that runs from the beginning of the settlement of the Territory until there is a sufficiency of people to make a State Constitution—all that portion of time popular sovereignty is given up. The seal is absolutely put down upon it by the Court decision, and Judge Douglas puts his own upon the top of that, yet he is appealing to the people to give him credit for his devotion to popular sovereignty. [Applause]

. . . "I suppose that Judge Douglas will claim in a little while, that he is the inventor of the idea that people shall govern themselves: [cheers and laughter]; that nobody even thought of such a thing until he brought it forward."

The Lecompton Constitution,
Opposed by Republicans Before Douglas

"The Lecompton Constitution connects itself with this question, for it is in this matter . . . that our friend Judge Douglas claims such vast credit. I agree that in opposing the Lecompton Constitution so far as I can perceive, he was right. I do not deny that at all; and gentlemen, you will readily see why I could not deny it, even if I wanted to. But I do not wish to; for all the Republicans in the nation opposed it, . . . They had all taken ground against it long before he did. Why, the reason that he urges against that Constitution, I urged against him a year before. I have the printed speech in my hand. . . . I pointed out . . . that no fair chance was to be given to the people. . . .

. . . "Ground was taken against it by the Republicans long before Douglas did it. The proportion of opposition to that measure is about five to one."

A voice—"Why don't they come out on it?"

Mr. Lincoln—"You don't know what you are talking about, my friend. I am willing to answer any gentleman in the crowd who asks an *intelligent* question." . . .

Explains House Divided Allegory Upon Scripps' Advice

Scripps advised Lincoln to explain his meaning of his "house divided against itself" allegory in order to correct the preposterous applications of it being made by Douglas. After quoting his statement he at first half apologetically defended it.

> . . . "In this paragraph which I have quoted in your hearing, and to which I ask the attention of all, Judge Douglas thinks he discovers great political heresy. . . . He says I am in favor of making all the States of this Union uniform in all their internal relations; . . . in all their domestic concerns. . . . He draws this inference from the language I have quoted to you. He says I am in favor of making war by the North upon the South for the extinction of Slavery; that I am also in favor of inviting (as he expresses it) the South to a war upon the North, for the purpose of nationalizing slavery. Now, it is singular enough, if you will carefully read that passage over, that I did not say that I was in favor of anything in it. I only said what I expected would take place. I made a prediction only — it may have been a foolish one perhaps. I did not even say that I desired slavery should be put in course of ultimate extinction. I do say so now, however, [great applause] so there need be no longer any difficulty about that. It may be written down in the next speech." [Applause and laughter.]

Lincoln's "house divided" representation of the dangerous schism then developing in the nation over the bitter contradiction of the rights of freedom versus the rights of slavery had clarified and crystalized the sentiment of the opponents of slavery. Within two weeks the tide of national approval had gained such headway that it could no longer be checked. Concomitantly, it aroused intense proslavery resentment. Douglas persisted in denouncing it as a declaration of intention to end slavery by force if necessary and Lincoln was forced as persistently to defend it lest it be made to boomerang against him.

> "Gentlemen, Judge Douglas informed you that this speech of mine was probably carefully prepared. I admit that it was. I am not master of language; I have not a fine education; I am not capable of entering into a disquisition upon dialectics, as I believe you call it; but I do not believe the language I employed bears any such construction as Judge Douglas put upon it. But I don't care about a quibble in regard to words. I know what I meant, and I will not leave this crowd in doubt, if I can explain it to them, what I really meant in the use of that paragraph.
>
> "I am not, in the first place, unaware that this Government has endured, eighty-two years, half slave and half free. I know that. [This statement was ignored by Douglas and other critics of Lincoln.] I am tolerably well acquainted with the history of the country, and I know that it has endured eighty-two years, half slave and half free.

I *believe*—and that is what I meant to allude to there—I *believe* it has endured because, during all that time, until the introduction of the Nebraska Bill, the public mind did rest, all the time, in the belief that slavery was in course of ultimate extinction. (Applause.)

"The adoption of the Constitution and its attendent history led the people to believe so; . . . And now, when I say . . . that I think the opponents of slavery will resist the farther spread of it, and place it where the public mind shall rest with the belief that it is in the course of ultimate extinction, I only mean to say, that they will place it where the founders of this Government originally placed it.

"I have said a hundred times, and I have now no inclination to take it back, that I believe there is no right, and ought to be no inclination in the people of the free States to enter into the slave States, and interfere with the question of slavery at all. I have said that always. Judge Douglas has heard me say it—if not quite a hundred times, at least as good as a hundred times; and when it is said that I am in favor of interfering with slavery where it exists, I know it is unwarranted by anything I have ever *intended,* and, as I believe, by anything I have ever *said.* If, by any means, I have ever used language which could be so construed, (as, however, I believe I never have,) I now correct it.

"So much, then, for the inference that Judge Douglas draws that I am in favor of setting the sections at war with one another. I know that I never meant any such thing, and I believe that no fair mind can infer any such thing from anything I have ever said."

Although Lincoln earnestly repeated this explanation of his constitutional position on slavery in nearly every speech throughout the campaign, Douglas persisted in charging him with wanting to abolish it even though it would involve the North and South in war.

. . . "I have said, very many times, in Judge Douglas' hearing, that no man believed more than I in the principle of self-government; that it lies at the bottom of all my ideas of just government, from beginning to end. I have denied that his use of the term applies properly . . . I believe each individual is naturally entitled to do as he pleases with himself and the fruit of his labor, so far as it in no wise interferes with any other man's rights—[applause]—that each community, as a State, has a right to do exactly as it pleases with all the concerns within that State that interfere with the rights of no other State, and that the general government, upon principle, has no right to interfere with anything other than that general class of things that does concern the whole." . . .

Justified His Criticism of Dred Scott Decision

Lincoln justified his criticism of the Supreme Court's Dred Scott decision as not being "a resistance to the decision," as charged by Douglas, but as "refusing to obey it as a political rule."

"If I were in Congress, and a vote should come up on a question whether slavery should be prohibited in a new territory, in spite of that Dred Scott decision, I would vote that it should." [Applause] . . .

"Judge Douglas said last night, that before the decision he might advance his opinion, and it might be contrary to the decision when it was made; but after it was made he would abide by it until it was reversed. . . . Somebody has to reverse it since it is made, and we mean to reverse it, and we mean to do it peaceably . . . we mean to do what we can to have the court decide the other way. That is one thing we mean to try to do.

"The sacredness that Judge Douglas throws around this decision, is a degree of sacredness that has never been thrown around any other decision. I have never heard of such a thing. Why, decisions apparently contrary to that decision, or that good lawyers thought were contradictory to that decision, have been made by that very court before. It is the first of its kind; it is an astonisher in legal history. . . . It is based upon falsehood in the main as to the facts— allegations of fact upon which it stands are not facts at all in many instances, and no decision made on any question—the first instance of a decision made under so many unfavorable circumstances—thus placed has ever been held by the profession as law, and it has always needed confirmation before lawyers regarded it as settled law."

Lincoln's repeated statements that he would do what he could to have the Supreme Court reverse its decision because it was based on a falsification of historical facts, excited intense resentment in the slave states.

After extolling the men who fought the Revolution under the Declaration of Independence and founded our constitutional government, and the pride of their descendants in their achievements, Lincoln took advantage of Douglas' prejudices:

. . . "We have besides these men—descended by blood from our ancestors—among us perhaps half of our people who are not descendants at all of these men, they are men who have come from Europe—German, Irish, French and Scandinavian . . . or whose ancestors have come hither and settled here, finding themselves our equals in all things. If they look back through this history to trace their connections with those days by blood, they find they have none, they cannot carry themselves back into that glorious epoch and make themselves feel that they are part of us, but when they look through that old Declaration of Independence they find that those old men say 'We hold these truths to be self-evident, that all men are created equal,' and then they feel that that moral sentiment taught in that day evidences their relations to those men, that it is the father of all moral principle in them, and that they have a right to claim it as though they were the blood of the blood, the flesh of the flesh of the men who wrote the Declaration, [loud and long continued applause] and so they are. That is the electric cord in that Declaration that links the hearts of patriotic and liberty-loving men together, and will link those patriotic hearts as long as the love of freedom exists in the minds of men throughout the world. [Applause.]

"Now, sirs, for the purpose of squaring things with this idea of 'don't care if slavery is voted up or voted down,' for sustaining the Dred Scott decision, for holding that the Declaration of Independence did not mean anything at all, we have Judge Douglas giving his exposition of what the Declaration of Independence means, and we have him saying that the people of America are equal to the people of England. According to his construction, you Germans are not connected with it. Now I ask you in all soberness, if all these things, if indulged in, if ratified, if confirmed and endorsed, if taught our children, and repeated to them, do not tend to rub out the sentiment of liberty in the country, and to transform this Government into . . . some other form. Those arguments that are made, that the inferior race are to be treated with as much allowance as they are capable of enjoying, that as much is to be done for them as their condition will allow. What are these arguments? They are the arguments that kings have made for enslaving the people in all ages of the world. You will find that the arguments in favor of king-craft were of this class; they always bestrode the necks of people, not that they wanted to do it, but because the people were better off being ridden. . . . Turn in whatever way you will—whether it come from the mouth of a King, an excuse for enslaving the people of his country, or from the mouth of the men of one race as a reason for enslaving the men of another race, it is all the same old serpent, and I hold if that course of argumentation that is made for the purpose of convincing the public mind that we should not care about this, should be granted, it does not stop with the negro. Where will it stop? . . . If that declaration [of independence] is not the truth, let us go the the Statute book, in which we find it and tear it out! Who is so bold as to do it! [Voices "me," "no one," etc.] If it is not true let us tear it out! [Cries "no, no,"] let us stick to it then, [cheers] let us stand firmly by it then. [Applause.]

"It may be argued that there are certain conditions that make necessities and impose them upon us, and to the extent that a necessity is imposed upon a man he must submit to it. I think that was the condition in which we found ourselves when we established this government. We had slavery among us, we could not get our constitution unless we permitted them to remain in slavery, we could not secure the good we did secure if we grasped for more, and having by necessity submitted to that much, it does not destroy the principle that is the charter of our liberties. Let that charter stand as our standard."

Practical Morality

"My friend has said to me that I am a poor hand to quote Scripture. I will try it again, however. It is said in one of the admonitions of the Lord, 'As your Father in Heaven is perfect, be ye also perfect.' The Saviour, I suppose, did not expect that any human creature could be perfect as the Father in Heaven; but he said, 'As your Father in Heaven is perfect, be ye also perfect.' He set that up as a Standard, and he who did most towards reaching that standard, attained the highest degree of moral perfection. So I say in relation to the principle that all men are created equal, let it be as nearly reached as we can. If we cannot give freedom to every creature, let us do nothing that will impose slavery upon any other creature. Let us then turn this government back into the channel in which the framers of the constitution originally placed it." . . .

Made Douglas Adopt More Liberal Policy

The political philosophies of the North and the South involved the Constitution in a contradiction of principles on the moral and economic rights of man which had become irreconcilable and must eventually resolve itself all one way or the other. Lincoln realized this better than anyone and was determined to obtain consistency and unity through adopting educational methods that would lead to the extinction of slavery. His eloquent reassurance that the founders of the Government meant equality of citizenship for all immigrants and their descendants, with the descendants of the Dutch and English colonists who fought the Revolution, won for him their loyal support throughout the remainder of his political career. Douglas, by attempting the demagoguery of reducing the meaning of legal equality of all men, to British colonial descendants with that of British subjects, won the enmity of people who felt the injustice of his discrimination. Its hypocrisy, however, appealed to the Know-Nothings who were still active.

Happy with Success

The Chicago speech was Lincoln's first major effort after his nomination for the Senate in 1858. Never had he seen such big, vociferous crowds, such brass and parade in a political rally as had greeted Douglas the night before. When he had suggested to his own party leaders that he wanted to answer Douglas the next evening, the Republican organization had sent out announcements and succeeded in getting up a surprisingly large and enthusiastic audience, including many people who had attended the Douglas speech.

The reasonableness and fairness of his argument aroused vigorous newspaper and public approval, and Lincoln, feeling encouraged and elated, expressed his confidence in a letter a few days later to his friend, G.P. Koerner, (6, 15, 1858):

. . . "I have just returned from Chicago, Douglas took nothing by his motion there. In fact, by his rampant indorsement of the Dred Scott decision he drove back a few Republicans who were favorably inclined towards him. His tactics just now, in part is, to make it appear that he is having a triumphal entry into; and march throughout the country; but it is all as bombastic and hollow as Napoleon's bulletins sent back from his campaign in Russia. I was present at his reception in Chicago, and it certainly was very large and imposing; but judging from the opinions of others better acquainted with faces there, and by the strong call for me to speak, when he closed, I really believe we could have voted him down in that very crowd. Our meeting, twentyfour hours after, called only twelve hours before it came together and got up without trumpery, was nearly as large, and five times as enthusiastic.

"I write this, for your private eye, to assure you that there is no solid shot, in these bombastic parades of his."

At Bloomington, Illinois

On July 15, Lincoln attended Douglas' speech at Bloomington and as soon as the Judge retired the crowd persisted in calling for a speech from him. He finally went upon the stand and was greeted with louder cheers than had been given to Douglas. "This meeting," he said, "was called by the friends of Judge Douglas, and it will be improper for me to address it." He then retired amid loud cheering. (From the Bloomington *Pantagraph*.)

At Atlanta, Illinois

Lincoln heard Douglas' speech on July 16th at Atlanta, and again when the Judge finished the crowd called for "Lincoln!" "Lincoln!!" "Lincoln!!!" He stepped before the audience, and remarked that feelings of delicacy prompted him to refrain from addressing them. (Bloomington *Pantagraph*.)

Springfield Reply to Douglas

Lincoln's speech in Springfield on the evening of July 17th, 1858, in reply to one made there by Douglas in the afternoon, was regarded by him and his friends as the clearest and most coherent exposition of his views that he had presented up to this time. He later wrote to G.P. Koerner (8, 6, 1858), who urged him to have it printed for distribution:

"I went at once to the Journal office here, and set them to work to print me in English, fifty dollars worth of my last speech at Springfield. . . . For that sum they will furnish about 7000; they will, at the same time print some more, on their own account, and keep the type standing for a while. I also wrote to Judd yesterday, to get the same speech done up there in German." . . .

This Springfield speech is presented in full because of Lincoln's estimation of its importance. When we compare it with the extemporaneous speech of the previous week at Chicago we find a remarkable improvement in thoughtful preparation, and simplicity, clarity, logic, and coherence of statement. The literary style is Lincoln's at his best, and it is evident that he prepared this speech with great enthusiasm and care after the vigorous response of the wildly cheering audience and the press in Chicago. (Captions inserted.)

"Fellow Citizens:—Another election, which is deemed an important one, is approaching, and, as I suppose, the Republican party will, without much difficulty elect their State ticket. But in regard to the Legislature, we, the Republicans, labor under some disadvantages. In the first place, we have a Legislature to elect upon an apportionment of the representation made several years ago, when the proportion of the population was far greater in the South (as compared with the North) than it now is; and inasmuch as our opponents hold almost entire sway in the South, and we a correspondingly large majority in the North, the fact that we are now to be represented as we were years ago, when the population was different, is to us a very great disadvantage. We had, in the year 1855, according to law, a census or enumeration of the inhabitants, taken for the purpose of a new apportionment of representation. We know what a fair apportionment of representation upon that census would give us. We know that it could not if fairly made, fail to give the Republican party from six to ten more members of the Legislature than they can probably get as the law now stands. It so happened at the last session of the Legislature, that our opponents, holding the control of both branches of the Legislature, steadily refused to give us such an apportionment as we were rightfully entitled to have upon the census already taken. . . . The Legislature would pass no bill upon that subject, except as was at least as unfair to us as the old one, and in which, in some instances, two men in the Democratic regions were allowed to go as far towards sending a member to the Legislature as three were in the Republican regions. Comparison was made at the time as to representative and senatorial districts, which completely demonstrated that such was the fact. Such a bill was passed, and tendered to the Republican Governor for his signature; but principally for the reasons I have stated, he withheld his approval, and the bill fell without becoming a law.

"Another disadvantage under which we labor is, that there are one or two Democratic Senators who will be members of the next Legislature, and will vote for the election of Senator, who are holding over in districts in which we could, on all reasonable calculation, elect men of our own, if we only had the chance of an election. When we consider that there are but twenty five Senators in the Senate, taking two from the side where they rightfully belong and adding them to the other, is to us a disadvantage not to be lightly regarded. Still, so it is; we have this to contend with. Perhaps there is no ground of complaint on our part. In attending to the many things involved in the last general election for President, Governor, Auditor, Treasurer, Superintendent of Public Instruction, Members of Congress, of the Legislature, County officers, and so on, we allowed these things to happen by want of sufficient attention, and we have no cause to complain of our adversaries, so far as this matter is concerned. But we have some cause to complain of the refusal to give us a fair apportionment."

Nobody Has Ever Expected Me to Be President

"There is still another disadvantage under which we labor, and to which I will ask your attention. It arises out of the relative positions of the two persons who stand before the State as candidates for the Senate. Senator Douglas is of world wide renown. All the anxious politicians of his party, or who have been of his party for years past, have been looking upon him as certainly, at no distant day, to be the President of the United States. They have seen in his round, jolly, fruitful face, postoffices, landoffices, marshalships, and cabinet appointments, chargeships and foreign missions, bursting and sprouting out in wonderful exuberance ready to be laid hold of by their greedy hands. [Great laughter.] And as they have been gazing upon this attractive picture so long they cannot, in the little distraction that has taken place in the party, bring themselves to give up the charming hope; but with greedier anxiety they rush about him, sustain him, and give him marches, triumphal entries, and receptions beyond what even in the days of his highest prosperity they could have brought about in his favor. On the contrary nobody has ever expected me to be President. In my poor, lean, lank, face, nobody has ever seen that any cabbages were sprouting out. [Tremendous cheering and laughter.] These are disadvantages all, taken together, that the Republicans labor under. *We* have to fight this battle upon principle, and upon principle alone. I am, in a certain sense, made the standard-bearer in behalf of the Republicans. I was made so merely because there had to be some one so placed—I being in no wise, preferable to any other one of the twenty-five—perhaps a hundred we have in the Republican ranks. Then I say I wish it to be distinctly understood and borne in mind, that we have to fight this battle without many—perhaps without any—of the external aids which are brought to bear against us. So I hope those with whom I am surrounded have principle enough to nerve themselves for the task and leave nothing undone, that can be fairly done, to bring about the right result."

Napoleon Douglas

"After Senator Douglas left Washington, as his movements were made known by the public prints, he tarried a considerable time in the city of New York; and it was heralded that, like another Napoleon, he was lying by, and framing the plan of his campaign. It was telegraphed to Washington City, and published in the *Union,* that he was framing his plan for the purpose of going to Illinois to pounce upon and annihilate the treasonable and disunion speech which Lincoln had made here on the 16th of June. Now, I do suppose that the Judge really spent some time in New York maturing the plan of the campaign, as his friends heralded for him. I have been able, by noting his movements since his arrival in Illinois, to discover evidences confirmatory of that allegation. I think I have been able to see what are the material points of that plan. I will, for a little while, ask your attention to some of them. What I shall point out, though not showing the whole plan, are nevertheless, the main points, as I suppose.

"They are not very numerous. The first is Popular Sovereignty. The second and third are attacks upon my speech made on the 16th of June. Out of these three points—drawing within the range of Popular Sovereignty the question of the Lecompton Constitution— he makes his principal assault. Upon this matter of Popular Sovereignty I wish to be a little careful. Auxiliary to these main points, to be sure, are their thunderings of cannon, their marching and music, their fizzlegigs and firewords; but I will not waste time with them. They are but the little trappings of the campaign."

Defines Popular Sovereignty

"Coming to the substance—the first point—'Popular Sovereignty.' It is to be labelled upon the cars in which he travels; put upon the hacks he rides in; to be flaunted upon the arches he passes under, and the banners which wave over him. It is to be dished up in as many varieties as a French cook can produce soups from potatoes. Now, as this is so great a staple of the plan of the campaign, it is worth while to examine it carefully; and if we examine only a very little, and do not allow ourselves to be misled, we shall be able to see that the whole thing is the most arrant Quixotism that was ever enacted before a community. What is the matter of Popular Sovereignty? The first thing, in order to understand it is to get a good definition of what it is, and after that to see how it is applied.

"I suppose almost every one knows, that in this controversy, whatever has been said, has had reference to the question of negro slavery. We have not been in a controversy about the right of the people to govern themselves in the ordinary matters of domestic concern in the States and Territories. Mr. Buchanan in one of his late messages, (I think when he sent up the Lecompton Constitution,) urged that the main points to which the public attention had been directed, was not in regard to the great variety of small domestic matters, but was directed to the question of negro slavery; and he asserts, that if the people had had a fair chance to vote on that question, there was no reasonable ground of objection in regard to minor questions. Now, while I think that the people had *not* had given, or offered them, a fair chance upon that slavery question; still, if there had been a fair submission to a vote upon that main question, the President's proposition would have been true to the uttermost. Hence, when hereafter, I speak of popular sovereignty, I wish to be understood as applying what I say to the question of slavery only, not to other minor domestic matters of a Territory or a State."

How Douglas Opposes and Sustains Popular Sovereignty

"Does Judge Douglas, when he says that several of the past years of his life have been devoted to the question of 'popular sovereignty,' and that all the remainder of his life shall be devoted to it, does he mean to say that he has been devoting his life to securing to the people of the territories the right to exclude slavery from the territories? If he means so to say, he means to deceive; because he and every one knows that the decision of the Supreme Court, which he approves and makes especial ground of attack upon me for disapproving, forbids the people of a territory to exclude slavery. This covers the whole ground, from the settlement of a territory till it reaches the degree of maturity entitling it to form a State Constitution. So far as all that ground is concerned, the Judge is not sustaining popular sovereignty, but absolutely opposing it. He sustains the decision which declares that the popular will of the territories has no constitutional power to exclude slavery during their territorial existence. [Cheers.] This being so, the period of time from the first settlement of a territory till it reaches the point of forming a State Constitution, is not the thing that the Judge has fought for or is fighting for, but on the contrary, he has fought for, and is fighting for, the thing that annihilates and crushes out that same popular sovereignty.

"Well, so much being disposed of, what is left? Why, he is contending for the right of the people, when they come to make a State Constitution, to make it for themselves, and precisely as best suits themselves. I say again, that is Quixotic. I defy contradiction when I declare that the Judge can find no one to oppose him on that proposition. I repeat, there is nobody opposing that proposition on *principle*. Let me not be misunderstood. I know that, with reference to the Lecompton Constitution, I may be misunderstood; but when you understand me correctly, my proposition will be true and accurate. Nobody is opposing, or has opposed, the right of the people, when they form a Constitution, to form it for themselves. Mr. Buchanan and his friends have not done it; they, too, as well as the Republicans and the Anti-Lecompton Democrats, have not done it; but, on the contrary, they together have insisted on the right of the people to form a constitution for themselves. The difference between the Buchanan men on the one hand, and the Douglas men and the Republicans on the other, has not been on a question of principle, but on a question of *fact*.

Lecompton—Matter of Fact

"The dispute was upon the question of fact, whether the Lecompton Constitution had been fairly formed by the people or not. Mr. Buchanan and his friends have not cotended for the contrary principle any more than the Douglas men or the Republicans. They have insisted that whatever of small irregularities existed in getting up the Lecompton Constitution, were such as happen in the settlement of all new Territories. The question was, was it a fair emanation of the people? It was a question of fact, and not of principle. As to principle, all were agreed. Judge Douglas voted with the Republicans upon that matter of fact.

"He and they, by their voices and votes, denied that it was a fair emanation of the people. The Administration affirmed that it was.

With respect to the evidence bearing upon that question of fact, I readily agree that Judge Douglas and the Republicans had the right on their side, and that the Administration was wrong. But I state again that as a matter of principle there was no dispute upon the right of a people in a Territory, merging into a State to form a Constitution for themselves without outside interference from any quarter. This being so, what is Judge Douglas going to spend his life for? Is he going to spend his life in maintaining a principle that nobody on earth opposes? [Cheers] Does he expect to stand up in majestic dignity, and go through his *apotheosis* and become a god, in the maintaining of a principle which neither a man nor a mouse in all God's creation is opposing? [Tremendous cheering.] Now something in regard to the Lecompton Constitution more specially; for I pass from this other question of popular sovereignty as the most errant humbug that has ever been attempted on an intelligent community.

"As to the Lecompton Constitution, I have already said that on the question of fact as to whether it was a fair emanation of the people or not, Judge Douglas with the Republicans and some Americans had greatly the argument against the Administration; and while I repeat this, I wish to know what there is in the opposition of Judge Douglas to the Lecompton Constitution that entitles him to be considered the only opponent to it—as being *par excellence* the very *quintessence* of that opposition. I agree to the rightfulness of his opposition. He in the Senate and his class of men there formed the number *three* and no more. In the House of Representatives his class of men—the anti Lecompton Democrats—formed a number of about twenty to defeat the measure against one hundred and twelve. Of the votes of that one hundred and twenty, Judge Douglas' friends furnished twenty, to add to which, there were six Americans and ninety-four Republicans, I do not say that I am precisely accurate in their numbers, but I am sufficiently so for any use I am making of it.

"Why is it that twenty shall be entitled to all the credit of doing that work, and the hundred none of it? Why, if, as Judge Douglas says, the honor is to be divided and due credit is to be given to other parties, why is just so much given as is consonant with the wishes, the interests and advancement of the twenty? My understanding is, when a common job is done, or a common enterprise prosecuted, if I put in five dollars to your one, I have a right to take out five dollars to your one. But he does not so understand it. He declares the dividend of credit for defeating Lecompton upon a basis which seems unprecedented and incomprehensible."

Why Credit Douglas

"Let us see. Lecompton in the raw was defeated. It afterwards took a sort of cooked up shape, and was passed in the English bill. It is said by the Judge that the defeat was a good and proper thing. If it was a good thing, why is he entitled to more credit than others, for the performance of that good act, unless there was something in the antecedents of the Republicans that might induce every one to expect them to join in that good work, and at the same time, something leading them to doubt that he would? Does he place his superior claim to credit, on the ground that he performed a good act which was never expected of him? He says I have a proneness for quoting scripture. If I should do so now, it occurs that perhaps he places himself somewhat upon the ground of the parable of the lost sheep which went astray upon the mountains, and when the owner of the hundred sheep found the one that was lost, and threw it upon his shoulders, and came home rejoicing, it was said that there was more rejoicing over the one sheep that was lost and had been found, than over the ninety and nine in the fold. [Great cheering, and renewed cheering.] The application is made by the Saviour in this parable, thus, 'Verily, I say unto you, there is more rejoicing in heaven over one sinner that repenteth, than over ninety and nine just persons that need no repentence.' [Cheering.]

"And now, if the Judge claims the benefit of this parable, *let him repent.* [Vociferous applause.] Let him not come up here and say: I am the only just person; and you are the ninety-nine sinners! *Repentence,* before *forgiveness* is a provision of the Christian system, and on that condition alone will the Republicans grant his forgiveness. [Laughter and cheers.]

"How will he prove that we have ever occupied a different position in regard to the Lecompton Constitution or any principle in it? He says he did not make his opposition on the ground as to whether it was a free or slave constitution, and he would have you understand that the Republicans made their opposition because it ultimately became a slave constitution. To make proof in favor of himself on this point, he reminds us that he opposed Lecompton before the vote was taken declaring whether the State was to be free or slave. But he forgets to say that our Republican Senator Trumbull, made a speech against Lecompton, even before he did.

"Why did he oppose it? Partly, he declares, because the members of the Convention who framed it were not fairly elected by the people; that the people were not allowed to vote unless they had been registered; and that the people of whole counties, in some instances, were not registered. For these reasons he declares the constitution was not an emanation, in any true sense, from the people. He also has an additional objection as to the mode of submitting the constitution back to the people. But bearing on the question of whether the delegates were fairly elected, a speech of his, made something more than twelve months ago, from this stand, becomes important. It was made a little while before the election of the delegates who made Lecompton. In that speech he declared there was every reason to hope and believe the election would be fair; and if any one failed to vote, it would be his own culpable fault.

"I, a few days after, made a sort of answer to that speech. In that answer, I made, substantially, the very argument with which he combatted his Lecompton adversaries in the Senate last winter. I pointed to the facts that the people could not vote without being registered, and that the time for registering had gone by. I commented on it as wonderful that Judge Douglas could be ignorant of these facts which every one else in the nation so well knew.

"I now pass from popular sovereignty and Lecompton, I may have occasion to refer to one or both."

"Make No Inferences That Do Not Appear True"

"When he was preparing his plan of campaign, Napoleon like, in New York, as appears by two speeches I have heard him deliver since his arrival in Illinois, he gave special attention to a speech of mine, delivered here on the 16th of June last. He says that he carefully read that speech. He told us that at Chicago a week ago last night, and he repeated it at Bloomington last night. Doubtless, he repeated it again to-day, though I did not hear him. In the first two places— Chicago and Bloomington—I heard him; to-day I did not. [A voice— Yes; he said the same thing.] He said he had carefully examined that speech; *when*, he did not say; but there is no reasonable doubt it was when he was in New York preparing his plan of campaign. I am glad he did read it carefully. He says it was evidently prepared with great care. I freely admit it was prepared with care. I claim not to be more free from errors than others—perhaps scarcely so much, but I was very careful not to put anything in that speech as a matter of fact, or make any inferences which did not appear to me to be true, and fully warrentable. If I had made any mistake I was willing to be corrected; if I had drawn any inference in regard to Judge Douglas, or any one else, which was not warrented, I was fully prepared to modify it as soon as discovered. I planted myself upon the truth, and the truth only, so far as I knew it, or could be brought to know it."

A Gentlement in Substance but Not of Polish

"Having made that speech with the most kindly feeling towards Judge Douglas, as minifested therein, I was gratified when I found that he had carefully examined it, and had detected no error of fact, nor any inference against him, nor any misrepresentations, of which he thought fit to complain. In neither of the two speeches I have mentioned, did he make any such complaint. I will thank any one who will inform me that he, in his speech today, pointed out anything I had stated, respecting him, as being erroneous. I presume there is no such thing. I have reason to be gratified that the care and caution used in that speech, left it so that he, most of all others interested in discovering error, has not been able to point out one thing against him which he could say was wrong. He seizes upon the doctrines he supposes to be included in that speech, and declares that upon them will turn the issues of this campaign. He then quotes, or attempts to quote, from my speech. I will not say that he wilfully misquotes, but he does fail to quote accurately. His attempt at quoting is from a passage which I believe I can quote accurately from memory. I shall make the quotation now, with some comments upon it, as I have already said, in order that the Judge shall be left entirely without excuse for misrepresenting me. I do so now, as I hope, for the last time. I do this in great caution, in order that if he repeats his misrepresentation, it shall be plain to all that he does so wilfully. If, after all, he still persists, I shall be compelled to reconstruct the course I have marked out for myself, and draw upon such humble resources as I have, for a new course, better suited to the real exigencies of the case. I set out in this campaign, with the intention of conducting it strictly as a gentleman, in substance at least, if not in the outside polish. The latter I shall never be, but that which constitutes the inside of a gentleman I hope I understand, and am not less inclined to practice than others. [Cheers.] It was my purpose and expectations that this canvass would be conducted upon principle, and with fairness on both sides; and it shall not be my fault, if this purpose and expectation shall be given up."

Douglas Charges I Invite War

"He charges, in substance, that I invite a war of sections; that I propose all the local institutions of the different States shall become consolidated and uniform. What is there in the language of that speech which expresses such purpose, or bears such construction? I have again and again said that I would not enter into any of the States to disturb the institution of slavery. Judge Douglas said, at Bloomington, that I used language most able and ingenious for concealing what I really meant; and that while I had protested against entering into the slave States, I nevertheless did mean to go on the banks of Ohio and throw missiles into Kentucky to disturb them in their domestic institutions.

"I said, in that speech, and I meant no more, that the institution of slavery ought to be placed in the very attitude where the framers of this Government placed it, and left it. I do not understand that the framers of our Constitution left the people of the free States in the attitude of firing bombs or shells into the slave States. I was not using that passage for the purpose which he infers I did use it. I said:

" 'We are now far advanced into the fifth year since a policy was created for the avowed object and with the confident promise of putting an end to slavery agitation. Under the operation of that policy that agitation has not only not ceased, but has constantly augmented. In my opinion it will not cease till a crisis shall have been reached and passed. 'A house divided against itself can not stand.' I believe that this government cannot endure permanently half slave and half free. It will become all one thing or all the other. Either the opponents of slavery will arrest the further spread of it, and place it where the public mind shall rest in the belief that it is the course of ultimate extinction, or its advocates will push it forward till it shall become alike lawful in all the States, old as well as new, North as well as South.' "

"Now you all see, from that quotation, I did not express my *wish* on anything. In that passage I indicated no wish or purpose of my own; I simply expressed my *expectation*. Cannot the

Judge perceive the distinction between a *purpose* and an *expectation*. I have often expressed an expectation to die, but I have never expressed a *wish* to die. I said at Chicago, and now repeat, that I am quite aware this government has endured, half slave and half free, for eighty-two years. I understand that little bit of history. I expressed the opinion I did, because I perceived—or thought I perceived—a new set of causes introduced. I did say, at Chicago, in my speech there, that I do wish to see the spread of slavery arrested and to see it placed where the public mind shall rest in the belief that it is in course of ultimate extinction. I said that because I supposed, when the public mind shall rest in that belief, we shall have peace on the slavery question. I have believed—and now believe—the public mind did rest on that belief up to the introduction of the Nebraska bill."

Ultimate Extinction of Slavery

"Although I have ever been opposed to slavery, so far I rested in the hope and belief that it was in course of ultimate extinction. For that reason, it had been a minor question with me. I might have been mistaken; but I had believed, and now believe, that the whole public mind, that is the mind of the great majority, had rested in that belief up to the repeal of the Missouri compromise. But upon that event, I became convinced that either I had been resting in a delusion, or the institution was being placed on a new basis—a basis for making it perpetual, national and universal. Subsequent events have greatly confirmed me in that belief. I believe that bill to be the beginning of a conspiracy for that purpose. So believing, I have since then considered that question a paramount one. So believing, I have thought the public mind will never rest till the power of Congress to restrict the spread of it, shall again be acknowledged and exercised on the one hand, or on the other, all resistance be entirely crushed out. I have expressed that opinion, and I entertain it to-night. It is denied that there is any tendency to the nationalization of slavery in these States.

"Mr. Brooks, of South Carolina, in one of his speeches, when they were presenting him with canes, silver plate, gold pitchers and the like, for assaulting Senator Sumner, distinctly affirmed his opinion that when this Constitution was formed, it was the belief of no man that slavery would last to the present day.

"He said, what I think, that the framers of our Constitution placed the institution of slavery where the public mind rested in the hope that it was in course of ultimate extinction. But he went on to say that the men of the present age, by their experience, have become wiser than the framers of the Constitution; and the invention of the cotton gin had made the perpetuity of slavery a necessity in this country.

"As another piece of evidence tending to the same point:—Quite recently in Virginia, a man—the owner of slaves—made a will providing that after his death certain of his slaves should have their freedom if they should so choose, and go to Liberia, rather than remain in slavery. They chose to be liberated. But the persons to whom they would descend as property, claimed them as slaves. A suit was instituted, which finally came to the Supreme Court of Virginia, and was therein decided against the slaves, upon the ground that a negro cannot make a choice—that they had no legal power to choose—could not perform the condition upon which their freedom depended.

"I do not mention this with any purpose of criticising, but to connect it with the arguments as affording additional evidence of the change of sentiment upon this question of slavery in the direction of making it perpetual and national. I argue now as I did before, that there is such a tendency, and I am backed not merely by the facts, but by the open confession in the Slave States."

Ridicules Douglas' Criticism

"And now as to the Judge's inference, that because I wish to see slavery placed in the course of ultimate extinction—placed where our fathers originally placed it—I wish to annihilate the State Legislatures—to force cotton to grow upon the tops of the Green Mountains—to freeze ice in Florida—to cut lumber on the broad Illinois prairies—that I am in favor of all these ridiculous and impossible things.

"It seems to me it is a complete answer to all this, to ask, if, when Congress did have the fashion of restricting slavery from free territory; when courts did have the fashion of deciding that taking a slave into a free country made him free—I say it is a sufficient answer to ask, if any of this ridiculous nonsense about consolidation, and uniformity, did actually follow. Who heard of any such thing, because of the Ordinance of '87? because of the Missouri Restriction?" because of the numerous court decisions of that character?"

Political Rejection of Dred Scott Decision

"Now, as to the Dred Scott Decision; for upon that he makes his last point at me. He boldly takes ground in favor of that decision.

"This is one-half the onslaught, and one-third of the entire plan of the campaign. I am opposed to that decision in a certain sense, but not in the sense which he puts on it. I say that in so far as it decided in favor of Dred Scott's master and against Dred Scott and his family, I do not propose to disturb or resist the decision.

"I have never proposed to do any such thing. I think, that in respect for judicial authority, my humble history would not suffer in a comparison with that of Judge Douglas. He would have the citizen conform his vote to that decision; the Member of Congress, his; the President, his use of the veto power. He would make it a rule of political action for the people and all the departments of the government. I would not. By resisting it as a political rule, I disturb no right of property, create no disorder, excite no mobs.

"When he spoke at Chicago, on Friday evening of last week, he made this same point upon me. On Saturday evening I replied and reminded him of a Supreme Court decision which he opposed for at least several years. Last night, at Bloomington, he took some notice of that reply; but entirely forgot to remember that part of it.

"He renews his onslaught upon me, forgetting to remember that I have turned the tables against himself on that very point. I renew the effort to draw his attention to it. I wish to stand erect before the country as well as Judge Douglas, on this question of judidical authority; and therefore I add something to the authority in favor of my own position. I wish to show that I am sustained by authority, in addition to that heretofore presented. I do not expect to convince the Judge. It is part of the plan of his campaign, and he will cling to it with a desperate gripe. Even, turn it upon him— turn the sharp point against him, and gaff him through—he will still cling to it till he can invent some new dodge to take the place of it."

Danger of Despotic Oligarchy

"In public speaking it is tedious reading from documents; but I must beg to indulge the practice to a limited extent. I shall read from a letter written by Mr. Jefferson in 1820, and now to be found in the seventh volume of his correspondence, at page 177. It seems he had been presented by a gentleman of the name of Jarvis with a book, or essay, or periodical, called "Republican," and he was writing in acknowledgment of the present, and noting some of its contents. After expressing the hope that the work will produce a favorable effect upon the minds of the young, he proceeds to say:

" 'That it will have this tendency may be expected, and for that reason I feel an urgency to note what I deem an error in it, the more requiring notice as your opinion is strengthened by that of many others. You seem in pages 84 and 148, to consider the judges as the ultimate arbiters of all constitutional questions—a very dangerous doctrine indeed and one which would place us under the despotism of an oligarchy. Our judges are as honest as other men, and not more so. They have, with others, the same passions for party, for power, and the privilege of their corps. Their maxim is, 'boni judicis est ampliare jurisdictionem;' and their power is the more dangerous as they are in office for life, and not responsible, as the other functionaries are, to the elective control. The Constitution has erected no such single tribunal, knowing that to whatever hands confided, with the corruptions of time and party, its members would become despots. It has more wisely made all the departments co-equal and co-sovereign within themselves.'

"Thus we see the power claimed for the Supreme Court by Judge Douglas, Mr. Jefferson holds, would reduce us to the despotism of an oligarchy.

"Now, I have said no more than this—in fact, never quite so much as this—at least I am sustained by Mr. Jefferson.

"Let us go a little further. You remember we once had a national bank. Some one owed the bank a debt; he was sued and sought to avoid payment, on the ground that the bank was unconstitutional. The case went to the Supreme Court, and therein it was decided that the bank was constitutional. The whole Democratic party revolted against that decision. General Jackson himself asserted that he, as President, would not be bound to hold a national bank to be constitutional, even though the Court had decided it to be so.

He fell in precisely with the view of Mr. Jefferson, and acted upon it under his official oath, in vetoing a charter for a national bank. The declaration that Congress does not possess this constitutional power to charter a bank, has gone into the Democratic platform at their national conventions, and was brought forward and re-affirmed in their last convention at Cincinnati. They have contended for that declaration, in the very teeth of the Supreme Court, for more than a quarter of a century. In fact, they have reduced the decision to an absolute nullity. That decision, I repeat, is repudiated in the Cincinnati platform; and still, as if to show that effrontery can go no farther, Judge Douglas vaunts in the very speeches in which he denounces me for opposing the Dred Scott decision, that he stands on the Cincinnati platform."

Douglas Is for What He Likes

"Now, I wish to know what the Judge can charge upon me, with respect to decisions of the Supreme Court which does not lie in all its length, breadth, and proportions at his own door. The plain truth is simply this: Judge Douglas is *for* Supreme Court decisions when he likes and against them when he does not like them. He is for the Dred Scott decision because it tends to nation-alize slavery—because it is part of the original combination for that object. It so happens, singularly enough, that I never stood opposed to a decision of the Supreme Court till this. On the contrary, I have no recollection that he was ever particularly in favor of one till this. He never was in favor of any, nor opposed to any, till the present one, which helps to nationalize slavery."

Judge Ye between Him and Me

"Free men of Sangamon—free men of Illinois—free men everywhere—judge ye between him and me, upon this issue.

"He says this Dred Scott case is a very small matter at most—that it has no practical effect; that at best, or rather, I suppose, at worst, it is but an abstraction. I submit that the proposition that the thing which determines whether a man is free or a slave, is rather *concrete* than *abstract*. I think you would conclude that it was, if your liberty depended upon it, and so would Judge Douglas if his liberty depended upon it. But suppose it was on the question of spreading slavery over the new territories that he con-siders it as being merely an abstract matter, and one of no practical importance. How has the planting of slavery in new countries always been effected? It has now been decided that slavery cannot be kept out of our new territories by any legal means. In what does our new territories now differ in this respect, from the old colonies when slavery was first planted within them? It was planted as Mr. Clay once declared, and as history proves true, by individual men in spite of the wishes of the people; the mother government refusing to prohibit it, and withholding from the people of the colonies the authority to prohibit it for themselves. Mr. Clay says this was one of the great and just causes of complaint against Great Britain by the colonies, and the best apology we can now make for having the institution amongst us. In that precise condition our Nebraska politicians have at last succeeded in placing our own new territories; the government will not prohibit slavery within them, nor allow the people to prohibit it.

"I defy any man to find any difference between the policy which originally planted slavery in these colonies and that policy which now prevails in our own new Territories. If it does not go into them, it is only because no individual wishes it to go. The Judge indulged himself, doubtless, today, with the question as to what I am going to do with or about the Dred Scott decision. Well, Judge, will you please tell me what you did about the Bank decision? Will you not graciously allow us to do with the Dred Scott decision precisely as you did with the Bank decision? You succeeded in breaking down the moral effect of that decision; did you find it necessary to amend the Constitution? or to set up a court of negroes in order to do it?"

Douglas Affects Clay

"There is one other point, Judge Douglas has a very affectionate leaning towards the Americans and old Whigs. Last evening, in a sort of weeping tone, he described to us a death bed scene. He had been called to the side of Mr. Clay, in his last moments, in order that the genius of 'popular sovereignty' might duly descend from the dying man and settle upon him, the living and most worthy successor. He could do no less than promise that he would devote the remainder of his life to 'popular sovereignty;' and then the great statesman departs in peace. By this part of the 'plan of the campaign,' the Judge has evidently promised himself that the tears shall be drawn down the cheeks of all old Whigs, as large as half grown apples.

"Mr. Webster, too, was mentioned; but it did not quite come to a death-bed scene, as to him. It would be amusing, if it were not disgusting, to see how quick these compromise-breakers administer on the political effects of their dead adversaries, trumping up claims never before heard of, and dividing the assets among themselves. If I should be found dead tomorrow morning, nothing but my insignificance could prevent a speech being made on my authority, before the end of next week. It so happens that in that 'popular sovereignty' with which Mr. Clay was identified, the Missouri Compromise was expressly reserved; and it was a little singular if Mr. Clay cast his mantle upon Judge Douglas on purpose to have that compromise repealed.

"Again, the Judge did not keep faith with Mr. Clay when he first brought in his Nebraska bill. He left the Missouri Compromise unrepealed, and in his report accompanying the bill, he told the world he did it on purpose. The manes of Mr. Clay must have been in great agony, till thirty days later, when 'popular sovereignty' stood forth in all its glory."

Douglas Shifts from British to Europeans

"One more thing. Last night Judge Douglas tormented himself with horrors about my disposition to make negroes perfectly equal with white men in social and political relations. He did not stop to show that I have said any such thing, or that it legitimately follows from any thing I have said, but he rushes on with his assertions. I adhere to the Declaration of Independence. If Judge Douglas and his friends are not willing to stand by it, let them come up and amend it. Let them make it read that all men are created equal except negroes. Let us have it decided, whether the Declaration of Independence, in this blessed year of 1858, shall be thus amended. In his construction of the Declaration last year he said it only meant that Americans in America were equal to Englishmen in England. Then, when I pointed out to him that by that rule he excludes the Germans, the Irish, the Portuguese, and all the other people who have come amongst us since the Revolution, he reconstructs his construction. In his last speech he tells us it meant Europeans.

"I press him a little further, and ask if it meant to include the Russians in Asia? or does he mean to exclude that vast population from the principles of our Declaration of Independence? I expect ere long he will introduce another amendment to his definition. He is not at all particular. He is satisfied with any thing which does not endanger the nationalization of negro slavery. It may draw white men down, but it must not lift negroes up. Who shall say, 'I am the superior, and you are the inferior?' "

Equal Rights to Liberty for All Men

"My declarations upon this subject of negro slavery may be misrepresented, but can not be misunderstood. I have said that I do not understand the Declaration to mean that all men were created equal in all respects. They are not our equal in color; but I suppose it does mean to declare that all men are equal in some respects; they are equal in their right to life, liberty, and the pursuit of happiness.' Certainly the negro is not our equal in color—perhaps not in many other respects; still, in the right to put into his mouth the bread that his own hands have earned, he is the equal of every other man, white or black. In pointing out that more has been given you, you can not be justified in taking away the little which has been given him. All I ask for the negro is that if you do not like him, let him alone. If God gave him but little, that little let him enjoy.

"When our Government was established, we had the institution of slavery among us. We were in a certain sense compelled to tolerate its existence. It was a sort of necessity. We had gone through our struggle and secured our own independence. The framers of the Constitution found the institution of slavery amongst their other institutions at the time. They found that by an effort to eradicate it, they might lose much of what they had already gained. They were obliged to bow to the necessity. They gave power to Congress to abolish the slave trade at the end of twenty years. They also prohibited it in the Territories where it did not exist. They did what they could and yielded to the necessity for the rest. I also yield to all which follows from that necessity. What I would most desire would be the separation of the white and black races."

Recharges Conspiracy

"One more point on this Springfield speech which Judge Douglas says he has read so carefully. I expressed my belief in the existence of a conspiracy to perpetuate and nationalize slavery. I did not profess to know it, nor do I now. I showed the part Judge Douglas had played in the string of facts, constituting to my mind, the proof of that conspiracy. I showed the parts played by others.

"I charged that the people had been deceived into carrying the last Presidential election, by the impression that the people of the Territories might exclude slavery if they chose, when it was known in advance by the conspirators, that the Court was to decide that neither Congress nor the people could so exclude slavery. These charges are more distinctly made than any thing else in the speech.

"Judge Douglas has carefully read and re-read that speech. He has not, so far as I know, contradicted those charges. In the two speeches which I heard he certainly did not. On his own tacit admission I renew the charge. I charge him with having been a party to that conspiracy and to that deception for the sole purpose of nationalizing slavery." [Mr. Lincoln sat down amidst loud and continued cheering.]

"I Hope You Perceive I Am Improving"

John Mathers, a brick manufacturer and prominent citizen of Jacksonville, Ill., had advised Lincoln to adopt a more aggressive and less defensive attitude in his speeches. Lincoln's reply (7, 20, 1858) shows his eagerness to improve his methods:

"Your suggestions as to placing one's self on the offensive, rather than the *defensive,* are certainly correct. That is a point which I shall not disregard. I spoke here on Saturday-night. The speech, not very well reported, appears in the State Journal of this morning. You, doubtless, will see it; and I hope you will perceive in it, that I am already improving."

Factual Analysis—Realistic Synthesis

Lincoln differed from most political leaders in that they generally judged possibilities wishfully from impressions, whereas he held close to what he could gather from what the people, in everyday life, were saying *for* and *against* candidates and their political principles and policies. An excellent example of this is shown in his letter of advice to his old friend Joseph Gillespie (7, 16, 1858):

"I write this to say that from the specimens of Douglas democracy we occassionally see here in Madison, we learn that they are making very confident calculation of beating both you, and your friends for the lower House in that county. They offer to bet upon it. . . . If they do so, it can only be done by carrying the Fillmore men of 1856, very differently from what they seem to be going in other parts. Below is the vote of 1856, in your district.

	Buc.	Fre.	Fill.
Bond	607	153	659
Madison	1451	1111	1658
Montg.	992	162	686
	3050	1426	3003

"By this you will see, if you go through the calculation, that if *they* get one quarter of the Fillmore and *you* get three quarters, they will beat you by 125 votes. If they get one *fifth* and you four fifths, you beat them 179. In Madison alone if our friends get 1000 of the Fillmore votes, and their opponents the remainder—658, we win by just two votes.

"This shows the whole field, on the basis of the election of 1856. Whether, since then, any Buchanan men, or Fremonters have shifted ground, and how the majority of *new* voters will go, you can judge better than I.

"Of course you, *on* the ground, can better determine your line of tactics, than any one off the ground; but it behooves you to be wide awake, and actively working." . . .

Will to Win

Gillespie replied (7, 18) that Douglas would carry at least half of the American Know-Nothing vote and that he (Gillespie) would be beaten for the State Senate by virtue of having been in too long.

Lincoln's answer (7, 25, 1858) bespeaks the remarkable vigor and tenacity of his driving powers to win.

"Your doleful letter of the 18th. was received on my return from Chicago last night. I do hope you are worse scared than hurt, though you ought to know best. We must not lose that district. We must make a job of it, and save it. Lay hold of the proper agencies and secure all the Americans you can, at once. I do hope, on closer inspection, you will find they are not half gone. Make a little test. Run down one of the pool-books of the Edwardsville precinct, and take the first hundred known American names. Then quietly ascertain how many of them are actually going for Douglas. I think you will find less than fifty. But even if you find find [sic] fifty, make sure of the other fifty—that is, make sure of all you can at all events. We will set other agencies to work, which shall compensate for the loss of a good many Americans. Don't fail to check the stampede at once." . . .

Gillespie's predictions eventually proved true in Illinois. Douglas, through his demogogic claim that the declaration of equality referred to Americans of English descent, gained much of the Know-Nothing vote, whereas Lincoln's claim that it meant all men, regardless of nationality or race, prejudiced that secretly hypocritical "American for Americans" sentiment that broods in degenerating families.

To G. P. Koerner (7, 25, 1858) he wrote:

> . . . "I learn we are in great danger in Madison. It is said half of the Americans are going for Douglas; and that slam will ruin us if not counteracted. It appears to me this fact of itself, would make it, at least no harder for us to get accessions from the Germans. . . . Can not you, Canisius [Dr. T., editor of the Alton Free Press], and some other influential Germans set a plan on foot that shall gain us accessions from the Germans, and see that, at the election, none are cheated in their ballots? . . . Nothing must be left undone. Elsewhere things look reasonably well." . . .

Lincoln was *thoroughly factualistic in analysis and realistic in synthesis.* He abhorred loose guesses and wishful generalizations as misleading and untrustworthy. He must always see the ground on which he stood and foresee where his steps were going. This habitually cautious attitude was a protective compensation against his ever present tendency to develop anxiety when he became involved in unavoidable conflicting conditions that required making decisive discriminations and irreversible decisions.

Chapter XXIX

PREDETERMINANTS OF
LINCOLN-DOUGLAS DEBATES

The great debates of 1858 between Lincoln and Douglas followed naturally from preceding events. Twenty years past when ambitious young men gathered in Speed's store and discussed the problems of the nation, two young lawyers, Abe Lincoln and Steve Douglas, were almost certain to hold opposite views on every important issue.

We have seen that, in 1839, Lincoln and Douglas held a formal public debate in Springfield on Democratic versus Whig policies in regard to the national currency. We have seen that inspired Lincoln followed Douglas about in the campaigns of 1854 and 1856 and how, on one occasion, the people succeeded in getting up a debate after Douglas spoke in the afternoon by inviting Lincoln, who was present, to reply. When he accepted for that evening, Douglas declared that he would stay and hear him and make a rebuttal the next day.

We have seen how Lincoln continued to follow Douglas from one speech to the next in the campaign of 1858 and how the crowds shouted for a speech from him after Douglas had finished. By public demand it became necessary that these two men should debate their political principles before the same audiences in order that the people might better judge their values on federal versus states' rights, and the moral as well as economic rights and wrongs involved in Southern efforts to extend slavery against Northern efforts to prevent it, and, not least, to gather in great showy crowds to have a good time. Western pioneers loved a good debate as much as a good fight or horse race and never missed a chance to make the most of it.

Exchange of Letters Arranging the Debates

On July 24, 1858 Lincoln wrote to Douglas:

"Will it be agreeable to you to make an arrangement for you and myself to divide time, and address the same audiences during the present canvass? Mr. [N. B.] Judd, who will hand you this, is authorized to receive your answer; and, if agreeable to you, to enter into terms of such arrangement."

Douglas replied immediately but Lincoln did not receive it until the 29th. Douglas said:

566

"Your note of this date, in which you inquire if it would be agreeable to me to make an arrangement to divide the time and address the same audiences during the present canvass, was handed me by Mr. Judd.

"Recent events have interposed difficulties in the way of such an arrangement."

He then cited the schedule prepared by the Democratic State Central Committee which arranged for himself and other candidates of his party to appear together on the same program.

"It is evident," he continued, "that these various candidates, in connection with myself, will occupy the whole time of the day and evening and leave no opportunity for other speeches.

"Besides, there is another consideration which should be kept in mind. It has been suggested recently that an arrangement had been made to bring out a third candidate for the U. S. Senate, who, with yourself, should canvass the state in opposition to me, and with no other purpose than to insure my defeat by dividing the Democratic party for your benefit. If I should make the arrangement with you, it is more than probable that this other candidate, who has common object with you, would desire to become a party to it and claim the right to speak from the same stand; so that he and you in concert might be able to take the opening and closing speech in every case.

"I cannot refrain from expressing my surprise, if it was your original intention to invite such an arrangement that you should have waited until after I had made my appointments, inasmuch that as we were both here in Chicago together for several days after my arrival, and again at Bloomington, Atlanta, Lincoln and Springfield, where it was well known I went for the purpose of consulting with the State Central Committee and agreeing upon the plan of campaign.

"While under these circumstances I do not feel at liberty to make an arrangement that would deprive the Democratic candidates for Congress, State offices and the Legislature from participating in the discussion, at the various meetings designated by the Democratic State Central Committee, I will in order to accomodate you in so far as it is in my power to do so, take the responsibility for making an arrangement with you for a discussion between us at one prominent point in each congressional district in the state, excepting the second and sixth districts, where we have both spoken in each of which cases you had the concluding speech. If agreeable to you I will indicate the following places as the most suitable in the several congressional districts at which we should speak, to wit, Freeport, Ottawa, Galesburg, Quincy, Alton, Jonesboro and Charleston.

"I will confer with you at the earliest convenient opportunity in regard to the mode of conducting the debate and the times of meeting at the several places subject to the conditions that where appointments have already been made by the Democratic State

Central Committee at any of those places I must insist upon your meeting me at the times specified. Very respectfully, Your obd't Servant."

Lincoln promptly answered on the same day at considerable length. The letters show that he and Douglas regarded each other with friendly respect and admiration as men, although each disagreed vigorously with most of the political principles of his opponent. The two letters are historical examples of democracy at work between rival candidates who are self-respecting gentlemen.

"Yours of the 24th. in relation to an arrangement to divide and address the same audiences, is received; and, in apology for not sooner replying, allow me to say that when I sat by you at dinner yesterday I was not aware that you had answered my note, nor certainly, that my own note had been presented to you. An hour after I saw a copy of your answer in the Chicago Times; and, reaching home, I found the original awaiting me. Protesting that your insinuations of attempted unfairness on my part are unjust; and with the hope that you did not very considerately make them, I proceed to reply. To your statement that 'It has been suggested recently that an arrangement had been made to bring out a third candidate for the U. S. Senate who, with yourself, should canvass the state in opposition to me &.' I can only say that such suggestion must have been made by yourself; for certainly none such has been made by, or to me; or otherwise, to my knowledge. Surely you did not *deliberately* conclude, as you insinuate, that I was expecting to draw you into an arrangement, of terms to be agreed upon by yourself, by which a third candidate, and my self, in concert, might be able to take the opening and closing speech in every case.'

"As to your surprise that I did not sooner make the proposal to divide time with you, I can only say I made it as soon as I resolved to make it. I did not know but that such proposal would come from you; I waited respectfully to see. It may have been well known to you that you went to Springfield for the purpose of agreeing upon the plan of campaign; but it was not so known to me. When your appointments were announced in the papers, extending only to the 21st. of August, I, for the first time, considered it certain that you would make no proposal to me; and then resolved, if my friends concurred, I would make one to you. As soon thereafter as I could see and consult with friends satisfactorily, I did make the proposal. It did not occur to me that the proposed arrangement could derange your plan, after the latest of your appointments already made. After that, there was, before the election, largely over two months of clear time.

"For you to say that we have already spoken at Chicago and Springfield, and that on both occasions I had the concluding speech, is hardly a fair statement. The truth rather is this. At Chicago, July 9th, you made a carefully prepared conclusion on my speech of June 16th.; twenty-four hours after I made a hasty conclusion on yours of the 9th.; you had six days to prepare, and concluded on me again at Bloomington on the 16th., twenty-four hours after I concluded on you again at Springfield. In the mean time you had made another conclusion on me at Springfield, which I did not hear, and of the contents of which I knew nothing when I spoke; so that your speech made in day-light, and mine at night of the 17th. at Springfield were both made in perfect independence of each other. The dates of making all these speeches, will show, I think, that in the matter of time for preparation, the advantage has all been on your side; and that none of the external circumstances have stood to my advantage.

"I agree to an arrangement for us to speak at the seven places you have named, and at your own times, provided you name the times at once, so that I, as well as you, can have to myself the time not covered by the arrangement. As to other details, I wish perfect reciprocity, and no more. I wish as much time as you, and that conclusions shall alternate. That is all. Your obedient servant

"P.S. As matters now stand, I shall be at no more of your exclusive meetings; and for about a week from today a letter from you will reach me at Springfield."

The arrangements for the debates were finally completed upon Linoln's reply to Douglas of July 31:

"Yours of yesterday, naming places, times and terms, for joint discussions between us, was received this morning. Although by the terms, as you propose, you take *four* openings and closes to my three, I accede, and thus close the arrangement. . . . I shall try to have both your letter and this, appear in the Journal and Register on Monday morning."

Keen Insight and Comprehensive Foresight

It is obvious from the preceding letters exchanged by Douglas and Lincoln, that the former worked in close cooperation with the old, thoroughly well tried and organized, Democratic state and national committees, whereas the latter had then only a loose state Republican organization, hardly worth referring to for arranging a speaking itinerary and advising him on campaign tactics. Lincoln depended entirely on a few confidential friends and the common sense and fairness of his appeal.

His letter to Henry Asbury, a Quincy attorney and trusted friend (7, 31, 1858) shows how well Lincoln knew Douglas and how far ahead he foresaw that the logical course of political events had two great potentialities which he must plan to discuss in the debates.

"The points you propose to press upon Douglas, he will be very hard to get up to. But I think you labor under a mistake when you say no ones cares how he answers. This implies that it is equal with him whether he is injured here or at the South. That is a mistake. He cares nothing for the South—he knows he is already dead there. He only leans Southward now to keep the Buchanan party from growing in Illinois. You shall have hard work to get him directly to the point whether a territorial Legislature has or has not the power to exclude slavery. But if you succeed in bringing him to it, though he will be compelled to say it possesses no such power; he will instantly take ground that slavery can not actually exist in the territories, unless the people desire it, and so give it protective territorial legislation. If it offends the South he will let it offend them; as at all events he means to hold on to his chances in Illinois."

We will see later, in the Debates, that Lincoln finally succeeded in cornering Douglas so that he had to answer this and other questions, and how, in so doing, it split the Democratic party into irreconcilable pro- and anti-Douglas factions and made possible the election of Lincoln, two years later, as President of the United States.

Definition of Democracy

Lincoln's much quoted definition of democracy is supposed to have been written in August 1858:

"As I would not be a *slave,* so I would not be a *master.* This expresses my idea of democracy. Whatever differs from this, to the extent of the difference, is no democracy."

Douglas Objects to Lincoln's "Intrusions"

The people were so persistent in calling for Lincoln after Douglas had finished speaking that he was privately informed that his presence at Democratic rallies embarrassed Douglas, who desired that he would refrain from attending them.

To J.T. Eccles he wrote (8, 2, 1858):

"I should be at your town today with Judge Douglas, had he not strongly intimated in his letter, which you have seen in the newspapers, that my presence on the days or evenings of his meetings would be considered an intrusion. Before long I shall publish a string of appointments following upon his present track."

He wrote similar letters on the same day to three other friends in communities where he had planned to be with Douglas.

Lincoln Provokes Douglas

In speeches at Beardstown and Havana, in August, Lincoln continued to charge Douglas with being in a "conspiracy" to nationalize slavery. Douglas had ignored the whole allegation as ridiculous, but Lincoln's persistent reiteration tried his patience and in pretended or righteous indignation he publicly condemned the ethics of a man who would publicly cast dishonorable reflections upon another man's character. Lincoln persisted in these charges, although on highly doubtful basis of evidence, until their friendly relations grew strained.

At Beardstown (8, 12, 1858) Lincoln said:

. . . "Well, seeing that Douglas had had the process served on him, and that he had taken notice of such service, that he had come into court and pleaded to a part of the complaint, but had ignored the main issue, I took a default on him. I held that he had no plea to make to the general charge. So, when I was called on to reply to him twenty-four hours afterwards, I renewed the charge as explicitly as I could. My speech was reported and published on the following morning, and of course Judge Douglas saw it. He went from Chicago to Bloomington, and there made another and longer speech, and yet took no notice of the 'conspiracy charge.' He then went to Springfield and made another elaborate argument, but was not prevailed upon to know anything about the outstanding indictment. I made another speech in Springfield—this time taking it for granted that Judge Douglas was satisfied to take his chances in the campaign with the imputation of the conspiracy hanging over him. It was not until he went into a small town (Clinton) in DeWitt county, where he delivered his fourth or fifth regular speech, that he found it convenient to notice this matter at all. At that place (I was standing in the crowd when he made his speech) he bethought himself that he was charged with something: (laughter;) and his reply was that 'his self-respect alone prevented his calling it a falsehood.' Well, my friends, perhaps he so far lost his self-respect in Beardstown as to actually call it a falsehood!" (Great laughter—Douglas had called it "an infamous lie.")

Two days later at Havana, Lincoln again pestered Douglas.

"I am informed, that my distinguished friend yesterday became a little excited, nervous perhaps, (laughter) and he said something about *fighting,* as though referring to a pugilistic encounter between him and myself. Did anybody in the audience hear him use such language? (Cries of "yes.") . . . Well I merely desire to say that I shall fight neither Judge Douglas nor his second. (Someone had offered to fight Lincoln for the Judge.) I shall not do this for two reasons, which I will now explain. In the first place a fight would *prove* nothing which is in issue in this contest. It might establish that Judge Douglas is a more muscular man than myself, or it might demonstrate that I am a more muscular man than Judge Douglas. (Great laughter.) Neither result would prove him right or wrong. And so of the gentleman who volunteered to do his fighting for him. If my fighting Judge Douglas would not prove anything, it certainly would prove nothing for me to fight his bottle-holder. (Continued laughter.)

"My second reason for not having a personal encounter with the Judge is, that I don't believe he wants it himself. (Laughter.) He and I are the best of friends in the world, and when we get together he would no more think of fighting me than of fighting his wife. Therefore, ladies and gentlemen, when the Judge talked about fighting, he was not giving vent to any ill-feeling of his own, but merely to excite—well, *enthusiasm* against me on the part of the audience. And as I find he was tolerably successful we will call it quits." (Cheers and laughter.) But he did not quit.

Lincoln's Soliloquy Before the Debates

In the coming series of debates Lincoln felt that at last the supreme opportunity had come to disprove the political philosophy of his great rival.

In the following private notes (8, 21, 1858) he analyses his attitude and his reasons again for the controversial position he has taken. He soliloquizes remarkably in the way of Hamlet, even to the meter of his sentences (to be read slowly). His notes indicate that his mind worked habitually as if addressing an audience (captions inserted).

"When Douglas ascribes such to me, he does so, not by argument, but by mere burlesque on the art and name of argument—by such fantastic arrangements of words as prove 'horse-chestnuts to be chestnut horses.' In the main I shall trust an intelligent community to learn my objects and aims from what I say and do myself, rather than what Judge Douglas may say of me. But I must not leave the judge just yet. When he has burlesqued me into a position which I never thought of assuming myself, he will, in the most benevolent and patronizing manner imaginable, compliment me by saying 'he has no doubt I am perfectly conscientious in it.' I thank him for the word 'conscientious.' It turns my attention to the wonderful evidences of conscience he manifests. When he assumes to be the first discoverer and sole advocate of the right of a people to govern themselves, he is conscientious. When he affects to understand that a man, putting a hundred slaves through under the lash, is simply governing himself, he is more conscientious. When he affects not to know that the Dred Scott decision forbids a territorial legislature to exclude slavery, he is most conscientious. When, as in his last Springfield speech, he declares that I say, unless I shall play my batteries successfully, so as to abolish Slavery in every one of the States, the Union shall be dissolved, he is absolutely bursting with conscience. It is nothing that I have never said any such thing. With some men it might make a difference; but consciences differ in different individuals. Judge Douglas has a greater conscience than most men. It corresponds with his other points of greatness."

On Prophets

"Judge Douglas amuses himself by saying I wish to go into the Senate on my qualifications as a prophet. He says he has known some other prophets, and does not think very well of them. Well, others of us have also known some prophets. We know who nearly five years ago prophesied that the 'Nebraska Bill' would put an end to slavery agitation in next to no time—one who has renewed that prophesy at least as often as quarter-yearly ever since; and still the prophesy has not been fulfilled. That one might very well go out of the Senate on his qualifications as a false prophet."

"Why I Am in This Campaign"

"Allow me now, in my own way, to state with what aims and objects I did enter this campaign. I claim no extraordinary exemption from personal ambition. That I like preferment as well as the average of men may be admitted. But I protest I have not entered upon this hard contest solely, or even chiefly, for a mere personal object. I clearly see, as I think, a powerful plot to make slavery universal and perpetual in this nation. The effort to carry that plot through will be persistent and long continued, extending far beyond the senatorial term for which Judge Douglas and I are just now struggling. I enter upon the contest to contribute my humble and temporary mite in opposition to that effort.

"At the Republican State convention at Springfield I made a speech. That speech has been considered the opening of the canvass on my part. In it I arrange a string of incontestable facts which, I think, prove the existence of a conspiracy to nationalize slavery. The evidence was circumstantial only; but nevertheless it seemed inconsistent with every hypothesis, save that of the existence of such conspiracy. I believe the facts can be explained to-day on no other hypothesis. Judge Douglas can so explain them if any one can. From warp to woof his handiwork is everywhere woven in."

"Douglas Perverts Me"

"At New York he finds this speech of mine, and devises his plan of assault upon it. At Chicago he develops that plan. Passing over, unnoticed, the obvious purport of the whole speech, he cooks up two or three issues upon points not discussed by me at all, and then authoritatively announces that these are to be the issues of the campaign. Next evening I answer, assuring him that he misunderstands me—that he takes issues which I have not tendered. In good faith I try to set him right. If he really has misunderstood my meaning, I give him language that can no longer be misunderstood. He will have none of it. At Bloomington, six days later, he speaks again, and perverts me even worse than before. He seems to have grown confident and jubilant, in the belief that he has entirely diverted me from my purpose of fixing a conspiracy upon him and his co-workers. Next day he speaks again at Springfield, pursuing the same course, with increasing confidence and recklessness of assertion. At night of that day I speak again. I tell him that as he has carefully read my speech making the charge of conspiracy, and has twice spoken of the speech without noticing the charge, upon his own tacit admission I renew the charge against him. I call him, and take a default upon him. At Clifton, ten days after, he comes in with a plea. The substance of that plea is that he never passed a word with Chief Justice Taney as to what his decision was to be in the Dred Scott case; that I ought to know that he who affirms what he does not know to be true falsifies as much as he who affirms what he does know to be false; and that he would pronounce the whole charge of conspiracy a falsehood, were it not for his own self-respect!"

"I Have a Right to Prove"

"Now I demur to this plea. Waiving objection that it was not filed till after default, I demur to it on the merits. I say it does not meet the case. What if he did not pass a word with Chief Justice Taney? Could he not have as distinct an understanding, and play his part as well, without directly passing a word with Taney, as with it? But suppose we construe this part of the plea more broadly than he puts it himself—suppose we construe it, as in an answer to chancery, to be a denial of all knowledge, information, or belief of such conspiracy. Still I have the right to prove the conspiracy, even against his answer; and there is much more than the evidence of two witnesses to prove it by. Grant that he has no knowledge, information, or belief of such a conspiracy, and what of it? That does not disturb the facts in evidence. It only makes him the dupe, instead of a principal, of conspirators.

"What if a man may not affirm a proposition without knowing it to be true? I have not affirmed that a conspiracy does exist. I have only stated the evidence, and affirmed my belief in its existence. If Judge Douglas shall assert that I do not believe what I say, then he affirms what he cannot know to be true, and falls within the condemnation of his own rule.

"Would it not be much better for him to meet the evidence, and show, if he can, that I have no good reason to believe the charge? Would not this be far more satisfactory than merely vociferating an intimation that he may be provoked to call somebody a liar?"

"So far as I know, he denies no fact which I have alleged. Without now repeating all those facts, I recall attention to only a few of them. A provision of the Nebraska bill, penned by Judge Douglas, is in these words:

" 'It being the true intent and meaning of this act not to legislate slavery into any Territory or State, nor exclude it therefrom, but to leave the people thereof perfectly free to form and regulate their domestic institutions in their own way, subject only to the Constitution of the United States.'

"In support of this the argument, evidently prepared in advance, went forth: 'Why not let the people of a Territory have or exclude slavery just as they choose? Have they any less sense or less patriotism when they settle in the Territories than when they lived in the States?'

Did Douglas Conspire to Exclude Slavery

"Now the question occurs: Did Judge Douglas, even then intend that the people of a Territory should have the power to exclude slavery? If he did, why did he vote against an amendment expressly declaring they might exclude it? With men who then knew and intended that a Supreme Court decision should soon follow, declaring that the people of a Territory could not exclude slavery, voting down such an amendment was perfectly rational. But with men not expecting or desiring such a decision, and really wishing the people to have such power, voting down such an amendment, to my mind, is wholly inexplicable.

"That such an amendment was voted down by the friends of the bill, including Judge Douglas, is a recorded fact of the case. There was some real reason for so voting it down. What that reason was, Judge Douglas can tell. I believe that reason was to keep the way clear for a court decision, then expected to come, and which has since come, in the case of Dred Scott. If there was any other reason for voting down that amendment, Judge Douglas knows of it and can tell. Again, in the before-quoted part of the Nebraska bill, what means the provision that the people of the "State" shall be left perfectly free, subject only to the Constitution. Congress was not therein legislating for, or about, States or the people of States. In that bill the provision about the people of "States" is the odd half of something, the other half of which was not yet quite ready for exhibition. What is that other half to be? Another Supreme Court decision, declaring that the people of a State cannot exclude slavery, is exactly fitted to be that other half. As the power of the people of the Territories and of the States is cozily set down in the Nebraska bill as being the same; so the constitutional limitations on that power will then be judicially held to be precisely the same in both Territories and States—that is, that the Constitution permits neither a Territory nor a State to exclude slavery.

"With persons looking forward to such additional decision, the inserting of a provision about States in the Nebraska bill was perfectly rational; but to persons not looking for such decision it was a puzzle. There was a real reason for inserting such provision. Judge Douglas inserted it, and therefore knows, and can tell what that real reason was."

My Belief Not Lessened

"Judge Douglas's present course by no means lessens my belief in the existence of a purpose to make slavery alike lawful in all the States. This can be done by a Supreme Court decision holding that the United States Constitution forbids a State to exclude slavery; and probably it can be done in no other way. The idea of forcing slavery into a free State, or out of a slave State, at the point of the bayonet, is alike nonsensical. Slavery can only become extinct by being restricted to its present limits, and dwindling out. It can only become national by a Supreme Court decision. To such a decision, when it comes, Judge Douglas is fully committed. Such a decision acquiesced in by the people affects the whole object. Bearing this in mind, look at what Judge Douglas is doing every day. For the first sixty-five years under the United States Constitution, the practice of government had been to exclude slavery from the new free Territories. About the end of that period Congress, by the Nebraska bill, resolved to abandon this practice; and this was rapidly succeeded by a Supreme Court decision holding the practice to have always been unconstitutional. Some of us refuse to obey this decision as a political rule. Forthwith Judge Douglas espouses the decision, and denounces all opposition to it in no measured terms. He adheres to it with extraordinary tenacity, and under rather extraordinary circumstances. He espouses it not on any opinion of his that it is right within itself. On this he forbears to commit himself. He espouses it exclusively on the ground of its binding authority on all citizens—a ground which commits him as fully to the next decision as to this. I point out to him that Mr. Jefferson and General Jackson were both against him on the binding political authority of the Supreme Court decisions. No response. I might as well preach Christianity to a grizzly bear as to preach Jefferson and Jackson to him.

"I tell him I have often heard him denounce the Supreme Court decision in favor of a national bank. He denies the accuracy of my recollection—which seems strange to me, but I let it pass."

This Douglas Cannot Deny

"I remind him that he, even now, indorses the Cincinnati platform, which declares that Congress has no constitutional power to charter a bank; and that in the teeth of a Supreme Court decision that Congress has such power. This he cannot deny; and so he remembers to forget it.

"I remind him of a piece of Illinois history about Supreme Court decisions—of a time when the Supreme Court of Illinois, consisting of four judges, because of one decision made, and one expected to be made, were overwhelmed by the adding of five new judges to their number; that he, Judge Douglas, took a leading part in that onslaught, ending in his sitting down on the bench as one of the five added judges. I suggest to him that as to his questions how far judges have to be catechized in advance, when appointed under such circumstances, and how far a court, so constituted, is prostituted beneath the contempt of all men, no man is better posted to answer than he, having once been entirely through the mill himself."

Public Sentiment Is Everything

"Still no response, except 'Hurrah for the Dred Scott decision!' These things warrant me in saying that Judge Douglas adheres to the Dred Scott decision under rather extraordinary circumstances— circumstances suggesting the question, 'Why does he adhere to it so pertinaciously? Why does he thus belie his whole past life? Why, with a long record more marked for hostility to judicial decisions than almost any living man, does he cling to this with a devotion that nothing can baffle?' In this age, and this country, public sentiment is every thing. *With* it, nothing can fail; *against* it, nothing can succeed. Whoever moulds public sentiment, goes deeper than he who enacts statutes, or pronounces judicial decisions. He makes possible the inforcement of these, else impossible."

Dangerous Douglas Propaganda

"Judge Douglas is a man of large influence. His bare opinion goes far to fix the opinion of others. Besides this, thousands hang their hopes upon forcing their opinions to agree with his. It is a party necessity with with them to *say* they agree with him; and there is danger they will repeat the saying till they really come to believe it. Others dread, and shrink from his denunciations, his sarcasms, and his ingenious misrepresentations. The susceptable young hear lessons from him, such as their fathers never heared [*sic*] when they were young.

"If, by all these means, he shall succeed in moulding public sentiment to a perfect accordance with his own—in bringing all men to indorse all court decisions, without caring to know whether they are right or wrong— in bringing all tongues to as perfect a silence as his own, as to there being any wrong in slavery—in bringing all to declare, with him, that they care not whether slavery be voted down or voted up—that if any people want slaves they have a right to have them—that negroes are not men— have no part in the Declaration of Independence—that there is no moral question about slavery—that liberty and slavery are perfectly consistent— indeed, necessary accompaniaments—that for a strong man to declare himself the *superior* of a weak one, and thereupon enslave the weak one, is the very *essence* of liberty—the most sacred right of self-government— when, I say, public sentiment shall be brought to all this, in the name of heaven, what barrier will be left against slavery being made lawful every where? Can you find *one* word of his, opposed to it? Can you *not* find many strongly favoring it? If for his life—for his eternal salvation—he was solely striving for that end, could he find any means so well adapted to reach the end?

"If our Presidential election, by a mere plurality, and of doubtful significance, brought one Supreme Court decision, that no power can exclude slavery from a Territory; how much much [*sic*] more shall a public sentiment, in exact accordance with the sentiments of Judge Douglas bring another that no power can exclude it from a State?

"And then, the negro being doomed, and damned, and forgotten, to everlasting bondage, is the white man quite certain that the tyrant demon will not turn upon him too?"

Personal Characteristics of Lincoln in 1858

Lincoln's "base," Herndon (1889) said,

"was plain common sense, direct statement, and the inflexibility of logic. In physical make-up he was cold—at least not magnetic—and made no effort to dazzle people by his bearing. He cared nothing for a following, though he had often before struggled for a political prize, yet in his efforts he never had strained his well-known spirit of fairness or open love of the truth. He analyzed everything, laid every statement bare, and by dint of his broad reasoning powers and manliness of admission inspired his hearers with deep conviction of his earnestness and honesty. Douglas may have electrified the crowds with his eloquence or charmed them with his majestic bearing and dexterity in debate, but as each man, after the meetings were over and the applause had died away, went to his home, his head rang with Lincoln's logic and appeal to manhood.

"Aside from the sad, pained look due to habitual melancholy, his face had no characteristic or fixed expression. . . . He never acted for stage effect. He was cool, considerate, reflective—in time self-possessed and self-reliant. His style was clear, terse, and compact. In argument he was logical, demonstrative, and fair. . . . As he moved along in his speech he became freer and less uneasy in his movements; to that extent he was graceful. He had a perfect naturalness, a strong individuality; and to that extent he was dignified. He despised glitter, shows, set forms, and shams. He spoke with effectiveness and to move the judgment as well as the emotions of men. There was a world of meaning and emphasis in the long, bony finger of his right hand as he dotted the ideas on the minds of his hearers. Sometimes, to express joy or pleasure, he would raise both hands at an angle of about fifty degrees, the palms upward, as if desirous of embracing the spirit of that which he loved. If the sentiment was one of detestation—denunciation of slavery, for example—both arms, thrown upward and fists clenched, swept through the air, and he expressed an execration that was truly sublime. This was one of his most effective gestures, and signified most vividly a fixed determination to drag down the object of his hatred and trample it in the dust. . . . In his defense of the Declaration of Independence—his greatest inspiration—he was [quoting Horace White] 'tremendous in the directness of his utterances; he rose to impassioned eloquence, . . . as his soul was inspired with the thought of human right and Divine justice.' His little gray eyes flashed in a face aglow with the fire of his profound thoughts; and his uneasy movements and diffident manner sunk themselves beneath the wave of righteous indignation that came sweeping over him. Such was Lincoln the orator."

Lincoln's style, as a speaker and writer, was entirely consistent with his attitude as a man. His dress, walk, and speech showed this. He was slow, deliberate, forethoughtful, objective, factual, and clear, logical, ever reasonable and reasoning in manner, ever in search of words for the most simple and economical, easily intelligible and completely expressive thought. His great sources of inspiration were the Virginian Thomas Jefferson and the Kentuckian Henry Clay, both of whom were opposed to the extension of slavery. In his hat he carried, as if ever to remind him, the following quotation from Henry Clay: "I repeat it, Sir, I never can, and never will, and no earthly power will make me vote, directly or indirectly, to spread slavery over territory where it does not exist. Never while reason holds her seat in my brain—never while my heart sends vital fluid through my veins—NEVER."

Personal Characteristics of Douglas in 1858

Stephen A. Douglas was born in 1813, in Vermont, where he lived among the Green Mountain descendants of the Revolution who practiced a form of popular sovereignty as a democratic institution. All through his childhood and youth Douglas saw evidence of the efficiency, in community, and state government, of people meeting freely in their homes, churches and town halls to discuss and vote approval or disapproval on questions of local, state and national political interest.

He well learned cabinet making in his youth from a master craftsman, and studied at Canandaiga Academy. Like many ambitious young men he went West and after several trials settled in Winchester, Ill., where he taught school. He was admitted to the bar in 1834 and elected to the State legislature in 1836. He was always a member of the Democratic party and highly active in its organization and political determination. He was defeated for Congress in 1838; appointed secretary of state of Illinois in 1840-41; and in 1841, at 28 years of age, became a member of the state supreme court. He was elected to Congress for three successive terms, from 1843 to 1847, and to the United States Senate in 1846, 1852, and 1858. Through his great capacity as an orator and leader he dominated the Democratic membership of the Senate for many years and became a prominent candidate for the Democratic nomination for the presidency in 1852, 1856, and 1860.

In 1847 he married Martha Martin, the beautiful daughter of Colonel Robert Martin, a North Carolina planter who owned some 150 slaves. Upon her father's death Mrs. Douglas inherited the slaves with other property—a liability to her husband's political interests even though he never owned slaves.

Senator Douglas moved to Chicago in 1847 and, with strong faith in the future of that city, invested largely in real estate and became identified with commercial institutions promoting the greater development of the city and its railroad connections with the South and West.

His young wife died in 1853 and he grew depressed and embittered, alcoholic, ill-tempered, slovenly, careless of his duties and indifferent to his friends. He traveled for a season in Europe for relief, and recovered his mental integrity.

The issue of slavery in the Northwest territories grew stormy as the people and the railroads pushed westward, and demands for a solution gave Senator Douglas, as chairman of the Committee on Territories, increasing prominence and power in national politics. He held consistently that slavery was a domestic institution to be established and regulated, or prohibited, by the people of each territory separately and not by Congress.

In 1856 Douglas married Adele Cutts, the charming daughter of J. Madison Cutts. She was the belle of Washington and great niece of historically famous Dolly Madison. Although he was much older, she chose him from many admirable suitors—evidence of his masculine virility and unusual attractiveness to women. He was then at the height of his power in the Senate and enjoyed great political influence in the North and South. She became the mother of two sons and a devoted partner and counselor. Through his remarkable conviviality and the means of her wealth and social connections, the hospitality of Douglas in Washington became proverbial and the progressive younger men and women of the South and North followed him eagerly as their leader.

When President Buchanan tried in 1857 to force through the Senate adoption of the notorious, proslavery Lecompton constitution of Kansas, Douglas, fully aware of the consequences for himself, attacked and defeated the scheme. The South then turned bitterly against him and the Democratic press became set for his destruction. His friends were thrown out of office to wreck his patronage and influence, but he fought with such eloquent intelligence, courage, and fortitude that he defeated Buchanan and forced him into decline of political influence.

"Douglas," as Herndon (1889) described his personality, "was polite and affable, but fearless. He had that unique trait, magnetism, fully developed in his nature, and that attracted a host of friends and readily made him a popular idol. He had had extensive experience in debate, and had been trained by contact for years with the great minds and orators of Congress. He was full of political history, well informed on general topics, eloquent almost to the point of brilliancy, self-confident to the point of arrogance, and a dangerous competitor in every respect. What he lacked in ingenuity he made up in strategy, and if in debate he could not tear down the structure of his opponent's argument by a direct and violent attack, he was by no means reluctant to resort to a strained restatement of the latter's position or to the extravagence of ridicule. . . .

"An erroneous impression has grown up in recent years concerning Douglas' ability and standing as a lawyer. One of the latest biographies of Lincoln credits him with many of the artifices of the 'shyster.' This is not only unfair, but decidedly untrue. I always found Douglas at the bar to be a broad, fair, and liberal-minded man. Although not a thorough student of the law his large fund of good commonsense kept him in the front rank. He was equally generous and courteous, and he never stooped to gain a case. I know that Lincoln entertained the same view of him. It was only in politics that Douglas demonstrated any want of inflexibility and rectitude, and then only did Lincoln manifest a lack of faith in his morals."

The Greatest Show on Earth

In accepting the challenge to debate, Douglas has been said by historians to have made a tactical error. However, the popular demand was so strong that it could not be ignored by him. He was a man of great reputation in the state and union, whereas Lincoln was still not highly regarded except in his district and party. Wherever Douglas spoke, crowds of people of all classes gathered. Where Lincoln spoke on his own reputation only a small handful of poor radicals stopped to listen. But Douglas was so sure of his superior oratorical powers, and of his ability to put the quietus on Lincoln's philosophy of equal rights for all people and reestablish himself with the Southern Democrats, that he eagerly accepted the challenge.

So popular was the first debate at Ottawa (8, 21, 1858) as a political show that the anticipation of the next six accumulated into a crescendo. The schedule included Freeport (8, 27), Jonesboro (9, 15), Charleston (9, 18), Galesburg (10, 7), Quincy (10, 13), and Alton (10, 15). Both men made numerous speeches between these dates and afterwards, in which they repeated their arguments.

The people swarmed in excursion trains and excursion boats, carriages and wagons, on horseback and on foot, arrayed in clothing ranging from the stylish finery of ladies and gentlemen to the buckskins and boots of backwoodsmen. Both parties outdid each other in parading with brass bands, symbolical floats, patriotic songs, political clubs in costumes, torch light parades and firing guns and cannon. The delight and fascination of the people of Illinois for the big show, in which they were players as well as audience, extended rapidly all over the nation. Attracted by its dramatic and sporting features for entertainment, people and representatives of the press came from every state to report the arguments and sallies of wit, generally in burning praise or vitriolic condemnation of one or the other contestant's statements, manners, and decorum.

Douglas and his great coterie of political friends traveled in a special train provided by George B. McClellan, general superintendent of the Illinois Central Railway. Lincoln traveled any way he could in passenger trains, freight caboose or carriage.

The natural physical and personal characteristics of the rival speakers contrasted so dramatically that no vaudeville impressario or movie director could have added a touch to improve their entertaining attractions.

The more masculine, more extroverted Douglas generally adopted the aggressive, offensive affirmative, and the less masculine, more introverted Lincoln generally replied in a more defensive but often surprising aggressiveness that seized any advantage and, like a skilled wrestler, suddenly turned and unexpectedly threw his opponent on the defensive.

Lincoln, now 49, was six feet four, lanky and more studious in attitude, average of head, long of face, crowned with wild, nervously fingered, coarse black hair, supported by a long scrawny neck and sloping shoulders, with narrow, flat chest and stooping back, grotesquely long arms and legs, awkward and angular in movement, always humble and careless in attitude, wearing a long, black, unpressed coat and tall, old, green-black stove-pipe hat, and carrying a huge, baggy, cotton umbrella. He was deliberate with drawling speech whether sedate or humorous, with high pitched, raspy, nervous voice, purposely temperate, cool, good natured, patient and kindly, ever surprisingly alert and witty when seeming, weakly, to give precious advantages, naturally provincial and simple in choice of words, but inexorably analytical, factual, and logical in thought, with a confident cleverness for analagy, quotation, and moral story that would excite his audience to laughter or tears as he designed. He argued with fearless masterly skill, always toward impressing the people to remember the priceless value of their constitutional heritage giving equal rights of freedom to all men, and that the interpretations of the meanings of the Constitution by the Supreme Court were questionable and reversible.

Douglas, now 45, energetic, cordial, abundant hair, deep, hoarse voice, proudly self-confident, well dressed and pompous in manner, hot headed and impulsive, intemperate in habits, erudite and polished in speech, dogmatic and opportunistic in thinking, the Senate's most sophisticated, brilliant, and forceful orator, adept in all of the tricks of invective and ineuendo, bold, aggressive, vigorous, merciless, sarcastic and caustic in argument, utterly fearless and fully as earnest as Lincoln, maintained persistently that the laws of Congress and the rights of the people are limited under the Constitution as interpreted by the Supreme Court, and that he cared not whether the people of a state or territory voted slavery up or down.

The Issues

In the first debate at Ottawa the differences in policy on the issues involved in the slavery question were all brought out definitely and argued skilfully by both men. The main issues were the natural relations between the white and black races: what to do with the Negroes if freed, how popular sovereignty applied, the implications of the repeal of the Missouri Compromise and the substitution of the Kansas-Nebraska Act, the implications of the Dred Scott decision, the propriety of challenging the Supreme Court decision, and Lincoln's charge that Douglas was involved in a conspiracy to extend slavery throughout the nation and Douglas' charge that Lincoln and Trumbull had allied to defeat him.

The material of the debates, when measured many years later in relation to other policies of government confronting the people at that time, was, according to Beveridge (1928), neglectful of many problems that were important. However, from what followed in the next three years, Lincoln and Douglas both seem to have talked about the issues of greatest interest to most of the people of the state and nation. Because of the profound influence Douglas had on the development of Lincoln's political attitude and philosophy of human relations, we quote the essential statements in the debates of both men to each other.

Douglas, as a renewal candidate for the United States Senate, and the leading man for the Democratic nomination for the presidency in 1860, had the more complex task of the two. He must continue to hold both Illinois and his national position as the favorite of northern and southern Democrats, and many liberal Republicans. He had learned in Vermont how popular sovereignty had been applied successfully through public discussions in community houses for many generations and he earnestly believed that it could be applied lawfully to slavery as well as other public issues in the territories under the Supreme Court's ruling. Thereby, as will be seen, he gave Lincoln, although defeating him for the Senate, the opportunity to split the Democratic party and eventually gain the Republican leadership and defeat him for the Presidency.

Chapter XXX

THE DEBATES—OTTAWA

The debates, as presented here, are taken from Illinois newspapers, as repeated in *The Collected Works*. Since they were approved by Lincoln and Douglas in 1859 for publication in book form, we give the statements of each speaker in quotations. Captions and comments are inserted. Audience reactions as given by the Press are in parenthesis.

All of the important issues had been discussed in previous speeches and were repeated in all of the debates, but with more spirit and wit in some than others. Hence the seven debates are treated here as one continuous argument and broken up into issues, with selections of the best statements and rebuttals of each speaker in order to give the development of Lincoln's presentation of his political philosophy under the vigorous, ingenious, uncompromising criticisms of his opponent. Douglas, more than any other contemporary, had not only the greatest influence, through antagonistic antithesis, on Lincoln's mind but also, up to the presidency, he aroused the most intense Southern prejudice against Lincoln's political principles.

Ottawa

At Ottawa (8, 21, 1858) Senator Stephen A. Douglas, as the first speaker, began:

> "Ladies and Gentlemen: I appear before you to-day for the purpose of discussing the leading political topics which now agitate the public mind. By arrangement with Mr. Lincoln and myself, we are present here today for the purpose of having a joint discussion as the representatives of the two great political parties of the State and Union, upon the principles in issue between these parties and this vast concourse of people, shows the deep feeling which pervades the public mind in regard to the questions dividing us."

Douglas Charges Lincoln with Political Sectionalism and Plot

Douglas sketched the history of the two parties in a loose, breezy way that praised the Democrats and old Whigs and excoriated the young Republican party.

> "Prior to 1857, this country was divided into two great political parties, known as the Whig and Democratic parties. Both were national and patriotic, advocating principles that were universal in their application. An old line Whig could proclaim his principles in Louisiana and Massachusetts alike. Whig principles had no boundary sectional line, they were not limited by the Ohio river, nor by the

Potomac, nor by the line of the free and slave States, but applied and were proclaimed wherever the Constitution ruled or the American flag waved over the American soil. [Hear him, and three cheers.] So it was, and so it is with the great Democratic party, which, from the days of Jefferson until this period, has proved itself to be the historic party of this nation. While the Whig and Democratic parties differed in regard to a bank, the tariff, distribution, the specie circular and the sub-treasury, they agreed on the great slavery question which now agitates the Union. I say that the Whig party and the Democratic party agreed on this slavery question while they differed on those matters of expediency to which I have referred. The Whig party and the Democratic party jointly adopted the Compromise measures of 1850 as the basis of a proper and just solution of this slavery question in all its forms. Clay was the great leader, with Webster on his right and Cass on his left, and sustained by the patriots in the Whig and Democratic ranks, who had devised and enacted the Compromise measures of 1850.

"In 1851, the Whig party and the Democratic party united in Illinois in adopting resolutions endorsing and approving the principles of the compromise measures of 1850, as the proper adjustment of that question. In 1852, when the Whig party assembled in Convention at Baltimore for the purpose of nominating a candidate for the Presidency, the first thing it did was to declare the compromise measures of 1850, in substance and in principle, a suitable adjustment of that question. [Here the speaker was interrupted by loud and long continued applause.] My friends, silence will be more acceptable to me in the discussion of these questions than applause. I desire to address myself to your judgment, your understanding, and your consciences, and not to your passions or your enthusiasm. When the Democratic convention assembled in Baltimore in the same year, for the purpose of nominating a Democratic candidate for the Presidency, it also adopted the compromise measures of 1850 as the basis of Democratic action. Thus you see that up to 1853-54, the Whig party and the Democratic party both stood on the same platform with regard to the slavery question. That platform was the right of the people of each State and each Territory to decide their local and domestic institutions for themselves, subject only to the federal constitution.

"During the session of Congress of 1853-'54, I introduced into the Senate of the United States a bill to organize the Territories of Kansas and Nebraska on that principle which had been adopted in the compromise measures of 1850, approved by the Whig party and the Democratic party in Illinois in 1851, and endorsed by the Whig party and the Democratic party in national convention in 1852. In order that there might be no misunderstanding in relation to the principle involved in the Kansas and Nebraska bill, I put forth the true intent and meaning of the act in these words: 'It is the true intent and meaning of this act not to legislate slavery into any State or Territory, or to exclude it therefrom, but to leave the people thereof perfectly free to form and regulate their domestic institutions in their own way, subject only to the federal constitution.' Thus, you see, that up to 1854, when the Kansas and Nebraska bill was brought into

Congress for the purpose of carrying out the principles which both parties
had up to that time endorsed and approved, there had been no division
in this country in regard to that principle except the opposition of the
abolitionists. In the House of Representatives of the Illinois Legislature,
upon a resolution asserting that principle, every Whig and every Democrat
in the House voted in the affirmative, and only four men voted against it,
and those four were old line Abolitionists. [Cheers.]

"In 1854, Mr. Abraham Lincoln and Mr. Trumbull entered into an
arrangement, one with the other, and each with his respective friends, to
dissolve the old Whig party on the one hand, and to dissolve the old Democratic party on the other, and to connect the members of both into an
Abolition party under the name and disguise of a Republican party. [Laugh-
ter and cheers, hurrah for Douglas.] The terms of that arrangement between
Mr. Lincoln and Mr. Trumbull have been published to the world by Mr.
Lincoln's special friend, James H. Matheny, Esq., and they were that Lincoln
should have Shield's place in the U.S. Senate, which was then about to become
vacant, and that Trumbull should have my seat when my term expired.
[Great laughter.] Lincoln went to work to abolitionize the Old Whig party
all over the State, pretending that he was then as good a Whig as ever;
[laughter] and Trumbull went to work in his part of the State preaching
Abolitionism in its milder and lighter form, and trying to abolitionize the
Democratic party, and bring old Democrats handcuffed and bound hand
and foot into the Abolition camp. ["Good," "Hurrah for Douglas," and
cheers.] In pursuance of the arrangement, the parties met at Springfield in
October, 1854, and proclaimed their new platform. Lincoln was to bring
into the Abolition camp the old line Whigs and transfer them over to . . .
their new faith. They laid down on that occasion a platform for their new
Republican party, which was to be thus constructed. I have the resolutions
of their State convention then held, which was the first mass State Convention
ever held in Illinois by the Black Republican party, and I now . . . will read
a part of them. Here is the most important and material resolution of this
Abolition platform.

" '1. *Resolved,* That we believe this truth to be self-evident, that when
parties become subversive of the ends for which they are established or incapable of restoring the government to the true principles of the constitution,
it is the right and duty of the people to dissolve the political bands by which
they may have been connected therewith, and to organize new parties upon
such principles and with such views as the circumstances and exigencies of
the nation may demand.
" '2. *Resolved,* That the times imperatively demand the reorganization
of parties, and repudiating all previous party attachments, names and predi-
lections, we unite ourselves together in defence of the liberty and constitution
of the country, and will hereafter co-operate as the Republican party, pledged
to the accomplishment of the following purposes: to bring the administration
of the government back to the control of first principles; to restore Nebraska
and Kansas to the position of free territories; that, as the constitution of the
United States, vests in the States, and not in Congress, the power to legislate
for the extradition of fugitives from labor, *to repeal and entirely abrogate
the fugitive slave law; to restrict slavery to those States in which it exists;
to prohibit the admission of any more slaves in the District of Columbia;
to exclude slavery from all the territories over which the general govern-*

ment has exclusive jurisdiction; and to resist the acquirement of any more territories unless the practice of slavery therein forever shall have been prohibited. *

" '3. *Resolved,* That in furtherance of these principles we will use such constitutional and lawful means as shall seem best adapted to their accomplishment, and that we will support no man for office, under the general or State government, who is not positively and fully committed to the support of these principles, and whose personal character and conduct is not a guaranty that he is reliable, and who shall not have abjured old party allegiance and ties.

[The resolutions, as they were read, were cheered throughout.]

Douglas Catechises Lincoln

"Now, gentlemen, your Black Republicans have cheered every one of those propositions, ["good and cheers,"] and yet I venture to say that you cannot get Mr. Lincoln to come out and say that he is now in favor of each one of them. [Laughter and applause. Hit him again."] That these propositions, one and all, constitute the platform of the Black Republican party of this day, I have no doubt, ["good"] and when you were not aware of what purpose I was reading them, your Black Republicans cheered them as good Black Republican doctrines. ["That's it," etc.] My object in reading these resolutions, was to put the question to Abraham Lincoln this day, whether he now stands and will stand by each article in that creed and carry it out. ["Good." "Hit him again."] I desire to know whether Mr. Lincoln to-day stands as he did in 1854, in favor of the unconditional repeal of the fugitive slave law. I desire him to answer whether he stands pledged to-day, as he did in 1854, against the admission of any more slave States into the Union, even if the people want them. I want to know whether he stands pledged against the admission of a new State into the Union with such a constitution as the people of that State may see fit to make. ["That's it;" "put it at him."] I want to know whether he stands to-day pledged to the abolition of slavery in the District of Columbia. I desire him to answer whether he stands pledged to the prohibition of the slave trade between the different States. ["He does."] I desire to know whether he stands pledged to prohibit slavery in all the territories of the United States, North as well as South of the Missouri Compromise line, ["Kansas too."] I desire him to answer whether he is opposed to the acquisition of any more territory unless slavery is first prohibited therein. I want his answer to these questions. Your affirmative cheers in favor of this Abolition platform is not satisfactory. I ask Abraham Lincoln to answer these questions, in order that when I trot him down to lower Egypt [southern Illinois] I may put the same questions to him. [Enthusiastic applause.] My principles are the same everywhere. [Cheers, and "hark."] I can proclaim them alike in the North, the South, the East, and the West. My principles will apply wherever the Constitution prevails and the American flag waves. ["Good," and applause.] I desire to know whether Mr. Lincoln's principles will bear transplanting from Ottawa to Jonesboro? I put these questions to him to-day distinctly, and ask an

*The resolutions which Lincoln had refused to adopt are given here in italics. On August 5th he had written to H.E. Dummer, "I do not understand the Republican party to be committed to the proposition 'No more slave States.'

answer. I have a right to an answer ["that's so," "he can't dodge you," etc.], for I quote from the platform of the Republican party, made by himself and others at the time that party was formed, and the bargain made by Lincoln to dissolve and kill the old Whig party, . . ."

Lincoln Denies Plot—Demands Proof

We give here Lincoln's Ottawa reply to these points of attack on him by Douglas, before presenting other parts of their speeches. His record of public statements in favor of a fugitive slave law and against radical abolitionism had been utterly disregarded by Douglas in order to force him on the defensive. We will see in the following Freeport speech how he turned Douglas' quiz tricks to a fateful advantage.

"MY FELLOW CITIZENS: When a man hears himself somewhat misrepresented, it provokes him—at least, I find it so with myself; but when the misrepresentation becomes very gross and palpable, it is more apt to amuse him. [Laughter.] The first thing I see fit to notice, is the fact that Judge Douglas alleges, after running through the history of the old Democratic and the old Whig parties, that Judge Trumbull and myself made an arrangement in 1854, by which I was to have the place of Gen. Shields in the United States Senate, and Judge Trumbull was to have the place of Judge Douglas. Now all I have to say upon that subject is, that I think no man—not even Judge Douglas—can prove it, *because it is not true.* [Cheers.] I have no doubt he is *'conscientious'* in saying it. [Laughter.] As to those resolutions that he took such a length of time to read, as being the platform of the Republican party in 1854, I say I never had anything to do with them, and I think Trumbull never had. (Renewed laughter.) Judge Douglas cannot show that either of us ever had anything to do with them. I believe *this* is true about those resolutions: There was a call for a Convention to form a Republican party at Springfield, and I think that my friend Mr. Lovejoy, who is here upon this stand, had a hand in it. I think this is true, and I think if he will remember accurately, he will be able to recollect that he tried to get me into it, and I would not go in. [Cheers and laughter.] I believe it is also true, that I went away from Springfield when the Convention was in session, to attend court in Tazewell County.* It is true they did place my name, though without authority, upon the Committee, and afterwards wrote me to attend the meeting of the Committee, but I refused to do so, and I never had anything to do with that organization. This is the plain truth about all that matter of the resolutions.

"Now, about this story that Judge Douglas tells of Trumbull bargaining to sell out the old Democratic party, and Lincoln agreeing to sell out the old Whig party, I have the means of *knowing* about that; [laughter] Judge Douglas cannot have; and I know there is no substance to it whatever. [Applause.] Yet I have no doubt he is *'conscientious'* about it. [Laughter.] I know that after Mr. Lovejoy got into the Legislature that winter, he complained of me that I had told all the old Whigs in his district that the old Whig party was good enough for them, and some of them voted against him because I told them so. Now I have no means of totally disproving

*This statement was later verified by Herndon (1889).

such charges as this which the Judge makes. A man cannot prove a negative charge, he must offer some proof to show the truth of what he says. I certainly cannot introduce testimony to show the negative about things, but I have a right to claim that if a man says he *knows* a thing, then he must show *how* he knows it. I always have a right to claim this, and it is not satisfactory to me that he may be 'conscientious' on the subject. [Cheers and Laughter.]

"Now gentlemen, I hate to waste my time on such things, but in regard to that general abolition tilt that Judge Douglas makes, when he says that I was engaged at that time in selling out and abolitionizing the old Whig party—I hope you will permit me to read a part of a printed speech that I made then at Peoria, [presented entirely in a previous chapter] which will show altogether a different view of the position I took in that contest of 1854."

Lincoln then read that part of the speech in which he had protested against the repeal of the Missouri Compromise and declared it wrong for letting slavery into Kansas and Nebraska.

> " 'It is wrong in its prospective principle, allowing it to spread to every other part of the wide world, where man can be found inclined to take it. This *declared* indifference, but as I must think, covert *real* zeal for the spread of slavery, I cannot but hate. I hate it because of the monstrous injustice of slavery. I hate it because it deprives our republican example of its just influence on the rest of the world . . .
>
> . . . " 'I have no prejudice against the Southern people. They are just what we would be in their situation. . . . [When they] tell us they are no more responsible for the origin of slavery then we; I acknowledge the fact. . . . If all earthy power were given me, I should not know what to do, as to the existing institution. My first impulse would be to free all the slaves, and send them to Liberia,—to their own native land. But a moment's reflection would convince me, that . . . its . . . sudden execution is impossible. . . . What then? Free them all, and keep them among us as underlings? Is it quite certain that this betters their condition? I think I would not hold one in slavery, at any rate; . . . What next? Free them and make them politically and socially, our equals? My own feelings will not admit of this; and if mine would, we well know that those of the great mass of white people will not. . . . A universal feeling, whether well or ill-founded, can not be safely disregarded. We can not, then, make them equals. It does seem to be that systems of gradual emancipation might be adopted. . . .
>
> " 'When they [Southern people] remind us of their constitutional rights, I acknowledge them, not grudgingly, but fully, and fairly; and I would give them any legislation for the reclaiming of their fugitives,' " . . .
>
> " 'But all this; . . . furnishes no more excuse for permitting slavery to go into our free territory, than it would for reviving the African slave trade by law.' "

"I have reason to know that Judge Douglas *knows* that I have said this. I think he has the answer here to one of the questions he put to me. I do not mean to allow him to catechise me unless he pays back for it in kind. I will not answer questions one after another unless he reciprocates, but as he made this inquiry and I have answered it before, he has got it without my getting anything in return. He has got my answer on the Fugitive Slave Law.

"Now gentlemen, I don't want to read at any greater length, but this is the true complexion of all I have ever said in regard to the institution of slavery and the black race. This is the whole of it, and anything that argues me into his idea of perfect social and political equality with the negro, is but a specious and fantastic arrangement of words, by which a man can prove a horse chestnut to be a chestnut horse." [Laughter.]

Douglas Satirizes Lincoln

"In the remarks I have made on this platform, and the position of Mr. Lincoln upon it, I meant nothing personally disrespectful or unkind to that gentleman. I have known him for nearly twenty-five years. There were many points of sympathy between us when we first got acquainted. We were both comparatively boys, and both struggling with poverty in a strange land. I was a school-teacher in the town of Winchester, and he a flourishing grocery-keeper in the town of Salem. [Applause and laughter.] He was more successful in his occupation than I was in mine, and hence more fortunate in this world's goods. Lincoln is one of those peculiar men who perform with admirable skill everything which they undertake. I made as good a school-teacher as I could and when a cabinet maker I made a good bedstead and tables, although my old boss said I succeeded better with bureaus and secretaries than anything else;* [cheers,] but I believe that Lincoln was always more successful in business than I, for his business enabled him to get into the Legislature. I met him there, however, and had a sympathy with him, because of the up hill struggle we both had in life. He was then just as good at telling an anecdote as now. ["No doubt."] He could beat any of the boys wrestling, or running a foot race, in pitching quoits or tossing a copper, could ruin more liquor† than all the boys of the town together, [uproarious laughter,] and the dignity and impartiality with which he presided at a horse race or fist fight, excited the admiration and won the praise of everybody that was present and participated. [Renewed laughter.] I sympathized with him because he was struggling with difficulties and so was I. Mr. Lincoln served with me in the Legislature in 1836, when we both retired, and he subsided, or became submerged, and he was lost sight of as a public man for some years. In 1846, when Wilmot introduced his celebrated proviso, and the Abolition tornado swept over the country, Lincoln again turned up as a member of Congress from the Sangamon district. I was then in the Senate of the United States, and was glad to welcome my old friend and companion. Whilst in Congress, he distinguished himself by his opposition to the Mexican War, taking the side of the common enemy against his own country; ["that's true,"] and when he returned home he found that the indignation of the people followed him everywhere, and he was again sub-

---

*Lincoln and Douglas both made house furniture but the latter was far better trained and more skilful.

†The arrogant satire of Douglas' personal comparisons becomes evident when we recall that Lincoln was a failure as a storekeeper and had to sell out heavily burdened with debt. He was a total abstainer except for taking a glass of beer occasionally, whereas Douglas was an habitual user of whiskey. Lincoln by 1858 had paid off all debts but was not wealthy, whereas Douglas had married— the first time a woman of wealthy Southern slaveholding family and the second time another woman of wealth — and was at this time a prosperous owner of Chicago real estate. The reader will notice how Douglas ruthlessly falsified Lincoln's record under the guise of amusing exaggeration.

merged or obliged to retire into private life, forgotten by his former friends. ["And will be again."] He came up again in 1854, just in time to make this Abolition or Black Republican platform, in company with Giddings, Lovejoy, Chase, and Fred Douglass [a free, able negro lectuer] for the Republican party to stand upon. (Laughter, "Hit him again," etc.) Trumbull, too, was one of our own contemporaries. . . . . He became noted as the author of the scheme to repudiate a large portion of the State debt of Illinois, which, if successful, would have brought infamy and disgrace upon the fair escutcheon of our glorious State. The odium of that measure consigned him to oblivion for a time. I helped to do it. I walked into a public meeting in the hall of the House of Representatives and replied to his repudiating speeches, and resolutions were carried over his head denouncing repudiation, and asserting the moral and legal obligation of Illinois to pay every dollar of the debt she owed and every bond that bore her seal. ["Good," and cheers.] Trumbull's malignity has followed me since I thus defeated his infamous scheme."

Lincoln Discredits Douglas' "Conscience"

"The Judge is woefully at fault about his early friend Lincoln being a "grocery keeper." [Laughter.] I don't know as it would be a great sin, if I had been, but he is mistaken. Lincoln never kept a grocery anywhere in the world.* [Laughter.] It is ture that Lincoln did work the latter part of one winter in a small still house, up at the head of a hollow. [Roars of laughter.]

"And so I think my friend, the Judge is equally at fault when he charges me at the time when I was in Congress of having opposed our soldiers who were fighting in the Mexican War. The Judge did not make his charge very distinctly but I can tell you what he can prove by referring to the record. You remember I was an old Whig, and whenever the Democratic party tried to get me to vote that the war had been righteously begun by the President, I would not do it. But whenever they asked for any money, or land warrents, or anything to pay the soldiers there, during all that time, I gave the same votes that Judge Douglas did. [Loud applause.] You can think as you please as to whether that was consistent. Such is the truth; and the Judge has the right to make all he can out of it. But when he, by a general charge, conveys the idea that I withheld supplies from the soldiers who were fighting in the Mexican War, or did anything else to hinder the soldiers, he is, to say the least, grossly and altogether mistaken, as a consultation of the records will prove to him."

*Lincoln's pointed statement that he had "never kept a grocery anywhere in the world" in denial of Douglas' assertion has aroused no little dispute of its truth and meaning among biographers and readers since. In his New Salem years it was customary for a general store to sell also whiskey and beer in bulk to be taken from the premises before consumption. The term "grocery keeper" was used then much like that of "saloon keeper" today. It meant the keeper of a store had a special license to sell "spiritous" liquors in quantities less than a quart and beer less than two gallons for consumption on the premises. Since the license was issued to Berry in the names of the partnership of Berry and Lincoln, and Lincoln's name was not in his handwriting, and Lincoln sold out to Berry a few months later, it seems that he had disapproved of Berry's actions and that he meant as exactly true that he never had "kept a grocery anywhere in the world."

Douglas Condemns Lincoln's "House Divided" Doctrine

Douglas repeated the following attack in every speech regardless of Lincoln's explanations of his meaning.

"Having formed this new party for the benefit of deserters from Whiggery, and deserters from Democracy, and having laid down the Abolition platform which I have read, Lincoln now takes his stand and proclaims his Abolition doctrines. Let me read a part of them. In his speech at Springfield to the convention which nominated him for the Senate, he said:

" 'In my opinion it will not cease until a crisis shall have been reached and passed 'A house divided against itself cannot stand.' I believe this Government *cannot endure permanently half Slave and half Free.* I do not expect the house to fall—*but I do expect it will cease to be divided.* It will become all one thing, or all the other. Either the opponents of Slavery *will arrest the further spread of it* and place it where the public mind shall rest in the belief *that it is in the course of ultimate extinction;* or its advocates *will push it forward till it shall become alike lawful in all the States*—old as well as new, North as well as South.'

("Good," "good," and cheers.)

"I am delighted to hear you Black Republicans say "good." (Laughter and cheers.) I have no doubt that doctrine expresses your sentiments ["hit them again," "that's it,"] and I will prove to you now, if you will listen to me, that it is revolutionary and destructive of the existence of this Government. [Hurrah for Douglas," "good," and cheers.] Mr. Lincoln, in the extract from which I have read, says that this Government cannot endure permanently in the same condition in which it was made by its framers—divided into free and slave States. He says that it has existed for about seventy years divided, and yet he tells you that it cannot endure permanently on the same principles and in the same relative condition in which our fathers made it. ["Neither can it."] Why can it not exist divided into free and slave States? Washington, Jefferson, Franklin, Madison, Hamilton, Jay, and the great men of that day, made this Government divided into free States and slave States, and left each State perfectly free to do as it pleased on the subject of slavery. ["Right, right."] Why can it not exist on the same principles on which our fathers made it?" ["It can."] They knew when they framed the Constitution that in a country as wide and broad as this, with such a variety of climate, production and interest, the people necessarily required different laws and institutions in different localities. They knew that the laws and regulations which would suit the granite hills of New Hampshire would be unsuited to the rice plantations of South Carolina, ["right, right"] and they, therefore, provided that each State should retain its own Legislature, and its own sovereignty with the full and complete power to do as it pleased within its own limits, in all that was local and not national. [Applause.] One of the reserved rights of the States, was the right to regulate the relations between Master and Servant, on the slavery question. At the time the Constitution was formed, there were thirteen States in the Union, twelve of which were slaveholding States and one a free State. Suppose this doctrine of uniformity preached by Mr. Lincoln, that the States should all be free or all be slave had prevailed and what would have been the result? Of course, the twelve slaveholding States would have overruled the one free State, and slavery would have been fastened by a Constitutional provision on every inch of the American Republic, instead of bing left as our fathers wisely left it, to each State to decide for itself. ["Good, good," and three cheers for Douglas.] Here I assert that uniformity in the local laws and institutions of the different states in neither possible or desirable. If uniformity had been adopted when the government was established, it must inevitably have been the uniformity of slavery everywhere, or else the uniformity of negro citizenship and negro equality everywhere."

Lincoln Shows Historically and Morally
Why a House Divided Cannot Stand

"He [Douglas] has read from my speech in Springfield, in which I say that 'a house divided against itself cannot stand.' Does the Judge say it *can* stand? [Laughter.] I don't know whether he does or not. The Judge does not seem to be attending to me just now, but I would like to know if it is his opinion that a house divided against itself *can stand.* If he does, then there is a question of veracity, not between him and me, but between the Judge and an authority of somewhat higher character* [Laughter and applause.]

"Now, my friends, I ask your attention to this matter for the purpose of saying something seriously. I know that the Judge may readily agree with me that the maxim which was put forth by the Saviour is true, but he may allege that I misapply it; and the Judge has a right to urge that, in my application, I do misapply it, and then I have a right to show that I do *not* misapply it. When he undertakes to say that because I think this nation, so far as the question of Slavery is concerned, will all become one thing or all the other, I am in favor of bringing about a dead uniformity in the various States, in all their institutions, he argues erroneously. The great variety of the local institutions in the States, springing from differences in the soil, differences in the face of the country, and in the climate, are bonds of Union. They do not make 'a house divided against itself,' but they make a house united. If they produce in one section of the country what is called for by the wants of another section, and this other section can supply the wants of the first, they are not matters of discord but bonds of union, true bonds of union. But can this question of slavery be considered as among *these* varieties in the institutions of the country? I leave it to you to say whether, in the history of our government, this institution of slavery has not always failed to be a bond of union, and, on the contrary, been an apple of discord and an element of division in the house. [Cries of "Yes, yes," and applause.] I ask you to consider whether, so long as the moral constitution of men's minds shall continue to be the same, after this generation and assemblage shall sink into the grave, and another race shall arise, with the same moral and intellectual development we have— whether, if that institution is standing in the same irritating position in which it now is, it will not continue an element of division? [Cries of "Yes, Yes."] If so, then I have a right to say that in regard to this question, the Union is a house divided against itself, and when the Judge reminds me that I have often said to

*Lincoln was a master of considerate understatement, thereby holding the mind of his audience interested in completing the thought, whereas Douglas was a master of opportunistic overstatement to force uncritical acceptance of his ideas.

him that the institution of slavery has existed for eighty years in some States, and yet it does not exist in some others, I agree to the fact, and I account for it by looking at the position in which our fathers originally placed it— restricting it from the new Territories where it had not gone, and legislating to cut off its source by the abrogation of the slave trade, thus putting the seal of legislation *against its spread*. The public mind *did* rest in the belief that it was in the course of ultimate extinction. [Cries of "Yes, yes."] But lately, I think— and in this I charge nothing on the Judge's motives—lately, I think, that he, and those acting with him, have placed that institution on a new basis, which looks to the *perpetuity and nationalization of slavery*. [Loud cheers.] And while it is placed upon this new basis, I say, and I have said, that I believe we shall not have peace upon the question until the opponents of slavery arrest the further spread of it, and place it where the public mind shall rest in the belief that it is in the course of ultimate extinction; or, on the other hand, that its advocates will push it forward until it shall become alike in all the States, old as well as new, North as well as South. Now, I believe if we could arrest the spread, and place it where Washington, and Jefferson, and Madison placed it, it *would be* in the course of ultimate extinction, and the public mind *would*, as for eighty years past, believe that it was in the course of ultimate extinction. The crisis would be past and the institution might be let alone for a hundred years, if it should live so long, in the States where it exists, yet it would be going out of existence in the way best for both the black and the white races." [Great cheering.]

Douglas Holds Negroes Inferior— Without Constitutional Rights

"We are told by Lincoln that he is utterly opposed to the Dred Scot decision, and will not submit to it, for the reason that he says it deprives the negro of the rights and privileges of citizenship. [Laughter and applause.] That is the first and main reason which he assigns for his warfare on the Supreme Court of the United States and its decision.* I ask you, are you in favor of conferring upon the negro the rights and privileges of citizenship? ["No, no."] Do you desire to strike out of our State Constitution that clause which keeps slaves and free negroes out of the State, and allow the free negroes to flow in, ["never,"] and cover your prairies with black settlements? Do you desire to turn this beautiful State into a free negro colony, ["no, no,"] in order that when Missouri abolishes slavery she can send one hundred thousand emancipated slaves into Illinois, to become citizens and voters, on an equality with yourselves? ["Never," "no."] If you desire negro citizenship, if you desire to allow them to come into the State and settle with the white man, if you desire them to vote on an equality with yourselves, and to make them eligible to office, to serve on juries, and to adjudge your rights, then support Mr. Lincoln and the Black Republican party, who are in favor of the citizenship of the negro. ["Never, never."] For one, I am opposed to negro citizenship in any and every form. [Cheers.] I believe this government was made on the white basis. ["Good."] I believe it was made by white men, for the benefit of white men and their posterity for ever, and I am in favor of confining citizenship to white men, men of European birth and descent, instead of conferring it up-

*This was a typical Douglas bludgeoning generalization designed, although illogical and untrue, to excite thoughtless prejudice against his opponent.

on negroes, Indians and other inferior races. ["Good for you." "Douglas forever."]

"Mr. Lincoln, following the example and lead of all the little Abolition orators, who go around and lecture in the basements of schools and churches, reads from the Declaration of Independence, that all men were created equal, and then asks how can you deprive a negro of that equality which God and the Declaration of Independence awards to him. He and they maintain that negro equality is guarantied by the laws of God, and that it is asserted in the Declaration of Independence. If they think so, of course they have a right to say so, and so vote. I do not question Mr. Lincoln's conscientious belief that the negro was made his equal, and hence is his brother, [laughter] but for my own part, I do not regard the negro as my equal, and positively deny that he is my brother or any kin to me whatever. ["Never," "Hit him again," and cheers.] Lincoln has evidently learned by heart Parson Lovejoy's catechism. [Laughter and applause.] He can repeat it as well as Farnsworth, and he is worthy of a medal from father Giddings and Fred Douglas for his Abolitionism. [Laughter.] He holds that the negro was born his equal and yours, and that he was endowed with equality by the Almighty, and that no human law can deprive him of these rights which were guarantied to him by the Supreme ruler of the Universe. Now, I do not believe that the Almighty ever intended the negro to be the equal of the white man. ["Never, never."] If he did, he has been a long time demonstrating the fact. ["Cheers."] For thousands of years the negro has been a race upon the earth, and during all that time, in all latitudes and climates, wherever he has wandered or been taken, he has been inferior to the race which he has there met. He belongs to an inferior race, and must always occupy an inferior position. ["Good," "that's so," etc.] I do not hold that because the negro is our inferior that therefore he ought to be a slave. By no means can such a conclusion be drawn from what I have said. On the contrary, I hold that humanity and christianity both require that the negro shall have and enjoy every right, every privilege, and every immunity consistent with the safety of the society in which he lives. ["That's so."] On that point, I presume, there can be no diversity of opinion. You and I are bound to extend to our inferior and dependent being every right, every privilege, every facility and immunity consistent with the public good. The question then arises what rights and privileges are consistent with the public good. This is a question which each State and each Territory must decide for itself— Illinois has decided for herself. We have provided that he shall not be a citizen, but protect him in his civil rights, in his life, his person and his property, only depriving him of all political rights whatsoever, and refusing to put him on an equality with the white man." ["Good."]

Lincoln Holds Negroes Inferior—But with Equal Constitutional Rights

"I have no purpose directly or indirectly to interfere with the institution of slavery in the States where it exists. I believe I have no lawful right to do so, and I have no inclination to do so. I have no purpose to introduce political and social equality between the white and black races. There is a physical difference between the two, which in my judgment will probably forever forbid their living together upon the footing of perfect equality, and inasmuch as it becomes a necessity that there must be a difference, I, as well as Judge Douglas, am in favor of the race to which I belong, having the superior position. I have never said anything to the contrary, but I hold that notwithstanding all this, there is no reason in the world why the negro is not entitled to all the natural rights enumerated in the Declaration of Independence, the right to life, liberty and the pursuit of happiness. [Loud cheers.] I hold that he is as much entitled to these as the white man. I agree with Judge Douglas he is not my equal in many respects— certainly not in color, perhaps not in moral or intellectual endowment. But in the right to eat the bread, without leave of anybody else, which his own hand earns, *he is my equal and the equal of Judge Douglas, and the equal of every living man.*" [Great applause.]

The view held by Lincoln and Douglas and most civilized peoples of that time, that the negro race was inferior to the white, was based on the vast differences in their native cultures. The ability of many negroes and mulattoes to develop, in three generations, intellectual and cultural levels equaling those of their white contemporaries, when given equal opportunities, has been amply demonstrated in Europe and America. The general superiority of white children who have well educated, prosperous, ethically minded parents, over white children of less mentally endowed and economically fortunate parents has been amply demonstrated by modern psychology and anthropology. Hence it is now believed, and probably Lincoln and Douglas would now also believe from such indications, that the capacity of the negro race to develop a high state of civilization in successive generations of reproductive selection, upon being given equal opportunity, is potentially equal to that of any other race.

Douglas on States' Rights and Popular Sovereignty

. . . "Republicans say that he [negro] ought to be made a citizen, and when he becomes a citizen he becomes your equal, with all your rights and privileges. ["He never shall."] They assert the Dred Scott decision to be monstrous because it denies that the negro is or can be a citizen under the Constitution. Now, I hold that Illinois had a right to abolish and prohibit slavery as she did, and I hold that Kentucky has the same right to continue and protect slavery that Illinois had to abolish it. I hold that New York had as much right to abolish slavery as Virginia has to continue it, and that each and every State of this Union is a sovereign power, with the right to do as it pleases upon this question of slavery, and upon all its domestic institutions. Slavery is not the only question which comes up in this controversy. There is a far more important one to you, and that is, what shall be done with the free negro? We have settled the slavery question as far as we are concerned; we have prohibited it in Illinois forever, and in doing so, I think we have done wisely, and there is no man in the State who would be more strenuous in his opposition to the introduction of slavery than I would; [cheers] but when we settled it for ourselves, we exhausted all our power over that subject. We have done our whole duty, and can do no more. We must leave each and every other State to decide for itself the same question. In relation to the policy to be pursued towards the free negroes, we have said that they shall

not vote; whilst Maine, on the other hand, has said that they shall vote.
Maine is a sovereign State, and has the power to regulate the qualifications
of voters within her limits. I would never consent to confer the right of voting
and citizenship upon a negro, but still I am not going to quarrel with Maine
for differing from me in opinion. . . . So with the State of New York. She
allows the negro to vote provided he owns two hundred an fifty dollars'
worth of property, but not otherwise. While I would not make any distinction
whatever between a negro who held property and one who did not; yet if the
sovereign State of New York chooses to make that distinction it is her business and not mine, and I will not quarrel with her for it. She can do as she
pleases on this question if she minds her own business, and we will do the
same thing. Now, my friends, if we will only act conscientiously and rigidly
upon this great principle of popular sovereignty which guarantees to each
State and Territory the right to do as it pleases on all things local and domestic instead of Congress interfering, we will continue at peace one with another.
Why should Illinois be at war with Missouri, or Kentucky with Ohio, or Virginia with New York, merely because their institutions differ? Our fathers intended that our institutions should differ. They knew that the North and the
South having different climates, productions and interests, required different
institutions. This doctrine of Mr. Lincoln's of uniformity among the institutions of the different States is a new doctine, never dreamed of by Washington, Madison, or the framers of this Government. Mr. Lincoln and the
Republican party set themselves up as wiser than these men who made this
government, which has flourished for seventy years under the principle of
popular sovereignty, recognizing the right of each State to do as it pleased.
Under that principle, we have grown from a nation of three or four millions
to a nation of about thirty millions of people; we have crossed the Allegheny
mountains and filled up the whole North West, turning the prairie into a
garden, and building up churches and schools, thus spreading civilization
and christianity where before there was nothing but savege-barbarism.
Under that principle we have become from a feeble nation, the most powerful on the face of the earth, and if we only adhere to that principle, we can
go forward increasing in territory, in power, in strength and in glory until
the Republic of America shall be the North Star that shall guide the friends
of freedom throughout the civilized world. ["Long may you live," and great
applause.] And why can we not adhere to the great principle of self-
government, upon which our institutions were originally based. ["We
can."] I believe that this new doctrine preached by Mr. Lincoln and his party
will dissolve the Union if it succeeds. They are trying to array all the Northern States in one body against the South, to excite a sectional war between
the free States and the slave States, in order that the one or the other may be
driven to the wall."

Lincoln on States' versus Federal Rights and Popular Sovereignty

Douglas' argument on the constitutional rights of the people of a territory, under the Dred Scott decision, to abolish or establish slavery and
determine the legal and political rights of free negroes had, since defeating
President Buchanan's Lecompton scheme, made him the most popular and
influential political leader in the West as well as the East. His argument

PLATE 14. Abraham Lincoln, Debater. Courtesy of the Library of Congress.

PLATE 15. Stephen A. Douglas, Debater. Courtesy of the Lincoln National Life Foundation.

now proved to be his most popular card in the campaign for the Senate, Lincoln tried, at first defensively, to demonstrate its sophistry and injustice.

> "What is Popular Sovereignty? [Cries of "A humbug," "a humbug."] Is it the right of the people to have Slavery or not have it, as they see fit, in the territories? I will state— and I have an able man to watch me— my understanding is that Popular Sovereignty, as now applied to the question of Slavery, does allow the people of a Territory to have Slavery if they want to, but does not allow them *not* to have it if they *do not* want it. [Applause and laughter.] I do not mean that if this vast concourse of people were in a Territory of the United States, any one of them would be obliged to have a slave if he did not want one; but I do say that, as I understand the Dred Scott decision, if any one man wants slaves, all the rest have no way of keeping that one man from holding them.
>
> "When I made my speech at Springfield, of which the Judge complains, and from which he quotes, I really was not thinking of the things which he ascribes to me at all. I had no thought in the world that I was doing anything to bring about a war between the free and slave States. I had no thought in the world that I was doing anything to bring about a political and social equality of the black and white races. It never occurred to me that I was doing anything or favoring anything to reduce to a dead uniformity all the local institutions of the various States. But I must say, in all fairness to him, if he thinks I am doing something which leads to these bad results, it is none the better that I did not mean it. It is just as fatal to the country, if I have any influence in producing it, whether I intend it or not. But can it be true, that placing this institution upon the original basis— the basis upon which our fathers placed it— can have any tendency to set the Northern and the Southern States at war with one another, or that it can have any tendency to make the people of Vermont raise sugar cane, because they raise it in Louisiana, or that it can compel the people of Illinois to cut pine logs on the Grand Prairie, where they will not grow, because they cut pine logs in Maine, where they do grow? [Laughter.] The Judge says this is a new principle started in regard to this question. Does the Judge claim that he is working on the plan of the founders of government? I think he says in some of his speeches— indeed I have one here now— that he saw evidence of a policy to allow slavery to be south of a certain line, while north of it it should be excluded, and he saw an indisposition on the part of the country to stand upon that policy, and therefore he set about studying the subject upon *original principles*, and upon *original principles* he got up the Nebraska bill! I am fighting it upon these 'original principles'— fighting it in the Jeffersonian, Washingtonian, and Madisonian fashion." [Laughter and applause.]

By stressing the practical application of popular sovereignty, Lincoln was, with consummate foresight, forcing Douglas into a self-contradictory position. He maintained that the Supreme Court's decision that slave owners had the right to take their slave property into the territories as a matter of states' rights violated the principle of popular sovereignty in the territories wherever people objected to slavery before they adopted a constitution and became admitted as a state. Since the people were unable to maintain their political rights Congress must, under its constitutional requirement, pass laws regulating them. This had been done under the Ordinance of 1787 and the Missouri Compromise but was repealed by the Nebraska Act of 1854. The basic political issue now became: Does Congress have the constitutional power to prevent the extension of slavery in the territories or do the people of the slave states have the constitutional right to take their slaves there regardless of congressional regulations? Thereby the slavery problem was made, by these two men, by far the most important confronting the nation. It now involved questions of Federal versus States' rights, and the powers conferred upon Congress by the Constitution, and the historic basis of the Supreme Court's decision.

Lincoln Charges Douglas with "Conspiracy"

"Now my friends I wish you to attend for a little while to one or two other things in that Springfield speech. My main object was to show, as far as my humble ability was capable of showing to the people of this country, what I believed was the truth— that there was a *tendency*, if not a conspiracy among those who have engineered this slavery question for the last four or five years, to make slavery perpetual and universal in this nation. Having made that speech principally for that object, after arranging the evidences that I thought tended to prove my proposition, I concluded with this bit of comment:

" 'We cannot absolutely know that these exact adaptations are the result of pre-concert, but when we see a lot of framed timbers, different portions of which we know have been gotten out at different times and places, and by different workmen, Stephen, Franklin, Roger and James, for instance— and when we see these timbers joined together, and see they exactly make the frame of a house or a mill, all the tenons and mortices exactly fitting and all the lengths and proportions of the different pieces exactly adapted to their respective places and not a piece too many or too few—not omitting even the scaffolding— or if a single piece be lacking we see the place in the frame exactly fitted and prepared yet to bring such piece in—in such a case we feel it impossible not to believe that Stephen and Franklin, and Roger and James, all understood one another from the beginning, and all worked upon a common plan or draft before the first blow was struck.' [Great cheers.]

"When my friend, Judge Douglas, came to Chicago, on the 9th of July, this speech having been delivered on the 16th of June, he made an harangue there, in which he took hold of this speech of mine, showing that he had carefully read it; and while he paid no attention to *this* matter at all, but complimented me as being a 'kind, amiable, and intelligent gentleman,' notwithstanding I had said this; he goes on and eliminates, or draws out, from my speech this tendency of mine to set the States at war with one another, to make all the institutions uniform, and set the niggers and white people to marrying together. [Laughter.] Then, as the Judge had complimented me with these pleasant titles, (I must confess to my weakness,) I was a little 'taken,' [laughter] for it came from a great man. I was not very much accustomed to flattery, and it came the sweeter to me. I was rather like the Hoosier, with the gingerbread, when he said he reckoned he loved it better than any other man, and got less of it. [Roars of laughter.] As the Judge had so flattered me, I could not make up my mind that he meant to deal unfairly with me; so I went to work to show him that he misunderstood the whole scope of my speech, and that I really never intended to set the people at war with one another. As an illustration, the next time I met him, which was at Springfield, I used this expression, that I claimed no right under the Constitution, nor had I any inclination, to enter into the Slave States and interfere with the institutions of Slavery. He says upon that: Lincoln will not enter into the Slave States, but will go to the banks of the Ohio, on this side, and shoot over! [Laughter.] He runs on, step by step, in the horse-chestnut style of argument, until in the Springfield speech, he says, 'Unless he shall be successful in firing his batteries until he shall have extinguished slavery in all the States, the Union shall be dissolved.' Now I don't think that was exactly the way to treat a kind, amiable, intelligent gentleman. [Roars of laughter.] I know if I had asked the Judge to show when or where it was I had said that, if I didn't succeed in firing into the Slave States until slavery should be extinguished, the Union should be dissolved, he could not have shown it. I understand what he would do. He would say, 'I don't mean to quote from you, but this was the *result* of what you say.' But I have the right to ask, and I do ask now, did you not put it in such a form that an ordinary reader or listener would take it as an expression *from me?** [Laughter.]

"In a speech at Springfield, on the night of the 17th, I thought I might as well attend to my own business a little, and I recalled his attention as well as I could to this charge of conspiracy to nationalize Slavery. I called his attention to the fact that he had acknowledged, in my hearing twice, that he had carefully read the speech, and, in the language of the lawyers, as he had twice read the speech, and still had put in no plea or answer, I took a default on him. I insisted that I had a right then to renew that charge of conspiracy. Ten days afterwards, I met the Judge at Clinton—that is to say, I was on the ground, but not in the discussion—and heard him make a speech. Then he comes in with his plea to this charge, for the first time, and his plea when put in, as well as I can recollect, amounted to this: that he never had any talk with Judge Taney or the President of the United States with regard to the Dred Scott decision before it was made. I (Lincoln) ought to know that the man who makes a charge without knowing it to be true, falsifies as much as he who knowingly tells a falsehood;† and lastly, that he would pronounce the whole thing a falsehood; but he would make no personal application of the charge of falsehood, not because of any regard for the 'kind, amiable, intelligent gentleman,' but because of his own personal self-respect! (Roars of laughter.) I have understood since then, (but [turning to Judge Douglas] will not hold the Judge to it if he is not willing) that he has broken through the 'self-respect' and has got to saying the thing *out*. The Judge nods to me that it is so. [Laughter.] It is fortunate for me that I can keep as good-humored as I do, when the Judge acknowledges that he has been trying to make a question of veracity with me. I know the Judge is a great man, while

---

*Lincoln seems, on Douglas' charge against him of design for abolishing slavery, to have justified in his own mind the value of pushing the countercharge on Douglas of conspiracy to nationalize slavery.

†In a previous chapter we quoted Lincoln, as holding this moral principle to be basic in the practice of law.

I am only a small man, but *I feel that I have got him*. [Tremendous cheering.] I demur to that plea. I waive all objections that it was not filed till after default was taken, and demur to it upon the merits. What if Judge Douglas never did talk with Chief Justice Taney and the President, before the Dred Scott decision was made, does it follow that he could not have had as perfect an understanding without talking, as with it? I am not disposed to stand upon my legal advantage. I am disposed to take his denial as being an answer in chancery, that he neither had any knowledge, information or belief in the existence of such a conspiracy. I am disposed to take his answer as being as broad as though he had put it in these words. And now, I ask, even if he has done so, have not I a right to *prove it on him,* and to offer the evidence of more than two witnesses, by whom to prove it; and if the evidence proves the existence of the conspiracy, does his broad answer denying all knowledge, information, or belief, disturb the fact? It can only show that he was *used* by conspirators, and was not a *leader* of them." [Vociferous cheering.]

Lincoln Justifies Morality of His Charge

"Now in regard to his reminding me of the moral rule that persons who tell what they do not know to be true, falsify as much as those who knowingly tell falsehoods. I remember the rule, and it must be borne in mind that in what I have read to you, I do not say that I *know* such a conspiracy to exist. To that, I reply I *believe it*. If the Judge says that I do *not* believe it, then *he* says what *he* does not know, and falls within his own rule, that he who asserts a thing which he does not know to be true, falsifies as much as he who knowingly tells a falsehood. I want to call your attention to a little discussion on that branch of the case, and the evidence which brought my mind to the conclusion which I expressed as my *belief*. If, in arraying that evidence, I had stated anything which was false or erroneous, it needed but that Judge Douglas should point it out, and I would have taken it back with all the kindness in the world. I do not deal in that way. If I have brought forward anything not a fact, if he will point it out, it will not even ruffle me to take it back. But if he will not point out anything erroneous in the evidence, is it not rather for him to show, by a comparison of the evidence that I have *reasoned* falsely, than to call the 'kind, amiable, intelligent gentleman' a liar? [Cheers and laughter.] If I have reasoned to a false conclusion, it is the vocation of an able debater to show by argument that I have wandered to an erroneous conclusion. I want to ask your attention to a portion of the Nebraska Bill, which Judge Douglas has quoted: 'It being the true intent and meaning of this act, not to legislate slavery into any Territory or State, nor to exclude it therefrom, but to leave the people thereof perfectly free to form and regulate their domestic institutions in their own way, subject only to the Constitution of the United States.' Thereupon Judge Douglas and others began to argue in favor of 'Popular Sovereignty' the right of the people to have slaves if they wanted them, and to exclude slavery if they did not want them. 'But,' said, in substance, a Senator from Ohio, (Mr. Chase, I believe,) 'we more than suspect that you do not mean to allow the people to exclude slavery if they wish to, and if you do mean it, accept an amendment which I propose expressly authorizing the people to exclude slavery.' I believe I have the amendment here before me, which was offered, and under which the people of the

Territory, through their proper representatives, might if they saw fit, prohibit the existence of slavery therein. And now I state it as a *fact*, to be taken back if there is any mistake about it, that Judge Douglas and those acting with him, *voted that amendment down.* [Tremendous applause.] I now think that those men who voted it down, had a *real reason* for doing so. They know what that reason was. It looks to us, since we have seen the Dred Scott decision pronounced holding that 'under the Constitution' the people cannot exclude slavery—I say it looks to outsiders, poor, simple, 'amiable, intelligent gentlemen,' (great laughter,) as though the niche was left as a place to put that Dred Scott decision in— [laughter and cheers]—a niche which would have been spoiled by adopting the amendment. And now, I say again, if *this* was not the reason, it will avail the Judge much more to calmly and good-humoredly point out to these people what that *other* reason was for voting the amendment down, than, swelling himself up, to vociferate that he may be provoked to call somebody a liar. [Tremendous applause.]

"Again: there is in that same quotation from the Nebraska bill this clause—'It being the true intent and meaning of this bill not to legislate slavery into any Territory or *State.*' I have always been puzzled to know what business the word 'State' had in that connection. Judge Douglas knows. *He put it there.* He knows what he put it there for. We outsiders cannot say what he put it there for. The law they were passing was not about States, and was not making provisions for States. What was it placed there for? After seeing the Dred Scott decision, which holds that the people cannot exclude slavery from a *Territory*, if another Dred Scott decision shall come, holding that they cannot exclude it from a *State*, we shall discover that when the word was originally put there, it was in view of something which was to come in due time, we shall see that it was the *other half* of something. [Applause.] I now say again, if there is any different reason for putting it there, Judge Douglas, in a good-humored way, without calling anybody a liar, *can tell what the* reason was." [Renewed cheers.]

Lincoln Shows Douglas Made Similar Charges against Buchanan

"When the Judge spoke at Clinton, he came very near making a charge of falsehood against me. He used, as I found it printed in a newspaper, which I remember was very nearly like the real speech, the following language:

" 'I did not answer the charge [of conspiracy] before, for the reason that I did not suppose there was a man in America with a heart so corrupt as to believe such a charge could be true. I have too much respect for Mr. Lincoln to suppose he is serious in making the charge.'

"I confess this is rather a curious view, that out of respect for me he should consider I was making what I deemed rather a grave charge in fun. [Laughter.] I confess it strikes me rather strangely. But I let it pass. As the Judge did not for a moment believe that there was a man in America whose heart was so 'corrupt' as to make such a charge, and as he places me among the 'men in America' who have hearts base enough to make such a charge, I hope he will excuse me if I hunt out another charge very like this; and if it should turn out that in hunting I should find that other, and it should turn out to be Judge Douglas himself who made it, I hope he will reconsider this question of the deep corruption of heart he has thought fit to ascribe to me. [Great applause and laughter.] In Judge Douglas' speech of March 22d, 1858, which I hold in my hand he says:

" 'In this connection there is another topic to which I desire to allude. I seldom refer to the course of newspapers, or notice the articles which they publish in regard to myself; but the course of the Washington *Union* has been so extraordinary, for the last two or three months, that I think it well enough to make some allusion to it. It has read me out of the Democratic party every other day, at least for two or three months, and keeps reading me out, [laughter;] and, as if it had not succeeded still continues to read me out, using such terms as 'traitor,' 'renegade,' 'deserter,' and other kind and polite epithets of that nature. Sir, I have no vindication to make of my democracy against the Washington *Union,* or any other newspapers. I am willing to allow my history and action for the last twenty years to speak for themselves as to my political principles, and my fidelity to political obligations. The Washington *Union* has a personal grievance. When its editor was nominated for Public Printer I declined to vote for him, and stated that at some time I might give my reasons for doing so. Since I declined to give that vote, this scurrilous abuse, these vindictive and constant attacks have been repeated almost daily on me. Will my friend from Michigan read the article to which I allude.'

"This is part of the speech. You must excuse me from reading the entire article of the Washington *Union,* as Mr. Stuart [Senator C. E. Stuart] read it for Mr. Douglas. The Judge goes on and sums up, as I think correctly:

" 'Mr. President, you find here several distinct propositions advanced boldly by the Washington *Union* editorially and apparently *authoritatively,* and every man who questions any of them is denounced as an Abolitionist, a Free-Soiler, a fanatic. The propositions are, first, that the primary object of all government at its original institution is the protection of person and property; second, that the Constitution of the United States declares that the citizens of each State shall be entitled to all the privileges and immunities of citizens in the several States; and that, therefore, thirdly, all State laws, whether organic or otherwise, which prohibit the citizens of one State from settling in another with their slave property, and especially declaring it forfeited, are direct violations of the original intention of the Government and Constitution of the United States; and fourth, that the emancipation of the slaves of the northern States was a gross outrage on the rights of property, inasmuch as it was involuntarily done on the part of the owner.
" 'Remember that this article was published in the *Union* on the 17th of November, and on the 18th appeared the first article giving the adhesion of the *Union* to the Lecompton constitution. It was in these words:
" *'Kansas and her Constitution.* — The vexed question is settled. The problem is solved. The dread point of danger is passed. All serious trouble to Kansas affairs is over and gone. . . .

"I pass over some portions of the speech, and I hope that any one who feels interested in this matter will read the entire section of the speech, and see whether I do the Judge injustice. He proceeds:

" 'When I saw that article in the *Union* of the 17th of November, followed by the glorification of the Lecompton Constitution on the 18th of

November, and this clause in the Constitution asserting the doctrine that a State has no right to prohibit slavery within its limits, I saw that there was a fatal blow being struck at the sovereignty of the States of this Union.'

"I stop the quotation there, again requesting that it may all be read. I have read all of the portion I desire to comment upon. What is this charge that the Judge thinks I must have a very corrupt heart to make? It was a purpose on the part of certain high functionaries to make it impossible for the people of one State to prohibit the people of any other State from entering it with their "property," so called, and making it a slave State. In other words, it was a charge implying a design to make the institution of slavery national. And now I ask your attention to what Judge Douglas has himself done here. I know he made that part of the speech as a reason why he had refused to vote for a certain man for public printer, but when we get at it, the charge itself is the very one I made against him, that he thinks I am so corrupt for uttering. Now whom does he make that charge against? Does he make it against that newspaper editor merely? No; he says it is identical in spirit with the Lecompton Constitution, and so the framers of that Constitution are brought in with the editor of the newspaper in that 'fatal blow being struck.' He did not call it a 'conspiracy.' In his language it is a 'fatal blow being struck.' And if the words carry the meaning better when changed from a 'conspiracy' into a 'fatal blow being struck,' I will change *my* expression and call it a 'fatal blow being struck.' [Cheers and laughter.] We see the charge made not merely against the editor of the *Union* but all the framers of the Lecompton Constitution; and not only so, but the article was an *authoritative* article. By whose authority? Is there any question but he means it was by the authority of the President, and his Cabinet—the Administration?

"Is there any sort of question but he means to make that charge? Then there are the editors of the *Union,* the framers of the Lecompton Constitution, the President of the United States and his Cabinet, and all the supporters of the Lecompton Constitution in Congress and out of Congress, who are all involved in this 'fatal blow being struck.' I commend to Judge Douglas' consideration the question of *how corrupt a man's heart must be to make such a charge!"* [Vociferous cheering.]

Lincoln Shows How Slavery Can Be Nationalized

"Now my friends . . . I ask the attention of the people here assembled and elsewhere, to the course that Judge Douglas is pursuing every day as bearing upon this question of making slavery national. Not going back to the records but taking the speeches he makes, the speeches he made yesterday and the day before and makes constantly all over the country—I ask your attention to them. In the first place what is necessary to make the institution national? Not war. There is no danger that the people of Kentucky will shoulder their muskets and with a young nigger stuck on every bayonet march into Illinois and force them upon us. There is no danger of our going over there and making war upon them. Then what is necessary for the nationalization of slavery? It is simply the next Dred Scott decision. It is merely for the Supreme Court to decided that no *State* under the Constitution can exclude it, just as they have already decided that under the Constitution neither Congress nor the Territorial Legislature can do it. When that is decided and acquiesed in, the whole thing is done. This being true, and this being the way as I think that slavery is to be made national, let us consider what Judge Douglas is doing every day to that end. In the first place, let us see what influence he is exerting on public sentiment."

Evaluates Public Sentiment

"In this and like communities, public sentiment is everything. With public sentiment, nothing can fail; without it nothing can succeed. Consequently he who moulds public sentiment, goes deeper than he who enacts statutes or pronounces decisions. He makes statutes and decisions possible or impossible to be excuted. This must be borne in mind, as also the additional fact that Judge Douglas is a man of vast influence, so great that it is enough for many men to profess to believe anything, when they once find out that Judge Douglas professed to believe it. Consider also the attitude he occupies at the head of a large party—a party which he claims has a majority of all the voters in the country. This man sticks to a decision which forbids the people of a Territory from excluding slavery, and he does so not because he says it is right in itself—he does not give any opinion on that—but because it has been *decided by the court,* and being decided by the court, he is, and you are bound to take it in your political action as *law*—not that he judges at all of its merits, but because a decision of the court is to him a *'Thus saith the Lord.'* [Applause.] He places it on that ground alone, and you will bear in mind that thus committing himself unreservedly to this decision, *commits him to the next one* just as firmly as to this. He did not commit himself on account of the merit or demerit of the decision, but it is a *Thus saith the Lord.* The next decision, as much as this, will be a *thus saith the Lord.* There is nothing that can divert or turn him away from this decision."

Political Rejection of Supreme Court Decision

"It is nothing that I point out to him that his great prototype, Gen. Jackson, did not believe in the binding force of decisions. It is nothing to him that Jefferson did not so believe. I have said that I have often heard him approve of Jackson's course in disregarding the decision of the Supreme Court pronouncing a National Bank constitutional. He says, I did not hear him say so. He denies the accuracy of my recollection. I say he ought to know better than I, but I will make no question about this thing, though it still seems to me that I heard him say it twenty times. [Applause and laughter.] I will tell him though, that he now claims to stand on the Cincinnati platform, which affirms that Congress *cannot* charter a National Bank, in the teeth of that old standing decision that Congress *can* charter a bank." (Loud applause.)

Reminds Douglas of his "Overslaughing" of State Supreme Court Decision

"And I remind him of another piece of history on the question of respect for judicial decisions, and it is a piece of Illinois history, belonging to a time when the large party to which Judge Douglas belonged, were displeased with a decision of the Supreme Court of Illinois because they had decided that a Governor could not remove a secretary of state . . . and I know that Judge

Douglas will not deny that he was then in favor of overslaughing that decision by the mode of adding five new Judges, so as to vote down the four old ones. Not only so, but it ended in *the Judges's sitting down on that very bench as one of the five new Judges to break down the four old ones.* [Cheers and laughter.] It was in this way precisely that he got his title of Judge. Now, when the Judge tells me that men appointed conditionally to sit as members of a court, will have to be catechised beforehand upon some subject, I say 'You know Judge; you have tried it.' [Laughter.] When he says a court of this kind will lose the confidence of all men, will be prostituted and disgraced by such a proceeding, I say, 'You know best, Judge; you have been through the mill.' [Great laughter.] But I cannot shake Judge Douglas' teeth loose from the Dred Scott decision. Like some obstinate animal (I mean no disrespect,) that will hang on when he has once got his teeth fixed, you may cut off a leg, or you may tear away an arm, still he will not relax his hold. And so I may point out to the Judge, and say that he is bespattered all over, from the beginning of his political life to the present time, with attacks upon judicial decisons—I may cut off limb after limb of his public record, and strive to wrench him from a single dictum of the Court—yet I cannot divert him from it. He hangs to the last, to the Dred Scott decision. [Loud cheers.] These things show there is a purpose *strong as death and eternity* for which he adhered to this decision, and for which he will adhere to *all other decisions* of the same Court." [Vociferous applause.]

Douglas in Bludgeoning Rebuttal Catechised Lincoln Again

Douglas proceeded as if Lincoln had evaded his questions when actually he had said that he would submit to them if Douglas would in fair play answer an equal number. He began with the declaration that Lincoln had refused to say whether or not he approved of each article of the platform adopted by the Republican party in 1854. Here the audience interrupted so vigorously that the chairman of the Republican committee had to appeal for silence. It became now clear that the people would demand that each man answer the other's questions in later debates.

"The point," said Douglas, "I am going to remind Mr. Lincoln of is this: that after I had made my speech in 1854, during the fair, he gave me notice that he was going to reply to me the next day. I was sick at the time, but I staid over in Springfield to hear his reply and to reply to him. On that day this very convention, the resolutions adopted by which I have read, was to meet in the Senate chamber. He spoke in the hall of the House; and when he got through his speech—my recollection is distinct, and I shall never forget it—Mr. Codding walked in as I took the stand to reply, and gave notice that the Republican State Convention would meet instantly in the Senate chamber, and called upon the Republicans to retire and go into this very convention, instead of remaining and listening to me. [Three cheers for Douglas.]

MR. LINCOLN, interrupting, excitedly and angrily [according to the Democratic *Times*]. "Judge, add that I went along with them."

MR. DOUGLAS—"Gentlemen, Mr. Lincoln tells me to add that he went along with them to the Senate chamber. I will not add that, because I do not know whether he did or not.

MR. LINCOLN, again interrupting—"I know he did not."

MR. DOUGLAS—"I do not know whether he knows it or not, my point is this, and I will bring him to his milk on this point." [The *Times* reported that Lincoln grew so excited that his friends had to restrain him from interrupting again. The *Press* and *Tribune* did not mention such an episode.]

"But my friends, this denial of his that he did not act on the committee is a miserable quibble to avoid the main issue, [applause.] ["That's so,"] which is that this Republican platform declares in favor of the unconditional repeal of the Fugitive Slave Law. Has Lincoln answered whether he endorsed that or not? [No, no.] I called his attention to it when I first addressed you and asked him for an answer and I then predicted that he would not answer. [Bravo, glorious and cheers.] How does he answer? Why that he was not on the committee that wrote the resolutions.* [Laughter.] I then repeated the next proposition contained in the resolutions, which was to restrict slavery in those states in which it exists and asked him whether he endorsed it. Does he answer yes, or no? He says in reply, 'I was not on the committee at the time; I was up in Tazewell.' The next question I put to him was, whether he was in favor of prohibiting the admission of any more slave States into the Union. I put the question to him distinctly, whether, if the people of the Territory, when they had sufficient population to make a State, should form their constitution recognizing slavery, he would vote for or against its admission. ["That's it."] He is a candidate for the United States Senate, and it is possible, if he should be elected, that he would have to vote directly on that question. ["He never will."] I asked him to answer me and you whether he would vote to admit a State into the Union, with slavery or without it, as its own people might choose. ["Hear him," "That's the doctrine," and applause.] He did not answer that question. ["He never will."] He dodges that question also, under the cover that he was not on the Committee at the time, that he was not present when the platform was made. I want to know if he should happen to be in the Senate when a State applied for admission, with a constitution acceptable to her own people, he would vote to admit that State, if slavery was one of its institutions. ["That's the question."] He avoids the answer."

Here Lincoln is reported by the *Times* to have interrupted Douglas with the answer, "No, Judge."

Douglas continued: "It is true he gives the abolitionists to understand by a hint that he would not vote to admit such a State. . . . What is the meaning of that? That he is not in favor of each State having the right to do as it pleases on the slavery question? ["Stick it to him," "don't spare him," and applause.] I will put the question to him again and again, and I intend to force it out of him.† [Immense applause.]

Douglas Tries to Maneuver Lincoln Out of Republican Party

"Then again, this platform which was made at Springfield by his own

---

*The reader will recall that Lincoln had stated repeatedly in this debate that he recognized the constitutionality of the Fugitive Slave Law.

†Lincoln's position as opposing the admission of any more slave States into the Union, except Southwestern, was strongly approved by some anti-slavery factions in the State and Nation, and as strongly opposed by pro-slavery factions, becoming thereby a decisive factor later in the States' Rights secession movement against him.

party, when he was it's acknowledged head, provides that Republicans will insist on the abolition of slavery in the District of Columbia, and I asked Lincoln specifically whether he agreed with them in that? Did you get an answer? ["No, no."] He is afraid to answer it. . . . The convention . . goes a little further, and pledges itself to exclude slavery from all the Territories over which the general government has exclusive jurisdiction north of 36 deg. 30 min., as well as South. Now I want to know whether he approves that provision. . . . I want to know . . . whether he will redeem the pledge of this platform and resist the acquirement of any more territory unless slavery therein shall be forever prohibited. . . . Each of the questions I have put to him are practical questions, questions based upon the fundamental principles of the Black Republican party, and I want to know whether he is the first, last and only choice of a party with whom he does not agree in principle." ["Great applause,"] ["Rake him down,"] . . .

Douglas, sensing the popularity of his attack, repeated it several times and then read resolutions of the Republican convention which demanded allegiance to its platform from its candidates.

"The Black Republican party stands pledged that they will never support Lincoln until he has pledged himself to that platform, [tremendous applause, men throwing up their hats, and shouting, "you've got him."] but he cannot devise his answer; he has not made up his mind, whether he will or not. [Great laughter.] He talked about everything else he could think of to occupy his hour and a half, and when he could not think of anything more to say, without an excuse for refusing to answer these questions, he sat down long before his time was out." [Cheers.]

Douglas Declares Conspiracy Charge an "Infamous Lie."

"In relation to Mr. Lincoln's charge of conspiracy against me, I have a word to say. . . . He . . . said that when he made it he did not know whether it was true or not [laughter], but inasmuch as Judge Douglas had not denied it, although he had replied to the other parts of his speech three times, he repeated it as a charge of conspiracy against me, thus charging me with moral turpitude. When he put it in that form I did say that inasmuch as he repeated the charge simply because I had not denied it, I would deprive him of the opportunity of ever repeating it again, by declaring that it was in all its bearings and infamous lie. [Three cheers for Douglas.] He says he will repeat it until I answer his folly, and nonsense about Stephen, and Franklin, and Roger, and Bob, and James.

"He studied that out, prepared that one sentence with the greatest care, committed it to memory, and put it in his first Springfield speech, and now he carries that speech around and reads that sentence to show how pretty it is. [Laughter.] . . . All I have to say is, that I am not green enough to let him make a charge which he acknowledges he does not know to be true, and then take up my time in answering it, when I know it to be false and nobody else knows it to be true. [Cheers.]

"I have not brought a charge of moral turpitude against him. When he, or any other man, brings one against me, instead of disproving it, I will say that it is a lie, and let him prove it if he can. [Enthusiastic applause.]

"I have lived twenty-five years in Illinois. I have served you with all the fidelity and ability which I possess, ["That's so," "good," and cheers,] and Mr. Lincoln is at liberty to attack my public action, my votes, and my conduct; but when he dares to attack my moral integrity, by a charge of conspiracy between myself, Chief Justice Taney, and the Supreme Court and two Presidents of the United States, I will repel it. ["Three cheers for Douglas."]

"Mr. Lincoln has not character enough for integrity and truth merely on his own *ipse dixit* to arraign President Buchanan, President Pierce, and nine judges of the Supreme Court, not one of whom would be complimented by being put on an equality with him. ["Hit him again, three cheers" etc.] There is an unpardonable presumption in a man putting himself up before thousands of people, and pretending that his *ipse dixit,* without proof, without fact and without truth, is enough to bring down and destroy the purest and best of living men." ["Hear him," "Three cheers."]

Douglas Explains Vote Against Chase Amendment

Senator Chase had offered a proviso to the Nebraska Bill which implied that the people could prohibit slavery by not introducing it. When he refused to modify it so as to provide that the people might prohibit or introduce slavery, and thus make it fair and equal to both sides, Douglas and his allies voted it down.

The word "State" as well as "Territory" was put in the Nebraska Bill, Douglas said, in answer to Lincoln's question, "to meet just such false arguments as he had been adducing. That first, not only the people of the territories should do as they pleased, but that when they came to be admitted as States, they should come into the Union with or without slavery, as the people determined. I meant to knock in the head this Abolition doctrine of Mr. Lincoln's, that there shall be no more slave States, even if the people want them."

Douglas closed with expounding the virtues of popular sovereignty and the danger of war in trying to make the States of the Union all slave or all free.

Chapter XXXI

THE DEBATES—FREEPORT,
JONESBORO, CHARLESTON

In the next six debates the speakers largely repeated the arguments made at Ottawa. Each criticised the other for ignoring his statements as well as answers to questions. But it must be said for Lincoln that he treated with meticulous care each question and argument made by Douglas. Lincoln said after the campaign that the second debate (held at Freeport) proved to be the most important in the series, for in it he succeeded in putting a question to Douglas, the answer of which split the Democratic party. Lincoln opened this debate and assumed a restrained offensive argument which he continued throughout the series. We present in this chapter the material of the next three debates as they developed the issues introduced at Ottawa. For lack of space, only the stinging assertions by Douglas are given that built up in Lincoln's mind an irrepressible, anti-Douglas political complex. (Captions and comments inserted.)

Lincoln Traps Douglas

"LADIES AND GENTLEMEN—On Saturday last, Judge Douglas and myself first met in public discussion. . . . In the course of that argument Judge Douglas proposed to me seven distinct interrogatories. In my speech of an hour and a half, I attended to some other parts of his speech, and incidentally, as I thought, answered one of the interrogatories then. I distinctly intimated to him that I would answer the rest of his interrogatories on condition only that he should agree to answer as many from me. He made no intimation at the time of the proposition, nor did he in his reply allude at all to that suggestion of mine. I do him no injustice in saying that he occupied at least half of his reply in dealing with me as though I had *refused* to answer his interrogatories. I now propose that I will answer any of the interrogatories, upon condition that he will answer questions from me not exceeding the same number. I give him an opportunity to respond. The Judge remains silent. I now say to you that I will answer his interrogatories, whether he answers mine or not; [applause] and that after I have done so, I shall propound mine to him." [Applause.]

By this highly popular maneuver in which Lincoln gave prepared answers to known questions, he forced Douglas to answer studied questions defensively, without preparation. Lincoln took advantage of the will of the people better than Douglas.

Answers Douglas' Interrogatories

"I have supposed myself, since the organization of the Republican party at Bloomington, in May, 1856, bound as a party man by the platforms of the

party, then and since. If in any interrogatories which I shall answer I go beyond the scope of what is within these platforms it will be perceived that no
one is responsible but myself.

"Having said this much, I will take up the Judge's interrogatories as I find
them printed in the Chicago *Times,* and answer them *seriatim.* In order that
there may be no mistake about it, I have copied the interrogatories in writing,
and also my answers to them. The first one of these interrogatories is in these
words:

"Question 1. 'I desire to know whether Lincoln today stands, as he did
in 1854, in favor of the unconditional repeal of the fugitive slave law?'

"Answer. 'I do not now, nor ever did, stand in favor of the unconditional
repeal of the fugitive slave law. [Cries of 'Good,' 'Good,']

"Q. 2. 'I desire him to answer whether he stands pledged today, as he did
in 1854, against the admission of any more slave States into the Union, even
if the people want them?'

"A. I do not now, nor ever did, stand pledged against the admission of
any more slave States into the Union.

"Q. 3. 'I want to know whether he stands pledged against the admission
of a new State into the Union with such a Constitution as the people of that
State may see fit to make.'

"A. I do not stand pledged against the admission of a new State into the
Union, with such a Constitution as the people of that State may see fit to
make. [Cries of "good," "good."]

"Q. 4. 'I want to know whether he stands to-day pledged to the abolition
of slavery in the District of Columbia?'

"A. I do not stand to-day pledged to the abolition of slavery in the District of Columbia.

"Q. 5. 'I desire him to answer whether he stands pledged to the prohibition of the slave trade between different States.'

"A. I do not stand pledged to the prohibition of the slave trade between
the different States.

"Q. 6. 'I desire to know whether he stands pledged to prohibit slavery in
all the Territories of the United States, North as well as South of the Missouri Compromise line.'

"A. I am impliedly, if not expressly, pledged to a belief in the *right* and
duty of Congress to prohibit slavery in all the United States Territories.
[Great applause.]

"Q. 7. 'I desire him to answer whether he is opposed to the acquisition
of any new territory unless slavery is first prohibited therein.'

"A. I am not generally opposed to honest acquisition of territory; and,
in any given case, I would or would not oppose such acquisition, according
as I might think such acquisition would or would not agravate the slavery
question among ourselves. [Cries of good, good.]

Lincoln Upholds Fugitive Slave Law

"Now, my friends, it will be perceived upon an examination of these
questions and answers, that so far I have only answered that I was not pledged
to this, that or the other. The Judge has not framed his interrogatories to ask
me anything more than this, and I have answered in strict accordance with

the interrogatories, and have answered truly that I am not *pledged* at all upon any of the points to which I have answered. But I am not disposed to hang upon the exact form of his interrogatory. I am rather disposed to take up at lease some of these questions, and state what I really think upon them."

Lincoln then declared again that he thought "under the Constitution of the United States, the people of the Southern States are entitled to a Congressional Fugitive Slave Law" and the existing law "should have been so framed as to be free from some of the objections that pertain to it, without lessening its efficiency."

Upholds Free Popular Sovereignty

About the admission of more slave States into the Union he said:

"I state to you frankly that I would be exceedingly sorry to be put in a position of having to pass upon that question. I should be exceedingly glad to know that there would never be another slave State admitted into the Union; [applause]; but I must add, that if slavery shall be kept out of the Territories during the territorial existence of any one given Territory, and then the people shall, having a fair chance and a clear field, when they come to adopt the Constitution, do such an extraordinary thing as to adopt a Slave Constitution, uninfluenced by the actual presence of the institution among them, I see no alternative, if we own the country, but to admit them into the Union." [Applause.]

This was Lincoln's practical idea of popular sovereignty at work. It differed from that of Douglas who would let slaves be brought into all territories before they adopted a State Constitution.

Lincoln Would Abolish Slavery in District of Columbia with Compensation to Owners

"The third interrogatory is answered by the answer to the second, it being, as I conceive, the same as the second.

"The fourth one is in regard to the abolition of slavery in the District of Columbia. In relation to that, I have my mind very distinctly made up. I should be exceedingly glad to see slavery abolished in the District of Columbia. [Cries of "good, good."] I believe that Congress possesses the constitutional power to abolish it. Yet as a member of Congress, I should not with my present views, be in favor of *endeavoring* to abolish slavery in the District of Columbia, unless it would be upon these conditions. *First,* that the abolition should be gradual. *Second,* that it should be on a vote of the majority of qualified voters in the District, and *third,* that compensation should be made to unwilling owners. With these conditions, I confess I would be exceedingly glad to see Congress abolish slavery in the District of Columbia, and, in the language of Henry Clay, 'sweep from our Capital that foul blot upon our nation.' " [Loud applause.]

Congressman Lincoln held these views and later as President he continued to urge the justice of compensating the owners of slaves when deprived of them by law.

Lincoln Opposes Abolition of Interstate Slave
Trade as Unconstitutional

"In regard to the fifth interrogatory, I must say here, that as to the question of the abolition of Slave Trade between the different States, I can truly answer, as I have, that I am pledged to nothing about it. It is a subject to which I have not given that mature consideration that would make me feel authorized to state a position so as to hold myself entirely bound by it. In other words, that question has never been prominently enough before me to investigate whether we really have the Constitutional power to do it. I could investigate it if I had sufficient time, to bring myself to a conclusion upon that subject, but I have not done so, and I say so frankly to you here, and to Judge Douglas. I must say, however, that if I should be of opinion that Congress does possess the Constitutional power to abolish the slave trade among the different States, I should still not be in favor of the exercise of that power unless upon some conservative principle as I conceive it, akin to what I have said in relation to the abolition of slavery in the District of Columbia. . . .

"Now in all this, the Judge has me and he has me on the record. I suppose he flattered himself that I was really entertaining one set of opinions for one place and another set for another place—that I was afraid to say at one place what I uttered at another. What I am saying here I suppose I say to a vast audience as strongly tending to Abolitionism as any audience in the State of Illinois, and I believe I am saying that which, if it would be offensive to any persons and render them enemies to myself, would be offensive to persons in this audience."

Lincoln Questions Douglas

"I now proceed to propound to the Judge the interrogatories, so far as I have framed them. I will bring forward a new installment when I get them ready. [Laughter.] I will bring them forward now, only reaching to number four.

"The first one is—

"Question 1. If the people of Kansas shall, by means entirely unobjectionable in all other respects, adopt a State Constitution, and ask admission into the Union under it, *before* they have the requisite number of inhabitants according to the English Bill—some ninety-three thousand—will you vote to admit them? (Applause.)

"Q. 2. Can the people of a United States Territory, in any lawful way, against the wish of any citizen of the United States, exclude slavery from its limits prior to the formation of a State Constitution?" [Renewed applause.]

Joseph Medill, a publisher of the Chicago *Tribune,* was asked by Lincoln before the debate at Freeport for his opinion on the four questions he intended "to spear at" Douglas. Medill advised against the second because it provided an opportunity for Douglas to placate many Illinoisians who had turned against him after he annulled the Missouri Compromise. Although other Republican leaders also tried to persuade Lincoln not to ask the second question, he persisted in his plan to make Douglas commit himself. If he answered in the affirmative he would win the election but negate the Supreme Court Dred Scott decision and lose the South and the next Democratic presidential nomination. If he answered in the negative he would win the South but probably lose the election to the Senate.

"Q. 3. If the Supreme Court of the United States shall decide that States can not exclude slavery from their limits, are you in favor of acquiescing in, adopting and following such decision as a rule of political action? [Loud applause.]

"Q. 4. Are you in favor of acquiring additional territory, in disregard of how such acquisition may affect the nation on the slavery question?" [Cries of "good," "good."]

Lincoln Reprimands Douglas

The Resolutions which Douglas had read at Ottawa, as having been passed by a Republican State Convention at Springfield in 1854, and used by him as a basis for the interrogatories he designed to make Lincoln answer and discredit himself in his own party, were shown by Lincoln, at Freeport, not to have been passed by any convention in 1854 "calling itself a Republican State Convention."

"I understand that it was from that set of resolutions that he deduced the interrogatories he propounded to me. . . . Now I say here to-day that I do not answer his interragoratories because of their springing at all from that set of resolutions which he read. I answered them because Judge Douglas saw fit to ask them. I do not now, nor never did recognize any responsibility upon myself in that set of resolutions. . . . I repeat here today, that I never in any possible form had any thing to do with that set of resolutions. It turns out, I believe, that those resolutions were never passed in any Convention held in Springfield. . . . So little did I really know of the proceedings of that Convention, or what set of resolutions they had passed, though having a general knowledge that there had been such an assemblage of men there, that when Judge Douglas read the resolutions, I really did not know but they had been the resolutions passed then and there. I did not question that they were the resolutions adopted. For I could not bring myself to suppose that Judge Douglas could say what he did upon this subject without *knowing* that it was true. [Cheers and laughter.] I contented myself, on that occasion, with denying, as I truly could, all connection with them, not denying or affirming whether they were passed at Springfield. Now it turns out that he had got hold of some resolutions passed at some Convention or public meeting in Kane County. [Renewed laughter.] I wish to say here that I can't conceive that in any fair and just mind this discovery relieves me at all. . . . I am just as much responsible for the resolutions at Kane County as those at Springfield, the amount of responsibility being exactly nothing in either case; . . ."

"I allude to this extraordinary matter in this canvass for some further purpose than anything yet advanced. Judge Douglas did not make his statement upon that occasion as matters that he believed to be true, but he stated them roundly as *being true*, in such form as to pledge his veracity for their truth. When the whole matter turns out as it does . . . it is *most extraordinary* that he should so far forget all the suggestions of justice to an adversary, or prudence to himself, as to venture upon the assertion of that which the slightest investigation would have shown to be wholly false. [Cheers.] . . . And I may add that another extraordinary feature of the Judge's conduct in this canvass—made more extraordinary by this incident—is that he is in the habit, in almost all the speeches he makes, of charging falsehood upon his adversaries—myself and others."

Douglas Answers Lincoln's Questions

"I am glad that at last I have brought Mr. Lincoln to the conclusion that he had better define his position on certain political questions to which I called his attention at Ottawa. He there showed no disposition, no inclination to answer them. I did not present idle questions for him to answer merely for my gratification. I laid the foundation for those interrogatories by showing that they constituted the platform of the party whose nominee he is for the Senate. I did not presume that I had the right to catechise him as I saw proper, unless I showed that his party, or a majority of it stood upon the platform and were in favor of the propositions upon which my questions were based. I desired simply to know, inasmuch as he had been nominated as the first, last, and only choice of his party, whether he concurred in the platform which that party had adopted for its government. In a few moments I will proceed to review the answers which he has given to these interrogatories; but in order to relieve his anxiety I will first respond to those which he has presented to me. Mark you, he has not presented interrogatories which have ever received the sanction of the party with which I am acting, and hence he has no other foundation for them than his own curiosity." ["That's a fact."]

In reply to Lincoln's first question Douglas said:

"I hold it to be a sound rule of universal application to require a territory to contain the requisite population (93,420) for a member of Congress, before it is admitted as a State into the Union. I made that proposition in the Senate in 1856, and I renewed it during the last session, in a bill providing that no territory of the United States should form a constitution and apply for admission until it had the requisite population."

Congress had made an exception of Kansas to this proposition and Douglas justified it with the comment, "it having been decided that Kansas has people enough for a slave State, I hold she has enough for a free State." He then continued that since Senator Trumbull had voted against the admission of Oregon as a free State, because of insufficient population, although greater than that of Kansas, he must also oppose the admission of Kansas, and since Trumbull was supporting Lincoln's candidacy, he would ask Lincoln to answer his own question.

The Fateful Question and Answer

In reply to Lincoln's second question, "Can the people of a United States Territory, in any lawful way, against the wish of any citizen of the United States, exclude slavery from its limits prior to the formation of a State Constitution?" Douglas said:

> "I answer emphatically, as Mr. Lincoln has heard me answer a hundred times from every stump in Illinois, that in my opinion the people can, by lawful means, exclude slavery from their limits prior to the formation of a State Constitution. [Enthusiastic applause.] Mr. Lincoln knew that I had answered that question over and over again. . . . and he has no excuse for pretending to be in doubt as to my position on that question. *It matters not what way the Supreme Court may hereafter decide as to the abstract question whether slavery may or may not go into a territory under the constitution, the people have the lawful means to introduce it or exclude it as they please, for the reason that slavery cannot exist a day or an hour anywhere, unless it is supported by local police regulations.* [Right, right.] [Italics inserted.] These police regulations can only be established by the local legislature, and if the people are opposed to slavery they will elect representatives to that body who will by unfriendly legislation effectually prevent the introduction of it into their midst. If, on the contrary, they are for it, their legislation will favor its extension. Hence, no matter what the decision of the Supreme Court may be on that abstract question, still the right of the people to make a slave territory or a free territory is perfect and complete under the Nebraska bill."

Douglas' answers rang the bell of public approval. The Democrats shouted themselves hoarse while the Republicans remained gloomily silent. "Lincoln was very uneasy; he could not sit still, nor would his limbs sustain him while standing. He was shivering, quaking, trembling, and his agony during the last fifteen minutes of Judge Douglas' speech was positively painful to the crowd. (Chicago Times, Dem.) The Democratic papers of Illinois quoted the reply as a triumph for popular sovereignty.

Douglas Condemns Lincoln's Attitude About Supreme Court

Lincoln's third question, "If the Supreme Court . . . shall decide that States can not exclude slavery from their limits, are you in favor of acquiescing in, adopting and following such decisions as a rule of political action?" was distorted by Douglas into "If the Supreme Court shall decide that a State of this Union cannot exclude slavery from its own limits will I submit to it?" Ignoring the point about accepting or rejecting such decision as "a rule of political action," he charged:

> "[Mr. Lincoln] casts an imputation upon the Supreme Court of the United States by supposing that they would violate the Constitution of the United States. I tell him that such a thing is not possible. [Cheers.] It would be an act of moral treason that no man on the bench could ever descend to."

Lincoln's much disputed assertion that Chief Justice Taney and other justices of the Supreme Court could nationalize slavery by deciding, in an appropriate case, that owners can take slaves as property into all states, became a double edged sword that was used effectively by Douglas against him. It produced the conviction in the South, two years later, of Lincoln's intention to appoint members to the Court who would favor the national abolition of slavery.

To the fourth question, on the acquisition of more territory, Douglas gave a popular reply. He said he was for it, and when we acquire it he would leave the people, according to the Nebraska bill, free to do as they please on the subject of slavery.

Douglas Puts Lincoln on "the Spot."

"I have a word to say on Mr. Lincoln's answer to the interrogatories contained in my speech at Ottawa, and which he had pretended to reply to here to-day. Mr. Lincoln makes a great parade of the fact that I quoted a platform as having been adopted by the Black Republican party at Springfield in 1854, which, it turns out, was adopted at another place. Mr. Lincoln loses sight of the thing itself in his ecstasies over the mistake I made in stating the place where it was done. He thinks that that platform was not adopted on the right 'spot.' [Laughter and applause.] Lincoln and his political friends are great on 'spots.' [Renewed laughter.] In Congress, as a representative of this State, he declared the Mexican war to be unjust and infamous, and would not support it, or acknowledge his own country to be right in the contest, because he said that American blood was not shed on American soil in the 'right spot.' "

Not until many years after the Mexican War did Lincoln succeed in living down the derisive reference to him in Democratic circles as "Spot" Lincoln, and Douglas now used this opportunity to revive the old prejudice.

Douglas Tries Again to Split Republicans

In reply to Lincoln's disowning of the resolutions passed in 1854 by a pre-Republican Convention in Kane County, Douglas substituted another set that had been passed at Rockford in the same year by another county convention. "This platform," he said, "was adopted in nearly every county that gave a Black Republican majority to the Legislature in that year." The resolutions were intensely abolitionistic. They denounced "the increasing aggressions of slavery in our country" as "destructive of the best rights of free people." They would restore Kansas and Nebraska to free territories, repeal the fugitive slave law, restrict slavery to those states where it exists, prohibit the admission of any more slave states into the Union, exclude slavery from all territories and resist the acquisition of new territories unless the introduction of slavery therein forever shall have been prohibited, and it would support no man for office who is not positively committed for the support of these principles.

Knowing very well that Lincoln was opposed to most of the radical abolition policies as being unconstitutional, Douglas hoped to split the

Republicans and induce the conservative antislavery Whigs to adopt his leadership. The resolutions show the sentiment Lincoln had to contend with in his own party as well as among Democrats.

"You Whigs," Douglas coyly appealed in distinction from Black Republicans, "and we Democrats differed about the bank, the tariff, distribution, the specie circular and the subtreasury, but we agreed on this slavery question and the true mode of preserving the peace and harmony of the Union."

Tom Turner, an active committeeman in the Republican organization, interrupted Douglas to say that he and not Lincoln was the author of the Rockford resolutions. "They are our creed exactly." he said.

"When the bargain between Lincoln and Trumbull was completed for abolitionizing the Whig and Democratic parties," Douglas continued, working on the old prejudice, . . . "they played the part that 'decoy ducks' play down on the Potomac river. In that part of the country they make artificial ducks and put them on the water in places where the wild ducks are to be found for the purpose of decoying them. Well, Lincoln and Trumbull played the part of these 'decoy ducks' and deceived enough Old Line Whigs and Old Line Democrats to elect a Black Republican Legislature. When that Legislature met, the first thing it did was to elect as Speaker of the House the very man who is now boasting that he wrote the Abolition platform on which Lincoln will not stand."

Douglas developed so skilfully this old line of accusation that Lincoln grew obviously embarrassed by it. He continued to charge that Lincoln and Trumbull had worked out an understanding between themselves whereby in 1854 they would align Whigs and Democrats "to abolitionize the two parties and defeat Senator Shields, and Trumbull would then withdraw and Lincoln would be elected, and in 1858 they would repeat the scheme and defeat Douglas, and Trumbull would get the office.

Douglas insisted; "the bargain was that Lincoln was to have had Shield's place and Trumbull was to have waited for mine, but that Trumbull having the control of a few abolitionized Democrats, he prevented them from voting for Lincoln" and eventually had himself elected. "Well, Trumbull having cheated Lincoln, his friends made a fuss, and in order to keep them and Lincoln quiet, the party were obliged to come forward, in advance, at the last State election, and . . . make a pledge that they would go for Lincoln and nobody else."

The clamor of the audience grew so intense here that Douglas had to appeal for fair play. "The object of the opposition is to occupy my attention in order to prevent me from giving the whole evidence and nailing this double dealing on the Black Republican party," He then read another set of resolutions drawn up by Republican legislators the day previous to the election of a senator in 1855. In it they asked Congress to pass an act prohibiting slavery in the territories, and to oppose the admission of new slave states into the Union, and to repeal the fugitive slave law and failing in that to pass an act providing that persons claimed as owing service or labor shall have the right of *habeas corpus* and trial by jury by regularly constituted authorities in all States.

"Either Mr. Lincoln," Douglas insisted, "was then pledged to each one of those propositions, or else every Black Republican representative from this Congressional District violated his pledge of honor to his constituents by voting for him. I ask you which horn of the dilemma will you take? . . . There is no dodging the question, I want Lincoln's answer. He says he was not pledged to repeal the fugitive slave law, . . . but he does not tell us what he is for, or what he will vote for. . . .

"In regard to there being no more slave States, he is not pledged to that. . . . the true intent and inevitable conclusion to be drawn from his first Springfield speech is, that he is opposed to the admission of any more slave States under any circumstances. . . . If he believes this Union cannot endure divided into free and slave States, that they must all become free in order to save the Union, he is bound, as an honest man, to vote against any more slave States. . . . Show me that it is my duty in order to save the Union to do a particular act, and I will do it if the constitution does not prohibit it. I am not for the dissolution of the Union under any circumstances. I will pursue no course of conduct that will give just cause for the dissolution of the Union."

These statements by Douglas proved remarkably anticipatory of the trend of anti-Lincoln sentiment that was developing in Illinois.

Dissolves Dilemma

Lincoln had succeeded in the Bloomington Republican state convention of 1856 and again in the Springfield convention of 1858 in inducing the adoption of a platform that was entirely constitutional and free from the radical abolitionism maintained by earlier county conventions.

"It is true," he said in reply to Douglas, "that many of these resolutions are at variance with the positions I have here assumed. All I have to ask is that we talk reasonably and rationally about it. . . . I have never tried to conceal my opinions, nor tried to deceive any one in reference to them. He [Douglas] may go and examine all the members who voted for me for United States Senator in 1855, after the election of 1854. They were pledged to certain things here at home, and were determined to have pledges from me, and if he will find any of these persons who will tell him anything inconsistent with that I say now, I will resign, or rather retire from the race, and give him no more trouble. The plain truth is this: At the introduction of the Nebraska policy, we believed there was a new era being introduced in the history of the Republic, which tended to the spread and perpetuation of slavery. But in our opposition to that measure we did not agree with one another in everything. The people in the north end of the State were for stronger measures of opposition than we of the central and southern portions of the State, but we were all opposed to the Nebraska doctrine. . . . You at the north met in your Conventions and passed your resolutions. We in the middle of the State and further south did not hold such Conventions and pass the same resolutions. . . . So that these meetings which the Judge has alluded to, and the resolutions he has read from were local and did not spread over the whole State. We at last met together in 1856 [Bloomington] from all parts of the

State, and we agreed upon a common platform. You, who held more extreme notions either yielded these notions, or if not wholly yielding them, agreed to yield to them practically, for the sake of embodying the opposition to the measures which the opposite party were pushing forward at that time. We met then, and if there was anything yielded, it was for practical purposes. We agreed then upon a platform for the party throughout the entire State of Illinois, and now we are all bound as a party, *to that platform.*"

Lincoln Compares His and Douglas' Answers

"I say here to you, if any one expects of me—in the case of my election—that I will do anything not signified by our Republican platform and my answers here today, I tell you very frankly that person will be deceived. I do not ask for the vote of any one who supposes that I have secret purposes or pledges that I dare not speak out." . . .

"The Judge complains that I did not fully answer his questions. If I have the sense to comprehend and answer those questions, I have done so fairly. If it can be pointed out to me how I can more fully and fairly answer him, I aver I have not the sense to see how it is to be done. He says I do not declare I would in any event vote for the admission of a slave State into the Union. If I have been fairly reported he will see that I did give an explicit answer to his interrogatories. I did not merely say that I would dislike to be put to the test; but I said clearly, if I were put to the test, and a Territory from which slavery had been excluded should present herself with a State Constitution sanctioning slavery—a most extraordinary thing and wholly unlikely ever to happen—I did not see how I could avoid voting for her admission. But he refuses to understand that I said so, and he wants his audience to understand that I did not say so. Yet it will be so reported in the printed speech that he cannot help seeing it.

"He says if I should vote for the admission of a Slave State I would be voting for a dissolution of the Union, because I hold that the Union can not permanently exist half slave and half free. I repeat that I do not believe this Government *can* endure permanently half slave and half free, yet I do not admit, nor does it at all follow, that the admission of a single Slave State will permanently fix the character and establish this as a universal slave nation. The Judge is very happy indeed at working up these quibbles. [Laughter and cheers.] Before leaving the subject of answering questions I aver as my confident belief, when you come to see our speeches in print, that you will find every question which he has asked me more fairly and boldly and fully answered than he has answered those which I put to him. Is not that so?" [Cries of yes, yes.]

Concludes by Exposing Douglas' Republican Aspirations

Lincoln quoted, as evidence of a plot to nationalize slavery by the Democratic administration, from a speech by Judge Douglas (3, 22, 1858) made before the Senate against the Lecompton Constitution in which he said:

" 'When I saw that article in the *Union* [Washington] of the 17th of November, followed by the glorification of the Lecompton Constitution on the 18th of November, and this clause in the Constitution asserting the doctrine that a State has no right to prohibit slavery within its limits, I saw there was a *fatal blow* being struck at the sovereignty of the States of this Union.' . . .

"Out of respect to Judge Douglas' good sense," Lincoln summarily stated, "I must believe he didn't manufacture his idea of the 'fatal' character of that blow out of such a miserable scapegrace as he represents that editor to be. But the Judge's eye is farther south now. Then, it was very peculiarly and decidedly North. His hope rested on the idea of visiting the great 'Black Republican' party, and making it the tail of his new kite. He knows he was then expecting from day to day to turn Republican and place himself at the head [of] our organization."

Who Was Winning the Debates?

There is little question but that in the Freeport debate the clear, simple, logical, lucid, factual pedestrian-argument of Lincoln gained a decisive popular preference over the ambivalent generalizations of Douglas, in the minds of the people who were opposed to slavery. Lincoln had skilfully led Douglas to commit himself in favor of a slavery-privileged form of popular sovereignty in the Territories that, however, could in practice either support or obliterate the constitutional rights of slave holders. He had also successfully exposed the double political game Douglas was playing to win control of the Republicans and Northern Democrats. Douglas, on the other hand, had failed in his efforts to show that Lincoln's slavery policies ignored the principles established by the Republican state conventions of 1856 and 1858.

Greatly encouraged by the enormous increase in support he was obtaining from freedom-loving people, Lincoln made an amazing number of speeches before the next debate. At Clinton (8, 2, 1858) he is credited with having given a warning to Douglas that has become an historical doctrine of practical democracy.

> *"You can fool all the people some of the time, and some of the people all of the time, but you cannot fool all of the people all of the time."*

Lincoln Becomes Inspired

To William Fithian, Republican State legislator, he wrote (9, 3, 1858):

> "You will see by the Journal that I have appointed to speak at Danville on the 22nd. of Sept.—the day *after* Douglas speaks there. My recent experience shows that speaking at the same place the next day after D. is the very thing—it is, in fact, a concluding speech on him."

Lincoln's philosophy of common sense set a new precedent in American politics: *rebuttal,* in order to be effective, must be given without delay. His letter to J. C. Bagby (9, 6) 1858) shows that his "soul was on fire."

> "Mr. Hatch tells me you write rather in a discouraged tone as to your own election. That wont do. You *must* be elected. *Must* is the word. Make known to the committee at Chicago the *amount* and *nature* of the help you can make available, and I expect they will furnish it. But, by all means, dont say 'if I can'; say 'I will.' "

The speeches at Paris, Edwardsville and Greenville show that Lincoln's conception of the principles involved in the Constitutional solution of the slavery problem was evolving from state to national appeal. The ideas expressed here were restated with increasing effectiveness. He shattered Douglas' claim of having originated the principle of popular sovereignty by showing that the Constitution established it when it stated that "all men are created equal," . . . and "endowed with certain inalienable rights" to secure which "governments were instituted among men, *deriving their just powers from the* consent of the governed." "Was not this the origin of Popular Sovereignty?"

At Edwardsville, he said:

> "I have been requested to give a concise statement, as I understand it, of the difference between the Democratic and the Republican parties on the leading issues of this campaign. The question has just been put to me by a gentlemen whom I do not know. I do not even know whether he is a friend of mine or a supporter of Judge Douglas in this contest; nor does that make any difference. His question is a pertinent one and, though it has not been asked me anywhere in the State before, I am very glad that my attention has been called to it today. Lest I should forget it, I will give you my answer before proceeding with the line of argument I have marked out for discussion.

Lincoln's impromptu answer to this basic question shows that he did not have an indecisive, vacillating mind that could not form a conviction promptly, as Douglas and many biographers have said. He had an unusual analytical grasp of basic principles and applied them immediately and constantly in everyday life wherever he was informed of both sides of an issue.

> "The difference between the Republican and Democratic parties on the leading issue of this contest, as I understand it, is, that the former consider slavery a moral, social and political wrong, while the latter *do not* consider it either a moral, social or political wrong; and the action of each, as respects the growth of the country and the expansion of our population, is squared to meet these views. I will not allege that the Democratic party consider slavery morally, socially and politically *right;* though their tendency to that view has, in my opinion, been constant and unmistakable for the past five years. I prefer to take, as the accepted maxim of the party, the idea put forth by Judge Douglas, that he 'don't care whether slavery is voted down or voted up.'

Lincoln Analyzes Douglas' Double Talk

In notes prepared for the Jonesboro debate Lincoln analyzed the self-contradiction Douglas made by upholding the Supreme Court's Dred Scott decision, that the people of a territory had no right to exclude slave property and the Missouri Compromise was unconstitutional, while he also proclaimed that by applying popular sovereignty the people could keep slavery in or out of their communities before forming a State constitution.

Lincoln's notes for these speeches show that he wrote them in all seriousness as if he were addressing an audience. The logical analysis of each step or factor in a proposition for both its relative positive and negative values to every other in forming a whole principle of legal or political action had become, under Douglas' vitriolic catechizing, an indispensable requisite for the organization of his ideas. We find in the notes for the Jonesboro and later debates that his compulsion to prove himself to be right and Douglas wrong now turned decisively towards interpreting and applying the meaning of the Constitution, as its founders meant it, for political action. It was this specific, conditional qualification of his compulsion to prevent the extension of social injustice in the form of slavery, and defeat the arrogant opportunism of Douglas, that gave him increasing national prominence. In pattern, this bivalent compulsion is an extension of the attitude of his youth which accepted and upheld the just claims of his father but resented and condemned his opportunistic arrogance and injustice.

"At Freeport I propounded," he wrote in his Jonesboro notes (about 9, 15, 1858), "four distinct interrogations to Judge Douglas, all of which he assumed to answer. I say he assumed to answer them; for he did not very distinctly answer any of them. . . .

"To my second interrogatory . . . 'Can the people of a United States Territory, in any lawful way, against the wish of any citizen of the United States, exclude slavery from their limits, prior to the formation of a State constitution?' The Judge answers that they can, and he proceeds to show how they can exclude it. The how, as he gives it, is by withholding friendly legislation and adopting unfriendly legislation. As he thinks, the people still can, by doing nothing to help slavery and by a little unfriendly leaning against it, exclude it from their limits. That is his position. This position and the Dred Scott decision are absolutely inconsistent. The judge furiously endorses the Dred Scott decision; and that decision holds that the United States Constitution guarantees to the citizens of the United States the right to hold slaves in the Territories, and that neither Congress nor a territorial legislature can destroy or abridge that right. In the teeth of this, where can the judge find room for his unfriendly legislation against their right? The members of a territorial legislature are sworn to support the Constitution of the United States. How dare they legislate unfriendly to a right guaranteed by that Constitution? And if they should how quickly would the courts hold their work to be unconstitutional and void! But doubtless the judge's chief reliance to sustain his proposition that the people can exclude slavery, is based upon non-action—upon withholding friendly legislation. But can members of a territorial legislature, having sworn to support the United States Constitution, conscientiously withhold necessary legislative protection to a right guaranteed by that Constitution?

"Again, will not the courts, without territorial legislation, find a remedy for the evasion of a right guaranteed by the United States Constitution? It is a maxim of the courts that 'there is no right without a remedy.' But as a matter of fact, non-action, both legislative and judicial, will not exclude slavery from any place. It is of record that Dred Scott and his family were held in actual slavery in Kansas without any friendly legislation or judicial assistance. It is well known that other negroes were held in actual slavery at the military post in Kansas under practically the same circumstances. This was not only done without any friendly legislation, but in direct disregard of the congressional prohibition,—the Missouri Compromise,— then supposed to be valid, thus showing that it requires positive law to be both made and executed to keep actual slavery out of any Territory where any owner chooses to take it. Slavery having actually gone into a territory to some extent, without local legislation in its favor, and against congressional prohibition, how much more will it go there now that by a judicial decision that congressional prohibition is swept away, and the constitutional guaranty of property declared to apply to slavery in the Territories.

"But this is not all. Slavery was originally planted on this continent without the aid of friendly legislation. History proves this. After it was actually in existence to a sufficient extent to become, in some sort, a public interest, it began to receive legislative attention, but not before. How futile, then, is the proposition that the people of a Territory can exclude slavery by simply not legislating in its favor. Learned disputants use what they call the *argumentum ad hominem*—a course of argument which does not intrinsically reach the issue, but merely turns the adversary against himself. There are at least two arguments of this sort which may easily be turned against Judge Douglas' proposition that the people of a Territory can lawfully exclude slavery from their limits prior to forming a State constitution. In his report of the 12th of March, 1856, on page 28, Judge Douglas says: 'The sovereignty of a Territory remains in abeyance, suspended in the United States, in trust for the people, until they shall be admitted into the Union as a State.' If so,— if they have no active living sovereignty, — how can they readily enact the Judge's unfriendly legislation to slavery?

"But in 1856, on the floor of the Senate, Judge Trumbull asked Judge Douglas the direct question, 'Can the people of a Territory exclude slavery prior to forming a State constitution?'—and Judge Douglas answered, 'That is a question for the Supreme Court.' I think he made the same answer to the same question more than once. But now, when the Supreme Court has decided that the people of a Territory cannot so exclude slavery, Judge Douglas shifts his ground, saying the people can exclude it, and thus virtually saying it is not a question for the Supreme Court.

"I am aware Judge Douglas avoids admitting in direct terms that the Supreme Court have decided against the power of the people of a Territory to exclude slavery. He also avoids saying directly that they have not so decided; but he labors to leave the impression that he thinks they have not so decided. For instance, in his Springfield speech of July 17, 1858, Judge Douglas, speaking of me says: 'He infers that it [the court] would decide that the territorial legislatures could not prohibit slavery. I will not stop to inquire whether the courts will carry the decision that far or not.' The court has already carried the decision exactly that far, and I must say I think Judge Douglas very well knows it has. After stating that Congress cannot prohibit slavery in the Territories, the court adds: 'And if Congress itself cannot do this, if it be beyond the powers conferred on the Federal Government, it will be admitted, we presume, that it could not authorize a territorial government to exercise them, it could confer no power on any local government, established by its authority, to violate the provisions of the Constitution.'

"Can any mortal man misunderstand this language? Does not Judge Douglas equivocate when he pretends not to know that the Supreme Court has decided that the people of a Territory cannot exclude slavery prior to forming a State constitution?

Analyzes the Fifth Amendment of the Constitution

"My third interrogatory to the judge is in these words: 'If the Supreme Court of the United States shall decide that States cannot exclude slavery from their limits, are you in favor of acquiescing in, adopting, and following such decision as a rule of political action?' To this question the judge gives no answer whatever. He disposes of it by an attempt to ridicule the idea that the Supreme Court will ever make such a decision. When Judge Douglas is drawn up to a distinct point, there is significance in all he says, and in all he omits to say. In this case he will not, on the one hand, face the people and declare he will support such a decision when made, nor on the other hand will he trammel himself by saying he will not support it.

"Now I propose to show, in the teeth of Judge Douglas' ridicule, that such a decision does logically and necessarily follow the Dred Scott decision. In that case the court holds that Congress can legislate for the Territories in some respects, and in others it cannot; that it cannot prohibit slavery in the Territories, because to do so would infringe on the 'right of property' guaranteed to the citizen by the fifth amendment to the constitution, which provides that 'no person shall be deprived of life, liberty, or property without due process of law.' Unquestionably there is such a guaranty in the Constitution, whether or not the court rightfully apply it in this case. I propose to show, beyond the power of quibble, that that guaranty applies with all the force, if not more, to States than it does to Territories. The answers to two questions fix the whole thing: to whom is this guaranty given? and against whom does it protect those to whom it is given? The guaranty makes no distinction between persons in the States and those in the Territories; . . .

"Against whom does this guaranty protect the rights of property? Not against Congress alone, but against the world—against State constitutions and laws, as well as against acts of Congress. The United States Constitution is the supreme law of the land; this guaranty of property is expressly given in that Constitution, in that supreme law; and no State constitution or law can override it. It is not a case where power over the subject is reserved to the States, because it is not expressly given to the General Government; it is a case where the guaranty is expressly given to the individual citizen, in and by the organic law of the General Government; and the duty of maintaining that guaranty is imposed upon that General Government, overriding all obstacles.

"The following is the article of the Constitution containing the guaranty of property upon which the Dred Scott decision is based.

" 'Article V. No person shall be held to answer for a capital or otherwise infamous crime, unless on a presentment or indictment by a grand jury, except in cases arising in the land or naval forces, or in the militia when in actual service, in time of war or public danger; nor shall any person be subject for the same offense to be twice put in jeopardy of life or limb; nor shall be compelled, in any criminal case, to be a witness against himself, nor be deprived of life, liberty, or property without due process of law; nor shall private property be taken for public use without just compensation.'

"Suppose, now, a provision in a State constitution should negative all the above propositions, declaring directly or substantially that 'any person may be deprived of life, liberty, or property without due process of law,' a direct contradiction— collison— would be pronounced between the United States Constitution and such State constitution. And can there be any doubt but that which is declared to be the supreme law would prevail over the other to the extent of the collision? Such State constitution would be unconstitutional.

"There is no escape from this conclusion but in one way, and that is to deny that the Supreme Court, in the Dred Scott case, properly applies this constitutional guaranty of property. The Constitution itself impliedly admits that a person may be deprived of property by 'due process of law,' and the Republicans hold that if there be a law of Congress or territorial legislature telling the slaveholder in advance that he shall not bring his slave into the Territory upon pain of forfeiture, and he still will bring him, he will be deprived of his property in such slavery by 'due process of law.' And the same would be true in the case of taking a slave into a State against a State constitution or law prohibiting slavery."

Such Euclidian analysis of the meaning and application of the articles and amendments of the Constitution, in regard to federal powers and state and individual rights, reveals the kindly, solemn dignity which Lincoln's mind was developing with enduring strength of self-reliance, against criticism and ridicule. This self-cultural method was to convince him within two years that he was fit to serve as President.

Douglas Agitates War Potentials at Jonesboro

Douglas, in his opening speech at Jonesboro (9, 15, 1858), repeated his old harangue of freely interpreted historical generalizations in order to make the people believe that the Republican party was a sectional organization of antislavery Whigs and Democrats, who "based all their hopes on the single fact that the North was the stronger division of the nation, and hence, if the North could be combined against the South, a sure victory awaited their efforts." The effect being "to combine all the free States in hostile array against the slave States."

"I am doing no more than justice to the truth of history when I say that in this State Abraham Lincoln, on behalf of the Whigs, and Lyman Trumbull, on behalf of the Democrats, were the leaders who undertook to perform this grand scheme of abolitionizing the two parties to which they belonged."

Again he brought forth his array of assumptions to show that Lincoln and Trumbull had plotted to defeat State Senator Shields and himself, and that Lincoln had been double crossed by Turnbull. According to Douglas' reporters Lincoln grew "nervous," looked "miserable," "as if he had not a friend on earth." Again Douglas attacked Lincoln's political doctrine that "a house divided can not stand:"

"He [Lincoln] says to the North, 'You must not be content with regulating your own affairs and minding your own business, but if you desire to maintain your freedom, you must invade the Southern states, abolish slavery there and everywhere, in order to have the States all one thing or all the other.' I say that this is the inevitable and irresistible result of Mr. Lincoln's argument inviting warfare between the North and the South, to be carried on with ruthless vengence, until one section or the other shall be driven to the wall and become the victim of the rapacity of the other." . . .

"If we wish to preserve our institutions in their purity, and transmit them unimpaired to our latest posterity, we must preserve with religious good faith that great principle of self government which guarantees to each and every State, old and new, the right to make just such constitutions as they deserve, and come into the Union with their own constitution and not one palmed upon them. [Cheers.] Whenever you sanction the doctrine that Congress may crowd a constitution down the throats of an unwilling people against their consent, you will subvert the great fundamental principle upon which all our free institutions rests." . . .

Lincoln Again Upholds States' Rights

Lincoln replied:

"There is very much in the principles that Judge Douglas has here enunciated that I most cordially approve, and over which I shall have no controversy with him. In so far as he has insisted that all the States have the right to do exactly as they please about all their domestic relations, including that of slavery, I agree entirely with him. He places me wrong in spite of all I can tell him, though I repeat it again and again, insisting that I have no difference with him upon this subject. I have made a great many speeches, some of which have been printed, and it will be utterly impossible for him to find anything that I have ever put in print contrary to what I now say upon this subject. I hold myself under constitutional obligations to allow the people in all the States without interference,

direct or indirect, to do excactly as they please, and I deny that I have any
inclination to interfere with them, . . .

    . . . "Judge Douglas . . . says, 'Why can't this Union endure per-
manently, half slave and half free?' I have said that I supposed it could not,
and I will try, before this new audience, to give briefly some of the reasons
for entertaining that opinion. Another form of his question is, 'Why can't
we let it stand as our fathers placed it?' That is the exact difficulty between
us, I say that Judge Douglas and his friends have changed them from the
position in which our fathers originally placed it. I say in the way our
fathers originally left the slavery question, the institution was in the course
of ultimate extinction, and the public mind rested in the belief that it *was*
in the course of ultimate extinction. I say when this government was first
established it was the policy of its founders to prohibit the spread of
slavery into the new Territories of the United States, where it had not
existed. But Judge Douglas and his friends have broken up that policy and
placed it upon a new basis by which it is to become national and perpetual.
All I have asked or desired anywhere is that it should be placed back again
upon the basis that the fathers of our government originally placed it upon.
I have no doubt that it *would* become extinct, for all time to come, if
we but re-adopted the policy of the fathers by restricting it to the limits
it has already covered—restricting it from the new Territories."

Although Lincoln repeated this simple justification of his famous
doctrine in every debate in answer to Douglas' charges against it and
later in his Cooper Institute and other speeches, proslavery sentiment
throughout the Nation fed on the Douglas prejudice, whereas antislavery
sentiment upheld Lincoln. This schism was to become one of the basic
drives to secession and war.

Characterizes Douglas as "Crazy"

"Now, fellow citizens, in regard to this matter about a contract . . .
between Judge Trumbull and myself, . . . I wish simply to say what I have
said to him before, that he cannot know whether it is true or not, and
I *do know* that there is not a word of truth in it. And I have told him
so before. I don't want any harsh language indulged in, but I do not know
how to deal with this persistent insisting on a story that I know to be
utterly without truth. It used to be a fashion amongst men that when a
charge was made some sort of proof was brought forward to establish it,
and if no proof was found to exist, the charge was dropped. I don't know
how to beat this kind of an argument. I don't want to have a fight with
Judge Douglas, and I have no way of making an argument up into the
consistency of a corn-cob and stopping his mouth with it. (Laughter and
applause.) All I can do is, good-humoredly to say that from the beginning
to the end of all that story about a bargain between Judge Trumbull and
myself, *there is not a word of truth in it.*"

Douglas said as much in reply to Lincoln's assertion that he believed
the two Democratic Presidents, the Chief Justice and himself were involved in a plan to nationalize slavery. But it must be said with due
respect for Lincoln that he said he "believed" it as indicated by their

official actions even though he had "no proof" of it, whereas Douglas made his charges without the qualification of admissable doubt.

Lincoln was embarrassed by the slick, irrepressible manner in which Douglas had twisted and exaggerated the meaning of his having been carried off in triumph on the shoulders of some ardent Republicans after the debate at Ottawa.

"Now, my fellow citizens," he closed his speech at Jonesboro:
"I find a report of a speech made by Judge Douglas at Joliet, since we last met at Freeport—published I believed in the *Missouri Republican*—on the 9th of this month, in which Judge Douglas says:

> " 'You know at Ottawa, I read this platform, and asked him if he con-curred in each and all of the principles set forth in it. He would not answer these questions. At last I said frankly, I wish you to answer them because when I get them up here where the color of your principles is a little darker than in Egypt, I intend to trot you down to Jonesboro. The very notice that I was going to take him down to Egypt made him tremble in the knees so that he had to be carried from the platform. He laid up seven days, and in the meantime held a consultation with his political physicians, they had Lovejoy and Farnsworth and all the leaders of the Abolition party, they consulted it all over, and at last Lincoln came to the conclusion that he would answer. So he came up to Freeport last Friday.'

"Now that statement altogether furnishes a subject for philosophical contemplation. [Laughter.] I have been treating it in that way, and I have really come to the conclusion that I can explain it in no other way than by believing the Judge is crazy. [Renewed laughter.] If he was in his right mind, I cannot conceive how he would have risked disgusting the four or five thousand of his own friends who stood there, and knew, as to my having been carried from the platform, that there was not a word of truth in it.

JUDGE DOUGLAS—"Didn't they carry you off?"

Mr. LINCOLN—"There; that question illustrates the character of this man Douglas, exactly. He smiles now and says, 'Didn't they carry you off?' But he says then, *'He had to be carried off;'* and he said it to convince the country that he had so completely broken me down by his speech that I had to be carried away. Now he seeks to dodge it, and asks, 'Didn't they carry you off?' Yes, they did. *But, Judge Douglas, why didn't you tell the truth?* [Great laughter and cheers.] I would like to know why you didn't tell the truth about it. [Continued laughter.] And then, 'He laid up seven days.' He puts this in print for the people of the country to read as a serious document. I think if he had been in his sober senses he would not have risked that barefacedness in the presence of thousands of his own friends, who knew that I made speeches within six of the seven days at Henry, Marshall County; Augusta, Hancock County; and Macomb, McDonough County, including all the necessary travel to meet him again at Freeport at the end of the six days. Now, I say, there is no charitable way to look at that statement, except to conclude that he is actually crazy. [Laughter.] There is another thing in that statement that alarmed me very greatly as he states it, that he was going to 'trot me down to Egypt.' Thereby he would have you to infer that I would not come to Egypt unless he forced

Special Publications New York Academy of Sciences

me—that I could not be got here, unless he, giant-like, had hauled me down here. [Laughter.] That statement he makes, too, in the teeth of the knowledge that I had made the stipulation to come down here, *and that he himself had been very reluctant to enter into the stipulation.* [Cheers and laughter.] More than all this, Judge Douglas, when he made that statement must have been crazy, and wholly out of his sober senses, or else he would have known that when he got me down here—that promise—that windy promise—of his powers to annihilate me, wouldn't amount to anything. Now, how little do I look like being carried away trembling? Let the Judge go on, and after he is done with his half hour, I want you all, if I can't go home myself, to let me stay and rot here; and if anything happens to the Judge, if I cannot carry him to the hotel and put him to bed, let me stay here and rot. [Great laughter.] I say, then, there is something *extraordinary* in this statement? I ask you if you know any other living man who would make such a statement? . . . But really I have talked about this matter perhaps longer than I ought, for it is no great thing, and yet the smallest are often the most difficult things to deal with. The Judge has set about seriously trying to make the impression that when we meet at different places I am literally in his clutches—that I am a poor, helpless, decrepit mouse, and that I can do nothing at all. This is one of the ways he has taken to create that impression. I don't know any other way to meet it, except this. I don't want to quarrel with him—to call him a liar—but when I come to square up to him I don't know what else to call him, if I must tell the truth out. [Cheers and laughter.] I want to be at peace, and reserve all my fighting powers for necessary occasions. My time, now is very nearly out, and I give up the trifle that is left to the Judge to let him set my knees trembling again, if he can."

Despite this correction of Douglas' maliciously humorous version of the Ottawa episode, the Democratic press continued to cite it as evidence of Lincoln's unfitness to be elected because of cowardly nervous weakness and, even today, many people having read the Douglas version, believe it.

Douglas Persists in Ridiculing Lincoln

"I did say in a playful manner," Douglas justified himself in rebuttal, "that when I put these questions to Mr. Lincoln at Ottawa he failed to answer, and that he trembled and had to be carried off the stand, and required seven days to get his reply. That he did not walk of the stand he will not deny. That when the crowd went away from the stand with me, a few persons carried him home on their shoulders and laid him down, he will admit. I wish to say to you whenever I degrade my friends and myself by allowing them to carry me on their backs along through the public streets when I am able to walk I am willing to be deemed crazy."

Herein is a typical example of the extroverted, opportunistic, self-righteous egotism of Douglas and how, by tricky use of words and half truths, he tried to put his rival in ridiculously humiliating positions. This attitude was constitutionally founded and continued so throughout his life; hence we get some idea of how probably he had "playfully" humiliated Lincoln during their rivalry in courting Mary Todd. In his next speech, at Pekin, Ill. (10, 5, 1858) Lincoln said in reply to the same barrage of Douglas' assertions, that he had "known Judge Douglas for twenty-five years, and was not now to be astonished by any statement he might make, no matter what it might be."

Lincoln Enlarges upon Douglas' Fateful Self-Contradiction

We have seen how Lincoln, in his notes prepared for the Jonesboro debate, analyzed the self-contradictory position Douglas had assumed in replying to the second question. With meticulous care, step by step, he clearly and logically showed at Jonesboro that Douglas was both opposing the decision of the Supreme Court, although clamoring to uphold it, and violating the Constitution with his version of popular sovereignty. This argument has been said by many historians to have established Lincoln nationally as an authoritative interpreter of the Constitution and constituted a turning point in his political comprehension. It has become historically one of his most important statements. The following presentation is taken from the Jonesboro speech.

"The Supreme Court of the United States has decided that any Congressional prohibition of slavery in the Territories is unconstitutional—that they have reached this proposition as a conclusion from their former proposition that the Constitution of the United States expressly recognizes property in slaves, and from that other constitutional provision that no person shall be deprived of property without due process of law. Hence they reach the conclusion that as the Constitution of the United States expressly recognizes property in slaves, and prohibits any person from being deprived of property without due process of law, to pass an act of Congress by which a man who owned a slave on one side of a line would be deprived of him if he took him on the other side, is depriving him of that property without due process of law. That I understand to be the decision of the Supreme Court. I understand also that Judge Douglas adheres most firmly to that decision; and the difficulty is, how is it possible for any power to exclude slavery from the Territory unless in violation of that decision? That is the difficulty.

"In the Senate of the United States in 1856 . . . the Judge said that whether the people could exclude slavery prior to the formation of a constitution or not *was a question to be decided by the Supreme Court.* . . . I maintain that when he says, after the Supreme Court have decided the question, that the people may yet exclude slavery by any means whatever, he does virtually say, that it is *not* a question for the Supreme Court. He shifts his ground. I appeal to you whether he did not say it was a question for the Supreme Court. Has not the Supreme Court decided that question? When he now says the people *may* exclude slavery, does he not make it a question for the people? Does he not virtually shift his ground and say that it is *not* a question for the Court, but for the people? This is a very simple proposition—a very plain and naked one. It seems to me that there is no difficulty in deciding it. In a variety of ways he said that it was a question for the Supreme Court. He did not stop then to tell us that whatever the Supreme Court decides the people can by withholding necessary 'police regulations' keep slavery out. He did not make any such answer. I submit to you now, whether the new state of the case has not induced the Judge to sheer away from his original ground. [Applause.] Would not this be the impression of every fair-minded man?

"I hold that the proposition that slavery cannot enter a new country without police regulations is historically false. It is not true at all. I hold that the history of this country shows that the institution of slavery was originally planted in this continent *without* these 'police regulations,' which the Judge now thinks necessary for the actual establishment of it. Not only so, but is there not another fact—how came this Dred Scott decision to be made? It was made upon the case of a negro being taken and actually held in slavery in Minnesota Territory, claiming his freedom because the act of Congress prohibited his being so held there. *Will the Judge pretend that Dred Scott was not held there without police regulations?* There is at least one matter of record as to his having been held in slavery in the Territory, not only without police regulations, but in the teeth of Congressional legislation supposed to be valid at the time. This shows that there is vigor enough in Slavery to plant itself in a new country even against unfriendly legislation. It takes not only law but the *enforcement* of law to keep it out. That is the history of this country upon the subject.

"I wish to ask one other question. It being understood that the Constitution of the United States guarantees property in slaves in the Territories, if there is any infringement of the right of that property, would not the United States Courts, organized for the government of the Territory, apply such remedy as might be necessary in that case? It is a maxim held by the Courts, that there is no wrong without its remedy; and the Courts have a remedy for whatever is acknowledged and treated as a wrong.

"Again: I will ask you, my friends, if you were elected members of the Legislature, what would be the first thing you would have to do before entering upon your duties? *Swear to support the Constitution of the United States.* Suppose you believe, as Judge Douglas does, that the Constitution of the United States guarantees to your neighbor the right to hold slaves in that Territory—that they are his property—how can you clear your oaths unless you give him such legislation as is necessary to enable him to enjoy that property? What do you understand by supporting the Constitution of a State or of the United States? Is it not to give such constitutional helps to the rights established by that Constitution as may be practically needed? Can you, if you swear to support the Constitution, and believe that the Constitution establishes a right, clear your oath, without giving it support? Do you support the Constitution if, knowing, or believing there is a right established under it which needs specific legislation, you withhold that legislation? Do you not violate and disregard your oath? I can conceive of nothing plainer in the world. There can be nothing in the words 'support the constitution,' if you may run counter to it by refusing support to any right established under the constitution. And what I say here will hold with still more force against the Judge's doctrine of 'unfriendly legislation.' How could you, having sworn to support the Constitution, and believing it guaranteed the right to hold slaves in the Territories, assist in legislation *intended to defeat that right?* That would be violating your own view of the constitution. Not only so, but if you were to do so, how long would it take the courts to hold your votes unconstitutional and void? Not a moment.

"Lastly I would ask—is not Congress, itself, under obligation to give legislative support to any right that is established under the United States Constitution? I repeat the question—is not Congress, itself, bound to give legislative support to any right that is established in the United States Constitution ? A member of Congress swears to support the Constitution of the United States, and if he sees a right established by that Constitution which needs specific legislative protection, can he clear his oath without giving that protection? Let me ask you why many of us who are opposed to slavery upon principle give our acquiescence to a fugitive slave law? Why do we hold ourselves under obligations to pass such a law, and abide by it when it is passed. Because the Constitution makes provision that the owners of slaves shall have the right to reclaim them. It gives the right to reclaim slaves, and that right is, as Judge Douglas says, a barren right, unless there is legislation that will enforce it.

"The mere declaration 'No person held to service or labor in one State under the laws thereof, escaping into another, shall in consequence of any law or regulation therein be discharged from such service or labor, but shall be delivered up on claim of the party to whom such service or labor may be due' is powerless without specific legislation to enforce it. Now on what ground would a member of Congress who is opposed to slavery in the abstract vote for a fugitive law, as I would deem it my duty to do? Because there is a Constitutional right which needs legislation to enforce it. And although it is distasteful to me, I have sworn to support the Constitution, and having so sworn I cannot conceive that I do support it if I withheld from that right any necessary legislation to make it practical. And if this is true in regard to a fugitive slave law, is the right to have fugitive slaves reclaimed any better fixed in the Constitution than the right to hold slaves in the Territories? For this decision is a just exposition of the Constitution as Judge Douglas thinks. Is the one right any better than the other? Is there any man who while a member of Congress would give support to the one any more than the other? If I wished to refuse to give legislative support to slave property in the Territories, if a member of Congress, I could not do it holding the view that the Constitution establishes that right. If I did it at all, it would be because I deny that this decision properly construes the Constitution. But if I acknowledge with Judge Douglas that this decision properly construes the Constitution, I cannot conceive that I would be less than a perjured man if I should refuse in Congress to give such protection to that property as in its nature it needed.

The Fifth Question

"At the end of what I have said here I propose to give the Judge my fifth interrogatory which he may take and answer at his leisure. My fifth interrogatory is this: If the slaveholding citizens of a United States Territory should need and demand Congressional legislation for the protection of their slave property in such territory, would you, as a member of Congress, vote for or against such legislation? . . .

"I am aware that in some of the speeches Judge Douglas has made, he has spoken as if he did not know or think that the Supreme Court had decided that a territorial Legislature cannot exclude slavery. Precisely what the Judge would say upon the subject—whether he would say definitely that he does not understand they have so decided, or whether he would say he does understand that the Court have so decided, I do not know; but I know that in his speech at Springfield he spoke of it as a thing they had not decided yet; and in his answer to me at Freeport, he spoke of it so far again as I can comprehend it, as a thing that had not yet been decided. Now I hold that if the Judge does entertain that view I think he is not mistaken in so far as it can be said that the Court has not decided anything save the mere question of jurisdiction. I know the legal arguments that can be made—that after a court has decided that it cannot take a jurisdiction of a case, it then has decided all that is before it, and that is the end of it. A plausible argument can be made in favor of that proposition, but I know that Judge Douglas has said in one of his speeches that the court went forward *like honest men as they were* and decided all the points in the case. If any points are really extrajudicially decided because not necessarily before them, then this one as to the power of the Territorial Legislature to exclude slavery is one of them, as also the one that the Missouri Compromise was null and void. They are both extra-judicial or neither is according as the Court held that they had no jurisidiction in the case between the parties, because of want of capacity of one party to maintain a suit in that Court. I want, if I have sufficient time, to show that the Court did *pass its opinion,* but that is the only thing actually done in the case. If they did not decide, they showed what they were ready to decide whenever the matter was before them. What is that opinion? After having argued that Congress had no power to pass a law excluding slavery from a United States Territory, they then used language to this effect:—that inasmuch as Congress itself could not exercise such a power, it followed as a matter of course that it could not authorize a territorial government to exercise it, for the Territorial Legislature can do no more than Congress could do. Thus it expressed its opinion emphatically against the power of a Territorial Legislature to exclude slavery, leaving us in just as little doubt on that point as upon any other point they really decided."

Douglas Answers the Fifth Question

"I answer him that it is a fundamental article in the Democratic creed that there should be non-interference and non-intervention by Congress with the slavery in the States or territories. . . . I stand on that platform now. (Cheer after cheer was here given for Douglas.)

"Now I desire to call your attention to the fact that Lincoln did not define his own position in his own question. . . . He put the question to me at Freeport whether or not I would vote to admit Kansas into the Union before she had 93,420 inhabitants. I answered him at once that it having been decided that Kansas had now population enough for a slave State, she had population enough for a free State.

"I answered the question unequivocally, and then I asked him whether he would vote for or against the admission of Kansas before she had 93,420 inhabitants, and he would [not] answer me. . . . He now puts a question in relation [to] Congressional interference in the territories to me. I answer him direct, and yet he has not answered the question himself. I ask you whether a man has any right, in common decency, to put questions in these public discussions, to his opponent, which he will not answer himself, when they are pressed home to him. I have asked him three times, whether he would vote to admit Kansas whenever the people applied with a constitution of their own making and their own adoption, under circumstances that were fair, just and unexceptionable, but I cannot get an answer from him."

Douglas Treats Slave Property Like Other Property

"It is the fundamental principles of the judiciary that its decisons are final. It is created for that purpose so that when you cannot agree among yourselves on a disputed point you appeal to the judicial tribunal which steps in and decides for you, and that decision is then binding on every good citizen. It is the law of the land just as much with Mr. Lincoln against it as for it. . . . Well, if you [turning to Mr. Lincoln] are not going to resist the decision, if you obey it, and do not intend to array mob law against the constituted authorities, then, according to your own statement, you will be a perjured man if you do not vote to establish slavery in these territories. My doctrine is, that even taking Mr. Lincoln's view that the decision recognizes the right of a man to carry his slaves into the territories of the United States, if he pleases, yet after he gets there he needs affirmative law to make that right of any value. The same doctrine not only applies to slave property, but all other kinds of property. Chief Justice Taney places it upon the ground that slave property is on an equal footing with other property. Suppose one of your merchants should move to Kansas and open a liquor store; he has a right to take groceries and liquors there, but the mode of selling them, and the circumstances under which they shall be sold, and all the remedies must be prescribed by local legislation, and if that is unfriendly it will drive him out just as effectually as if there was a constitutional provision against the sale of liquor. So the absence of local legislation to encourage and support slave property in a territory excludes it practically just as effectually as if there was a positive constitutional provision against it. Hence, I assert that under the Dred Scott decision you cannot maintain slavery a day in a territory where there is an unwilling people and unfriendly legislation. If the people are opposed to it, our right is a barren, worthless, useless right, and if they are for it, they will support and encourage it. We come right back, therefore, to the practical question, if the people of a territory want slavery they will have it and if they do not want it you cannot force it on them. And this is the practical question, the great principle upon which our institutions rests."

Lincoln Apoligizes to a Friend

In his reply to Douglas at Jonesboro Lincoln mentioned the name of a friend, a former Republican candidate for Congress, in a manner that later produced a depressing after-effect upon himself. He said, "when Judge Douglas and myself spoke at Freeport in joint discussion . . . there was poor Martin P. Sweet standing on the platform, trying to help poor me to be elected." The next day (9, 16) he wrote to Sweet in a manner that indicates he must have had some anxiety over the slip.

> "Yesterday . . . a very trifling thing occurred which gives me a little uneasiness. I was, at the suggestion of friends, putting in, some resolutions and the like of abolition caste, passed by Douglas friends, some time ago, as a Set-off to his attempts of a like character against me. Among others I put the questions to T. Campbell and his answers to them, in 1850 when you and he ran for Congress. As my attention was divided, half lingering upon that case, and half advancing to the next one, I mentioned your name, as Campbell's opponent, in a confused sentence, which, when I heard it myself, struck me as having something disparaging to you in it. I instantly corrected it, and asked the reporters to suppress it; but my fear now is that those villainous reporters Douglas has with him will try to make something out of it. I do not myself exactly remember what it was, so little connection had it with any distinct thought in my mind, and I really hope no more may be heard of it; but if there should, I write this to assure you that nothing can be farther from me than to *feel,* much less, intentionally *say* anything disrespectful to you."

This letter shows incidentally that Lincoln had unusual self-analytical insight and used the salutary, confessional, apologetic method of relieving his conscience when worried about having wronged anyone.

Fourth Debate, at Charleston

At Charleston (9, 18, 1858) Lincoln and Douglas more definitely expressed the essential differences between their views on the legal involvement of the Supreme Court's decision. Lincoln held consistently that the people, having formed and agreed upon a Constitution, must live and abide by it, and their properly elected representatives in Government are bound under oath to preserve it and make and execute laws under jurisdiction of its courts. He interpreted the history of the founding of the Constitution as showing that it was the intention to give Congress the power to make laws prohibiting or sanctioning slavery in the territories. He challenged the constitutionality of the ruling by the Supreme Court that denied Congress such powers. Douglas upheld this ruling but claimed that citizens of the territories could make local laws for the benefit or hindrance of slavery.

The political principles of the two men were consistent in claiming that negroes as a people were mentally too inferior to be given all the rights of citizenship, but they differed uncompromisingly in predicting the consequences of emancipation of negroes.

Lincoln Opposes Negro Citizenship

"I am not, nor ever have been in favor of bringing about in any way the social and political equality of the white and black races, [applause] . . . I am not nor ever have been in favor of making voters or jurors of negroes, nor of qualifying them to hold office, nor to intermarry with white people; and I will say in addition to this that there is a physical difference between the white and black races which I believe will ever forbid the two races living together on terms of social and political equality. And inasmuch as they cannot so live, while they do remain together there must be the position of superior and inferior, and I as much as any other man am in favor of having the superior position assigned to the white race. I say upon this occasion I do not perceive that because the white man is to have the superior position the negro should be denied everything. I do not understand that because I do not want a negro woman for a slave I must necessarily want her for a wife. [Cheers and laughter.] My understanding is that I can just let her alone. I am now in my fiftieth year, and I certainly never have had a black woman for either a slave or a wife. So it seems to me quite possible for us to get along without making either slaves or wives of negroes. I will add to this that I have never seen to my knowledge a man, woman or child who was in favor of producing a perfect equality, social and political, between negroes and white men.

. . . "I have never had the least apprehension that I or my friends would marry negroes if there was no law to keep them from it, [laughter]— but as Judge Douglas and his friends seem to be in great apprehension that they might, if there were no law to keep them from it, [roars of laughter] I give him the most solemn pledge that I will to the very last stand by the law of this State, which forbids the marrying of white people with negroes. [Continued laughter and applause.] . . . I do not understand there is any place where an alteration of the social and political relations of the negro and the white man can be made except in the State Legislature—not in the Congress of the United States—and as I do not really apprehend the approach of any such thing myself, and as Judge Douglas seems to be in constant horror that some such danger is rapidly approaching, I propose as the best means to prevent it that the Judge be kept at home and placed in the State Legislature to fight the measure." [Uproarious laughter and applause.]

Lincoln's position in regard to the solution of the racial problem after the liberation of the negro was consistent in 1858 with that of most, earnest, public minded citizens of his time. We will see later how rapidly his views enlarged to include legal rights to education and holding government office and serving on juries. In his rejoinder to Senator Douglas' question whether or not he was in favor of Negro citizenship, he said: "I tell him very frankly that I am not in favor of negro citizenship."

"Now my opinion is that the different States have the power to make the negro a citizen under the Constitution of the United States if they choose. The Dred Scott decision decides that they have not that power. If the State of Illinois had that power I should be opposed to the exercise of it. . . .

. . . "There is no way of putting an end to the slavery agitation amongst us but to put it back upon the basis where our fathers placed it. . . . Then the public mind *will* rest in the belief that it is in the course of ultimate extinction. . . .

"The other way is for us to surrender and let Judge Douglas and his friends have their way and plant slavery over all the States—cease speaking of it as in any way a wrong—regard slavery as one of the common matters of property, and speak of negroes as we do of our horses and cattle. But while it drives on in its state of progress as it is now driving, and as it has driven for the last five years, I have ventured the opinion, and I say to-day, that we will have no end to the slavery agitation until it takes one turn or the other. [Applause.] I do not mean that when it takes a turn towards ultimate extinction it will be in a day, nor in a year, nor in two years. I do not suppose that in the most peaceful way ultimate extinction would occur in less than a hundred years at the least; but that it will occur in the best way for both races in God's own good time, I have no doubt."

Chapter XXXII

THE GENIUS OF LINCOLN—
GALESBURG, QUINCY

Only the more important developments of argument in the next two debates are presented here.

In the Galesburg debate (10, 7, 1858) Douglas cited that Jefferson and other eminent framers of the Declaration of Independence owned slaves and that it was evidently not their intention to include negroes as "men" or "people." Lincoln replied:

> "I believe that the entire records of the world, from the date of the Dec-laration of Independence up to within three years ago, may be searched in vain for one single affirmation, from one single man, that the negro was not included in the Declaration of Independence. . . . the necessities of this present policy of the Democratic party, in regard to slavery, had to invent that affirmation. [Tremendous applause.] . . . While Mr. Jefferson was the owner of slaves he said 'that he trembled for his country when he remembered that God is just.' " . . .

Lincoln maintained consistently throughout his political career that the statement in the Declaration which said: "We hold these truths to be self-evident, that all men are created free and equal, that they are endowed by their Creator with certain inalienable Rights, that among these are Life, Liberty, and the pursuit of Happiness" included all of mankind, regardless of race, age, sex, education, creed or mental and physical ability. Douglas has modified his political argument that the statement, "inalienable rights" of "all men" in the Declaration, referred to people of English extraction, to include people of European extraction, as it had turned Northern public sentiment against him and enabled Lincoln to cultivate public sentiment in favor or moral justice for people of all nationalities and races.

Lincoln Predicts the Political Fate of Douglas

In the Galesburg debate (10, 7, 1858) Douglas tried again to make the most of his claim that the Democratic Party was the only truly national party, represented and organized in every State of the Union, whereas the Republican party was a sectional party established only in the Northern free states. To this troublesome prejudice Lincoln replied:

> "The Judge . . . in regard to the distinction between his party and our party . . . assumes [his] to be a national party—ours, a sectional one. He does this in asking the question whether this country has any interest in the maintenance of the Republican party? He assumes that our party is altogether sectional— that the party to which he adheres is national; and the argument is, that no party can be a rightful party—can be based upon rightful prin-

ciples—unless it can announce its principles everywhere. . . . Is it the true test of the soundness of a doctrine, that in some places people won't let you proclaim it? [No, no, no,] Is that the way to test the truth of any doctrine? [No, no, no.] Why, I understood that at one time the people of Chicago would not let Judge Douglas preach a certain favorite doctrine of his. [Laughter and cheers.] I commend to his consideration the question, whether he takes that as a test of the unsoundness of what he wanted to preach. [Loud cheers.]

    . . . "What has always been the evidence brought forward to prove that the Republican party is a sectional party? The main one was that in the southern portion of the Union the people did not let the Republicans proclaim their doctrine amongst them. That has been the main evidence brought forward—that they had no supporters, or substantially none, in the Slave States. The South have not taken hold of our principles as we announce them; nor does Judge Douglas now grapple with those principles. We have a Republican State Platform, laid down in Springfield in June last, stating our position all the way through the questions before the country. We are now far advanced in this canvass. Judge Douglas and I have made perhaps forty speeches apiece, and we have now for the fifth time met face to face in debate, and up to this day I have not found either Judge Douglas or any friend of his taking hold of the Republican platform or laying his finger upon anything in it that is wrong. [Cheers.] I ask you all to recollect that. Judge Douglas turns away from the platform of principles to the fact that he can find people somewhere who will not allow us to announce those principles. [Applause.] If he had great confidence that our principles were wrong, he would take hold of them and demonstrate them to be wrong. But he does not do so.

The only evidence he has of their being wrong is in the fact that there are people who won't allow us to preach them. I ask again, is that the way to test the soundness of a doctrine? [Cries of "No," "No."]

    "I ask his attention also to the fact that by the rule of nationality he is himself fast becoming sectional. [Great cheers and laughter.] I ask his attention to the fact that his speeches would not go as current now south of the Ohio River as they have formerly gone there. [Loud cheers.] I ask his attention to the fact that he felicitates himself to-day that all the Democrats of the Free States are agreeing with him, [applause,] while he omits to tell us that the Democrats of any Slave State agree with him. If he has not thought of this, I commend to his consideration the evidence in his own declaration, on this day, of his becoming sectional too. [Immense cheering.] I see it rapidly approaching. Whatever may be the result of this ephemeral contest between Judge Douglas and myself, I see the day rapidly approaching when his pill of sectionalism, which he has been thrusting down the throats of Republicans for years past, will be crowded down his own throat." [Tremendous applause.]

Two years later (1860) Douglas was a candidate for the Democratic Party's nomination for President and rejected in Convention at Charleston South Carolina by the Slave States. Later he was nominated by a "rump" convention of northern Free State Democrats at Baltimore.

The Opinion of a Very Humble Man

Lincoln presented the reasons for his planned question which Douglas had answered evasively: "If the Supreme Court of the United States shall decide that the States cannot exclude slavery from their limits, are you in favor of acquiescing in, adhering to and following such decision, as a rule of political action?

"To this interrogatory Judge Douglas made no answer. He contented himself with sneering at the thought that it was possible for the Supreme Court ever to make such a decision."

"In the second clause of the sixth article, I believe it is of the Constitution of the United States, we find the following language: 'This Constitution and the laws of the United States which shall be made in pursuance thereof; and all treaties made or which shall be made under the authority of the United States, shall be the supreme law of the land; and the judges in every State shall be bound thereby anything in the Constitution or laws of any State to the contrary notwithstanding.'

"The essence of the Dred Scott case is compressed into the sentence which I will now read: 'Now, as we have already said in an earlier part of this opinion, upon a different point, the right of property in a slave is distinctly and expressly affirmed in the Constitution.' I repeat it, *'The right of property in a slave is distinctly and expressly affirmed in the Constitution!'* What is it to be 'affirmed' in the Constitution? Made firm in the Constitution—so made that it cannot be separated from the Constitution without breaking the Constitution—durable as the Constitution, and part of the Constitution. Now, remembering the provision of the Constitution which I have read, affirming that that instrument is the supreme law of the land; that the Judges of every State shall be bound by it, any law or constitution of any State to the contrary notwithstanding; that the right of property in a slave is affirmed in that Constitution, is made, formed into and cannot be separated from it without breaking it; durable as the instrument; part of the instrument; —what follows as a short and even syllogistic argument from it? I think it follows, and I submit to the consideration of men capable of arguing, whether as I state it in syllogistic form the argument has any fault in it:

"Nothing in the Constitution or laws of any State can destroy a right distinctly and expressly affirmed in the Constitution of the United States.

"The right of property in a slave is distinctly and espressly affirmed in the Constitution of the United States;

"Therefore, nothing in the Constitution or laws of any State can destroy the right of property in a slave.

"I believe that no fault can be pointed out in that argument; assuming the truth of the premises, the conclusion, so far as I have capacity at all to understand it, follows inevitably. There is a fault in it as I think, but the fault is not in the reasoning; but the falsehood in fact is a fault of the premises. I believe that the right of property in a slave *is not* distinctly and expressly affirmed in the Constitution, and Judge Douglas thinks it *is.* I believe that the Supreme Court and the advocates of that decision may search in vain for the place in the Constitution where the right of property in a slave is distinctly and expressly affirmed. I say, therefore, that I think one of the premises is not true in fact. But it is true with Judge Douglas. It is true with the Supreme Court who pronounced it. They are estopped from denying it, and being estopped from denying it, the conclusion follows that the Constitution of the United States being the supreme law, no constitution or law can interfere with it. It being affirmed in the decision that the right of property in a slave is distinctly and expressly affirmed in the Constitution, the conclusion inevitably follows that no State law or constitution can destroy that right. I then say to Judge Douglas and to all others, that I think it will take a better answer than a sneer to show that those who have said that the right of property in a slave is distinctly and expessly affirmed in the Constitution, are not prepared to show that no constitution or law can destroy that right. I say I believe it will take a far better argument than a mere sneer to show to the minds of intelligent men that whoever has said so, is not prepared, whenever public sentiment is so far advanced as to justify it, to say the other. ['That's so.'] This is but an opinion, and the opinion of one very humble man; but it is my opinion that the Dred Scott decision, as it is, never would have been made in its present form if the party that made it had not been sustained previously by the elections. My own opinion is, that the new Dred Scott decision, deciding against the right of the people of the States to exclude slavery, will never be made, if that party is not sustained by the elections. [Cries of "Yes, yes."] I believe, further, that it is just as sure to be made as to-morrow is to come, if that party shall be sustained. ["We won't sustain it, never, never."] I have said, upon a former occasion, and I repeat it now, that the course of argument that Judge Douglas makes use of upon this subject, (I charge not his motives in this), is preparing the public mind for that new Dred Scott decision. I have asked him again to point out to me the reasons for his firm adherence to the Dred Scott decision as it is. I have turned his attention to the fact that General Jackson differed from him in regard to the political obligation of a Supreme Court decision. I have asked his attention to the fact that Jefferson differed from him in regard to the political obligation of a Supreme Court decision. Jefferson said, that 'Judges are as honest as other men, and not more so.' And he said, substantially, that 'whenever a free people should give up in absolute submission to any department of government, retaining for themselves no appeal from it, their liberties were gone.' " . . .

Public Sentiment the Basis of Freedom

"So far in this controversy I can get no answer at all from Judge Douglas upon these subjects. Not one can I get from him, except that he swells himself up and says, 'All of us who stand by the decision of the Supreme Court are the friends of the Constitution; all you fellows that dare question it in any way, are the enemies of the Constitution.' [Continued laughter and cheers.] Now, in this very devoted adherence to this decision, in opposition to all the great political leaders whom he has recognized as leaders—in opposition to his former self and history, there is something very marked. And the manner in which he adheres to it—not as being right upon the merits, as he conceives (because he did not discuss that at all), but as being absolutely obligatory upon every one simply because of the source from whence it comes —as that which no man can gainsay, whatever it may be,—this is another marked feature of his adherence to that decision. It marks it in this respect, that it commits him to the next decision, whenever it comes, as being as obligatory as this one, since he does not investigate it, and won't inquire whether this opinion is right or wrong. So he takes the next one without inquiring whether *it* is right or wrong. [Applause.] He teaches men this doctrine, and in so doing prepares the public mind to take the next decision when it comes, without any inquiry. In this I think I argue fairly (without questioning motives at all) that Judge Douglas is most ingeniously and powerfully preparing the public mind to take that decision when it comes; and not only so, but he is doing it in various other ways. In these general maxims about liberty—in his assertions that he 'don't care whether Slavery is voted up or voted down;' that 'whoever wants Slavery has a right to have it;' that 'upon principles of equality it should be allowed to go everywhere;' that 'there is no inconsistency between free and slave institutions.' In this he is also preparing (whether purposely or not), the way for making the institution of Slavery national! [Cries of "Yes," "Yes," "That's so."] I repeat again, for I wish no misunderstanding, that I do not charge that he means it so; but I call upon your minds to inquire, if you were going to get the best instrument you could, and then set it to work in the most ingenious way, to prepare the public mind for this movement, operating in the free States, where there is now an abhorrence of the institution of Slavery, could you find an instrument so capable of doing it as Judge Douglas? or one employed in so apt a way to do it?" [Great cheering. Cries of "Hit him again," "That's the doctrine."]

On Expansion and Internationalization of Slavery

"Among the interrogatories that Judge Douglas propounded to me at Freeport, there was one in about this language: 'Are you opposed to the acquisition of any further territory to the United States, unless slavery shall first be prohibited therein?' I answered as I thought, in this way, that I am not generally opposed to the acquisition of additional territory, and that I would support a proposition for the acquisition of additional territory, according as my supporting it was or was not calculated to aggravate this slavery question amongst us. I then proposed to Judge Douglas another interrogatory, which was correlative to that: 'Are you in favor of acquiring additional territory in disregard as to how it may affect us upon the slavery question?' Judge Douglas answered, that is, in his own way he answered it. . . . The substance of his answer was, that this country would continue to expand—that it would need additional territory—that it was . . . absurd to suppose that we could continue upon our present territory, enlarging in population as we are . . . he was in favor of the acquisition of further territory, as fast as we might need it, in disregard of how it might affect the slavery question. I do not say this as giving his exact language, but he said so substantially, and he would leave the question of slavery where the territory was acquired, to be settled by the people of the acquired territory. ["That's the doctrine."] May be it is; let us consider that for a while. This will probably, in the run of things, become one of the concrete manifestations of this slavery question. If Judge Douglas's policy upon this question succeeds, and gets fairly settled down, until all opposition is crushed out, the next thing will be a grab for the territory of poor Mexico, an invasion of the rich lands of South America, then the adjoining islands will follow, each one of which promises additional slave fields. And this question is to be left to the people of those countries for settlement. . . .

"It is to be remembered . . . that this power of acquiring additional territory is a power confided to the President and Senate of the United States. It is a power not under the control of the Representatives of the people any further than they, the President and the Senate can be considered the representatives of the people. Let me illustrate that by a case we have in our history. When we acquired the territory from Mexico in the Mexican war, the House of Representatives, composed of the immediate representatives of the people all the time insisted that the territory thus to be acquired should be brought in upon condition that slavery should be forever prohibited therein, upon the terms and in the language that slavery had been prohibited from coming into this country. That was insisted upon constantly, and never failed to call forth an assurance that any territory thus acquired would have that prohibition in it, so far as the House of Representatives was concerned. But at last the President and the Senate acquired the territory without asking the House of Representatives anything about it, and took it without that prohibition. They have the power of acquiring territory without the immediate representatives of the people being called upon to say anything about it, and thus furnishing a very apt and powerful means of bringing new territory into the Union, and when it is once brought into the country, involving us anew in this slavery agitation. It is therefore, as I think, a very important question for the consideration of the American people, whether the policy of bringing in additional territory, without considering at all how it will operate upon the safety of the Union in reference to this one great disturbing element in our national politics, shall be adopted as the policy of the country. You will bear in mind that it is to be acquired, according to the Judge's view, as fast as it is needed, and the indefinite part of this proposition is that we have only Judge Douglas and his class of men to decide how fast it is needed. . . . Whoever wants wider slave fields, feels sure that some additional territory is needed as slave territory. Then it is as easy to show the necessity of additional slave territory as it is to assert anything that is incapable of absolute demonstration. Whatever motive a man or a set of men may have for making annexation of property or territory, it is very easy to assert, but much less easy to disprove, that it is necessary for the wants of the country.

"And now it only remains for me to say that I think it is a very grave question for the people of this Union to consider whether, in view of the fact that this Slavery question has been the only one that has ever endangered our republican institutions—the only one that has ever threatened or menaced a dissolution of the Union—that has ever disturbed us in such a way as to make us fear for the perpetuity of our liberty—in view of these facts, I think it is an exceedingly interesting and important question for this people to consider, whether we shall engage in the policy of acquiring additional territory, discarding altogether from our consideration, while obtaining new territory, the question how it may affect us in regard to this the only endangering element to our liberties and national greatness."

Tides of Freedom versus Slavery in Government

Lincoln's prophetic anticipation of proslavery's tendency to nationalize and internationalize itself has been criticised by some historians as fantastic but ingenious for exciting abolitionism. Other historians have held that it was the potential consequence of an immoral public attitude that must continue to grow until stopped by a stronger opposing moral force. Lincoln continued to hold substantially the preceding view when President. The modern study of interracial and international cultures in social organization has shown that public opinion moves insidiously in great tides of economically directed contagious sentiment, from unilateral legalistic dominance by organized minorities over unorganized masses, with exploitation tending to poverty, serfdom and slavery, and then turning to equilaterally intended legalistic organization in which exploitation is restricted and special privileges prohibited, as the people become sufficiently differentiated and organized in occupational systems so as to prevent dominance by any one group—only again to reverse itself

In his sixth debate, at Quincy (10, 13, 1858), the masterly genius of Abraham Lincoln grew eloquent in comprehensive, discriminating statesmanship, in serene, sympathetic, dignified presentation of the moral fundamentals of democracy and foresight of the inevitable consequences of the political maneuvres of Douglas. In the debates and in the other speeches of this campaign Lincoln rarely made a reference to himself except to defend his record against the defamation of unfounded charges by Douglas. He never presented a self-laudatory account of his personal qualifications for the Senate as Douglas did in each speech. Once he did speak of his youth along the Ohio River in southern Indiana as evidence of his ability to understand the river people of nearby "Egypt" (southern Illinois). On a few occasions he referred to himself as a man of "humility," as if in contrast to the arrogant pride displayed by Douglas.

Lincoln's speech at Quincy is regarded as one of the great political orations of all time. When we compare its carefully studied defensive understatements and aggressive counterattacks with the contradictions of facts in Douglas' commitment of political principles, we can feel the tension of Lincoln's egoistic attitude as he designed to destroy his rival's national influence. The paternal maturation of Lincoln's attitude now contrasts with that of Douglas who remained fixed at a querulous narcissistic level. Lincoln's literary style becomes here magnificently sage-heroic, in the simplicity of phrasing and wisdom of statement of understanding moral obligations required of man in democratic social organization.

The human mind, like other living things, grows in spurts under disposing conditions of trial and stimulation. The care with which Lincoln prepared his statements under the repetitive excitation of debating with an ingenious, implacable critic, the one man in the world that he envied and wanted to conquer, before an aroused, judicial public, is evident in his choice and definition of essential issues.

Carl Schurz (1907), a well educated German liberal and naturalized citizen of the United States, has given, as a news reporter, the most intimate portrait of Lincoln at Quincy:

"On the evening before the day of the debate, I was on a railroad train bound for Quincy. The car in which I travelled was full of men who discussed the absorbing question with great animation. A member of the Republican State Committee accompanied me and sat by my side.

"All at once, after the train had left a way station, I observed a great commotion among my fellow passengers, many of whom jumped from their seats and pressed eagerly around a tall man who had just entered the car. They addressed him in the most familiar style: Hello, Abe! How are you? and so on. And he responded in the same manner: 'Good evening, Ben! How are you, Joe? Glad to see you, Dick!' and there was much laughter at some things he said, which in the confusion of voices, I could not understand. 'Why,' exclaimed my companion, the committeeman, 'there's Lincoln himself!' He pressed through the crowd and introduced me to Abraham Lincoln, whom I then saw for the first time.

"I must confess that I was somewhat startled by his appearance. There he stood, overtopping by several inches all those surrounding him. Although measuring something over six feet myself, I had, standing quite near to him, to throw my head backward in order to look into his eyes. That swarthy face with its strong features, its deep furrows, and its benignant, melancholy eyes, is now familiar to every American. . . . At that time it was clean-shaven, and looked even more haggard and careworn than later when it was framed in whiskers.

"On his head he wore a somewhat battered stovepipe hat. His neck emerged, long and sinewy, from a white collar turned down over a thin black necktie. His lank, ungainly body was clad in a rusty black dress coat with sleeves that should have been longer; but his arms appeared so long that the sleeves of a store coat could hardly be expected to cover them all the way down to the wrists. His black trousers, too, permitted a very full view of his large feet. On his left arm he carried a gray woolen shawl, which evidently served him for an overcoat in chilly weather. His left hand held a cotton umbrella of the bulging kind, and also a cloth satchel that bore the marks of long and hard usage. His right he had kept free for handshaking, of which there was no end until everybody in the car seemed to be satisfied. I had seen in Washington and in the West, several public men of rough appearance; but none whose looks seemed quite so uncouth, not to say grotesque, as Lincoln's.

"He received me with an offhand cordiality, like an old acquaintance, having been informed of what I was doing in the campaign, and we sat down together. In a somewhat high-pitched but pleasant voice he began to talk to me, telling me much about the points he and Douglas had made in the debates at different places, and about those he intended to make at Quincy on the morrow.

. . . "He talked in so simple and familiar a strain, and his manner and homely phrase were so absolutely free from any semblance of selfconsciousness or pretension to superiority, that I soon felt as if I had known him all my life and we had long been close friends. He interspersed our conversation with all sorts of quaint stories, each of which had a witty point applicable to the subject in hand, . . . He seemed to enjoy his own jests in a childlike way, for his unusually sad-looking eyes would kindle with a merry twinkle, and he himself led in the laughter; and his laugh was so genuine, hearty, and contagious that nobody could fail to join in it. . . .

"The next morning the country people began to stream into town for the great meeting, some singly, on foot or on horseback, or small parties of men and women, and even children, in buggies or farm wagons; while others were marshaled in solemn procession from outlying towns or districts with banners and drums, many of them headed by maidens in white with tricolored scarfs, who represented the Goddess of Liberty and the different States of the Union, . . . On the whole the Democratic displays were much more elaborate and gorgeous than those of the Republicans, and it was said that Douglas had plenty of money to spend for such things. He himself also travelled in what was called in those days 'great style,' with a secretary and servants and a numerous escort of somewhat loud companions, moving from place to place by special train with cars specially decorated for the occasion, all of which contrasted strongly with Lincoln's extremely modest simplicity. There was no end of cheering and shouting and jostling on the streets of Quincy that day. But in spite of the excitement created by the political contest, the crowds remained very good-natured, and the occasional jibes flung from one side to the other were uniformly received with a laugh.

"The great debate took place in the afternoon on the open square, where a large, pine-board platform had been built for the committee of arrangements, the speakers, and the persons they wished to have with them. I thus was favored with a seat on that platform. In front of it many thousands of people were assembled, Republicans and Democrats standing peaceably together, only chaffing one another now and then in a good-tempered way.

"As the champions arrived they were demonstratively cheered by their adherents. The presiding officer agreed upon by the two parties called the meeting to order and announced the program of proceedings. Mr. Lincoln was to open with an allowance of one hour. . . . His voice was not musical, rather high-keyed, and apt to turn into a shrill treble in moments of excitement; but it was not positively disagreeable. It had an exceedingly penetrating, far-reaching quality. The looks of the audience convinced me that every word he spoke was understood at the remotest edges of the vast assemblage. His gesture was awkward. He swung his long arms sometimes in a very ungraceful manner. Now and then he would, to give particular emphasis to a point, bend his knees and body with a sudden downward jerk, and then shoot up again with a vehemence that raised him to his tiptoes and made him look much taller than he really was—a manner of enlivening a speech which at that time was . . . not unusual in the West. . . .

"There was, however, in all he said, a tone of earnest truthfulness, of elevated, noble sentiment, and of kindly sympathy, which added greatly to the strength of his argument, and became, as in the course of his speech he touched upon the moral side of the question in debate, powerfully impressive." . . .

Mr. Lincoln's Speech at Quincy (Captions inserted)

"LADIES AND GENTLEMEN:- I have had no immediate conference with Judge Douglas, but I will venture to say he and I will perfectly agree that your entire silence both when I speak and when he speaks will be most agreeable to us.

"In the month of May, 1856, the elements in the State of Illinois, which have since been consolidated into the Republican party, assembled together in a State Convention at Bloomington. They adopted at that time what, in political language, is called a platform. In June of the same year, the elements of the Republican party in the nation assembled together in a National Convention at Philadelphia. They adopted what is called the National Platform. In June, 1858— the present year— the Republicans of Illinois re-assembled at Springfield, in State Convention, and adopted again their platform, as I suppose not differing in any essential particular from either of the former ones, but perhaps adding something in relation to the new developments of political progress in the country."

Lincoln, characteristically, gave indication of a *supposition*, when he made one. To impatient people, who like to be impressed by the positiveness of demagoguery, this sounded weak and inconclusive. Actually it was a logical source of strength in that he characteristically took pains to combine suppositions and negatives with their relative positives based on demonstrable facts. Thereby, in comparison with the arts of *ad lib*, prejudicial harangue used by Douglas and most political speakers, Lincoln, through conscientious self-education, had developed the method of reasoning used by science, which bilaterally considers the relative values of specific positives with general negatives and *vice versa*.

Lincoln's Republican Platform

"The Convention that assembled in June last did me the honor, if it be one, and I esteem it such, to nominate me as their candidate for the United States Senate. I have supposed that in entering upon this canvass I stood generally upon these platforms. We are now met together on the 13th of October of the same year, only four months from the adoption of the last platform, and I am unaware that in this canvass, from the beginning until to-day, any one of our adversaries has taken hold of our platforms or laid his finger upon anything that he calls wrong in them.

"In the very first one of these joint discussions between Senator Douglas and myself, Senator Douglas, without alluding at all to these platforms, or any one of them, of which I have spoken, attempted to hold me responsible for a set of resolutions passed long before the meeting of either one of these Conventions of which I have spoken. And as a ground for holding me responsible for these resolutions, he assumed that they had been passed at a State Convention of the Republican party, and that I took part in that Convention. It was discovered afterwards that this was erroneous, that the resolutions which he endeavored to hold me responsible for, had not been passed by any State Convention anywhere— had not been passed at Springfield, where he supposed they had, or assumed that they had, and that they had been passed in no Convention in which I had taken part. The Judge, nevertheless, was not willing to give up the point that he was endeavoring to make upon me, and he therefore thought to still hold me to the point that he was endeavoring to make, by showing that the resolutions that he read, had been passed at a local convention in the northern part of the State, although it was not a local Convention that embraced my residence at all, nor one that reached, as I suppose, nearer than 150 or 200 miles of where I was when it met, nor one in which I took any part at all. He also introduced other resolutions passed at other meetings, and by combining the whole, although they were all antecedents to the two State Conventions, and the one National Convention I have mentioned, still he insisted and now insists, as I understand, that I am in some way responsible for them."

Differentiates Constitutional Rights and State Limitations of Negroes

"At Jonesboro, on our third meeting, I insisted to the Judge that I was in no way rightfully held responsible for the proceedings of this local meeting or convention in which I had taken no part, and in which I was in no way embraced; but I insisted to him that if he thought I was responsible for every man and every set of men everywhere, who happen to be my friends, the rule ought to work both ways, and he ought to be responsible for the acts and resolutions of all men or sets of men who were or are now his supporters and friends, ["good." "good"] and gave him a pretty long string of resolutions, passed by men who are now his friends, and announcing doctrines for which he does not desire to be held responsible.

"This still does not satisfy Judge Douglas. He still adheres to his proposition, that I am responsible for what some of my friends in different parts of the State have done; but that he is not responsible for what his have done. At least so I understand him. But in addition to that, the Judge at our meeting in Galesburg, last week, undertakes to establish that I am guilty of a species of double-dealing with the public—that I make speeches of a certain sort in the North, among the Abolitionists, which I would not make in the South, and that I make speeches of a certain sort in the South which I would not make in the North. I apprehend in the course I have marked out for myself that I shall not have to dwell at very great length upon this subject.

"As this was done in the Judge's opening speech at Galesburg, I had an opportunity, as I had the middle speech then, of saying something in answer to it. He brought forward a quotation or two from a speech of mine delivered at Chicago, and then to contrast with it he brought forward an extract from a speech of mine at Charleston, in which he insisted that I was greatly inconsistent, and insisted that his conclusion followed that I was playing a double part, and speaking in one region one way and in another region another way. I have not time now to dwell on this as long as I would like, and I wish only now to requote that portion of my speech at Charleston which the Judge quoted, and then make some comments upon it. This he quotes from me as being delivered at Charleston, and I believe correctly: 'I will say, then, that I am not, nor ever have been, in favor of bringing about in any way the social and political equality of the white and black races— that I am not nor ever have been in favor of making voters or jurors of negroes, nor of qualifying them to hold office, nor to intermarry with white people; and I will say in addition to this that there is a physical difference between the white and black races which will ever forbid the two races living together on terms of social and political equality. And inasmuch as they cannot so live, while they do remain together, there must be the position of superior & inferior. I am as much as any other man in favor of having the superior position assigned to the white race.' ["Go͞od," "Good," and loud cheers.] This, I believe, is the entire quotation from the Charleston speech as the Judge made it. His comments are as follows:

" 'Yes, here you find men who hurrah for Lincoln, and say he is right when he discards all distinction between the races, or when he declares that he discards the doctrine that there is such a thing as a superior and inferior race; and Abolitionists are required and expected to vote for Mr. Lincoln because he goes for the equality of the races, holding that in the Declaration of Independence the white man and the negro were declared equal, and endowed by Divine law with equality. And down South with the Old Line Whigs, with the Kentuckians, the Virginians, and the Tennesseeans, he tells you that there is a physical difference between the races, making the one superior, the other inferior, and he is in favor of maintaining the superiority of the white race over the negro.' "

"My Sentiments Were Long Entertained and Openly Expressed"

"Those are the Judge's comments. Now I wish to show you, that a month, or only lacking three days of a month, before I made the speech at Charleston, which the Judge quotes from, he had himself heard me say substantially the same thing. It was in our first meeting, at Ottawa—and I will say a word about where it was and the atmosphere it was in, after a while—but, at our first meeting, at Ottawa, I read an extract from an old speech of mine, made nearly four years ago, not merely to show my sentiments, but to show that my sentiments were long entertained and openly expressed; in which extract I expressly declared that my own feelings would not admit a social and political equality between the white and black races, and that even if my own feelings would admit of it, I still knew that the public sentiment of the country would not, and that such a thing was an utter impossibility, or substantially that. That extract from my old speech the reporters, by some sort of accident, passed over, and it was not reported. I lay no blame upon anybody. I suppose they thought that I would hand it over to them, and dropped reporting while I was reading it, but afterwards went away without getting it from me. At the end of that quotation from my old speech, which I read at Ottawa, I made the comments which were reported at that time, and which I will now read, and ask you to notice how very nearly they are the same as Judge Douglas says were delivered by me down in Egypt. After reading I added these words:

'Now, gentlemen, I don't want to read at any great length, but this is the true complexion of all I have ever said in regard to the institution of slavery or the black race, and this is the whole of it; and anything that argues me into his idea of perfect social and political equality with the negro is but a specious and fantastical arrangement of words by which a man can prove a horse-chestnut to be a chestnut horse. I will say here, while upon this subject, that I have no purpose directly or indirectly to interfere with the institution in the States where it exists. I believe I have no right to do so. I have no inclination to do so. I have no purpose to introduce political and social equality between the white and black races. There is a physical difference between the two, which, in my judgment, will probably forever forbid their living together on the footing of perfect equality, and inasmuch as it becomes a necessity that there must be a difference, I as well as Judge Douglas am in favor of the race to which I belong having the superior position. [Cheers, "That's the doctrine."] I have never said anything to the contrary, but I hold that, notwithstanding all this, there is no reason in the world why the negro is not entitled to all the rights enumerated in the Declaration of Independence—the right of life, liberty and the pursuit of happiness. I hold that he is as much entitled to these as the white man. I agree with Judge Douglas that he is not my equal in many respects, certainly not in color— perhpas not in intellectual and moral endowments; but in the right to eat the bread without leave of anybody else which his own hand earns, he is my equal and the equal of Judge Douglas, and the equal of every other man.' (Loud cheers.)

Consistent Principles, North and South

"I have chiefly introduced this for the purpose of meeting the Judge's charge that the quotation he took from my Charleston speech was what I would say down south among the Kentuckians, the Virginians, &., but would not say in the regions in which was supposed to be more of the Abolition element. I now make this comment: That speech from which I have now read the quotation, and which is there given correctly, perhaps too much so for good taste, was made away up north in the Abolition district of this State *par excellence*—in the Lovejoy District—in the personal presence of Lovejoy, for he was on the stand with us when I made it. It had been made and put in print in that region only three days less than a month before the speech made at Charleston, the like of which Judge Douglas thinks I would not make where there was any abolition element. I only refer to this matter to say that I am altogether unconscious of having attempted any double dealing anwhere—that upon once occasion I may say one thing and leave other things unsaid, and *vice versa;* but that I have said anything on one occasion that is inconsistent with what I have said elsewhere, I deny— at least I deny it so far as the intention is concerned. I find that I have devoted to this topic a larger portion of my time than I had intended. I wished to show, but I will pass it upon this occasion, that in the sentiment I have occasionally advanced upon the Declaration of Independence, I am entirely borne out by the sentiments advanced by our old Whig leader, Henry Clay, and I have the book here to show it from; but because I have already occupied more time than I intended to do on that topic, I pass over it."

"Very Hard to Affirm a Negative"

"At Galesburg, I tried to show that by the Dred Scott decision, pushed to its legitimate consequences, slavery would be established in all the States as well as in the Territories. I did this because, upon a former occasion, I had asked Judge Douglas whether, if the Supreme Court should make a decision declaring that the States had not the power to exclude slavery from their limits, he would adopt and follow that decision as a rule of political action; and because he had not directly answered that question, but had merely contented himself with sneering at it, I again introduced it, and tried to show that the conclusion that I stated followed inevitably and logically from the proposition already decided by the court. Judge Douglas had the privilege of replying to me at Galesburg, and again he gave me no direct answer as to whether he would or would not sustain such a decision if made. I give him this third chance to say yes or no. He is not obliged to do either—

probably he will not do either—[laughter] but I give him the third chance. I tried to show then that this result—this conclusion inevitably followed from the point already decided by the court. The Judge, in his reply, again sneers at the thought of the court making any such decision, and in the course of his remarks upon this subject, uses the language which I will now read. Speaking of me the Judge says:

" 'He goes on and insists that the Dred Scott Decision would carry slavery into the Free States, notwithstanding the decision itself says the contrary.' And he adds: 'Mr. Lincoln knows that there is no member of the Supreme Court that holds that doctrine. He knows that every one of them in their opinions held the reverse.'

"I especially introduce this subject again for the purpose of saying that I have the Dred Scott Decision here, and I will thank Judge Douglas to lay his finger upon the place in the entire opinions of the court where any one of them 'says the contrary.' It is very hard to affirm a negative with entire confidence. I say, however, that I have examined that decision with a good deal of care, as a alwyer examines a decision, and so far as I have been able to do so, the Court has no where in its opinions said that the States have the power to exclude slavery, nor have they used other language substantially that. I also say, so far as I can find, not one of the concurring Judges has said that the States can exclude slavery, nor said anything that was substantially that. The nearest approach that any one of them made to it, so far as I can find, was by Judge Nelson, and the approach he made to it was exactly, in substance, the Nebraska Bill—that the States had the exclusive power over the question of slavery, so far as they are not limited by the Constitution of the United States. I asked the question, therefore, if the non-concurring Judges, McLean or Curtis, had asked to get an express declaration that the States could absolutely exclude slavery from their limits, what reason have we to believe that it would not have been voted down by the majority of the Judges, just as Chase's amendment was voted down by Judge Douglas and his compeers when it was offered to the Nebraska Bill." (Cheers.)

"I Am Not a Daring Man"

"Also at Galesburg, I said something in regard to those Springfield Resolutions that Judge Douglas had attempted to use upon me at Ottawa, and commented at some length upon the fact that they were, as presented, not genuine. Judge Douglas in his reply to me seemed to be somewhat exasperated. He said he would never have believed that Abraham Lincoln, as he kindly called me, would have attempted such a thing as I had attempted upon that occasion; and among other expressions which he used toward me, was that I dared to say forgery—that I had *dared* to say forgery [turning to Judge Douglas]. Yes, Judge, I did dare to say forgery. [Loud applause.] But in this political canvass, the Judge ought to remember that I was not the first who *dared* to say forgery. At Jacksonville Judge Douglas made a speech in answer to something said by Judge Trumbull, and at the close of what he said upon that subject, he *dared* to say that Trumbull had forged his evidence. He said, too, that he should not concern himself with Trumbull any more, but thereafter he should hold Lincoln responsible for the slanders upon him. [Laughter.] When I met him at

Charleston after that, although I think that I should not have noticed the subject if he had not said he would hold me responsible for it, I spread out before him the statements of the evidence that Judge Trumbull had used, and I asked Judge Douglas, piece by piece, to put his finger upon one piece of all that evidence that he would say was a forgery! When I went through with each and every piece, Judge Douglas did not *dare* then to say that any piece of it was a forgery. [Laughter, and cries of "good, good."] So it seems that there are some things that Judge Douglas dares to do, and some that he dares not to do. [Great applause and laughter.]

A VOICE—It's the same thing with you.

MR. LINCOLN—Yes, sir, it's the same thing with me. I do dare to say forgery, when it's true, and I don't dare to say forgery when it's false. [Thunders of applause. Cries of "Hit him again," "Give it to him, Lincoln."] Now, I will say here to this audience and to Judge Douglas, I have not dared to say he committed a forgery, and I never shall until I know it; but I did dare to say—just to suggest to the Judge—that a forgery had been committed, which by his own showing had been traced to him and two of his friends. [Roars of laughter and loud cheers.] I dared to suggest to him that he had expressly promised in one of his public speeches to investigate that matter, and I dared to suggest to him that there was an implied promise that when he investigated it he would make known the result. I dared to suggest to the Judge that he could not expect to be quite clear of suspicion of that fraud, for since the time that promise was made he had been with those friends, and had not kept his promise in regard to the investigation and the report upon it. [Loud laughter. Cries of "Good, good," "Hit him hard."] I am not a very daring man, [laughter] but I dared that much, Judge, and I am not much scared about it yet." (Uproarious laughter and applause.)

"My Truthfulness and My Honor"

"When the Judge says he wouldn't have believed of Abraham Lincoln that he would have made such an attempt as that, he reminds me of the fact that he entered upon this canvass with the purpose to treat me courteously; that touched me somewhat. [Great laughter.] It sets me to thinking. I was aware, when it was first agreed that Judge Douglas and I were to have these seven joint discussions, that they were the successive acts of a drama— perhaps I should say, to be enacted not merely in the face of audiences like this, but in the face of the nation, and to some extent, by my relation to him, and not from anything in myself, in the face of the world; and I am anxious that they should be conducted with dignity and in the good temper which would be befitting the vast audience before which it was conducted. But when Judge Douglas got home from Washington and made his first speech in Chicago, the evening afterwards I made some sort of a reply to it. His second speech was made at Bloomington, in which, he commented upon my speech at Chicago, and said that I had used language ingeniously contrived to conceal my intentions, or words to that effect. Now, I understand that this is an imputation upon my veracity and my candor. I do not know what the Judge understood by it; but in our first disucssion at Ottawa, he led off by charging a bargain, somewhat corrupt in its character, upon Trumbull and myself—that we had entered into a bargain, one of the terms of which was that Trumbull was to abolitionize the old Democratic party, and I (Lincoln) was to abolitionize the old Whig party—I pretending to be as good an Old Line Whig as ever. Judge Douglas may not understand that he implicated my truthfulness and my honor, when he said I was doing one thing and pretending another; and I misunderstood him if he thought he was treating me in a dignified way, as a man of honor and truth, as he now claims he was disposed to treat me. Even after that time, at Galesburg, when he brings forward an extract from a speech made at Chicago, and an extract from a speech made at Charleston, to prove that I was trying to play a double part—that I was trying to cheat the public, and get votes upon one set of principles at one place and upon another set of principles at another place—I do not understand but what he impeaches my honor, my veracity and my candor, and because *he* does this, I do not understand that I am bound, if I see a truthful ground for it, to keep my hands off him. As soon as I learned that Judge Douglas was disposed to treat me in this way, I signified in one of my speeches that I should be driven to draw upon whatever of humble resources I might have—to adopt a new course with him. I was not entirely sure that I should be able to hold my own with him, but I at least had the purpose made to do as well as I could upon him; and now I say that I will not be the first to cry 'hold.' I think it originated with the Judge, and when he quits, I probably will. [Roars of laughter.] But I shall not ask any favors at all. He asks me, or he asks the audience, if I wish to push this matter to the point of personal difficulty. I tell him, no. He did not make a mistake, in one of his early speeches, when he called me an 'amiable' man, though perhaps he did when he called me an 'intelligent' man. [Laughter.] It really hurts me very much to suppose that I have wronged anybody on earth. I again tell him, no! I very much prefer, when this canvass shall be over, however it may result, that we at least part without any bitter recollections of personal difficulties.

"The Judge, in his concluding speech at Galesburg, says that I was pushing this matter to a personal difficulty, to avoid the responsiblity for the enormity of my principles. I say to the Judge and to this audience now, that I will again state our principles as well as I hastily can in all their enormity, and if the Judge hereafter chooses to confine himself to a war upon these principles, he will probably not find me departing from the same course."

"Our Principles—in All Their Enormity"

"We have in this nation this element of domestic slavery. It is a matter of absolute certainty that it is a disturbing element. It is the opinion of all the great men who have expressed an opinion upon it, that it is a dangerous element. We keep up a controversy in regard to it. That controversy necessarily springs from difference of opinion, and if we can learn exactly—can reduce to the lowest elements—what that difference of opinion is, we perhaps shall be better prepared for discussing the different systems of policy that we would propose in regard to that disturbing element. I suggest that the difference of opinion, reduced to its lowest terms, is no other than the difference between the men who think slavery a wrong and those who do not think it wrong. The Republican party think it wrong—we think it is a moral, a social and a political wrong. We think it is a wrong not confining itself merely to the persons or the States where it exists, but that it is a wrong in its tendency, to say the least, that extends itself to the existence of the whole nation.

Because we think it wrong, we propose a course of policy that shall deal with it as a wrong. We deal with it as with any other wrong, in so far as we can to prevent its growing any larger, and so deal with it that in the run of time there may be some promise of an end to it. We have a due regard to the actual presence of it amongst us and the difficulties of getting rid of it in any satisfactory way, and all the constitutional obligations thrown about it. I suppose that in reference both to its actual existence in the nation, and to our constitutional obligations, we have no right at all to disturb it in the States where it exists, and we profess that we have no more inclination to disturb it than we have the right to do."

Proposes Gradual Emancipation with Compensation

"We go further than that; we don't propose to disturb it where, in one instance, we think the Constitution would permit us. We think the Constitution would permit us to disturb it in the District of Columbia. Still we do not propose to do that, unless it should be in terms which I don't suppose the nation is very likely soon to agree—the terms of making the emancipation gradual and compensating the unwilling owners. Where we suppose we have the constitutional right, we restrain ourselves in reference to the actual existence of the instution and the difficulties thrown about it. We also oppose it as an evil so far as it seeks to spread itself. We insist on the policy that shall restrict it to its present limits. We don't suppose that in doing this we violate anything due to the actual presence of the institution, or anything due to the constitutional guarantees thrown around it."

Proposes Political Demand for Reversal of Supreme Court Decision

"We oppose the Dred Scott decision in a certain way, upon which I ought perhaps to address you a few words. We do not propose that when Dred Scott has been decided to be a slave by the court, we, as a mob, will decide him to be free. We do not propose that, when any other one, or one thousand, shall be decided by that court to be slaves, we will in any violent way disturb the rights of property thus settled; but we nevertheless do oppose that decision as a political rule which shall be binding on the voter, to vote for nobody who thinks it wrong, which shall be binding on the members of Congress or the President to favor no measure that does not actually concur with the principles of that decision. We do not propose to be bound by it as a political rule in that way, because we think it lays the foundation not merely of enlarging and spreading out what we consider an evil, but it lays the foundation for spreading that evil into the States themselves. We propose so resisting it as to have it reversed if we can, and a new judicial rule established upon this subject."

Disbelievers—Ought to Leave Us

"I will add this, that if there be any man who does not believe that slavery is wrong in the three aspects which I have mentioned, or in any one of them, that man is misplaced, and ought to leave us. While, on the other hand, if there be any man in the Republican party who is impatient over the necessity springing from its actual presence, and is impatient of the constitutional guarantees thrown around it, and would act in disregard of these, he too is misplaced standing with us. He will find his place somewhere else; for we have a due regard, so far as we are capable of understanding them, for all these things. This, gentlemen, as well as I can give it, is a plain statement of our principles in all their enormity."

Douglas Never Says Slavery Is Wrong

"I will say now that there is a sentiment in the country contrary to me—a sentiment which holds that slavery is not wrong, and therefore it goes for policy that does not propose dealing with it as a wrong. That policy is the Democratic policy, and that sentiment is the Democratic sentiment. If there be a doubt in the mind of any one of this vast audience that this is really the central idea of the Democratic party, in relation to this subject, I ask him to bear with me while I state a few things tending, as I think, to prove that proposition. In the first place, the leading man—I think I may do my friend Judge Douglas the honor of calling him such—advocating the present Democratic policy, never himself says it is wrong. He has the high distinction, so far as I know, of never having said slavery is either right or wrong. [Laughter.] Almost everybody else says one or the other, but the Judge never does. If there be a man in the Democratic party who thinks it is wrong, and yet clings to that party I suggest to him in the first place that his leader don't talk as he does, for he never says that it is wrong. In the second place, I suggest to him that if he will examine the policy proposed to be carried forward, he will find that he carefully excludes the idea that there is anything wrong in it. If you will examine the arguments that are made on it, you will find that every one carefully excludes the idea that there is anything wrong in slavery. Perhaps that Democrat who says he is as much opposed to slavery as I am, will tell me that I am wrong about this. I wish him to examine his own course in regard to this matter a moment, and then see if his opinion will not be changed a little. You say it is wrong; but don't you constantly object to anybody else saying so? Do you not constantly argue that this is not the right place to oppose it? You say it must not be opposed in the free States, because slavery is not there; it must not be opposed in the slave States, because it is there; it must not be opposed in politics, because that will make a fuss; it must not be opposed in the pulpit, because it is not religion. [Loud cheers.] Then where is the place to oppose it? There is no suitable place to oppose it. There is no place in the country to oppose this evil overspreading the continent, which you say yourself is coming. Frank Blair and Gratz Brown tried to get up a system of gradual emancipation in Missouri, had an election in August and got beat, and you, Mr. Democrat, threw up your hat, and halloed 'hurrah for Democracy.'" [Enthusiastic cheers.]

How to End Slavery Agitation

"So I say again that in regard to the arguments that are made, when Judge Douglas says he 'don't care whether slavery is voted up or voted down,' whether he means that as individual expression of sentiment, or only as a sort of statement of his views on national policy, it is alike true to say that he can thus argue logically if he don't see anything wrong in it; but he cannot say so logically if he admits that slavery is wrong. He cannot say that he would as soon see a wrong voted up as voted down. When Judge Douglas says that whoever, or whatever community, wants slaves, they have a right to have them, he is perfectly logical if there is nothing wrong in the institution; but if you admit that it is wrong, he cannot logically say that anybody has a right to do wrong. When he says that slave property and horse and hog property are alike to be allowed to go into the Territories, upon the principles of equality, he is reasoning truly, if there is no difference between them as property; but if the one is property, held rightfully, and the other is wrong, then there is no equality between the right and wrong; so that, turn it in any way you can, in all the arguments sustaining the Democratic policy, and in that policy itself, there is a careful, studied exclusion of the idea that there is anything wrong in slavery. Let us understand this. I am not, just here, trying to prove that we are right and they are wrong. I have been stating where we and they stand, and trying to show what is the real difference between us; and I now say that whenever we can get the question distinctly stated—can get all these men who believe that slavery is in some of these respects wrong, to stand and act with us in treating it as a wrong—then, and not till then, I think we will in some way come to an end of this slavery agitation." [Prolonged cheers.]

Douglas Misrepresents Lincoln's Charge of Conspiracy

Douglas, in his reply at Quincy, repeated ruthlessly the counter-attack that he had made at Galesburg. Unfortunately we can only give here the part that nettled Lincoln most:

"I stated with entire fairness, as soon as it was made known to me, that there was a mistake about the spot where the resolutions had been adopted, although their truthfulness, as a declaration of the principles of the Republican party, had not and could not be questioned. . . . I wish Mr. Lincoln could show that he has acted with equal fairness, and truthfulness, when I have convinced him that he has been mistaken." [Hit him again, and cheers.] I will give you an illustration to show you how he acts in a similar case: In a speech at Springfield, he charged Chief Justice Taney, and his associates, President Pierce, President Buchanan, and myself, with having entered into a conspiracy at the time the Nebraska bill was introduced, by which the Dred Scott decision was to be made by the Supreme Court, in order to carry slavery everywhere under the Constitution. I called his attention to the fact, that at the time alluded to, to wit: the introduction of the Nebraska bill, it was not possible that such a conspiracy could have been entered into, for the reason that the Dred Scott case had never been taken before the Supreme Court, and was not taken before it for a year after; and I asked him to take back that charge. Did he do it? [No.] I showed him that it was impossible that the charge could be true, I proved it by the record, and I then called upon him to retract his false charge. What was his answer? Instead of coming out like an honest man and doing so, he reiterated the charge, and said that if the case had not gone up to the Supreme Court from the courts of Missouri at the time he charged that the Judges of the Supreme Court entered into the conspiracy, yet, that there was an understanding with the Democratic owners of Dred Scott, that they would take it up. I have since asked him who the Democratic owners of Dred Scott were, but he could not tell, and why? Because there were no such Democratic owners in existence. Dred Scott at the time was owned by the Rev. Dr. Chaffee, an Abolition member of Congress, of Springfield, Massachussetts, in right of his wife. He was owned by one of Lincoln's friends, and not by Democrats at all; [immense cheers, "give it to him," etc.] his case was conducted in court by Abolition lawyers, so that both the prosecution and the defense were in the hands of the Abolition political friends of Mr. Lincoln. [Renewed cheering.] Notwithstanding I thus proved by the record that his charge against the Supreme Court was false, instead of taking it back, he resorted to another false charge to sustain the infamy of it. [Cheers.] He also charged President Buchanan with having been a party to the conspiracy. I directed his attention to the fact that the charge could not possibly be true, for the reason that at the time specified, Mr. Buchanan was not in America, but was three thousand miles off, representing the United States at the Court of St. James, and had been there for a year previous, and did not return until three years afterwards. Yet, I never could get Mr. Lincoln to take back his false charge, although I have called upon him over and over again. He refuses to do it, and either remains silent, or, resorts to other tricks to try and palm his slander off on the country." [Cheers.]

Lincoln "Skins" Douglas in Rebuttal

"I wish to return to Judge Douglas my profound thanks for his public annunciation here to-day, to be put on record, that his system of policy in regard to the institution of slavery *contemplates that it shall last forever.* [Great cheers and cries of "Hit him again."] We are getting a little nearer the true issue of this controversy, and I am profoundly grateful for this one sentence. Judge Douglas asks you 'why cannot the institution of slavery, or rather, why cannot this nation, part slave and part free, continue as our fathers made it forever?' In the first place, I insist that our fathers *did not* make this nation half slave and half free, or part slave and part free. [Applause, and "That's so."] I insist that they found the institution of slavery existing here. They did not make it so, but they left it so because they knew of no way to get rid of it at that time. ["Good," "Good," "That's true."] When Judge Douglas undertakes to say that as a matter of choice the fathers of the government made this nation part slave and part free, he *assumes what is historically* a falsehood. [Long continued applause.] More than that; when the fathers of the government cut off the source of slavery by the abolition of the slave trade, and adopted a system of restricting it from the new Territories where it had not existed, I maintain that they placed it where they understood, and all sensible men understood, it was in the course of ultimate extinction ["That's so."]; and when Judge Douglas asks me why it cannot continue as our fathers made it, I ask him why he and his friends could not let it remain as our fathers made it? [Tremendous cheering.]

"It is precisely all I ask of him in relation to the institution of slavery, that it shall be placed upon the basis that our fathers placed it upon. . . .

"I hope nobody has understood me as trying to sustain the doctrine that we have a right to quarrel with . . . any of the slave States, about the institution of slavery—thus giving the Judge an opportunity to make himself

eloquent and valiant against us in fighting for their rights. I expressly declared in my opening speech, that I had neither the inclination to exercise,
nor the belief in the existence of the right to interfere with the States . . .
in doing as they pleased with slavery or any other existing institution. Then
what becomes of all his eloquence in behalf of the rights of States, which are
assailed by no living man? [Applause, "He knows it's all humbuggery."] . . .

"Now in regard to the matter of the Dred Scott decision I wish to say a
word or two. After all, the Judge will not say whether, if a decision is made
holding that the people of the *States* cannot exclude slavery, he will
support it or not. He obstinately refuses to say what he will do in that case.
The Judges of the Supreme Court as obstinately refused to say what
they would do on this subject. Before this I reminded him that at Galesburg
he had said the Judges had expressly declared the contrary, and you remember that in my opening speech I told him I had the book containing
the decision here, and I would thank him to lay his finger on the place where
any such thing was said. He occupied his hour and a half and he has not
ventured to try to sustain his assertion. [Loud cheers.] *He never will.* [Re-
newed cheers.] But he is desirous of knowing how we are going to reverse
the Dred Scott decision. Judge Douglas ought to know how. Did not he and
his political friends find a way to reverse the decision of that same Court in
favor of the constitutionality of the National Bank? [Cheers and laughter.]
Didn't they find a way to do it so effectually that they have reversed it as
completely as any decision was ever reversed— so far as its practical operation
is concerned? [Cheers, and cries of "good," "good."] And let me ask you,
didn't Judge Douglas find a way to reverse the decision of our Supreme
Court, when it decided that Carlin's father—old Governor Carlin—had not the
constitutional power to remove a Secretary of State? [Great cheering and
laughter.] Did he not appeal to the 'MOBS' as he calls them? Did he not
make speeches in the lobby to show how villainous that decision was, and
how it ought to be overthrown? Did he not succeed too in getting an act
passed by the Legislature to have it overthrown? And didn't he himself sit
down on that bench as one of the five added judges, who were to overslaugh
the four old ones—getting his name of 'Judge' in that way and no other?
[Thundering cheers and laughter.] If there is a villainy in using disrespect or
making opposition to Supreme Court decisions, I commend it to Judge
Douglas' earnest consideration. [Cheers and laughter.] I know of no man
in the State of Illinois who ought to know so well about *how much* villainy it takes to oppose a decision of the Supreme Court, as our honorable
friend, Stephen A. Douglas. [Long continued applause.]

"Judge Douglas also makes the declaration that I say the Democrats are
bound by the Dred Scott decision while the Republicans are not. In the
sense in which he argues, I never said it; but I will tell you what I have said
and what I do not hesitate to repeat today. I have said that as the Democrats believe that decision to be correct and that the extension of slavery
is affirmed in the National Constitution, they are bound to support it as
such; and I will tell you here that General Jackson once said that each man
was bound to support the Constitution 'as he understood it.' Now, Judge
Douglas understands the Constitution according to the Dred Scott decision,
and he is bound to support it as he understands it. [Cheers.] I understand it
another way, and therefore I am bound to support it in the way in which I

understand it. [Prolonged applause.] And as Judge Douglas believes that decision to be correct, I will remake that argument if I have time to do so. Let me talk to some gentleman down there among you who looks me in the face. We will say you are a member of the Territorial Legislature, and like Judge Douglas, you believe that the right to take and hold slaves there is a constitutional right. The first thing you do is to *swear you will support the Constitution* and all rights guaranteed therein; that you will, whenever your neighbor needs your legislation to support his constitutional rights, not withhold that legislation. If you withhold that necessary legislation for the support of the Constitution and constitutional rights, do you not commit perjury? [Cries of "Yes."] I ask every sensible man, if that is not so? ["Yes, yes"—"That's a fact."] That is undoubtedly just so, say what you please. Now that is precisely what Judge Douglas says, that this is a constitutional right. Does the Judge mean to say that the Territorial Legislature in legislating may by withholding necessary laws, or by passing unfriendly laws, *nullify that constitutional right?* Does he mean to say that? Does he mean to ignore the proposition so long known and well established in the law, that what you cannot do directly, you cannot do indirectly? Does he mean that? The truth about the matter is this: Judge Douglas has sung paeans to his 'Popular Sovereignty' doctrine until his Supreme Court cooperating with him has *squatted* his Squatter Sovereignty out. [Uproarious laughter and applause.] But he will keep up this species of humbuggery about Squatter Sovereignty. He has at last invented this sort of *do nothing Sovereignty*—[renewed laughter]—that the people may exclude slavery by a sort of 'Sovereignty' that is exercised by doing nothing at all. [Continued laughter.] Is not that running his Popular Sovereignty down awfully? [Laughter.] Has it not got down as thin as the homoeopathic soup that was made by boiling the shadow of a pigeon that had starved to death? (Roars of laughter and cheering.) But at last, when it is brought to the test of close reasoning, there is not even that thin decoction of it left. It is a presumption impossible in the domain of thought. It is precisely no other than putting of that most unphilosophical proposition, that two bodies may occupy the same space at the same time. The Dred Scott decision covers the whole ground, and while it occupies it, there is no room even for the shadow of a starved pigeon to occupy the same ground." [Great cheering and laughter.] . . .

"He [Douglas] says, when he discovered there was a mistake in that case [of Republican conventions], he came forward magnanimously, without my calling his attention to it, and explained it. I will tell you how he became so magnanimous. When the newspapers of our side had discovered and published it, and put it beyond his power to deny it, then he came forward and made a virtue of necessity by acknowledging it." [Great applause.] . . .

. . . "he wants to know why I won't withdraw the charge in regard to a conspiracy to make slavery national, as he has withdrawn the one he made. May it please his worship, I will withdraw it *when it is proven false on me as that was proved false on him.* [Shouts of applause and laughter.] I will add a little more than that. I will withdraw it whenever a reasonable man shall be brought to believe that the charge is not true. [Renewed applause.]

The belief became general in the Free States that a conspiracy existed among the leaders of the Democratic party to nationalize slavery. It was now becoming a double edged sword threatening secession and war in that it was one of the strongest incentives for the organization of the Republican party around the restriction of slavery leading eventually to extinction; and, in retaliation, it excited the southern Democrats into an intensely resentful organization to defend the Constitutional rights of the Slave States as defined by the Supreme Court.

"I have asked Judge Douglas' attention to certain matters of fact tending to prove the charge of a conspiracy to nationalize slavery, and he says he convinced me that this is all untrue because Buchanan was not in the country at that time, and because the Dred Scott case had not then got into the Supreme Court; and he says that I say the *Democratic* owners of Dred Scott got up the case. I never did say that. [Applause.] I defy Judge Douglas to show that I ever said so *for I never uttered it.* [One of Mr. Douglas' reporters gesticulated affirmatively at Mr. Lincoln.] I don't care if your hireling does say I did, I tell you myself that *I never said the 'Democratic' owners of Dred Scott got up the case.* [Tremendous enthusiasm.] I have never pretended to know whether Dred Scott's owners were Democrats or Abolitionists, or Free Soilers or Border Ruffians. I have said that there is evidence about the case tending to show that it was a made up case, for the purpose of getting that decision. I have said that evidence was strong in the fact that when Dred Scott was declared to be a slave, the owner of him made him free, showing that he had had the case tried and the question settled for such use as could be made of that decision; he cared nothing about the property thus declared to be his by that decision." [Enthusiastic applause.]

We have seen in Lincoln's previous notes and speeches that he was fully informed on the Abolitionists' promotion of Dred Scott's suit for freedom in the United States Supreme Court after the Missouri State Supreme Court had decided against him. Hence his denial of Douglas' misrepresentation that he had said the Democrats had promoted the suit in the Supreme Court is consistent and acceptable.

By the statement, "I never pretended to know whether Dred Scott's owners were Democrats, Abolitionists, or Free Soilers, or Border Ruffians," Lincoln obviously meant that he had not expressed himself on this point in any of his speeches.

The preceding lines of argument proved so effective in arousing public moral interpretation of the intent of the fathers of the Constitution that Lincoln presented them with increasing ardor in every major speech in the next two years, reaching their full development in his Cooper Union address. It is interesting to see how his realization of their truth and effectiveness continued to grow.

Excessive Nervous Tension in Debate

Lincoln's predisposition to nervousness was well known, and made the subject of derogatory comments by Democratic newspapers during the campaign. His speech at Quincy was his supreme effort at clarifying the political agitation and confusion over the question of slavery around the opportunistic assertions, claims and half-truths of Douglas. The cost in nervous energy was excessive and he broke down after closing, in a serious state of nervous distress and exhaustion. Lincoln seems to have had a nervous chill, for his friends took him to a hotel room. Ever retaining his wise sense of humor he commented that he was "mighty nigh petered out" and might have to give up the race. Various ministrations were tried without success until he was given hot ginger tea, seated in a chair, covered with blankets and steamed with burning rum until he sweated copiously and relaxed. After a refreshing sleep he recovered his spirits fully and praised his friends for the rum treatment. Lincoln's thin, tired body and nervous face showed the effects of working under great strain of his constant nervous disability. He had made over 50 speeches and travelled, generally alone, under most fatiguing, unrestful conditions. Two days later, at Alton, he had fully recovered and was in much better physical and mental condition than Douglas.

Chapter XXXIII

LINCOLN MASTERS DOUGLAS' ARROGANCE

Lincoln's personality matured observably in wisdom of self-restraint, patient consideration, and firmly moral and keenly analytical understanding, under the pressure of the long series of 20 years of repetitions of critical arguments with his old, arrogant, ambitious, opportunistic rival, Douglas, to win public approval on the best ways of developing the constitutional rights of the people and carrying on government.

Last Debate, at Alton (10, 15, 1858)

Gustave Koerner (1909), a lawyer and close political friend of Mr. Lincoln, attended the debate at Alton and visited the Lincolns on the morning of that day. He said he found both Mr. and Mrs. Lincoln "rather dispirited." They had come from Springfield that morning and gone to the hotel without a reception committee to greet them. In contrast, the arrival of Senator Douglas was celebrated with a great parade and the whistling of a steamboat from St. Louis loaded with a gay, cheering party of a thousand Democrats. Douglas, he said, greeted everyone cordially, but his bronzed, bloated face and tired, haggard eyes and voice so hoarse that he could scarcely speak above a whisper, gave evidence of worry, overwork, and excessive whiskey.

> Mr. Lincoln, "although sunburned, was as fresh as if he had just entered the campaign, and as cool and collected as ever. Without any apparent effort he stated his propositions clearly and tersely, and his whole speech was weighted with noble deep thoughts. There was no appeal to passion or prejudice."

When we read this speech analytically, however we find in it certain worried, defensive arguments attended by vigorous counter-attacks against the ruthless, untruthful charges of Douglas. When correlated with similar reactions in previous debates and Lincoln's speeches of 1859 and 1860, we find that they express the repetitive resentment of an unhappy man against an opponent's false injustice.

Lincoln's Wit in Debate

Douglas assumed the affirmative with his usual broadsides of generalized statements and accusations. Lincoln's reply to his doctrines and self-praises was perhaps the wittiest speech he ever made. We present here only the parts of importance bearing on future political relations.

"LADIES AND GENTLEMEN:

"I have been somewhat, in my own mind, complimented by a large portion of Judge Douglas' speech—I mean that portion which he devotes to the controversy between himself and the present Administration. [Cheers and laughter.] This is the seventh time Judge Douglas and myself have met in these joint discussions, and he has been gradually improving in regard to his war with the Administration. [Laughter.] At Quincy, day before yesterday, he was a little more severe upon the Administration than I had heard him upon any former occasion, and I took pains to compliment him for it. I then told him to 'Give it to them with all the power he had;' and as some of them were present I told them I would be very much obliged if they would *give it to him* in about the same way. [Uproarious laughter and cheers.] I take it he has now vastly improved upon the attack he made then upon the Administration. I flatter myself he has really taken my advice on this subject. All I can say now is to recommend to him and to them what I then commended—to prosecute the war against one another in the most vigorous manner. I say to them again—'Go it, husband! Go it bear!' [Great Laughter.]

"There is one other thing I will mention before I leave this branch of the discussion— although I do not consider it much of my business, any way. I refer to that part of the Judge's remarks where he undertakes to involve Mr. Buchanan in an inconsistency. He reads something from Mr. Buchanan, from which he undertakes to involve him in an inconsistency; and he gets something of a cheer for having done so. I would only remind the Judge that while he is very valiantly fighting for the Nebraska bill and the repeal of the Missouri Compromise, it has been but a little while since he was the *valiant advocate* of the Missouri Compromise. [Cheers.] I want to know if Buchanan has not as much right to be inconsistent as Douglas has? [Loud applause and laughter; "Good, good!" "Hurrah for Lincoln!"] Has Douglas the *exclusive right*, in this country, of being *on all sides of all questions*? Is nobody allowed that high privilege but himself? Is he to have an entire *monopoly* on that subject?" [Great laughter.]

Analyzes Douglas' "Predetermination to Misrepresent Me"

"So far as Judge Douglas addressed his speech to me, or so far as it was about me, it is my business to pay some attention to it. I have heard the Judge state two or three times what he has stated to day—that in a speech which I made at Springfield, Illinois, I had in a very especial manner, complained that the Supreme Court in the Dred Scott case had decided that a negro could never be a citizen of the United States. I have omitted by some accident heretofore to analyze this statement, and it is required of me to notice it now. In point of fact it is *untrue*. I never have complained *especially* of the Dred Scott decision because it held that a negro could not be a citizen, and the Judge is always wrong when he says I ever did complain of it. I have the speech here, and I will thank him or any of his friends to show where I said that a negro should be a citizen, and complained especially of the Dred Scott decision because it declared he could not be one.

I have done no such thing, and Judge Douglas' so persistently insisting that I have done so, has strongly impressed me with the belief of a predetermination on his part to misrepresent me. He could not get his foundation for insisting that I was in favor of this negro equality anywhere else as well as he could by assuming that untrue proposition."

Lincoln then repeated the three major points of his argument in the Springfield speech: "I was then endeavoring to prove that the Dred Scott decision was a portion of a system or scheme to make slavery national in this country. . . . I mentioned as a fact that they had decided that a negro could not be a citizen,—that they had done so, as I supposed, to deprive the negro, under all circumstances, of the remotest possibility of ever becoming a citizen and claiming the rights of a citizen of the United States under a certain clause of the Constitution." . . . The Court would not decide whether a negro was made free or not by the owner bringing him into a free state; but it did decide that "taking him into a United States Territory where slavery was prohibited by an act of Congress, did not make him free because that act of Congress as they held was unconstitutional." . . .

"Out of this, Judge Douglas builds up his beautiful fabrication—of my purpose to introduce a perfect, social, and political equality between the white and black races. His assertion that I made an 'especial objection' (that is his exact language) to the decision on this account, is untrue in point of fact."

"The True Idea I Intended to Convey"

"I desire to place myself, in connection with Mr. Clay, as nearly right before this people as may be. He knows that we are before an audience, having strong sympathies southward by relationship, place of birth, and so on. He desires to place me in an extremely Abolition attitude. He read upon a former occasion, and alludes without reading today, to a portion of a speech which I delivered in Chicago. In his quotations from that speech as he has made them upon former occasions, the extracts were taken in such a way, as I suppose, brings them within the definition of what is called *garbling*— taking portions of a speech which, when taken by themselves, do not present the entire sense of the speaker as expressed at the time. I propose, therefore, out of that same speech, to show how one portion of it which he skipped over (taking an extract before and an extract after) will give a different idea and the true idea I intended to convey."

After reading his Springfield statement on holding the Constitution "the inviolate charter of our liberties," Lincoln said, "Now I have upon all occasions declared as strongly as Judge Douglas against the disposition to interfere with the existing institution of slavery. You hear me read it from the same speech from which he takes garbled extracts for the purpose of proving upon me a disposition to interfere with the institution of slavery, and establish a perfect social and political equality between negroes and white people." . . .

He then read further from another speech, on the intent of the Declaration of Independence:

" 'I think the authors of that notable instrument intended to include *all* men, but they did not mean to declare all men equal *in all respects.* They did not mean to say all men were equal in color, size, intellect, moral development or social capacity. They defined with tolerable distinctinctness in what they did consider all men created equal—equal in certain inalier.able rights, among which are life, liberty and the pursuit of happiness.' . . .

" 'They meant to set up a standard maxim for free society which should be familiar to all; constantly looked to, constantly labored for, and even though never perfectly attained, constantly approximated and therby constantly spreading and deepening its influence and augmenting the happiness and value of life to all people, of all colors, everywhere.' "

"There again are the statements I have expressed in regard to the Declaration of Independence upon a former occasion—sentiments which have been put in print and read wherever anybody cared to know what so humble an individual as myself chose to say in regard to it."

"I Combat the Tendency to Dehumanize the Negro"

"At Galesburg the other day, I said in answer to Judge Douglas, that three years ago there never had been a man, so far as I knew or believed, in the whole world, who had said that the Declaration of Independence did not include negroes in the term 'all men.' I re-assert it to-day. . . . Do not let me be misunderstood. I know that more than three years ago there were men who, finding this assertion constantly in the way of their schemes to bring about the ascendancy and perpetuation of slavery, *denied the truth of it.* . . . But I say . . . I believe the first man who ever said it was Chief Justice Taney in the Dred Scott case, and the next after him was our friend Stephen A. Douglas. And now it has become the catch-word of the entire party, I would like to call upon his friends everywhere to consider how they have come in so short a time to view this matter in a way so entirely different from their former belief? to ask whether they are not being borne along by an irresistible current—whither, they know not? [Great applause.] . . .

"When this new principle,—this new proposition that no human being thought of three years ago,—is brought forward, *I combat it* as having a tendency to dehumanize the negro—to take away from him the right of ever striving to be a man. I combat it as being one of the thousand things constantly done in these days to prepare the public mind to make property, and nothing but property of the *negro in all the States of the* Union." [Tremendous applause.]

Laying the Foundation of New Free Societies

Lincoln frequently quoted Henry Clay's statement on slavery in laying the foundation of new societies: "If a state of nature existed, and we were about to lay the foundations of society, *no man would be more strongly opposed than I should be, to incorporating the institution of slavery among its elements."*

"The principle upon which I have insisted in this canvass," Lincoln said, "is in relation to laying the foundations of new societies. I have never sought to apply these principles to the old States for the purpose of abolishing slavery in those States. It is nothing but a miserable perversion of what I *have* said, to assume that I have declared Missouri, or any other slave State shall emancipate her slaves."

Demonstrates That Constitution Refers to Slaves as "Persons"

Douglas, in each of the debates and in most of his speeches, attacked the doctrine, that "a house divided against itself cannot stand," so artfully as to make it seem to mean that Lincoln would try to bring about total emancipation if elected. This greatly embarrassed the Republicans as it became one of the chief causes of distrust of Lincoln's policy among Southern sympathizers.

No phrase in American history obtained so much press notice and discussion, became so pregnant in meaning, and so popular and so condemned.

"Judge Douglas has again referred to a Springfield speech in which I said 'a house divided against itself cannot stand' " . . . .

After quoting the entire statement he continued:

"That extract and the sentiments expressed in it, have been extremely offensive to Judge Douglas. He has warred upon them as Satan does upon the Bible. His perversions upon it are endless. Here now are my views in brief.

"I said we were now far into the fifth year since a policy was initiated with the avowed object and confident promise of putting an end to the slavery agitation. Is it not so? When that Nebraska bill was brought forward four years ago last January, was it not for the 'avowed object' of putting an end to the slavery agitation? We were to have no more agitation in Congress; it was all to be banished to the Territories. . . . We were for a little while *quiet* on the troublesome thing and that very allying plaster of Judge Douglas', stirred it up again. [Applause and laughter.] . . . In every speech you heard Judge Douglas made, until he got into this 'imbroglio,' as they call it, with the Administration about the Lecompton Constitution, every speech on that Nebraska bill was full of his felicitations that we were *just at the end* of the slavery agitation. The last tip of the last joint of the old serpent's tail was just drawing out of view. [Cheers and laughter.] But has it proved so? I have asserted that under that policy that agitation 'has not only not ceased, but has constantly augmented.' When was there ever a greater agitation in Congress than last winter? When was it as great in the country as to-day?

"There was a collateral object in the introduction of that Nebraska policy which was to clothe the people of the Territories with a superior degree of self-government, beyond what they had ever had before. . . . In its main policy, and in its collateral object, it *has been nothing but a living, creeping lie from the time of its introduction, till to-day.* [Loud cheers.]

"I have intimated that I thought the agitation would not cease until a crisis should have been reached and passed. I have stated in what way I thought it would be reached and passed. I have said that it might go one way or the other. We might, by arresting the further spread of it and placing it where the fathers originally placed it, put it where the public mind should rest in the belief that it was in the course of ultimate extinction. Thus the agitation may cease. It may be pushed forward until it shall become alike lawful in all the States, old as well as new, North as well as South. I have said, and I repeat, my wish is that the further spread of it may be arrested, and that it may be placed where the public mind shall rest in the belief that it is in the course of ultimate extinction. [Great applause.] I have expressed that as my wish. I entertain the opinion upon evidence sufficient to my mind, that the fathers of this Government placed that institution where the public mind *did* rest in the belief that it was in the course of ultimate extinction. Let me ask why they made provision that the source of slavery—the African slave trade—should be cut off at the end of twenty years? Why did they make provision that in all the new territory we owned at that time slavery should be forever inhibited? Why stop its spread in one direction and cut off its source in another, if they did not look to its being placed in the course of ultimate extinction?

"Again; the institution of slavery is only mentioned in the Constitution of the United States two or three times, and in neither of these cases does the word 'slavery' or 'negro race' occur; but covert language is used each time, and for a purpose full of significance. What is the language in regard to the prohibition of the African slave trade? It runs in about this way: 'The migration or importations of such persons as any of the States now existing shall think proper to admit, shall not be prohibited by the Congress prior to the year one thousand eight hundred and eight.'

"The next allusion in the Constitution to the question of slavery and the black race, is on the subject of the basis of representation, and there the language used is, 'Representatives and direct taxes shall be apportioned among the several States which may be included within this Union, according to their respective numbers, which shall be determined by adding to the whole number of free persons, including those bound to service for a term of years, and excluding Indians not taxed—three fifths of all other persons.'

"It says 'persons,' not slaves, not negroes; but this 'three-fifths' can be applied to no other class amoung us than negroes.

"Lastly, in the provision for the reclamation of fugitive slaves it is said: 'No person held to service or labor in one State under the laws thereof escaping into another, shall in consequence of any law or regulation therein, be discharged from such service or labor, but shall be delivered up, on claim of the party to whom such service or labor may be due.' There again there is no mention of the word 'negro' or of slavery. In all three of these places, being the only allusions to slavery in the instrument, covert language is used. Language is used not suggesting that slavery existed or that the black race were among us. And I understand the contemporaneous history of those times to be that covert language was used with a purpose, and that purpose was that in our Constitution, which it was hoped and is still hoped will endure forever—when it should be read by intelligent and patriotic men, after the institution of slavery had passed from among us—there should be nothing on the face of the great charter of liberty suggesting that such a thing as negro slavery had ever existed among us. [Enthusiastic applause.] This is part of the evidence that the fathers of the Government expected and intended the institution of slavery to come to an end. They expected and intended that it should be in the course of ultimate extinction. And when I say that I desire to see the further spread of it arrested I only say I desire to see that done which the fathers have first done. When I say I desire to see it placed where the public mind will rest in the belief that it is in the course of ultimate extinction, I only say I desire to see it placed where they placed it. It is not true that our fathers, as Judge Douglas assumes, made this government part slave and part free. Understand the sense in which he puts it. He assumes that slavery is a rightful thing within itself,—was introduced by the framers of the Constitution. The exact truth is, that they found the institution existing among us, and they left it as they found it. But in making the government they left this institution with many clear marks of disapprobation upon it. They found slavery among them and they left it among them because of the difficulty—the absolute impossibility of its immediate removal. And when Judge Douglas asks me why we cannot let it remain part slave and part free as the fathers of the government made, he asks a question based upon an assumption which is itself a falsehood; and I turn upon him and ask him the question, when the policy that the fathers of the government had adopted in relation to this element among us was the best policy in the world—the only wise policy—the only policy that we can ever safely continue upon—that will ever give us peace unless this dangerous element masters us all and becomes a national institution—*I turn upon him and ask him why he could not let it alone?* [Great and prolong cheering.] I turn and ask him why he was driven to the necessity of introducing a *new policy* in regard to it? He has himself said he introduced a new policy. He said so in his speech on the 22nd of March of the present year, 1858. I ask him why he could not let it remain where our fathers left it? I ask you when he infers that I am in favor of setting the free and slave States at war, when the institution was placed in that attitude by those who made the constitution, *did they make any war?* ["No;" "no;" and cheers.] If we had no war out of it when thus placed, wherein is the ground of belief that we shall have war out of it if we return to that policy? ["No, no."] I maintain that we have not. I have proposed nothing more than a return to the policy of the fathers."

"The Quotation I Happened to Make"

"I confess, when I propose a certain measure of policy, it is not enough for me that I do not intend anything evil in the result, but it is incumbent on me to show that it has not a *tendency* to that result. I have met Judge Douglas in that point of view. I have not only made the declaration that I do not *mean* to produce a conflict between the States, but I have tried to show by fair reasoning, and I think I have shown to the minds of fair men, that I propose nothing but what has a most peaceful tendency. The quotation that I happened to make in that Springfield speech that 'a house divided against itself cannot stand,' and which has proved so offensive to the Judge, was part and parcel of the same thing. He tried to show that variety in the domestic institutions of the different States is necessary and indispensable. I do not dispute it. I have no controversy with Judge Douglas about that. I shall very readily agree with him that it would be foolish for us to insist upon having a cranberry law here, in Illinois, where we have no cranberries, because they have a cranberry law in Indiana, where they have cranberries." [Laughter, "good, good."] . . .

This conciliatory qualification of, until then, the most impressive political statement that Lincoln had made shows that he had yet to learn how it was resounding in his favor through the homes of the Northern states towards establishing solidarity of the Union, and in the Southern states towards secession.

Lincoln's Natural Defensive Offensive

"I understand as well as Judge Douglas, or anybody else, that . . . mutual accomodations are the cements which bind together the different parts of the Union, . . . they are the props of the house tending always to hold it up.

"But when I have admitted all this, I ask if there is any parallel between these things and this institution of slavery? . . . When have we had perfect peace in regard to this thing which I say is an element of discord in this Union? We have sometimes had peace, but when was it? It was when the institution of slavery remained quite where it was. We have had difficulty and turmoil whenever it has made a struggle to spread itself where it was not. I ask then, if experience does not speak in thunder tones, telling us that the policy which has given peace to the country heretofore, being returned to, gives the greatest promise of peace again."

The Only Serious Danger That Has Threatened Our Institutions

"Is it true that all the difficulty and agitation we have in regard to this institution of slavery springs from office seeking—from the mere ambition of politicians? Is that the truth? How many times have we had danger from this question? Go back to the day of the Missouri Compromise. Go back to the Nullification question, at the bottom of which lay this slavery question. Go back to the time of the Annexation of Texas. Go back to the troubles that led to the Compromise of 1851. You will find that every time, with the single exception of the Nullification question, they sprung from an endeavor to spread this institution. There never was a party in the history of this country, and there probably never will be of sufficient strength to disturb the general peace of the country. Parties themselves may be divided and quarrel on minor questions, yet it extends not beyond the parties themselves. But does *not* this question make a disturbance outside of political circles? Does it not enter into the churches and rend them asunder? What divided the great Methodist Church into two parts, North and South? What has raised this constant disturbance in every Presbyterian General Assembly that meets? What disturbed the Unitarian Church in this very city two years ago? What has jarred and shaken the great American Tract Society recently, not yet splitting it, but sure to divide it in the end. Is it not this same mighty, deep seated power that somehow operates on the minds of men, exciting and stirring them up in every avenue of society—in politics, in religion, in literature, in morals, in all the manifold relations of life? (Applause.) Is this the work of politicians? Is that irresistible power which for fifty years has shaken the government and agitated the people to be stilled and subdued by pretending that it is an exceedingly simple thing, and we ought not to talk about it? [Great cheers and laughter.] If you will get everybody else to stop talking about it, I assure I will quit before they have half done so. [Renewed laughter.] But where is the philosophy of statesmanship which assumes that you can quiet that disturbing element in our society which has disturbed us for more than half a century, which has been the only serious danger that has threatened our institutions—I say, where is the philosophy or the statesmanship based on the assumption that we are to quit talking about it [applause], and that the public mind is all at once to cease being agitated by it? Yet this is the policy here in the North that Douglas is advocating— that we are to care nothing about it! I ask you if it is not a false philosophy? Is it not a false statesmanship that undertakes to build up a system of policy upon the basis of caring nothing about *the very thing that every body does care the most about?* ["Yes, yes," and applause]—a thing which all experience has shown we care a very great deal about?" [Laughter and applause.]

Federal versus States' Rights

"The Judge alludes very often in the course of his remarks to the exclusive right which the States have to decide the whole thing for themselves. I agree with him very readily that the different States have that right. He is but fighting a man of straw when he assumes that I am contending against the right of the States to do as they please about it. Our controversy with him is in regard to the new Territories. We agree that when the States come in as States they have the right and the power to do as they please. We have no power as citizens of the free States or in our federal capacity as members of the Federal Union through the general government, to disturb slavery in the States where it exists. We profess constantly that we have no more inclination than belief in the power of the Government to disturb it; yet we are driven constantly to defend ourselves from the assumption that we are warring upon the rights of the *States.* What I insist upon is, that the new Territories shall be kept free from it while in the Territorial condition. Judge Douglas assumes that we have no interest in them—that we have no right whatever to interfere. I think we have some interest. I think that as white men we have. Do we not wish for an outlet for our surplus population, if I may so express myself? Do we not feel an interest in getting to that outlet with such institutions as we would like to have prevail there? If *you* go to the Territory opposed to slavery and another man comes upon the same ground with his slave, upon the assumption that the things are equal, it turns out that he has the equal right all his way and you have no part of it your way. If he goes in and makes it a slave Territory, and by consequence a slave State, is it not time that those who desire to have it a free State were on equal ground. Let me suggest it in a different way. How many Democrats are there about here ["a thousand"] who have left slave States and come into the free State of Illinois to get rid of the institution of slavery. [Another voice—"a thousand and one."] I reckon there are a thousand and one. [Laughter.] I will ask you if the policy you are now advocating had prevailed when this country was in a Territorial condition, where would you have gone to get rid of it? [Applause.] Where would you have found your free State or Territory to go to? And when hereafter, for any cause, the people in this place shall desire to find new homes, if they wish to be rid of the instituion, where will they find the place to go to?"* (Loud cheers.)

"Now irrespective of the moral aspect of this question as to whether there is a right or wrong in enslaving a negro, I am still in favor of our new Territories being in such a condition that white men may find a home—may find some spot where they can better their condition—where they can settle upon new soil and better their condition in life. [Great and continued cheering.] I am in favor of this not merely, (I must say it here as I have elsewhere,) for our own people who are born amongst us, but as an outlet for *free white people everywhere,* the world over—in which Hans and Baptiste and Patrick, and all other men from all the world, may find new homes and better their conditions in life." [Loud and long continues applause.]

The Real Issue—Is Slavery Morally Right or Wrong

"I have stated upon former occasions, and I may as well state again, what I understand to be the real issue in this controversy between Judge Douglas and myself. On the point of my wanting to make war between the free and the slave States, there has been no issue between us. So, too, when he assumes that I am in favor of introducing a perfect social and political equality between the white and black races. These are false issues, upon which Judge Douglas has tried to force the controversy. There is no foundation in truth for the charge that I maintain either of these propositions. The real issue in this controversy—the one pressing upon every mind—is the sentiment on the part of one class that looks upon the institution of slavery *as a wrong,* and of another class that *does not* look upon it as a wrong. The sentiment that contemplates the institution of slavery in this country as a wrong is the sentiment of the Republican party. It is the sentiment around which all their actions—all their arguments circle—from which all their propositions radiate. They look upon it as being a moral, social and political wrong; and while they contemplate it as such, they nevertheless have due regard for its actual existence among us, and the difficulties of getting rid of it in any satisfactory way and to all the constitutional obligations thrown about it. Yet having a due regard for these, they desire a policy in regard to it that looks to its not creating any more danger. They insist that it should as far as may be, *be treated* as a wrong, and one of the methods of treating it as a wrong is to *make provision that it shall grow no larger.* [Loud applause.] They also desire a policy that looks to a peaceful end of slavery at sometime, as being wrong. . . . .

"On this subject of treating it as a wrong, and limiting its spread, let me say a word. Has any thing ever threatened the existence of this Union save and except this very institution of Slavery? What is it that we hold most dear amongst us? Our own liberty and prosperity. What has ever threatened our liberty and prosperity save and except this institution of Slavery? If this is true, how do you propose to improve the condition of things by enlarging Slavery—by spreading it out and making it bigger? . . . You see this peaceful way of dealing with it as a wrong—restricting the spread of it and not allowing it to go into new countries where it has not already existed. That is the

---

*It should be recalled here that Lincoln's father moved his family from Kentucky to Indiana in order to live in a free State.

peaceful way, the old-fashioned way, the way in which the fathers themselves set us the example.

"On the other hand, I have said there is a sentiment which treats it as *not* being wrong. That is the Democratic sentiment of this day. I do not mean to say that every man who stands within that range positively asserts that it is right. That class will include all who positively assert that it is right, and all who like Judge Douglas treat it as indifferent and do not say it is either right or wrong. These two classes of men fall within the general class of those who do not look upon it as a wrong."

Public sentiment, in the Northern and in the Southern states, at this time and leading up to and during the Civil War divided into intensely antislavery and proslavery and straddling groups. This complicated the division of sentiment between the preservation of the Union *versus* States' Rights to Secession, and confused the effort to prevent war and later to conduct it successsfully.

. . . "The Democratic policy in regard to that institution will not tolerate the merest breath, the slightest hint, of the least degree of wrong about it. Try it by some of Judge Douglas' arguments. He says he 'don't care whether it is voted up or voted down' in the Territories. I do not care myself in dealing with that expression, whether it is intended to be expressive of his individual sentiments on the subject, or only of the national policy he desires to have established. It is alike valuable for my purpose. Any man can say that who does not see anything wrong in slavery, but no man can logically say it who does see a wrong in it; because no man can logically say he don't care whether a wrong is voted up or voted down. He may say he don't care whether an indifferent thing is voted up or down, but he must logically have a choice between a right thing and a wrong thing. He contends that whatever community wants slaves has a right to have them. So they have if it is not a wrong. But if it is a wrong, he cannot say people have a right to do wrong. He says that upon the score of equality, slaves would be allowed to go [be taken] in a new Territory, like other property. This is strictly logical if there is no difference between it and other property. If it and other property are equal, his argument is entirely logical. But if you insist that one is wrong and the other right, there is no use to institute a comparison between right and wrong. You may turn over everything in the Democratic policy from beginning to end, whether in the shape it takes on the statute book, in the shape it takes in the Dred Scott decision, in the shape it takes in conversation or the shape it takes in short maxim-like arguments— it everywhere carefully excludes the idea that there is anything wrong in it."

We have previously called attention to Lincoln's habit since boyhood, of stating mathematical and other logical conclusions directly and in reverse or indirectly, as if to verify or fix them in his mind against doubt. This method of argument made his ideas stick in the minds of his audience.

"That is the real issue. That is the issue that will continue in this country when these poor tongues of Judge Douglas and myself shall be silent. It is the eternal struggle between these two principles— right and wrong— throughout the world. They are the two principles that have stood face to face from the beginning of time; and will ever continue to struggle. The one is the common right of humanity and the other the divine right of kings. It is the same principle in whatever shape it develops itself. It is the same spirit that says, 'you work and toil and earn bread, and I'll eat it.' [Loud applause.] No matter in what shape it comes, whether from the mouth of a king who seeks to bestride the people of his own nation and live by the fruit of their labor, or from one race of man as an apology for enslaving another race, it is the same tyrannical principle."

Douglas used the art of repetitive aggressive suggestion that his ideas on the regulation of Slavery were right and practical by Constitution and Supreme Court judgment, and Lincoln's were wrong both ways and impractical, as causes of war. Douglas' philosophy, like that of Chief Justice Taney and slavery's defenders, in holding that slaves were property and not "people," virtually maintained that might makes right. Lincoln adhered religiously to the logic of equal Federal constitutional rights for negroes as persons, although he held citizenship to be conditional on State constitutional decision. While he lost in immediate appeal in the senatorial race, his moral philosophy continued to grow in impressiveness, in the free States in his favor and in the slave States against him.

Lincoln Predicts Rightly and Wrongly

"I was glad to express my gratitude at Quincy, and I re-express it here to Judge Douglas— *that he looks to no end of the institution of slavery.* That will help the people to see where the struggle really is. It will hereafter place with us all men who really do wish the wrong may have an end. And whenever we can get rid of the fog which obscures the real question— when we can get Judge Douglas and his friends to avow a policy looking to its perpetuation— we can get out from among them that class of men and bring them to the side of those who treat it as a wrong. Then there will soon be an end of it, and that end will be its 'ultimate extinction.' Whenever the issue can be distinctly made, and all extraneous matter thrown out so that men can fairly see the real difference between the parties, this controversy will soon be settled, and it will be done peaceably too. There will be no war, no violence. It will be placed again where the wisest and best men of the world, placed it. . . . I now say that willingly or unwillingly, purposely or without purpose, Judge Douglas has been the most prominent instrument in changing the position of the institution of slavery which the fathers of the government expected to come to an end ere this— *and putting it upon Brooks' cotton gin basis,* (great applause,)— placing it where he openly confesses he has no desire there shall ever be an end of it." [Renewed applause.]

Lincoln Rebukes Douglas' "Monstrous Talk"

When the United States was organized twelve of the thirteen states had legalized slavery. Within a few years thereafter New Hampshire, Vermont, Massachusetts, Rhode Island, Connecticut, New York and Pennsylvania abolished the institution. The transition of public sentiment in opposition to slavery did not move from above downward through legislative action but developed in the form of sporadic community religious and moral revulsions of sentiment which increased in number until, as an allied force, it was able to dominate the proslavery vote of the State. Herein Douglas, as a young Vermonter, had intimate contact with the ways of working of the will-of-people in communities, and his argument was neither impractical nor illogical when applied to States' rights. However, as Lincoln held, it was illegal when applied to Territories, which did not have the right of self-government. Lincoln's acumen in making this legal discrimination gave him top rank as a constitutional lawyer and political philosopher.

"Judge Douglas [has] constantly said, before the decision, that whether they could or not [exclude slavery], *was a question for the Supreme Court.* (Cheers.) But after the Court has made the decision he virtually says it is *not* a question for the Supreme Court, but for the people. [Renewed applause.] And how is it he tells us they can exclude it? He says it needs 'police regulations,' and that admits of 'unfriendly legislation.' Although it is a right established by the constitution of the United States to take a slave into a Territory of the United States and hold him as property, yet unless the Territorial Legislature will give friendly legislation, and, more especially, if they adopt unfriendly legislation, they can practically exclude him. Now without meeting this proposition as a matter of fact, I pass to consider the real constitutional obligation. Let me take the gentleman who looks me in the face before me, and let us suppose he is a member of the Territorial Legislature. The first thing he will do will be to swear that he will support the Constitution of the United States. His neighbor by his side in the Territory has slaves and needs Territorial legislation to enable him to enjoy that constitutional right. Can he withhold the legislation which his neighbor needs for the enjoyment of a right which is fixed in his favor in the Constitution of the United States which he has sworn to support? Can he withhold it without violating his oath? And more especially, can he pass unfriendly legislation to violate his oath? Why this is a *monstrous* sort of talk about the Constitution of the United States! (Great applause.) *There has never been as outlandish or lawless a doctrine from the mouth of any respectable man on earth.* [Tremendous cheers.] I do not believe it is a constitutional right to hold slaves in a Territory of the United States. I believe the decision was improperly made and I go for reversing it. Judge Douglas is furious against those who go for reversing a decision. But he is for legislating it out of all force while the law itself stands. I repeat that there has never been so monstrous a doctrine uttered from the mouth of a respectable man. [Loud cheers.]

"I suppose most of us, (I know it of myself,) believe that the people of the Southern States are entitled to a Congressional fugitive slave law—that it is a fixed right in the Constitution. But it cannot be made available to them without Congressional legislation. In the Judge's language, it is a 'barren right' which needs legislation before it can become efficient and valuable to the persons to whom it is guaranteed. And as the right is constitutional I agree that the legislation shall be granted to it—and that not that we like the institution of slavery. We profess to have no taste for running and catching niggers—at least I profess no taste for that job at all. Why then do I yield support to a fugitive slave law? Because I do not understand that the Constitution, which guarantees that right, can be supported without it. And if I believed that the right to hold a slave in a Territory was equally fixed in the Constitution with the right to reclaim fugitives, I should be bound to give it the legislation necessary to support it. I say that no man can deny his obligation to give the necessary legislation to support slavery in a Territory, who believes it is a constitutional right to have it there. No man can, who does not give the Abolitionist an argument to deny the obligation enjoined by the constitution to enact a fugitive slave law. Try it now. It is the strongest abolition argument ever made. I say if that Dred Scott decision is correct then the right to hold slaves in a Territory is equally a constitutional right with the right of a slaveholder to have his runaway returned. No one can show the distinction between them. The one is express, so that we cannot deny it. The other is construed to be in the constitution, so that he who believes the decision to be correct believes in the right. And the man who argues that by unfriendly legislation, in spite of that constitutional right, slavery may be driven from the Territories, cannot avoid furnishing an argument by which Abolitionists may deny the obligation to return fugitives, and claim the power to pass laws unfriendly to the right of the slaveholder to reclaim his fugitive. I do not know how such an argument may strike a popular assembly like this, but I defy anybody to go before a body of men whose minds are educated to estimating evidence and reasoning, and show that there is an iota of difference between the constitutional right to reclaim a fugitive, and the constitutional right to hold a slave, in a Territory, provided this Dred Scott decision is correct. (Cheers.) I defy any man to make an argument that will justify unfriendly legislation to deprive a slaveholder of his right to hold his slave in a Territory, that will not equally, in all its length, breadth and thickness furnish an argument for nullifying the fugitive slave law. Why there is not such an Abolitionist in the nation as Douglas, after all." [Loud and enthusiastic applause.]

As the campaign drew to a close Lincoln and Douglas continued to make speeches almost daily, each repeating the claims, charges and arguments he used in the debates without accepting his opponent's rebuttals and denials.

"What I Most Dread"

To N.B. Judd (10, 20, 1858) Lincoln wrote:

"I now have a high degree of confidence that we shall succeed, if we are not over-run with fradulent votes to a greater extent than usual. . . .

"What I most dread is that they will introduce into the doubtful districts numbers of men who are legal voters in all respects except *residence* and who will swear to residence and thus put it beyond our power to exclude them. They can & I fear will swear falsely on that point, because they know it is next to impossible to convict them of Perjury upon it."

To Judd again (10, 24, 1858): "Just out of Hancock. Spoke three times in that county. *Tight,* with chances slightly in our favor."

Corrects an Ugly Douglas Imputation

Douglas made ugly imputations that Lincoln favored the evasion of taxes by the Central Railroad. Lincoln's reply is a gem of moral confidence, with dignity, simplicity, clarity, economy and honesty of statement that ends with placing "the saddle on the other horse" by demonstrating the false prejudice of his opponent. In a speech at Carthage (10, 22, 1858) he said (as reported by the Chicago *Press and Tribune*):

"I learned that Judge Douglas had been imputing to me and my friends a purpose to release the Central Railroad Company from paying into the State Treasury the seven per cent, upon their gross earnings, which, by law, they are now bound to do. I learn he repeated the same imputations at Pekin, Oquawka, Monmouth and this place, though he has never mentioned it at any of our joint meetings, or elsewhere in my presence. I mention it now to correct any false impression that may have been made. I understand the Judge states, among other things, that I once received a fee of $5,000 from that Company. My partner and I did receive such fee under the following circumstances: By their charter, the Company are bound to make periodical payments into the State Treasury, in exemption of all other taxes. This exempts them from county and city taxes. The Legislature intended, as I understand, in consideration of the large land grant, to make the Company pay about as much as they could bear; and to make them pay it into the State Treasury, so that the *whole* people could share the benefit, instead of paying any to the counties through which the road passes, to the exclusion of those through which it does not pass. This was a fair way of dealing with the whole people, as was thought. The county of McLean, one of the counties through which the road passes, claimed that the exemption was unconstitutional, and that the Company was bound to pay county taxes on their property within the limits of the county; and the parties went to Court to try the question. The Railroad Company employed me as one of their lawyers in the case, the county having declined to employ me. The decision, I thought, and still think, was worth half a million dollars to them. I wanted them to pay me $5,000, and they wanted to pay me about $500. I sued them and got the $5,000. This is the whole truth about the fee; and what tendency it has to prove that I received any of the people's money, or that I am on very cozy terms with the Railroad Company, I do not comprehend.

"It is a matter of interest to you that the Company shall not be released from their obligations to pay money into the State Treasury. Every dollar they so pay relieves the whole people of just so much in the way of taxation. I am a candidate for no office wherein I could release them, if elected. The State Legislature alone can release them. Therefore, all you need to do is to know your candidates for the Legislature, how they will vote on the question of release, if elected. I doubt not every candidate who is a friend of mine is ready to show his hand; and perhaps it would be well to have Judge Douglas' friends show their hands also. See to your members of the Legislature, and you are beyond the power of all others as to releasing the Central Railroad from its obligations. This is your perfect security."

Last Speech of the Campaign

In his last speech of the campaign, at Springfield (10, 30, 1858), serenity, sweetness and light and love of peace and friendship characterized
Lincoln's attitude, much as it did in his immortal farewell address to the
people of Springfield two years later. We note how with paternal fortitude
and heroic cadence he balances, in Shakespearean manner, *essentials*
with *avoidants* in his statement of political principles.

> "My friends, today closes the discussions of this canvass. The planting
> and the culture are over; and there remains but the preparation, and the
> harvest.
> "I stand here surrounded by friends— some *political, all personal* friends,
> I trust. May I be indulged, in this closing scene, to say a few words of myself.
> I have borne a laborious, and, in some respects to myself, a painful part in
> the contest. Through it all, I have neither assailed, nor wrestled with any
> part of the constitution. The legal right of the Southern people to reclaim
> their fugitives I have constantly admitted. The legal right of Congress to
> interfere with their institution in the States, I have constantly denied. In
> resisting the spread of slavery to new territory, and with that, what appears
> to me to be a tendency to subvert the first principle of free government
> itself my whole effort has consisted. To the best of my judgment I have
> labored *for*, and not *against* the Union. As I have not felt, so I have not
> expressed any harsh sentiment towards our Southern bretheren. I have con-
> stantly declared, as I really believe, the only difference between them and us,
> is the difference of circumstances.
> "I have meant to assail the motives of no party, or individual; and if I
> have, in any instance (of which I am not conscious) departed from my
> purpose, I regret it.
> "I have said that in some respects the contest has been painful to me.
> Myself, and those with whom I act have been constantly accused of a pur-
> pose to destroy the Union; and bespattered with every imaginable odious
> epithet; and some who were friends, as it were but yesterday have made
> themselves most active in this. I have cultivated patience, and made no
> attempt at a retort.
> "Ambition has been ascribed to me. God knows how sincerely I prayed
> from the first that this field of ambition might not be opened. I claim no
> insensibility to political honors; but today could the Missouri restriction be
> restored, and the whole slavery question replaced on the old ground of
> 'toleration' by *necessity* where it exists, with unyielding hostility to the
> spread of it, on principle, I would, in consideration, gladly agree, that Judge
> Douglas should never be *out*, and I never *in*, an office, so long as we both
> or either, live."

The *Illinois State Journal* (11, 1, 1858), from which the preceding
copy is taken, commented: "The conclusion of the speech was one of
the most eloquent appeals ever addressed to the American people. It was
received with spontaneous bursts of enthusiasm unequaled by any thing
ever before enacted in this city."

Lincoln's conscious cultivation of patient endurance and avoidance of intolerant retort, in fighting against odious epithet for the principles of free government, were conducive to wholesome personal maturation as well as reaping a harvest of Northern supporters. He had greatly increased in personal integrity and the mastery of his old tendency to develop nervous melancholia and anxiety under unjust accusation and fatigue; he had developed a style of expression that the people loved for its dignity, simplicity, clarity, logic and honesty of statement; and he had at last arrived, in his own mind, at a definite comprehension of the critical issues in the public mind that demanded somehow to be solved.

History's Verdict on the Debates

An unbiased reconsideration of history, on the positions and arguments of Lincoln and Douglas, shows that they were in fundamental agreement on most questions of political policy. Douglas was bolder and more opportunistic in his statement of principles than Lincoln, who was generally more cautious, logical and moral. Douglas was more bludgeoning and ridiculing and Lincoln more sedate and serious but at times satirically witty. Both men neglected other political issues and policies which were then nationally important and talked as if there were only one question before the people, the extension or prevention of slavery in the territories.

Douglas' argument on community sovereignty within the State proved for the time to be more convincing to Illinois voters, as the practical means, under the Constitution, of solving territorial problems of slavery. Lincoln's argument that such popular sovereignty violated the intent of the Constitution when it opposed the Supreme Court's decision; and that the Supreme Court's Dred Scott decision was in violation of the intent of the Constitution; and that a conspiracy existed, involving Douglas, President Buchanan and Chief Justice Taney, to extend slavery throughout the nation was then less impressive. Illinois, like every state and territory in the Union, was seething with plots to abolish slavery and counterplots to extend it. Douglas won the election and is credited by some historians as having won the debates.

The arguments were inconclusive and accomplished little in solving the national slavery problem, but they gained for both speakers national publicity. This was invaluable to Lincoln, the locally known Illinois lawyer whose cautious policy of advocating the retention of slavery in the states where it existed and the justice of the fugitive slave law, while urging its prohibition in the territories, won the support of many Republicans, old Whigs, Free Soilers, Abolitionists and antislavery Democrats. The potential influence of this following was to be felt in the next two years.

"The Emotions of Defeat"

The allotment of counties in districts for the election of members to the State legislature gave Douglas a majority vote here, insuring his election, although Lincoln obtained a majority of 4,000 in the popular vote. Lincoln had forseen this disadvantage and derived no little encouragement in defeat from the popular strength of his political principles.

Douglas is said to have spent over $50,000 to carry on the campaign whereas Lincoln spent about $500. We get some idea of how he felt about the election from the following comments in his letters.

Publication, early in the campaign, in the Missouri *Republican* of a letter by Senator J. J. Crittenden of Frankfort, Kentucky, expressing approval of Senator Douglas for reelection had caused Lincoln to write him in protest (see previous chapter). After the election he wrote again to Crittenden (11, 4, 1858) to assure him that he did not harbor resentment for his defeat.

> "The emotions of defeat, at the close of a struggle in which I felt more than merely a selfish interest, and to which defeat the use of your name contributed largely, are fresh upon me; but, even in this mood, I can not for a moment suspect you of anything dishonorable."

"Two Years Hence—I Shall Fight in the Ranks"

Two weeks later he wrote humorously to the Republican State Committee chairman, Hon. N. B. Judd (11, 15, 1858). The letter indicates that he had not yet thought of himself as a potential presidential candidate in 1860.

> "I have the pleasure to inform you that I am convalescent and hoping these lines may find you in the same improving state of health. Doubtless you have suspected for some time that I entertain a personal wish for a term in the US Senate; and had the suspicion taken the shape of a direct charge, I think I could not have truthfully denied it. But let the past as nothing be.
>
> "For the future my view is that the fight must go on. The returns here are not yet completed, . . . we have some hundred and twenty thousand clear Republican votes. That pile is worth keeping together. It will elect a state trustee [treasurer?] two years hence.
>
> "In that day I shall fight in the ranks, but I shall be in no ones way for any of the places. I am especially for Trumbulls reelection; and by the way this brings me to the principal object of this letter. Can you not take your draft of an apportionment law, and carefully revise it till it shall be strictly & obviously just in all particulars, & then by an early & persistent effort get enough of the enemies men to enable you to pass it. I believe if you & Peck [E] make a job of it begin early & work earnestly & quietly, you can succeed in it. Unless something be done Trumbull is eventually beaten two years hence. Take this into serious consideration."

Lincoln continued to believe that the most effective method of winning public approval and votes was to go among the people and work early, earnestly and quietly from man to man. Later, as President, he used daily a large part of his time in talking with people individually to get their ideas and sentiments on the great problems confronting his administration.

"I Am Willing to Pay According to My Ability"

The Republican debts of the campaign (totaling about $2,500) had to be paid and Lincoln's letter to Judd (11, 16, 1858) reveals his economic status and prompt willingness to pay on it.

"Yours of the 15th. is just received. I *wrote* you the same day. As to the pecuniary matter, I am willing to pay according to my ability; but I am the poorest hand living to get others to pay. I have been on expences so long without earning any thing that I am absolutely without money now for even household purposes. Still, if you can put in two hundred and fifty dollars for me towards discharging the debt of the Committee, I will allow it when you and I settle the private matter between us. This, with what I have already paid, and with an outstanding note of mine, will exceed my subscription of five hundred dollars. This too, is exclusive of my ordinary expences during the campaign, all which being added to my loss of time and business, bears pretty heavily upon one no better off in world's goods than I; but as I had the post of honor, it is not for me to be over-nice.

"You are feeling badly. *'And this too shall pass away.'* Never fear."

This last bit of consoling advice to a friend was Lincoln's own personal axiom, applied constantly to himself. It was much like that he gave his friend Speed, 17 years past, to reassure him against depressive anxiety over getting married.

"I Am Glad I Made the Race"

In a letter (11, 19, 1858) to his old friend and personal confidant, Dr. A. G. Henry, now living in Oregon, Lincoln expressed his most intimate thoughts on the campaign:

"You doubtless have seen, ere this, the result of the election here. Of course I *wished*, but I did not much *expect* a better result. The popular vote [of the St]ate is with us; . . . John and George Weber and several such old democrats were furiously for me. As a general rule, out of Sangamon, as well as in it, much of the plain old democracy is with us. while nearly all the old exclusive silk-stocking whiggery is against us. I do not mean nearly all the old whig party; but nearly all of the nice exclusive sort. And why not? There has been nothing in politics since the Revolution so congenial to their nature, as the present position of the great democratic party.

"I am glad I made the late race. It gave me a hearing on the great and durable question of the age, which I could have had in no other way; and though I now sink out of view, and shall be forgotten, I believe I have made some marks which will tell for the cause of civil liberty long after I am gone."

"Seed Has Been Sown That Will Yet Produce Fruit"

In a letter (11, 19, 1858) to Illinois Legislator Anson Miller Lincoln made a prediction that indicated the attitude of prophetic expectancy he would hold from now on.

"Your very kind and complimentary letter of the 15th. was received yesterday; and for which I sincerely thank you. In the last canvass I strove to do my whole duty both to our cause, and to the kind friends who had assigned me the post of honor; and now if those friends find no cause to regret that they did not assign that post to other hands, I have none for having made the effort, even though it has ended in personal defeat. I hope and believe seed has been sown that will yet produce fruit. The fight must go on. Douglas managed to be supported both as the best means to *break down,* and to *uphold* the slave power. No ingenuity can long keep those opposing elements in harmony. Another explosion will come before a great while."

To E. A. Paine he wrote (11, 19, 1858) in the same vein: "Well, the election is over; and, in the main point, we are beaten. Still, my view is that the fight must go on. Let no one falter. The *question* is not half settled. New splits and divisions will soon be upon our adversaries; and we shall [have] fun again."

"My Scrap-Book"

"I wish to preserve a Set of the late debates (if they may be called so) between Douglas and myself," Lincoln wrote to Dr. C. H. Ray (11, 20, 1858). "To enable me to do so, please get two copies of each number of your paper containing the whole, and send them to me by Express; and I will pay you for the papers & for your trouble. I wish the two sets, in order to lay one away in the raw, and to put the other in a Scrap-book. Remember, if part of any debate is on *both* sides of one sheet, it will take two sets to make a scrap book.

"I believe, according to a letter of yours to Hatch you are 'feeling like h—ll yet.' Quit that, You will soon feel better. Another 'blow-up' is coming; and we shall have fun again. Douglas managed to be supported as both the best instrument to *put down* and to *uphold* the slave power; but no ingenuity can long keep these antagonisms in harmony."

Lincoln's negotiations a year later (3, 26, 1859) with W. A. Ross, for the joint publication of the speeches by himself and Douglas, reflect the equalitarian sportmanship of the thoroughgoing gentleman.

"I would really be pleased with a publication substantially as you propose. But I would suggest a few variations from your plan. I would not include the Republican platform; because that would give the work a onesided & party cast, unless the democratic platform was also included.

"I would not take *all* the speeches from the *Press & Tribune,* but I would take mine from that paper; and those of Judge Douglas from the Chicago *Times.* This would represent each of us, as reported by his own friends, and thus be mutual, and fair. I would take the speeches alone; rigidly excluding all comments of the newspapers.

"I would include the correspondance between Judge Douglas and myself which led to the joint discussions."

After describing his own scrap-book and naming the speeches it contained, he continued:

"In my own speeches I have corrected only a few small typographical errors. The other speeches I have not touched; but merely pasted them in from the papers in which they were reported.

"Judge Douglas would have the right to correct typographical errors in his, if he desired; but I think the necessity, in his case, would be less than in mine; because he had two hired reporters travelling with him, and probably revised their manuscripts before they went to press; while I had no reporter of my own, but depended on a very excellent one sent by the Press & Tribune; but who never waited to show me his notes or manuscripts; so that the first I saw of my speeches, after delivering them, was in the Press & Tribune precisely as they now stand.

"My Scrap-book would be the best thing to print from; still, as it cost me a good deal of labor to get it up, and as I am very desirous to preserve the substance of it permanently, I would not let it go out of my own control. If an arrangement could be made to print it in Springfield, under my own supervision, I would allow the Scrap-book to be used, and would claim no share in any profit that could be made out of the publication."

Instructions to Publish without Changes or Comment

G. M. Parsons of Ohio arranged with Lincoln and Douglas to publish their joint debates. To Parsons Lincoln instructed (12, 19, 1859):

"Your letter of the 7th inst. accompanied by a similar one from the governor elect, the Republican State officers, and the Republican members of the State Board of Equalization of Ohio, both requesting of me, for publication in permanent form, copies of the political debates between Senator Douglas and myself, last year, has been received. With my grateful acknowledgements to both you and them, for the very flattering terms in which the request is communicated, I transmit you the copies. The copies I send you are reported and printed, by the respective friends of Senator Douglas and myself, at the time—that is, his by his friends, and mine by mine. It would be an unwarrantable liberty for us to change a word or a letter in his, and the changes I have made in mine, you perceive, are verbal only, and very few in number. I wish the reprint to be precisely as the copies I send, without any comment whatever."

Not Justifiable to Change Arguments

James W. Sheahan, editor of the Chicago *Times,* requested copies of the speeches in the Debates, and, it seems, he assumed that naturally extensive revisions had been made of some of the statements. Lincoln answered (1, 24, 1860):

"Yours of the 21st., requesting copies of my speeches now in progress of publication in Ohio, is received. I have no such copies now at my control; having sent the only sett I ever had, to Ohio. Mr. Geo. M. Parsons has taken an active part among those who have the matter in charge, in Ohio; and I understand Messrs. Follett, Foster & Co are to be the publishers. I make no objection to any satisfactory arrangement you may make with Mr. Parsons and the publishers; and, if it will facilitate you, you are at liberty to show them this note.

"You labor under a mistake, somewhat injurious to me, if you suppose I have *revised* the speeches, in any just sense of the word. I only made some small verbal corrections, most such as an intelligent reader would make for himself; not feeling justified to do more, when republishing the speeches along with those of Senator Douglas—his and mine being mutually answers and replies to one another."

"As You Have Complimented Me"

When Abraham Jonas applied for a copy of the debates he received the following warm reply (2, 4, 1860):

"Yours of the 3rd. inquiring how you can get a copy of the debates now being published in Ohio, is received. As you are one of my most valued friends, and have complimented me by the expression of a wish for the book, I propose doing myself the honor of presenting you with one, as soon as I can. By the arrangement our Ohio friends have made with the publishers, I am to have one hundred copies gratis. When I shall receive them I will send you one by Express. I understand they will not be out before March; and I probably shall be absent about that time, so that you must not be disappointed if you do not receive yours before about the middle of that month."

Chapter XXXIV

PAVING THE WAY TO
NATIONAL RECOGNITION

With amazing energy, Senator Douglas, the dominant leader of his party, began immediately after his election to work for the Democratic nomination for President in 1860. He made numerous speeches in the principal cities of the South and North, ever advocating a form of popular sovereignty in the Territories that permitted the introduction of slavery, without moral prejudice as to whether it was right or wrong, before the residents could vote for its acceptance or rejection.

This policy, based on the reasoning of Chief Justice Taney in expressing the Dred Scott decision, had the approval of the leading Southern Democrats, including Jefferson Davis and Alexander Stevens, as well as many Northern Democrats in President Buchanan's administration.

In opposition to this policy, Northern abolitionism grew stronger and more aggressive, and its intolerant demands were being countered with Southern claims of States's Rights and threat of secession, which in turn excited talk of war on both sides. Leading Eastern Republicans, like Horace Greeley, alarmed at the danger of war and looking for a just, peaceful compromise, were favorably impressed with Douglas as the man who could resolve the conflict over slavery.

Lincoln Predicts Fate of Douglas' Double Strategy

Lincoln's foresight of the logical steps ahead in Douglas' strategy to win the coming Democratic nomination for President proved amazingly accurate. It showed an unusual capacity for analyzing the nature and predicting the course of allied and antagonistic political forces in government.

"Douglas has gone South, making characteristic speeches, and seeking to re-instate himself in that section." Lincoln wrote to Senator Trumbull (12, 11, 1858). "The majority of the democratic politicians of the nation mean to kill him; but I doubt whether they will adopt the aptest way to do it. Their true way is to present him with no new test, let him into the Charleston Convention, and then outvote him, and nominate another. In that case he will have no pretext for bolting the nomination, and will be as powerless as they can wish. On the other hand, if they push a Slave code upon him, as a test, he will bolt at once, turn upon us, as in the case of Lecompton, and claim that all Northern men shall make common cause in electing him President as the best means of breaking down the Slave power. In that case, the democratic party go into a minority inevitably; and the struggle in the whole North will be, as it was in Illinois last summer and fall, whether the Republican party can maintain it's identity, or be broken up to form the tail of Douglas' new kite. Some of our great Republican doctors will then have a splendid chance to swallows the pills they so eagerly prescribed for us last Spring. Still I hope they will not swallow them; and although I do not feel that I owe the said doctors much, I will help them, to the best of my ability, to reject the said pills. The truth is, the Republican principle can, in no wise live with Douglas; and it is arrant folly now, as it was last Spring, to waste time, and scatter labor already performed in dallying with him."

To Alexander Sympson (12, 12, 1858): "I have an abiding faith that we shall beat them in the long run. Step by step the objects of the leaders will become too plain for the people to stand on. I write merely to let you know that I am neither dead nor dying."

Those Who Support Douglas "Cut Their Own Throats"

In a reply (1, 8, 1859) to an inquiry from W. H. Wells of Pennsylvania, a young printer, Lincoln expressed his feeling about Douglas' policy most vividly.

"I regret to say that the joint discussions between Judge Douglas and myself have been published in no shape except in the newspaper reports; and that I have no copy of them, or even of the single one at Freeport, which I could send you. By dint of great labor since the election, I have got together a nearly, (not quite) complete single set to preserve myself. I shall preserve your address, and if I can, in a reasonable time, lay my hand on an old paper containing the Freeport discussion, I will send it to you.

"All dallying with Douglas by Republicans, who are such at heart, is, at the very least, time, and labor lost; and all such, who so dally with him, will yet bite their lips in vexation for their own folly. His policy, which rigorously excludes all idea of there being any *wrong* in slavery, does lead inevitably to the nationalization of the institution; and all who deprecate that consummation, and yet are seduced into his support, do but cut their own throats."

Reassures Senator Trumbull

Douglas Democrats tried repeatedly to excite bad feeling and distrust between the antislavery Democrats and Abolitionists and Whigs that had united to form the Republican party. Lincoln as a leader of the latter element reassured Trumbull, the leader of the Democratic division, of his loyalty (2, 3, 1859).

"The article mentioned by you, prepared for the Chicago Journal, I have not seen; nor do I wish to see it, though I heard of it a month, or more, ago. Any effort to put enmity between you and me, is as idle as the wind. I do not for a moment doubt that you, Judd, Cook, Palmer, and the republicans generally, coming from the old democratic ranks, were as sincerely anxious for my success in the late contest, as I myself, and the old whig republicans were. And I beg to assure you, beyond all possible cavil, that you can scarcely be more anxious to be sustained two years hence than I am that you shall be so sustained. I can not conceive it possible for me to be a rival of yours, or to take sides against you in favor of any rival. Nor do I think there

is much danger of the old democratic and whig elements of our party breaking
into opposing factions. They certainly shall not, if I can prevent it."

"Our Principles Will Live Under All Circumstances"

Letters to close political friends show how Lincoln's mind, after his
defeat by Douglas, was becoming definitely set upon treating slavery
as a moral political issue and organizing the young Republican party
around this principle. In his speech at Chicago (3, 1, 1859) before a
Republican rally, he boldly separated the sheep from the goats and
warned those who believed in the straddling policies of Douglas, including Horace Greeley and the New York *Tribune,* of their political
fate unless they turned steadfastly to the right.

In this first political speech after his defeat Lincoln expressed his
gratitude for the support given him by the Republicans of Chicago
and other communities of Illinois in the recent senatorial canvass, and
ingeniously appealed to all members of his party to unite with him for
the coming campaign of 1860:

"I am afraid of the result upon organized action where great results are
in view, if any of us allow ourselves to seek out minor or separate points
on which there may be difference of views as to policy and right, and let
them keep us from uniting in action upon a great principle in a cause on
which we all agree; or are deluded into the belief that all can be brought to
consider alike and agree upon every minor point before we unite and press
forward in organization, asking the cooperation of all good men in that
resistance to the extension of slavery upon which we all agree. I am afraid
that such methods would result in keeping the friends of liberty waiting
longer than we ought to. I say this for the purpose of suggesting that we
consider whether it would not be better and wiser, so long as we all agree
that this matter of slavery is a moral, political and social wrong, and ought
to be treated as a wrong, not to let anything minor or subsidiary to that
main principle and purpose make us fail to cooperate.

"One other thing, and that again I say in no spirit of unkindness.
There was a question amongst Republicans all the time of the canvass of
last year, and it has not quite ceased yet, whether it was not the true and
better policy for the Republicans to make it their chief object to reelect
Judge Douglas to the Senate of the United States. Now, I differed with
those who thought that the true policy, but I have never said an unkind
word of any one entertaining that opinion. I believe most of them were as
sincerely the friends of our cause as I claim to be myself; yet I thought they
were mistaken, and I speak of this now for the purpose of justifying the course
that I took and the course of those who supported me. In what I say now
there is no unkindness even towards Judge Douglas. I have believed, that
in the Republican situation in Illinois, if we, the Republicans of this State,
had made Judge Douglas our candidate for the Senate of the United States
last year and had elected him, there would to-day be no Republican party
in this Union. I believed that the principles around which we have rallied
and organized that party would live; they will live under all circumstances,

while we will die. They would reproduce another party in the future. But in the meantime all the labor that had been done to build up the present Republican party would be entirely lost, and perhaps twenty years of time, before we would again have formed around that principle as solid, extensive, and formidable an organization as we have, standing shoulder to shoulder to-night in harmony and strength around the Republican banner.

"It militates not at all against this view to tell us that the Republicans could make something in the State of New York by electing to Congress John B. Haskin, who occupied a position similar to Judge Douglas, or that they could make something by electing Hickman, of Pennsylvania, or Davis, of Indiana. It think it likely that they could and do make something by it; but it is false logic to assume that for that reason anything could be gained by us in electing Judge Douglas in Illinois. And for this reason: It is no disparagement to these men, Hickman and Davis, to say that individually they were comparatively small men, and the Republican party could take hold of them, use them, elect them, absorb them, expel them, or do whatever it pleased with them, and the Republican organization be in no wise shaken. But it is not so with Judge Douglas. Let the Republican party of Illinois dally with Judge Douglas; let them fall in behind him and make him their candidate, and they do not absorb him; he absorbs them. They would come out at the end all Douglas men, all claimed by him as having indorsed every one of his doctrines upon the great subject with which the whole nation is engaged at this hour—that the question of negro slavery is simply a question of dollars and cents, that the Almighty has drawn a line across the continent, on one side of which labor—the cultivation of the soil—must always be performed by slaves. It would be claimed that we, like him, do not care whether slavery is voted up or voted down. Had we made him our candidate and given him a great majority, we should have never heard an end of declarations by him that we had indorsed all these dogmas. Try it by an example.

"You all remember that at the last session of Congress there was a measure introduced in the Senate by Mr. Crittenden, which proposed that the pro-slavery Lecompton constitution should be left to a vote to be taken in Kansas, and if it and slavery were adopted Kansas should be at once admitted as a slave State. That same measure was introduced into the House by Mr. Montgomery, and therefore got the name of the Crittenden-Montgomery bill; and in the House of Representatives the Republicans all voted for it under the peculiar circumstances in which they found themselves placed. You may remember also that the New York *Tribune,* which was so much in favor of our electing Judge Douglas to the Senate of the United States, has not yet got through the task of defending the Republican party, after that one vote in the House of Representatives, from the charge of having gone over to the doctrine of popular sovereignty. Now, just how long would the New York *Tribune* have been in getting rid of the charge that the Republicans had abandoned their principles, if we had taken up Judge Douglas, adopted all his doctrines and elected him to the Senate, when the single vote upon that one point so confused and embarrassed the position of the Republicans that it has kept the *Tribune* one entire year arguing against the effect of it?"

The Central Republican Principle

"This much being said on that point, I wish now to add a word that has a bearing on the future. The Republican principle, the profound central truth that slavery is wrong and ought to be dealt with as a wrong, though we are always to remember the fact of its actual existence amongst us and faithfully observe all the constitutional guarantees—the unalterable principle never for a moment to be lost sight of that it is a wrong and ought to be dealt with as such, cannot advance at all upon Judge Douglas' ground—that there is a portion of the country in which slavery must always exist; that he does not care whether it is voted up or voted down, as it is simply a question of dollars and cents. Whenever, in any compromise or arrangement or combination that may promise some temporary advantage, we are led upon that ground, then and there the great living principle upon which we have organized as a party is surrendered. The proposition now in our minds that this thing is wrong being once driven out and surrendered, then the institution of slavery necessarily becomes national.

"One or two words more of what I did not think of when I arose. Suppose it is true that the Almighty has drawn a line across this continent, on the south side of which part of the people will hold the rest as slaves; that the Almighty ordered this; that it is right, unchangeably right, that men ought there to be held as slaves, and that their fellow men will always have the right to hold them as slaves. I ask you, this once admitted, how can you believe that it is not right for us, or for them coming here, to hold slaves on this other side of the line? Once we come to acknowledge that it is right, that it is the law of Eternal Being, for slavery to exist on one side of that line, have we any sure ground to object to slaves being held on the other side? Once admit the position that a man rightfully holds another man as property on one side of the line, and you must, when it suits his convenience to come to the other side, admit that he has the same right to hold his property there. Once admit Judge Douglas's proposition and we must all finally give way. Although we may not bring ourselves to the idea that it is to our interest to have slaves in this Northern country, we shall soon bring ourselves to admit that, while we may not want them, if any one else does he has the moral right to have them. Step by step—south of the Judge's moral climate line in the States, then in the Territories everywhere, and then in all the States—it is thus that Judge Douglas would lead us inevitably to the nationalization of slavery. Whether by his doctrines of squatter sovereignty, or by the ground taken by him in his recent speeches in Memphis and through the South,—that wherever the climate makes it the interest of the inhabitants to encourage slave property, they will pass a slave code—whether it is covertly nationalized, by Congressional legislation, or by the Dred Scott decision, or by the sophistical and misleading doctrine he has last advanced, the same goal is inevitably reached by the one or the other device. It is only travelling to the same place by different roads."

Judge Douglas, the Great Danger

"In this direction lies all the danger that now exists to the Republican cause. I take it that so far as concerns forcibly establishing slavery in the

Territories by Congressional legislation, or by virtue of the Dred Scott decision, that day has passed. Our only serious danger is that we shall be led upon this ground of Judge Douglas, on the delusive assumption that it is a good way of whipping our opponents, when in fact, it is a way that leads straight to final surrender. The Republican party should not dally with Judge Douglas when it knows where his proposition and his leadership would take us, nor be disposed to listen to it because it was best somewhere else to support somebody occupying his ground. That is no just reason why we ought to go over to Judge Douglas, as we were called upon to do last year. Never forget that we have before us this whole matter of the right or wrong of slavery in this Union, though the immediate question is as to its spreading out into new Territories and States."

Stand by Your Principles

"I do not wish to be misunderstood upon this subject of slavery in this country. I suppose it may long exist, and perhaps the best way for it to come to an end peaceably is for it to exist for a length of time; But I say that the spread and strengthening and perpetuation of it is an entirely different proposition. There we should in every way resist it as a wrong, treating it as a wrong, with the fixed idea that it must and will come to an end. If we do not allow ourselves to be allured from the strict path of our duty by such a device as shifting our ground and throwing ourselves into the rear of a leader who denies our first principle, denies that there is an absolute wrong in the institution of slavery, then the future of the Republican cause is safe and victory is assured. . . . All you have to do is to keep the faith, to remain steadfast to the right, to stand by your banner. Nothing should lead you to leave your guns. Stand together, ready, with match in hand. Allow nothing to turn you to the right or to the left. Remember how long you have been in setting out on the true course; how long you have been in getting your neighbors to understand and believe as you now do. Stand by your principles; stand by your guns; and victory complete and permanent is sure at the last."

So entered Lincoln from the Right onto the war-inclined stage of national politics.

In Tribute to Thomas Jefferson's Axioms of Freedom

Lincoln's speech in Chicago had warned the Republicans effectively against being absorbed by Douglas and beguiled into an indifferent, unmoral, economic acceptance of slavery in the Territories. It aroused an enthusiastic response in the Puritan center of freedom in the nation and he was invited to address a great festival in Boston in honor of Thomas Jefferson. His letter declining the honor shows how keenly he was dissecting the origins and changes in the major philosophical principles of American political history. The letter was given wide publicity in eastern Republican papers.

Messrs. Henry L. Pierce, & Others
Gentlemen

Springfield, Ills.
April 6, 1859

"Your kind note inviting me to attend a Festival in Boston, on the 13th. Inst. in honor of the birth-day of Thomas Jefferson, was duly received. My engagements are such that I can not attend.

"Bearing in mind that about seventy years ago, two great political parties were first formed in this country, that Thomas Jefferson was the head of one of them, and Boston the head-quarters of the other, it is both curious and interesting that those supposed to descend politically from the party opposed to Jefferson, should now be celebrating his birthday in their own original seat of empire, while those claiming political descent from him have nearly ceased to breathe his name everywhere.

"Remembering too, that the Jefferson party were formed upon their supposed superior devotion to the *personal* rights of men, holding the rights of property to be secondary only, and greatly inferior, and then assuming that the so-called democracy of to-day, are the Jefferson, and their opponents, the anti-Jefferson parties, it will be equally interesting to note how completely the two have changed hands as to the principle upon which they were originally supposed to be divided.

"The democracy of to-day hold the *liberty* of one man to be absolutely nothing, when in conflict with another man's right of *property*. Republicans, on the contrary, are for both the *man* and the *dollar;* but in cases of conflict, the man *before* the dollar.

"I remember once being much amused at seeing two partially intoxicated men engage in a fight with their great-coats on, which fight, after a long, and rather harmless contest, ended in each having fought himself *out* of his own coat, and *into* that of the other. If the two leading parties of this day are really identical with the two in the days of Jefferson and Adams, they have performed about the same feats as the two drunken men.

"But soberly, it is no child's play to save the principles of Jefferson from total overthrow in this nation.

"One would start with great confidence that he could convince any sane child that the simpler propositions of Euclid are true; but, nevertheless, he would fail, utterly, with one who should deny the definitions and axioms. The principles of Jefferson are the definitions and axioms of free society. And yet they are denied, and evaded, with no small show of success. One dashingly calls them 'glittering generalities'; another bluntly calls them 'self evident lies'; and still others insidiously argue that they apply only to 'superior races.'

"These expressions, differing in form, are identical in object and effect—the supplanting the principles of free government, and restoring those of classification, caste, and legitimacy. They would delight a convocation of crowned heads, plotting against the people. They are the van-guard—the miners, and sappers—of returning despotism. We must repulse them, or they will subjugate us.

"This is a world of compensations; and he who would *be* no slave, must consent to *have* no slave. Those who deny freedom to others, deserve it not for themselves; and, under a just God, can not long retain it.

"All honor to Jefferson—to the man who, in the concrete pressure of a struggle for national independence by a single people, had the coolness, forecast, and capacity to introduce into a merely revolutionary document, an abstract truth, applicable to all men and all times, and so to embalm it there, that to-day, and in all coming days, it shall be a rebuke and a stumbling-block to the very harbingers of re-appearing tyranny and oppression. Your obedient Servant

A. Lincoln—

Lincoln's letter to Pierce, with comments on Jefferson's axioms of freedom, reveals unintentionally by word association a cardinal subconscious conditioning determinant, in his own experience, of his own political philosophy. He conceived equal *personal rights* and *equal property rights* to be cornerstones in the organization of democratic government but in cases of conflict between them he placed "the man before the dollar." He, like Jefferson, distrusted and hated the dictations and usurpations of tyranny for "it plotted," as he said, against the people and supplanted the principles of free government with "classification, caste and legitimacy." His association of "legitimacy" as a prerequisite condition of tyrannical caste systems, indicates how deeply he felt the taboo cast upon him by "silk-stocking aristocracy." Unlike Jefferson, who was a descendant of an old, aristocratic, wealthy family, Lincoln was born, as he said, "in the most humble walks of life." The American pioneers loved freedom and equality of legal rights more passionately than security, and people were measured by what they could do and believed more than by the reputations of their ancestors. Although his people condoned illegitimacy, Lincoln's mother's illegitimate birth marked him as an outcast with a limited political future in a socially graded system that made legitimacy one of the prerequisites of social recognition. It seems, as his letters will indicate shortly, that silk stocking whiggery had rejected him because of his mother's family.

Jefferson, in his experience in England and as ambassador to France during the revolution, which he supported, learned to distrust and hate the usurpation of privilege under hereditary titular systems of fixed ruling classes. Determined to prevent, if possible, the development of similar usurpations of privilege in the new republic through the repetition of old political tricks, he based the constitution on the free will of "the people."

Lincoln, the commoner, and Jefferson, the aristocrat, saw that the common people, under free, unlimited and unprejudiced education, would best serve themselves and, in so doing, best serve the majority and preserve the political institutions of democracy from exploitation by a self-anointed organized minority.

We have seen how Lincoln almost completely adopted Jefferson's political philosophy, not only for its basic humanitarian premises and sound logic but because his heart felt right in doing so, giving him vigorous inspiration to carry on the great moral fight for freedom for all mankind.

First Suggestion of Lincoln for President

T. J. Pickett, editor in 1859 of the Rock Island *Register,* launched a plan among Republican editors of Illinois to simultaneously announce and promote in their papers Lincoln's candidacy for the party's nomination for President. Lincoln's reply to Pickett's request for permission to take this bold step is the earliest evidence of how casually he at first regarded the efforts of his friends to make him a candidate for President.

> "Yours of the 13th. is just received. My engagements are such that I can not, at any very early day, visit Rock-Island, to deliver a lecture, or for any other object.
> "As to the other matter you kindly mention, I must, in candor, say I do not think myself fit for the Presidency. I certainly am flattered, and gratified, that some partial friends think of me in that connection; but I really think it best for our cause that no concerted effort, such as you suggest, should be made.
> "Let this be considered confidential."

Lincoln's letter to Pickett, written ten days after his letter to Pierce, indicates that he seems to have continued to think of himself as being unfit for the Presidency, but not for lack of legal ability to interpret and apply the meaning of the Constitution.

Grateful Lincoln Deferentially Advises Chase

Ex-Senator Salmon P. Chase, old Whig and now Republican Governor of Ohio, a leader of antislavery policies and a national figure in his party, was laying fences to corral the Republican nomination for the Presidency. Governor Chase of Ohio, Senator and Ex-Governor W. H. Seward of New York, and Senator Simon Cameron of Pennsylvania were by early 1859 the most prominent prospective candidates in the race. Lincoln's letters to Chase at this time show how greatly he had valued the personal interest of the Governor in his race with Douglas.

> (4, 30, 1859) "Allow me also to thank you as being one of the very few distinguished men, whose sympathy we in Illinois did receive last year, of all those whose sympathy we thought we had reason to expect.
> "Of course I would have preferred success; but failing in that, I have no regrets for having rejected all advice to the contrary, and resolutely made the struggle. Had we thrown ourselves into the arms of Douglas, as re-electing him by our votes would have done, the Republican cause would have been anihilated in Illinois, and, as I think, demoralized, and prostrated everywhere for years, if not forever. As it is, . . . 'we are clean' and the Republican star gradually rises higher everywhere."

Chase, when a lawyer in Cincinnati, had gained a national reputation through successfully defending escaped slaves against the fugitive slave law. As Governor of Ohio he was now declaring the fugitive slave law to be unconstitutional.

"Please pardon the liberty I take in addressing you, as I now do," Lincoln wrote to Chase (6, 9, 1859). "It appears by the papers that the late Republican State convention of Ohio adopted a platform, of which the following is one plank. 'A repeal of the atrocious Fugitive Slave Law.'

"This is already damaging us here. I have no doubt that if that plank be even *introduced* into the next Republican National convention, it will explode it. Once introduced, its supporters and its opponents will quarrel irreconcilably. The latter believe the U. S. constitution declares that a fugitive slave *'shall be delivered up;'* and they look upon the above plank as dictated by the spirit which declares a fugitive slave *'shall not be delivered up.'*

"I enter no argument one way or the other; but I assure you the cause of Republicanism is hopeless in Illinois, if it be in any way made responsible for that plank. I hope you can, and will, contribute something to relieve us from it."

In reply to the above letter Chase held that the Fugitive Slave Act was unconstitutional and its repeal indispensable. Hoping that the party in Illinois would accept this view, he asked Lincoln for his interpretation of the constitution on it. Chase's extreme, abolitionistic position on this issue defeated him a year later for the Republican nomination. Lincoln's commonsense interpretation of the Constitution, as expressed in his answer to Chase (6, 20, 1858) might be said here to have been one of the factors that contributed to his national recognition and Republican nomination.

"You say you would be glad to have my views. Although I think congress has constitutional authority to enact a Fugitive Slave law, I have never elaborated an opinion upon the subject. My view has been, and is, simply this: The U. S. constitution says the fugitive slave *'shall be delivered up'* but it does not expressly say *who* shall deliver him up. Whatever the constitution says *'shall be done'* and has omitted stating who shall do it, the government established by that constitution, *ex vi termini,* is vested with the power of doing; and congress is, by the constitution, expressly empowered to make all laws which shall be necessary and proper for carrying into execution all powers vested by the constitution in the government of the United States. This would be my view, on a simple reading of the constitution; and it is greatly strengthened by the historical fact that the constitution was adopted, in great part, in order to get a government which could execute it's own behests, in contradistinction to that under the Articles of confederation, which depended, in many respects, upon the States, for its' execution; and the other fact that one of the earliest congresses, under the constitution, did enact a fugitive Slave law.

"But I did not write you on this subject, with any view of discussing the constitutional question. My only object was to impress you with what I believe is true, that the introduction of a proposition for repeal of the Fugitive Slave law, into the next Republican Nattional convention, will explode the convention and the party."

Staunch Friend of the South

It is clear from the foregoing letters that Lincoln would fight in his party and with any other party to the bitter end to make all political resolutions and federal laws conform to the articles of the Constitution. He desired only that the Missouri Compromise and the legal idea of the "Fathers of the Constitution" be restored. He continued to believe that peace between the opposing factions would thereby be reestablished, and slavery could take "a hundred years" if necessary for its gradual extinction with just compensation under individual State, and perhaps Federal, legislation. Bearing this in mind we can understand the consistency of his remarkably catholic letter to M. W. Delahay, a Kansas lawyer, who was urging him to speak in Kansas.

> In a previous letter to Delahay's encouraging statement—"you have more friends in Kansas and better friends than any living man"—Lincoln had replied:"It will push me hard to get there without injury to my own business, but I shall *try* to do it, though I am not quite certain when I shall succeed."
>
> He finally wrote (5, 14, 1859): "I find it impossible for me to attend your Republican convention at Ossawatan [Ossawatomie] on the 18th. It would have afforded me much personal gratification to see your fine new country and to meet the good people who have cast their lot there; and still more, if I could thereby contribute any thing to the Republican cause. You probably will adopt resolutions in the nature of a platform; and, as I think, the only danger will be the temptation to lower the Republican Standard in order to gather recruits. In my judgement such a step would be a serious mistake—would open a gap through which more would pass *out* than pass *in.* And this would be the same, whether the letting down should be in deference to Douglasism, or to the southern opposition element. Either would surrender the o[b]ject of the Republican organization—the preventing the *spread* and *nationalization* of Slavery. This object surrendered, the organization would go to pieces. I do not mean by this, that no southern man must be placed upon our Republican National ticket for 1860. There are many men in the slave states for any one of whom I would cheerfully vote to be either President or Vice President provided he would enable me to do so with *safety* to the Republican cause—without lowering the Republican Standard. This is the indispensable condition of a union with us. It is idle to think of any other. Any other would be as fruitless to the South, as distasteful to the North, the whole ending in common defeat. Let a union be attempted on the basis of ignoring the Slavery question, and magnifying other questions which the people just now are really caring nothing about, and it will result in gaining no single electoral vote in the South and losing ev[e]ry one in the North."

Some later historians and biographers have narrowly held that Lincoln ingeniously overemphasized the danger of nationalizing slavery with neglect of other important questions in order to give the Republican party sufficient reason for existing. This letter indicates that he was regarding himself as an agent for compromising the difficulties between the two great, intensely hostile factions of the nation over a social, religious and political issue that threatened its existence.

"I am Opposed to Whatever Degrades Men"

When Massachusetts passed legislation that discriminated against the rights of naturalized citizens, Theodore Canisius, German born editor of the *Illinois Staats-Anzeiger,* asked Lincoln for his attitude toward the law. Lincoln's answer (5, 17, 1859) treated the problem with such commonsense comprehension of the equality of rights of native born and naturalized citizens in a democracy that it won for him in the foreign born population of the nation great faith in his widom and courage as a leader of men. The letter was published in the *Illinois Staats-Anzeiger* and the *Illinois State Journal* and copied by many newspapers. The opinions repeated what he had previously said in contempt for the prejudices of the Know-Nothings and Douglas against naturalized Europeans.

"Your note asking, in behalf of yourself and other german citizens, whether I am for or against the constitutional provision in regard to naturalized citizens, lately adopted by Massachusetts; and whether I am for or against the fusion of the republicans, and other opposition elements, for the canvass of 1860, is received.

"Massachusetts is a sovereign and independent state; and it is no privilege of mine to scold her for what she does. Still, if from what she *has done,* an inference is sought to be drawn as to what I *would do,* I may, without impropriety, speak out. I am against it's adoption in Illinois, or in any other place, where I have a right to oppose it. Understanding the spirit of our institutions to aim at the *elevation* of men, I am opposed to whatever tends to *degrade* them. I have some little notoriety for commiserating the oppressed condition of the negro; and I should be strangely inconsistent if I could favor any project for curtailing the existing rights of *white men,* even though born in different lands, and speaking different languages from myself.

"As to the matter of fusion, I am for it, if it can be had on republican grounds; and I am not for it on any other terms. A fusion on any other terms, would be as foolish as unprincipled. It would lose the whole North, while the common enemy would still carry the whole South. The question of *men* is a different one. There are good patriotic men, and able statesmen, in the South whom I would cheerfully support, if they would now place themselves on republican ground. But I am against letting down the republican standard a hair's breadth."

Sacredness of Personal Contracts

The most sacred thing in the relations of free men, Lincoln held, was the promise or contract freely made. We have seen that he analyzed and defined the proprieties, qualifications and limitations in the legal statements of contracts with meticulous care. We have traced the origin of this almost obsessive mental attitude to the painful childhood experience when he saw his father lose his home and farm in Kentucky because of discrepancies in the deed. He regarded the obligation of contracts as fundamental, not only to business, but to the very existence of organized government, and he conceived the Constitution to be a contract between the governments of the respective states in forming the Federal government, a conception that was soon to become of the utmost importance in preserving the Union.

Greatly impressed by the intense passion with which the German immigrants in Illinois, Indiana, Wisconsin and other mid-western States regarded freedom and equality for all men under the guarantees of the Constitution and how they abhorred slavery in America after their revolutionary defiance against tyranny in their own fatherland, Lincoln made one of the most unusual ventures of his life. He purchased from T. Canisius for $400 late in May 1859 the type and press of the *Illinois Staats-Anziger,* a Springfield newspaper printed in German.

The enthusiastic reception given his answer of the 17th to the question by editor Canisius, of his attitude towards the rights of naturalized citizens, seems to have suggested the idea of developing this field of political influence and the purchase of the paper. The contract he made (5, 30, 1859) with T. Canisius shows thoroughgoing tenacity to have and to hold.

> "This instrument witnesseth that the Printing-press, german types &c. purchased of John Burkhardt, belong to Abraham Lincoln; that Theodore Canissius is to have immediate possession of them, and is to commence publishing in Springfield, Illinois, a Republican newspaper, to be chiefly in the german language, with occasional translations into English at his option; the first number to issue in the ensuing month of June, and to continue thenceforward issuing weekly or oftener, at the option of said Cannissius, he, said Cannissius, bearing all expences, and charges, and taking all income and profits; said paper, in political sentiment, not to depart from the Philadelphia and Illinois Republican platforms; and for a material departure in that respect, or a failure of said paper to issue as often as weekly, or any attempt to remove said press, types &c, from Springfield, or to print with them any thing opposed to, or designed to injure the Republican party, said Lincoln may, at his option, at once take possession of said press, types &c, and deal with them as his own. On the contrary, if said Canissius shall issue a newspaper, in all things conformable hereto, until after the Presidential election of 1860, then said press, types &c are to be his property absolutely, not, however, to be used against the Republican party; nor to be removed from Springfield without the consent of said Lincoln."

It is clear that by June 1859 Lincoln had become determined to have a prominent part in directing the national policies of the Republican party. He had now advocated a series of strong principles upholding the sacredness of the Constitution, equal legal rights of all of its citizens, native or foreign born, moral wrong of slavery, justice for slave holders, real popular sovereignty and restriction of slavery.

Taming Radicals

Nathan Sargent, an old Whig who had served as sergeant-at-arms in the House of Representatives during Lincoln's term in Congress, advocated weak compromising methods of solving the slavery conflict and tried to induce Lincoln to adopt them. For his pains he received the following sage advice (6, 23, 1859):

> "Of course I would be pleased to see all the elements of opposition united for the approaching contest of 1860; but I confess I have not much hope of seeing it. You state a platform for such union in these words '*Opposition to the opening of Slave-trade; & eternal hostility to the rotten democracy.*' You add, by way of comment 'I say, if the republicans would be content with this, there will be no obstacle to a union of the *opposition*. But this should be distinctly understood, before Southern men are asked to join them in a National convention.' Well, I say such a platform, unanamously adopted by a National convention, with two of the best men living placed upon it as candidates, would probably carry Maryland, and would certainly not carry a single other state. It would gain nothing in the South, and lose every thing in the North. . . . You could not help perceiving this, if you would but reflect that the republican party is utterly pow[er]less everywhere, if it will, by any means, drive from it all those who came to it from the democracy for the sole object of preventing the spread, and nationalization of slavery. Whenever this object is waived by the organization, they will drop the organization; and the organization itself will dissolve into thin air. Your platform proposes to allow the spread, and nationalization of slavery to proceed without let or hindrance, save only that it shall not receive supplies directly from Africa. Surely you do not seriously believe the Republicans can come to any such terms.
> "From the passage of the Nebraska-bill up to date, the Southern opposition have constantly sought to gain an advantage over the rotten democracy, by running ahead of them in extreme opposition to, and vilifacation and misrepresentation of black republicans. It will be a good deal, if we fail to remember this in malice, (as I hope we shall fail to remember it;) but it is altogether too much to ask us to try to stand with them on the platform which has proved altogether insufficient to sustain them alone.
> "If the rotten democracy shall be beaten in 1860, it has to be done by the North; no human invention can deprive them of the South. I do not deny that there are as good men in the South as the North; and I guess we will elect one of them if he will allow us to do so on Republican ground. I think there can be no other ground of Union. For my single self I would be willing to risk some Southern men without a platform; but I am satisfied that it is not the case with the Republican party generally."

I. N. Coltrin, editor of the *Central Transcript*, a Republican paper published in Clinton, Illinois, had taken an extremely radical, controversial position in a series of agitating articles on candidates for the Republican nomination for governor. Lincoln, fearing disaster to the party wrote Coltrin a personal letter (6, 3, 1859) correcting his extreme statements and advising the adoption of a more restrained and dignified attitude.

"I think it unjust and impolitic. Why manufacture slang to be used against us by our enemies? . . . I plead in . . . my great anxiety that we shall have harmony and not discord; have candidates by agreement, and not by force; *help* one another instead of trying to *hurt* one another."

"We Should Look Beyond Our Noses"

Schuyler Colfax, representative to Congress from Indiana and a leading organizer of the Republican party in his state held views similar to Lincoln's on consolidating the antislavery sentiment of the nation. In a homely letter (7, 6, 1859) to him, Lincoln gave the gist of his idea of practical politics:

. . . "to hedge against divisions in the Republican ranks generally and particularly for the contest of 1860." "The point of danger is the temptation in different localities to '*platform*' for something which will be popular just there, but which, nevertheless, will be a firebrand elsewhere, and especially in a National convention. As instances, the movement against foreigners in Massachusetts; in New Hampshire, to make obedience to the Fugitive Slave law, punishable as a crime; in Ohio, to repeal the Fugitive Slave law; and squatter sovereignty in Kansas. In these things there is explosive matter enough to blow up half a dozen national conventions, if it gets into them; and what gets very rife outside of conventions is very likely to find it's way into them. What is desirable, if possible, is that in every local convocation of Republicans, a point should be made to avoid everything which will distract republicans elsewhere. Massachusetts republicans should have looked beyond their noses; and then they could not have failed to see that tilting against foreigners would ruin us in the whole North-West. New Hampshire and Ohio should forbear tilting against the Fugitive Slave law in such a way as [to] utterly overwhelm us in Illinois with the charge of enmity to the constitution itself. Kansas, in her confidence that she can be saved to freedom on 'squatter sovereignty'—ought not to forget that to prevent the spread and nationalization of slavery is a national concern, and must be attended to by the nation. In a word, in every locality we should look beyond our noses; and at least say *nothing* on points where it is probable we shall disagree.

"I write this for your eye only; hoping however that if you see danger as I think you do, you will do what you can to avert it. Could not suggestions be made to the leading men in the congressional conventions; and so avoid, to some extent at least, these apples of discord?"

In a land now torn with violence-inciting accusations and declarations, efforts to keep peace through compromise was to become characteristic of Lincoln's political efforts.

Still Thinks Himself Unfit for the Presidency

Samuel Galloway, a prominent attorney and leading Republican of Columbus, Ohio, and Lincoln had exchanged letters on legal business but had never met personally. On July 23, Galloway wrote a political letter enthusiastically suggesting that Lincoln become a candidate for President. Lincoln answered (7, 28, 1859):

"Your very complimentary, not to say flattering letter of the 23rd. Inst. is received. Dr. Reynolds [a mutual friend] had induced me to expect you here; and I was disappointed, not a little, by your failure to come. And yet I fear you have formed an estimate of me which can scarcely be sustained on a personal acquaintance.

"Two things done by the Ohio Republican Convention—the repudiation of Judge Swan,* and the 'plank' for a repeal of the Fugitive Slave law—I very much regretted. These two things are of a piece; and they are viewed by many good men, sincerely opposed to slavery, as a struggle against, and in disregard of, the constitution itself. And it is the very thing that will greatly endanger our cause, if it be not kept out of our national convention. There is another thing our friends are doing which gives me some uneasiness. It is their leaning towards 'popular sovereignty.' There are three substantial objections to this. First, no party can command respect which sustains this year, what it opposed last. Secondly, Douglas, (who is the most dangerous enemy of liberty, because the most insidious one) would have little support in the North, and by consequence, no capital to trade on in the South, if it were not for our friends thus magnifying him and his humbug. But lastly, and chiefly, Douglas' popular sovereignty, accepted by the public mind, as a just principle, nationalizes slavery, and revives the African Slave-trade, inevitably. Taking slaves into new territories, and buying slaves in Africa, are identical things—identical *rights* or identical *wrongs*—and the argument which establishes one will establish the other. Try a thousand years for a sound reason why congress shall not hinder the people of Kansas from having slaves, and when you have found it, it will be an equally good one why congress should not hinder the people of Georgia from importing slaves from Africa.

"As to Gov. Chase, I have a kind side for him. He was one of the few distinguished men of the nation who gave us, in Illinois, their sympathy last year. I never saw him, suppose him to be able, and right-minded; but still he may not be the most suitable as a candidate for the Presidency.

"I must say I do not think myself fit for the Presidency. As you propose a correspondance with me, I shall look for your letters anxiously."

The personal opinion of Abraham Lincoln on the political necessity of maintaining the Constitution as a whole, as the inviolate law of the nation in all of its articles including the rights of slavery, and that of Gov. Salmon O. Chase who would, through party edict and public opinion demand repeal of the Fugitive Slave Law as unconstitutional—without regard to jeopardizing the remainder of the Constitution, expressed more than contradictions in political philosophy. They were characteristic of the personal attitude of each man toward the Constitution which must, as will be seen later, conflict again on this question when President and Secretary of the Treasury.

*Chief Justice J. R. Swan of the Ohio Supreme Court upheld the constitutionality of the fugitive slave law in a *habeas corpus* case.

Chapter XXXV

WINNING NATIONAL RECOGNITION

In August, 1859 Lincoln went to Council Bluffs, Iowa, to look after his interest in a tract of land that had been deeded to him in payment of a debt. The Republicans got up an impromptu meeting for him to address. The Council Bluffs *Bugle* said: "He was listened to with much attention, for his Waterloo defeat by Douglas has magnified him into quite a lion here." This tempered, though favorable reception in Iowa is representative of the degree of esteem that was growing for Lincoln in western antislavery circles outside of his state. His ideas on the organization of the Republican party and control of slavery and his criticism of the deliberate misstatements of Douglas in an article in *Harpers* for September (1859) seem to have stimulated him to prepare notes for additional speeches in Wisconsin, Ohio, Minnesota and other states that were now sending him urgent invitations.

What Will Douglas do Now?

Douglas was now on the high road to winning the Democratic nomination for President. He had yet, however, to reconcile the Northern antislavery and Southern proslavery factions in his party. Lincoln's habit of analyzing political situations for basic motives in order to foresee their future consequences is evinced with beautiful clarity and logic in the following notes made in September in preparation for speeches in Ohio.

[I]

"What will Douglas do now. "He does not quite know himself. Like a skilful gambler he will play for all the chances. His first wish is to be the nominee of the Charleston convention, without any new test. The democratic party proper do not wish to let it go just that way. They are thinking of getting up a Slave code test for him. They better not. Their true policy is to let him into the convention, beat him then, and give him no plausible excuse to bolt the nomination. But if they pass the Slave code test upon him, he will not take it; but, as in the case of Lecompton, will appeal to the North on his bravery in opposing it. True the logic of his position, as an indorser of the Dred Scott decision imperatively requires him to go the Slave code. Honestly believing in that decision, he can not, without perjury, refuse to go the Slave code. But he will refuse. He never lets the logic of principle, displace the logic of success. And then, when he thus turns again to the North, we shall have the Lecompton phase of politics reproduced on a larger scale. It will then be a question of whether the Republican party of the Nation shall make him President, in magnanimous

703

gratitude for having opposed the Slave code, just as it was, last year, a question whether the Illinois Republicans should re-elect him Senator, in magnanimous gratitude for having opposed Lecompton. Some larger gentlemen will then have a chance of swallowing the same pill which they somewhat persistently prescribed for us little fellows last year. I hope they will not swallow it. For the sake of the *cause,* rather than the *men,* I hope they will not swallow it. The Republican cause can not live by Douglas' position. His position, whether for or against a slave code, for or against Lecompton, leads inevitably to the nationalizing and perpetuity of slavery, and the Republican cause can not live by it. Dallying with Douglas is, at best, for Republicans, only loss of labor, and loss of time. Wander with him however long, at last they must turn back and strike for a policy, which shall deal with slavery as a wrong, restrain it's enlargement, and look to its termination.

[II]

"The effort to prove that our fathers who framed the government under which we live, understood that a proper division of local from federal authority, and some provision of the constitution, both forbid the federal government to control slavery in the federal territories, is as if, when a man stands before you, so that you see him, and lay your hand upon him, you should go about examining his tracks, and insisting therefrom, that he is not present, but somewhere else. They *did,* through the federal government, control slavery in the federal territories. They did the identical thing, which D. insists they understood they ought not to do.

[III]

"Negro equality! Fudge!! How long, in the government of a God, great enough to make and maintain the Universe, shall there continue knaves to vend, and fools to gulp, so low a piece of demagougeism as this."

Lincoln's foresight of Douglas' political moves proved to be remarkably accurate. His contempt for him as an opportunistic political gambler without logical consistency his apprehension of him as the most insidious enemy of freedom, who would fool the people into giving away their constitutional rights in order to be President, and his fear of him as the most beguiling danger to the Republican party and its cause, drove Lincoln to revive their old arguments and expose the self-centered designs of his opponent.

Douglas, we recall, in the later debates with Lincoln, had adopted a catch phrase that excited popular approval. He claimed that his principle of popular sovereignty was restoring the plan adopted by "our fathers who framed the government under which we live." He had elaborated this claim in an article in *Harper's,* and Lincoln again seized the bull by the horns. From now on he missed no opportunity to show with historical evidence that Douglas' statements were utterly false and intentionally misleading of an uninformed public.

Critical Speeches in Ohio

Lincoln made in two days two great extemporaneous speeches in Ohio besides two lesser ones at Dayton and Hamilton. The first at Columbus (9, 16, 1859) and the second at Cincinnati (9, 17, 1859) were directed particularly at the policies and offensive charges of Douglas who had previously spoken in both cities. These speeches were practically a continuation of the debates and gained wide publicity, leading to the invitation to address a New York audience at Cooper Institute. In the Columbus, Cincinnati, and New York speeches and all the other speeches of 1859 and 1860, Lincoln largely repeated the ideas he had expressed in the debates. However, it is necessary, in order to appreciate his rapidly developing political genius for upholding moral principles, to read the speeches in their order, as reported in the *Illinois State Journal,* for in them he presented the same ideas in different, highly original ways to fit the cultural conditions of each audience.

At Columbus

With innate modesty, humility and diffidence Lincoln pressed on cautiously, but earnestly, always forward. His introductory sentences give us a warmly intimate appreciation of the man thinking and feeling his way through the intricacies of speaking on a desperately serious question before a strange, critical audience. (Captions inserted.)

> "I cannot fail to remember that I appear for the first time before an audience in this now great State—an audience that is accustomed to hear such speakers as Corwin, and Chase, and Wade, and many other renowned men; and, remembering this, I feel that it will be well for you, as for me, that you should not raise your expectations to that standard to which you would have been justified in raising them had one of these distinguished men appeared before you. You would perhaps be only preparing a disappointment for yourselves, and, as a consequence of your disappointment, mortification to me. I hope, therefore, you will commence with very moderate expectations; and perhaps, if you will give me your attention, I shall be able to interest you to a moderate degree.

> "Appearing here for the first time in my life, I have been somewhat embarrassed for a topic by way of introduction to my speech; but I have been relieved from that embarrassment by an introduction which the Ohio *Statesman* newspaper gave me this morning. In this paper I have read an article, in which, among other statements, I find the following:

>> " 'In debating with Senator Douglas during the memorable contest of last fall, Mr. Lincoln declared in favor of negro suffrage, and attempted to defend that vile conception against the Little Giant.'

> "I mention this now, at the opening of my remarks, for the purpose of making three comments upon it. The first I have already announced—it furnishes me an introductory topic; the second is to show that the gentleman is mistaken; thirdly, to give him an opprotunity to correct it. [A voice—"That he won't do."]

"In the first place, in regard to this matter being mistaken. I have found that it is not entirely safe, when one is misrepresented under his very nose, to allow the misrepresentation to go uncontradicted. I therefore purpose, here at the outset, not only to say that this is a misrepresentation, but to show conclusively that it is so; and you will bear with me while I read a couple of extracts from that very 'memorable' debate with Judge Douglas, last year, to which this newspaper refers. In the first pitched battle which Senator Douglas and myself had, at the town of Ottawa, I used the language which I will now read."

Lincoln then read what he considered to be the most concise and effective statement that he had made on equal rights for negroes. Since this has been previously given in full it is sufficient here to repeat only the sentences that have since become famous.

" 'This is the true complexion of all I have ever said in regard to the institution of slavery and the black race. This is the whole of it, and anything that argues me into his idea of perfect social and political equality with the negro, is but a specious and fantastic arrangement of words, by which a man can prove a horse chestnut to be a chestnut horse. . . . I have no lawful right . . . no inclination . . . and no purpose to introduce political and social equality between the white and the black races. There is a physical difference between the two which in my judgment will probably forever forbid their living together upon the footing of perfect equality, and inasmuch as it becomes a necessity that there must be a difference, I, as well as Judge Douglas, am in favor of the race to which I belong, having the superior position. . . . notwithstanding all this, there is no reason in the world why the negro is not entitled to all the natural rights enumerated in the Declaration of Independence, the right to life, liberty and the pursuit of happiness. I hold that he is as much entitled to these as the white man. I agree with Judge Douglas, he is not my equal in many respects . . . but in the right to eat the bread, without leave of anybody else, which his own hand earns, *he is my equal and the equal of Judge Douglas and the equal of every living man.*' "

" ' . . . I am not, nor ever have been in favor of making voters or jurors of negroes, nor of qualifying them to hold office, or intermarry with white people, . . . I do not perceive that because the white man is to have the superior position, the negro should be denied everything. I do not understand that because I do not want a negro woman for a slave, I must necessarily want her for a wife. I am now in my fiftieth year, and I certainly never had a black woman for either a slave or a wife. . . . I will add to this that I have never seen to my knowledge a man, woman, or child, who was in favor of producing perfect equality, socially and politically, between negroes and white men. . . . I have never had the least apprehension that I or my friends would marry negroes, if there was no law to keep them from it; but as Judge Douglas and his friends seem to be in great apprehension that they might, if there were no law to keep them from it, I give the most solemn pledge that I will to the very last stand by the law of the State, which forbids the marrying of white people with negroes.' "

"There, my friends, you have briefly what I have, upon former occasions, said upon the subject to which this newspaper, to the extent of its ability, [laughter] has drawn the public attention. In it you not only perceive as a probability that in that contest I did not at any time say I was in favor of negro suffrage; but the absolute proof that twice—once substantially and once expressly—I declared against it. Having shown you this, there remains but a word of comment on that newspaper article. It is this: that I presume the editor of that paper is an honest and truth-loving man, [a voice—"that's a great mistake,"] and that he will be very greatly obliged to me for furnishing him thus early an opportunity to correct the misrepresentation he has made, before it has run so long that the malicious people can call him a liar. [Laughter and applause.]"

G. W. Manypenny, the author of the aforementioned statement, replied in the Ohio *Statesman:* "We give Mr. Lincoln the benefit of the denial, and yet we are not satisfied but that he did in some parts of Illinois preach that doctrine in the campaign of 1858."

There are now (1964) probably few pure bred Negroes in the Americas, and the enormous progress in mental and social development that these people have made in the past hundred years is due to their political and social freedom. The recent ban against segregation of negro school children will no doubt be conducive to much more rapid and much greater progress. Lincoln, later, when President, began to foresee this possibility and changed his mind about the future of the negro in government and education.

That Insidious Douglas Popular Sovereignty

Lincoln continued:

"The Giant himself has been here recently. [Laughter.] I have seen a brief report of his speech. If it were otherwise unpleasant to me to introduce the subject of the negro as a topic for discussion, I might be somewhat relieved by the fact that he dealt exclusively in that subject while he was here. I shall, therefore, without much hesitation, or diffidence, enter upon this subject.

"The American people, on the first day of January, 1854, found the African slave trade prohibited by a law of Congress. In a majority of the States of this Union, they found African slavery, or any sort of slavery, prohibited by State constitutions. They also found a law existing, supposed to be valid, by which slavery was excluded from almost all the territory the United States then owned. This was the condition of the country, with reference to the institution of slavery, on the 1st of January, 1854. A few days after that, a bill was introduced into Congress, which ran through its regular course in the two branches of the National Legislature, and finally passed into a law in the month of May, by which the act of Congress prohibiting slavery from going into the territories of the United States was repealed. In connection with the law itself, and, in fact, in the terms of the law, the then existing prohibition was not only repealed, but there was a declaration of a purpose on the part of Congress never thereafter to exercise any power that they might have, real or supposed, to prohibit the extension or spread of slavery. This was a very great change; for the law thus repealed was of more than thirty years' standing. Following rapidly upon the heels of this action of Congress, a decision of the Supreme Court is made, by which it is declared that Congress, if it desires to prohibit the spread of slavery into the territories, has no constitutional power to do so. Not only so, but that decision lays down principles, which, if pushed to their logical conclusion—I say pushed to their logical conclusion—would decide that the constitutions of the Free States, forbidding slavery, are themselves unconstitutional. Mark me, I do not say the judge[s?] said this, and let no man say that I affirm the judge[s?] used these words; but I only say it is my opinion that what they did say, if pressed to its logical conclusion, will inevitably result thus. [Cries of "Good! Good!"]

"Looking at these things, the Republican party, as I understand its principles and policy, believe that there is a great danger of the institution of slavery being spread out and extended, until it is ultimately made alike lawful in all the States of this Union; so believing, to prevent that incidental and ultimate consummation, is the original and chief purpose of the Republican organization. I say 'chief purpose' of the Republican organization; for it is certainly true that if the national House shall fall into the hands of the Republicans, they will have to attend to all the other matters of national house-keeping, as well as this. This chief and real purpose of the Republican party is eminently conservative. It proposes nothing save and except to restore this government to its original tone in regard to this element of slavery, and there to maintain it, looking for no further change, in reference to it, than that which the original framers of the government themselves expected and looked forward to.

"The chief danger to this purpose of the Republican party is not just now the revival of the African slave trade, or the passage of a Congressional slave code, or the declaring of a second Dred Scott decision, making slavery lawful in all the States. These are not pressing us just now. They are not quite ready yet. The authors of these measures know that we are too strong for them; but they will be upon us in due time, and we will be grappling with them hand to hand, if they are not now headed off. They are not now the chief danger to the purpose of the Republican organization; but the most imminent danger that now threatens that purpose is that insidious Douglas Popular Sovereignty. This is the miner and sapper. While it does not propose to revive the African slave trade, nor to pass a slave code, nor to make a second Dred Scott decision, it is preparing us for the onslaught and charge of these ultimate enemies when they shall be ready to come on and the word of command for them to advance shall be given. I say this Douglas Popular Sovereignty—for there is a broad distinction, as I now understand it, between that article and a genuine popular sovereignty.

Lincoln Compares His Idea of Popular Sovereignty

"I believe there is a genuine popular sovereignty. I think a definition of genuine popular sovereignty, in the abstract, would be about this: That each man shall do precisely as he pleases with himself, and with all those things which exclusively concern him. Applied to government, this principle would be, that a general government shall do all those things which pertain to it, and all the local governments shall do precisely as they please in respect to those matters which exclusively concern them. I understand that this government of the United States, under which we live, is based upon this principle; and I am misunderstood if it is supposed that I have any war to make upon that principle.

"Now, what is Judge Douglas' Popular Sovereignty? It is, as a principle, no other than that, if one man chooses to make a slave of another man, neither that other man nor anybody else has a right to object. [Cheers and laughter.] Applied in government, as he seeks to apply it, it is this: If, in a new territory into which a few people are beginning to enter for the purpose of making their homes, they choose to either exclude slavery from their limits, or to establish it there, however one or the other may affect the persons to be enslaved, or the infinitely greater number of persons who are afterward to inhabit that territory, or the other members of the families of communities, of which they are but an incipient member, or the general head of the family of States as parent of all—however their action may affect one or the other of these, there is no power or right to interfere. That is Douglas' popular sovereignty applied."

Criticises Douglas' Essay in Harpers

"He has a good deal of trouble with his popular sovereignty. His explanations explanatory of explanations explained are interminable. (Laughter.) The most lengthy, and, as I suppose, the most maturely considered of his long series of explanations, is his great essay in Harper's Magazine. [Laughter.] I will not attempt to enter upon any very thorough investigation of his argument, as there made and presented. I will nevertheless occupy a good portion of your time here in drawing your attention to certain points in it. Such of you as may have read this document will have perceived that the Judge, early in the document, quotes from two persons, as belonging to the Republican party, without naming them, but who can readily be recognized as being Gov. Seward of New York and myself. It is true, that exactly fifteen months ago this day, I believe, I for the first time expressed a sentiment upon this subject, and in such a manner that it should get into print, that the public might see it beyond the circle of my hearers; and my expression of it at that time is the quotation that Judge Douglas makes. He has not made the quotation with accuracy, but justice to him requires me to say that it is sufficiently accurate not to change its sense.

"The sense of that quotation condensed is this—that this slavery element is a durable element of discord among us, and that we shall probably not have perfect peace in this country with it until it either masters the free principle in our government, or is so far mastered by the free principle as for the public mind to rest in the belief that it is going to its end. This sentiment, which I now express in this way, was, at no great distance of time, perhaps in different language, and in connection with some collateral ideas, expressed by Gov. Seward. Judge Douglas had been so much annoyed by the expression of that sentiment that he has constantly, I believe, in almost all his speeches since it was uttered, been referring to it. I find he alluded to it in his speech here, as well as in the copy-right essay. [Laughter.] I do not now enter upon this for the purpose of making an elaborate argument to show that we were right in the expression of that sentiment.

In other words, I shall not stop to say all that might properly be said upon this point; but I only ask your attention to it for the purpose of making one or two points upon it.

"If you will read the copy-right essay, you will discover that Judge Douglas himself says a controversy between the American Colonies and the government of Great Britian began on the slavery question in 1699, and continued from that time until the Revolution; and, while he did not say so, we all know that it has continued with more or less violence ever since the Revolution.

"Then we need not appeal to history, to the declarations of the framers of the government, but we know from Judge Douglas himself that slavery began to be an element of discord among the white people of this country as far back as 1699, or one hundred and sixty years ago, or five generations of men—counting thirty years to a generation. Now it would seem to me that it might have occurred to Judge Douglas, or anybody who had turned his attention to these facts, that there was something in the nature of that thing, Slavery, somewhat durable for mischief and discord. [Laughter.]

"There is another point I desire to make in regard to this matter, before I leave it. From the adoption of the constitution down to 1820 is the precise period of our history when we had comparative peace upon this question— the precise period of time when we came nearer to having peace about it than any other time of that entire one hundred and sixty years, in which he says it began, or of the eighty years of our own constitution. Then it would be worth our while to stop and examine into the probable reason of our coming nearer to having peace then than at any other time. This was the precise period of time in which our fathers adopted, and during which they followed a policy of restricting the spread of slavery, and the whole Union was acquiescing in it. The whole country looked forward to the ultimate extinction of the institution. It was when a policy had been adopted and was prevailing, which led all just and right-minded men to suppose that slavery was gradually coming to an end, and that they might be quiet about it, watching it as it expired. I think Judge Douglas might have perceived that too, and whether he did or not, it is worth the attention of fair-minded men, here and else where, to consider whether that is not the truth of the case. If he had looked at these two facts, that this matter has been an element of discord for one hundred and sixty years among this people, and that the only comparative peace we have had about it was when that policy prevailed in this government, which he now wars upon, he might then, perhaps, have been brought to a more just appreciation of what I have said fifteen months ago—that 'a house divided against itself cannot stand. I believe that this government cannot endure permanently half slave and half free. I do not expect the house to fall. I do not expect the Union to dissolve; but I do expect it will cease to be divided. It will become all one thing or all the other. Either the opponents of slavery will arrest the further spread of it, and place it where the public mind will rest in the belief that it is in the course of ultimate extinction; or its advo- cates will push it forward, until it shall become alike lawful in all the States, old as well as new, north as well as south.' That was my sentiment at that time. In connection with it, I said, 'we are now, far into the fifth year since a policy was inaugurated with the avowed object and confident

promise of putting an end to slavery agitation. Under the operation of
the policy, that agitation has not only not ceased, but has constantly
augmented.' I now say to you here that we are advanced still farther into
the sixth year since that policy of Judge Douglas—that Popular Sovereignty
of his, for quieting the Slavery question—was made the national policy.
Fifteen months more have been added since I uttered that sentiment, and I
call upon you, and all other right-minded men to say whether that fifteen
months have belied or corroborated my words. ["Good, good! that's the
truth!"]

"While I am here upon this subject, I cannot but express gratitude
that this true view of this element of discord among us—as I believe it is—
is attracting more and more attention. I do not believe that Gov. Seward
uttered that sentiment because I had done so before, but because he reflected upon this subject and saw the truth of it. Nor do I believe, because
Gov. Seward or I uttered it, that Mr. Hickman of Pennsylvania, in different language, since that time, has declared his belief in the utter antagonism which exists between the principles of liberty and slavery. You see we are
multiplying. [Applause and laughter.] Now, while I am speaking of Hickman, let me say, I know but little about him. I have never seen him, and
know scarcely anything about the man; but I will say this much of him:
Of all the Anti-Lecompton Democracy that have been brought to my
notice, he alone has the true, genuine ring of the metal. And now, without
endorsing anything else he has said, I will ask this audience to give three
cheers for Hickman. [The audience responded with three rousing cheers for
Hickman.]

"Another point in the copy-right essay to which I would ask your
attention, is rather a feature to be extracted from the whole thing, than
from any express declaration of it at any point. It is a general feature of
that document, and, indeed, of all of Judge Douglas' discussions of this
question, that the territories of the United States and the States of this
Union are exactly alike—that there is no difference between them at all—
that the constitution applies to the territories precisely as it does to the
States—and that the United States Government, under the constitution,
may not do in a State what it may not do in a territory, and what it must
do in a State, it must do in a territory. Gentlemen, is that a true view of
the case? It is necessary for this squatter sovereignty; but is it true?

"Let us consider. What does it depend upon? It depends altogether upon
the proposition that the States must, without the interference of the general
government, do all those things that pertain *exclusively* to themselves—
that are local in their nature, that have no connection with the general
government. After Judge Douglas has established this proposition, which
nobody disputes or ever has disputed, he proceeds to assume, without
proving it, that slavery is one of those little, unimportant, trivial matters
which are of just about as much consequence as the question would be to
me, whether my neighbor should raise horned cattle or plant tobacco
[laughter]; that there is no moral question about it, but that it is altogether
a matter of dollars and cents; that when a new territory is opened for
settlement, the first man who goes into it may plant there a thing which,
like the Canada thistle, or some other of those pests of the soil, cannot
be dug out by the millions of men who will come thereafter; that it is one

of those little things that is so trivial in its nature that it has no effect upon anybody save the few men who first plant upon the soil; that it is not a thing which in any way affects the family of communities composing these States, nor any way endangers the general government. Judge Douglas ignores altogether the very well known fact, that we have never had a serious menace to our political existence, except it sprang from this thing which he chooses to regard as only upon a par with onions and potatoes. [Laughter.]

"Turn it, and contemplate it in another view. He says, that according to his Popular Sovereignty, the general government may give to the territories governors, judges, marshals, secretaries, and all the other chief men to govern them, but they must not touch upon this other question. Why? The question of who shall be governor of a territory for a year or two, and pass away, without his track being left upon the soil, or an act which he did for good or for evil being left behind, is a question of vast national magnitude. It is so much opposed in its nature to locality, that the nation itself must decide it; while this other matter of planting slavery upon a soil— a thing which once planted cannot be eradicated by the succeeding millions who have as much right there as the first comers or if eradicated, not without infinite difficulty and a long struggle— he considers the power to prohibit it, as one of these little, local, trivial things that the nation ought not to say a word about; that if affects nobody save the few men who are there.

"Take these two things and consider them together, present the question of planting a State with the Institution of slavery by the side of a question of who shall be Governor of Kansas for a year or two, and is there a man here,— is there a man on earth, who would not say that the Governor question is the little one, and the slavery question is the great one? I ask any honest Democrat if the small, the local, and the trivial and temporary question is not, who shall be Governor? While the durable, the important and the mischievous one is, shall this soil be planted with slavery?"

On the Nature of the Man Douglas

"This is an idea, I suppose, which has arisen in Judge Douglas' mind from his peculiar structure. I suppose the institution of slavery really looks small to him. He is so put up by nature that a lash upon his back would hurt him, but a lash upon anybody else's back does not hurt him. [Laughter.] That is the build of the man, and consequently he looks upon the matter of slavery in this unimportant light.

"Judge Douglas ought to remember when he is endeavoring to force this policy upon the American people that while he is put up in that way a good many are not. He ought to remember that there was once in this country a man by the name of Thomas Jefferson, supposed to be a Democrat— a man whose principles and policy are not very prevalent amongst Democrats to-day, it is true; but that man did not take exactly this view of the insignificance of the element of slavery which our friend Judge Douglas does. In contemplation of this thing, we all know he was led to exclaim, 'I tremble for my country when I remember that God is just!' We know how he looked upon it when he thus expressed himself. There was danger to this country—danger of the avenging justice of God in that little unimportant popular sovereignty question of Judge Douglas. He supposed there was a question of God's eternal justice wrapped up in the enslaving of any race of men, or any man, and that those who did so braved the arm of Jehovah—that when a nation thus dared the Almighty every friend of that nation had cause to dread His wrath. Choose ye between Jefferson and Douglas as to what is the true view of this element among us. [Applause.]

"There is another little difficulty about this matter of treating the Territories and States alike in all things, to which I ask your attention, and I shall leave this branch of the case. If there is no difference between them, why not make the Territories States at once? What is the reason that Kansas was not fit to come into the Union when it was organized into a Territory, in Judge Douglas' view? Can any of you tell any reason why it should not have come into the Union at once? They are fit, as he thinks, to decide upon the slavery question—the largest and most important with which they could possibly deal—what could they do by coming into the Union that they are not fit to do, according to his view, by staying out of it? Oh, they are not fit to sit in Congress and decide upon the rates of postage, or questions of *ad valorem* or specific duties on foreign goods, or live oak timber contracts [laughter]; they are not fit to decide these vastly important matters, which are national in their import, but they are fit, 'from the jump,' to decide this little negro question. But gentlemen, the case is too plain; I occupy too much time on this head, and I pass on."

Douglas' Internal Policy

"Near the close of the copyright essay, the Judge, I think, comes very near kicking his own fat into the fire [laughter]. I did not think, when I commenced these remarks, that I would read from that article, but now believe I will:

> " 'This exposition of the history of these measures, shows conclusively that the authors of the Compromise Measures of 1850 and of the Kansas-Nebraska act of 1854, as well as the members of the Continental Congress of 1774, and the founders of our system of government subsequent to the Revolution, regarded the people of the Territories and Colonies as political communities which were entitled to a free and exclusive power of legislation in their provisional [provincial?] legislatures, where their representation could alone be preserved, in all cases of taxation and internal polity.'

"When the Judge saw that putting the word 'slavery' would contradict his own history, he put in what he knew would pass as synonymous with it: 'internal polity.' Whenever we find *that* in one of his speeches, the substitute is used in this manner; and I can tell you the reason. It would be too bald a contradiction to say slavery, but 'internal polity' is a general phrase, which would pass in some quarters, and which he hopes will pass with the reading community for the same thing.

> " 'This right pertains to the people collectively, as a law-abiding and peaceful community, and not in the isolated individuals who may wander upon the public domain in violation of the law. It can only be exercised

where there are inhabitants sufficient to constitute a government, and capable of performing its various functions and duties, a fact to be ascertained and determined by'—

"Who do you think? Judge Douglas says 'By Congress!' [Laughter.]

" 'Whether the number shall be fixed at ten, fifteen or twenty thousand inhabitants does not affect the principle.'

"Now I have only a few comments to make. Popular Sovereignty, by his own words, does not pertain to a few persons who wander upon the public domain in violation of law. We have his words for that. When it does pertain to them, is when they are sufficient to be formed into an organized political community, and he fixes the minimum for that at 10,000, and the maximum at 20,000. Now I would like to know what is to be done with the 9,000? Are they all to be treated, until they are large enough to be organized into a political community, as wanderers upon the public land in violation of law? And if so treated and driven out at what point of time would there ever be ten thousand? [Great laughter.] If they were not driven out, but remained there as trespassers upon the public land in violation of the law, can they establish slavery there? No,—the Judge says Popular Sovereignty don't pertain to them then. Can they exclude it then? No, Popular Sovereignty don't pertain to them then. I would like to know, in the case covered by the Essay, what condition the people of the Territory are in before they reach the number of ten thousand?

"But the main point I wish to ask attention to is, that the question as to when they shall have reached a sufficient number to be formed into a regular organized community, is to be decided 'by Congress.' Judge Douglas says so. Well, gentlemen, that is about all we want. [Here someone in the crowd made a remark inaudible to the reporter, whereupon Mr. Lincoln continued.] No, that is all the Southerners want. That is what all those who are for slavery want. They do not want Congress to prohibit slavery from coming into the new territories, and they do not want Popular Sovereignty to hinder it; and as Congress is to say when they are ready to be organized, all that the south has to do is to get Congress to hold off. Let Congress hold off until they are ready to be admitted as a State, and the south has all it wants in taking slavery into and planting it in all the territories that we now have, or hereafter may have. In a word, the whole thing, at a dash of the pen, is at last put in the power of Congress; for if they do not have this Popular Sovereignty until Congress organizes them, I ask if it at last does not come from Congress? If, at last it amounts to anything at all, Congress gives it to them. I submit this rather for your reflection than for comment. After all that is said, at last by a dash of the pen, everything that has gone before is undone, and he puts the whole question under the control of Congress. After fighting through more than three hours, if you undertake to read it, he at last places the whole matter under the control of that power which he had been contending against, and arrives at a result directly contrary to what he had been laboring to do. He at last leaves the whole matter to the control of Congress."

Douglas' Historical Inaccuracies

"There are two main objects, as I understand it, of this Harper's Magazine essay. One was to show, if possible, that the men of our revolutionary times were in favor of his popular sovereignty; and the other was to show that the Dred Scott Decision had not entirely squelched out this popular sovereignty. I do not propose, in regard to this argument drawn from the history of former times, to enter into a detailed examination of the historical statements he has made. I have the impression that they are inaccurate in a great many instances. Sometimes in positive statement but very much more inaccurate by the suppression of statements that really belong to the history. But I do not propose to affirm that this is so to any very great extent; or to enter into a very minute examination of his historical statements. I avoid doing so upon this principle—that if it were important for me to pass out of this lot in the least period of time possible and I came to that fence and saw by a calculation of my known strength and agility that I could clear it at a bound, it would be folly for me to stop and consider whether I could or [could?] not crawl through a crack. [Laughter.] So I say of the whole history, contained in his essay, where he endeavored to link the men of the revolution to popular sovereignty. It only requires an effort to leap out of it—a single bound to be entirely successful. If you read it over you will find that he quotes here and there from documents of the revolutionary times, tending to show that the people of the colonies were desirous of regulating their own concerns in their own way, that the British Government should not interfere; that at one time they struggled with the British Government to be permitted to exclude the African slave trade; if not directly, to be permitted to exclude it indirectly by taxation sufficient to discourage and destroy it. From these and many things of this sort, Judge Douglas argues that they were in favor of the people of our own territories excluding slavery if they wanted to, or planting it there if they wanted to, doing just as they pleased from the time they settled upon the territory. Now, however his history may apply, and whatever of his argument there may be that is sound and accurate or unsound and inaccurate, if we can find out what these men did themselves do upon this very question of slavery in the territories, does it not end the whole thing? If, after all this labor and effort to show that the men of the revolution were in favor of his popular sovereignty and his mode of dealing with slavery in the territories, we can show that these very men took hold of that subject, and dealt with it, we can see for ourselves *how* they dealt with it. It is not a matter of argument or inference, but we know what they thought about it.

"It is precisely upon that part of the history of the country, that one important omission is made by Judge Douglas. He selects parts of the history of the United States upon the subject of slavery, and treats it as the whole; omitting from his historical sketch the legislation of Congress in regard to the admission of Missouri, by which the Missouri Compromise was established, and slavery excluded from a country half as large as the present United States. All this is left out of his history, and in no wise alluded to by him, so far as I remember, save once, when he makes a remark, that upon his principle the Supreme Court were authorized to pronounce a decision that the act called the Missouri Compromise was unconstitutional. All that history has been left out. But this part of the history of the country was not made by the men of the Revolution.

"There was another part of our political history made by the very men who were the actors in the Revolution, which has taken the name of the ordinance of '87. Let me bring that history to your attention. In 1784, I believe, this same Mr. Jefferson drew up an ordinance for the government of the country upon which we now stand; or rather a frame or draft of an ordinance for the government of this country, here in Ohio; our neighbors in Indiana; us who live in Illinois; our neighbors in Wisconsin and Michigan. In that ordinance, drawn up not only for the government of that territory, but for the territories south of the Ohio River, Mr. Jefferson expressly provided for the prohibition of slavery. Judge Douglas says, and perhaps is right, that that provision was lost from that ordinance. I believe that is true. When the vote was taken upon it, a majority of all present in the Congress of the Confederation voted for it; but there was [were?] so many absentees that those voting for it did not make the clear majority necessary, and it was lost. But three years after that the Congress of the Confederation were together again, and they adopted a new ordinance for the government of this northwest territory, not contemplating territory south of the river, for the States owning that territory had hitherto refrained from giving it to the general Government; hence they made the ordinance to apply only to what the Government owned. In that, the provision excluding slavery *was inserted and passed unanimously,* or at any rate it passed and became a part of the law of the land. Under that ordinance we live. First here in Ohio you were a territory, then an enabling act was passed authorizing you to form a constitution and State government, provided it was republican and not in conflict with the ordinance of '87. When you framed your constitution and presented it for admission, I think you will find the legislation upon the subject, it will show that, 'whereas you had formed a constitution that was republican and not in conflict with the ordinance of '87,' therefore you were admitted upon equal footing with the original States. The same process in a few years was gone through with in Indiana, and so with Illinois, and the same substantially with Michigan and Wisconsin.

"Not only did that ordinance prevail, but it was constantly looked to whenever a step was taken by a new territory to become a State. Congress always turned their attention to it, and in all their movements upon this subject, they traced their course by that ordinance of '87. When they admitted new States they advertised them of this ordinance as a part of the legislation of the country. They did so because they had traced the ordinance of '87 throughout the history of this country. Begin with the men of the Revolution, and go down for sixty entire years, and until the last scrap of that territory comes into the Union in the form of the State of Wisconsin—everything was made to conform with the ordinance of '87 excluding slavery from that vast extent of country.

"I omitted to mention in the right place that the Constitution of the United States was in process of being framed when that ordinance was made by the Congress of the Confederation; and one of the first acts of Congress itself under the Confederation itself was to give force to that ordinance by putting power to carry it out into the hands of the new officers under the Constitution, in place of the old ones who had been legislated out of existence by the change in the government from the Confederation to the Constitution. Not only so, but I believe Indiana once or twice, if not Ohio, petitioned the general government for the privilege of suspending that provision and allowing them to have slaves. A report made by Mr. Randolph of Virginia, himself a slaveholder, was directly against it, and the action was to refuse them the privilege of violating the ordinance of '87.

"This period of history which I have run over briefly, is, I presume, as familiar to most of this assembly as any other part of the history of our country. I suppose that few of my hearers are not as familiar with that part of history as I am, and I only mention it to recall your attention to it at this time. And hence I ask how extraordinary a thing it is that a man who has occupied a position upon the floor of the Senate of the United States, who is now in his third term, and who looks to see the government of this whole country fall into his hands, pretending to give a truthful and accurate history of the slavery question in this country, should so entirely ignore the whole of that portion of our history—the most important of all. Is it not a most extraordinary spectacle that a man should stand up and ask for any confidence in his statements, who sets out as he does with portions of history calling upon the people to believe that it is a true and fair representation, when the leading part, and controlling feature of the whole history, is carefully suppressed.

"But the mere leaving out is not the most remarkable feature of this remarkable essay. His proposition is to establish that the leading men of the revolution were for his great principle of non-intervention by the government in the question of slavery in the territories, while history shows that they decided in the cases actually brought before them, in exactly the contrary way, and he knows it. Not only did they so decide at that time, but they stuck to it during sixty years, through thick and thin, as long as there was one of the revolutionary heroes upon the stage of political action. Through their whole course, from first to last, they clung to freedom. And now he asks the community to believe that the men of the revolution were in favor of his great principle, when we have the naked history that they themselves dealt with this very subject matter of his principle, and utterly repudiated his principle, acting upon a precisely contrary ground. It is as impudent and absurd as if a prosecuting attorney should stand up before a jury and ask them to convict A as the murderer of B, while B was walking alive before them. [Cheers and laughter.]

"I say again, if Judge Douglas asserts that the men of the Revolution acted upon principles by which, to be consistent with themselves, they ought to have adopted his popular sovereignty, then, upon a consideration of his own argument, he had a right to make you believe that they understood the principles of government, but misapplied them—that he has arisen to enlighten the world as to the just application of this principle. He has a right to try to persuade you that he understands their principles better than they did, and therefore he will apply them now, not as they did, but as they ought to have done. He has a right to go before the community, and try to convince them of this; but he has no right to attempt to impose upon any one the belief that the men themselves approved of his great principle.

There are two ways of establishing a proposition. One is by trying to demonstrate it upon reason; and the other is, to show that great men in former times have thought so and so, and thus to pass it by the weight of pure authority. Now, if Judge Douglas will demonstrate somehow that this is popular sovereignty—the right of one man to make a slave of another, without any right in that other, or any one else, to object—demonstrate it as Euclid demonstrated propositions—there is no objection. But when he comes forward, seeking to carry a principle by bringing to it the authority of men who themselves utterly repudiate that principle, I ask that he shall not be permitted to do it." [Applause.]

How Our Fathers Understood This Question

"I see, in the Judge's speech here, a short sentence in these words, 'Our fathers, when they formed this government under which we live, understood this question just as well and even better than we do now.' That is true; I stick to that. [Great cheers and laughter.] I will stand by Judge Douglas in that to the bitter end. [Renewed laughter.] And now, Judge Douglas, come and stand by me, and truthfully show how they acted, understanding it better than we do. All I ask of you, Judge Douglas, is to stick to the propostion that the men of the revolution understood this proposition, that the men of the revolution understood this subject better than we do now, *and with that better understanding they acted better than you are trying to act now.* [Applause and laughter.]

"I wish to say something now in regard to the Dred Scott decision, as dealt with by Judge Douglas. In that 'memorable debate' between Judge Douglas and myself last year, the Judge thought fit to commence a process of catechising me, and at Freeport I answered his questions, and propounded some to him. Among others propounded to him was one that I have here now. The substance, as I remember it, is, 'Can the people of a United States Territory, under the Dred Scott decision, in any lawful way, against the wish of any citizen of the United States, exclude slavery from its limits, prior to the formation of a State Constitution?' He answered that they could lawfully exclude slavery from the United States territories, notwithstanding the Dred Scott decision. There was something about that answer that has probably been a trouble to the Judge ever since. (Laughter.)

"The Dred Scott decision expressly gives every citizen of the United States a right to carry his slaves into the United States' Territories. And now there was some inconsistency in saying that the decision was right, and saying too, that the people of the Territory could lawfully drive slavery out again. When all the trash, the words, the collateral matter was cleared away from it; all the chaff was fanned out of it, it was a bare absurdity— *no less than a thing may be lawfully driven away from where it has a lawful right to be.* (Cheers and laughter.) Clear it of all the verbiage, and that is the naked truth of his proposition—that a thing may be lawfully driven from the place where it has a lawful right to stay. Well, it was because the Judge couldn't help seeing this, that he has had so much trouble with it; and what I want to ask your especial attention to, just now, is to remind you, if you have not noticed the fact, that the Judge does not any longer say that the people cannot [can?] exclude slavery. He does not say so in the copyright essay; he did not say so in the speech that he made here, and so far as I know, since his re-election to the Senate, he has never said as he did at Freeport, that the people of the Territories can exclude slavery. He desires that you, who wish the Territories to remain free, should believe that he stands by that position, but he does not say it himself. He escapes to some extent the absurd position I have stated by changing his language entirely. What he says now is something different in language, and we will consider whether it is not different in sense too. It is now that the Dred Scott decision, or rather the Constitution under that decision, does not carry slavery into the Territories beyond the power of the people of the Territories *to control it as other property.* He does not say the people can drive it out, but they can control it as other property. The language is different, we should consider whether the sense is different. Driving a horse out of this lot, is too plain a proposition to be mistaken about; it is putting him on the other side of the fence. [Laughter.] Or it might be a sort of exclusion of him from the lot if you were to kill him and let the worms devour him; but neither of these things is the same as 'controlling him as other property.' That would be to feed him, to pamper him, to ride him, to use and abuse him, to make the most money out of him 'as other property'; but, please you, what do the men who are in favor of slavery want more than this? [Laughter and applause.] What do they really want, other than that slavery being in the Territories, shall be controlled as other property. [Renewed applause.]

"If they want anything else, I do not comprehend it. I ask your attention to this, first for the purpose of pointing out the change of ground the Judge has made; and, in the second place, the importance of the change—that that change is not such as to give you gentlemen who want his popular sovereignty the power to exclude the institution or drive it out at all. I know the Judge sometimes squints at the argument that in controlling it as other property by unfriendly legislation they may control it to death, as you might in the case of a horse, perhaps, feed him so lightly and ride him so much that he would die. [Cheers and laughter.] But when you come to legislative control, there is something more to be attended to. I have no doubt, myself, that if the people of the territories should undertake to control slave property as other property—that is, control it in such a way that it would be the most valuable as property, and make it bear its just proportion in the way of burdens as property—really deal with it as property —the Supreme Court of the United States will say, 'God speed you and amen.' But I undertake to give the opinion, at least, that if the territories attempt by any direct legislation to drive the man with his slave out of the territory, or to decide that his slave is free because of his being taken there, the Supreme Court will unhesitatingly decide all such legislation uncon-stitutional, as long as that Supreme Court is constructed as the Dred Scott Supreme Court is. The first two things they have already decided, except there is a little quibble among lawyers between the words *dicta* and decision. They have already decided a negro cannot be made free by ter-ritorial legislation."

Fallacy of Indirect Legislation

"What is that Dred Scott decision? Judge Douglas labors to show that it is one thing, while I think it is altogether different. It is a long opinion, but it is all embodied in this short statement: 'The Constitution of the United States forbids Congress to deprive a man of his property, without due process of law; the right of property in slaves is distinctly and expressly affirmed in that Constitution; therefore, if Congress shall undertake to say that a man's slave is no longer his slave, when he crosses a certain line into a territory, that is depriving him of his property without due process of law, and is unconstitutional.' There is the whole Dred Scott decision. They add that if Congress cannot do so itself, Congress cannot confer any power to do so, and hence any effort by the Territorial Legislature to do either of these things is absolutely decided against. It is a foregone conclusion by that court.

"Now, as to this indirect mode by 'unfriendly legislation,' all lawyers here will readily understand that such a proposition cannot be tolerated for a moment, because a legislature cannot indirectly do that which it cannot accomplish directly. Then I say any legislation to control this property, as property, for its benefit as property, would be hailed by this Dred Scott Supreme Court, and fully sustained; but any legislation driving slave property out, or destroying it as property, directly or indirectly, will most assuredly, by that court, be held unconstitutional. . . .

"Another feature of the Judge's argument about the Dred Scott case is, an effort to show that that decision deals altogether in declarations of negatives; that the constitution does not affirm anything as expounded by the Dred Scott decision, but it only declares a want of power—a total absence of power, in reference to the territories. It seems to be his purpose to make the whole of that decision to result in a mere negative declaration of a want of power in Congress to do anything in relation to this matter in the territories. I know the opinion of the Judges states that there is a total absence of power; but that is, unfortunately, not all it states; for the Judges add that the right of property in a slave is distinctly and expressly affirmed in the constitution. It does not stop at saying that the right of property in a slave is recognized in the constitution, is declared to exist somewhere in the constitution, but says it is *affirmed* in the constitution. Its language [is?] equivalent to saying that it is embodied and so woven into that instrument that it cannot be detached without breaking the constitution itself. In a word, it is part of the constitution.

"Douglas is singularly unfortunate in his effort to make out that decision to be altogether negative, when the express language at the vital part is that this is distinctly affirmed in the Constitution. I think myself, and I repeat it here, that this decision does not merely carry slavery into the Territories, but by its logical conclusion it carries it into the States in which we live. One provision of that Constitution is, that it shall be the supreme law of the land—I do not quote the language—any Constitution or law of any State to the contrary notwithstanding. This Dred Scott decision says that the right of property in a slave is affirmed in that Constitution, which is the supreme law of the land, any State Constitution or law notwithstanding. Then I say that to destroy a thing which is distinctly affirmed and supported by the supreme law of the land, even by a State Constitution or law, is a violation of that supreme law and there is no escape from it. In my judgment there is no avoiding that result, save that the American people shall see that Constitutions are better construed than our Constitution is construed in that direction. They must take care that it is more faithfully and truly carried out than it is there expounded."

Danger of Nationalization of Slavery

"I must hasten to a conclusion. Near the beginning of my remarks, I said that this insidious Douglas popular sovereignty is the measure that now threatens the purpose of the Republican party, to prevent slavery from being nationalized in the United States. I propose to ask your attention for a little while to some propositions in affirmation of that statement. Take it just as it stands, and apply it as a principle; extend and apply that principle elsewhere and consider where it will lead you. I now put this proposition that Judge Douglas' popular sovereignty applied will re-open the African slave trade; and I will demonstrate it by any variety of ways in which you can turn the subject and look at it.

"The Judge says that the people of the territories have the rights, by his principle, to have slaves, if they want them. Then I say that the people of Georgia have the right to buy slaves in Africa, if they want them, and I defy any man on earth to show any distinction between the two things—to show that the one is either more wicked or more unlawful; to show, on original principles, that one is better or worse than the other; or to show by the constitution, that one differs a whit from the other. He will tell me, doubtless, that there is no constitutional provision against people taking slaves into the new territories, and I tell him that there is equally no constitutional provision against buying slaves in Africa. He will tell you that a people, in the exercise of popular sovereignty, ought to do as they please about that thing, and have slaves if they want them; and I tell you that the people of Georgia are as much entitled to popular sovereignty and to buy slaves in Africa, if they want them, as the people of the territory are to have slaves if they want them. I ask any man, dealing honestly with himself, to point out a distinction.

"I have recently seen a letter of Judge Douglas', in which without stating that to be the object, he doubtless endeavors, to make a distinction between the two. He says he is unalterably opposed to the repeal of the laws against the African Slave trade. And why? He then seeks to give a reason that would not apply to his popular sovereignty in the territories. What is that reason? 'The abolition of the African slave trade is a compromise of the constitution.' I deny it. There is no truth in the proposition that the abolition of the African slave trade is a compromise of the constitution. No man can put his finger on anything in the constitution, or on the line of history which shows it. It is a mere barren assertion, made simply for the purpose of getting up a distinction between the revival of the African slave trade and his 'great principle.'

"At the time the constitution of the United States was adopted it was expected that the slave trade would be abolished. I should assert, and insist upon that, if Judge Douglas denied it. But I know, that it was equally expected that slavery would be excluded from the territories and I can show by history, that in regard to these two things, public opinion was exactly alike, while in regard to positive action, there was more done in the Ordinance of '87, to resist the spread of slavery than was ever done to abolish the foreign slave trade. Lest I be misunderstood, I say again that at the time of the formation of the constitution, public expectation was that the slave trade would be abolished, but no more so than the spread of slavery in the territories should be restrained. They stand alike, except that in the Ordinance of '87 there was a mark left by public opinion showing that it was more committed against the spread of slavery in the territories than against the foreign slave trade.

"Compromise! What word of compromise was there about it. Why the public sense was then in favor of the abolition of the slave trade; but there was at the time a very great commercial interest involved in it and extensive capital in that branch of trade. There were doubtless the incipient stages of improvement in the South in the way of farming, dependent on the slave trade, and they made a proposition to the Congress to abolish the trade after allowing it twenty years, a sufficient time for the capital and commerce engaged in it to be transferred to other channels. They made no provision that it should be abolished [in?] twenty years; I do not doubt that they expected it would be; but they made no bargain about it. The public sentiment left no doubt in the minds of any that it would be done away. I repeat there is nothing in the history of those times, in favor of that matter being a *compromise* of the Constitution. It was the public expectation at the time, manifested in a thousand ways, that the spread of slavery should be restricted.

"Then I say if this principle is established, that there is no wrong in slavery, and whoever wants it has a right to have it, is a matter of dollars and cents, a sort of question as to how they shall deal with brutes, that between us and the negro here there is no sort of question, but that at the South the question is between the negro and the crocodile. That is all. It is a mere matter of policy; there is a perfect right according to interest to do just as you please—when this is done, where this doctrine prevails, the miners and sappers will have formed public opinion for the slave trade. They will be ready for Jeff. Davis and Stephens and other leaders of that company, to sound the bugle for the revival of the slave trade, for the second Dred Scott decision, for the flood of slavery to be poured over the free states, while we shall be here tied down and helpless and run over like sheep.

"It is to be a part and parcel of this same idea, to say to men who want to adhere to the Democratic party, who have always belonged to that party, and are only looking about for some excuse to stick to it, but nevertheless hate slavery, that Douglas' Popular Sovereignty is as good a way as any to oppose slavery. They allow themselves to be persuaded easily in accordance with their previous dispositions, into this belief, that it is about as good a way of opposing slavery as any, and we can do that without straining our old party ties or breaking up old political associations. We can do so without being called negro worshippers. We can do that without being subjected to the jibes and sneers that are so readily thrown out in place of argument where no argument can be found; so let us stick to this Popular Sovereignty—this insidious Popular Sovereignty—. Now let me call your attention to one thing that has really happened, which shows this gradual and steady debauching of public opinion, this course of preparation for the revival of the slave trade, for the territorial slave code, and the new Dred Scott decision that is to carry slavery into the free States. Did you ever five years ago, hear of anybody in the world saying that the negro had no share in the Declaration of National Independence; that it did not mean negroes at all; and when 'all men' were spoken of negroes were not included?

"I am satisfied that five years ago that proposition was not put upon paper by any living being anywhere. I have been unable at any time to find a man in an audience who would declare that he had ever known any body saying so five years ago. But last year there was not a Douglas popular sovereign in Illinois who did not say it. Is there one in Ohio but declares his firm belief that the Declaration of Independence did not mean negroes at all? I do not know how this is; I have not been here much; but I presume you are much alike everywhere. Then I suppose that all now express the belief that the Declaration of Independence never did mean negroes. I call upon one of them to say that he said it five years ago.

"If you think that now, and did not think it then, the next thing that strikes me is to remark that there has been a *change* wrought in you [Laughter and applause], and a very significant change it is, being no less than changing the negro, in your estimation, from the rank of a man to that of a brute. They are taking him down, and placing him, when spoken of, among reptiles and crocodiles, as Judge Douglas himself expresses it."

"Public Opinion Is Everything"

"Is not this change wrought in your minds a very important change? Public opinion in this country is everything. In a nation like ours this popular sovereignty and squatter sovereignty have already wrought a change in the public mind to the extent I have stated. There is no man in this crowd who can contradict it.

"Now, if you are opposed to slavery honestly, as much as anybody I ask you to note that fact, and the like of which is to follow, to be plastered on, layer after layer, until very soon you are prepared to deal with the negro everywhere as with the brute. If public sentiment has not been debauched already to this point, a new turn of the screw in that direction is all that is wanting; and this is constantly being done by the teachers of this insidious popular sovereignty. You need but one or two turns further until your minds, now ripening under these teachings will be ready for all these things, and you will receive and support, or submit to, the slave trade; revived with all its horrors; a slave code enforced in our territories, and a new Dred Scott decision to bring slavery up into the very heart of the free North. This, I must say, is but carrying out those words prophetically spoken by Mr. Clay, many, many years ago. I believe more than thirty years when he told an audience that if they would repress all tendencies to liberty and ultimate emancipation, they must go back to the era of our independence and muzzle the cannon which thundered its annual joyous return on the fourth of July; they must blow out the moral lights around us; they must penetrate the human soul and eradicate the love of liberty; but until they did these things, and others eloquently enumerated by him, they could not repress all tendencies to ultimate emancipation.

"I ask attention to the fact that in a pre-eminent degree these popular sovereigns are at this work; blowing out the moral lights around us, teaching that the negro is no longer a man but a brute; that the Declaration has nothing to do with him; that he ranks with the crocodile and the reptile; that man, with body and soul, is a matter of dollars and cents. I suggest to this portion of the Ohio Republicans, or Democrats if there be any present, the serious consideration of this fact, that there is now going on among you a steady process of debauching public opinion on this subject. With this my friends, I bid you adieu."

Chapter XXXVI

LINCOLN ADRESSES
THE SOUTHERN PEOPLE

Southern editors, orators and statesmen were now vigorously threatening secession if a Republican was elected President. This attempt to
intimidate Democratic antislavery voters from supporting the Republican
candidate was advanced by Douglas as a reason for ending the Republican party. It excited equally radical retaliation among Northern abolitionists. Lincoln would probably have accepted an invitation to speak in
any important Southern city had it been offered and no doubt he would
have presented compromising suggestions to both sides for restoring
peace. Cincinnati, then the largest and most important city west of the
Allegheny Mountains, with a population composed largely of Germans
and Kentuckians, and lying just across the Ohio River from Kentucky,
presented an opportunity for speaking directly to the Southern people.

Lincoln's notes written in September, 1859 for speeches in Ohio and
Kansas show the energy of his anti-Douglas, restrict slavery drive, and
how far he had progressed in forming a political philosophy for the
Republican party amid the scheming, turmoil, and shouting of hundreds
of political bosses, government officials, editors, ministers and sociol-
ogists who offered platforms and panaceas for the slavery question. Some
were sensibly considerate of the rights of Southern and Northern people,
but most were wildly prejudiced and unconstitutional. The notes show
even better than his speeches, how his thoughts were turning on the
greatest issue of the time, as forced toward a crises by the endless
pressure of the presidential ambitions of Douglas (Author's captions
except those quoted.)

"Introduction

"Purpose of the Republican organization

"The Republican party believe there is danger that slavery will be further
extended, and ultimately made national in the United States; and to prevent this incidental, and final consummation, is the *purpose* of their
organization.

"Chief danger to that purpose

"A congressional slave code, for the territories, and the revival of the
African Trade and a second Dred Scott decision, are not, just now the chief
danger to our purpose. These will press us in due time, but they are not
quite ready yet— they know that, as yet, we are too strong for them. The

insidious Douglas popular sovereignty, which prepares the way for this ultimate danger, it is, which just now constitutes our chief danger.

"Popular Sovereignty.

"I say Douglas popular sovereignty; for there is a broad distinction between *real* popular Sovereignty and Douglas popular sovereignty. That the nation shall control what concerns it; that a state, or any minor political community, shall control what exclusively concerns it; and that an individual shall control what exclusively concerns him, is a *real* popular sovereignty, which no republican opposes.

"But this is not Douglas popular sovereignty. Douglas popular sovereignty, as a matter of principle, simply is 'If one man would enslave another, neither that other, nor any third man, has the right to object.'

"Douglas popular sovereignty, as he practically applies it, is 'If any organized political community, however new and small, would enslave men, or forbid their being enslaved within its own territorial limits; however the doing the one or the other, may affect the men sought to be enslaved, or the vastly superior number of men who are afterwards to come within those limits; or the family of communities of which it is but a member, or the head of that family, as the parent, and common guardian of the whole— however any, or all, these are to be effected, neither any nor all may interfere'

"This is Douglas popular sovereignty.

"He has great difficulty with it. His speeches and letters, and essays, and explanations, explanatory of explanations explained, upon it, are legion. The most lengthy, and, as I suppose, the most maturely considered, is that recently published in Harper's Magazine. It has too *[sic]* leading objects —the first, to appropriate the authority and reverence, due the great and good men of the revolution, to his popular sovereignty; and secondly, to show that the Dred Scott decision has not entirely squelched his popular sovereignty.

"Before considering these main objects, I wish to consider a few minor points of the copy-right essay.

"Last year Gov. Seward and myself, at different times and occasions, expressed the opinion that slavery is a durable element of discord, and that we shall not have peace with it, until it either masters, or is mastered by, the free principle. This gave great offence to Judge Douglas; and his denunciations of it, and absurd inferences from it have never ceased. Almost at the very beginning of the copy-right essay he quotes the language respectively of Seward and myself (not quite accurately, but substantially in my case) upon this point, and repeats his absurd and extravagent inference. For lack of time I omit much which I might say here with propriety; and content myself with two remarks only upon this point. The first is that, inasmuch as Douglas, in this very essay, tells us slavery agitation began in this country, in 1699, and has not yet ceased—has lasted through a hundred and sixty years—through ten entire generations of men—it might have occurred to even him that slavery, in its tendency to agitation and discord, has something slightly durable about it. The second remark is that Judge Douglas might have noted, if he would while he was diving so deeply into history—the historical fact that the only comparative peace we have had with slavery during that hundred and sixty years, was in the period from the Revolution to 1820—precisely the period through which we were closing out the African slave-trade, abolishing slavery in several of the states, and restraining the spread of it into new ones, by the ordinance of '87—precisely the period in which the public mind had reason to rest, and did rest, in the belief that slavery was in course of ultimate extinction.

"Another point, which for the present I shall touch only hastily, is Judge Douglas' assumption that the states and territories differ only in the fact that the States are *in* the Union, and the territories are not in it. But if this be the only difference, why not instantly bring the territories in? Why keep them out? Do you say they are unfitted for it? What unfits them? Especially what unfits them for any duty in the Union, after they are fit, if they choose, to plant the soil they sparsely inhabit, with slavery, beyond the power of their millions of successors to eradicate it; and to the durable discord of the Union? What function of sovereignty, out of the Union or in it, is so portentous as this? What function of government requires such perfect maturity in numbers, and everything else, among those who exercise it? It is a concealed assumption of Douglas' popular sovereignty that slavery is a little, harmless, indifferent thing, having no wrong in it, and no power for mischief about it. If all men looked upon it as he does, his policy in regard to it might do. But neither all, nor half the world, so look upon it."

The Power of Congress

"Near the close of the essay Douglas tells us that his popular sovereignty pertains to a people only after they are regularly organized into a political community; and that congress, in its discretion, must decide when they are fit, in points of numbers, to be so organized. Now I should like for him to point out, in the constitution any clause conferring that discretion upon congress, which, when pointed out, will not be equally a power in congress to govern them, in it's discretion, till they are admitted as a State. Will he try? He intimates that before the exercise of that discretion, their number must be ten, fifteen, or twenty thousand. Well, what is to be done for them, or with them, or by them, before they number ten thousand? If any one of them desires to have slaves, is any other one bound to help him, or at liberty to hinder him? Is it his plan that any time before they reach the required number, those who are on hand shall be driven out as trespassers? If so, it will probably be a good while before a sufficient number to organize, will get in.

"But plainly enough this conceding to congress the discretion as to *when* a community shall be organized, is a total surrender of his popular sovereignty. He says himself it does not pertain to a people until they are organized; and that *when* they shall be organized is in the discretion of congress. Suppose congress shall choose to not organize them, until they are numerous enough to come into the Union as a State. By his own rule, his popular sovereignty is derived from Congress, and can not be exercised by the people till congress chooses to confer it. After toiling through nineteen mortal pages of Harper, to show that congress can not keep the people of a new country from excluding slavery, in a single closing paragraph he makes the whole thing depend on congress at last. And should congress refuse to organize, how will that affect the question of planting slavery in a new country? If individuals choose to plant it, the people can not prevent them, for they are not yet clothed with popular sovereignty. If it be said that it can not be planted, in fact, without protective law, that is already falsified by history; for it was originally planted on this continent without protective law.

"And, by the way, it is probable that no act of territorial organization could be passed by the present Senate; and almost certainly not by both the Senate and the House of Representatives. If an act declared the right of congress to exclude slavery, the Republicans would vote for it, and both wings of the democracy against it. If it denied the power to either exclude or protect it, the Douglasites would vote for it, and both the Repulicans and slave-coders against it. If it denied the power to exclude, and asserted the power to protect, the slave-coders would vote for it, and the Republicans and Douglasites against it."

To the People of Kansas

"You are now a part of a people of a Territory, but that territory is soon to be a state of the Union. Both in your individual, and collective capacities, you have the same interest in the past, the present, and the future, of the United States, as any other portion of the people. Most of you came from the states, and all of you soon will be citizens of the common Union. What I shall now address to you will have neither greater nor less application to you, than to any other people of the nation.

"You are gathered, to-day, as a Republican convention—republican, in the party sense, and, as we hope, in the true, original, sense of the word republican.

"I assume that Republicans, throughout the nation, believe they are right, and are earnest, and determined in their cause."

Danger of Nationalization of Slavery

"Let them, then, keep constantly in view that the chief object of their organization is to prevent the *spread* and *Nationalization,* of Slavery. With this ever distinctly before us we can always better see at what point our cause is most in danger.

"We are, as I think, in the present temper, or state of public sentiment, in no danger from the open advocates of a congressional slave code for the territories, and of the revival of the African slave-trade. As yet we are strong enough to meet, and master any combination openly formed on those grounds. It is only the insidious position of Douglas, that endangers our cause. That position is simply an ambuscade. By entering into contest with our open enemies, we are to be lured into his train; and then, having lost our own organization, and arms, we are to be turned over to those same open enemies.

"Douglas' position leads to the *nationalization* of Slavery as surely as does that of Jeff. Davis and Mason of Virginia. The two positions are but slightly different roads to the same place—with this difference, that the nationalization of slavery *can* be reached by Douglas' route, and never can by the other.

"I have said that in our present moral tone and temper, we are strong enough for our open enemies; and so we are. But the chief effect of Douglasism, is to change that tone and temper. Men who support the measures of a political leader do, almost of necessity, adopt the reasoning and sentiments the leader advances in support of them. The reasoning and sentiments advanced by Douglas in support of his policy as to slavery, all spring from the view that slavery is not wrong. In the first place he never says it is *wrong*. He says he does not care whether it shall be voted *down* or voted *up*. He says whoever wants slavery has a right to have it. He says the question whether people will have it or not is simply a question of dollars and cents. He says the Almighty has drawn a line across the continent, on *one side* of which the soil *must* be cultivated by slave labor.

"Now, let the people of the free-states adopt these sentiments, and they will be unable to see a single reason for maintaining their prohibitions of slavery in their own states. 'What! Do you mean to say that anything in these sentiments requires us to believe it will be the *interest* of the Northern states to have slavery?' No, I do mean to say, that although it is not the interest of the Northern states to grow *cotton*, none of them have, or need, any law against it; and it would be tyranny to deprive any one man of the privilege to grow cotton in Illinois. There are many individual men in all the free-states who desire to have slaves; and if you admit that slavery is not wrong, it is absolute tyranny to deny them the privilege. It is no just function of government to prohibit what is *not wrong*.

"Again, if slavery is right—ordained by the Almighty—on *one side* of a line, dividing sister states of a common Union, then it is positively wrong to harrass, and bedevil the owners of it, with constitutions, and laws, and prohibitions of it, on the other side of the line.

"In short, there is no justification for prohibiting slavery anywhere, save only in the assumption that slavery is *wrong*. And whenever the sentiment, that slavery is wrong, shall give way in the North, all legal prohibitions of it will also give way.

"If it be insisted that men may support Douglas' measures, without adopting his sentiments, let it be tested by what is actually passing before us. You can, even now, find no Douglas man who will disavow any one of these sentiments; and none but will actually indorse them, if pressed to the point.

"Five years ago no living man had placed on record, nor, as I believe verbally expressed, a denial that negroes have, a share in the Declaration of Independence. Two or three years since Douglas began to deny it; and now every Douglas man in the nation denies it.

"To the same effect is the absurdity compounded of *support* to the Dred Scott decision, and *unfriendly* legislation, to Slavery, by the territories—the absurdity which asserts that a thing may be *lawfully* driven from a place, at which place it has a *lawful* right to remain. That absurd position will not be long maintained by any one. The Dred Scott half of it, will soon master the other half. The process will probably be about this: some territorial legislature will adopt *unfriendly legislation;* the Supreme court will decide that legislation to be unconstitutional, and then the advocates of the present 'compound['] absurdity, will acquiesce in the decision. The only effect of that position now is, to prepare it's advocates for such acquiescence when the time comes. Like wood for ox-bows, they are

merely being *soaked* in it, preparatory to the bending. The advocates of
a slave code are not now strong enough to master us; and they never will
be, unless recruits enough to make them so, be tolled in through the gap
of Douglasism. Douglas, on the sly, is affecting more for them, than all
their open advocates. He has reason to be provoked, that they will not understand him, and recognize him as their best friend. He can not be *more*
plain, without being *so* plain, as to lure no one into their trap—so plain,
as to lose his power to serve them profitably. . . .

"At Memphis Douglas told his audience that he was for the negro
against the crocodile, but for the white man against the negro. This was
not a sudden thought spontaneously thrown off at Memphis. He said the
same thing many times in Illinois last summer and autumn, though I
am not sure it was reported then. It is a carefully framed illustration of the
estimate he places upon the negro and the manner he would have him dealt
with. It is a sort of proposition in proportion. 'As the negro is to the
crocodile, *so* the white man is to the negro.' As the negro ought to treat
the crocodile as a beast, so the white man ought to treat the negro as a
beast. Gentlemen of the South, is not that satisfactory? Will you give
Douglas no credit for impressing that sentiment on the Northern mind for
your benefit? Why, you should magnify him to the utmost, in order that
he may impress it the more deeply, broadly, and surely."

In Order to Unite

"A hope is often expressed that all the elements of opposition to the
so-called democracy may unite in the next presidential election; and to
favor this, it is suggested that at least *one* candidate on the opposition
national ticket, must be resident in the slave states. I strongly sympathize
with this hope; and the particular suggestion presents no difficulty with me.
There are very many men in the slave states who, *as* men, and statesmen,
and patriots, are quite acceptable to me for either President or Vice-
President. But there is a difficulty of another sort; and I think it most
prudent for us to face that difficulty at once. *Will* those good men of the
South occupy any ground upon which we of the free-states *can* vote for
them? There's the rub. They seem to labor under a huge mistake in regard
to us. They say they are *tired* of slavery *agitation.* We think the slaves,
and free white laboring men too, have more reason to be tired of *slavery,*
than masters have to be tired of *agitation* about it. In Kentucky a
democratic candidate for congress takes the ground *against* a congressional slave code for the territories; whereupon his opponent, in full hope
to unite with Republicans in 1860, takes ground *in favor* of such slave
code. Such hope, under such circumstances, is delusion gross as insanity
itself. Rational men can only entertain it, in the strange belief that Republicans are not in earnest for their principles—that they are really devoted
to no principle of their own, but are ready for, and anxious to jump to,
any position not occupied by the democracy. This mistake must be dispelled.
For the sake of their principles, in forming their party, they broke and
sacraficed, the strongest mere party ties and advantages which can exist.
Republicans believe that slavery is wrong; and they insist, and will continue
to insist upon a national policy which recognizes it, and deals with it, as a
wrong. There *can* be no letting down about this. Simultaneously with

such letting down, the republican organization itself would go to pieces, and half it's elements go in a different direction, leaving an easy victory to the common ene[my]. No ingenuity of political trading could possibly hold it together. About this there is no joke, and can be no trifling. Understanding this, that Republicanism can never mix with territorial slave-codes, becomes self evident."

Mere Men Are Nothing

"In this contest, mere men are nothing. We could come down to Douglas, quite as well, as to any other man standing *with* him; and better then to any other standing below, or beyond him. The simple problem is, will any good and capable man of the South, allow the Republicans to elect him, on their own platform? If such man can be found, I believe the thing can be done. It can be done, in no other way.

"But what do *we* gain, say you, by such a union? Certainly not everything; but still *something,* and quite *all* that we, for our lives, can possibly give. In yielding a share of the high honors and offices to you, you gain the assurance that ours is not a mere struggle to secure those honors and offices for one section. You gain the assurance that we mean no *more* than we say in our platforms; else we would not make one of you the executor of the laws, and commander of the Army and Navy.

"As a matter of mere partizan policy, there is no reason *for,* and much *against,* any letting down of the Republican platform in order to form a union with the Southern opposition. By no possibility can a union ticket secure a simple electoral vote in the South, unless the Republican platform be so far let down as to lose every electoral vote in the North; and even at that, not a single vote would be secured in the South, unless, by bare possibility, those of Maryland.

"There is no successful basis of union, but for some good Southern man to allow us of the North to elect him square on *our* platform. Plainly, it is that, or nothing."

I Am Not Wedded to the Formal Platform System

"The St. Louis Intellig[enc]er is out in favor of a *good man* for President, to be run *without* a platform. Well, I am not wedded to the formal written platform system; but a thousand to one, the editor is not himself in favor of his plan, except with the qualification, that he and his sort, are to select and name the *'good man.'* To bring him to the test, is he willing to take *Seward* without a platform? O, no; Seward's antecedents exclude him, say you. Well, is your *good man*, without antecedents? If he is, how shall the nation know that he is a good man? The sum of the matter is that, in the absence of formal written platforms, the antecedents of candidates become their platforms. On just such platforms, all our earlier and better Presidents were elected; but this by no means facilitates a union of men who differ in principles.

"Nor do I believe we can ever *advance* our *principles,* by supporting *men* who *oppose* our principles. Last year, as you know, we republicans in Illinois, were advised by numerous, and respectable outsiders to reelect Douglas to the Senate by our votes. I never questioned the motives

of such advisers; nor the devotion to the republican cause of such as professed to be republicans. But I never, for a moment, thought of following
the advice; and have never yet regretted that we did not follow it. True,
Douglas is back in the Senate in spite of us; but we are *clear* of *him,*
and *his* principles; and, we are uncrippled and ready to fight both him
and them straight along till they shall be finally 'closed out.' Had we
followed the advice, there would now be no Republican party in Illinois,
and none, to speak of, anywhere else. The whole thing would now be
floundering along after Douglas, upon the Dred Scott and crocodile theory.
It would have been the grandest *'haul'* for slavery, ever yet made. Our
principles would still live, and ere long would produce a party; but we
should have lost all our past *labor,* and twenty years of *time,* by the
folly.

"Take an illustration. About a year ago, all the republicans in congress
voted for what was called the Crittenden-Montgomery-bill; and forthwith
Douglas claimed, and still claims, that they were all committed to his
'gur-reat pur-rinciple.' And republicans have been so far embarrassed by
the claim, that they have ever since been protesting that they were not so
committed, and trying to explain why. Some of the very newspapers
which advised Douglas' return to the Senate by republican votes, have been
largely and continuously engaged in these protests, and explanations.
For such, let us state a question in the Rule of Three. If voting for the
Crittenden-Montgomery bill, entangle the republicans with Douglas' dogmas for one year, how long would voting for Douglas himself, so entangle,
them?

"It is nothing to the contrary, that republicanism gained something by
electing Haskin, Hickman and Davis. They were comparatively *small* men.
I mean no disrespect; they may have large merit; but Republicans can dally
with them, and absorb, or expel them, at pleasure. If they dally with
Douglas, he absorbs them."

Preview of Republican Platform of 1860

"We want, and must have, a national policy, as to slavery, which deals
with it as being a wrong. Whoever would prevent slavery becoming national
and perpetual, yields all when he yields to a policy which treats it either
as being *right,* or as being a matter of indifference.

"We admit that the U. S. general government is not charged with the
duty of redressing, or preventing, all the wrongs in the world. But that
government rightfully may, and, subject to the constitution, ought to,
redress and prevent, all wrongs, which are wrongs to the nation itself. It is
expressly charged with the duty of providing for the general welfare. We
think slavery impairs, and endangers the general welfare. Those who do not
think this are not of us, and we can not argue with them. We must shape
our own course by our own judgment.

"We must not disturb slavery in the states where it exists, because the
constitution, and the peace of the country, both forbid us. We must not
withhold an efficient fugitive slave law, because the constitution demands it.

"But we must, by a national policy, prevent the spread of slavery into
new territories, or free states, because the constitution does not forbid us,

and the general welfare does demand such prevention. We must prevent the revival of the African slave trade, because the constitution does not forbid us, and the general welfare does require the prevention. We must prevent these things being done by either *congresses* or *courts.* The people—the people—are the rightful masters of both congresses, and courts—not to overthrow the constitution, but to overthrow the men who pervert it.

"To effect our main object, we have to employ auxiliary means. We must hold conventions, adopt platforms, select candidates, and carry elections. At every step we must be true to the main purpose. If we adopt a platform, falling short of our principle, or elect a man rejecting our principle, we not only take nothing affirmative by our success; but we draw upon us the positive embarrassment of seeming ourselves to have abandoned our principle.

"That our principle, however baffled, or delayed, will finally triumph, I do not permit myself to doubt. Men will pass away—die—die, politically, and naturaly; but the principle will live, and live forever. Organizations, rallied around that principle, may, by their own dereliction, go to pieces, thereby losing all their time and labor. But the principle will remain, and will reproduce another, and another, till the final triumph will come.

"But to bring it *soon,* we must save our labor already performed—our organization, which has cost so much time and toil to create. We must keep our principle constantly in view, and never be false to it.

"And as to men, for leaders, we must remember that 'He that is not *for* us, is against us; and he that gathereth not with us scattereth.' "

These notes of September, 1859 indicate clearly that his attitude was changing from believing himself unfit to being fit for the Presidency.

Making Free States Out of Slave States

Douglas repeated his old assertion at Dayton, Ohio that the ordinance of 1787 (prohibiting slavery in the Northwest Territories) had never made a free state, and that Ohio had been made free solely by the action of its people

Lincoln replied in the same city, as on numerous other occasions, that after slavery was established in a territory it was extremely difficult to abolish it. Through the ordinance of 1787 the people of the territory of Ohio were free to draft a free state constitution in 1802 without difficulty. In contrast, the adjacent territory of Kentucky with the same climate was not protected by that ordinance and slavery became so extensively established that it adopted a proslavery constitution.

The history of the original states of the nation corroborates Lincoln's view that slavery, after being legally adopted by a state can only be eradicated with difficulty by the people. Maine was the only one of the original states that had prohibited slavery when the Union was formed. Vermont, New Hampshire, Massachusetts, Rhode Island, Connecticut, New York, Pennsylvania and New Jersey abolished slavery later but not without painful, internal political struggles.

Speech at Cincinnati (9, 17, 1859)

The following account of the Cincinnati speech is taken from *Collected Works*. The speech appeared in the *Illinois State Journal* (10, 7, 1859) after correction and revision, by Lincoln, of the text as it appeared in the Cincinnati *Gazette*. The captions in *Collected Works* have not been used. I have, instead, inserted others to mark the statements of Lincoln's ethical principles in political philosophy. He was now determined to force Douglas into such an untruthful, immoral, ambivalent slavery position that it would no longer be possible for him to get control of the Republican party. After thoroughly deflating his popular sovereignty balloon he offered him ironically to the Southern states as their best presidential candidate, knowing very well that Douglasism had become anathema there.

"*My fellow-citizens of the State of Ohio:* This is the first time in my life that I have appeared before an audience in so great a city as this. I therefore—though I am no longer a young man—make this appearance under some degree of embarrassment. But, I have found that when one is embarrassed, usually the shortest way to get through with it is to quit talking or thinking about it, and go at something else." [Applause.]

On Douglas' Agitation of War

"I understand that you have had recently with you, my very distinguished friend, Judge Douglas, of Illinois, [laughter] and I understand, without having had an opportunity, (not greatly sought to be sure), of seeing a report of the speech, that he made here, that he did me the honor to mention my humble name. I suppose that he did so for the purpose of making some objection to some sentiment at some time expressed by me. I should expect, it is true, that Judge Douglas had reminded you, or informed you, if you had never before heard it, that I had once in my life declared it as my opinion that this government cannot 'endure permanently half slave and half free; that a house divided against itself cannot stand,' and, as I had expressed it, I did not expect the house to fall; that I did not expect the Union to be dissolved; but that I did expect that it would cease to be divided; that it would become all one thing or all the other, that either the opponents of Slavery would arrest the further spread of it, and place it where the public mind would rest in the belief that it was in the course of ultimate extinction; or the friends of Slavery will push it forward until it becomes alike lawful in all the States, old or new, Free as well as Slave. I did, fifteen months ago express the opinion, and upon many occasions Judge Douglas denounced it, and has greatly, intentionally or unintentionally, misrepresented my purpose in the expression of that opinion.

"I presume, without having seen a report of his speech, that he did so here. I presume that he alluded also to that opinion in different language, having been expressed at a subsequent time by Governor Seward of New York, and that he took the two in a lump and denounced them; that he tried to point out that there was something couched in this opinion which led to the making of an entire uniformity of the local institutions of the various

States of the Union, in utter disregard of the different States, which in their nature would seem to require a variety of institutions, and a variety of laws, conforming to the differences in the nature of the different States.

"Not only so; I presume he insisted that this was a declaration of war between the Free and Slave States—that it was the sounding to the onset of continual war between the different States, the Slave and Free States.

"This charge, in this form, was made by Judge Douglas on, I believe, the 9th of July, 1858, in Chicago, in my hearing. In the next evening, I made some reply to it. I informed him that many of the inferences he drew from that expression of mine were altogether foreign to any purpose entertained by me, and in so far as he should ascribe those inferences to me, as my purpose, he was entirely mistaken; and in so far as he might argue that whatever might be my purpose, actions, conforming to my views, would lead to these results, he might argue and establish if he could; but, so far as purposes were concerned, he was totally mistaken as to me."

Upholds States' Rights To Slavery

"When I made that reply to him—when I told him, on the question of declaring war between the different States of the Union, that I had not said I did not expect any peace upon this question until Slavery was exterminated, that I had only said I expected peace when that institution was put where the public mind should rest in the belief that it was in course of ultimate extinction; that I believed from the organization of our government, until a very recent period of time, the institution had been placed and continued upon such a basis, that we had had comparative peace upon that question through a portion of that period of time, only because the public mind rested in that belief in regard to it, and that when we returned to that position in relation to that matter, I supposed we should again have peace as we previously had. I assured him, as I now assure you, that I neither then had, nor have, or ever had, any purpose in any way of interfering with the institution of Slavery, where it exists. [Long continued applause.] I believe we have no power, under the Constitution of the United States; or rather under the form of government under which we live, to interfere with the institution of Slavery, or any other of the institutions of our sister States, be they Free or Slave States. [Cries of "Good," and applause.] I declared then and I now re-declare, that I have as little inclination to so interfere with the institution of Slavery where it now exists, through the instrumentality of the general Government, or any other instrumentality, as I believe we have no power to do so. [A voice—"You're right."] I accidentally used this expression: I had no purpose of entering into the Slave States to disturb the institution of Slavery! So, upon the first occasion that Judge Douglas got an opportunity to reply to me, he passed by the whole body of what I had said upon that subject, and seized upon the particular expression of mine, that I had no purpose of entering into the Slave States to disturb the institution of Slavery! 'Oh, no,' said he, 'he [Lincoln] won't enter into the Slave States to disturb the institution of Slavery; he is too prudent a man to do such a thing as that; he only means that he will go on to the line between the Free and Slave States, and shoot over at them. [Laughter.] This is all he means to do. He means to do them all the harm he can, to disturb them all he can, in such a way as to keep his own hide in perfect safety.' [Laughter.]

"Well, now, I did not think, at that time, that that was either a very dignified or very logical argument; but so it was, I had to get along with it as well as I could.

"It has occurred to me here to-night, that if I ever do shoot over the line at the people on the other side of the line into a Slave State, and purpose to do so, keeping my skin safe, that I have now about the best chance I shall ever have. [Laughter and applause.] I should not wonder that there are some Kentuckians about this audience, we are close to Kentucky, and whether that be so or not, we are on elevated ground, and by speaking distinctly, I should not wonder if some of the Kentuckians would hear me on the other side of the river. [Laughter.] For that reason, I propose to address a portion of what I have to say to the Kentuckians."

Addresses Kentuckians and All Southerners

"I say then, in the first place, to the Kentuckians, that I am what they call, as I understand it, a 'Black Republican.' [Applause and laughter.] I think Slavery is wrong, morally, and politically. I desire that it should be no further spread in these United States, and I should not object if it should gradually terminate in the whole Union. [Applause.] While I say this for myself, I say to you, Kentuckians, that I understand you differ radically with me upon this proposition; that you believe Slavery is a good thing; that Slavery is right; that it ought to be extended and perpetuated in this Union. Now, there being this broad difference between us, I do not pretend in addressing myself to you, Kentuckians, to attempt proselyting you; that would be a vain effort. I do not enter upon it. I only propose to try to show you that you ought to nominate for the next Presidency, at Charleston, my distinguished friend Judge Douglas. [Applause.] In all that there is a difference between you and him, I understand he is as sincerely for you, and more wisely for you, than you are for yourselves. [Applause.] I will try to demonstrate that proposition. Understand now, I say that I believe he is as sincerely for you, and more wisely for you, than you are for yourselves."

Lincoln Nominates Douglas for Proslavery President

"What do you want more than anything else to make successful your views of Slavery,— to advance the outspread of it, and to secure and per- petuate the nationality of it? What do you want more than anything else? What is needed absolutely? What is indispensable to you? Why! if I may be allowed to answer the question, it is to retain a hold upon the North—it is to retain support and strength from the Free States. If you can get this support and strength from the Free States, you can succeed. If you do not get this support and this strength from the Free States, you are in the minority, and you are beaten at once.

"If that proposition be admitted, and it is undeniable, then the next thing I say to you, is that Douglas of all men in this nation is the only man that affords you any hold upon the Free States; that no other man can give you any strength in the Free States. This being so, if you doubt the other branch of the proposition, whether he is for you—whether he is really for you as I have expressed it, I propose asking your attention for awhile to a few facts.

"The issue between you and me, understand, is that I think Slavery is wrong, and ought not to be outspread, and you think it is right and ought to be extended and perpetuated. [A voice, "oh, Lord."] That is my Kentuckian I am talking to now. [Applause.]

"I now proceed to try to show you that Douglas is as sincerely for you and more wisely for you than you are for yourselves."

Importance of Public Opinion

"In the first place we know that in a Government like this, in a Government of the people, where the voice of all the men of the country, substantially enter into the execution,—or administration rather—of the Government—in such a Government, what lies at the bottom of all of it, is public opinion. I lay down the proposition, that Douglas is not only the man that promises you in advance a hold upon the North, and support in the North, but that he constantly moulds public opinion to your ends; that in every possible way he can, he constantly moulds the public opinion of the North to your ends; and if there are a few things in which he seems to be against you—a few things which he says that appear to be against you, and a few that he forbears to say which you would like to have him say—you ought to remember that the saying of the one, or the forbearing to say the other, would loose his hold upon the North, and, by consequence, would lose his capacity to serve you. [A Voice, "That is so."]

"Upon this subject of moulding public opinion, I call your attention to the fact—for a well-established fact it is—that the Judge never says your institution of Slavery is wrong; he never says it is right, to be sure, but he never says it is wrong. [Laughter.] There is not a public man in the United States, I believe, with the exception of Senator Douglas, who has not, at some time in his life, declared his opinion whether the thing is right or wrong; but, Senator Douglas never declared it is wrong. He leaves himself at perfect liberty to do all in your favor which he would be hindered from doing if he were to declare the thing to be wrong. On the contrary, he takes all the chances that he has for inveigling the sentiment of the North, opposed to Slavery, into your support, by never saying it is right. [Laughter.] This you ought to set down to his credit. [Laughter.] You ought to give him full credit for this much, little though it be, in comparison to the whole which he does for you."

Douglas' Political Opportunism

"Some other things I will ask your attention to. He said upon the floor of the United States Senate, and he has repeated it as I understand, a great many times, that he does not care whether Slavery is 'voted up or voted down.' This again shows you, or ought to show you, if you would reason upon it, that he does not believe it to be wrong, for a man may say, when he sees nothing wrong in a thing, that he does not care whether it be voted up or voted down, but no man can logically say that he cares not whether a thing goes up or goes down, which to him appears to be wrong. You therefore have a demonstration in this, that to Douglas' mind your favorite institution which you would have spread out, and made perpetual, is no wrong.

"Another thing he tells you, in a speech made at Memphis in Tennessee, shortly after the canvass in Illinois, last year. He there distinctly told the people, that there was a 'line drawn by the Almighty across this continent, on the one side of which the soil must always be cultivated by slaves,' that he did not pretend to know exactly where that line was, [laughter and applause,] but that there was such a line. I want to ask your attention to that proposition again; that there is one portion of this continent where the Almighty has designed the soil shall always be cultivated by slaves; that its being cultivated by slaves at that place is right; that it has the direct sympathy and authority of the Almighty. Whenever you can get these Northern audiences to adopt the opinion that Slavery is right on the other side of the Ohio; whenever you can get them, in pursuance of Douglas' views, to adopt that sentiment, they will very readily make the other argument, which is perfectly logical, that that which is right on that side of the Ohio, cannot be wrong on this, [laughter;] and that if you have that property on that side of the Ohio, under the seal and stamp of the Almighty, when by any means it escapes over here, it is wrong to have constitutions and laws, 'to devil' you about it. So Douglas is moulding the public opinion of the North, first to say that the thing is right in your State over the Ohio river, and hence to say that that which is right there is not wrong here, [at this moment the cannon was fired; to the great injury of sundry panes of glass in the vicinity,] and that all laws and constitutions here, recognizing it as being wrong, are themselves wrong, and ought to be repealed and abrogated. He will tell you, men of Ohio, that if you choose here to have laws against Slavery it is in conformity to the idea that your climate is not suited to it, that your climate is not suited to slave labor, and therefore you have constitutions and laws against it.

"Let us attend to that argument for a little while and see if it be sound. You do not raise sugar cane—(except the new fashioned sugar cane, and you won't raise that long) but they do raise it in Louisiana. You don't raise it in Ohio because you can't raise it profitably, because the climate don't suit it. [Here again the cannon interrupted. Its report was followed by another fall of window glass.] They do raise it in Louisiana because there it is profitable. Now, Douglas will tell you that is precisely the Slavery question. That they do have slaves there because they are profitable, and you don't have them here because they are not profitable. If that is so, then it leads to dealing with the one precisely as with the other. Is there anything in the Constitution or laws of Ohio against raising sugar cane? Have you found it necessary to put any such provision in your law? Surely not! No man desires to raise sugar cane in Ohio; but, if any man did desire to do so, you would say it was a tyrannical law that forbid his doing so, and whenever you shall agree with Douglas, whenever your minds are brought to adopt his argument, as surely you will have reached the conclusion, that although Slavery is not profitable in Ohio, if any man wants it, it is wrong to him not to let him have it.

"In this matter Judge Douglas is preparing the public mind for you of Kentucky, to make perpetual that good thing in your estimation, about which you and I differ."

The Changes in Five Years

"In this connection let me ask your attention to another thing. I believe it is safe to assert that five years ago, no living man had expressed the opinion that the negro had no share in the Declaration of Independence. Let me state that again: five years ago no living man had expressed the opinion that the negro had no share in the Declaration of Independence. If there is in this large audience any man who ever knew of that opinion being put upon paper as much as five years ago, I will be obliged to him now or at a subsequent time to show it.

"If that be true I wish you then to note the next fact; that within the space of five years Senator Douglas, in the argument of this question, has got his entire party, so far as I know, without exception, to join in saying that the negro has no share in the Declaration of Independence. If there be now in all these United States, one Douglas man that does not say this, I have been unable upon any occasion to scare him up. Now if none of you said this five years ago, and all of you say it now, that is a matter that you Kentuckians ought to note. That is a vast change in the Northern public sentiment upon that question.

"Of what tendency is that change? The tendency of that change is to bring the public mind to the conclusion that when men are spoken of, the negro is not meant; that when negroes are spoken of, brutes alone are contemplated. That change in public sentiment has already degraded the black man in the estimation of Douglas and his followers from the condition of a man of some sort, and assigned him to the condition of a brute. Now, you Kentuckians ought to give Douglas credit for this. That is the largest possible stride that can be made in regard to the perpetuation of your thing of Slavery."

A Voice— "Speak to Ohio men, and not to Kentuckians."

Mr. Lincoln— "I beg permission to speak as I please." [Laughter.]

The Bible's Justification of Slavery

"In Kentucky, perhaps, in many of the Slave States certainly, you are trying to establish the rightfulness of Slavery by reference to the Bible. You are trying to show that slavery existed in the Bible times by Divine ordinance. Now Douglas is wiser than you, for your own benefit, upon that subject. Douglas knows that whenever you establish that Slavery was right by the Bible, it will occur that that Slavery was the Slavery of the *white* man— of men without reference to color—and he knows very well that you may entertain that idea in Kentucky as much as you please, but you will never win any Northern support upon it. He makes a wiser argument for you; he makes the argument that the slavery of the *black* man, the slavery of the man who has a skin of a different color from your own, is right. He thereby brings to your support Northern voters who could not for a moment be brought by your own argument of the Bible-right of slavery. Will you not give him credit for that? Will you not say that in this matter he is more wisely for you than you are for yourselves.

"Now having established with his entire party this doctrine—having been successful in that branch of his efforts in your behalf; he is ready for another."

White Man vs. Negro vs. Crocodile

"At this same meeting at Memphis, he declared that while in all contests between the negro and the white man, he was for the white man, but that in all questions between the negro and the crocodile, he was for the negro. [Laughter.] He did not make that declaration accidentally at Memphis. He made it a great many times in the canvass in Illinois last year, (though I don't know that it was reported in any of his speeches there,) but he frequently made it. I believe he repeated it at Columbus, and I should not wonder if he repeated it here. It is, then, a deliberate way of expressing himself upon that subject. It is a matter of mature deliberation with him thus to express himself upon that point of his case. It therefore requires some deliberate attention.

"The first inference seems to be that if you do not enslave the negro you are wronging the white man in some way or other, and that whoever is opposed to the negro being enslaved is in some way or other against the white man. Is not that a falsehood? If there was a necessary conflict between the white man and the negro, I should be for the white man as much as Judge Douglas; but I say there is no such necessary conflict. I say that there is room enough for us all to be free, [loud manifestations of applause,] and that it not only does not wrong the white man that the negro should be free, but it positively wrongs the mass of the white men that the negro should be enslaved; that the mass of white men are really injured by the effect of slave labor in the vicinity of the fields of their own labor. [Applause.]

"But I do not desire to dwell upon this branch of the question more than to say that this assumption of his is false, and I do hope that that fallacy will not long prevail in the minds of intelligent white men. At all events, you Kentuckians ought to thank Judge Douglas for it. It is for your benefit it is made.

"The other branch of it is, that in a struggle between the negro and the crocodile, he is for the negro. Well, I don't know that there is any struggle between the negro and the crocodile, either. [Laughter.] I suppose that if a crocodile (or as we old Ohio boatsmen used to call them, alligators) should come across a white man, he would kill him if he could, and so he would a negro. But what, at last, is this proposition? I believe it is a sort of proposition in proportion, which may be stated thus: As the negro is to the white man, so is the crocodile to the negro, and as the negro may rightfully treat the crocodile as a beast or reptile, so the white man may rightfully treat the negro as a beast or reptile. [Applause.] That is really the 'knip' of all that argument of his.

"Now, my brother Kentuckians, who believe in this, you ought to thank Judge Douglas for having put that in a much more taking way than any of yourselves have done." [Applause.]

Popular Sovereignty and Slave Trade

"Again, Douglas' *great principle,* 'Popular Sovereignty,' as he calls it, gives you, by natural consequence, the revival of the Slave-trade whenever you want it. If you question this, listen a while, consider a while, what I shall advance in support of that proposition.

"He says that it is the sacred right of the man who goes into the Territories, to have Slavery if he wants it. Grant that for argument's sake. Is it not the sacred right of the man that don't go there equally to buy slaves in Africa, if he wants them? Can you point out the difference? The man who goes into the Territories of Kansas and Nebraska, or any other new Territory, with the sacred right of taking a slave there which belongs to him, would certainly have no more right to take one there than I would who own no slave, but who would desire to buy one and take him there. You will not say—you, the friends of Douglas—but that the man who does not own a slave, has an equal right to buy one and take him to the Territory, as the other does?"

A Voice. "I want to ask a question. Don't foreign nations interfere with the Slave-trade?"

Mr. Lincoln. "Well! I understand it to be a principle of Democracy to whip foreign nations whenever they interfere with us." [Laughter and applause.]

Voice. "I only asked for information. I am a Republican myself."

Mr. Lincoln. "You and I will be on the best terms in the world, but I do not wish to be diverted from the point I was trying to press.

"I say that Douglas' Popular Sovereignty, establishing a sacred right in the people, if you please, if carried to its logical conclusion, gives equally the sacred right to the people of the States or the Territories themselves to buy slaves, wherever they can buy them cheapest; and if any man can show a distinction, I should like to hear him try it. If any man can show how the people of Kansas have a better right to slaves because they want them, than the people of Georgia have to buy them in Africa, I want him to do it. I think it cannot be done. If it is 'Popular Sovereignty' for the people to have slaves because they want them, it is Popular sovereignty for them to buy them in Africa, because they desire to do so."

"I Think I know" What Framers of Constitution Wanted

"I know that Douglas has recently made a little effort—not seeming to notice that he had a different theory—has made an effort to get rid of that. He has written a letter addressed to somebody, I believe, who resides in Iowa, declaring his opposition to the repeal of the laws that prohibit the African Slave Trade. He bases his opposition to such repeal upon the ground that these laws are themselves one of the compromises of the Constitution of the United States. Now it would be very interesting to see Judge Douglas or any of his friends turn to the Constitution of the United States and point out that compromise, to show where there is any compromise in the Constitution or provision in the Constitution, express or implied, by which the Administrators of that Constitution are under any obligation to repeal the African Slave-trade. I know, or at least I think I know, that the framers of that Constitution did expect that the African Slave-trade would be abolished at the end of twenty years, to which time their prohibition against its being abolished extended. I think there is abundant contemporaneous history to show that the framers of the Constitution expected it to be abolished. But while they so expected, they gave nothing for that expectation, and they put no provision in the Constitution requiring it should be so abolished. The migration or importation of such persons as the States shall see fit to admit shall not be prohibited, but a certain tax might be levied upon such importation. But what was to be done after that time? The Constitution is as silent about that, as it is silent personally about myself. There is absolutely nothing in it about that subject—there is only the expectation of the framers of the Constitution that the Slave-trade would be abolished, owing to public sentiment, before that time, and they put that provision in, in order that it should not be abolished before that time, for reasons which I suppose they thought to be sound ones, but which I will not now try to enumerate before you.

"But while they expected the Slave-trade would be abolished at that time, they expected that the spread of Slavery into the new Territories should also be restricted. It is as easy to prove that the framers of the Constitution of the United States, expected that Slavery should be prohibited from extending into the new Territories, as it is to prove that it was expected that the Slave-trade should be abolished. Both these things were expected. One was no more expected than the other. There was nothing said in the Constitution in regard to the spread of Slavery into the Territory. I grant that, but there was something very important said about it by the same generation of men in the adoption of the old Ordinance of '87, through the influence of which you here in Ohio, our neighbors in Indiana, we in Illinois, our neighbors in Michigan and Wisconsin are happy, prosperous, teeming millions of free men. [Continued applause.] That generation of men, though not to the full extent members of the Convention that framed the Constitution, were to some extent members of that Convention, holding seats, at the same time in one body and the other, so that if there was any compromise on either of these subjects, the strong evidence is that that compromise was in favor of the restriction of Slavery from the new territories.

"But Douglas says that he is unalterably opposed to the repeal of those laws; because, in his view, it is a compromise of the Constitution. You Kentuckians, no doubt, are somewhat offended with that! You ought not to be! You ought to be patient! You ought to know that if he said less than that, he would lose the power of 'lugging' the Northern States to your support. Really, what you would push him to do would take from him his entire power to serve you. And you ought to remember how long, by precedent, Judge Douglas holds himself obliged to stick by compromises. You ought to remember that by the time you yourselves think you are ready to inaugurate measures for the revival of the African Slavetrade that sufficient time will have arrived by precedent, for Judge Douglas to break through that compromise. He says now nothing more strong than he said in 1849 when he declared in favor of the Missouri Compromise—that precisely four years and a quarter after he declared that compromise to be a sacred thing, which 'no ruthless hand would ever dare to touch,' he, himself, brought forward the measure, ruthlessly to destroy it. [A voice—"hit him again.'" Applause.] By a mere calculation of time it will only be four years more until he is ready to take back his profession about the sacredness of the Compromise abolishing the slave trade. Precisely as soon as you are ready to have his services in that direction, by fair calculation you may be sure of having them." [Applause and laughter.]

Ingenious Agitation of Democratic Schism

"But you remember and set down to Judge Douglas' debit, or discredit, that he, last year, said the people of the Territories can, in spite of the Dred

Scott decision, exclude your slaves from those territories; that he declared by 'unfriendly legislation,' the extension of your property into the new Territories may be cut off in the teeth of the decision of the Supreme Court of the United States.

"He assumed that position at Freeport on the 27th of August, 1858. He said that the people of the Territories can exclude Slavery in so many words. You ought, however, to bear in mind that he has never said it since. [Laughter.] You may hunt in every speech that he has since made, and he has never used that expression once. He has never seemed to notice that he is stating his views differently from what he did then; but, by some sort of accident, he has always really stated it differently. He has always since then declared that 'the Constitution does not carry Slavery into the Territories of the United States beyond the power of the people legally to control it, as other property.' Now, there is a difference in the language used upon that former occasion and in this latter day. There may or may not be a difference in the meaning, but it is worth while considering whether there is not also a difference in meaning.

"What is it to exclude? Why, it is to drive it out. It is in some way to put it out of the Territory. It is to force it across the line, or change its character, so that as property it is out of existence. But what is the controlling of it 'as other property?' Is controlling it as other property the same thing as destroying it, or driving it away? I should think not. I should think the controlling of it as other property would be just about what you in Kentucky should want. I understand the controlling of property means the controlling of it for the benefit of the owner of it. While I have no doubt the Supreme Court of the United States would say 'God speed' to any of the Territorial legislatures that should thus control slave property, they would sing quite a different tune if by the pretense of controlling it they were to undertake to pass laws which virtually excluded it, and that upon a very well known principle to all lawyers, that what a legislature cannot directly do, it cannot do by indirection; that as, the legislature has not the power to drive slaves out, they have no power by indirection, by tax or by imposing burdens in any way on that property, to effect the same end, and that any attempt to do so would be held by the Dred Scott Court unconstitutional.

"Douglas is not willing to stand by his first proposition that they can exclude it, because we have seen that that proposition amounts to nothing more nor less than the naked absurdity, that you may lawfully drive out that which has a lawful right to remain. He admitted at first that the slave might be lawfully taken into the Territories under the Constitution of the United States, and yet asserted that he might be lawfully driven out. That being the proposition, it is the absurdity I have stated. He is not willing to stand in the face of that direct, naked and impudent absurdity; he has, therefore, modified his language into that of being *'controlled as other property.'*

Why Douglas Swears by the Court

"The Kentuckians don't like this in Douglas! I will tell you where it will go. He now swears by the Court. He was once a leading man in Illinois to break down a Court, because it had made a decision he did not like. But he now not only swears by the Court, the courts having got to working for you, but he denounces all men that do not swear by the Courts, as unpatriotic, as bad citizens. When one of these acts of unfriendly legislation shall impose such heavy burdens as to, in effect, destroy property in slaves in a Territory and show plainly enough that there can be no mistake in the purpose of the Legislature to make them so burdensome, this same Supreme Court will decide that law to be unconstitutional, and he will be ready to say for your benefit, 'I swear by the Court; I give it up;' and while that is going on he has been getting all his men to swear by the Courts, and to give it up with him. In this again he serves you faithfully, and as I say, more wisely than you serve yourselves.

Pryor, Lincoln, Seward, on House Divided

"Again! I have alluded in the beginning of these remarks to the fact, that Judge Douglas has made great complaint of my having expressed the opinion that this Government 'cannot endure permanently half slave and half free.' He has complained of Seward for using different language, and declaring that there is an 'irrepressible conflict' between the principles of free and slave labor.

[A voice— "He says it is not original with Seward. That it is original with Lincoln."]

"I will attend to that immediately sir. Since that time, Hickman, of Pennsylvania expressed the same sentiment. He has never denounced Mr. Hickman: why? There is a little chance, notwithstanding, that opinion in the mouth of Hickman, that he may yet be a Douglas man. That is the difference! It is not unpatriotic to hold that opinion, if a man is a Douglas man.

"But neither I nor Seward, nor Hickman, is entitled to the enviable or unenviable distinction of having first expressed that idea. That same idea was expressed by the Richmond *Enquirer* in Virginia, in 1856; quite two years before it was expressed by the first of us. And while Douglas was pluming himself, that in his conflict with my humble self, last year, he had 'squelched out' that fatal heresy, as he delighted to call it, and had suggested that if he only had had a chance to be in New York and meet Seward he would have 'squelched' it there also, it never occurred [to him?] to breathe a word against Pryor.* I don't think that you can discover that Douglas ever talked of going to Virginia to 'squelch' out that idea there. No. More than that. That same Roger A. Prior was brought to Washington City and made the editor of the *par excellence* Douglas paper, after making use of that expression, which, in us, is so unpatriotic and heretical. From all this, my Kentucky friends may see that this opinion is heretical in his view only when it is expressed by men suspected of a desire that the country shall all become free and not when expressed by those fairly known to entertain the desire that the whole country shall become slave. When expressed by that class of men, it is in no wise offensive to him. In this again, my friends of Kentucky, you have Judge Douglas with you."

---

*Roger A. Pryor was editor of the Richmond *Enquirer*.

Nominate Douglas at Charleston

"There is another reason why you Southern people ought to nominate Douglas at your convention at Charleston. That reason is the wonderful capacity of the man; [laughter] the power he has of doing what would seem to be impossible. Let me call your attention to one of these apparently impossible things.

"Douglas had three or four very distinguished men of the most extreme anti-slavery views of any men in the Republican party, expressing their desire for his re-election to the Senate last year. That would, of itself, have seemed to be a little wonderful, but that wonder is heightened when we see that Wise of Virginia, a man exactly opposed to them, a man who believes in the Divine right of slavery, was also expressing his desire that Douglas should be re-elected, that another man that may be said to be kindred to Wise, Mr. Breckenridge, the Vice President, and of your own State, was also agreeing with the anti-slavery men in the North; that Douglas ought to be re-elected. Still, to heighten the wonder, a senator from Kentucky, whom I have always loved with an affection as tender and endearing as I have ever loved any man, who was opposed to the anti-slavery men for reasons which seemed sufficient to him, and equally opposed to Wise and Breckenridge, was writing letters into Illinois to secure the re-election of Douglas.* Now that all these conflicting elements should be brought, while at dagger's points, with one another, to support him, is a feat that is worthy for you to note and consider. It is quite probable, that each of these classes of men thought by the re-election of Douglas, their peculiar views would gain something, it is probable that the antislavery men thought their views would gain something that Wise and Breckenridge thought so too, as regards their opinions, that Mr. Crittenden thought that his views would gain something, although he was opposed to both these other men. It is probable that each and all of them thought that they were using Douglas, and it is yet an unsolved problem whether he was not using them all. If he was, then it is for you to consider whether that power to perform wonders, is one for you lightly to throw away."

South, Take Douglas or Be Defeated

"There is one other thing that I will say to you in this relation. It is but my opinion, I give it to you without a fee. It is my opinion that it is for you to take him or be defeated; and that if you do take him you may be beaten. You will surely be beaten if you do not take him. We, the Republicans and others forming the Opposition of the country, intend to 'stand by our guns,' to be patient and firm, and in the long run to beat you whether you take him or not. [Applause.] We know that before we fairly beat you, we have to beat you both together. We know that you are 'all of a feather,' [loud applause,] and that we have to beat you altogether, and we expect to do it. [Applause.] We don't intend to be very impatient about it. We mean to be as deliberate and calm about it as it is possible to be, but as firm and resolved, as it is possible for men to be. When we do as

*This statement gives some idea of the complexity of public opinion in the North and South for and against the extension of slavery.

we say, beat you, you perhaps want to know what we will do with you. [Laughter.]

"I will tell you, as far as I am authorized to speak for the Opposition, what we mean to do with you. We mean to treat you as near as we possibly can, like Washington, Jefferson and Madison treated you. [Cheers.] We mean to leave you alone, and in no way to interfere with your institution; to abide by all and every compromise of the constitution, and, in a word, coming back to the original proposition, to treat you, so far as degenerated men (if we have degenerated) may, according to the examples of those noble fathers—Washington, Jefferson and Madison. [Applause.] We mean to remember that you are as good as we; that there is no difference between us other than the differences of circumstances. We mean to recognise and bear in mind always that you have as good hearts in your bosoms as other people, or as we claim to have, and treat you accordingly. We mean to marry your girls when we have a chance—the white ones I mean—[laughter] and I have the honor to inform you that I once did have a chance in that way." [A voice, "Good for you," and applause.]

South, You Cannot Master Us

"I have told you what we mean to do. I want to know, now, when that thing takes place, what you mean to do. I often hear it intimated that you mean to divide the Union whenever a Republican, or anything like it, is elected President of the United States. [A voice, "That is so."] 'That is so,' one of them says. I wonder if he is a Kentuckian? [A voice, "He is a Douglas man."] Well, then, I want to know what you are going to do with your half of it? [Applause and laughter.] Are you going to split the Ohio [River] down through, and push your half off a piece? Or are you going to keep it right alongside of us outrageous fellows? Or are you going to build up a wall some way between your country and ours, by which that moveable property of yours can't come over here any more, to the danger of your losing it? Do you think you can better yourselves on that subject, by leaving us here under no obligation whatever to return those specimens of your moveable property that come hither? You have divided the Union because we would not do right with you as you think, upon that subject; when we cease to be under obligations to do anything for you, how much better off do you think you will be? Will you make war upon us and kill us all? Why, gentlemen, I think you are as gallant and as brave men as live; that you can fight as bravely in a good cause, man for man, as any other people living; that you have shown yourselves capable of this upon various occasions; but, man for man, you are not better than we are, and there are not so many of you as there are of us. [Loud cheering.] You will never make much of a hand at whipping us. If we were fewer in numbers than you, I think that you could whip us; if we were equal it would likely be a drawn battle; but inferior in numbers, you will make nothing by attempting to master us."

How Ohio, Indiana and Illinois Became Free States

"But perhaps I have addressed myself as long, or longer, to the Kentuckians than I ought to have done inasmuch as I have said that whatever course you take we intend in the end to beat you. I propose to address a few remarks to our friends by way of discussing with them the best means of keeping that promise, that I have in good faith made. [Long continued applause.]

"It may appear a little episodical for me to mention the topic of which I shall speak now. It is a favorite proposition of Douglas' that the interference of the General Government, through the Ordinance of '87, or through any other act of the General Government, never has made or ever can make a Free State; that the Ordinance of '87 did not make Free States of Ohio, Indiana or Illinois. That these States are free upon his 'great principle' of Popular Sovereignty, because the people of those several States have chosen to make them so. At Columbus, and probably here, he undertook to compliment the people that they themselves have made the State of Ohio free and that the Ordinance of '87 was not entitled in any degree to divide the honor with them. I have no doubt that the people of the State of Ohio did make her free according to their own will and judgment, but let the facts be remembered.

"In 1802, I believe, it was you who made your first constitution, with the clause prohibiting slavery, and you did it I suppose very nearly unanimously, but you should bear in mind that you—speaking of you as one people—that you did so unembarrassed by the actual presence of the institution amongst you; that you made it a Free State, not with the embarrassment upon you of already having among you many slaves, which if they had been here, and you had sought to make a Free State, you would not know what to do with. If they had been among you, embarrassing difficulties, most probably, would have induced you to tolerate a slave constitution instead of a free one, as indeed these very difficulties have constrained every people on this continent who have adopted slavery.

"Pray what was it that made you free? What kept you free? Did you not find your country free when you came to decide that Ohio should be a Free State? It is important to enquire by what reason you found it so? Let us take an illustration between the States of Ohio and Kentucky. Kentucky is separated by this river Ohio, not a mile wide. A portion of Kentucky, by reason of the course of the Ohio, is further north than this portion of Ohio in which we now stand. Kentucky is entirely covered with slavery—Ohio is entirely free from it. What made that difference? Was it climate? No! A portion of Kentucky was further north than this position of Ohio. Was it soil? No! There is nothing in the soil of the one more favorable to slave labor than the other. It was not climate or soil that caused one side of the line to be entirely covered with slavery and other side free of it. What was it? Study over it. Tell us, if you can, in all the range of conjecture, if there be anything you can conceive of that made that difference, other than that there was no law of any sort keeping it out of Kentucky? while the Ordinance of '87 kept it out of Ohio. If there is any other reason than this, I confess that it is wholly beyond my power to conceive of it. This, then, I offer to combat the idea that that ordinance has never made any State free.

"I don't stop at this illustration. I come to the State of Indiana; and what I have said as between Kentucky and Ohio I repeat as between Indiana and Kentucky; it is equally applicable. One additional argument is applicable also to Indiana. In her Territorial condition she more than once petitioned Congress to aborgate the ordinance entirely, or at least so far as to suspend its operation for a time, in order that they should exercise the 'Popular Sovereignty' of having slaves if they wanted them. The men then controlling the General Government, imitating the men of the Revolution, refused Indiana that privilege. And so we have the evidence that Indiana supposed she could have slaves, if it were not for that ordinance that she besought Congress to put that barrier out of the way; that Congress refused to do so, and it all ended at last in Indiana being a Free State. Tell me not, then, that the Ordinance of '87 had nothing to do with making Indiana a free state, when we find some men chafing against and only restrained by that barrier.

"Come down again to our State of Illinois. The great Northwest Territory including Ohio, Indiana, Illinois, Michigan and Wisconsin, was acquired, first I believe by the British Government, in part at least, from the French. Before the establishment of our independence, it became a part of Virginia, enabling Virginia afterwards to transfer it to the general government. There were French settlements in what is now Illinois, and at the same time there were French settlements in what is now Missouri— in the tract of country that was not purchased till about 1803. In these French settlements negro slavery had existed for many years— perhaps more than a hundred, if not as much as two hundred years— at Kaskaskia in Illinois, and at St. Genevieve, or Cape Girardeau, perhaps, in Missouri. The number of slaves was not very great, but there was about the same number in each place. They were there when we acquired the Territory. There was no effort made to break up the relation of master and slave and even the Ordinance of 1787 was not so enforced as to destroy that slavery in Illinois; nor did the Ordinance apply to Missouri at all.

"What I want to ask your attention to, at this point, is that Illinois and Missouri came into the Union about the same time, Illinois in the latter part of 1818, and Missouri, after a struggle, I believe some time in 1820. They had been filling up with American people about the same period of time; their progress enabling them to come into the Union [at] about the same [time]. At the end of that ten years, in which they had been so preparing, (for it was about that period of time) the number of slaves in Illinois had actually decreased; while in Missouri, beginning with very few, at the end of that ten years, there were about ten thousand. This being so, and it being remembered that Missouri and Illinois are, to a certain extent, in the same parallel of lattitude— that the Northern half of Missouri and the Southern half of Illinois are in the same parallel of lattitude— so that climate would have the same effect upon one as upon the other, and that in the soil there is no material difference so far as bears upon the question of slavery being settled upon one or the other— there being none of those natural causes to produce a difference in filling them, and yet there being a broad difference in their filling up, we are led again to inquire what was the cause of that difference.

"It is most natural to say that in Missouri there was no law to keep that country from filling up with slaves, while in Illinois there was the Ordinance of '87. The Ordinance being there, slavery decreased during that ten years— the Ordinance not being in the other, it increased from a few to ten thousand. Can anybody doubt the reason of the difference?

Douglas' Fallacy

"I think all these facts most abundantly prove that my friend Judge Douglas's proposition, that the Ordinance of '87 or the national restriction of slavery, never had a tendency to make a free State, is a fallacy—a proposition without the shadow or substance of truth about it.

"Douglas sometimes says that all the States (and it is part of this same proposition I have been discussing) that have become free, have become so upon his 'great principle'—that the State of Illinois itself came into the Union as a slave State, and that the people upon the 'great principle' of Popular Sovereignty have since made it a Free State. Allow me but a little while to state to you what facts there are to justify him in saying that Illinois came into the Union as a Slave State.

"I have mentioned to you that there were a few old French slaves there. They numbered, I think, one or two hundred. Besides that there had been a Territorial law for indenturing black persons. Under that law in violation of the Ordinance of '87, but without any enforcement of the Ordinance to overthrow the system, there had been a small number of slaves introduced as indentured persons. Owing to this the clause for the prohibition of slavery, was slightly modified. Instead of running like yours, that neither slavery nor involuntary servitude, except for crime of which the party shall have been duly convicted, should exist in the State, they said that neither slavery nor involuntary servitude should thereafter be introduced, and that the children of indentured servants should be born free; and nothing was said about the few old French slaves. Out of this fact, that the clause for prohibiting slavery was modified because of the actual presence of it, Douglas asserts again and again that Illinois came into the Union as a Slave State. How far the facts sustain the conclusion that he draws, it is for intelligent and impartial men to decide. I leave it with you with these remarks, worthy of being remembered, that that little thing, those few indentured servants being there, was of itself sufficient to modify a Constitution made by a people ardently desiring to have a free Constitution; showing the power of the actual presence of the institution of slavery to prevent any people, however anxious to make a Free State, from making it perfectly so.

"I have been detaining you longer perhaps than I ought to do. [Long and repeated cries of "go on."]

Compares Douglas and Himself on Popular Sovereignty

"I am in some doubt whether to introduce another topic upon which I could talk awhile. [Cries of "Go on," and "Give us it."] It is this then. Douglas' Popular Sovereignty as a principle, is simply this: If one man chooses to make a slave of another man, neither that other man or anybody else has a right to object. [Cheers and laughter.] Apply it to government, as he seeks to apply it and it is this—if, in a new Territory, into which a few people are beginning to enter for the purpose of making their homes, they choose to either exclude slavery from their limits, or to establish it there, however one or the other may effect the persons to be enslaved, or the infinitely greater number of persons who are afterwards to inhabit that Territory, or the other members of the family of communities, of which they are but an incipient member, or the general head of the family of states as parent of all—however their action may affect one or the other of these, there is no power or right to interfere. That is Douglas' Popular Sovereignty applied. Now I think that there is a real popular sovereignty in the world. I think a definition of popular sovereignty, in the abstract, would be about this—that each man shall do precisely as he pleases with himself, and with all those things which exclusively concern him. Applied in government, this principle would be, that a general government shall do all those things which pertain to it, and all the local governments shall do precisely as they please in respect to those matters which exclusively concern them.

"Douglas looks upon slavery as so insignificant that the people must decide that question for themselves, and yet they are not fit to decide who shall be their Governor, Judge or secretary, or who shall be any of their officers. These are vast national matters in his estimation but the little matter in his estimation, is that of planting slavery there. That is purely of local interest, which nobody should be allowed to say a word about. [Applause.]

"Labor is the great source from which nearly all, if not all, human comforts and necessities are drawn. There is a difference in opinion about the elements of labor in society. Some men assume that there is a necessary connection between capital and labor, and that connection draws within it the whole of the labor of the community. They assume that nobody works unless capital excites them to work. They begin next to consider what is the best way. They say that there are but two ways; one is to hire men and to allure them to labor by their consent; the other is to buy the men and drive them to it, and that is slavery. Having assumed that, they proceed to discuss the question of whether the laborers themselves are better off in the condition of slaves or of hired laborers, and they usually decide that they are better off in the condition of slaves.

"In the first place, I say, that the whole thing is a mistake. That there is a certain relation between capital and labor, I admit. That it does exist, and rightfully exists, I think is true. That men who are industrious, and sober, and honest in the pursuit of their own interests should after a while accumulate capital, and after that should be allowed to enjoy it in peace, and also if they should choose when they have accumulated it to use it to save themselves from actual labor and hire other people to labor for them is right. In doing so they do not wrong the man they employ for they find men who have not of their own land to work upon, or shops to work in, and who are benefited by working for others, hired laborers, receiving their capital for it. Thus a few men that own capital, hire a few others, and these establish the relation of capital and labor rightfully. A relation of which I make no complaint. But I insist that that relation after all does not embrace more than one-eighth of the labor of the country."

The speaker [reporter's reference to Lincoln] proceeded to argue that the hired laborer with his ability to become an employer, must have every precedence over him who labors under the inducement of force. He continued:

The Right National Policy

"I have taken upon myself in the name of some of you to say, that we expect upon these principles to ultimately beat them. In order to do so,

I think we want and must have a national policy in regard to the institution of slavery, that acknowledges and deals with that institution as being wrong. (Loud cheering.) Whoever desires the prevention of the spread of slavery and the nationalization of that institution, yields all, when he yields to any policy that either recognizes slavery as being right, or as being an indifferent thing. Nothing will make you successful but setting up a policy which shall treat the thing as being wrong. When I say this, I do not mean to say that this general government is charged with the duty of redressing or preventing all the wrongs in the world; but I do think that it is charged with the duty of preventing and redressing all wrongs which are wrongs to itself. This government is expressly charged with the duty of providing for the general welfare. We believe that the spreading out and perpetuity of the institution of slavery impairs the general welfare. We believe—nay, we know, that that is the only thing that has ever threatened the perpetuity of the Union itself. The only thing which has ever menaced the destruction of the government under which we live, is this very thing. To repress this thing, we think is providing for the general welfare. Our friends in Kentucky differ from us. We need not make our argument for them, but we who think it is wrong in all its relations, or in some of them at least, must decide as to our own actions, and our own course, upon our own judgment.

"I say that we must not interfere with the institution of slavery in the states where it exists, because the constitution forbids it, and the general welfare does not require us to do so. We must not withhold an efficient fugitive slave law because the constitution requires us, as I understand it, not to withhold such a law. But we must prevent the outspreading of the institution, because neither the constitution nor general welfare requires us to extend it. We must prevent the revival of the African slave trade and the enacting by Congress of a territorial slave code. We must prevent each of these things being done by either Congresses or courts. The people of these United States are the rightful masters of both Congresses and courts (applause) not to overthrow the constitution, but to overthrow the men who pervert that constitution. [Applause.]

"To do these things we must employ instrumentalities. We must hold conventions; we must adopt platforms if we conform to ordinary custom; we must nominate candidates, and we must carry elections. In all these things, I think that we ought to keep in view our real purpose, and in none do anything that stands adverse to our purpose. If we shall adopt a platform that fails to recognize or express our purpose, or elect a man that declares himself inimical to our purpose, we not only take nothing by our success, but we tacitly admit that we act upon no [other] principle than a desire to have 'the loaves and fishes' by which, in the end our apparent success is really an injury to us.

"I know that it is very desirable with me, as with everybody else, that all the elements of the Opposition shall unite in the next Presidential election and in all future time. I am anxious that that should be, but there are things seriously to be considered in relation to that matter. If the terms can be arranged, I am in favor of the Union. But suppose we shall take up some man and put him upon one end or the other of the ticket, who declares himself against us in regard to the prevention of the spread of slavery—who turns up his nose and says he is tired of hearing anything about it, who is more against us than against the enemy, what will be the issue? Why he will get no slave states after all—he has tried that already until being beat is the rule for him. If we nominate him upon that ground, he will not carry a slave state; and not only so, but that portion of our men who are high strung upon the principle we really fight for, will not go for him, and he won't get a single electoral vote anywhere, except, perhaps, in the state of Maryland. There is no use in saying to us that we are stubborn and obstinate, because we won't do some such thing as this. We cannot do it. We cannot get our men to vote it. I speak by the card, that we cannot give the state of Illinois in such case by fifty thousand. We would be flatter down than the 'Negro Democracy' themselves have the heart to wish to see us."

Proposes a Southerner for President

"After saying this much, let me say a little on the other side. There are plenty of men in the slave states that are altogether good enough for me to be either President or Vice President, provided they will profess their sympathy with our purpose, and will place themselves on the ground that our men, upon principle, can vote for them. There are scores of them, good men in their character for intelligence and talent and integrity. If such a one will place himself upon the right ground I am for his occupying one place upon the next Republican or Opposition ticket. [Applause.] I will heartily go for him. But, unless he does so place himself, I think it a matter of perfect nonsense to attempt to bring about a union upon any other basis; that if a union be made, the elements will scatter so that there can be no success for such a ticket, nor anything like success. The good old maxims of the Bible are applicable, and truly applicable to human affairs, and in this as in other things, we may say here that he who is not for us is against us; he who gathereth not with us scattereth. [Applause] I should be glad to have some of the many good, and able, and noble men of the south to place themselves where we can confer upon them the high honor of an election upon one or the other end of our ticket. It would do my soul good to do that thing. It would enable us to teach them that inasmuch as we select one of their own number to carry out our principles, we are free from the charge that we mean more than we say.

"But, my friends I have detained you much longer than I expected to do. I believe I may do myself the compliment to say that you have stayed and heard me with great patience, for which I return you my most sincere thanks."

Chapter XXXVII

BECOMING FIT TO BE PRESIDENT

The speeches in Illinois, Iowa, Ohio, Indiana, Wisconsin and Kansas consolidated for Lincoln intense public approval in the states descended from the Northwestern territories. We have followed the presentation of his principles through Ohio, and now continue with him through Indiana, Wisconsin and Kansas in order to see how they enabled him to react effectively and immediately to new crises as they developed. The increasing vigor of his expressed abhorrence of slave labor and determination to prevent its extension beyond the slave states, and his pointed determination to preserve the Union as an eternally binding contract between all of its member states, aroused a center of contagious enthusiasm in these states for making him the leader of the Republican party and its candidate for President.

Free Labor Has the Inspiration of Hope

Lincoln's notes repeat, from many different points of view for different audiences, the same social and political principles. They show how, before and after a speech, ideas on these principles would keep automatically reverberating in his mind so persistently that he would keep writing them over and again in one way and then another. A fragment of notes written in mid-September, 1859 contains the following comments.

"*Equality* in society, alike beats *inequality,* whether the latter be of the British aristocratic sort, or of the domestic slavery sort.

"We know; Southern men declare that their slaves are better off than hired laborers among us. How little they *know,* whereof they speak! There is no permanent class of hired laborers amongst us. Twentyfive years ago, I was a hired laborer. The hired laborer of yesterday, labors on his own account today; and will hire others to labor for him to-morrow. Advancement— improvement in condition— is the order of things in a society of equals. As Labor is the common *burthen* of our race, so the effort of *some* to shift their share of the burthen on to the shoulders of *others,* is the great, durable, curse of the race. Originally a curse for transgression upon the whole race, when, as by slavery, it is concentrated on a part only, it becomes the double-refined curse of God upon his creatures.

"Free labor has the inspiration of hope; pure slavery has no hope. The power of hope upon human exertion, and happiness, is wonderful. The slave-master himself has a conception of it; and hence the system of *tasks* among slaves. The slave whom you can not drive with the lash to break seventy-five pounds of hemp in a day, if you will task him to break a hundred, and promise him pay for all he does over, he will break you a hundred and fifty. You have substituted *hope,* for the *rod.* And yet perhaps it does not occur to you, that to the extent of your gain in the case, you have given up the slave system, and adopted the free system of labor."

The scientific investigations of modern psychology and sociology have shown that Lincoln's humanitarian principle of an organized society based on equal rights of free people has proven sound, as shown by the enormous superiority in mental development, material productivity, longevity and the pursuit of happiness of democratic peoples over all others. Here labor is free to work to acquire monetary returns commensurate with the immediate economic value of its output, and prevent frustration and exploitation under capitalistic control of supply and demand designed to increase private income. Organized free labor, through duly elected representatives in government, is now able to counterbalance the influence of organized capital, in having laws passed to regulate and equilibrate the rights of contract and income of both labor and capital for the greatest common good. The natural tendency of each man to exploit the labor of his fellows for his own benefit, through getting more for less, is not necessarily "the curse of God" but a psychological result of the processes of competitive evolution whereby is produced greater development of the human mind and human society. However, when uncontrolled by law, self-centered dominance of either capital or labor leads to gangsterism in which organized minorities control government and exploit unorganized masses. When the struggle for dominance is controlled by fairly adjudicated law, it produces a greater humanitarian society of equalitarian rights and fair economic opportunities, without undue privileges and oppressions.

Lincoln saw, in the pseudomoral self-justification of slave owners in America, an identification with the religiously moral assumption of divine rights by the British, hereditary titular, ruling class, to exploit legally the labor of its own people at home and in its colonies of subjected peoples. The former originated in the early British colonization of America, and continued in the South after slavery had undergone gradual extinction in the British Empire. In his notes on free labor, written probably in September 1859, Lincoln stated why he preferred it to domestic slavery and, we might add here, they indicate why he would have preferred that the state should belong to the people rather than the principle of absolute monarchy or communism, that all people belong to the state hence must submit abjectly to the dictations of a permanent, self-appointed circle of government officials.

At Indianapolis

We have observed in Lincoln's letters and speeches that he had an unusual sense of his personal relations with people as individuals and as groups. Although afflicted with a trying nervous disability he never spared himself time or energy in cultivating sympathetic, cooperative relations whenever possible. He disliked personal conflicts but never shirked them when the cause of human rights required him to take issue. But, whatever he had to say was given with the considerate respect for his opponent and himself characteristic of the thoroughgoing gentleman and sportsman.

At Indianapolis (9, 19, 1859) he addressed his audience as "Fellow citizens of the State of Indiana," and began with recounting briefly his life until 20 in Spencer County as evidence of his fond ties for the people of the state. He discussed largely the same issues presented in Ohio, and dwelt at considerable length on the division of the Northwest Territory into the states of Ohio, Indiana, Illinois, Wisconsin and Michigan and their admission into the Union as free states. He frankly reminded his audience that Indiana, when a territory, had petitioned Congress to abrogate the ordinance of 1787 in order that the people might exercise popular sovereignty and admit slaves. The petition was refused and Indiana and the other Northwestern Territories were prevented from becoming slave states. In the case of Missouri there was no law to prevent the introduction of slavery and it increased so rapidly that it became a slave state, whereas in the adjacent territory of Illinois, where the ordinance of 1787 applied, the number of slaves steadily decreased.

Lincoln's argument at Indianapolis was further devoted to showing that the "fathers" of the Constitution and of the ordinance of 1787 were largely the same men. Their attitudes of tolerance of slavery as decided by the various states and prohibition in the Territories expressed their dislike of slavery and hope for its gradual, but ultimate extinction. This argument so convincingly refuted Douglas' claim, that the ordinance of 1787 and the national restriction of slavery were never intended to make a free state, that he found himself becoming in public opinion the most impressive, authoritative interpreter of the Constitution in the nation.

On Agriculture and Labor

Lincoln's address before the Wisconsin State Agricultural Society, in Milwaukee (9, 30, 1859), constituted a diversion from political argument but was not without political influence in a nation now highly agitated over the immoral injustice and economic incompetence of slave labor. This speech should not be neglected in the study of the development of Lincoln's political philosophy. Although it lacks the inspiration characteristic of his political speeches, it reveals the breadth of his interest in human welfare. Later when President, he established a Department of Agriculture. (Captions inserted.)

"Members of the Agricultural Society and Citizens of Wisconsin:* Agricultural Fairs are becoming an institution of the country; they are

---

*This paper is taken from the Milwaukee *Sentinel* and Chicago *Press and Tribune* of October 1, 1859, as reproduced in *Collected Works.* It was published from a manuscript, originally prepared by Lincoln.

useful in more ways than one; they bring us together, and thereby make us
better acquainted, and better friends than we otherwise would be."

Culture of Sympathetic Friendship Basic for Civilization

"From the first appearance of man upon the earth, down to very recent
times, the words 'stranger' and 'enemy' were *quite* or *almost*, synonymous. Long after civilized nations had defined robbery and murder as
high crimes, and had affixed severe punishments to them, when practiced
among and upon their own people respectively, it was deemed no offence,
but even meritorious, to rob, and murder, and enslave *strangers*, whether
as nations or as individuals. Even yet, this has not totally disappeared. The
man of the highest moral cultivation, in spite of all which abstract principle
can do, likes him whom he *does* know, much better than him whom
he does *not* know. To correct the evils, great and small, which spring
from want of sympathy, and from positive enmity, among *strangers*, as
nations, or as individuals, is one of the highest functions of civilization. To
this end our Agricultural Fairs contribute in no small degree. They make
more pleasant, and more strong, and more durable, the bond of social and
political union among us. Again, if, as Pope declares, 'happiness is our
being's end and aim,' our Fairs contribute much to that end and aim, as
occasions of recreation—holidays. Constituted as man is, he has positive
need of occasional recreation; and whatever can give him this, associated
with virtue and advantage, and free from vice and disadvantage, is a positive
good. Such recreation our Fairs afford. They are a present pleasure, to be
followed by no pain, as a consequence; they are a present pleasure, making
the future more pleasant."

Chief Use of Agricultural Fairs

"But the chief use of agricultural fairs is to aid in improving the great
calling of *agriculture,* in all it's departments, and minute divisions—to
make mutual exchange of agricultural discovery, information and knowledge; so that, at the end, *all* may know every thing, which may have
been known to but *one,* or to but a *few,* at the beginning—to bring
together especially all which is supposed to not be generally known, because
of recent discovery, or invention.

"And not only to bring together, and to impart all which has been
accidentally discovered or invented upon ordinary motive; but, by exciting emulation, for premiums, and for the pride and honor of success—of
triumph, in some sort—to stimulate that discovery and invention into extraordinary activity. In this, these Fairs are kindred to the patent clause in the
Constitution of the United States; and to the department, and practical
system, based upon that clause.

"One feature, I believe, of every fair, is a regular *address.* The Ag-
gricultural Society of the young, prosperous, and soon to be, great State
of Wisconsin, has done me the high honor of selecting me to make that
address upon this occasion—an honor for which I make my profound, and
grateful acknowledgement."

Farmer's Interest Should Be Cultivated

"I presume I am not expected to employ the time assigned me, in the mere flattery of the farmers, as a class. My opinion of them is that, in proportion to numbers, they are neither better nor worse than other people. In the nature of things they are more numerous than any other class; and I believe there really are more attempts at flattering them than any other; the reason of which I cannot perceive, unless it be that they can cast more votes than any other. On reflection, I am not quite sure that there is not cause of suspicion against you, in selecting me, in some sort a politician, and in no sort a farmer, to address you.

"But farmers, being the most numerous class, it follows that their interest is the largest interest. It also follows that their interest is most worthy of all to be cherished and cultivated—that if there be inevitable conflict between that interest and any other, that other should yield.

"Again, I suppose it is not expected of me to impart to you much specific information on Agriculture. You have no reason to believe, and do not believe, that I possess it—if that were what you seek in this address, any one of your own number, or class, would be more able to furnish it.

"You, perhaps, do expect me to give some general interest to the occasion; and to make some general suggestions, on practical matters. I shall attempt nothing more. And in such suggestions by me, quite likely very little will be new to you, and a large part of the rest possibly already known to be erroneous."

Relativity of Labor and Production

"My first suggestion is an inquiry as to the effect of greater *thoroughness* in all the departments of Agriculture than now prevails in the North-West—perhaps I might say in America. To speak entirely within bounds, it is known that fifty bushels of wheat, or one hundred bushels of Indian corn can be produced from an acre. Less than a year ago I saw it stated that a man, by extraordinary care and labor, had produced of wheat, what was equal to two hundred bushels from an acre. But take fifty of wheat, and one hundred of corn, to be the possibility, and compare with it the actual crops of the country. Many years ago I saw it stated in a Patent Office Report that eighteen bushels was the average crop throughout the wheat growing region of the United States; and this year an intelligent farmer of Illinois, assured me that he did not believe the land harvested in that State this season, had yielded more than an average of eight bushels to the acre. The brag crop I heard of in our vicinity was two thousand bushels from ninety acres. Many crops were thrashed, producing no more than three bushels to the acre; much was cut, and then abandoned as not worth threshing; and much was abandoned as not worth cutting. As to Indian corn, and, indeed, most other crops, the case has not been much better. For the last four years I do not believe the ground planted with corn in Illinois, has produced an average of twenty bushels to the acre. It is true, that heretofore we have had better crops, with no better cultivators; but I believe it is also true that the soil has never been pushed up to one-half of its capacity.

"What would be the effect upon the farming interest, to push the soil up to something near its full capacity? Unquestionably it will take more labor to produce *fifty* bushels from an acre, than it will to produce *ten* bushels from the same acre. But will it take more labor to produce fifty bushels from *one* acre, than from *five?* Unquestionably, thorough cultivation will require more labor to the *acre;* but will it require more to the *bushel?* If it should require just as *much* to the bushel, there are some *probable,* and several *certain,* advantages in favor of the thorough practice. It is probable it would develope these unknown causes, or develope unknown cures for those causes, which of late years have cut down our crops below their former average. It is almost certain, I think, that in the deeper plowing, analysis of soils, experiments with manures, and varieties of seeds, observance of seasons, and the like, these cases [causes?] would be found. It is certain that thorough cultivation would spare half or more than half, the cost of land, simply because the same product would be got from half, or from less than half the quantity of land. This proposition is self-evident, and can be made no plainer by repetitions or illustrations. The cost of land is a great item, even in new countries; and constantly grows greater and greater, in comparison with other items, as the country grows older.

"It also would spare a large proportion of the making and maintaining of inclosures—the same, whether these inclosures should be hedges, ditches, or fences. This again, is a heavy item—heavy at first, and heavy in its continual demand for repairs. I remember once being greatly astonished by an apparently authentic exhibition of the proportion the cost of inclosures bears to all the other expenses of the farmer; though I can not remember exactly what that proportion was. Any farmer, if he will, can ascertain it in his own case, for himself.

"Again, a great amount of 'locomotion' is spared by thorough cultivation. Take fifty bushels of wheat, ready for the harvest, standing upon a *single* acre, and it can be harvested in any of the known ways, with less than half the labor which would be required if it were spread over *five* acres. This would be true, if cut by the old hand sickle; true, to a greater extent if by the scythe and cradle; and to a still greater extent, if by the machines now in use. These machines are chiefly valuable, as a means of substituting animal power for the power of men in this branch of farm work. In the highest degree of perfection yet reached in applying the horse power to harvesting, fully nine-tenths of the power is expended by the animal in carrying himself and dragging the machine over the field, leaving certainly not more than one-tenth to be applied directly to the only end of the whole operation—the gathering in the grain, and clipping of the straw. When grain is very thin on the ground, it is always more or less intermingled with weeds, chess and the like, and a large part of the power is expended in cutting these. It is plain that when the crop is very thick upon the ground, the larger proportion of the power is directly applied to gathering in and cutting it; and the smaller, to that which is totally useless as an end. And what I have said of harvesting is true, in a greater or less degree of mowing, plowing, gathering in of crops generally, and, indeed, of almost all farm work."

Every Man Is Proud of What He Does Well

"The effect of thorough cultivation upon the farmer's own mind, and, in reaction through his mind, back upon his business, is perhaps quite equal to any other of its effects. Every man is proud of what he does *well;* and no man is proud of what he does *not* do well. With the former, his heart is in his work; and he will do twice as much of it with less fatigue. The latter performs a little imperfectly, looks at it in disgust, turns from it, and imagines himself exceedingly tired. The little he has done, comes to nothing, for want of finishing.

"The man who produces a good full crop will scarcely ever let any part of it go to waste. He will keep up the enclosure about it, and allow neither man nor beast to trespass upon it. He will gather it in due season and store it in perfect security. Thus he labors with satisfaction, and saves himself the whole fruit of his labor. The other, starting with no purpose for a full crop, labors less, and with less satisfaction; allows his fences to fall, and cattle to trespass; gathers not in due season, or not at all. Thus the labor he has performed, is wasted away, little by little, till in the end, he derives scarcely anything from it.

"The ambition for broad acres leads to poor farming, even with men of energy. I scarcely ever knew a mammoth farm to sustain itself; much less to return a profit upon the outlay. I have more than once known a man to spend a respectable fortune upon one; fail and leave it; and then some man of more modest aims, get a small fraction of the ground, and make a good living upon it. Mammoth farms are like tools or weapons, which are too heavy to be handled. Ere long they are thrown aside, at a great loss."

Suggestions for a Steam Plow

"The successful application of *steam power,* to farm work is a *desideratum*— especially a Steam Plow. It is not enough, that a machine operated by steam, will really plow. To be successful, it must, all things considered, plow *better* than can be done with animal power. It must do all the work as well, and *cheaper;* or more *rapidly,* so as to get through more perfectly *in season;* or in some way afford an advantage over plowing with animals, else it is no success. I have never seen a machine intended for a Steam Plow. Much praise, and admiration, are bestowed upon some of them; and they may be, for aught I know, already successful; but I have not perceived the demonstration of it. I have thought a good deal, in an abstract way, about a Steam Plow. That one which shall be so contrived as to apply the larger proportion of its power to the cutting and turning the soil, and the smallest, to the moving itself over the field, will be the best one. A very small stationary engine would draw a large gang of plows through the ground from a short distance to itself; but when it is not stationary, but has to move along like a horse, dragging the plows after it, it must have additional power to carry itself; and the difficulty grows by what is intended to overcome it; for what adds power also adds size, and weight to the machine, thus increasing again, the demand for power. Suppose you should construct a machine so as to cut a succession of short furrows, say a rod in length, transversely to the course the machine is locomoting, something like the shuttle in weaving. In such case the whole machine would move North only the width of a furrow, while in length, the furrow would be a rod from East to West. In such case, a very large proportion of the power, would be applied to the actual plowing. But in this, too, there would be a difficulty, which would be the getting of the plow *into,* and *out of,* the ground, at the ends of all these short furrows.

"I believe, however, ingenious men will, if they have not already, over-come the difficulty I have suggested. But there is still another, about which I am less sanguine. It is the supply of *fuel,* and especially of *water,* to make steam. Such supply is clearly practicable, but can the expense of it be borne? Steamboats live upon the water, and find their fuel at stated places. Steam mills, and other stationary steam machinery, have their sta-tionary supplies of fuel and water. Railroad locomotives have their regular wood and water station. But the steam plow is less fortunate. It does not live upon the water; and if it be once at a water station, it will work away from it, and when it gets away can not return, without leaving its work, at a great expense of its time and strength. It will occur that a wagon and horse team might be employed to supply it with fuel and water; but this, too, is expensive; and the question recurs, 'can the expense be borne?' When this is added to all other expenses, will not the plowing cost more than in the old way?

"It is to be hoped that the steam plow will be finally successful, and if it shall be, *'thorough cultivation'*—putting the soil to the top of its capacity—producing the largest crop possible from a given quantity of ground—will be most favorable to it. Doing a large amount of work upon a small quan-tity of ground, it will be, as nearly as possible, stationary while working, and as free as possible from locomotion; thus expending its strength as much as possible upon its work, and as little as possible in travelling.* Our thanks, and something more substantial than thanks, are due to every man engaged in the effort to produce a successful steam plow. Even the unsuccessful will bring something to light, which, in the hands of others, will contribute to the final success. I have not pointed out difficulties, in order to discourage, but in order that being seen, they may be the more readily overcome."

Derides the "Mud-Sill" Theory of Labor

"The world is agreed that *labor* is the source from which human wants are mainly supplied. There is no dispute upon this point. From this point, however, men immediately diverge. Much disputation is maintained as to the best way of applying and controlling the labor element. By some it is assumed that labor is available only in connection with capital—that nobody labors, unless somebody else, owning capital, somehow, by the use of that capital, induces him to do it. Having assumed this, they proceed to consider whether it is best that capital shall *hire* laborers, and thus induce them to work by their own consent; or *buy* them, and drive them to it without their consent. Having proceeded so far they naturally conclude that all laborers are necessarily either *hired* laborers, or *slaves*. They further assume that whoever is once a *hired* laborer, is fatally fixed

*Lincoln's suggestion for a steam plow never proved feasible. However, a practical steam tractor was developed that pulled a series of plows attached in parallel in a frame.

in that condition for life; and thence again that his condition is as bad as, or worse than that of a slave. This is the 'mud-sill' theory.

"But another class of reasoners hold the opinion that there is no *such* relation between capital and labor, as assumed; and that there is no such thing as a freeman being fatally fixed for life, in the condition of a hired laborer, that both these assumptions are false, and all inferences from them groundless. They hold that labor is prior to, and independent of, capital; that, in fact, capital is the fruit of labor, and could never have existed if labor had not *first* existed— that labor can exist without capital, but that capital could never have existed without labor. Hence they hold that labor is the superior— greatly the superior— of capital.

"They do not deny that there is, and probably always will be, *a* relation between labor and capital. The error, as they hold, is in assuming that the *whole* labor of the world exists within that relation. A few men own capital, and that few avoid labor themselves, and with their capital, hire, or buy, another few to labor for them. A large majority belong to neither class— neither work for others, nor have others working for them. Even in all our slave States, a large majority are neither *hirers* nor *hired*. Men, with their families—wives, sons and daughters—work for themselves, on their farms, in their houses and in their shops, taking the whole product to themselves, and asking no favors of capital on the one hand, nor of hirelings or slaves on the other. It is not forgotten that a considerable number of persons mingle their own labor with capital; that is, labor with their own hands, but also buy slaves or hire freemen to labor for them; but this is only a *mixed*, and not a *distinct* class. Again, as has already been said, the opponents of the 'mud-sill' theory insist that there is not, of necessity, any such thing as the free hired laborer being fixed to that condition for life. There is demonstration for saying this. Many independent men, in this assembly, doubtless a few years ago were hired laborers. And their case is almost if not quite the general rule."

Labor and Education

"The prudent, penniless beginner in the world, labors for wages awhile, saves a surplus with which to buy tools or land, for himself; then labors on his own account another while, and at length hires another new beginner to help him. This, say its advocates, is *free* labor—the just and generous, and prosperous system, which opens the way for all—gives hope to all, and energy, and progress, and improvement of condition to all. If any continue through life in the condition of the hired laborer, it is not the fault of the system, but because of either a dependent nature which prefers it, or improvidence, folly, or singular misfortune. I have said this much about the elements of labor generally, as introductory to the consideration of a new phase which that element is in process of assuming. The old general rule was that *educated* people did not perform manual labor. They managed to eat their bread, leaving the toil of producing it to the uneducated. This was not an insupportable evil to the working bees, so long as the class of drones remained very small. But *now*, especially in these free States, nearly all are educated— quite too nearly all, to leave the labor of the uneducated, in any wise adequate to the support of the whole. It follows from this that henceforth educated people must labor. Otherwise, education itself would become a positive and intolerable evil. No country can sustain, in idleness, more than a small percentage of its numbers. The great majority must labor at something productive. From these premises the problem springs, 'How can *labor* and *education* be the most satisfactorily combined?'

"By the *mud-sill* theory it is assumed that labor and education are incompatible; and any practical combination of them impossible. According to that theory, a blind horse upon a tread-mill, is a perfect illustration of what a laborer should be—all the better for being blind, that he could not tread out of place, or kick understandingly. According to that theory, the education of laborers, is not only useless, but pernicious, and dangerous. In fact, it is, in some sort, deemed a misfortune that laborers should have heads at all. Those same heads are regarded as explosive materials, only to be safely kept in damp places, as far as possible from that peculiar sort of fire which ignites them. A Yankee who could invent a strong *handed* man without a head would receive the everlasting gratitude of the 'mud-sill' advocates.

"But Free Labor says 'no!' Free Labor argues that, as the Author of man makes every individual with one head and one pair of hands, it was probably intended that heads and hands should cooperate as friends; and that that particular head, should direct and control that particular pair of hands. As each man has one mouth to be fed, and one pair of hands to furnish food, it was probably intended that that particular pair of hands should feed that particular mouth—that each head is the natural guardian, director, and protector of the hands and mouth inseparably connected with it; and that being so, every head should be cultivated, and improved, by whatever will add to its capacity for performing its charge. In one word Free Labor insists on universal education.

"I have so far stated the opposite theories of 'Mud-Sill' and 'Free Labor' without declaring any preference of my own between them. On an occasion like this I ought not to declare any. I suppose, however, I shall not be mistaken, in assuming as a fact, that the people of Wisconsin prefer free labor, with its natural companion, education."

Nothing So Pleasant as Discovery

"This leads to the further reflection, that no other human occupation opens so wide a field for the profitable and agreeable combination of labor with cultivated thought, as agriculture. I know of nothing so pleasant to the mind, as the discovery of anything which is at once *new* and *valuable*—nothing which so lightens and sweetens toil, as the hopeful pursuit of such discovery. And how vast, and how varied a field is agriculture, for such discovery. The mind, already trained to thought, in the country school, or higher school, cannot fail to find there an exhaustless source of profitable enjoyment. Every blade of grass is a study; and to produce two, where there was but one, is both a profit and a pleasure. And not grass alone; but soils, seeds, and seasons—hedges, ditches, and fences, draining, droughts, and irrigation—plowing, hoeing, and harrowing—reaping, mowing, and threshing—saving crops, pests of crops, diseases of crops, and what will prevent or cure them—implements, utensils, and machines, their relative merits, and [how] to improve them—hogs, horses, and cattle—sheep, goats, and poultry—

trees, shrubs, fruits, plants, and flowers—the thousand things of which these are specimens— each a world of study within itself.

"In all this, book-learning is available. A capacity, and taste, for reading, gives access to whatever has already been discovered by others. It is the key, or one of the keys, to the already solved problems. And not only so. It gives a relish, and facility, for successfully pursuing the unsolved ones. The rudiments of science, are available, and highly valuable. Some knowledge of Botany assists in dealing with the vegetable world—with all growing crops. Chemistry assists in the analysis of soils, selection, and application of manures, and in numerous other ways. The mechanical branches of Natural Philosophy, are ready help in almost everything; but especially in reference to implements and machinery."

Value of Thorough Work

"The thought recurs that education—cultivated thought—can best be combined with agricultural labor, or any labor, on the principle of *thorough* work— that careless, half performed, slovenly work, makes no place for such combination. And thorough work, again, renders sufficient the smallest quantity of ground to each man. And this again, conforms to what must occur in a world less inclined to wars, and more devoted to the arts of peace, than heretofore. Population must increase rapidly—more rapidly than in former times—and ere long the most valuable of all arts, will be the art of deriving a comfortable subsistence from the smallest area of soil. No community whose every member possesses this art, can ever be the victim of oppression in any of its forms. Such community will be alike independent of crowned-kings, money-kings, and land-kings.

"But, according to your programme, the awarding of premiums awaits the closing of this address. Considering the deep interest necessarily pertaining to that performance, it would be no wonder if I am already heard with some impatience. I will detain you but a moment longer. Some of you will be successful, and such will need but little philosophy to take them home in cheerful spirits; others will be disappointed, and will be in a less happy mood. To such, let it be said, 'Lay it not too much to heart.' Let them adopt the maxim, 'Better luck next time;' and then, by renewed exertion, make that better luck for themselves.

"And by the successful, and the unsuccessful, let it be remembered, that while occasions like the present, bring their sober and durable benefits, the exultations and mortifications of them, are but temporary; that the victor shall soon be the vanguished, if he relax in his exertion; and that the vanguished this year, may be victor the next, in spite of all competition."

This Shall Not Pass Away

"It is said an Eastern monarch once charged his wise men to invent him a sentence, to be ever in view, and which should be true and appropriate in all times and situations. They presented him the words: *'and this, too, shall pass away.'* How much it expresses! How chastening in the hour of pride!— how consoling in the depths of affliction! 'And this, too shall pass away.' And yet let us hope it is not *quite* true. Let us hope, rather, that by the best cultivation of the physical world, beneath and around us; and the intellectual and moral world within us, we shall secure an individual, social, and political prosperity and happiness, whose course shall be onward and upward, and which, while the earth endures, shall not pass away."

Importance of Making Correct Statements

Lincoln kept himself so thoroughly informed on the policies and records of influential politicians and legislators of all parties and the reactions of the public that he could discuss them accurately years later without need of verification. He kept his mind remarkably free from personally wishful and resentful impediments and distortions of thinking, in a field where sentiment, for or against a man, is easily aroused and readily turned in prejudicial directions; where estimations of trends in public opinion are based more on impressions and intuitions of attitudes than on tangible facts.

A letter (7, 3, 1859) to J. N. Coltrin, editor of the *Central Transcript* of Clinton, Ill., shows how vigorously Lincoln demanded true statement of fact and justice of opinion and abhorred prejudiced, loose generalizations.

"Your paper of the 1st. which I presume you sent me is received. Put me on your subscription list, and I will pay at fall court.

"I cut a slip from this number and return it with a word of comment. I shall heartily support for Governor whoever shall be nominated by a Republican State convention; and no one more heartily than any one of the five you name. But is not the fling you make at our Northern bretheren both unjust to them, and dangerous to our cause? You open by saying, 'A strong controversy is going on between the Chicago papers as to who shall be the next Republican nominee for Governor.' I was unaware of this. I have not seen in any Chicago paper, a man named, or pointed to, whom such paper declares for it's candidate for Governor. Have you? Again, ought you to say, as you do that 'the matter will be entirely controlled by the Central and Southern portions of the State? Surely, on reflection, you will agree that the matter must be controlled, in due proportions, by all parts of the state. Again, you say, 'The defeat of Mr. Lincoln may be attributed to the course pursued by these Northerners in putting none but the most ultra men on the track, as candidates for the most important state and Federal offices, etc.' This statement is, indeed, strange. The Republican party, since its organization in Illinois, has gone through two general elections—in 1856 and 1858; and 'these Northerners' have not even had a single candidate for a State office, or a Federal office, commensurate with the state, either residing within their section, or holding their supposed ultra views. In 1856 they put on the track, Bissell, of Bellville, for Governor, Hatch of Pike Co, for Secretary of State; Dubois, of Lawrence Co, for Auditor; Miller, of Bloomington, for Treasurer; Powell of Peoria for School Superintendent; and Wood of Quincy, for Lieutenant Governor; and they elected all of them. In 1858, all these, but two, held over, and one of them, Mr. Miller was again put upon the track, and in lieu of Mr. [Powell], Mr. Bateman, still further South, was put on the track; and again, both elected. Now, can you, on reflection, say either of these men is an ultra man? or that 'these Northerners' could have had any peculiarly selfish reason for supporting them? Another very marked fact is that 'these Northerners' in the two past elections, gave nearly all the votes which carried them; and that the next election will be lost, unless 'these Northerners' do the same thing again. Your fling about men entangled with the 'Matteson Robbery' as you express it; and men indicted for stealing niggers and mail-bags, I think is unjust and impolitic. Why manufacture slang to be used against us by our enemies? The world knows who are alluded to by the mention of stealing niggers and mail-bags; and as to the Canal script fraud, the charge of being entangled with it, would be as just, if made against you, as against any other Republican in the State.

"Finally, can articles such as the inclosed, fail to weaken our party, and our cause?

"I beg your pardon for writing thus freely, without a better acquaintance with you; and I plead in excuse, my great anxiety that we shall have harmony and not discord; have candidates by agreement, and not by force;— *help* one another instead of trying to *hurt* one another.

"I do not write this for publication; and would not have written at all, had I expected a chance to see and talk with you soon."

Lincoln's antislavery, anti-Douglas argument was gaining supporting momentum in the Northeastern states and fully as intense opposition in the South. Repetitive misrepresentation of the meaning of his argument had, by October (1859), made him intolerable to the Southern people even though he continued to uphold the rights of the slave states to a fugitive slave law and their solution of their internal problems on slavery.

The newspaper reports of his speeches quoted little correctly of what he said, indulging rather in such editorial comments as "We have not space, of course, to give anything like a report of Mr. Lincoln's speech. Although entirely unpremeditated, it was in every respect one of the ablest we have ever heard him deliver," (Illinois *State Journal,* 10, 18, 1859). "He closed his eloquent and masterly exposition of the true intent of our cherished and time-honored principles and the sophistries and delusions of our enemies, amid the loud, prolonged and stentorian cheering of the vast audience, that made the rafters of the court-house ring," (Clinton *Weekly Central Transcript,* 10, 20, 1859.)

The young editor of the *Central Transcript* still could not resist the pleasures of loose overstatement, but he had evidently become a vigorous supporter of Abraham Lincoln for President.

Significance of Self-Assertion to Chase

As his political influence in the Northwestern States increased, Lincoln seemed to grow more inspired to mold Republican principles and assert himself as a leader. The rapid change of cautious self-restraint to a more self-reliant attitude becomes apparent when we compare his previous self-humbling, deferential letters to Governor Chase with the following (9, 21, 1859).

"My dear Sir—This is my first opportunity to express to you my great regret at not meeting you personally while in Ohio. However, you were at work in the cause, and that, after all, was better. It is useless for me to say to you (and yet I cannot refrain from saying it) that you must not let your approaching election in Ohio so result as to give encouragement to Douglasism. That ism is all which now stands in the way of an early and complete success of Republicanism; and nothing would help it or hurt us so much for Ohio to go over or falter just now. You must, one and all, put your souls into the effort."

At Beloit, Wis. (10, 1, 1859), Lincoln urged a stronger antislavery policy on the Republican party. Its underlying "life-giving principle" should be hatred of the institution of slavery; hatred of it in all its aspects, moral, social and political. The expression of this hatred should be made in every *legitimate, Constitutional way.* He closed his speech, the Beloit *Journal* reported, "with an eloquent passage from Mr. Clay, pointing out, with prophetic voice, the ruin which the adoption by the people of such principles as Douglas advocates would bring upon the country, and denouncing, in terrible language, the authors of such a change of public policy."

Speeches in Kansas

The people's attitude in the territory of Kansas towards the adoption of slavery was particularly important to Lincoln. He saw it as a test of Douglas' idea of popular sovereignty at work after the introduction of slavery under the Kansas-Nebraska act. A constitution prohibiting slavery had been adopted after five years of murderous fighting, and appeal had been made to Congress for admission into the Union as a State. The day before he spoke at Leavenworth (12, 3, 1859), the anti-slavery fanatic, John Brown, had been executed for treason after due trial and conviction in Charleston, Va., for his raid on the United States arsenal at Harper's Ferry, Va.

The abbreviated reports of his two speeches in the Leavenworth *Register* (12, 12, 1859) contain the usual Lincoln arguments on the principal questions on slavery of that time. Of particular interest are his advice to people of the territory still involved in bloody conflict, to settle their differences peaceably and prepare to assume the responsibilities of a state in the Union, and his warning to the Southern states against secession.

"You are, as yet, the people of a Territory; but you probably soon will be the people of a State of the Union. Then you will be in possession of new privileges, and new duties will be upon you. You will have to bear a part in all that pertains to the administration of the National Government. That government, from the beginning, has had, has now, and must continue to have a policy in relation to domestic slavery. It cannot, if it would, be without a policy upon that subject. And that policy must of necessity, take one of two directions. It must deal with the institution as being *wrong* or as *not* being wrong."

Kansas Proves Lincoln's Argument on Murderous Conflict of Popular Sovereignty over Slavery

After repeating his historical account of the adoption of the Constitution and the ordinance of 1787 to show that the founding Fathers regarded slavery as being wrong, he discussed the policies of the authors of the Kansas-Nebraska act, in regard to slavery as not being wrong.

"You, the people of Kansas, furnish the example of the first application of this new policy. At the end of about five years, after having almost continual struggles, fire and bloodshed, over this very question, and after having framed several State Constitutions, you have, at last, secured a Free State Constitution, under which you will probably be admitted into the Union. You have, at last, at the end of all this difficulty, attained what we, in the old North-western Territory, attained without any difficulty at all. Compare, or rather contrast, the actual working of this new policy with that of the old, and say whether, after all, the old way—the way adopted by Washington and his compeers—was not the better way." . . .

"If your first settlers had so far decided in favor of slavery, as to get five thousand slaves planted on your soil, you could, by no moral possibility, have adopted a Free State Constitution. Their owners would be influential voters among you as good men as the rest of you, and, by their greater wealth, and consequent, greater capacity to assist the more needy, perhaps the most influential among you. You could not wish to destroy, or injuriously interfere with their property. You would not know what to do with the slaves after you had made them free. You would not wish to keep them as underlings; nor yet to elevate them to social and political equality. You could not send them away. The slave States would not let you send them there; and the free States would not let you *send* them there. All the rest of your property would not pay for sending them to Liberia. In a word, you could not have made a free State, if the first half of your own numbers had got five thousand slaves fixed upon the soil. You could have disposed of, not merely five, but five hundred Governors easier. There they would have stuck, in spite of you, to plague you and your children, and your children's children, indefinitely."

We Are Not Trying to Destroy Slavery

Lincoln argued that those who thought slavery was right should unite on a policy which would deal with it as a right. It should try to revive the African slave trade, and carry the institution everywhere, into all the free states as well as the territories, and demand the surrender of all fugitive slaves in Canada.

"All shades of Democracy . . . are fully agreed that slaves are property, and only property. If Canada now had as many horses as she has slaves belonging to Americans, I should think it just cause of war if she did not surrender them on demand." . . .

"You claim that you are conservative; and we are not. We deny it. What is conservatism? Preserving the old against the new. And yet you are conservative in struggling for the new, and we are destructive in trying to maintain the old. Possibly you mean you are conservative in trying to maintain the existing institution of slavery. Very well; we are not trying to destroy it. The peace of society, and the structure of our government both require that we should let it alone, and we insist on letting it alone. If I might advise my Republican friends here, I would say to them, leave your Missouri neighbors alone. Have nothing whatever to do with their slaves. Have nothing whatever to do with the white people, save in a friendly way. Drop past differences, and so conduct yourselves that if you cannot be at peace with them, the fault shall be wholly theirs.

"You say we have made the question more prominent than heretofore. We deny it. It is more prominent; but we did not make it so. Despite of us, you would have a change of policy; we resist the change, and in the struggle, the greater prominence is given to the question. Who is responsible for that, you or we? If you would have the question reduced to its old proportions go back to the old policy. That will effect it."

Warns Against Secession

"But you are for the Union; and you greatly fear the success of the Republicans would destroy the Union. Why? Do the Republicans declare against the Union? Nothing like it. Your own statement of it is, that if the Black Republicans elect a President, you won't stand it. You will break up the Union. That will be your act, not ours. To justify it, you must show that our policy gives you just cause for such desperate action. Can you do that? When you attempt it, you will find that our policy is exactly the policy of the men who made the Union. Nothing more and nothing less. Do you really think you are justified to break up the government rather than have it administered by Washington, and other good and great men who made it, and first administered it? If you do you are very unreasonable; and more reasonable men cannot and will not submit to you. While you elect [the] President, we submit, neither breaking nor attempting to break up the Union. If we shall constitutionally elect a President, it will be our duty to see that you submit."

Comments on Old John Brown

"Old John Brown has just been executed for treason against a state. We cannot object, even though he agreed with us in thinking slavery wrong. That cannot excuse violence, bloodshed, and treason. It could avail him nothing that he might think himself right. So, if constitutionally we elect a President, and therefore you undertake to destroy the Union, it will be our duty to deal with you as old John Brown has been dealt with. We shall try to do our duty. We hope and believe that in no section will a majority so act as to render such extreme measures necessary."

John Brown, an old, Kansas, paranoid, religious, antislavery fanatic, had heard the voice of God urging him to lead the slaves in rebellion against their masters. In order to start the insurrection he had seized the United States Government arsenal at Harper's Ferry, Virginia, and then awaited the expected uprising, making no attempt to invade the South. He was promptly taken prisoner by the Federal Government and later tried in Virginia for treason. Judicial public opinion in the North condemned Brown for treason but judged the act as insane, whereas in the South it was misrepresented by radicals as a rebellious scheme incited by Republican antislavery morality. Brown conducted himself in the trial with such respectful dignity and bore the execution with such upright fortitude that he became the popular antislavery hero of the day in the North, his deed epitomized in song as glorious. "John Brown's body lies amouldering in the grave, his soul is marching on."

Advises Peace

The free application of popular sovereignty, Lincoln pointed out, had been limited by the Dred Scott decision and would have been crushed entirely had the decision been applied directly to Territorial government. Technically the so-called Supreme Court *decision* was really a *dictum,* and not a decision, for it had not been made in application to a specific condition.

He advised the people of Kansas not to interfere with the people of Missouri in the management of their slave problems although Missourians continued to try to impose slavery on Kansas. "Drop past differences, and so conduct yourselves that if you cannot be at peace with them, the fault shall be wholly theirs."

Lincoln held consistently throughout his career as a lawyer that all freely agreed and properly drawn contracts were sacred facts of life, not to be disregarded or broken without the consent of both parties. The most sacred of all contracts was the Union of States under the Constitution. By taking the bold step of warning the South that the Republican party would not tolerate secession and disunion he aroused the people of the northwestern states to patriotic fervor. Talk of Lincoln for President now appeared everywhere as if by spontaneous sympathy in need of a leader in a time of great danger.

Chapter XXXVIII

DARK HORSE "ON THE TRACK"

The constitutionally logical justice of Lincoln's political philosophy for the control of slavery and the preservation of the Union, as expressed in speeches in 1859, had aroused such vigorous public approval that a little group of lawyers, old friends of the circuit court (including Judge David Davis, W. H. Herndon, Leonard Swett, W. H. Lamon, Stephen T. Logan, Lyman Trumbull, Norman B. Judd and Editor Jesse W. Fell), began in the fall of that year to discuss the possibilities of Abraham Lincoln as a candidate for the Republican nomination for President.

First Mention of Lincoln for The Presidency

In 1858, ambitious Mrs. Lincoln had predicted that her husband would defeat Douglas for the Senate and later be elected President. He was defeated by Douglas, and his wife's unrestrained prophecies so amused him that he liked to repeat them to friends for a laugh. By late 1859 the pressure of conservative "restrict slavery" versus radical "abolish slavery" sentiment in the North had grown so intensely conflicting and the pressure for secession in the South was so ominous, that Lincoln's friends in Illinois decided to present him for the Republican nomination as the best balanced, middle-of-the-road man in the nation to lead the people out of the chaos.

Judge David Davis said, after Lincoln's death:

> "The first time I ever heard the name of Lincoln used in connection with the Presidency was from Lincoln himself. A group of lawyers were talking over the possible nominees and each name mentioned was passed off as having certain weak points. At last Lincoln spoke up: 'Why don't you run me? I can be nominated. I can be elected and I can run the government?' We all looked at him and saw that he was not joking. This was the first time I ever knew his name to have been suggested for the office."

Although Davis' recollection of Lincoln's interest in winning the nomination does not coincide in time with the record of its development; it gives an account of how the initial plans of the Judge and members of the bar started.

How could a man of Lincoln's intelligence—a successful, self-educated trial lawyer with no administrative or judicial experience and no more than elementary knowledge of the principles of economics and social organization—come to believe that he was able and fit to serve effectively as President of the most complex and chaotic government in the world? He seems to have believed that good presidential administration of a constitutional, democratic government was, after all, most dependent on the honest, courageous and impartial application of well-informed common sense. A man who understood the history, intent and meaning of the Constitution could apply it to the executive, legislative and judicial processes of government. He who knew politics and how to win the support of its major factions, who knew how to get the most reliable information from properly qualified officials on what the Federal and state governments needed, and from the common people on what they needed and wanted, likewise from leaders of capital and labor, religion, science and education, and from specialists on domestic and foreign relations, and who had the vision and wisdom to use it, could maintain responsible leadership with the exercise of impartial judgment and effectively promote equal rights and justice for all in recommending and executing the laws of Congress. He would serve the people better as President than most men who were committed to the biased obligations of a political party. Though deficient in education, with full confidence in his wisdom for finding right ways and avoiding wrong ways, and sure of his wit and courage to advise and command, he would summon to his aid the best available men of his time without fear of losing their respectful service.

Lincoln was a keen judge of the ambitions of men, working individually and in groups. He had uncanny ability for differentiating and estimating the moral and self-interested will of the people in politics. His speeches earned for him the national reputation of being the best balanced, most conservatively progressive, constitutionally correct leader of "stop the spread of slavery and save the Union" movement. Although the names of politically more famous and experienced and fortified men still took precedence over his, he estimated more accurately than anyone the comparative values of his and their arguments in the minds of people. He saw most clearly that the great political interests of the time had grown more moral than economic. Free people would willingly endure discomforts and hardships in order to enjoy their precious rights of freedom, and they could not long consistently preserve this way of life without logically extending and applying it to the last man, regardless of race, wealth, education and creed.

Abraham Lincoln was rapidly becoming a man of destiny. When we review the crossed political purposes at work that resulted in his nomination and election, although not the most popular candidate either way, we can see how he, having best read the social and political signs of his time, placed himself advantageously in the position offering the only logical constitutional compromise for the irrepressible conflict over slave labor. The young Republican party had been first patched together in New England out of the dissenting factions of old, ultraconservative Whiggism, wrecked over the failure to maintain a cooperative antislavery policy. It was only four years old, without traditions or principles—an aggregation of frustrated, jealous, unsympathetic, sectional political bosses, looking for a platform of workable ideas on how to stop the alarming extension of slavery and a leader best qualified to win the election. Most of the Northern political factions had declared oppostion to slavery and were eager to support a candidate who would counteract the concessions made by the spineless, proslavery, Democratic incumbent, President Buchanan, to the intolerant demands of the fiery advocates of slave labor.

Senator W. H. Seward of New York, Senator Simon Cameron of Pennsylvania, and Governor Salmon P. Chase of Ohio each had the support of wealthy, powerful political organizations in the coming race for the nomination. Eastern machine bosses were not impressed by the dark horse that was put "on the track" in the west.

Cultivating Second Choice in Pennsylvania

Pennsylvania, a mountainous state with vast iron, coal and limestone deposits, was rapidly developing a great iron manufacturing industry, rivalling that of Great Britain. It needed a protective tariff, like all young American manufacturing industries, in order to compete with European production. The Republican party in Pennsylvania was proposing its favorite son, Senator Simon Cameron for the nomination, more with the purpose of trading commitments than with the hope of having him nominated.

Lincoln was asked for his position on a protective tariff by Dr. Edward Wallace of Reading, Pa., through his brother Dr. William S. Wallace, who was Mrs. Lincoln's brother-in-law. His views (10, 11, 1859), consistent with those presented in earlier chapters on the needs of protective tariffs, proved so highly satisfactory to Pennsylvanian and other industrialists that they contributed largely to winning the advantageous position of second choice in eastern manufacturing states.

> "Dr. William S. Wallace showed me a letter of yours in which you kindly mention my name, inquire for my tariff views, and suggest the propriety of my writing a letter upon that subject.
> "I was an old Henry Clay tariff whig. In old times I made more speeches on that subject, than on any other. I have not since changed my views, I believe yet, if we would have a moderate, carefully adjusted, protective tariff, so far acquiesced in, as to not be a perpetual subject of political strife, squabbles, charges, and uncertainties, it would be better for us. Still, it is my opinion that, just now, the revival of that question, will not advance the cause itself, or the man who revives it. I have not thought much upon the subject recently; but my general impression is, that the necessity for a protective tariff will, ere long, force it's old opponents to take it up, and then it's old friends can join in, and establish it on a more firm and durable basis. We, the old whigs, have been entirely beaten out on the tariff question; and we shall not be able to re-establish the policy, until the absence of it, shall have demonstrated the necessity for it, in the minds of men heretofore opposed to it.

"With this view, I should prefer, to not now, write a public letter upon the subject. I therefo[re] wish this to be considered confidential."

We have seen in previous chapters that Lincoln, in the eighteen forties and early fifties, had urged the adoption of moderate special tariffs in order to encourage the development of manufacturing so as to make the nation economically more independent of Great Britain. Such measures, involving an increase of the cost of farm machinery and labor, without commensurate increase of returns for farm produce, aroused the political opposition of farmers, particularly in the South where prosperity was based on the production of cotton by slave labor and sold to British mills. Lincoln now wisely avoided increasing antagonism in the South to a Republican administration by not publicly advocating a tariff and he kept from exciting opposition to himself by Northern manufacturing through quietly expressing approval of a moderate, carefully adjusted protective tariff. These discretely measured considerations later won him the support of Pennsylvanian and other Eastern industrialists at the Republican convention.

Avoid Commitments and Prejudices

The general result of the election in Ohio and other states, he wrote (10, 17, 1859) to W. M. Dickson, Republican and prominent attorney of Cincinnati, "is, indeed, glorious. Now let our friends bear, and forbear, and not quarrel over the spoils."

"It is certainly important to secure Pennsylvania for the Republicans, in the next Presidential contest, and not unimportant to, also, secure Illinois," he wrote (11, 1, 1859) to W. E. Frazer of Pennsylvania, supporter of Senator Simon Cameron of that State for presidential nomination. "As to the ticket you name, I shall be heartily for it, *after* it shall have been fairly nominated by a Republican national convention; and I can not be committed to it *before*. For my single self, I have enlisted for the permanent success of the Republican cause; and, for this object, I shall labor faithfully in the ranks, unless, as I think not probable, the judgement of the party shall assign me a different position. If the Republicans of the great State of Pennsylvania, shall present Mr. Cameron as their candidate for the Presidency, such an indorsement of his fitness for the place, could scarcely be deemed insufficient. Still, as I would not like the *public* to know, so I would not like *myself* to know I had entered a combination with any man, to the prejudice of all others whose friends respectively may consider them preferable."

Cultivating Greeley

Horace Greeley, in his editorials in the New York *Tribune,* had advocated the reelection of Douglas over Lincoln for the United States Senate and for a time had urged the adoption of his leadership and policies by the Republican party as the best solution of the national conflict over slavery. Later Greeley recanted and grew more inclined towards upholding Lincoln's principles. A bitter enemy of the Seward-Weed political machine in New York, he was naturally a highly desirable friend for the advancement of Lincoln's interest.

William Kellogg, United States Representative from Illinois and a close friend of Lincoln, had attacked Greeley's pro-Douglas record in a speech before the House in December 1859 and Greeley had defended himself in a public letter against Kellogg's charges. Lincoln, fearing that an unnecessary feud might arise here, promptly wrote to Kellogg (12, 11, 1859) advising him to accept Greeley's change of attitude. The letter is again characteristic of Lincoln's desire and ability for arranging peaceful compromises between contenders.

> "I have been a good deal relieved this morning by a sight of Greeley's letter to you, published in the Tribune. Before seeing it, I much feared you had, in charging interviews between Douglas & Greely, stated what you *believed,* but did not certainly *know* to be true; and that it might be untrue, and our enemies would get an advantage of you. However, as G. admits the interviews, I think it will not hurt you that he denies conversing with D. about his re-[e]lection to the Senate. G. I think, will not tell a falsehood; and I think he will scarcely deny that he had the interviews with D. in order to assure himself from D's own lips, better than he could from his public acts & declarations, whether to try to bring the Republican party to his support generally, including his re-election to the Senate. What else could the interviews be for? Why immediately followed in the Tribune the advice that all anti-Lecompton democrats should be re-elected? The world will not consider it any thing that D's reelection to the Senate was not specifically talked of by him & G.
> "Now, mark, I do not charge that G. was corrupt in this. I do not think he was, or is. It was his judgment that the course he took was the best way of serving the Republican cause. For this reason, and for the further reason, that he is now pulling straight with us, I think, if I were you, I would not pursue him further than necessary to my own justification. If I were you I would however be greatly tempted [to] ask him if he really thinks D.'s advice to his friends to vote for a Lecompton & Slave code man, is very 'plucky'.
> "Please excuse what I have said, in the way of unsolicited a[d]vice. I believe you will not doubt the sincerity of my friendship for you."

Lincoln's advice to relax critical pressure on Greeley for his past pro-Douglas attitude enabled the editor to swing more gracefully into a stronger Republican, anti-Douglas position, later to the benefit of Lincoln's nomination and election to the Presidency.

Would Rather Be Senator Than President

Letters of late 1859 to political friends indicate that Lincoln's confidence in his administrative ability and Republican popularity was increasing so as to make him feel that he might, after all, be a successful candidate for the presidency.

N. B. Judd, lawyer and Democratic state legislator had managed the election of Trumbull (Democrat) over Lincoln (Whig) for the United States Senate in 1854. By 1856 he had combined with Senator Trumbull in opposing Douglasism and leading the antislavery Democrats of Illinois to form with Lincoln and other Whigs the new Republican party. He became chairman of the Republican State Central Committee and managed Lincoln's campaign against Douglas in 1858. He was now being blamed for Lincoln's defeat and the dishonorable misuse of funds, by Lincoln's law partner, W. H. Herndon, and other Republican leaders including prominent editors and business men of Chicago. They would depose him from the office of chairman.

Judd, proud and hot tempered, was deeply offended, for his honor and political integrity were at stake. He had sent a letter of protest and appeal for justification to Lincoln. The following answer (12, 9, 1859) shows characteristically how Lincoln measured men by their honesty, sincerity, beliefs, and practical intelligence.

"I have just reached home from Kansas and found your long letter of the 1st. inst. It has a tone of blame towards myself which I think is not quite just; but I will not stand upon that, but will consider a day or two, and put something in the best shape I can, and send it to you. A great difficulty is that they make no distinct charge against you, which I can contradict. You did vote for Trumbull against me; and, although I think, and have said a thousand times, that was no injustice to me, I cannot change the fact, nor compel people to cease speaking of it. Ever since that matter occurred, I have constantly labored, as I believe you know, to have all recollection of it dropped.

"The vague charge that you played me false last year, I believe to be false and outrageous; but, it seems, I can make no impression by expressing that belief. I made a special job of trying to impress that upon Baker, Bridges and Wilson, here last winter. They all well know that I believe no such charge against you. But they choose to insist that they know better about it than I do.

"As to the charge of your intriguing for Trumbull against me, I believe as little of that as any other charge. If Trumbull and I were candidates for the same office, you would have a right to prefer him, and I should not blame you for it; but all my acquaintance with you induces me to believe you would not *pretend* to be for me while really for him. But I do not understand Trumbull & myself to be rivals. You know I am pledged to not enter a struggle with him for the seat in the Senate now occupied by him; and yet I would rather have a full term in the Senate than in the Presidency.

"I have made this letter longer than I expected when I began. Your friend as ever

A. Lincoln

"P.S. I omitted to say that I have, in no single instance, permitted a charge against such as above alluded to, to go uncontradicted, when made in my presence."

Through the emotional economy of never bearing resentment against the free exercise of the right of other men to oppose him justly, Lincoln avoided the most common cause of neurotic anxiety that afflicts mankind and thereby kept reduced the excitation of his organic neurosis.

Defends the Honor of His Chairman

A group of influential Chicago Republicans (G. W. Dole, G. S. Hubbard, W. H. Brown) stated in a letter to Lincoln why they distrusted Judd and charged him with being unfit for chairman. He promptly seized the opportunity (12, 14, 1859) to quash their charges and assert his faith in his chairman.

"Your favor of the 12th. is at hand, and it gives me pleasure to be able to answer it. It is not my intention to take part in any of the rivalries for the Gubernatorial nomination; but the fear of being misunderstood upon that subject, ought not to deter me from doing justice to Mr. Judd, and preventing a wrong being done to him by the use of my name in connection with alleged wrongs to me.

"In answer to your first question as to whether Mr. Judd was guilty of any unfairness to me at the time of Senator Trumbull's election, I answer unhesitatingly in the negative. Mr. Judd owed no political allegiance to any party whose candidate I was. He was in the Senate, holding over, having been elected by a democratic constituency. He never was in any caucus of the friends who sought to make me U. S. Senator—never gave me any promises or pledges to support me—and subsequent events have greatly tended to prove the wisdom, politically, of Mr. Judd's course. The election of Judge Trumbull strongly tended to sustain and preserve the position of that portion of the Democrats who condemned the repeal of the Missouri compromise, and left them in a position of joining with us in forming the Republican party, as was done at the Bloomington convention in 1856.

"During the canvass of 1858 for the Senatorship my belief was, and still is, that I had no more sincere and faithful friend than Mr. Judd—certainly none whom I trusted more. His position as Chairman of the State Central committee, led to my greater intercourse with him, and to my giving him a larger share of my confidence, than with, or, to almost any other friend; and I have never suspected that that confidence was, to any degree, misplaced.

"My relations with Mr. Judd, since the organization of the Republican party, in our State, in 1856, and, especially since the adjournment of the legislature in Feb. 1857, have been so very intimate, that I deem it an impossibility that he could have been dealing treacherously with me. He has also, at all times, appeared equally true and faithful to the party. In his position, as Chairman of the Committee, I believe he did all that any man could have done. The best of us are liable to commit errors, which become apparant, by the subsequent developments; but I do not now know of a single error, even, committed by Mr. Judd, since he and I have acted together politically.

"I had occasionally heard these insinuations against Mr. Judd, before the receipt of your letter, and in no instance have I hesitated to pronounce them wholly unjust, to the full extent of my knowledge and belief. I have been, and still am, very anxious to take no part between the many friends, all good and true, who are mentioned as candidates for the Republican Gubernatorial nomination; but I can not feel that my own honor is quite clear, if I remain silent, when I hear any one of them assailed about matters of which I believe I know more than his assailants.

"I take pleasure in adding that of all the avowed friends I had in the canvass of last year, I do not suspect any of having acted treacherously to me, or to our cause; and that there is not one of them in whose honesty, honor, and integrity I, to-day, have greater confidence than I have in those of Mr. Judd.

"I dislike to appear before the public, in this matter, but you are at liberty to make such use of this letter as you may think justice requires."

Lincoln again Chooses Judd to Manage His Campaign

The vigorous, intimately personal defense of the trustworthy character, loyal friendship and political sagacity of Norman B. Judd was tantamount to Lincoln's choice of him to continue as chairman of the State Central Committee and thereby to manage his bid for the Republican nomination. He sent to Judd (12, 14, 1859) the letter of "our old whig friends" and a copy of his reply to them, and then went on to say:

"I find some of our friends here, attach more consequence to getting the National convention into our State than I did, or do. Some of them made me promise to say so to you. As to the *time*, it must certainly be after the Charleston fandango; and I think, within bounds of reason, the later the better.

"As to that matter about the Committee, in relation to appointing delegates by general convention, or by Districts, I shall attend to it as well as I know how, which G-d knows, will not be very well."

The next day he wrote to J. Grimshaw, "Judd has started East to attend the sitting of the National committee, at N.Y. the 21st. Previous to going he wrote that soon after his return he would call the State Committee together" . . . relative to the manner of appointing delegates to the National convention.

"I Suppose That There Is Not Much Of Me"

Lincoln's friends in Illinois, Ohio and Pennsylvania were, by December 1859, vigorously promoting him as a candidate. J. L. Lewis of Pennsylvania and editor Jesse W. Fell, of Bloomington, Ill., requested an autobiographical sketch to be used in the preparation of an article on his life for publication in Republican papers. Lincoln wrote it, as presented in a previous chapter on his family and childhood. His letter (12, 20, 1859) to Fell introducing it reveals the man's humble regard for himself and his origin.

"Herewith is a little sketch, as you requested. There is not much of it, for the reason, I suppose, that there is not much of me.

"If anything be made of it, I wish it to be modest, and not to go beyond the material. If it were thought necessary to incorporate anything from any of my speeches, I suppose there would be no objection. Of course it must not appear to have been written by myself."

Formal Proposal of Lincoln for President

Herndon (1889) has told us that by the beginning of 1860 Lincoln was being "freely mentioned in connection with the Republican nomination for the Presidency," although he had up to this time, "in all cases discouraged the attempt." His friends, O. M. Hatch, J. Grimshaw, N. B. Judd, E. Peck, W. H. Herndon and others, met in the State House in the rooms of the Secretary of State, early in February to obtain his permission to enter his name in the race. "With characteristic modesty," Herndon said, "he doubted whether he could get the nomination even if he wished it, and asked until the next morning to answer us whether his name might be announced. Late the next day he authorized us, if we thought proper to do so, to place him in the field."

When asked if he would accept the nomination for Vice-President if he failed to get the nomination for President, he answered, Herndon said, that "his name having been used for the office of President, he would not permit it to be used for any other offic,e however honorable it might be."

Judd was successful in getting the National Republican Committee to choose Chicago for holding its National Convention. This selection proved later to give a decisive advantage to Lincoln in the vigorous contest for the nomination.

Two letters written early in February, 1860 show that although Lincoln had now decided in his own mind to seek the nomination he worried more over the discredit of failing to obtain the support of the entire Illinois delegation than over winning it.

Herndon, continuing to suspect that Judd was untrustworthy, seems to have made unwise remarks about him that were carried to him and to Lincoln. That Herndon was firmly corrected by Lincoln is evident in a letter he wrote to Judd (2, 5, 1860).

"A day or so before you wrote about Mr. Herndon, Dubois told me that he, H, had been talking to William Jayne in the way you indicate. At first sight afterwards, I mentioned it to him; he rather denied the charge, and I did not press him about the past; but got his solemn pledge to say nothing of the sort in the future. I had done this before I received your letter. I impressed upon him as well as I could, first that such, was untrue, and unjust to you, and second, that *I* would be held responsible for what he said. Let this be private.

"Some folks are pretty bitter towards me about the Dole, Hubbard, & Brown letter."

Four days later (2, 9, 1860) he wrote again to Judd: "I am not in a position where it would hurt much for me to not be nominated on the national ticket; but I am where it would hurt some for me to not get the Illinois delegates. What I expected when I wrote the letter to Messrs Dole and others is now happening. Your discomfitted assailants are most bitter against me; and they will, for revenge upon me, lay to the Bates egg in the South, and to the Seward egg in the North, and go far towards squeezing me out in the middle with nothing. Can you not help me a little in this matter, in your end of the vineyard?"

The self-respect with which Lincoln must naturally have regarded his personal defense of Judd's honesty and integrity against slander indicates that he did not take Herndon's rash violation of his honorable self-commitment lightly. His explanation to Judd of having obtained Herndon's solemn promise to say nothing in the future is deeply characteristic of Lincoln's wisdom in adjusting differences with individual men. He accepted Herndon's denial of the charge and appeared to dismiss his past indiscretions but made him commit himself on the future. This past-forgiving, tolerantly correcting, future-committing personal characteristic repeated itself, later, time and again with his Cabinet, generals and the Southern people when President. Lincoln was singularly free of cravings for vindictive retribution for past injustice and was always kindly inclined to be practically reconstructive to safeguard the future.

Inspired Moral Crusade

In 1859 Lincoln had been an extremely busy man, carrying on the practice of law, writing numerous long, personal letters on political and legal questions, and making numerous speeches in the northwestern states, traveling thousands of miles over bumpy railroads, in stuffy, uncomfortable cars pulled by noisy, smoking engines. Despite irregular hours of uncomfortable sleeping and eating badly prepared food, he carried on with undiminished energy.

Lincoln did not have a nervous depression after his defeat by Douglas and he did not have a cyclically depressive constitution, as A. A. Brill and other psychiatrists have erroneously interpreted and reported. He was more inclined than other highly able and intensely active men, as we have shown, to become for a short time somewhat depressed upon exhaustion from overwork or too severe frustration and defeat. That he recovered more quickly than most such men has become increasingly evident. This persistently recurrent gloominess of outlook on life when not engaged in work to gain an exciting objective and the amazing resiliency of mental energy that he developed when so engaged was due, as I have shown, to the hypersensitivity and instability of his nervous system. He was now so thoroughly aroused by the argument of Douglas and so intensely determined to refute it as false and defeat him as the most dangerous man in America that he seems to have obtained almost complete relief from his old nostalgic attachment of affection to the memories of those he loved who were dead. Transference of affection to his three young sons and loyalty to his wife, and the grand fight of his life to uphold the right to legal justice and freedom under the Constitution for all people and preserve the Union, were activating in his personality logically allied, sublimely harmonized autonomic drives.

Promoters of the extension of slavery included not only many of the big slave owners and traders of the South but some of the most powerful financiers of the North. For the past 30 years this ruthless interest had been increasing, despite the abrogation of slavery by the State of New York, until it threatened to reach the proportions of a political tide. The rapid development of more efficient means of transportation and communication (steamboat, railroad and telegraph) destined the building of transcontinental railroads and a new era of agricultural expansion. The Southern Yanceys would seize and extend slavery to Cuba, the islands of the Caribbean Sea, Mexico, and vulnerable parts of Central and South America as well as all the western territories of the United States, with New Orleans as the metropolis. They would convert this vast area into a "new slave empire," based on the private ownership of labor. The soft headed Buchanan administration had been sympathetic in part to this scheme, and, with the abolition of the Missouri Compromise, it had gained intense and uncompromising momentum in the South, threatening secession if blocked. Many Northern politicians, editors and business men, Republicans as well as Democrats, advocated compromise and appeasement, rather than resistance, in order to avoid this crisis.

New York was the center of the vast, covert, slavery-promoting scheme, and Lincoln foresaw that "big business" and the Weed-Seward faction might combine with the Douglas Democrats in working out a compromise that would lead to the destruction of the young Republican party. He would prevent this.

The strength of his political position had been recently augmented by a sweeping indorsement of him for President by the Chicago *Press & Tribune* on February 16th as, "the peer of any man yet named."

Cooper Institute

Reverend Henry Ward Beecher, rector of the Plymouth Church in Brooklyn, N. Y., was instrumental in having an invitation extended to Abraham Lincoln to address an audience in his church. A stipend of $200 was promised and the possibility of giving a second lecture in New York was mentioned. Lincoln chose February 27, 1860 as the most suitable time for himself and announced that he preferred to make a "political" speech. Herndon (1889) has told us that Lincoln hesitated for some time in choosing his subject and that he prevailed upon him to make it political. Herndon was then in personal communication with Beecher, Parker and other eastern moral and political reformers and, appreciating their zeal, advised his partner wisely.

Before Lincoln arrived in New York the Young Men's Central Republican Union had taken charge and arranged, without his knowledge, for the speech to be delivered in Cooper Institute.

When Lincoln arrived in New York on Saturday, February 25 he went immediately to the office of the editor of the *Independent* who had charge of the program.

> "I am Abraham Lincoln," he said. "I am just in from Springfield, Illinois, and I am very tired. If you have no objection I will lie down on your lounge here and you can tell me about the arrangement for Monday night."

He learned that such influential men as Charles Sumner, Wendell Phillips, John P. Hale, H. W. Beecher, W. C. Bryant, Gideon Welles, and Horace Greeley would hear with sympathy his argument against the extension of slavery.

He attended Reverend Beecher's service on Sunday and seems to have been much impressed by an exchange of views with that famous orator for he sent word to the editor that he would not meet him and his friends at dinner. "You will have to excuse me from dining with you . . . I have not fully prepared the speech that I am to deliver Monday night. I must go over to the Astor House and work on it." Although he would speak on the same issues that he had presented a hundred times before, he must prepare his mind for each audience as if it were the first time. For this reason no one can understandingly sense the heartfelt drive and ingenuity of Lincoln who has not read his major speeches in sequence of delivery.

Lincoln worked under tireless compulsion to prepare his thoughts. His arguments, like his stories, must be told with all the freshness and vigor of a new event for each audience. Herein he had the indefatiguable inspiration of a great actor.

When the long, lean, lanky Westerner, with scrawny neck and oddly sloping shoulders, dressed in low, large, winged collar, black tie, new, badly wrinkled, long, black, loosely fitting coat and abbreviated breeches, began an address at the Cooper Institute on February 27, 1860, in a slow, drawling, high pitched, squeaky voice with provincial accent, he looked more humorous than serious. Titters of amusement greeted him from the audience. Without the least sign of embarrassment, he continued earnestly to present his address on the supreme issue of the time, with such good will and convincing gravity that within a few minutes his entire audience grew respectful of the pertinence of his facts and the humility, simplicity, clarity and logic of his argument, and then sympathetically spellbound by the force of his humanitarian inspiration. Many eager listeners showed by rapt attention that they realized they were hearing the homely wisdom of the ages being applied legally and factually to the most dangerous internal dissension ever to threaten the life of the nation. Before his audience Lincoln grew in intellectual stature, a noble man, profoundly thoughtful of finding a just way of prevennting the profiteering, unchristian spread of slavery and the heedles destruction of the Union.

This address is now considered by many historians to have been the decisive factor that won him the nomination and the presidency. It has become established, among free civilized peoples, as another of the great humanitarian orations of all times. It is not the scintillating product of spontaneous aspiration. It is the culmination of five years of endless study of the history of his subject, of the attitudes of his people towards it, and numerous speeches, debates and private essays on every point of issue. It is the apex of conscious creation based on an unusually sympathetic, eloquently expressive man born of a devoted, tragically fated mother and an unjustly domineering father, in a wilderness of endless needs, driving inspiration to work for truth, freedom and justice, reinforced by the results of a brain injury that made a personality so sensitive that it must have equitable legal conditions of living for itself and its fellow men in order to prevent gloomy futility of life. No one can get a true appreciation of the climax of Lincoln's career before his nomination and election as President without reading it entirely. Its moral justification of the cause for slavery and against slavery was far superior to anything that had yet been given by anyone to the people. It drew the East to his support, but it enraged the South into uncompromising resentment against him. The speech was acclaimed, and is still so held, as a masterful discussion of the history and intent of the Federal Constitution. Its array of evidence and logic of interpretation on the reasoning of the Founders repeated much of what he had said on this in the debates and other speeches, but he had grown in such philosophical wisdom and political acumen that he now made many people feel confident that, if he were President, they would have a leader who would not only be an authority on the Constitution but who would understand how to apply it justly in the control of slavery and the preservation of the Union in the event of secession.

With characteristic, almost apologetic humility he carefully defined the issue, and then, with persistent repetition, he hammered home the meaning of his facts (captions inserted):

The Portentious Issue

"Mr. President and Fellow Citizens of New York:— The facts with which I shall deal this evening are mainly old and familiar; nor is there anything new in the general use I shall make of them. If there shall be any novelty, it will be in the mode of presenting the facts, and the inferences and observations following that presentation.

"In his speech last autumn, at Columbus, Ohio, as reported in 'the New-York Times,' Senator Douglas said:

" *'Our fathers, when they framed the Government under which we live,* understood this question just as well, and even better, than we do now.'

"I fully indorse this, and I adopt it as a text for this discourse. I so adopt it because it furnishes a precise and an agreed starting point for a discussion between Republicans and that wing of the Democracy headed by Senator Douglas. It simply leaves the inquiry: *'What was the understanding those fathers had of the question mentioned?*

"What is the frame of government under which we live?

"The answer must be: 'The Constitution of the United States.' That Constitution consists of the original, framed in 1787, (and under which the present Government first went into operation), and twelve subsequently framed amendments, the first ten of which were framed in 1789.

"Who were our fathers that framed the Constitution? I suppose the 'thirty-nine' who signed the original instrument may fairly be called our fathers who framed that part of the present Government. It is almost exactly true to say they framed it, and it is altogether true to say they fairly represented the opinion and sentiment of the whole nation at that time. Their names, being familiar to nearly all, and accessible to quite all, need not be repeated.

"I take these 'thirty-nine,' for the present, as being 'our fathers who framed the government under which we live.'

"What is the question which, according to the text, those fathers understood 'just as well, and even better than we do now?'

"It is this: Does the proper division of local from Federal authority, or anything in the Constitution, forbid *our Federal Government* to control as to slavery in *our Federal Territories?*

"Upon this, Senator Douglas holds the affirmative, and Republicans the negative. This affirmative and denial form an issue; and this issue—this question—is precisely what the text declares our fathers understood 'better than we.'

"Let us now inquire whether the 'thirty-nine,' or any of them, ever acted upon this question; and if they did, how they acted upon it—how they expressed that better understanding?

"In 1784, three years before the Constitution—the United States then owning the Northwestern Territory, and no other, the Congress of the Confederation had before them the question of prohibiting slavery in that Territory; and four of the 'thirty-nine' who afterward framed the Constitution, were in that Congress, and voted on that question. Of these, Roger Sherman, Thomas Mifflin, and Hugh Williamson voted for the prohibition, thus showing that, in their understanding, no line dividing local from Federal authority, nor anything else, properly forbade the Federal Government to control as to slavery in federal territory. The other of four—James M'Henry—voted against the prohibition, showing that, for some cause, he thought it improper to vote for it.

"In 1787, still before the Constitution, but while the Convention was in session framing it, and while the Northwestern Territory still was the only territory owned by the United States, the same question of prohibiting slavery in the territory again came before the Congress of the Confederation; and two more of the 'thirty-nine' who afterward signed the Constitution, were in that Congress, and voted on the question. They were William Blount [North Carolina], William Few [Georgia]; and they both voted for the prohibition—thus showing that, in their understanding, no line dividing local from Federal authority, nor anything else, properly forbade the Federal Government to control as to slavery in federal territory. This time the prohibition became a law, being a part of what is now well known as the Ordinance of '87.*

Collected Works cites from the statement of Rufus King (Massachusetts) member of the Senate and committee that drafted the ordinance: "Not only Virginia, but North Carolina, South Carolina, and Georgia, by the unanimous votes of their delegates in the Old Congress, approved of the Ordinance of 1787, by which slavery is forever abolished in the Territory northwest of the river Ohio. Without the votes of these states the Ordinance could not have passed, and there is no recollection of an opposition from any of these States to the act of confirmation passed under the actual Constitution."

"The question of federal control of slavery in the territories, seems not to have been directly before the Convention which framed the original Constitution; and hence it is not recorded that the 'thirty-nine,' or any of them, while engaged on that instrument, expressed any opinion on that precise question.*

The Ordinance of '87

"In 1789, by the first Congress which sat under the Constitution, an act was passed to enforce the Ordinance of '87, including the prohibition of slavery in the Northwestern Territory. The bill for this act was reported by one of the 'thirty-nine,' Thomas Fitzsimmons, then a member of the House of Representatives from Pennsylvania. It went through all its stages without a word of opposition, and finally passed both branches without yeas and nays, which is equivalent to an unanimous passage. In this Congress there were sixteen of the thirty-nine fathers who framed the original Constitution. They were John Langdon, Nicholas Gilman, Wm. S. Johnson, Roger Sherman, Robert Morris, Thos. Fitzsimmons, William Few, Abraham Baldwin, Rufus King, William Patterson, George Clymer, Richard Bassett, George Read, Pierce Butler, Daniel Carroll, and James Madison.

"This shows that, in their understanding, no line dividing local from federal authority, nor anything in the Constitution, properly forbade Congress to prohibit slavery in the federal territory; else both their fidelity to correct principle, and their oath to support the Constitution, would have constrained them to oppose the prohibition."†

President Washington's Approval

"Again, George Washington, another of the 'thirty-nine,' was then President of the United States, and, as such, approved and signed the bill; thus completing its validity as a law, and thus showing that, in his understanding, no line dividing local from federal authority, nor anything in the Constitution, forbade the Federal Government, to control as to slavery in federal territory."

---

*Patrick Henry, before a Convention in Virginia, had definitely expressed the sentiment of his state on this. It was remarkably sympathetic with the views of his contemporaries Washington and Jefferson. "May not Congress enact that every black man must fight? Did we not see a little of this in the last war? We were not so hard pushed as to make emancipation general. But acts of Assembly passed, that every slave who would go to the army should be free. Another thing will contribute to bring this event about. Slavery is detested. We feel its fatal effects. We deplore it with all the pity of humanity. Let all these considerations press with full force upon the minds of Congress. . . . they will search that paper and see if they have the power of manumission. . . . The paper speaks to the point; they have the power in clear, unequivocal terms, and will clearly and certainly express it." (C. W., 3.)

†The extraordinary assertions of Chief Justice Taney, that "the example of Virginia was soon afterwards followed by other States" and that the power in the Constitution "to dispose of and make all needful rules and regulations respecting the Territory or other property belonging to the United States" was intended only "to transfer to the new Government the property then held in common," and has no reference whatever to any Territory or other property, which the new sovereignty might afterwards itself acquire" (C. W., 3), were correctly discredited as historically unfounded by Lincoln.

Southern Territories

"No great while after the adoption of the original Constitution, North Carolina ceded to the Federal Government the country now constituting the State of Tennessee; and a few years later Georgia ceded that which now constitutes the States of Mississippi and Alabama. In both deeds of cession it was made a condition by the ceding States that the Federal Government should not prohibit slavery in the ceded country. Besides this, slavery was then actually in the ceded country. Under these circumstances, Congress, on taking charge of these countries, did not absolutely prohibit slavery within them. But they did interfere with it—take control of it—even there, to a certain extent. In 1798, Congress organized the Territory of Mississippi. In the act of organization, they prohibited the bringing of slaves into the Territory, from any place without the United States, by fine, and giving freedom to slaves so brought. This act passed both branches of Congress without yeas and nays. In that Congress were three of the 'thirty-nine' who framed the original Constitution. They were John Langdon [New Hampshire], George Read [Delaware], and Abraham Baldwin [Georgia]. They all, probably, voted for it. Certainly they would have placed their opposition to it upon the record, if, in their understanding, any line dividing the local from federal authority, or anything in the Constitution, properly forbade the Federal Government to control as to slavery in federal territory."

Louisiana Territory

"In 1803, the Federal Government purchased the Louisiana country. Our former territorial acquisitions came from certain of our own States; but this Louisiana country was acquired from a foreign nation. In 1804, Congress gave a territorial organization to that part of it which now constitutes the State of Louisiana. New Orleans, lying within that part, was an old and comparatively large city. There were other considerable towns and settlements, and slavery was extensively and thoroughly intermingled with the people. Congress did not, in the Territorial Act, prohibit slavery; but they did interfere with it—take control of it—in a more marked and extensive way than they did in the case of Mississippi. The substance of the provision therein made, in relation to slaves, was:

"*First*: That no slave should be imported into the Territory from foreign parts.

"*Second*: That no slave should be carried into it who had been imported into the United States since the first day of May, 1798.

"*Third*: That no slave should be carried into it, except by the owner, and for his own use as a settler; the penalty in all cases being a fine upon the violator of the law, and freedom to the slave.

"This act also was passed without yeas and nays. In the Congress which passed it there were two of the 'thirty-nine.' They were Abraham Baldwin, and Jonathan Dayton [New Jersey]. As stated in the case of Mississippi, it is probable they both voted for it. They would not have allowed it to pass without recording their opposition to it, if, in their understanding, it violated either the line properly dividing local from Federal authority, or any provision of the Constitution."

The Missouri Question

"In 1819-20 came, and passed, the Missouri question. Many votes were taken, by yeas and nays, in both branches of Congress, upon the various phases of the general question. Two of the 'thirty-nine'—Rufus King and Charles Pinckney [South Carolina]—were members of that Congress. Mr. King steadily voted for slavery prohibition and against all compromises, while Mr. Pinckney as steadily voted against prohibition and against all compromises. By this, Mr. King showed that, in his understanding, no line dividing local from federal authority, nor anything in the Constitution, was violated by Congress prohibiting slavery in federal territory; while Mr. Pinckney, by his votes, showed that, in his understanding, there was some sufficient reason for opposing such prohibition in that case.

"The cases I have mentioned are the only acts of the 'thirty-nine,' or of any of them, upon the direct issue, which I have been able to discover.

"To enumerate the persons who thus acted, as being four in 1784, two in 1787, seventeen in 1789, three in 1798, two in 1804, and counting John Langdon, Roger Sherman, William Few, Rufus King, and George Read, each twice, and Abraham Baldwin, three times. The true number of those of the 'thirty-nine' whom I have shown to have acted upon the question, which, by the text, they understood better than we, is twenty-three,* leaving sixteen not shown to have acted upon it in any way.

"Here, then, we have twenty-three out of our thirty-nine fathers 'who framed the Government under which we live,' who have, upon their official responsibility and their corporal oaths, acted upon the very question which the text affirms they 'understood just as well, and even better than we do now;' and twenty-one of them—a clear majority of the whole 'thirty-nine'—so acting upon it as to make them guilty of gross political impropriety and wilful perjury, if, in their understanding, any proper division between local and federal authority, or anything in the Constitution they had made themselves, and sworn to support, forbade the Federal Government to control as to slavery in the federal territories. Thus the twenty-one acted; and, as actions speak louder than words, so actions, under such responsibility, speak still louder.

"Two of the twenty-three voted against Congressional prohibition of slavery in the federal territories, in the instances in which they acted upon the question. But for what reasons they so voted is not known. They may have done so because they thought a proper division of local from federal authority, or some provision or principle of the Constitution, stood in the way; or they may, without any such question, have voted against the prohibition, on what appeared to them to be sufficient grounds of expediency. No one who has sworn to support the Constitution, can conscientiously vote for what he understands to be an unconstitutional measure, however expedient he may think it; but one may and ought to vote against a measure which he deems constitutional, if, at the same time, he deems it inexpedient. It, therefore, would be unsafe to set down even the two who voted against prohibition, as having done so because, in their understanding, any proper division of local from federal authority, or anything in the Constitution, forbade the Federal Government to control as to slavery in federal territory.

*Twelve were from slave-holding states.

"The remaining sixteen of the 'thirty-nine,' so far as I have discovered, have left no record of their understanding upon the direct question of federal control of slavery on the federal territories. But there is much reason to believe that their understanding upon that question would not have appeared different from that of their twenty-three compeers, had it been manifested at all.

"For the purpose of adhering rigidly to the text, I have purposely omitted whatever understanding may have been manifested by any person, however distinguished, other than the thirty-nine fathers who framed the original Constitution; and, for the same reason, I have also omitted whatever understanding may have been manifested by any of the 'thirty-nine' even, on any other phase of the general question of slavery. If we should look into their acts and declarations on those other phases, as the foreign slave trade, and the morality and policy of slavery generally, it would appear to us that on the direct question of federal control of slavery in federal territories, the sixteen, if they had acted at all, would probably have acted just as the twenty-three did. Among that sixteen were several of the most noted anti-slavery men of those times—as Dr. Franklin, Alexander Hamilton and Gouverneur Morris—while there was not one now known to have been otherwise, unless it may be John Rutledge, of South Carolina.

"The sum of the whole is, that of our thirty-nine fathers who framed the original Constitution, twenty-one—a clear majority of the whole—certainly understood that no proper division of local from federal authority, nor any part of the Constitution, forbade the Federal Government to control slavery in the federal territories; while all the rest probably had the same understanding. Such, unquestionably, was the understanding of our fathers who framed the original Constitution; and the text affirms that they understood the question 'better than we.' "

Demolishes Douglas' Presumptions

"But, so far, I have been considering the understanding of the question manifested by the framers of the original Constitution. In and by the original instrument, a mode was provided for amending it; and, as I have already stated, the present frame of 'the Government under which we live' consists of that original and twelve amendatory articles framed and adopted since. Those who now insist that federal control of slavery in federal territories violates the Constitution, point us to the provisions which they suppose it thus violates; and, as I understand, they all fix upon provisions in these amendatory articles, and not in the original instrument. The Supreme Court, in the Dred Scott case, plant themselves upon the fifth amendment, which provides that no person shall be deprived of 'life, liberty or property without due process of law;' while Senator Douglas and his peculiar adherents plant themselves upon the tenth amendment, providing that 'the powers not delegated to the United States by the Constitution,' 'are reserved to the States respectively, or to the people.'

"Now, it so happens that these amendments were framed by the first Congress which sat under the Constitution—the identical Congress which passed the act already mentioned, enforcing the prohibition of slavery in the Northwestern Territory. Not only was it the same Congress, but they were the identical, same individual men who, at the same session, and at the same time within the session, had under consideration, and in progress towards maturity, these Constitutional amendments, and this act prohibiting slavery in all the territory the nation then owned. The Constitutional amendments were introduced before, and passed after the act enforcing the Ordinance of '87; so that, during the whole pendency of the act to enforce the Ordinance, the Constitutional amendments were also pending.

"The seventy-six members of that Congress, including sixteen of the framers of the original Constitution, as before stated, were preeminently our fathers who framed that part of 'the Government under which we live,' which is now claimed as forbidding the Federal Government to control slavery in the federal territories.

"Is it not a little presumptuous in any one at this day to affirm that the two things which that Congress deliberately framed, and carried to maturity at the same time, are absolutely inconsistent with each other? And does not such affirmation become impudently absurd when coupled with the other affirmation from the same mouth, that those who did the two things, alleged to be inconsistent, understood whether they really were inconsistent better than we—better than he who affirms that they are inconsistent?

"It is surely safe to assume that the thirty-nine framers of the original Constitution, and the seventy-six members of the Congress which framed the amendments thereto, taken together, do certainly include those who may be fairly called 'our fathers who framed the Government under which we live.' And so assuming, I defy any man to show that any one of them ever, in his whole life, declared that, in his understanding, any proper division of local from federal authority, or any part of the Constitution, forbade the Federal Government to control as to slavery in the federal territories. I go a step further. I defy any one to show that any living man in the whole world ever did, prior to the beginning of the present century, (and I might almost say prior to the beginning of the last half of the present century,) declare that, in his understanding, any proper division of local from federal authority, or any part of the Constitution, forbade the Federal Government to control as to slavery in the federal territories. To those who now so declare, I give, not only 'our fathers who framed the Government under which we live,' but with them all other living men within the century in which it was framed, among whom to search, and they shall not be able to find the evidence of a single man agreeing with them.

"Now, and here, let me guard a little against being misunderstood. I do not mean to say we are bound to follow implicitly in whatever our fathers did. To do so, would be to discard all the lights of current experience—to reject all progress—all improvement. What I do say is, that if we would supplant the opinions and policy of our fathers in any case, we should do so upon evidence so conclusive, and argument so clear that even their great authority, fairly considered and weighed, cannot stand; and most surely not in a case whereof we ourselves declare they understand the question better than we."

For This Republicans Contend

"If any man at this day sincerely believes that a proper division of local from federal authority, or any part of the Constitution, forbids the Federal Government to control as to slavery in the federal territories, he is right to say so, and to enforce his position by all truthful evidence and fair argument which he can. But he has no right to mislead others, who have less access to history, and less leisure to study it, into the false belief that 'our fathers, who framed the Government under which we live,' were of the same opinion— thus substituting falsehood and deception for truthful evidence and fair argument. If any man at this day sincerely believes 'our fathers who framed the Government under which we live,' used and applied principles, in other cases, which ought to have led them to understand that a proper division of local from federal authority or some part of the Constitution, forbids the Federal Government to control as to slavery in the federal territories, he is right, to say so. But he should, at the same time, brave the responsibility of declaring that, in his opinion, he understands their principles better than they did themselves; and especially should he not shirk the responsibility by asserting that they 'understood the question just as well, and even better, then we do now.'

"But enough! *Let all who believe that 'our fathers, who framed the Government under which we live, understood this question just as well, and even better, than we do now,' speak as they spoke, and act as they acted upon it. This is all Republicans ask—all Republicans desire—in relation to slavery. As those fathers marked it, so let it be again marked, as an evil not to be extended, but to be tolerated and protected only because of and so far as its actual presence among us makes that toleration and protection a necessity. Let all the guaranties those fathers gave it, be, not grudgingly, but fully and fairly maintained.* For this Republicans contend, and with this, so far as I know or believe, they will be content."

Lincoln repeated some 17 times, up to this part of his address, the same phrasing of the crux of his argument that no "proper division of local from Federal authority, or any part of the Constitution forbids the Federal Government to control as to slavery in the Federal territories." In previous chapters we have observed how he would repeat a decisive statement with discussion from every angle until he felt all misunderstanding had been overcome. We have shown how this impressive personal characteristic began naturally with freedom in self-education in childhood and continued through maturity.

Challenges Southern Opinion

"And now, if they would listen— as I suppose they will not— I would address a few words to the Southern people.

"I would say to them:— You consider yourselves a reasonable and a just people; and I consider that in the general qualities of reason and justice you are not inferior to any other people. Still, when you speak of us Republicans, you do so only to denounce us as reptiles, or, at the best, as no better than outlaws. You will grant a hearing to pirates or murderers, but nothing like it to 'Black Republicans.' In all your contentions with one another, each of you deems an unconditional condemnation of 'Black Republicans' as the first thing to be attended to. Indeed, such condemnation of us seems to be an indispensable prerequisite— license, so to speak— among you to be admitted or permitted to speak at all. Now, can you, or not, be prevailed upon to pause and to consider whether this is quite just to us, or even to yourselves? Bring forward your charges and specifications, and then be patient long enough to hear us deny or justify.

"You say we are sectional. We deny it. That makes an issue; and the burden of proof is upon you. You produce your proof; and what is it? Why, that our party has no existence in your section gets no votes in your section. The fact is substantially true; but does it prove the issue? If it does, then in case we would, without change of principle, begin to get votes in your section, we should thereby cease to be sectional. You cannot escape this conclusion; and yet, are you willing to abide by it? If you are, you will probably soon find that we have ceased to be sectional, for we shall get votes in your section this very year. You will then begin to discover, as the truth plainly is, that your proof does not touch this issue. The fact that we get no votes in your section, is a fact of your making, and not of ours. And if there be fault in that fact, that fault is primarily yours, and remains so until you show that we repel you by some wrong principle or practice. If we do repel you by any wrong principle or practice, the fault is ours; but this brings you to where you ought to have started—to a discussion of the right or wrong of our principle. If our principle, put in practice, would wrong your section for the benefit of ours, or for any other object, then our principle, and we with it, are sectional, and are justly opposed and denounced as such. Meet us, then, on the question of whether our principle, put in practice, would wrong your section; and so meet us as if it were possible that something may be said on our side. Do you accept that challenge? No! Then you really believe that the principle which 'our fathers who framed the Government under which we live' thought so clearly right as to adopt it, and indorse it again and again, upon their official oaths, is in fact so clearly wrong as to demand your condemnation without a moment's consideration."

Washington for a Confederation of Free States

"Some of you delight to flaunt in our faces the warning against sectional parties given by Washington in his Farewell Address. Less than eight years before Washington gave that warning, he had, as President of the United States, approved and signed an act of Congress, enforcing the prohibition of slavery in the Northwestern Territory, which act embodied the policy of the Government upon that subject up to and at the very moment he penned that warning; and about one year after he penned it, he wrote La Fayette that he considered that prohibition a wise measure, expressing in the same connection his hope that we should at some time have a confederacy of free States.*

"Bearing this in mind, and seeing that sectionalism has since arisen upon this same subject, is that warning a weapon in your hands against us, or in our hands against you? Could Washington himself speak, would he cast the blame of that sectionalism upon us, who sustain his policy, or upon you who repudiate it? We respect that warning of Washington, and we

---

*President Washington to Lafayette: "I have long considered it a most serious evil, both socially and politically, and I should rejoice in any feasible scheme to rid our states of such a burden. The Congress of 1787 adopted an ordinance which prohibits the existence of involuntary servitude in our Northwestern Territories forever. I consider it a wise measure. It meets with the approval and assent of nearly every member from the States more immediately interested in Slave labor." (C. W., 3)

commend it to you, together with his example of pointing to the right application of it."

What Is Conservatism

"But you say you are conservative— eminently conservative— while we are revolutionary, destructive, or something of the sort. What is conservatism? Is it not adherence to the old and tried, against the new and untried? We stick to, contend for, the identical old policy on the point in controversy which was adopted by 'our fathers who framed the Government under which we live;' while you with one accord reject, and scout, and spit upon that old policy, and insist upon substituting something new. True, you disagree among yourselves as to what that substitute shall be. You are divided on new propositions and plans, but you are unanimous in rejecting and denouncing the old policy of the fathers. Some of you are for reviving the foreign slave trade; some for a Congressional Slave-Code for the Territories; some for Congress forbidding the Territories to prohibit Slavery within their limits; some for maintaining Slavery in the Territories through the judiciary; some for the 'gur-reat pur-rinciple' that 'if one man would enslave another, no third man should object,' fantastically called 'Popular Sovereignty;' but never a man amoung you in favor of federal prohibition of slavery in federal territories, according to the practice of 'our fathers who framed the Government under which we live.' Not one of all your various plans can show a precedent or an advocate in the century within which our Government originated. Consider, then, whether your claim of conservatism for yourselves, and your charge of destructiveness against us, are based on the most clear and stable foundations."

Denies the John Brown Slander

"Again, you say we have made the slavery question more prominent than it formerly was. We deny it. We admit that it is more prominent, but we deny that we made it so. It was not we, but you, who discarded the old policy of the fathers. We resisted, and still resist, your innovation, and thence comes the greater prominence of the question. Would you have that question reduced to its former proportions? Go back to that old policy. What has been will be again, under the same conditions. If you would have the peace of the old times, readopt the precepts and policy of the old times.

"You charge that we stir up insurrections among your slaves. We deny it; and what is your proof? Harper's Ferry! John Brown!! John Brown was no Republican; and you have failed to implicate a single Republican in his Harper's Ferry enterprise. If any member of our party is guilty in that matter, you know it or you do not know it. If you do know it, you are inexcusable for not designating the man and proving the fact. If you do not know it, you are inexcusable for asserting it, and especially for persisting in the assertion after you have tried and failed to make the proof. You need not be told that persisting in a charge which one does not know to be true, is simply malicious slander.

"Some of you admit that no Republican designedly aided or encouraged the Harper's Ferry affair, but still insist that our doctrines and declarations necessarily lead to such results. We do not believe it. We know we hold to no doctrines, and make no declaration, which were not held to and made by 'our fathers who framed the Government under which we live.' You never dealt fairly by us in relation to this affair. When it occurred, some important State elections were near at hand, and you were in evident glee with the belief that, by charging the blame upon us, you could get an advantage of us in those elections. The elections came, and your expectations were not quite fulfilled. Every Republican man knew that, as to himself at least, your charge was a slander, and he was not much inclined by it to cast his vote in your favor. Republican doctrines and declarations are accompanied with a continual protest against any interference whatever with your slaves, or with you about your slaves. Surely, this does not encourage them to revolt. True, we do, in common with 'our fathers, who framed the Government under which we live,' declare our belief that slavery is wrong; but the slaves do not hear us declare even this. For anything we say or do, the slaves would scarcely know there is a Republican party. I believe they would not, in fact, generally know it but for your misrepresentations of us, in their hearing. In your political contests among yourselves, each faction charges the other with sympathy with Black Republicanism; and then, to give point to the charge, defines Black Republicanism to simply be insurrection, blood and thunder among the slaves.

"Slave insurrections are no more common now than they were before the Republican party was organized. What induced the Southampton* insurrection, twenty-eight years ago, in which at least, three times as many lives were lost as at Harper's Ferry? You can scarcely stretch your very elastic fancy to the conclusion that Southampton was 'got up by Black Republicanism.' In the present state of things in the United States, I do not think a general, or even a very extensive slave insurrection, is possible. The indispensable concert of action cannot be attained. The slaves have no means of rapid communication; nor can incendiary freemen, black or white, supply it. The explosive materials are everywhere in parcels; but there neither are, nor can be supplied, the indispensable connecting trains.

"Much is said by Southern people about the affection of slaves for their masters and mistresses; and a part of it, at least is true. A plot for an uprising could scarcely be devised and communicated to twenty individuals before some one of them, to save the life of a favorite master or mistress, would divulge it. This is the rule; and the slave revolution in Hayti was not an exception to it, but a case occurring under peculiar circumstances. The gunpowder plot of British history, though not connected with slaves, was more in point. In that case, only about twenty were admitted to the secret; and yet one of them, in his anxiety to save a friend, betrayed the plot to that friend, and, by consequence, averted the calamity. Occasional poisonings from the kitchen, and open or stealthy assassinations in the fields, and local revolts extending to a score or so, will continue to occur as the natural results of slavery; but no general insurrection of slaves, as I think, can happen in this country for a long time. Whoever much fears, or much hopes for such an event, will be alike disappointed."

---

*This was the eleventh large insurrection in the Southern States. (C. W., 3.)

Cites Jefferson

"In the language of Mr. Jefferson, uttered many years ago, 'It is still in our power to direct the process of emancipation, and deportation, peaceably, and in such slow degrees, as that the evil will wear off insensibly; and their places be, *pari passu,* filled up by free white laborers. If, on the contrary, it is left to force itself on, human nature must shudder at the prospect held up.'

"Mr. Jefferson did not mean to say, nor do I, that the power of emancipation is in the Federal Government. He spoke of Virginia, and, as to the power of emancipation, I speak of the slaveholding States only. The Federal Government, however, as we insist, has the power of restraining the extension of the institution—the power to insure that a slave insurrection shall never occur on any American soil which is now free from slavery.

Human Nature Cannot Be Changed

"John Brown's effort was peculiar. It was not a slave insurrection. It was an attempt by white men to get up a revolt among slaves, in which the slaves refused to participate. In fact, it was so absurd that the slaves, with all their ignorance, saw plainly enough it could not succeed. That affair, in its philosophy, corresponds with the many attempts, related in history, at the assassination of kings and emperors. An enthusiast broods over the oppression of a people till he fancies himself commissioned by Heaven to liberate them. He ventures the attempt, which ends in little else than his own execution. Orsini's attempt on Louis Napoleon, and John Brown's attempt at Harper's Ferry were, in their philosophy, precisely the same. The eagerness to cast blame on old England in the one case, and on New England in the other, does not disprove the sameness of the two things.

"And how much would it avail you, if you could, by the use of John Brown, Helper's Book, and the like, break up the Republican organization? Human action can be modified to some extent, but human nature cannot be changed. There is a judgment and a feeling against slavery in this nation, which cast at least a million and a half of votes. You cannot destroy that judgment and feeling—that sentiment—by breaking up the political organization which rallies around it. You can scarcely scatter and disperse an army which has been formed into order in the face of your heaviest fire; but if you could, how much would you gain by forcing the sentiment which created it out of the peaceful channel of the ballot-box, into some other channel? What would that other channel probably be? Would the number of John Browns be lessened or enlarged by the operation?"

Rule or Ruin

"But you will break up the Union rather than submit to a denial of your Constitutional rights.*

*At this time many Southern members of Congress, governors, editors and ministers were threatening secession if W. H. Seward or S. P. Chase or any representative of the Republican party was elected President (C. W., 3). Lincoln was not then considered by many to be a presidential possibility.

"That has a somewhat reckless sound; but it would be palliated, if not fully justified, were we proposing, by the mere force of numbers, to deprive you of some right, plainly written down in the Constitution. But we are proposing no such thing.

"When you make these declarations, you have a specific and well-understood allusion to an assumed Constitutional right of yours, to take slaves into the federal territories, and to hold them there as property. But no such right is specifically written in the Constitution. That instrument is literally silent about any such right. We, on the contrary, deny that such a right has any existence in the Constitution, even by implication.

"Your purpose, then, plainly stated, is, that you will destroy the Government, unless you be allowed to construe and enforce the Constitution as you please, on all points in dispute between you and us. You will rule or ruin in all events."

Challenges the Supreme Court's Decision

"This, plainly stated, is your language. Perhaps you will say the Supreme Court has decided the disputed Constitutional question in your favor. Not quite so. But waiving the lawyer's distinction between dictum and decision, the Court have decided the question for you in a sort of way. The Court have substantially said, it is your Constitutional right to take slaves into the federal territories, and to hold them there as property. When I say the decision was made in a sort of way, I mean it was made in a divided Court, by a bare majority of the Judges, and they not quite agreeing with one another in the reasons for making it, that it is so made as that its avowed supporters disagree with one another about its meaning, and that it was mainly based upon a mistaken statement of fact— the statement in the opinion that 'the right of property in a slave is distinctly and expressly affirmed in the Constitution.'

"An inspection of the Constitution will show that the right of property in a slave is not *'distinctly* and *expressly* affirmed' in it. Bear in mind, the Judges do not pledge their judicial opinion that such right is *impliedly* affirmed in the Constitution; but they pledge their veracity that it is *'distinctly* and *expressly'* affirmed there—'distinctly,' that is, not mingled with anything else—'expressly,' that is, in words meaning just that, without the aid of any inference, and susceptible of no other meaning.

"If they had only pledged their judicial opinion that such right is affirmed in the instrument by implication, it would be open to others to show that neither the word 'slave' nor 'slavery' is to be found in the Constitution, nor the word 'property' even, in any connection with language alluding to the things slave, or slavery, and that wherever in that instrument the slave is alluded to, he is called a 'person;'— and wherever his master's legal right in relation to him is alluded to, it is spoken of as 'service or labor which may be due,'— as a debt payable in service or labor. Also, it would be open to show, by contemporaneous history, that this mode of alluding to slaves and slavery, instead of speaking of them, was employed on purpose to exclude from the Constitution the idea that there could be any property in man.

"To show all this, is easy and certain.

"When this obvious mistake of the Judges shall be brought to their notice, is it not reasonable to expect that they will withdraw the mistaken statement, and reconsider the conclusion based upon it?

"And then it is to be remembered that 'our fathers, who framed the Government under which we live'—the men who made the Constitution— decided this same Constitutional question in our favor, long ago—decided it without division among themselves, when making the decision; without division among themselves, about the meaning of it after it was made, and, so far as any evidence is left, without basing it upon any mistaken statement of facts."

Challenges the Threat to Destroy the Union

"Under all these circumstances, do you really feel yourselves justified to break up this Government, unless such a court decision as yours is, shall be at once submitted to as a conclusive and final rule of political action? But you will not abide the election of a Republican President! In that supposed event, you say, you will destroy the Union; and then, you say, the great crime of having destroyed it will be upon us! That is cool. A highwayman holds a pistol to my ear, and mutters through his teeth, 'Stand and deliver, or I shall kill you, and then you will be a murderer!'

"To be sure, what the robber demanded of me—my money—was my own; and I had a clear right to keep it; but it was no more my own than my vote is my own; and the threat of death to me, to extort my money, and the threat of destruction to the Union, to extort my vote, can scarcely be distinguished in principle."

Moral Advice to Republicans

Lincoln closed his address by advising the Republicans on the attitude to take towards the South. It was, in its inexorable, prophetic logic, irritating to the proud, sensitive Southern people who were in moral conflict over being unable to justify slavery under the moral precepts of Christianity and unable to decide to give up its cheap service, as the foundation of their prosperity in agriculture.*

---

*It was popular in the South to proclaim the cultural improvement of the Negro savage under slavery as evidence of the moral virtues of slavery.

"I am satisfied that the mind of the South has undergone a change to this great extent, that it is now the almost *universal belief* in the South, not only that the condition of African slavery in their midst, is the best condition to which the African race has ever been subjected, but *it has the effect of enobling both races, the white and the black."*— *Senator Mason of Virginia.*

"I am a Southern States' Rights man; I am an African slave-trader. I am one . . . who believes that slavery is right— morally, religiously, socially, and politically. . . . I believe the African Slave-trader is a true missionary and a true Christian."— *Mr. Gaulden of Georgia.*

"I declare again . . . that in my opinion, slavery is a great moral, social and political blessing— a blessing to the slave, and a blessing to the master."— *Mr. Brown, in the Senate.*

"I insist that negro slavery is not unjust," said Mr. O'Connor; eminent New York lawyer and counsel for the State of Virginia, in a speech at Cooper Institute in 1859.

"A few words now to Republicans. *It is exceedingly desirable that all parts of this great Confederacy shall be at peace, and in harmony, one with another. Let us Republicans do our part to have it so. Even though much provoked, let us do nothing through passion and ill temper. Even though the southern people will not so much as listen to us, let us calmly consider their demands, and yield to them if, in our deliberate view of our duty, we possibly can.* Judging by all they say and do, and by the subject and nature of their controversy with us, let us determine, if we can, what will satisfy them.

"Will they be satisfied if the Territories be unconditionally surrendered to them? We know they will not. In all their present complaints against us, the Territories are scarcely mentioned. Invasions and insurrections are the rage now. Will it satisfy them, if, in the future, we have nothing to do with invasions and insurrections? We know it will not. We so know, because we know we never had anything to do with invasions and insurrections; and yet this total abstaining does not exempt us from the charge and the denunciation."

Is Slavery Morally Right or Wrong?

"The question recurs, what will satisfy them? Simply this: We must not only let them alone, but we must, somehow, convince them that we do let them alone. This, we know by experience, is no easy task. We have been so trying to convince them from the very beginning of our organization, but with no success. In all our platforms and speeches we have constantly protested our purpose to let them alone; but this has had no tendency to convince them. Alike unavailing to convince them, is the fact that they have never detected a man of us in any attempt to disturb them.

"These natural, and apparently adequate means all failing, what will convince them? This, and this only: cease to call slavery *wrong,* and join them in calling it *right.* And this must be done thoroughly—done in *acts* as well as in *words.* Silence will not be tolerated—we must place ourselves avowedly with them. Senator Douglas's new sedition law must be enacted and enforced, suppressing all declarations that slavery is wrong, whether made in politics, in presses, in pulpits, or in private. We must arrest and return their fugitive slaves with greedy pleasure. We must pull down our Free State constitutions. The whole atmosphere must be disinfected from all taint of opposition to slavery, before they will cease to believe that all their troubles proceed from us.

"I am quite aware they do not state their case precisely in this way. Most of them would probably say to us, 'Let us alone, *do* nothing to us, and *say* what you please about slavery.' But we do let them alone—so that, after all, it is what we say, which dissatisfies them. They will continue to accuse us of doing, until we cease saying.

"I am also aware they have not, as yet, in terms, demanded the overthrow of our Free-State Constitutions.* Yet those Consitutions declare the

---

*Claims that the constitutions of Connecticut, Maine, Massachusetts, Michigan, New Hampshire, Ohio, Rhode Island, Vermont and Wisconsin, excluding slavery, violated the Constitution of the United States had been made in the Senate by Senator Toombs of Georgia.

wrong of slavery, with more solemn emphasis, than do all other sayings against it; and when all these other sayings shall have been silenced, the overthrow of these Constitutions will be demanded, and nothing be left to resist the demand. It is nothing to the contrary, that they do not demand the whole of this just now. Demanding what they do, and for the reason they do, they can voluntarily stop nowhere short of this consummation. Holding, as they do, that slavery is morally right, and socially elevating, they cannot cease to demand a full national recognition of it, as a legal right, and a social blessing."

Defends Constitutional Rights of Slave States

"Nor can we justifiably withhold this, on any ground save our conviction that slavery is wrong. If slavery is right, all words, acts, laws, and constitutions against it, are themselves wrong, and should be silenced, and swept away. If it is right, we cannot justly object to its nationality—its universality; if it is wrong, they cannot justly insist upon its extension—it enlargement. All they ask, we could readily grant, if we thought slavery right; all we ask, they could as readily grant, if they thought it wrong. Their thinking it right, and our thinking it wrong, is the precise fact upon which depends the whole controversy. Thinking it right, as they do, they are not to blame for desiring its full recognition, as being right; but thinking it wrong, as we do, can we yield to them? Can we cast our votes with their view, and against our own? In view of our moral, social, and political responsibilities, can we do this?

"Wrong as we think slavery is, we can yet afford to let it alone where it is, because that much is due to the necessity arising from its actual presence in the nation; but can we, while our votes will prevent it, allow it to spread into the National Territories, and to overrun us here in these Free States? If our sense of duty forbids this then let us stand by our duty, fearlessly and effectively. Let us be diverted by none of those sophistical contrivances wherewith we are so industriously plied and belabored—contrivances such as groping for some middle ground between the right and the wrong, vain as the search for a man who should be neither a living man nor a dead man—such a policy of 'don't care' on a question about which all true men do care—such as Union appeals beseeching true Union men to yield to Disunionists, reversing the divine rule, and calling, not the sinners, but the righteous to repentance—such as invocations to Washington, imploring men to unsay what Washington said, and undo what Washington did.

"Neither let us be slandered from our duty by false accusations against us, nor frightened from it by menaces of destruction to the Government nor of dungeons to ourselves. LET US HAVE FAITH THAT RIGHT MAKES MIGHT, AND IN THAT FAITH, LET US, TO THE END, DARE TO DO OUR DUTY AS WE UNDERSTAND IT."

Chapter XXXIX

WINNING NEW ENGLAND

The Eastern Republican, Abolitionist, and Antislavery Democratic press vigorously approved Lincoln's New York speech. He had delivered the most successful oration of his career. Intensely antislavery, pro-Union, morally minded, freedom-loving, commercially minded New England responded immediately, and requests from her principal cities poured in for speeches. He accepted with inspiration and spoke with fresh spontaneity before each audience although necessarily repeating the arguments expressed previously.

At Providence, R. I., the *Journal* (2, 29, 1860) said he "triumphantly vindicated himself and the Republican party against the false charges which are so unscrupulously brought against them."

At Manchester, N. H., the *Daily American* (3, 2, 1860), intensely abolitionist, commented on his speech: "One of the best points of his speech, (and this was among the first,) was the answer to the question—What will satisfy the demands of the South upon the subject of Slavery?—Simply this, . . . we must not only let them alone, but we must convince them that we do let them alone." . . . "The speaker said, let us not be slandered from our duty by the false accusations against us, nor frightened from it by menaces of destruction of the Government, nor in dungeons to ourselves."

At Dover, N. H., the *Inquirer* said (3, 8, 1860): "Mr. Lincoln spoke nearly two hours and we believe he would have held his audience had he spoken all night. . . . We should not, he said, be diverted by trick or strategem, by a senseless clamor about 'popular sovereignty,' by any contrivances for groping for some middle ground between the right and the wrong—the 'don't care' policy of Douglas—or Union appeals to true Union men to yield, to the threat of Disunionists, which was reversing the divine rule, and calling, not the sinners but the righteous to repentence—none of these things should move or intimidate us; but having faith that right makes might, let us to the end, dare to do our duty."

Declines Speaking Invitations

Isaac Pomeroy of New York, a member of the Republican Young Men's Working Club, asked Lincoln to deliver a speech in Newark, N. J. His reply (3, 3, 1860) bespeaks the intense popularity of the reaction to his political philosophy that now was burning throughout the Northeastern states.

"Owing to my great itinerary in this region, yours of the 28th. ult has just reached me. I have already spoken five times, and am engaged to speak five more. By the time these engagements shall be fulfilled, I shall be so far worn down, and also will be carried so far beyond my allotted time, that an immediate return home will be a necessity with me. At this very sitting I am declining invitations to go to Philadelphia, Reading, and Pittsburgh in Pa. You perceive I treat you no worse than I do the others. The near approach of the elections in N. H. Conn. & R. I. has been the means of their getting me so deeply in here. I hope I may yet be able to visit New-Jersey & Pa. before the fall elections. While at New-York a Mr. William Silvey got a promise from me that I would write him whether I could visit, & speak at New-Ark. [Newark]. Will you please show him this?"

The fragment of a letter to a friend in New York, J. A. Briggs (3, 4, 1860) appeals: "Since I left New York I have spoken at Providence, R. I. and at Concord, Manchester, Dover & Exeter, in this State, and I still am to speak at Hartford, Meriden . . . Then I close, and start for home. . . . Much as I appreciate your kindness allow me to beg that you will make no arrangements to detain me." . . .

To Mrs. Lincoln he wrote (3, 4, 1860) from Exeter where he was visiting his son Robert who was attending the Phillips Exeter Academy: "I have been unable to escape this toil. If I had forseen it, I think I would not have come east at all. The speech at New York, being within my calculation before I started, went off passably well and gave me no trouble whatever. The difficulty was to make nine others, before reading audiences who had already seen all my ideas in print."

Evangelist of Political Christianity

Abraham Lincoln, the evangelist of equalitarian freedom and deliverer of his people from the inequities of slavery, had arrived. His orations, entirely his own expressions and not the products of hack writers, as in the modern manner, revealed to the people his strength of mind and character. His speeches demonstrated that his legal, ethical, moral and prophetic grasp, of the rising national conflict over the economic, social, political, religious and educational institutions built on slavery, was superior to that of any public man in the nation. In the North a rising tide of public opinion acclaimed him as its leader and in the South people foresaw that, through him, slavery was doomed.

Lincoln was charged by conservatives with being a fool who rushed in where angels feared to tread and he countered: "Yes, I have seized the bull by the horns."

At Hartford

Grimy and weary from the smoke and shaking of railroad travel when he reached Hartford, he was rushed out of the station to a large public meeting arranged to hear him. The twittering reaction of the prim minded Puritan audience to his disheveled appearance, lanky, awkward build and angular movements, squeaking voice, western pronunciation and simple, pedestrian form of expression repeated the reception he had received in New York. With characteristic enduring humility and earnestness of statement, he again won respectful attention and eventually gained important converts to the restriction of slavery and the preservation of the Union, as the commonsense application of the philosophy of equalitarianism in a constitutional democracy.

Gideon Welles, scholarly editor of the Hartford *Evening Journal,* honest and independent minded, uncompromising opponent of slavery, secession and political corruption, interviewed Lincoln for the press. The fresh estimation of this professional analyst of public men, on the personality and social and political views of the rising western lawyer, are evidence of the vigorous impression Lincoln then made on first acquaintance as an original thinker and potential leader of the people. Welles said;

> "This orator and lawyer has been caricatured. He is not an Apollo, but he is not a Caliban. He was made where the material for strong men is plenty; his loose tall frame is loosely thrown together. He is in every way large—brain included, but his countenance shows intellect, generosity, great good nature and keen discrimination. He is an effective speaker because he is earnest, strong, honest, simple in style and clear as crystal in his logic." (Welles, 1911).

Public Opinion Based on Property

"Whether we will have it so or not," Lincoln said at Hartford, "the slave question is the prevailing question before the nation. . . . It was rife before the Revolution, . . . it has been settled many times. . . . But . . . in 1854 it rose . . . higher than any former time. . . . Why can't this question which we all desire so much to be settled, be satisfactorily arranged? . . . I think our wisest men have made this mistake. They underrate its importance. . . . Now what is the difficulty? One-sixth of the population of the United States is slave. One man in every six, one woman in every six, one child of every six, is a slave. Those who own them look upon them as property, . . . and speak of them as such. . . . The entire value of the slave population of the United States is, at a moderate estimate, not less than $2,000,000,000. This amount of *property* has a vast influence upon the minds of those who own it. The same amount of property owned by Northern men has the same influence upon *their* minds. In this we do not assume that we are better than the people of the South— neither do we admit that they are better than we. . . . Public opinion is formed relative to a property basis. Therefore, the slaveholders battle any policy which depreciates their slaves as property. What increases the value of this property, they favor. When you tell them that slavery is immoral, they rebel, because they do not like to be told they are interested in an institution which is not a moral one. When you enter into a defence of slavery, they seize upon it, for they like justification. The result is, that public opinion is formed among them which insists upon the encouragement or protection, the enlargement or perpetuation of slavery—and secures them property in the slave.

"Now this comes in conflict with this proposition that we at the North view slavery as wrong. We understand that the 'equality of man' principle which actuated our forefathers . . . is right; and that slavery, being directly opposed to this, is morally wrong. I think that if anything can be proved by natural theology, it is that slavery is morally wrong. God gave man a mouth to receive bread, hands to feed it, and his hand has a right to carry bread to his mouth without controversy.

"We suppose slavery is wrong, and that it endangers the perpetuity of the Union. . . . Almost every man has a sense of certain things being wrong, and at the same time, a sense of its pecuniary value."

Lincoln's homely argument was sound. Psychology has since recognized that each person's efforts at self-preservation and the sense of security is based on his own economic resources. The personality develops integrity of organization through being free to work for economic stability and social respectability.

Supports the Right of Labor to Strike

The Hartford *Daily Courant* quoted Lincoln as saying: "I am glad to know that there is a system of labor where the laborer can strike if he wants to! I would to God that such a system prevailed all over the world."

The Hartford *Evening Press* said Mr. Lincoln treated the Massachusetts shoemakers' strike in a humorous and philosophical manner, and exposed to ridicule the foolish pretence of Senator Douglas—that the strike arose from 'this unfortunate sectional warfare.' . . . He said:

"I have heard that in consequence of this 'sectional warfare,' as Douglas calls it, Senator Mason of Va., had appeared in a *suit of homspun.* Now up in New Hampshire, the woolen and cotton mills are all busy, and there is no strike—they are busy making the very goods Senator Mason has quit buying! To carry out his idea, he ought to go *barefoot!* If that's the plan, they should begin at the *foundation,* and adopt the well-known 'Georgia costume' of a shirtcollar and a pair of spurs!" (Irrepressible laughter and applause.)

At New Haven

The speech at New Haven, Connecticut (3, 6, 1860), reported from manuscript, was the most complete of any given in the New England series and it was the most reproduced by contemporary newspapers. We repeat here parts from the New Haven *Daily Palladium* that best express Lincoln's views to the Puritans on the moral nature of the political conflict.

"If the Republican party of this nation shall ever have the national house entrusted to its keeping, it will be the duty of that party to attend to all the affairs of national house-keeping. Whatever matters of importance may come up, whatever difficulties may arise in the way of its administration of the government, that party will then have to attend to. It will then be compelled to attend to other questions, besides this question which now assumes an overwhelming importance—the question of Slavery. It is true that in the organization of the Republican party this question of Slavery was more important than any other; indeed, so much more important has it become that no other national question can even get a hearing just at present. The old question of tariff—a matter that will remain one of the chief affairs of national housekeeping to all time—the question of the management of financial affairs; the question of the disposition of the public domain— how shall it be managed for the purpose of getting it well settled, and of making these the homes of a free and happy people—these will remain open and require attention for a great while yet, and these questions will have to be attended to by whatever party has the control of the government. Yet, just now, they cannot even obtain a hearing, and I do not propose to detain you upon these topics, or what sort of hearing they should have when opportunity shall come."

Lincoln neatly indicated to New England's people by these brief introductory remarks that he believed in the necessity of a protective tariff, a national system of managing and stabilizing finance and improvements in the distribution of Federal lands to free settlers—all highly desirable, all highly important to the development of industry and agriculture.

Settle the Slavery Question

Lincoln was charged with being an antislavery agitator although he continued to hold strictly that the constitutional rights of the slave states to a fugitive slave law must be observed. He was not as radical as Chase, who continued to hold the fugitive slave law unconstitutional. He was more clearly defined than Seward, who was playing a noncommittal ambivalent policy, to compromise both factions.

"Whether we will or not, the question of Slavery is *the* question, the all absorbing topic of the day. It is true that all of us—and by that I mean, not the Republican party alone, but the whole American people, here and elsewhere—all of us wish this question settled—wish it out of the way. It stands in the way, and prevents the adjustment, and the giving of necessary attention to other questions of national house-keeping."

Lincoln's homely comparisons of the administration of the Federal government to "national house-keeping" were used frequently and are indicative of the self-suggestions made to reassure himself that he had sufficient administrative capacity, although never previously tested, to serve as President.

After calling attention to the growing agitation in the North and South after 1854 over the Kansas-Nebraska act and the tragedy of Kansas, he said:

. . . "This question is one of national importance and we cannot help dealing with it: we must do something about it, whether we will or not. We cannot avoid it; the subject is one we cannot avoid considering; we can no more avoid it than a man can live without eating. It is upon us; it attaches to the body politic as much and as closely as the natural wants attach to our natural bodies. Now I think it important that this matter should be taken up in earnest, and really settled. And one way to bring about a true settlement of the question is to understand its true magnitude.

"There have been many efforts to settle it. Again and again it has been fondly hoped that it was settled, but every time it breaks out afresh, and more violently than ever. It was settled, our fathers hoped, by the Missouri Compromise, but it did not stay settled. Then the compromises of 1850 were declared to be a full and final settlement of the question. The two great parties, each in National Convention, adopted resolutions declaring that the settlement made by the Compromise of 1850 was a finality—that it would last forever. Yet how long before it was unsettled again! It broke out again in 1854, and blazed higher and raged more furiously than ever before, and the agitation has not rested since.

"These repeated settlements must have some fault about them. There must be some inadequacy in their very nature to the purpose for which they were designed. We can only speculate as to where that fault—that inadequacy, is, but we may perhaps profit by past experience.

"I think that one of the causes of these repeated failures is that our best and greatest men have greatly underestimated the size of this question. They have constantly brought forward small cures for great sores—plasters too small to cover the wound. That is one reason that all settlements have proved so temporary— so evanescent." (Applause.)

He again emphasized the "magnitude of the subject" by pointing out, that one sixth of the nation's population are slaves, held as property and treated as property with an estimated value of two billion dollars and "this immense pecuniary interest has its influence on their [the owner's] minds."

In the North "it appears natural to think that slaves are human beings; *men,* not property; that some of the things, at least, stated about men in the Declaration of Independence apply to them as well as to us. (Applause.) I say, we think, most of us, that this Charter of Freedom applies to the slave as well as to ourselves, that the class of arguments put forward to batter down that idea, are also calculated to break down the very idea of a free government, even for white men, and to undermine the very foundations of free society. (Continued applause.) We think Slavery a great moral wrong, and while we do not claim the right to touch it where it exists, we wish to treat it as a wrong in the Territories, where our votes will reach it. We think that a respect for ourselves, a regard for future generations and for the God that made us, require that we put down this wrong where our votes will properly reach it. We think that species of labor an injury to free white men— in short, we think Slavery a great moral, social and political evil, tolerable only because, and so far as its actual existence makes it necessary to tolerate it, and that beyond that, it ought to be treated as a wrong.

"Now these two ideas, the property idea that Slavery is right, and the idea that it is wrong, come into collision, and do actually produce that irrepressible conflict which Mr. Seward has been so roundly abused for mentioning. The two ideas conflict, and must conflict.

. . . "What ever endangered this Union, save and except Slavery? Did any other thing ever cause a moment's fear? All men must agree that this thing alone has ever endangered the perpetuity of the Union. . . . Can any man believe that the way to save the Union is to extend and increase the only thing that threatens the Union, and to suffer it to grow bigger and bigger?'' (Great applause.)

Philosophical Solution

"Whenever this question shall be settled, it must be settled on some philosophical basis. No policy that does not rest upon some philosophical public opinion can be permanently maintained. And hence, there are but two policies in regard to Slavery that can be at all maintained. The first, based on the property view that Slavery is right, conforms to that idea throughout, and demands that we shall do everything for it that we ought to do if it were right. We must sweep away all opposition, for opposition to the right is wrong; we must agree that Slavery is right, and we must adopt the idea that property has persuaded the owner to believe—that Slavery is morally right and socially elevating. This gives a philosophical basis for a permanent policy of encouragement.

"The other policy is one that squares with the idea that Slavery is wrong, and it consists in doing everything that we ought to do if it is wrong. Now, I don't wish to be misunderstood, nor to leave a gap down to be misrepresented, even. I don't mean that we ought to attack it where it exists. To me it seems that if we were to form a government anew, in view of the actual presence of Slavery we should find it necessary to frame just such a government as our fathers did, giving to the slaveholder the entire control where the system was established, while we possessed the power to restrain it from going outside these limits. (Applause.) From the necessities of the case we should be compelled to form just such a government as our blessed fathers gave us; and, surely, if they have so made it, that adds another reason why we should let Slavery alone where it exists."

Southern slave traders were being encouraged by the Southern ministry to assert themselves as moral benefactors of the white and black races. Some actually claimed they made possible the cultivation of Christian civilized slaves out of pagan savages. Northern political philosophy replied that although the mental and physical welfare of most American slaves had been improved over that of their African ancestors, the improvement would be more rapid and far greater if they were made free with full constitutional rights.

Ridicules Douglasism as Untenable

After repeating the white man vs. Negro vs. crocodile order of preference as expounded by Douglasism he ridiculed his opponent's idea of popular sovereignty as being a plausible, sugar-coated name for indifference on whether slavery "voted up or voted down."

"This policy chiefly stands in the way of a permanent settlement of the question. I believe there is no danger of its becoming the permanent policy of the country, for it is based on a public indifference. There is nobody that 'don't care.' 'ALL THE PEOPLE DO CARE' one way or the other. (Great applause.) I do not charge that its author, when he says he 'don't care,' states his individual opinion; he only expresses his policy for the government. . . . Now such a policy . . . may spring up as necessary to the political prospects of some gentleman; but it is utterly baseless; the people are not indifferent; and it can therefore have no durability or permanence.

"But suppose it could! Then it could be maintained only by a public opinion that shall say 'we don't care.' There must be a change in public opinion, the public mind must be so far debauched as to square with this policy of caring not at all. . . .

"You are ready to say it cannot, but be not too fast! Rember what a long stride has been taken since the repeal of the Missouri Compromise! Do you know of any Democrat, of either branch of the party—do you know one who declares that he believes that the Declaration of Independence has any application to the negro? Judge Taney declares that it has not, and Judge Douglas even vilifies me personally and scolds me roundly for saying that the Declaration applies to all men, and that negroes are men. (Cheers.) Is there a Democrat here who does not deny that the Declaration applies to a negro? Do any of you know of one? Well, I have tried before perhaps fifty audiences, some larger and some smaller than this, to find one such Democrat, and never yet have I found one who said I did not place him right in that. I must assume that Democrats hold that, and now, *not one of these Democrats can show that he said that five years ago!* (Applause.) I venture to defy the whole party to produce one man that ever uttered the belief that the Declaration did not apply to negroes, before the repeal of the Missouri Compromise! Four or five years ago we all thought negroes were men, and that when 'all men' were named, negroes were included. But *the whole Democratic party has deliberately taken negroes from the class of men and put them in the class of brutes.* (Applause.) Turn it as you will, it is simply the truth! Don't be too hasty then in saying that the people cannot be brought to this new doctrine, but note that long stride. One more as long completes the journey, from where negroes are estimated as men to where they are estimated as mere brutes—as rightful property!" . . .

The Unspeakable Moral Issue

"What we want, and all we want, is to have with us the men who think slavery wrong. But those who say they hate slavery, and are opposed to it, but yet act with the Democratic party—where are they? Let us apply a few tests. You say that you think slavery is wrong, but you denounce all attempts to restrain it. . . . We must not call it wrong in the Free States, because it is *not* there, and we must not call it wrong in the Slave States because it *is* there; we must not call it wrong in politics because that is bringing morality into politics, and we must not call it wrong in the pulpit because that is bringing politics into religion; we must not bring it into the Tract Society or the other societies, because those are such unsuitable places, and there is no single place, according to you, where this wrong thing can properly be called wrong! (Continued laughter and applause.)

Party Loyalty Transcends Morality

"Perhaps you will plead that if the people of Slave States should themselves set on foot an effort for emancipation, you would wish them success, and bid them God-speed. Let us test that! In 1858, the emancipation party of Missouri, with Frank Blair at their head, tried to get up a movement for that purpose, and having started a party contested the State. Blair was beaten, apparently if not truly, and when the news came to Connecticut, you, who knew that Frank Blair was taking hold of this thing by the right end, and doing the only thing that you say can properly be done to remove this wrong—did you bow your heads in sorrow because of that defeat? Do you, any of you, know one single Democrat that showed sorrow over that result? Not one! On the contrary every man threw up his hat, and hallooed at the top of his lungs, 'hooray for Democracy!' " (Great laughter and applause.)

What the Republicans Desire

"Now, gentlemen, *the Republicans desire to place this great question of slavery on the very basis on which our fathers placed it, and no other.* (Applause.) It is easy to demonstrate that 'our Fathers, who framed the government under which we live,' looked on Slavery as wrong, and so framed it and everything about it as to square with the idea that it was wrong, so far as the necessities arising from its existence permitted. In forming the Constitution they found the slave trade existing; capital invested in it; fields depending upon it for labor, and the whole system resting upon the importation of slave-labor. They therefore did not prohibit the slave trade at once, but they gave the power to prohibit it after twenty years. Why was this? What other foreign trade did they treat in that way? Would they have done this if they had not thought slavery wrong?

"Another thing was done by some of the same men who framed the Constitution, and afterwards adopted as their own act by the first Congress held under that Constitution, of which many of the framers were members; they prohibited the spread of Slavery into Territories. Thus the same men, the framers of the Constitution, cut off the supply and prohibited the spread of Slavery, and both acts show conclusively that they considered that the thing was wrong."

Phraseology of the Constitution

"If additional proof is wanting it can be found in the phraseology of the Constitution. When men are framing a supreme law and chart of government, to secure blessings and prosperity to untold generations yet to come, they use language as short and direct and plain as can be found, to express their meaning. In all matters but this of Slavery the framers of the Constitution used the very clearest, shortest, and most direct language. But the Constitution alludes to Slavery three times without mentioning it once! The language used becomes ambiguous, roundabout, and mystical. They speak of the 'immigration of persons,' and mean the importation of slaves, but do not say so. In establishing a basis of representation they say 'all other persons,' when they mean to say slaves—why did they not use the shortest phrase? In providing for the return of fugitives they say 'persons held to service or labor.' If they had said slaves it would have been plainer, and less liable to misconstruction. Why didn't they do it. We cannot doubt that it was done on purpose. Only one reason is possible, and that is supplied us by one of the framers of the Constitution—and it is not possible for a man to conceive any other—they expected and desired that the system would come to an end, and meant that when it did, the Constitution should not show that there ever had been a slave in this good free country of ours!" [Great applause.]

Democratic Bushwacking

. . . "I see the signs of the approaching triumph of the Republicans in the bearing of their political adversaries. A great deal of their war with us now-a-days is mere bushwacking. (Laughter.) . . . The Democrats are in that sort of extreme desperation; it is nothing else. (Laughter.) I will take up a few of these *arguments*.

"There is 'THE IRREPRESSIBLE CONFLICT.' (Applause.) How they rail at Seward for that saying! They repeat it constantly; and although the proof has been thrust under their noses again and again, that almost every good man since the formation of our government has uttered that same sentiment, from Gen. Washington, who 'trusted that we should yet have a confederacy of Free States,' with Jefferson, Jay, Monroe, down to the latest days, yet they refuse to notice that at all, and persist in railing at Seward for saying it. Even Roger A. Pryor, editor of the Richmond Enquirer, uttered the same sentiment in almost the same language, and yet so little offence did it give the Democrats that he was sent for to Washington to edit the States—the Douglas organ there, while Douglas goes into hydrophobia and spasms of rage because Seward dared to repeat it. (Great applause.) This is what I call bushwacking, a sort of argument that they must know any child can see through.

"Another is John Brown! (Great laughter.) . . . John Brown was not a Republican! You have never implicated a single Republican in that Harper's Ferry enterprise. You never dealt fairly with us in relation to that affair—and I will say frankly that I know of nothing in your character that should lead us to suppose that you would. You had just been soundly thrashed in elections in several States, and others were soon to come. . . . you were rejoicing that by charging Republicans with this thing you might get an advantage of us in New York, and the other States. You pulled that string as tightly as you could, but your very generous and worthy expectations were not quite fulfilled. (Laughter.) Each Republican knew that the charge was a slander as to himself at least, and was not inclined by it to cast his vote in your favor. It was mere bushwacking, because you had nothing else to do. You are still on that track, and I say, go on! If you think you can slander a woman into loving you or a man into voting for you, try it till you are satisfied!" (Tremendouse applause.)

The Right of Labor to Strike

"Another specimen of this bushwacking, that 'shoe strike.' (Laughter.) Now be it understood that I do not pretend to know all about this matter. I am merely going to speculate a little about some of its phases. And at the outset, *I am glad to see that a system of labor prevails in New England under which laborers* CAN *strike* when they want to (Cheers,) where they are not obliged to work under all circumstances, and are not tied down and obliged to labor whether you pay them or not! (Cheers.) I *like* the system which lets a man quit when he wants to, and wish it might prevail everywhere. (Tremendous applause.) One of the reasons why I am opposed to Slavery is just here. What is the true condition of the laborer? I take it that it is best for all to leave each man free to acquire property as fast as he can. Some will get wealthy. I don't believe in a law to prevent a man from getting rich; it would do more harm than good. So while we do not propose any war on capital, we do wish to allow the humblest man an equal chance to get rich with everybody else. (Applause.) When one starts poor, as most do in the race of life, free society is such that he knows he can better his condition; he knows that there is no fixed condition of labor, for his whole life. I am not ashamed to confess that twenty five years ago I was a hired laborer, mauling rails, at work on a flatboat—just what might happen to any poor man's son! (Applause.) I want every man to have the chance—and I believe a black man is entitled to it—in which he *can* better his condition —when he may look forward and hope to be a hired laborer this year and the next, work for himself afterward, and finally to hire men to work for him! That is the true system."

Lincoln also ridiculed as "bushwacking" the attempt of Southern politicians to influence Northern manufacturers by preparing a list of "white" (Democratic) and "black" (Republican) concerns for the guidance of Southern purchasers.

. . . "I find a good many people who are very much concerned about the loss of Southern trade. Now either these people are sincere or they are not. (Laughter.) I will speculate a little about that. If they are sincere, and are moved by any real danger of the loss of Southern trade, they will simply get their names on the white list, and then, instead of persuading Republicans to do likewise, they will be glad to keep you away! Don't you see they thus shut off competiton? They would not be whispering around to Republicans to come in and share the profits with them. But if they are not sincere, and are merely trying to fool Republicans out of their votes, they will grow very anxious about *your* pecuniary prospects; they are afraid you are going to get broken up and ruined; they did not care about Democratic votes—*Oh no, no, no!* You must judge which class those belong to whom you meet; I leave it to you to determine from the facts."

Republicans Are not Sectional

. . . "You say we are sectional. We deny it. That makes an issue; and the burden of proof is upon you. You produce your proof; and what is it? Why, that our party has no existence in your section—gets no votes in your section. The fact is substantially true; but does it prove the issue? If it does, then in case we should, without change of principle, begin to get votes in your section, we should thereby cease to be sectional. You cannot escape this conclusion; and yet, are you willing to abide by it? If you are, you will probably soon find that we have ceased to be sectional, for we shall get votes in your section this very year. (Applause.) The fact that we get no votes in your section is a fact of your making, and not of ours. And if there be fault in that fact, that fault is primarily yours, and remains so until you show that we repel you by some wrong principle or practice. If we do repel you by any wrong principle or practice, the fault is ours; but this brings you to where you ought to have started—to a discussion of the right or wrong of our principle. If our principle, put in practice, would wrong your section for the benefit of ours, or for any other object, then our principle, and we with it, are sectional, and are just opposed and denounced as such. Meet us, then, on the question of whether our principle, put in practice, would wrong your section, and so meet it as if it were possible that something might be said on our side. Do you accept the challenge? No? Then you really believe that the principle which our fathers who framed the Government under which we live and thought so clearly right as to adopt it, and indorse it again and again, upon their official oaths, is, in fact, so clearly wrong as to demand your condemnation without a moment's consideration.

"Some of you delight to flaunt in our faces the warning against sectional parties given by Washington in his Farewell address. Less than eight years before Washington gave that warning, he had, as President of the United States, approved and signed an act of Congress, enforcing the prohibiton of Slavery in the northwestern Territory, which act embodied the policy of Government upon that subject, up to and at the very moment he penned that warning; and about one year after he penned it he wrote LaFayette that he considered that prohibition a wise measure, expressing in the same connection his hope that we should some time have a confederacy of Free States.

"Bearing this in mind, and seeing that sectionalism has since arisen upon this same subject, is that warning a weapon in your hands against us, or in our hands against you? Could Washington himself speak, would he cast the blame of sectionalism upon us, who sustain his policy, or upon you who repudiate it? We respect that warning of Washington, and we commend it to you, together with his example pointing to the right application of it." (Applause.)

Lincoln closed his New Haven speech with reading the deliniations he gave at Cooper Institute on who is conservative and what can be done and should be done to satisfy proslavery demands.

Chapter XL

WINNING THE REPUBLICAN NOMINATION

New England, the home of the new Republicanism and of Abolitionism, took Abraham Lincoln to its heart. Senator Seward had long established himself in New York, Connecticut, Massachusetts and other Eastern states as first choice for the Republican nomination but Lincoln, principally through his philosophy of constitutional regulation of slavery, as expressed in speeches in the East, won for himself popular recognition, as second choice. Before each audience he had complimented Seward as the author of the "irrepressible conflict" epigrammatic statement, abandoning for the time his own far more trenchant and popular, though much criticised, "house divided against itself cannot stand" allegory. As a prospective candidate he cultivated public approval for Seward as well as himself, contented to be for a time, it seems, the tail of the great kite.

We gain some idea of Lincoln's happy reaction to the enormous increase in public approval that he had earned by his Eastern speeches from letters he wrote in answer to inquiries and praises received after he returned to Springfield.

All Good Intelligent People Much Alike

To W. Gooding (4, 6, 1860), an old friend and construction engineer of the important Illinois-Michigan canal: "I found your very complimentary letter of March 21st.; for which, I sincerely thank you. Our down East friends did, indeed, treat me with great kindness, demonstrating what I before believed, that all good, intelligent people are very much alike."

To A. W. Harvey (3, 14, 1860): "Your despatch of the 27th. ult. to Mr. Greeley, asking if you could not have a speech from me on my return, was forwarded to me by Mr. G. reaching me at Exeter, N. H.

"The appointments I had then already made carried me so far beyond my alloted time that I could not consistently add another.

"I hope that I may yet be allowed to meet the good people of Buffalo before the close of the struggle in which we are engaged."

Popular Demand for Cooper Institute Address

. Reply to John Pickering (4, 6, 1860): "Pamphlet copies of my late speech at Cooper Institute, N. Y. can be had at the office of the N. Y. Tribune; at the Republican Club Room at Washington, and at the office of the Illinois Journal at this place. At which place they are cheapest, I do not certainly know.

"I have no difficulty in knowing who you are by the fact that I knew your father [William Pickering, Whig state representative] so very well. I shall be glad to hear from you at any time."

Cannot Enter the Ring on a Money Basis

The following letter (3, 16, 1860) to an old Kansas firend, Mr. W. Delahay, has excited praise of Lincoln's character by many biographers and malicious condemnation by others:

"I have just returned from the East. Before leaving, I received your letter of Feb. 6 and on my return I find those of the 17th and 19th, with Gen. Lane's note enclosed in one of them.

"I sincerely wish you would be elected one of the first Senators for Kansas; but how to help you I do not know. If it were permissable for me to interfere, I am not personally acquainted with a single member of your Legislature. If my known friendship for you could be of any advantage, that friendship was abundantly manifested by me last December while in Kansas. If any member had written me, as you say some have Trumbull, I would very readily answer him. I shall write Trumbull on the subject at this sitting. . . .

"As to your kind wishes for myself, allow me to say I cannot enter the ring on the money basis—first, because, in the main it is wrong; and, secondly, I have not, and cannot get the money. I say, in the main, the use of money is wrong; but for certain objects, in a political contest, the use of some, is both right, and indispensable. With me, as with yourself, this long struggle has been one of great pecuniary loss. I now distinctly say this. If you shall be appointed a delegate to Chicago, I will furnish one hundred dollars to bear the expenses of the trip. . . ."

This direct, personal offer by a candidate for nomination, to give 100 dollars towards defraying the expenses of a delegate who whould serve his cause has been criticised, although now common practice, as unethical for obligating allegiance to the sponsor. Lincoln, it seems, never lost sight of the helpful advantage of friendship in politics, as indicated by the "abundant manifestion of it." Practically all of his private political letters give evidence of how sympathetically he cultivated friendship in personal relations.

He wrote to Senator Trumbull on the same day as he had promised, urging him to assist Delahay, if he could do so, "without impropriety." Trumbull replied that he would be glad to help him but was unable to do so for none of the letters received from Kansas friends had mentioned his name.

Give No Offense and Keep Cool

It developed shortly thereafter that Delahay did not win an appointment to the Kansas Republican delegation. Furthermore, much to Lincoln's chagrin, after his seeming great popularity following his speeches there, the delegation was instructed to name Seward as its first choice. Under these baffling conditions, Lincoln advised Delahay (4, 14, 1860):

"You know I was in New-England. Some of the acquaintances I made while there, write me since the elections that the close vote in Conn. & the quasi defeat in R. I. are a drawback upon the prospects of Gov. Seward; and Trumbull writes Dubois to the same effect. Do not mention this as coming from

me. Both those states are safe enough for us in the fall. I see by the despatches
that since you wrote, Kansas has appointed Delegates and instructed them
for Seward. Don't stir them up to anger, but come along to the convention,
& I will do as I said about the expenses."

Three weeks later (5, 12, 1860) Lincoln followed up his instructions to
Delahay with:

"Yours informing me of your arrival in Chicago was duly received.
Dubois, our A [uditor, goes] to Chicago today; and he will hand you $[? .]
Remainder will come before you leave the s[tate.]
"Look to Minnesota and Iowa rather, especially Iowa. Be careful to give
no offence, and keep cool under all circumstances."

Lincoln was, no doubt, hard up for funds. The enormous amount of
time and expense given to travel and speaking in the past five years had
greatly reduced his law practice and income.

The Plague of Candidates

The announcement of Lincoln's candidacy for the nomination produced a plague of requests for money, ostensibly for use in arousing
favorable public opinion and influencing delegates in his support. His
good humored, shrewd avoidance of being taken in is typical of his character, as expressed to E. Stafford (3, 17, 1860):

"Thanking you very sincerely for your kind purposes toward me, I am
compelled to say the money part of the arrangement you propose is, with me,
an impossibility. I could not raise ten thousand dollars if it would save me
from the fate of John Brown. Nor have my friends, so far as I know, yet
reached the point of staking any money on my chances of success. I wish I
could tell you better things, but it is even so."

Estimates His Chances Late in March

It seems that nearly everyone who took the trouble to ask Lincoln
what he thought of his chances for the nomination received a respectful
answer. To S. Galloway, an important Lincoln advocate in Ohio he replied
(3, 24, 1860):

"Of course I am gratified to know I have friends in Ohio who are disposed
to give me the highest evidence of their friendship and confidence. Mr. Parrott
of the Legislature, had written me to the same effect. If I have any chance, it
consists mainly in the fact that the *whole* opposition would vote for me if
nominated. (I dont mean to include the pro-slavery opposition in the South,
of course.) My name is new in the field; and I suppose I am not the *first*
choice of a very great many. Our policy, then, is to give no offence to others—
leave them in a mood to come to us, if they shall be compelled to give up
their first love. This, too, is dealing justly with all, and leaving us in a mood
to support heartily whoever shall be nominated. I believe I have once before
told you that I especially wish to do no ungenerous thing towards Governor
Chase, because he gave us his sympathy in 1858, when scarcely any other

distinguished man did. Whatever you may do for me, consistently with these suggestions, will be appreciated, and gratefully remembered."

By "the whole opposition" Lincoln obviously meant the antislavery Democrats. His belief that his constitutionally founded antislavery philosophy had won the approval of more Northern Democrats than the ambivalent "don't care" straddling of Douglas and the noncommittal attitude of Seward eventually proved to be sound.

When Not a Great Man Is Mentioned for a Great Office

R. M. Corwine, a Cincinnati lawyer, wrote that the Ohio delegates were divided on Chase, Bates, Seward and McLean and asked whether Illinois would support McLean, Bates or Seward, adding that more votes could be turned to him [Lincoln] than to Seward. Lincoln humbly replied (4, 6, 1860):

> "Remembering that when not a very great man begins to be mentioned for a very great position, his head is very likely to be a little turned, I concluded I am not the fittest person to answer the questions you ask. Making due allowance for this, I think Mr. Seward is the very best candidate we could have for the North of Illinois, and the very *worst* for the South of it. The estimate of Gov. Chase here is neither better nor worse than that of Seward, except that he is a newer man. They are regarded as being almost the same, seniority giving Seward the inside track. Mr. Bates, I think, would be the best man for the South of our State, and the worst for the North of it. If Judge McLean was fifteen, or even ten years younger, I think he would be stronger than either, in our state, taken as a whole; but his great age, and the recollection of the deaths of Harrison and Taylor have, so far, prevented his being much spoken of here.
>
> "I really believe we can carry the state for either of them, or for any one who may be nominated; but doubtless it would be easier to do it with some than with others.
>
> "I feel disqualified to speak of myself in this matter. I feel this letter will be of little value to you; but I can make it no better, under the circumstances. Let it be strictly confidential, not that there is anything really objectionable in it, but because it might be misconstrued."

Significance of a Clear Party Victory

Lincoln's confidence that the Republicans would carry Illinois was based on the result of a recent election in Springfield. To Senator L. Trumbull he wrote (4, 7, 1860):

> "We have just had a clear party victory in our city election; and our friends are more encouraged, and our enemies cowed by it, than be anything else since the organization of the Republican party. Last year we carried the city; but we did it, not by our own strength; but by an open feud among our enemies. This year their feud was healed; and we beat them fairly by main strength."

"My Forte, a Statesman"

After his return to Springfield in March, Lincoln devoted his time to the practice of law and politics. As he expressed it to F. C. Herbruger (4, 7, 1860) upon declining an invitation to give a popular lecture: "What , time I can spare from my own business this season I shall be compelled to give to politics."

Ward H. Lamon, prosecuting attorney in Lincoln, Illinois, had written to Lincoln about his motion to quash an indictment that he had filed against a man for sending a threatening letter. Lincoln had written the indictment without including the letter and Lamon, an unusually close friend, who became later the President's personal body guard and confidant, had advised that "quashing on Indct. written by a prominent candidate for the Presidency of the U. S. by a *little court* like Col. David Davis' will not sound well in history." Lincoln replied (3, 28, 1860):

> "I think I had no authority but the Statute when I wrote the Indictment. In fact, I remember but little about it. . . . I think yet there is no necessity for setting out the letter in *haec verba*. Our Statute, as I think, relaxes the high degree of technical certainty formerly required.
> "I am so busy with our case on trial here, that I can not examine authorities near as fully as you can there.
> "If, after all, the indictment shall be quashed, it will only prove that my *forte* is as a Statesman, rather than as a Prossecutor."

Make No Denial and No Explanations to Enemies

Anti-Lincoln propaganda was trying to arouse public disapproval against him by charging that he had accepted pay for making a political speech. C. F. McNeill, lawyer and editor of the Middleport (Illinois) *Press,* had sent Lincoln a clipping from his paper to this effect. Lincoln's self-defense (4, 6, 1860) was characteristic of his attitude against the tricky twist of half true charges:

> "It is not true that I ever *charged* anything for a political speech in my life— but this much is true: Last October I was requested, by letter, to deliver some sort of speech in Mr. Beechers church, in Brooklyn, $200 being offered in the first letter. I wrote that I could do it in February, provided they would take a political speech, if I could find time to get up no other. They agreed, and subsequently I informed them the speech would have to be a political one. When I reached New York, I, for the first [time], learned that the place was changed to "Cooper Institute." I made the speech, and left for New Hampshire, where I have a son at school, neither asking for pay nor having any offered me. Three days after, a check for $200- was sent to me, at N.H., and I took it, *and did not know it was wrong.* My understanding now is, though I knew nothing of it at the time, that they did charge for admittance, at the Cooper Institute, and that they took in more than twice $200.
> "I have made this explanation to you as a friend; but I wish no explanation made to our enemies. What they want is a squabble and a fuss; and that they can have if we explain; and they can not have if we don't.

"When I returned through New York from New England I was told by the gentlemen who sent me the check, that a drunken vagabond in the Club, having learned something about the $200, made the exhibition out of which *The Herald* manufactured the article quoted by *The Press* of your town.

"My judgment is, and therefore my request is, that you give no denial and no explanations."

Last Political Speech

Upon his return from the East Lincoln had decided not to make another political speech before the Republican nomination, preferring to rest on what he had said. However, when urged by friends to do so he replied (4, 6, 1860):

"Your dispatch, requesting me to deliver a speech at Bloomington is received. I very much prefer to make no more speeches soon; but if, as friends of mine, you can not excuse me, it is not much odds when—say the evening of Tuesday the 10th. Inst."

Lincoln had become incensed at Douglas' insolent disrespect of his brother Senator, Trumbull from Illinois, in leaving the Senate chamber while the latter was making a speech, and by Douglas' attempt to force through Congress sedition laws to suppress free speech.

His speech at Bloomington (4, 10, 1860) is astonishing for the risk he took, in giving grounds to his enemies for turning public opinion against him through misconstruing his remarks on polygamy in Utah in relation to popular sovereignty. The following is abstracted from the Bloomington *Statesman.*

The speaker commented upon polygamy in Utah, and the recent action in the United States House of Representatives on that subject [in voting for a bill to punish the practice of polygamy] because of the views expressed there by gentlemen who upheld the doctrine of popular sovereignty but would suppress polygamy. These gentlemen, he said, were Southern Democrats who by voting for the antipolygamy bill implied that Congress could regulate slavery in the Territories. But the Illinois Democrats, although opposed to polygamy, dared not vote for the bill because it was opposed by Douglas.

Mr. McClernand, of Illinois, proposed to solve the political contradiction and suppress the evil of polygamy by dividing the territory and attaching the portions to other territories.

But why divide the territory at all? Lincoln asked. . . . Why is not an act dividing the territory as much against popular sovereignty as one for protecting polygamy. If you can put down polygamy in that way why can't you put down slavery? The friends of popular sovereignty would say— if they dared speak out— that polygamy was wrong and slavery right; and therefore one might be put down and the other not.

Lincoln also took the opportunity to condemn Douglas' proposed law against sedition as a device to suppress free speech and republicanism and republican meetings. "He addressed his remarks chiefly to Mr. Douglas, and throughout the speech seemed to consider him as the only man in the Democratic party who was worthy of attention."

Estimates Chances in Mid-April

J. F. Babcock, an important advocate of Lincoln for President, had asked him for names of influential men who were his confidential friends, to whom he might write. The reply given (4, 14, 1860) expresses the candidate's estimation in mid-April of his position in the race.

> "I was very anxious for the result in Connecticut and am much gratified that it is all safe.
>
> "As to the Presidential nomination, claiming no greater exemption from selfishness than is common, I still feel that my whole aspiration should be, and therefore must be, to be placed anywhere, or nowhere, as may appear most likely to advance our cause.
>
> "As to the names of confidential friends here, with whom you might correspond, I give you David Davis, Bloomington, Ills.
>
> Julius White, Chicago, Ills.
>
> Dr. I. A. W. Buck, Aurora, Ills.
>
> A. Sympson, Carthage, Ills.
>
> "I will add that Hon. J. W. Grimes & Hon. S. R. Curtis, Senator & Representative from Iowa, are very friendly to me, though I do not know that they favor my nomination. The following named gentlemen are probably for me— and would like to correspond with you.
>
> Hon. Saml. Galloway, Columbus, O.
>
> Hon. Robt. C. Schenck, Dayton, O.
>
> Hon. J. W. Gordon, Indianapolis, Ia. [Ind.]
>
> Hon. W. Y. Page, Esq. Evansville, Ia. [Ind.]
>
> Hon. Hawkins Taylor, Esq. Keokuk, Iowa.
>
> "Please do not understand that I wish to task you with the opening of a correspondance with all these gentlemen; I mean no more than to furnish you the names, and leave the rest to your pleasure."

Lincoln, in mid-April, seems to have regarded his chances for obtaining the Republican nomination as rather poor. Although Herndon (1889) said that he had instructed his friends to present his name for the Presidency and refuse the Vice-Presidency, we find, according to his own statement, that he was willing to serve "anywhere" that would "most likely . . . advance our cause." This attitude was also indicated by his play to Seward, in New England, who was then the most likely candidate. In April he was not yet sure of the attitudes of many of his best friends towards his candidacy. Seward had received at this time, in Lincoln's estimation, "draw backs" in Connecticut and Rhode Island but he had made an unexpected gain in Kansas. This very doubtful position made Lincoln write (4, 14, 1860) to S. Sturges, a Chicago banker who had offered him a room in his house during the convention:

"Whether I shall be able to attend the Chicago convention, I have not yet determined; and so, of course, I can not yet say whether I can accept your very kindly proffered hospitality."

The Taste Is in My Mouth a Little

Lincoln had, for more than eight years, seen through Douglas' schemes to win the Democratic nomination for President. Twice (1852, and 1856) Senator Douglas had been on the verge of realizing his great ambition only to lose it to a compromise candidate because of intense prejudices that had combined against him. This time he was the choice of the Northern Democrats but, through his avowed 'don't care' policy toward the popular acceptance or rejection of slavery by residents of territories, and his answer to Lincoln's question at Freeport that local legislation could control the adoption or rejection of slavery despite the decision of the Supreme Court, he was bitterly opposed by the Southern members of his party.

Lincoln's opinions on Douglas' precarious position, as expressed upon the eve of the Democratic National Convention, show how it influenced his own game in the approaching Republican National Convention.

To H. Taylor (4, 21, 1860): "Opinions here, as to the prospect of Douglas being nominated, are quite conflicting— some very confident he *will,* and others that he will *not* be. I think his nomination possible; but that the chances are against him."

To Senator L. Trumbull (4, 29, 1860) towards whom he must adopt a policy that would retain public support for himself and at the same time support Trumbull's candidacy for reelection to the Legislature:

"Yours of the 24th. was duly received; and I have postponed answering it, hoping by the result at Charleston, to know who is to lead our adversaries, before writing. But Charleston hangs fire, and I wait no longer.

"As you request, I will be entirely frank. The taste *is* in my mouth a little; and this, no doubt, disqualifies me, to some extent, to form correct opinions. You may confidently rely, however, that by no advice or consent of mine, shall my pretensions be pressed to the point of endangering our common cause.

"Now, as to my opinions about the chances of others in Illinois. I think neither Seward nor Bates can carry Illinois if Douglas shall be on the track; and that either of them can, if he shall not be. I rather think McLean could carry it with D. on or off— in other words, I think McLean is stronger in Illinois, taking all sections of it, than either S. or B; and I think S. the weakest of the three. I hear no objection to McLean, except his age; but that objection seems to occur to every one, and it is possible it might leave him no stronger than the others. By the way, if we should nominate him, how would we save to ourselves the chance of filling his vacancy in the Court? Have him hold up to the moment of his inauguration? Would that course be no draw-back upon us in the canvass?

"Recurring to Illinois, we want something here quite as much as, and which is harder to get than, the electoral vote— the Legislature. And it is exactly in this point that Seward's nomination could be hard upon us. Suppose he should gain us a thousand votes in Winnebago, it would not compensate for the loss of fifty in Edgar.

"A word now for your own special benefit. You better write no letters which can possibly be distorted into opposition, or quasi opposition to me. There are men on the constant watch for such things out of which to prejudice my peculiar friends against you. While I have no more suspicion of you than I have of my best friend living, I am kept in a constant struggle against suggestions of this sort. I have hesitated some to write this paragraph, lest you should suspect I do it for my own benefit, and not for yours; but on reflection I conclude you will not suspect me.

"Let no eye but your own see this— not that there is anything wrong, or even ungenerous, in it; but it would be misconstrued."

Lincoln's Prediction— Democrats Split— Nominate Douglas

Lincoln and his friends believed that only he could carry Illinois if Douglas was nominated by the Democrats. If the latter event transpired it would dispose to the Republican nomination of Lincoln.

The Democratic National Convention at Charleston, N.C., was threatening to disrupt in a storm of protest against the nomination of Douglas. Early in the morning of May 1st, Lincoln wrote to C. M. Allen, a lawyer of Vincennes, Ind.:

"Douglas is not yet nominated; but we suppose he certainly will be before sun-set to-day, a few of the smaller Southern states having seceded from the convention— just enough to permit his nomination, and not enough to hurt him much at the election. This puts the case in the hardest shape for us. But fight we must; and conquer we shall; in the end." On the same day he wrote to Senator Trumbull: "In my last letter to you I believe I said I thought Mr. Seward would be weaker in Illinois than Mr. Bates. I write this to qualify that opinion so far as to say I think S. weaker than B. in our close Legislative districts; but probably not weaker taking the whole State over. We now understand that Douglas will be nominated to-day by what is left of the Charleston convention. All parties here dislike it. Republicans and Danites, that he should be nominated at all; and Doug. Dem's that he should not be nominated by an undivided convention."

After Douglas had expressed his opinion in the debates on how popular sovereignty could control slavery in the territories, Southern Democratic opposition grew so intense that he lost the chairmanship of his committee, and his party split into proslavery and antislavery factions. In the Charleston National Democratic Convention (4, 23, 1860) he led on every one of 57 ballots but was unable to obtain the necessary two-thirds majority for the nomination. Alabama, Mississippi, Louisiana, South Carolina, Florida, Texas, and Arkansas withdrew, forcing an adjournment.

In June, after the Republican convention, the Northern Democrats held a convention in Baltimore and Douglas was nominated after Virginia, North Carolina, Tennessee, Kentucky and Maryland withdrew to join forces with their more Southern proslavery allies. The seceders then convened and nominated J. C. Breckenridge of Kentucky for President.

National political conventions had split up in disunion before this but never along such definite, geographical, economic, social, and moral lines, with such intensely intolerant pride and uncompromising demands. The Southerners would not accept a Northern man for President, whether Republican or Democrat.

Estimates Chances Early in May

Two weeks before the Republican Convention, with almost prospective certainty that the Democrats would split into Northern and Southern parties and the Northerners would nominate Douglas, the Republican need to carry Illinois and her neighboring states enormously increased Lincoln's chances for the nomination. His estimation (5, 2, 1860) to R. M. Corwine, a vigorous supporter of his position, proved remarkably accurate.

"After what you have said, it is perhaps proper I should post you, so far as I am able, as to the 'lay of the land.' First then, I think the Illinois delegation will be unanamous for me at the start; and no other delegation will. A few individuals in other delegations would like to go for me at the start, but may be restrained by their colleagues. It is represented to me, by men who ought to know, that the whole of Indiana might not be difficult to get. You know how it is in Ohio. I am certainly not the first choice there; and yet I have not heard that any one makes any positive objection to me. It is just so everywhere so far as I can perceive. Everywhere except in Illinois, and possibly Indiana, one or another is preferred to me, but there is no positive objection. This is the ground as it now appears. I believe you personally know C. M. Allen, of Vincennes, Ia. He is a delegate, and has notified me that the entire Ia. delegation will be in Chicago the same day you name— Saturday the 12th. My friends Jesse K. Dubois, our Auditor & Judge David Davis, will probably be there ready to confer with friends from other States. Let me hear from you again when anything occurs."

Personal Traits in 1860

The most precious and important personal relics of Lincoln, left to the nation, are the cast of his face made in 1860, a week before his presidential nomination, by Leonard Volk, and the cast made in 1864 by Clark Mills. The following abstraction of Volk's account of making his mask, written 20 years later for the *Century Magazine* (1881), is taken from Rankin (1916). It gives a vivid sketch of Lincoln's personality in this ascendent period. Volk first met Lincoln in 1858, when sculpturing a portrait of Douglas during the debates. He said that, upon being introduced:

> "[Lincoln] saluted me with his natural cordiality, grasping my hand in both his large hands with a vise-like grip and looking down into my face with his heavy, dull, eyes, said: 'How do you do? I am glad to meet you. I have read of you in the papers; you are making a statue of Judge Douglas for Governor Matheson's new house?'
>
> " 'Yes Sir,' I answered, 'and some time, when you are in Chicago and can spare the time I would like to have you sit for me for your bust.' "

It was Lincoln's philosophy of friendship to start pleasant relations with each new person whom he met by making, immediately, kind remarks that showed interest in him. He was obviously pleased with Volk's suggestion and consented to sit for him. Two years later, when in that city conducting a trial (May, 1860), a week before the Republican convention where he would be a candidate for the nomination, Volk called on him in the United States District Court Room.

> "I found him," he said, "his feet on the edge of the table, one of his fingers thrust in his mouth, and his long, dark hair standing out at every imaginable angle, apparently uncombed for a week."

Rankin, having known Lincoln personally for many years, questioned the accuracy of this recollection. He says that Lincoln probably did not have his finger in his mouth, for he was a clean, plain, simple-mannered man, who had no vulgar habits. He did habitually, when sitting, while in deep thought, rest his chin on his hand with his thumb under it and the index finger curved around it.

Lincoln's disheveled hair was due, Rankin said to his nervous habit of frequently thrusting his fingers, by a quick movement of one hand or the other, upward from the temple to the crown of his head. The cast of Lincoln's face was made after a haircut upon Volk's request, and is therefore not characteristic in this respect of Lincoln.

The first time Lincoln went to Volk's studio he was uneasy and self-conscious and wanted to know what was expected of him. The sculptor described his method of taking measurements and making a clay cast of the face. In order to put his subject at ease he told a story of his Italian helper, Michael, when he had a studio in Europe. Lincoln's reaction to the story makes it worth repeating. In Volk's absence a Swiss gentleman, with long hair and heavy beard, thinking Michael was the sculptor, asked to have a portrait made at once. Michael, who liked to think himself an artist, decided to take advantage of the opportunity and make a facial mask. Having often assisted his master in this operation, he put on the usual coating of wet clay but forgot to prepare the skin properly for its removal. When the clay had dried sufficiently he tried to loosen it and then remembered his mistake. Without explanation, he hurried out of the studio, leaving his subject to get the clay off his skin and out of his beard as best he could. A few days later the Swiss gentleman, still feeling enraged, returned to the studio and caned another Italian helper whom he mistook for Michael. Volk said Lincoln laughed so heartily at this story that tears actually trickled down his cheeks.

Spontaneous tears with laughter at such grotesque injustice, like reference in some of his speeches to "our blessed fathers," indicate that he had completely repressed his resentment against his father for the unjust whippings he had endured in boyhood. His patient, consciously unresentful attitude, naturally, thereafter, included all men, however he was abused by them, but it was well balanced in being ready to react with righteous indignation against injustice to defenseless people.

When shown photographs of the magnificent architecture of Rome and Florence Lincoln remarked; "These things must be very interesting to you, Mr. Volk, but the truth is I don't know much about history, and all I do know of it, I have learned from law books." Such frank revelations of lack of education and esthetic appreciation were characteristic.

We get another glimpse into Lincoln's personality from his comment to Volk on the friendship of General W. A. Richardson for Steve Douglas. He said: "I regard him as one of the truest men that ever lived; he sticks to Judge Douglas through thick and thin—never deserted him and never will. I admire such a man." It was a life-long characteristic of Lincoln to like to hold in abiding trust anyone who had won his confidence. This primitive trait cost him many humiliating and unhappy betrayals later, particularly by members of his Cabinet.

Rankin, like Herndon, saw in Lincoln *three irregularly alternating dominant "moods:" a remarkable concentration of attention to the work he was doing with complete disregard of persons around him; a blank, unapproachable melancholy mood, present in times of great trial and anxiety, that made him a person of unfathomable mystery and grandeur; and his most usual state of complete serenity and peace of mind, tending toward humorous conviviality; all without a trace of self-consciousness.* It seems evident that these three major attitudes of Lincoln's personality continued throughout his life.

Lincoln has been said by many biographers to have been without self-consciousness. While this ultra-free state of mind was usually characteristic, he was also healthfully introspective and conscientiously self-searching to know how he really felt on each controversial question that required his moral judgment. When being photographed he was so uncontrollably self-conscious and stiff that few candid portraits of his face were made and none showing him laughing happily, as is now the style with government officials, in pretension of being highly successful.

Lincoln was an artist withall, one who responded to real beauty, especially to the vivid expression of sublime thought with appropriate words. J. G. Wilson, editor of the *Chicago Record,* a monthly devoted to religion, literature and the fine arts, sent him a copy of Fitz Greene Halleck's poems and he received the following expression (5, 2, 1860), written during the intensely exciting and important preparations for the approaching convention.

"Many a month has passed since I have met with anything more admir-

able than his beautiful lines on Burns. With Alnwick Castle, Marco Boz-
zaris, and Red Jacket, I am also much pleased.

"It is wonderful that you should have seen and known a sister of
Robert Burns. You must tell me something of her when we meet again."

Abraham Lincoln. The Rail Candidate for President

The Republican State Convention met in Decatur, Ill., May 9, 1860
to choose delegates for the national convention and formally lauch the
candidacy of Abraham Lincoln for the nomination. At the ingenious
suggestion of Richard J. Oglesby, John Hanks, Lincoln's cousin and
friend, carried into the convention two fence rails, one of black walnut
and the other of yellow locust. At the same time, amid wild cheering,
shouting and laughter, a banner was presented having the inscription:

ABRAHAM LINCOLN
The Rail Candidate
For President in 1860
Two rails from a lot of 3000 made in 1830 by John Hanks and Abe Lincoln,
whose father was the first pioneer of Macon County.

The rails, expressing Lincoln's lowly origin and rise in the world
through honest, free labor, proved an eloquent symbol of his humble
personality and humanitarian philosophy. He became happily known
thereafter as "The Railsplitter," "Old Abe," and "Honest Old Abe."
The latter expression, with its implied reputation, he said later, elected
him President.

This clinched the sentiment of the convention and its delegation for
Lincoln for President. Instead of having a minority in the delegation for
Seward, it presented a united front. This was most important, for at this
time Lincoln expected Seward to win the nomination but a united delegation would protect his nomination for the Senate in 1864.

Leading Candidates

Senator W. H. Seward of New York, its precocious Governor at 33
and Senator since 1849, was politically the most prominent, tried and
experienced of the candidates. He had the support of the strongest, best
organized, wealthiest and largest, new Republican and old Whig following. Big financial interests supported his bid with no legal limitation on
political contributions and expenditures. The established Jacksonian precedent, victors get privileges and take spoils, made the alliance of politics
and business profitable. Thurlow Weed of Albany, N. Y. owner and editor
of the Albany *Evening Journal,* powerful, avaricious and unscrupulous
political boss and long intimate friend of Seward, was determined to make
him President.

Seward had taken the place of Daniel Webster as the leader of the
Northern antislavery movement in the minds of the people through skilful, well-timed expressions of policy. Personally likeable, socially mag-

netic, energetic and imaginative, well educated, a brilliant, witty orator, raconteur and writer, with the political merit of expressing himself in attractive, scholarly, resounding, highly idealized, cleverly noncommital, ambiguous phrases, he had become, with Douglas, one of the best known political figures in the nation. A keen observer of the tides of public opinion, he rarely missed an opportunity for advancing a policy to ride on the popular flood, or for discrediting it with the ebb.

Literary Styles of Lincoln and Seward Compared

Lincoln had previously crystallized Northern antislavery, pro-Union sentiment with his entirely original, magnificently simple, profoundly philosophical statement before the Republican state convention in Springfield in June, 1858, when he said:

> "A house divided against itself cannot stand. I believe this government cannot endure permanently, half slave and half free. I do not expect the house to fall—but I do expect it will cease to be divided. It will become all one thing or the other."

The nation was ringing with this quotation when Seward, four months later, repeated the same idea in his ebullient sytle.

> "It is an irrepressible conflict between opposing and enduring forces and it means that the United States must and will, sooner or later, become entirely a slave holding nation or entirely a free-labor nation. Either the cotton and rice fields of South Carolina and the sugar plantations of Louisiana will ultimately be tilled by free labor, or the rye fields and wheat fields of Massachusetts and New York must again be surrendered by their farmers to slave culture and to the products of slaves and Boston and New York become once more markets for trade in the bodies and souls of men."

Without realizing the subtle public inferences from his imitative effusion, the great political magician had advanced the reputation of an obscure Western lawyer. The two statements of the same idea, the first one to become immortal, constitute a remarkable comparison of the minds of the two men who were soon to lead the nation into and out of destructive chaos.

Seward's speeches as the leading opponent of slavery in the Senate made him politically far better known than Lincoln, but his half-commital ambiguities had aroused the hatred of the radical abolitionists, who distrusted him as an opportunistic pretender dominated by the unprincipled opportunist Boss Weed.

Seward had the largest Republican delegation, but his inveterate enemy, Governor Salmon P. Chase of Ohio, a radical and uncompromising, but earnest and straight-thinking abolitionist, equally ambitious for the nomination, was strong enough to block him from winning on the first ballot. In his extreme left position, Chase was too weak ever to attain a majority. Edward Bates of Missouri, a famous lawyer more friendly to

Lincoln than Seward, with strong western support, though not from a pivotal state, would be able to swing the vote in favor of any leading candidate.

A few weeks before the Republican national convention, Lincoln estimated with well-balanced, conservative common sense that he alone of all the candidates, was the least involved in political commitments, quarrels and entanglements and had most clearly expressed the constitutional basis for the two most important policies to be considered in the convention, the constitutional restriction of slavery and preservation of the Union. We have followed the development of this unusually careful and conservative, but earnest, sincere and aggressive social attitude through youth and manhood, as a self-protective compensation against nervous instability. We will see later how this attitude functioned as a kindly patriarchial President.

Lincoln's Personal Platform

Dr. Edward Wallace of Pennsylvania, to whom, upon request, Lincoln had previously given confidentially his idea on the value of a protective tariff (see previous chapter), planned to attend the national convention in order to promote Lincoln's candidacy and make known his attitude on the tariff. Lincoln's reply (5, 12, 1860), to his request for permission, shows how carefully he was playing an unobstrusive, noncommittal game in order to let the leading candidates, Seward and Chase, stalemate each other.

> "In the days of Henry Clay I was a Henry Clay-tariff-man; and my views have undergone no material change upon that subject. I now think the Tariff question ought not to be agitated in the Chicago convention; but that all should be satisfied on that point, with a presidential candidate, whose antecedents give assurance that he would neither seek to force a tarrif-law by Executive influence; nor yet arrest a reasonable one, by a veto, or otherwise. Just such a candidate I desire shall be put in nomination. I really have no objection to these views being publicly known; but I do wish to thrust no letter before the public now, upon any subject. Save me from the appearance of obtrusion; and I do not care who sees this, or my former letter."

Judge David Davis, leader of the Illinois delegation at the Chicago convention opened "Lincoln Headquarters" in the Tremont House. Lincoln had requested of his promoters "to give no offence to others—leave them in a good mood to come to us if they shall be compelled to give up their first love. This, too is dealing justly with all, and leaving us in a mood to support heartily whoever is nominated."

Lincoln seems to have been more inclined to like Seward's more lenient views on slavery better than the radical abolitionism of Chase, as being more constitutional and fitting to the present needs of a Republican presidential candidate. Although grateful to the latter for having given sympathetic encouragement in 1858 in his canvass against Douglas he had praised Seward's statement on the "irrepressible conflict" and the imperative need of finding a national solution. However, he disagreed with Seward on one cardinal principle which proved to be a turning point in his favor.

The day before the nomination Lincoln handed E. L. Baker, editor of the Springfield *Journal,* when about to depart for the Chicago convention, a copy of the Missouri *Democrat.* On a margin he had written in pencil: "I agree with Seward in his 'Irrepressible Conflict,' but I do not endorse his 'Higher Law' doctrine. *Make no contracts that will bind me.*"

Seward had declared in the Senate; "there is a higher law than the Constitution, which regulates our authority over the domain."

Lincoln held that the Constitution was the nation's highest law that regulates the government and the civil rights of the people. Thereby he subordinated all religious authoritative interpretations of Biblical moral law, as being also man made and of secondary importance to it.

Southern sectarianism, justifying slavery as being consistent with the morally elevating intent of Christianity, and Northern sectarianism, condemning it as an immoral violation of Christian principles leading to the degradation of master and slave, were overrriding interest in the Constitution and depressing respect for its supreme protection of the rights of free men, based on the dignity and consent of free men. Lincoln's pencil note on the margin of a newspaper held inviolate the Constitution as the highest law of the Union so long as it may endure.

Later, President Lincoln felt repeatedly that he must remind the civilized world that ethical political sentiment was sacred to man and therefore to God; reversing the ancient religious dogma that what is said by man to be sacred to God must be accepted by man.

The Republican National Convention

The Republican National Convention met in Chicago on May 16, 1860. It unanimously adopted a platform entirely in harmony with Lincoln's principles. It denied the right of any authority to legalize the enslavement of any man in the national territories, denounced Douglas' version of popular sovereignty, urged the admission of Kansas as a state, advocated protective tariffs, a homestead law, and the construction, with Federal aid, of a railroad to the Pacific.

The tremendous organization, personally conducted by Thurlow Weed, to present the candidacy of William H. Seward far outdid all the preparations of the other candidates. All of New York and much of New England and the Northwest rallied to his support. The Seward men abounded in confidence and many believed they would nominate their man on the first ballot. The only names presented that excited "tremendous applause" were Seward and Lincoln. Everybody soon felt that the fight was between them. When W. M. Evarts nominated Seward the applause was enthusiastic. When Mr. Judd finished his sentence nominating Lincoln, the response was prodigious, "rising and roaring far beyond the Seward shriek." Most of Chicago was for Lincoln and the Wigwam was packed with leather-lunged rooters who roared with delight upon signal. When Caleb B. Smith of Indiana seconded the nomination of Lincoln the response was "absolutely terrific." When Blair of Michigan seconded the nomination of Seward the shouting grew frantic, pandemonium reigned, and thousands of hats were hurled back and forth through the vast auditorium.

In the face of this new tide of enthusiasm for Seward, Mr. Delano of Ohio, "on behalf of a portion of the delegation of that State," unexpectedly seconded the nomination of Lincoln. The response now surpassed the uproar given to Seward. (From Angle, 1947.)

The Ballot

On the first ballot the overly confident Seward supporters were astonished by the following count. Seward $173\frac{1}{2}$, Lincoln 102, Cameron $50\frac{1}{2}$, Chase, 49, Bates 48, and other candidates scattering. Lincoln's strength was unexpected. The main chance had come. Davis and Swett wired Lincoln for advice. By making a few promisory deals they could get the support of Pennsylvania and Missouri. Lincoln replied, "Make no commitments," but his sponsors gambled on his good will and offered attractive promises, hinting at positions in the Cabinet. On the second ballot Lincoln gained 79 votes to Seward's 11. On the third ballot Lincoln received $231\frac{1}{2}$ votes, $1\frac{1}{2}$ minus the majority of 233 necessary for the nomination. Then five more Ohio delegates cast the deciding votes for him and, in the wildest pandemonium, the convention nominated him unanimously.

During the convention Lincoln stayed in Springfield. During the balloting he remained in his office where he received from his manager in Chicago numerous telegrams informing him of changes in the situation. Outwardly cool, inwardly nervous and restless, the strain was severe. He believed that if Seward was not nominated on the first ballot he might win. When the news reached him that Seward had failed he he exclaimed, "I've got him."

Before the day passed he listened to a crowd of excited people in the State House cheer itself hoarse in "ratification of the nomination." Finally worn out, Abe Lincoln quietly asked for the telegram of announcement and excused himself with "Gentlemen, there is a little, short woman at our house who is possibly more interested in this dispatch than I am; and if you will excuse me, I will take it up and let her see it."

The happy, exhilirated crowd spontaneously formed a parade to Lincoln's house to serenade him. He responded with a brief speech in which he said he appreciated that the people were expressing honor for him as the representative of a great political party.

Acceptance of Official Notification

When the Republican delegation arrived on the following day (5, 19, 1860) to inform him officially of his nomination, Lincoln met it in his house. Springfield friends had eagerly offered to supply "the drinks" but he refused with:

> "Gentlemen, I thank you for your very kind intentions, but must respectfully decline your offer. I have no liquors in my house, and have never been in the habit of entertaining my friends in that way. I cannot permit my friends to do for me what I will not myself do. I shall provide cold water—nothing else."

In this triumphant hour he remained constant, and without elation, but seemed visibly embarrassed and a little more staid and awkward than usual. Dressed in a long, black coat, he stood stiffly erect in front of the fireplace as the chairman, George Ashmun, read the official notification of his nomination. He shifted his weight like a nervous schoolboy from one foot to the other, humbly looking down at the floor under the searching, critical gaze of the delegation of eminent men, most of whom were strangers, doubtful of their new leader's fitness for the great office of President.

Then his whole attitude changed as it became his turn to speak. His brief, extemporaneous reply, Charles Carlton Coffin reported to the *Boston Journal,* was made in a sympathetic voice, with an indescribable charm in its tones. There was no studied inflection or cadence for effect, but a simplicity and sincerity which won instant confidence. He said:

> "Mr. Chairman and gentlemen of the committee, I tender [to] you, and through you [to] the Republican National Convention, and all the people represented in it, my profoundest thanks for the high honor done me, which you now formally announce.
>
> "Deeply, and even painfully sensible of the great responsibility which is inseparable from that honor—a responsibility which I could almost wish had fallen upon some one of the far more eminent men and experienced statesmen whose distinguished names were before the Convention, I shall, by your leave, consider more fully the resolutions of the Convention, denominated the platform, and without unseasonable delay, respond to you, Mr. Chairman, in writing—not doubting now, that the platform will be found satisfactory, and the nomination gratefully accepted.
>
> "And now, I will not longer defer the pleasure of taking you, and each of you, by the hand." (Illinois *State Journal,* 5, 21, 1860.)

With complete economy and simplicty of expression, with every word meaningful, he had humbly accepted the honor of the nomination, complimented the eminence of the statesmen that he had defeated and approved of the resolutions and platform of the party. His good taste and natural power of expression convinced all present that here was a master of men.

After the ceremony his formal manner gave way to that of the genial friend and host. A smile like sunshine lit up his homely features. Soon he was telling stories and comparing his height with the tallest men on the committee and all was merriment.

To Serve Truth, Justice and Humanity

On the day of the official notification Lincoln received an earnest letter from an old friend, J. R. Giddings, which said that he had been nominated because of his honesty and freedom from corrupt men and that he should not place himself under obligation to anyone.

His reply, written two days later (5, 21, 1860) indicates the nature of Lincoln's emotional reaction to the responsibilities of his new position:

> "Your very kind and acceptable letter of the 19th. was duly handed me by Mr. Tuck. It is indeed, most grateful to my feelings, that the responsible position assigned me, comes without conditions, save only such honorable ones as are fairly implied. I am not wanting in the purpose, though I may fail in the strength, to maintain my freedom from bad influences. Your letter comes to my aid in this point, most opportunely. May the Almighty grant that the cause of truth, justice, and humanity, shall in no wise suffer at my hands.
>
> "Mrs. L. joins me in sincere wishes for your health, happiness, and long life."

Formal Acceptance

Historians have agreed that Lincoln's nomination was the most surprising ever made in a national political convention. Poor men had been nominated before, but none had ever emerged from the "humblest walks of life" and none had retained so many of the provincial habits, mannerisms and pronunciations of his boyhood people. He differed from all other candidates in one essential quality, he was the epitome of freedom and courage in a pioneering democracy, and the personification of the rising power in American politics of the principle of equalitarian justice based on the will of the common people. His ability and desire, characteristic through youth and manhood, to work out honestly compromises between antagonists, with justice for all, without sacrifice on either side of honor and principle, gave him a cautiously confident attitude that, more than any other characteristic, held the faith of the people.

Lincoln carefully wrote out his letter of acceptance to the Republican party. In scarcely 150 words he declared his loyalty to the party's principles. Then he submitted it to his friend, Dr. Newton Bateman, State Superintendent of Education, for correction, saying:

> "Mr. Schoolmaster, here is my letter of acceptance. I am not very strong on grammar and I wish you to see if it is all right. I wouldn't like to have any mistake in it."

After reading the manuscript through Mr. Bateman replied: "There is only one change I would suggest, Mr. Lincoln. You have written, 'it shall be my care to not violate or disregard it in any part,' you should have written 'not to violate.' Never split an infinitive is the rule."

With school-boyish amusmenet Lincoln commented, "So you think I better put those two little fellows end to end, do you."

The acceptance said:

"Hon: George Ashmun: Springfield, Ills. May 23, 1860
"President of the Republican National Convention.

"Sir: I accept the nomination tendered me by the Convention over which you presided, and of which I am formally apprized in the letter of yourself and others, acting as a committee of the convention, for that purpose.

"The declaration of principles and sentiments, which accompanies your letter, meets my approval; and it shall be my care not to violate, or disregard it, in any part.

"Imploring the assistance of Divine Providence, and with due regard to the views and feelings of all who were represented in the convention; to the rights of all the states, and territories, and people of the nation; to the inviolability of the constitution, and the perpetual union, harmony and prosperity of all, I am most happy to co-operate for the practical success of the principles declared by the convention. Your obliged friend, and fellow citizen

"A. LINCOLN"

In a personal note to G. Ashmun (5, 28, 1860) he added: "Herewith is a copy of the Committee's letter to me, as you requested; together with my answer. The answer, I hope, is sufficiently brief to do no harm."

Chapter XLI

CAGEY CAMPAIGN

The extant letters written by Lincoln immediately after his nomination for President show how he began at once to make personal contacts and cultivate friendly political affiliations.

To Gov. Chase (5, 26, 1860):

> "My dear Sir: It gave me great pleasure to receive yours, mistakenly dated, May 17. Holding myself the humblest of all whose names were before the convention, I feel in especial need of the assistance of all; and I am glad—very glad—of the indication that you stand ready. It is a great consolation that so nearly all—all except Mr. Bates & Mr. Clay,* I believe,—of those distinguished and able men, are already in high position to do service in the common cause."

On the same day he wrote to Cassius M. Clay, Kentucky Abolitionist:

> "Yours of the 21st. is received, and for which I sincerely thank you. The humblest of all whose names were before the convention, I shall, in the canvass, and especially afterwards, if the result shall devolve the administration upon me, need the support of all the talent, popularity, and courage, North and South, which is in the party; and it is with sincere gratification that I receive this early indication of your unwavering purpose to stand for the right."

Schuyler Colfax, who had supported Edward Bates for the nomination, wrote to Lincoln, "I need not say how heartily I join with your original friends in their greeting to you." Lincoln replied (5, 26), "You distinguish between yourself and my *original* friends—a distinction which, by your leave, I propose to forget."

With like warmth he wrote (6, 18, 1860) to Carl Schurz, a friend since the campaign of 1858, who had, however, as a member of the National Republican Committee, supported the nomination of Seward:

> . . . "I beg you to be assured that your having supported Gov. Seward, in preference to myself in the convention, is not even remembered by me for any purpose, or the slightest u[n]pleasant feeling. I go not back of the convention, to make distinctions among its' members; and, to the extent of our limited acquaintance, no man stands nearer my heart than yourself."

The great rush of correspondence, which had to be answered by Lincoln's secretary, John G. Nicolay, or himself, in handwriting, necessitated making all but the most important letters brief.

---

*C. M. Clay, abolitionist of Kentucky, ran second to Senator H. Hamlin of Maine for Vice-President.

The Thing Starts Almost Too Well

In three personal letters written on the same day, one week after his nomination, Lincoln expressed the same cautiously optimistic sentiment, as in the public reception of his nomination.

> To C. B. Smith (5, 26): "I have found no time till now, to say a word in the way of answer. I am, indeed, much indebted to Indiana; and, as my home friends tell me, much to you personally. Your saying you no longer consider Ia. [Indiana] a doubtful state, is very gratifying. The thing starts well everywhere—too well, I almost fear, to last. But we are in, and stick or go through, must be the word."

With like cautious optimism he wrote to Senator Trumbull:

> "I have received three letters from you since the nomination, for all which I sincerely thank you. As you say, if we can not get our state up now, I do not see when we can. The nominations start well here, and everywhere else, so far as I have heard. We may have a back-set yet. Give my respects to the Republican Senators; and especially to Mr. Hamlin, Mr. Seward, Gen. Cameron, and Mr. Wade."

> To E. B. Washburne: "I have several letters from you written since the nomination; but, till now, have found no moment to say a word by way of answer. Of course I am glad that the nomination is well received by our friends, and I sincerely thank you for so informing me. So far as I can learn, the nominations start well everywhere; and, if they get no back-set, it would seem as if they are going through."

The attitude of resilient, cautiously aggressive optimism with which Lincoln reacted to his nomination, we will see from the record of his own statements, became the most constant characteristic of his personality throughout the campaign for election, the period after his election, and the Presidency. Never did he lapse into uncontrollable, cyclical periods of ineffective depression as many biographers, historians, and psychiatric commentators have said.

Fairness, All Men Shall Have

New York Boss, Thurlow Weed, editor of the Albany *Evening Journal* and Seward's political manager, had to endure the most bitter disappointment of his life when he failed to get Seward nominated. He had been willing to spend a fortune on the gamble of making him President perhaps not so much for the honor of the position it would bring him, as for the advantageous government contracts to be gained, even as when he made Seward Governor of New York.

Within a few days after the nomination of Lincoln, he had assimilated his disappointment and went resolutely to Springfield to make friends. Lincoln greeted him cordially but gave the wily politician no chance to initiate conditional proposals to aid in the coming campaign for election. He entertained Weed with humorous stories and sent him home convinced that he had met his master.

Under such easily misconstrued and misrepresented conditions as a political conference, Lincoln wisely protected himself by having present some trusted friend to serve as confidential adviser and witness.

Leonard Swett, a member of Judge Davis' circuit court and an old friend and legal conferee, was, naturally, chosen by Lincoln to serve as a personal communitator. It devolved upon him to manage the pressure of the Weed contingent and in doing so he had to write a letter suggestive of policy which he thought should be submitted to Lincoln for approval before sending. He received the following comments (5, 30 1860):

> "Your letter, written to go to N. Y. is long, but substantially right, I believe. You heard Weed converse with me, and you now have Putnams letter. It can not have failed to strike you that these men ask for just, the same thing—*fairness,* and fairness only. This is so far as in my power, they, and all others, shall have. If this suggests any modification of, or addition to, your letter, make it accordingly. Burn this, not that there is any thing wrong in it; but because it is best not to be known that I write at all."

Correct Grammar but Change Not Meaning "A Hair's Breath"

The Cooper Institute speech now became the most important of Lincoln's career, a best seller in great demand. C. C. Nott had charge of editing and publishing it. Lincoln's reply (5, 31, 1860) to a letter suggesting certain corrections shows that he gratefully accepted suggestions and corrections on his speeches and other statements, so long as they did not involve a change in expression of meaning or sentiment, which generally he made with particular care. Corrections that improved his grammar interested him most; herein, however, he proved himself a master of the definitive sentence.

> "Yours of the 23rd, accompanied by a copy of the speech delivered by me at the Cooper Institute, and upon which you have made some notes for emmendations, was received some days ago. Of course I would not object to, but would be pleased rather, with a more perfect edition of that speech.
> . . .
> "So far as it is intended merely to improve in grammar, and elegance of composition, I am quite agreed; but I do not wish the sense changed, or modified, to a hair's breadth. And you, not having studied the particular points so closely as I have, can not be quite sure that you do not change the sense when you do not intend it. For instance, in a note at bottom of first page, you proposed to substitute 'Democrats' for 'Douglas.' But what I am saying there is *true* of Douglas, and is not true of 'Democrats' generally; so that the proposed substitution would be a very considerable blunder. Your proposed insertion of 'residences' though it would do little or no harm, is not at all necessary to the sense I was trying to convey. On page 5 your proposed grammatical change would certainly do no harm. The *'impudently absurd'* I stick to. The striking out *'he'* and inserting *'we'* turns the sense exactly wrong. The striking out *'upon it'* leaves

the sense too general and incomplete. The sense is 'act as they acted *upon that question'*—not as they acted generally. . . .

. . . "I return your copy of the speech, together with the one printed here, under my own hasty supervising. That at New York was printed without any supervision by me. If you conclude to publish a new edition, allow me to see the proof-sheets.

"And now thanking you for your very complimentary letter, and your interest for me generally, I subscribe myself."

Steps In Destiny

The great pressure of conferences and correspondence compelled Lincoln to shorten most of his letters, and to adopt form letters to be sent by his personal assistants in reply to requests for photographs, autographs, and information on his personal life and previous speeches and political opinions.

In June 1860, upon request of J. L. Scripps, editor of the Chicago *Press and Tribune,* Lincoln wrote an autobiography for publication in Republican newspapers. He chose to express himself in the third person, as if written by another person about himself, in order that no mistake or misconstruction which might be made in transposition would create unfavorable public opinion against him.

The autobiography has excited endless discussion as an example of Lincoln's unusual way of thinking. It should be read as a brief presentation of the decisive steps in the life of a man who believed solemnly in his predestination to work for the liberation of his people and that the time was now at hand. So interpreted it is logical and not strange. It contains more data than the sketch written for Fell in 1859. It has been presented in sections in previous chapters of this book, to give his own ideas of special periods and events of his life. Here we repeat the parts that had most significance for Lincoln, and most public appeal from a candidate for President of the United States.

Lincoln had nothing to conceal from public prejudice except his mother's illegitimate birth and the immorality of her relatives. He had nothing of heroic quality in the record of his ancestors' families or of himself to mention with pride. The most important statements include the time and place of his birth, the origins and abodes of his Lincoln ancestry and some near relatives, and his father's work and lack of education. About his mother he merely said her name was Nancy Hanks, that she was born in Virginia and that his parents were married in 1806, and that some of her Hanks relatives were now residing in Coles, Adams, and Macon counties of Illinois, and also in Iowa. He attracted as little attention as possible to his mother's family.

He described briefly how in Kentucky, as a child, he attended A.B.C. schools for short periods, and that his father moved in 1816 to Indiana "partly on account of slavery, but chiefly on account of the difficulty in land titles in Kentucky." With a brief description of his life in

Indiana he mentioned only that "in the autumn of 1818 his mother died; and a year afterwards his father married Mrs. Sally Johnston," a widow who had three children. Then followed a brief account of attending A.B.C. schools "by littles" in Indiana "the aggregate of all his schooling" being less than one year. "What he has in the way of education, he has picked up." "After he was twentythree, and had separated from his father, he studied English grammar, imperfectly of course, but so as to speak and write as well as he now does."

The injection of the memory that he began to improve his grammar after separating from his father suggests that he thought dutiful submission to paternal prejudice had retarded his self-education.

The autobiography continued on his education: "He studied and nearly mastered the Six-books of Euclid, since he was a member of Congress. He regrets his want of education, and does what he can to supply the want." He then added as if an afterthought, "In his tenth year he was kicked by a horse, and apparently killed for a time."

He described his first flat-boat trip to New Orleans when 19 and how, when 21, the family migrated to Illinois, in "waggons drawn by ox-teams." "On the North side of the Sangamon river, at the junction of the timber-land and prairie," he said, they built a log-cabin and here they "made sufficient rails to fence ten acres of ground." "These are, or are supposed to be, the rails about which so much is being said just now, though they are far from being the first, or only rails ever made by A."

He recalled how he with John D. Johnston and John Hanks "hired themselves to one Denton Offutt," to take a cargo of produce on a flatboat to New Orleans "as soon as the snow should go off" and flood the county; and how, upon Offutt's failure to get a boat, "this lead to their hiring themselves at $12 per month, each;" to build a boat of timber cut on the Sangamon river. His inclusion of a description of a "ludicrous incident" that transpired on this trip was written with amusement. "Offutt bought thirty odd large fat live hogs. but found difficulty in driving them from where [he] purchased them to the boat, and thereupon conceived the whim that he could sew up their eyes and drive them where he pleased. No sooner thought of than decided, he put his hands, including A. at the job, which they completed—all but the driving. In their blind condition they could not be driven out of the lot or field they were in. This expedient failing, they were tied and hauled on carts to the boat." This humorous diversion to relieve the tension of a serious discussion was characteristic of the ingenuity of Lincoln—to become famous and infamous later when President.

With affectionate regard for Offutt he described how, upon their return from New Orleans he served as his clerk in charge of "a store and Mill at New-Salem." "A, stopped indefinitely, and, for the first time, as it were, by himself at New-Salem, . . . in July 1831. Here he rapidly made acquaintances and friends." Offutt's business failed and then came the Black Hawk War. How he enlisted as a volunteer and to his surprise was elected captain was written with obvious pleasure. "He says he has not since had any success in life which gave him so much satisfaction. He went [through] the campaign, served near three months, met the ordinary hardships of such an expedition, but was in no battle. He now owns in Iowa, the land upon which his own warrants for this service, were located."

Then followed an account of his return to New Salem and how:

. . . "encouraged by his great popularity among his immediate neighbors, he, the same year, ran for the Legislature and was beaten—his own precinct, however, casting it's votes 277 for and 7, against him. And this too while he was an avowed Clay man, and the precinct the autumn afterwards, giving a majority of 115 to Genl. Jackson over Mr. Clay. This was the only time A was ever beaten on a direct vote of the people."

The autobiography continued in pioneer's conversational idiom without paragraphing:

"He was now without means and out of business, but was anxious to remain with his friends who had treated him with so much generosity, especially as he had nothing elsewhere to go to. He studied what he should do—thought of learning the black-smith trade—thought of trying to study law—rather thought he could not succeed at that without a better education."

Then followed an account of his venture as a merchant with a partner in buying a store: "they did nothing but get deeper and deeper in debt;" how he got the appointment as Postmaster of New Salem—"the office being too insignificant, to make his politics an objection." The store finally "winked out" and the surveyor of Sangamon offered him work as a deputy. He "procured a compass and chain, studied Flint, and Gibson a little, and went at it. This procured bread, and kept soul and body together."

Lincoln's great pleasure in having many friends is shown again in the account of his service in the Legislature.

"The election of 1834 came, and he was then elected . . . by the highest vote cast for any candidate. Major John T. Stuart, then in full practice of the law, was also elected. During the canvass, in a private conversation he encouraged A [to] study law. After the election he borrowed books of Stuart, took them home with him, and went at it in earnest. He studied with nobody. He still mixed in the surveying to pay board and clothing bills. When the Legislature met, the law books were dropped, but were taken up again at the end of the session."

He mentioned his reelections in 1836, 1838, and 1840, his moving to Springfield to practice law in partnership with Stuart, and the signed protest against the Legislature's declared slavery policy which he entered with Dan Stone in the Illinois House Journal in March, 1837. It "briefly defined his position on the slavery question; and so far as it goes, it was then the same that it is now." He said he was proposed in 1838 and

1840 by his party for Speaker of the House, "but being in the minority, he was not elected." He declined reelection after 1840 and served "on the Harrison electoral ticket in 1840 and that of Clay in 1844, and spent much time and labor in both those canvasses." He never mentioned his partnership with Logan or Herndon, seeming to consider the first experience only as having political importance.

About his family he said briefly:

> "In Nov. 1842 he was married to Mary, daughter of Robert S. Todd, of Lexington, Kentucky. They have three living children, all sons—one born in 1843, one in 1850, and one in 1853. They lost one who was born in 1846."

In defense of his actions in Congress, now of critical importance from the renewal of bitter condemnation of his criticism of the Democratic President's policy, he said:

> "In 1846, he was elected to the lower House of Congress, and served one term only, commencing in Dec. 1847 and ending with the inauguration of Gen. Taylor, in March 1849. All the battles of the Mexican war had been fought before Mr. L. took his seat in Congress, but the American army was still in Mexico, and the treaty of peace was not fully and formally ratified till the June afterwards. Much has been said of his course in Congress in regard to this war. A careful examination of the Journals and Congressional Globe shows, that he voted for all the supply measures which came up, and for all the measures in any way favorable to the officers, soliders, and their families, who conducted the war through; with this exception that some of these measures passed without yeas and nays, leaving no record as to how particular men voted. The Journals and Globe also show him voting that the war was unnecessarily and unconstitutionally begun by the President of the United States. This is the language of Mr. Ashmun's amendment, for which Mr. L. and nearly or quite all, other whigs of the H. R. voted."

Not satisfied with letting this brief, factual statement of his Congressional record stand against "much that has been said about it," Lincoln repeated vigorously his charges against President J. K. Polk's Democratic administration.

> "Mr. L's reasons for the opinion expressed by this vote were briefly that the President had sent Genl. Taylor into an inhabited part of the country belonging to Mexico, and not to the U. S. and thereby had provoked the first act of hostility—in fact the commencement of the war; that the place, being the country bordering on the East bank of the Rio Grande, was inhabited by native Mexicans, born there under the Mexican government; and had never submitted to, nor been conquered by Texas, or the U. S. nor transferred to either by treaty—that although Texas claimed the Rio Grande as her boundary, Mexico had never recognized it, the people on the ground had never recognized it, and neither Texas nor the U. S. had ever enforced it—that there was a broad desert between that, and the country over which Texas had actual control—that the country where hos-

tilities commenced, having once belonged to Mexico, must remain so, until it was somehow legally transferred, which had never been done.

"Mr. L. thought the act of sending an armed force among the Mexicans, was *unnecessary,* inasmuch as Mexico was in no way molesting, or menacing the U. S. or the people thereof; and that it was *unconstitutional,* because the power of levying war is vested in Congress, and not in the President. He thought the principal motive for the act, was to divert public attention from the surrender of 'Fifty-four, forty, or fight' to Great Britain, on the Oregon boundary question."

The courageous repetition of his charges against President Polk characterized Lincoln as a man who held with uncompromising tenacity that he was then and was now right in maintaining that the Constitution was the highest law of the Nation, that the President had no authority to order the invasion of a foreign territory, and that Congress alone had the power to declare war and levy war. He continued to hold, despite the great popularity of the territorial acquisition at the expense of Mexico that it was an unlawful, immoral, and infamous act of aggression upon a weaker nation in order to divert the attention of the people from its Government's shameful surrender of northwestern territory to Great Britain. Despite his great care to make no political statements or speeches lest he might say something that would jeopardize his chance for election he came perilously close to it in renewing these old charges. But here he again seized the bull by the horns and beat the opposition by defensive attack.

He continued: "Mr. L. was not a candidate for re-election . . . in accordance with an understanding among whig friends," and "in 1848 . . . he advocated Gen. Taylor's nomination for the Presidency."

"Upon his return from Congress he went to the practice of the law with greater earnestness than ever before. In 1852 he was upon the Scott electoral ticket, and did something in the way of canvassing, but owing to the hopelessness of the cause in Illinois, he did less than in previous presidential canvasses.

"In 1854, his profession had almost superseded the thought of politics in his mind, when the repeal of the Missouri compromise aroused him as he had never been before.

"In the autumn of that year he took the stump with no broader practical aim or object that [than?] to secure, if possible, the reelection of Hon. Richard Yates to congress. His speeches at once attracted a more marked attention than they had ever before done. As the canvass proceeded, he was drawn to different parts of the state, outside of Mr. Yates' district. He did not abandon the law, but gave his attention, by turns, to that and politics. The State agricultural fair was at Springfield that year, and Douglass was announced to speak there."

It was Lincoln's critical reply to that speech by Douglas that renewed their 20-year-old argument on how best the government should serve the interests of the people, and led to the long series of attacks and rebuttals by each other in 1856 and 1858, culminating in 1860 in their becoming rival candidates for President. The curiously abrupt and brief manner in which Lincoln mentioned Douglas' speech at the Springfield fair leaves the reader with the feeling that he conceived it as marking the critical turning point in his destiny.

> "In the canvass of 1856, Mr. L. made over fifty speeches, no one of which, so far as he remembers, was put in print. One of them was made at Galena, but Mr. L. has no recollection of any part of it being printed; nor does he remember whether in that speech he said anything about a Supreme court decision. He may have spoken upon that subject; and some of the newspapers may have reported him as saying what is now ascribed to him but he thinks he could not have expressed himself as represented."*

"My Name Is Abraham"

Lincoln was addressed affectionately as "Abe," and referred to in conversation as "Honest Abe," and "Old Abe," by his intimate friends and neighbors. Under formal conditions of legal or political importance he was generally referred to as "Abraham" and sometimes as "Abram." This followed largely from his signature which was usually A. Lincoln. He had so signed his name to his formal letter of acceptance of the nomination by the Republican National Convention.

The official business of the Republican National Committee required the use of his Christian name and when Chairman Ashmun asked Lincoln for it he received the following reply (6, 4, 1860):

> "It seems as if the question whether my first name is "Abraham" or "Abram" will never be settled. It is *"Abraham"* and if the letter of acceptance is not yet in print, you may, if you think fit, have my signature thereto printed *"Abraham Lincoln."* Exercise your own judgment about this."

Embarrassed by Accusation of Cowardice

Samuel Haycraft, clerk of Elizabethtown, Ky., had sent to Lincoln in May 1860, a copy of a speech that he planned to deliver at the unveiling ceremonies of a statue of Daniel Boone. It gave an historical account of the history of the early settlers, including Lincoln's parents and his birthplace. This Lincoln corrected in a letter (5, 28, 1860) which has been presented in an earlier chapter for evidence of his remarkable memory.

Lincoln invited further correspondence from Haycraft and received a letter suggesting that he visit Kentucky. In answering (6, 4,) he expressed himself in a way that a mistaken or maliciously

---

*The Galena Weekly *North-Western Gazette,* 7, 29, 1856, had quoted Lincoln as saying, "The Supreme Court of the United States is the tribunal to decide such questions [the constitutionality of a law restricting slavery], and we will submit to its decisions . . ." Since he held consistently that Republicans should abide by the decision until reversed by the Court, he could not accept the Galena quotation as being entirely correct.

inclined reporter represented as evidence of cowardice. Lincoln had said with obvious humorous reflection of the reputation for feuding of politicians in Kentucky: "You suggest that a visit to the place of my nativity might be pleasant to me. Indeed it would. But would it be safe? Would not the people Lynch me?" . . .

A few weeks later the distortion of this humorously friendly statement appeared in the New York *Herald* much to Lincoln's annoyance. In order to have it corrected he wrote (8, 16) to G. G. Fogg, a friend in New York, to intercede with the Herald's editor:

> "I am annoyed some by the printed paragraph below, in relation to myself, taken from the N. Y. Herald's correspondance from this place of August 8th.
>
>> "'He had, he said, on one occasion been invited to go into Kentucky and revisit some of the scenes with whose history his father in his lifetime had been identified. On asking by letter whether Judge Lynch would be present, he received no response; and he therefore came to the conclusion that the invitation was a trap laid by some designing person to inveigle him into a slave State for the purpose of doing violence to his person.'
>
> "This is decidedly wrong. I did not say it. I do not impunge the correspondent. I suppose he misconceived the statement from the following incident. Soon after the Chicago nomination I was written to by a highly respectable gentleman of Hardin county, Ky, inquiring if I was a son of Thomas Lincoln, whom he had known long ago, in that county. I answered that I was, and that I was myself born there. He wrote again, and, among other things, (did not *invite* me but) simply *inquired* if it would not be agreeable to me to revisit the scenes of my childhood. I replied, among other things, 'It would indeed; but would you not Lynch me?' He did not write again.
>
> "I have, *playfully*, (and never otherwise) related this incident several times; and I suppose I did so to the Herald correspondent, though I do not remember it. If I did, it is all that I did say, from which the correspondent could have inferred his statement.
>
> "Now, I dislike, exceedingly, for Kentuckians to understand that I am charging them with a purpose to inveigle me, and do violence to me. Yet I can not go into the newspapers. Would not the editor of the Herald, upon being shown this letter, insert the short correction, which you find upon the inclosed scrap?
>
> "Please try him, unless you perceive some sufficient reason to the contrary. In no event, let my name be publicly used."

"CORRECTION" [For publication.]

"We have such assurance as satisfies us that our correspondent writing from Springfield, Ill., under date of Aug. 8—was mistaken in representing Mr. Lincoln as expressing a suspicion of a design to inveigle him into Kentucky for the purpose of doing him violence. Mr. Lincoln neither entertains, nor has intended to express any such suspicion."

Worried lest Haycraft would be offended by the New York paper's mean little intimations, Lincoln also wrote to him on the 16th:

"A correspondent of the New-York Herald, who was here a week ago, writing to that paper, represents me as saying I had been invited to visit Kentucky, but that I suspected it was a trap to inveigle me into Kentucky, in order to do violence to me.

"This is wholly a mistake. I said no such thing. I do not remember, but possibly I did mention my correspondence with you. But very certainly I was not guilty of stating, or insinuating, a suspicion of any intended violence, deception, or other wrong, against me, by you, or any other Kentuckian. Thinking this Herald correspondence might fall under your eye, I think it due to myself to enter my protest against the correctness of this part of it. I scarcely think the correspondent was malicious; but rather that he misunderstood what was said."

Haycraft replied (8, 19) that he had understood the playfulness of Lincoln's remark in the letter of June 4th, and was willing to make a statement to the *Herald* if desired. Upon receipt of this friendly assurance Lincoln answered immediately (8, 23):

"I now fear I may have given you some uneasiness by my last letter. I did not mean to intimate that I had, to any extent, been involved, or embarrassed, by you; nor yet to draw from you anything to relieve myself from difficulty. My only object was to assure you that I had not, as represented by the Herald correspondent, charged you with an attempt to inveigle me into Kentucky to do me violence. I believe no such thing of you, or of Kentuckians generally; and I dislike to be represented to them as slandering them in that way."

Fogg presented Lincoln's request to James G. Bennett, editor of the *Herald*. Although personally favoring Lincoln's candidacy, Bennett was prevented from complying with it, because of newspaper ethics, which disclaims responsibility for a correspondent's error, except under the condition that the correction be signed by Fogg or some other responsible person or by Lincoln himself. Fogg wisely decided to drop the matter. (C. W., 4.)

Upon receiving this information from Fogg, Lincoln replied (8, 29):

"You have done precisely right in that matter with the Herald. Do nothing further about it. Although it wrongs me, and annoys me some, I prefer letting it run it's course, to getting into the papers over my own name. I regret the trouble it has given you, and thank you also for having performed your part so cheerfully and correctly."

Despite Lincoln's annoyance and personal corrections, the sinister meaning attributed to his playful remark has been repeated by some biographers as evidence that he was at heart a suspicious, cowardly man who had unnecessarily charged innocent people with plotting to do him violence.

"I Will Not Swear I Will Make No Committals"

As the campaign developed and political bosses offered support for favorable commitments, Lincoln's firm resolution to make none seemed to waver, as his letter (6, 5, 1860) to Senator Trumbull shows:

"I see by the papers this morning, that Mr. Fillmore refuses to go with us. What do the New-Yorkers at Washington think of this? Gov. Reeder was here last evening direct from Pennsylvania. He is entirely confident of that state, and of the general result. I do not remember to have heard Gen. Cameron's opinion of Penn. Weed was here, and saw me; but he showed no signs whatever of the intriguer. He asked for nothing; and said N. Y. is safe, without condition.

"Remembering that Peter denied his Lord with an oath, after most solemnly protesting that he never would, I will not swear I will make no committals; but I do think I will not."

"I Do Not Wish to Be Diddled"

Mr. and Mrs. Lincoln, with their son Robert, had stayed at the Burnet House in Cincinnati in September 1859, during the time of his speech there. On June 5, 1860, he received, much to his surprise, an itemized bill for $53.50 from Johnson, Saunders & Co. that had not been paid by the Republican Committee. Two days later he sent the bill to his friend W. M. Dickson, whose wife was Mrs. Lincoln's cousin, to investigate the charges against him. The reasons given express his honest, practical, economical self and reflect with moderation, no doubt, the reinforcing opinion of Mrs. Lincoln.

"Now this may be right, but I have a slight suspicion of it, for two or three reasons. First, when I left, I called at the office of the Hotel, and was there distinctly told the bill "was settled" "was all right" or words to that effect. Secondly, it seems a little steep that 'Board & parlor['] from Saturday 7-1/2 P.M. to Monday 10-1/2 A.M. for a man woman and one small child, should be $37.50. Thirdly, we had no extra suppers, unless having tea at our room the first evening, was such. We were in the house over the time of five meals, three of which we took in the house. We did not once dine in the house. As to wines, liquors & cigars, we had none—absolutely none. These last may have been in room 15, by order of Committee, but I do not recollect them at all.

"Please look into this, and write me. I can and will pay it if it is right; but I do not wish to be 'diddled!['] Please do what you do quietly, having no fuss about it."

Dickson investigated the bill and his explanation (6, 9, 1860) cleared Lincoln. Members of the Ohio State Republican Committee, he said:

. . . "ordered an extra parlor and bed room . . . dined or supped with you and they ordered the liquor and cigars for the musicians, the extra suppers were for some of them. . . . Now the best course is to have it paid at once without a word so I have paid it. . . . At a proper

time and quietly some of my particular friends, republicans will share
the matter with me. For the honor of our city dont send me the money.
I would not have it said that we have invited you here & then made
you pay the expenses not only of yourself but of the committee too."
(C. W., 4.)

Lincoln replied graciously (6, 15, 1860):

"I sincerely thank you for your attention to this business. Let it
stand as it is for the present, with the distinct understanding that you
are not to ultimately lose the money."

Definitive Propriety

Prohibitionists were delighted over Lincoln's serving cold water only
in his home to the National Republican Nominating Committee, and
editors of several temperance journals wished to make the most of it.
When asked for verification of the report by J. Mason Haight of
Madison, Wis., for publication, Lincoln suppressed the movement
(6, 11, 1860):

"I think it would be improper for me to write, or say anything to,
or for, the public, upon the subject of which you inquire. I therefore
wish the letter I do write to be held as strictly confidential. Having
kept house sixteen years, and having never held the 'cup' to the lips
of my friends then, my judgment was that I should not, in my new
position, change my habit in this respect. What actually occurred upon
the occasion of the Committee visiting me, I think it would be better
for others to say."

Meticulously careful to be right in his statements, Lincoln wrote (6,
16, 1860) to J. L. Scripps, who was preparing his biography, to correct a statement that he had made in a speech six years past and
found to be erroneous:

"In the Peoria speech of 1854, I have said the prohibition of slavery
in the N. W. Territory was made a condition in the Virginia deed of
cession. That is an error. Such prohibition is not a condition of the
deed; and in any reprint of the speech, the text should be preserved,
but there should be a note stating the error."

Indignant, "I Authorize Nothing"

Lincoln had been advised by his close friends and campaign man-
agers before the nomination that he must not go to Chicago. They
wanted no incumbrance of their political trading and scheming by his
presence. After the nomination they urged him even more vigorously
to make no speeches and to write no letters that might contain
statements that could be used to excite some sectional prejudice
against him. The best laid plans, however, slipped up through the
efforts of overly enthusiastic biographers.

PLATE 16. Presidential Candidate, 1860. Ambrotype by P. Butler. Courtesy of the Illinois State Historical Library.

PLATE 17. Abraham Lincoln in 1860. Portrait by Edward J. Kempf, photographed with sculptor and author, by John B. Lawrence.

J. Q. Howard, a radical antislavery writer, had collected material in Springfield after the nomination, for a biography of Lincoln who had given desired information liberally with, however, the stipulation that it was not to be published as having been authorized by him. Despite these restrictions the publisher and the author issued the book as having been authorized. Samuel Galloway called this risky condition to Lincoln's attention and urged him or some friend to examine the proof lest it contain some statement that might be used against him. Lincoln's reply (6, 19, 1860) to Galloway shows his indignation at the presumptions of Howard and the publishers and how he expressed himself with characteristic self-reassuring self-restraint.

. . . "Messrs. Follett, Foster & Co's Life of me is *not* by my authority; and I have scarcely been so much astounded by anything, as by their public announcement that it is authorized by me. They have fallen into some strange misunderstanding. I certainly knew they contemplated publishing a biography, and I certainly did not object to their doing so, *upon their own responsibility*. I even took pains to facilitate them. But, at the same time, I made myself tiresome, if not hoarse, with repeating to Mr. Howard, their only agent seen by me, my protest that I *authorized nothing*—would be *responsible for nothing*. How, they could so misunderstand me, passes comprehension. As a matter, *wholly my own*, I would authorize no biography, without *time*, and *opertunity* to carefully examine and consider every word of it; and, in this case, in the nature of things, I can have no such time and opertunity. But, in my present position, when, by the lessons of the past, and the united voice of all discrete friends, I am neither [to] write or speak a word for the public, how dare I to send forth by my authority, a volume of hundreds of pages, for adversaries to make points upon without end. Were I to do so, the convention would have a right to reassemble, and substitute another name for mine.

"For these reasons, I would not look at the proof sheets. I am determined to maintain the position of truly saying I never saw the proof sheets, or any part of their work, before its's publication.

"Now, do not mistake me. I feel great kindness for Messrs. F. F. & Co—do not think they have intentionally done wrong. There may be nothing wrong in their proposed book. I sincerely hope there will not. I barely suggest that you, or any of the friends there, on the party account, look it over, & exclude what you may think would embarrass the party—bearing in mind, at all times, that I *authorize nothing*—will be *responsible* for *nothing*."

Time and again, aggressive politicians and editors, and, later, members of the Cabinet and of Congress, generals of the army, and leaders of the Confederacy would misinterpret Lincoln's considerate statements made in self-defense, as indicating weakness of self-doubt. Lincoln's mental habit of reassuring himself that he "could not have expressed himself as represented," followed by impartial consideration of all available facts and possible contingencies *for* and *against* his position, was, we have seen, characteristic of the self-defensive development of his mind since early childhood, augmented by the peculiar nature of the injury of his brain. Later, this seemingly weak characteristic influenced the decision of the Confederacy to attack Fort Sumter.

"I Appreciate the Danger"

J. R. Giddings, an active Republican campaigner, had written to Lincoln from the convention that he had been nominated because of his honesty and freedom from corrupt men and that he should avoid making obligations. In June he wrote again suggesting that he adopt the tactics of John Quincy Adams, answering no questions of policy to be adopted if elected, and, further, that each member of the Cabinet would appoint the assistants in his department (C. W., 4). Lincoln's reply (6, 26, 1860), contained the characteristic note of cautious self-doubt: "The suggestions you make are very important, and are duly appreciated by me. If I fail, it will be for lack of *ability,* and not of *purpose.*"

In similar vein he replied (6, 28, 1860) to W. C. Bryant, editor of the New York *Evening Post,* who wrote to warn him against self-interested politicians and to make pledges cautiously and no speeches or letters for publication:

> "Please accept my thanks for the honor done me by your kind letter of the 16th. I appreciate the danger against which you would guard me; nor am I wanting in the *purpose* to avoid it. I thank you for the additional strength your words give me, to maintain that purpose."

The Candidates and Their Policies

In June, Senator Stephen A. Douglas was nominated as candidate for President by the Northern delegates to the Baltimore Democratic Convention after the Southern delegates had withdrawn. John C. Breckenridge of Kentucky, incumbent Vice-President of the United States under President Buchanan had been nominated for President by the Southern delegates. Also Senator John Bell of Tennessee had been nominated for that office by the Constitutional Union Party, a cleavage of Southern sympathizers from the Republican party. The Union was now in a feverishly excited and confused crisscrossing and double crossing of uncompromising moral, economic, and political interests in each of the Northern and Southern states for and against Lincoln's Republican, Bell's Union, Douglas' Northern Democratic, and Breckenridge's Southern Democratic policies.

Douglas maintained throughout his campaign, as he had since he became chairman of the Senate Committee on Territories, a policy of compromise on the extension of slavery in the territories and states. He continued to hold that slave owners had the right of property to take slaves into the territories and denied the right of Congress to interfere, that the prohibition or adoption of slavery was to be decided by the vote of the people upon the adoption of a state constitution, and that community regulations could be applied without regard to the decisions of the Supreme Court. The South had acclaimed and supported the popular sovereignty of Douglas with great enthusiasm up to 1858, when, upon his bold assertions in the debates with Lincoln, it turned against him, and became uncompromisingly opposed after Kansas adopted a free constitution.

Breckenridge denied the constitutional right of Congress to interfere in the matter of slavery, and held, like Douglas, that every territory should be open to the introduction of slavery, and decide to establish or abolish it upon the adoption of a constitution to become a state, and he opposed the policy of secession then being threatened by the slave states in the event of the election of a Northern man, whether Democrat or Republican.

"Douglas' Rump Concern at Baltimore"

Lincoln's letter (7, 4, 1860) to his old friend and intimate personal adviser during his nervous depressions, Dr. Anson G. Henry, who was now residing in Oregon, gives his private, candid estimation of the political situation at this time.

"My dear Doctor:

"Your very aggreable letter of May 15th. was received three days ago. We are just now receiving the first sprinkling of your Oregon election returns—not enough, I think, to indicate the result. . . .

"Long before this you have learned who was nominated at Chicago. We know not what a day may bring forth; but, to-day, it looks as if the Chicago ticket will be elected. I think the chances were more than equal that we could have beaten the Democracy *united.* Divided, as it is, it's chance appears indeed very slim. But great is Democracy in resources; and it may yet give it's fortunes a turn. It is under great temptation to do something; but what can it do which was not thought of, and found impracticable, at Charleston and Baltimore? The signs now are that Douglas and Breckenridge will each have a ticket in every state. They are driven to this to keep up their bombastic claims of *nationality,* and to avoid the charge of *sectionalism* which they have so much lavished upon us.

"It is an amazing fact, after all Douglas has said about *nationality,* and *sectionalism,* that I had more votes from the Southern section at Chicago, than he had at Baltimore! In fact, there was more of the Southern section represented at Chicago, than in the Douglas rump concern at Baltimore!!

"Our boy, in his tenth year, (the baby when you left) has just had a hard and tedious spell of scarlet-fever; and he is not yet beyond all danger. I have a head-ache, and a sore throat upon me now, inducing me to suspect that I have an inferior type of the same thing.

"Our eldest boy, Bob, has been away from us nearly a year at school, and will enter Harvard University this month. He promises very well, considering we never controlled him much.

"Write again when you receive this. Mary joins me in sending our kindest regards to Mrs. H. yourself, and all the family."

Here is the letter of a devoted husband, a proud, affectionate father and a warm, unforgetful friend.

We may picture the memories of 20 years past this letter recalled to Dr. Henry's mind—memories of two, earnest, ambitious young lawyers in Speed's old Springfield store, personally opposed in almost everything, endlessly argumentative, but friends and jealous rivals for the attentions and affections of pretty, little, flirtatious Mary Todd; how one became engaged to her and in jealous depression broke the engagement and then finally married her and now the two men were rival candidates for another love, the Presidency of the United States.

"If My Record Would Hurt Any"

R. W. Thompson, a Terre Haute, Ind, Lawyer, and an old acquaintance, had asked for an interview with someone close to Lincoln in order to talk about something that should not be written. Lincoln replied (7, 10, 1860) cagily:

> "If my *record* would *hurt* any, there is no hope that it will be over-looked; so that if friends can *help* any with it, they may as well do so. Of course, due caution and circumspection, will be used. . . ."
>
> "When I shall have reflected a little, you will hear from me again."

Lincoln sent Nicolay with the following written instructions on what to interview Thompson about:

> "Ascertain what he wants.
> On what subjects he would converse with me.
> And the particulars if he will give them.
> Is an interview indispensable?
> Tell him my motto is 'Fairness to all,'
> But commit me to nothing."

and the following terse note: "This introduces my friend, J. G. Nicolay. Converse as freely with him as you would with me."

"Old Abe Is a Great Fellow"

An estimation of the common people's reactions to Lincoln's personality in July of 1860 was so well expressed in a letter to Leonard Swett by J. O. Putnam of Buffalo, N. Y., that Swett mailed it to Lincoln. It gave him so much pleasure and reassurance that he copied certain parts of it to keep for himself before returning the letter. On such roundabout conversational indications Lincoln often relied to orient himself on the regard of the people for his policies.

> "They have had large meetings," Putnam said, "and they begin to feel that 'Old Abe' is a great fellow. This opinion I share, as you see. Do you know, Swett, I think him one of the most remarkable speakers of English, living? In all that constitutes logical eloquence, straight-forwardness, clearness of statement, sincerity that commands your admiration and assent, and

a compact strength of argument, he is infintely superior to Douglas, I think. The truth is, I have read every thing I have been able to find that he has written or said, and the ring of the best metal is in them all. I dont wonder at your admiration."

Putnam's inspirational letter to Swett on Lincoln's use of English in expressing his philosophy of human relations was the prototype of the reactions of millions of people.

"Great Caution and Delicacy of Action Is Necessary"

Members of the Republican Central Committee of Pennsylvania were in such conflict over local interests as to jeopardize Lincoln's election, for he must carry that state. His advice to Swett (7, 16, 1860) is characteristic of his methods of compromising dissention for the sake of harmonious team work:

. . . "That matter, mentioned by Mr. Casey, about want of confidence in their Centrl. Com. pains me. I am afraid there is a germ of difficulty in it. Will not the men thus suspected, and treated as proposed, rebel, and make a dangerous explosion? When you write Mr. Casey, suggest to him that great caution and delicacy of action, is necessary in that matter."

Lincoln characteristically avoided the use of bludgeoning táctics to line up dissenters, preferring to appeal to reason and the common sense of mutual welfare under the principal of "fairness to all."

"You and I Ought to Get Acquainted"

Two months had passed since the Republican convention and Senator Hannibal Hamlin of Maine, who had been nominated as the candidate for Vice-President, had neglected the courtesy of taking the first step in establishing friendly communications with his chief. As time passed and Lincoln waited, their political affiliation grew increasingly incongruous. Finally Lincoln decided that he had better make the first step. With characteristic humility he wrote (7, 18, 1860):

"My dear Sir: It appears to me that you and I ought to be acquainted, and accordingly I write this as a sort of introduction of myself to you. You first entered the Senate during the single term I was a member of the House of Representatives, but I have no recollection that we were introduced. I shall be pleased to receive a line from you.

"The prospect of Republican success now appears very flattering, so far as I can perceive. Do you see anything to the contrary?"

Avoids Denial of Public Charges

The Democratic opposition in Kentucky had now revived the backwoods gossip of his mother Nancy Hanks' illegitimate birth and, attributing to her reputation the scandals of her aunt Nancy Hanks, whispered abroad (See Chapter II) that her son Abraham was also illegitimate. In Illinois it tried to connect his name with the disreputable, anti-foreign, anti-Catholic, anti-Jewish prejudices of the expired Know-Nothing party which he had loathed and publicly ridiculed. The Kentucky gossip he wisely ignored, but the Illinois accusation he answered (7, 21, 1860) in a confidential letter to a personal friend, A. Jonas:

"I suppose as good, or even better, men than I may have been in American, or Know-Nothing lodges; but in point of fact, I never was in one, at Quincy, or elsewhere. I was never in Quincy but one day and two nights, while Know-Nothing lodges were in existence, and you were with me that day and both those nights. I had never been there before in my life; and never afterwards, till the joint debate with Douglas in 1858. It was in 1854, when I spoke in some Hall there, and after speaking, you, with others took me to an oyster saloon, passed an hour there, and you walked with me to, and parted with me at, the Quincy-House, quite late at night. I left by stage for Naples before day-light in the morning, having come in by the same route, after dark, the evening previous to the speaking, when I found you waiting at the Quincy House to meet me. A few days after I was there, Richardson [W. A.], as I understood, started this same story about my having been in a Know-Nothing lodge. When I heard of the charge, as I did soon after, I taxed my recollection for some incident which could have suggested it; and I remembered that on parting with you the last night, I went to the Office of the Hotel to take my stage passage for the morning, was told that no stage office for that line was kept there, and that I must see the driver, before retiring, to insure his calling for me in the morning; and a servant was sent with me to find the driver, who after taking me a square or two, stopped me, and stepped perhaps a dozen steps farther, and in my hearing called to some one, who answered him apparently from the upper part of a building, and promised to call with the stage for me at the Quincy House. I returned and went to bed; and before day the stage called and took me. That is all.

"That I never was in a Know-Nothing lodge in Quincy, I should expect, could be easily proved, by respectable men, who were always in the lodges and never saw me there. An affidavit of one or two such would put the matter at rest.

"And now, a word of caution. Our adversaries think they can gain a point, if they could force me to openly deny this charge, by which some degree of offence would be given to the Americans. For this reason, it must not publicly appear that I am paying any attention to the charge."

"I Have Scarcely Felt Greater Pain in My Life"

Upon his visit to Robert in Exeter Academy, Lincoln developed a fatherly interest in George C. Latham, a Springfield boy, who was his son's roommate. Robert passed the examination successfully to enter Harvard but George failed and grew despondent. Robert sought the the advice of his father on how to best help him. Although so overtaxed with conferences and correspondence that he could not find time to answer many important letters from personal friends, he wrote (7, 22, 1860) the following letter straight from his heart to George. No other personal communication expresses more intimately the paternal solicitude and maturity of Lincoln's humanitarian philosophy.

"My dear George

"I have scarcely felt greater pain in my life than on learning yesterday from Bob's letter, that you had failed to enter Harvard University. And yet there is very little in it, if you will allow no feeling of *discouragement* to seize, and prey upon you. It is a *certain* truth, that you *can* enter, and graduate in, Harvard University; and having made the attempt, you *must* succeed in it. '*Must*' is the word.

"I know not how to aid you, save in the assurance of one of mature age, and much severe experience, that you *can* not fail, if you resolutely determine, that you *will* not.

"The President of the institution, can scarcely be other than a kind man; and doubtless he would grant you an interview, and point out the readiest way to remove, or overcome, the obstacles which have thwarted you.

"In your temporary failure there is no evidence that you may not yet be a better scholar, and a more successful man in the great struggle of life, than many others, who have entered college more easily.

"Again I say let no feeling of discouragement prey upon you, and in the end you are sure to succeed.

"With more than common interest I subscribe myself

Very truly your friend,
A. Lincoln"

This heartfelt letter was written, we can believe, with his own feelings in mind, of defeat and depression that he had experienced in the early years of his career, and how the paternal interest of Dr. Henry had saved him. Young Latham responded warmly with a will to succeed. A few months later he was a devoted member of President-elect Lincoln's party on the train to Washington for the inauguration.

Stern Defense of Conscientious Record

In contrast to the paternal solicitude and sympathetic encouragement Lincoln felt for young Latham we produce here parts of a letter he wrote with righteous indignation, but never mailed, to young John Hill, for publishing unfair misrepresentations of his record in regard to the abolition of slavery, in the State Legislature and in Congress. The letter expresses the meticulously self-righting characteristic of Lincoln's mind.

John Hill (as previously mentioned in Chapter VIII) was the son of Lincoln's old friend Sam Hill of New Salem, in whose store Lincoln had kept the postoffice. During the campaign of 1860, when old residents of New Salem were regaling each other with fond memories of their personal associations with their great hero, Abraham Lincoln, Hill had taken a negative turn against him and published in the Missouri *Republican* (7, 24, 1860) a signed article that was later circulated as a political pamphlet (C. W., 4). In it he claimed to have proven by the record that Lincoln had voted for abolitionist measures and against antiabolitionist measures in a manner that opposed the principles of Henry Clay.

Lincoln apparently planned his reply, as will be seen, so that it could be published as a letter over the name of some Republican official. It was addressed in September 1860, to John Hill Esq. and began:

"Sir: A pamphlet, over name, bearing the title of 'Opposing principles of Henry Clay, and Abraham Lincoln' is being circulated among the people. I quote from it as follows, towit:

SLAVERY IN THE DISTRICT OF COLUMBIA

In 1837, as a member of the Illinois Legislature, Mr. Lincoln, with only four others, voted against the following resolution:

"*Resolved,* That the Government cannot abolish slavery in the District of Columbia against the consent of the citizens of said District *without a manifest breach of good faith.*" [See House J., 1836-7, p. 240.]

In Congress, at the session of 1848-49, he voted to institute measures for the abolition of slavery in the District. In 1839, in the Illinois Legislature, he voted against a resolution to the effect—

"That as the General Government cannot do, directly, what it is clearly prohibited from doing indirectly, that it is the openly declared design of the Abolitionist of this nation to abolish slavery in the District of Columbia, with a view to its ultimate abolishment in the States; . . . and that, therefore, Congress ought not to abolish slavery in the District of Columbia." [House Jour., 1838-9, p. 329.]

"It is seen in this that you arraign Mr. Lincoln, first, for a vote in the Illinois Legislature of 1836-37—secondly for a vote in Congress in 1848-9, and thirdly for a vote in the Illinois Legislature of 1839.

"As authority for the first arraignment, you say ('See House Jour. p. 240.'). Now, I have that Journal, at this moment open before me, at page 240- and there is, upon that page, absolutely nothing upon that subject. But on pages 243 & 244 there is a series of resolutions, four in number, the third of which is very nearly, but not quite, such as you set out. But they were not voted upon that day; on the contrary, as appears by the same Journal, at pages 248 & 249, they were referred to a select committee. Seven days afterwards, as shown by the same Journal, at pages 309-310 & 311, the committee reported the resolutions back to the House, with an amendment proposed to *each* one of them; which amendments were all adopted by the House; and then the series, as amended, passed the House by Yeas and Nays, Mr. Lincoln, and five others voting against them.

"Now the point is, John, that the Journal does not show in what shape any of those resolutions stood, when Mr. Lincoln voted against them. It does show that they were all amended—were all changed from their original form; but what new shape they took does nowhere appear in the Journal. And hence, John, in stating that Mr. Lincoln voted against a resolution, in the shape you alledge he did, you state what is almost certainly false, and certainly what you do not know to be true.

"But, more than this, John: These resolutions went to the senate, and were passed by that body, as appears by the Senate Journal, of that session, at pages 277 & 297. They were not spread upon the Senate Journal either, so that their substance and form remains entirely uncertain.

"But again, John, Mr. Lincoln, with his colleague, Dan Stone, at the same session, and with reference to these identical resolutions, defined his position in relation to Slavery in the District of Columbia, by a written protest, entered upon the same Journal of the House of Representatives, at pages 817-818, and which entry and protest is as follows, towit."

Then follows a printed clipping of the resolutions (see Chapter IX) signed by himself and Dan Stone, which asserted that "slavery is founded on both injustice and bad policy, but that the promulgation of abolition doctrines tend rather to increase than abate its evils," and that Congress has no power under the constitution to interfere with slavery in the different states," but that "it has the power to abolish it in the District of Columbia but that that power ought not to be exercised unless at the request of the people of the District."

"And now, John, we know you had these Journals in your hands—were ransacking them. Why did you suppress them?"

Hill's second charge, that "in Congress . . . Lincoln voted to institute measures for the abolition of slavery in the District" was made without citation of authority. Lincoln showed from the record for that session in the *Congressional Globe,* that he "gave no such vote." He did, however, admit voting against granting Mr. Palfrey permission to introduce a bill to repeal acts that maintained slavery and the slave trade in the District of Columbia, and to voting for the tabling of a bill to authorize the people of the District "to express their desires as to the existence of slavery therein."

Hill had made his charge without citing evidence, for which Lincoln gravely censured him: "You were not very prudent, John, in stating a falsehood in this instance; but you were as prudent as possible, under the circumstances to quote no authority by which to prove it."

The letter then continued:

> "Although Mr. Lincoln gave no other *votes* on the question, it is true, that he drew up, and sought to get before the House of Representatives, at that session, a bill for the abolition of slavery in the District of Columbia, upon the conditions that the abolition should be gradual, and only upon a vote of the majority of the people of the District, and with compensation to unwilling owners, and also embracing a fugitive slave clause, and an exception in favor of Officers of the Government, while in the District on the public business; all which appears in the same volume of the congressional Globe."

In answer to the third charge, that Lincoln voted in the Illinois Legislature in 1839 against a resolution holding that Congress cannot abolish slavery, he showed from the record that he with others voted to lay it on the table.

Lincoln then showed that he had held consistently, throughout his career, as held in the debates with Douglas, that Congress possessed the power to abolish slavery in the District of Columbia but that it should be under three conditions. "*First,* the abolition should be gradual. *Second,* that it should be on the vote of the majority of the qualified voters of the District;" and "*third* that compensation should be made to unwilling owners." Under these conditions, he said, "I confess I would be exceedingly glad to see Congress abolish slavery in the District of Columbia, and, in the language of Henry Clay, 'sweep from the capitol that foul blot upon our nation.' "

Hill's article on Lincoln's record in the Legislature and in Congress on the abolition of slavery prejudicially maintained that Lincoln had been a radical abolitionist, whereas Clay was conservative on the restriction of slavery. In this extremity of assertion Hill was wrong and untruthful, for Lincoln, by his own record and admission, had consistently favored abolition in the District of Columbia under constitutionally proper and equably compensating conditions.

Lincoln did not have his stern letter published as he might have easily, but after more mature consideration filed it with additional notes, indicating that he had been considerably preoccupied with the wisdom of refuting the charges. Perhaps he was reminded of the articles and handbills that he had published over his own name or a pseudonym, when a young lawyer and legislator, wherein he had ridiculed the efforts and attacked the sincerity of political opponents. Perhaps he remembered a law suit that was brought against him in 1837 for libelous slander by John Adams; or how he was challenged to a duel in 1842 by James Shields for defamation of character; and how he was charged by Stephen A. Douglas in 1858 with making unethical accusations, without sufficient evidence to prove their truth, that the President, Chief Justice and he had plotted before the Dred Scott decision was delivered, to extend slavery.

Estimation of Political Situation in Mid-Summer

"From present appearances," he wrote to Caleb Smith (7, 23), we might succeed in the general result, without Indiana; but *with* it, failure is scarcely possible. Therefore put in your best efforts."

When F. E. Spinner, banker of Mohawk, N. Y., wrote Lincoln, with great enthusiasm, that if he would "resist the importunities of your own political and personal friends" it would compel his reelection (C. W., 4), he received the following serene reply (7, 27):

> "You will perhaps be pleased, as I have been, to know that many good men have tendered me substantially the same advice that you do (excepting as to re-election) and that no single man of any mark has, so far, tempted me to a contrary course."

Simeon Francis, former editor of the Springfield *Journal,* who, with his wife, Speed, and Dr. Henry, had managed the renewal of Lincoln's courtship of Mary Todd that led to their marriage, had joined the migration to Portland, Ore., where he published the Oregon *Farmer.* Three letters from him, written since the campaign began had gone unanswered until August. Then Lincoln gave an estimation of the current political situation:

"I hesitate to say it, but it really appears now, as if the success of the Republican ticket is inevitable. We have no reason to doubt any of the states which voted for Fremont. Add to these, Minnesota, Pennsylvania, and New-Jersey, and the thing is done. Minnesota is as sure as such a thing can be; while the democracy are so divided between Douglas and Breckenridge in Penn. & N.J. that they are scarcely less sure. Our friends are also confident in Indiana and Illinois. I should expect the same division would give us   fair chance in Oregon. Write me what you think on that point."

Afew days later (8, 10) he said humorously in a letter to Cassius Clay: "As to the inagural, I have not yet commenced getting it up; while it affords me great pleasure to be able to say the cliques have not yet commenced upon me."

"My Purpose Is to Make No Speeches"

An immense Republican rally gathered on August 8th at the Springfield Fair Grounds to be addressed by a number of speakers. The enthusiastic assemblage called for Mr. Lincoln and he obliged by appearing in a carriage. He was lifted bodily from it and carried to one of the stands. In response to the wild tumult, cheers and shouts of the people for a speech, he replied:

"*My Fellow Citizens:* I appear among you upon this occasion with no intention of making a speech.

"It has been my purpose, since I have been placed in my present position, to make no speeches. This assemblage having been drawn together at the place of my residence, it appeared to be the wish of those constituting this vast assembly to see me; and it is certainly my wish to see all of you. I appear upon the ground here at this time only for the purpose of affording myself the best opportunity of seeing you, and enabling you to see me.

"I confess with gratitude, be it understood, that I did not suppose my appearance among you would create the tumult which I now witness. I am profoundly gratified for this manifestation of your feelings. I am gratified, because it is a tribute such as can be paid to no man as a man. It is the evidence that four years from this time you will give a like manifestation to the next man who is the representative of the truth on the questions that now agitate the public. And it is because you will then fight for this cause as you do now, or with even greater ardor than now, though I be dead and gone. I most profoundly and sincerely thank you.

Having said this much, allow me now to say that it is my wish that you will hear this public discussion by others of our friends who are present for the purpose of addressing you, and that you will kindly let me be silent."

Lincoln's strength of human appeal lay, he believed, in being a "representative of the truth" on the questions that "agitate the public." But this representation, he felt even then, was involved with an ominous premonition: "Four years from now you will give like manifestation to the next man . . . you will then fight for this cause . . . with even greater ardor than now, though I be dead and gone."

Historical and anthropological investigation of the sacrificial religious practices and fanatical inspirations of primitive and civilized peoples to kill a moral reformer or savior, have shown that excited people tend to become so obsessed toward him who gives them such truth as to destroy old beliefs, superstitions, and established privileges. Lincoln, as a close student of human nature, felt the potentiality of such fate for himself. Now that he was being called to serve the cause of preservation of the Constitution and the Union and restriction of slavery, his subconscious mind apprehended his destiny instinctively the more he resolutely advanced his moral mission. Evidence of the persistence of this feeling we will see on the day of his election and again on his departure from Springfield, and several times as President.

Chapter XLII

WINNING THE ELECTION

As the Republicans were exploiting the Northern and Southern Democratic split, the Democrats made the most of the Republican and American (Union) rift. Whereas the latter was less involved in uncompromising differences of policy, Douglas, famous for his skill in fomenting political dissension and forming new combinations, tried to work out a fusion in the eastern states with Bell, the American party candidate. Thurlow Weed, Republican boss, and Senator Seward opposed this threat to their interests. Surprisingly loyal, Weed informed Lincoln that Douglas men believed with "absurd confidence" that Seward would eventually oppose him. New York and Pennsylvania, he reported, however, safe but Rhode Island doubtful.

"Douglas Is Managing With Great Adroitness"

Lincoln's reply (8, 17, 1860) shows how greatly he was impressed with Douglas' skill for political maneuvering.

> "Douglas is managing the Bell-element with great adroitness. He had his men, in Kentucky, to vote for the Bell candidate, producing a result which has badly alarmed and damaged Breckenridge, and, at the same time, has induced the Bell men to suppose that Bell will certainly be President, if they can keep a few of the Northern States away from us, by throwing them to Douglas. But you, better than I, understand all this.
>
> "I think there will be the most extraordinary effort ever made, to carry New-York for Douglas. You, and all others who write me from your state, think the effort can not succeed; and I hope you are right; still it will require close watching, and great effort on the other side. . . .
>
> "You have seen that Bell tickets have been put on the track, both here, and in Indiana. In both cases, the object has been, I think, the same as the Hunt movement in N.Y.—to throw the States to Douglas. In our state we know the thing is engineered by Douglas men; and we do not believe they can make a great deal out of it."

Among Friends, Never Espouse Quarrels on Either Side

The quarrel in Pennsylvania, between the Cameron and Curtin factions, for a time threatened the loss of the state to Douglas, until finally patched up. Upon being informed of this Lincoln commented (8, 31, 1860) to J. M. Pomeroy:

> . . . "I have not heard near so much upon that subject as you probably suppose; and I am slow to listen to criminations among friends, and never espouse their quarrels on either side."

Danger of Overconfidence

The Republicans were growing overconfident, and Senator Henry Wilson of Massachusetts had written to Lincoln urging more thorough organization and avoidance of overconfidence. Lincoln's reply (9, 1, 1860) shows that he, too, distrusted the situation.

"The point you press—the importance of thorough organization—is felt, and appreciated by our friends everywhere. And yet it involves so much more of dry, irksome labor, that most of them shrink from it—preferring parades, and shows, and monster meetings. I know not how this can be helped. I do what I can in my position, for organization; but it does not amount to so much as it should."

The Down-Hill Track

The distortion of an unpleasant possibility, upon being passed along through two or more gossiping minds, led to unexpected apprehensions by Lincoln on the progress of his campaign. He confided to his team mate Hannibal Hamlin (9, 4, 1860):

"I am annoyed some by a letter from a friend in Chicago, in which the following passage occurs: 'Hamlin has written Colfax that two members of Congress will, he fears, be lost in Maine.' . . .

"Such a result as you seem to have predicted in Maine, in your letter to Colfax, would, I fear, put us on the down-hill track, lose us the State elections in Pennsylvania and Indiana, and probably ruin us on the main turn in November."

On the same day he wrote to Joseph Medill, editor of the *Chicago Tribune:*

. . . "I have a letter from Gen. Cameron, dated Aug. 29th. in which, among other things, he says: 'You may as well be getting your inaugural address ready, so as to have plenty time to make it short. If possible we are daily becoming stronger in Pennsylvania, and in New-Jersey all is right.' "

After mentioning additional assurances from Cameron on Pennsylvania he continued:

"I am more annoyed by what you write me of Maine. Long ago I had heard about danger of two members of congress there; but at least six weeks since Mr. Hamlin wrote me 'all *is* safe in New-England'; and very recently Mr. Fogg of N.H. wrote from N. York saying: 'We are having a desperate fight in Maine; but it will end in a splendid triumph for us.' He had just come from Maine."

Base Forgery

Collected Works, Vol. IV, gives an example of the sordid reports about Lincoln that were being circulated by the Democratic newspapers. The *Illinois State Journal* (9, 6, 1860) published the following account of one and its denial, supposedly written by Lincoln or authorized by him.

> "In the Chicago *Times and Herald* of the 4th we find the following, purporting to be 'a quotation from a speech made by Mr. Lincoln in 1844,' as taken from the *Macomb Eagle.*

>> " 'Mr. Jefferson is a statesman whose praises are never out of the mouths of the Democratic party. Let us attend to this uncompromising friend of freedom whose name is continually invoked against the Whig party. The character of Jefferson was repulsive. Continually puling about liberty, equality, and the degrading curse of slavery, he brought his own children to the hammer, and made money of his debaucheries. Even at his death he did not manumit his numerous offspring, but left them soul and body to degradation and the cart whip. A daughter of this vaunted champion of Democracy was sold some years ago at public auction in New Orleans, and purchased by a society of gentlemen who wished to testify by her liberation their admiration of the statesman, who
>>> "Dreamt of freedom in a slave's embrace."
>> " 'This single line I have quoted gives more insight to the character of the man than whole volumes of panegyric. It will outlive his epitaph, write it who may.'

> "This is a bold and deliberate forgery, whether originating with the Chicago *Times and Herald* or the Macomb *Eagle.* Mr. Lincoln never used any such language in any speech *at any time.* Throughout the whole of his political life, Mr. Lincoln has ever spoken of Mr. Jefferson in the most kindly and respectful manner, holding him up as one of the ablest statesmen of his own or any other age, and constantly referring to him as one of the greatest apostles of freedom and free labor. This is so well known that any attempt, by means of fraud or forgery, to create the contrary impression, can only react upon the desperate politicians who are parties to such disreputable tactics."

The denial is in the manner of Lincoln's following written expression. On the day previous to its publication in the *Illinois State Journal* he wrote about the article to A. G. Chester, editor of the Buffalo, N. Y., *Commercial Advertiser:*

> "The extract upon a newspaper slip which you sent, and which I herewith return, is a base forgery, so far as its authorship is imputed to me. I never said anything like it, at any time or place. I do not recognize it as anything I have ever seen before, emanating from any source. I wish my name not to be used; but my friends will be entirely safe in denouncing the thing as a forgery, so far as it is ascribed to me."

Home Loving, Nation Loving

Lincoln was of all things a home loving, nation loving man. The latter developed in youth from the former as each interest protects the other. History shows that the integrity of the government of a nation is based upon the proportion of monogamous families among its officials and people. The constant family of loving parents is most conducive to the consistent, natural development of the minds and personalities of its children and their constructive interests in the home and state.

In preceding chapters, letters to various members of his family have been presented to show Lincoln's regard for his kin.

The following note to B. F. James, once his neighbor, by a deeply engrossed candidate for President reveals the proud father and husband:

> "How time gallops along with us! Look at these great big boys of yours and mine, when it is but yesterday that we and their mothers were unmarried."

To Nathaniel Grigsby of Missouri, who had been a boyhood friend when in Spencer County, Ind., Lincoln wrote (9, 20, 1860):

> "Your letter of July 19th was received only a few days ago, having been mailed by your brother at Gentryville, Ia, on the 12th. of this month. A few days ago, Gov. Wood, of Quincy told me he saw you, and that you said you had written me. I had not then received your letter.
>
> "Of our three families who removed from Indiana together, my father, Squire Hall, and John D. Johnston, are dead—and all the rest of us are yet living. Of course the younger ones are grown up, marriages contracted, and new ones born. I have three boys now, the oldest of which is seventeen years of age.
>
> "There is now a Republican electoral ticket in Missouri, so that you can vote for me if your neighbors will let you. I would advise you not to get into any trouble about it. Give my kindest regards to your brother Charles."

"Professor" D. P. Gardner, an itinerant soap manufacturer (C. W., 4) who had sent samples of his craft to the Lincolns, received the following humorous note (9, 28, 1860):

> "Some specimens of your Soap have been used at our house and Mrs. L. declares it is a superb article. She at the same time, protests that I have never given sufficient attention to the 'soap question' to be a competent judge."

John Hanks, the son of Dennis Hanks, had moved to Oregon, and upon the appeal of his lonely parents to return home, he wrote to his uncle Abe for advice, and received the following:

> "If your Father and Mother desire you to come home, it is a delicate matter for me to advise you not to do it. Still, as you ask my advice, it is that if you are doing well, you better stick to it. If you have a good start there, and should give it up, you might not get it again, here, or elsewhere. It can not be other than their first wish that you shall do well.
>
> "And now, as to politics, I am very much obliged to you for what you offer to do for me in Oregon. This side of the Rocky Mountains things appear reasonably well for the general result. In opposing David Logan, at the late congressional election in Oregon, I suppose you did what you thought was right; and when a man does what he thinks is right, he does the best he can. Still, I am sorry you did not think differently, as I knew David from his childhood, and he studied law in our office when his father and I were partners."

Campaign Portraits

Republican committees were harassed at not being able to get an attractive campaign photograph of Lincoln. His face, sallow, sad, and enigmatical, with the left side weak and the left eye turned upward out of focus, and the muscles of the right side under natural volitional control but constantly pulling the tip of the nose and lower lip to the right, carried the perplexed expression of an indecisive, gloomy, frustrated man. A three quarters presentation of the face from the right hid the involitional weakness of the left side. The mystifying expression of Lincoln's face, as the result of the injury of his brain, doubtless contributed greatly to the failure of political leaders to have confidence in the strength of his character.

Upon being shown, by J. F. Babcock, a picture of himself (made by Hessler in 1857) he commented wryly (9, 13, 1860):

> "The original of the picture you inclose, and which I return, was taken from life, and is *I* think, a very true one; though my wife, and many others, do not. My impression is that their objection arises from the disordered condition of the hair. My judgment is worth nothing in these matters. If your friend could procure one of the 'heads' 'busts' or whatever you call it, by Volk at Chicago, I should think it the thing for him."

The "Sign" of the Beard

Lincoln has told us a number of times that he believed superstitiously since childhood, that he was a son of destiny, chosen by God to serve somehow in improving personal freedom and understanding in human relations through processes of law, as had "Father" Abraham. The course of this destiny, he believed, was to be directed by "signs" to be received at critical times, to be followed as the feelings of his heart and conscience directed. Through listening to the goodness of this semi-clairvoyant subconscious voice in times of doubt he usually obtained the answer that he could best believe in and best carry out.

In the closing weeks of the campaign it became generally accepted by all four parties that Lincoln would be elected. In reaction to this expectation, radical politicians in the Southern states began to agitate for secession. Public apprehension of this grave turn in disunion sentiment brought upon Lincoln numerous demands for a new reassurance of policy that would relieve the emotional tension and threat of an economic depression.

L. M. Bond, a Philadelphia and New Orleans merchant, asked: "In the event of your election to the Presidency, and of the election of a majority of Republicans to the next congress, would you countenance radicalism to the extent of embittering the feelings of our Southern bretheren?"

Lincoln replied (10, 15, 1860):

"I certainly am in no temper, and have no purpose, to embitter the feelings of the South; but whether I am inclined to such a course as would, in fact, embitter their feelings, you can better judge by my published speeches, than by anything I would say in a short letter, if I were inclined now, as I am not, to define my position anew."

In this increasingly difficult situation a letter was received in mid-October from 11-year old Grace Bedell of Westfield, N. Y., that augmented his inclination to cultivate a more patriarchal appearance, attitude and manner of personal expression.

"Hon. A. B. Lincoln

"Dear Sir

"My father has just home from the fair and brought home your picture and Mr. Hamlin's. I am a little girl only eleven years old, but want you should be President of the United States very much so I hope you wont think me very bold to write to such a great man as you are. Have you any little girls about as large as I am if so give them my love and tell her to write to me if you cannot answer this letter. I have got 4 brother's and part of them will vote for you anyway and if you will let your whiskers grow I will try and get the rest of them to vote for you you would look a great deal better for your face is so thin. All the ladies like whiskers and they could tease their husband's to vote for you and then you would be President. My father is a going to vote for you and if I was a man I would vote for you to but I will try and get every one to vote for you that I can I think that rail fence around your picture makes it look very pretty I have got a little baby sister she is nine weeks old and is just as cunning as can be. When you direct your letter dir[e]ct to Grace Bedell Westfield Chatauque County New York.

"I must not write any more answer the letter right off Good bye

"Grace Bedell"

Lincoln loved this letter. It was of the very essence of life. Although crowded day and night by thousands of people for interviews he replied almost immediately (10, 19, 1860):

"Private

"Miss Grace Bedell

"My dear little Miss.

"Your very agreeable letter of the 15th is received. I regret the necessity of saying I have no daughters. I have three sons—one seventeen, one nine, and one seven, years of age. They, with their mother, constitute my whole family.

"As to the whiskers, having never worn any, do you not think people would call it a piece of silly affectation if I were to begin it now?

Your very sincere well-wisher

"A. Lincoln"

Lincoln's fear of being thought "silly" resisted the little girl's heart-felt suggestion, "if you will let your whiskers grow . . . you would look a great deal better for you face is so thin," but his paternalistic patriarchical attitude seized upon it, to better be itself. Shortly after his election he began to cultivate a beard. Probably this suggestion, coming from a little girl who had a sympathetic urge for helping other people much like his own, made his heart adopt it and her entirely. We will see later what his beard meant to President Lincoln and what he said to Grace personally when his train, on the way to Washington, stopped in her town.

"Mischievous Blunder"

On July 29 Lincoln had commented on the press report of a speech by J. O. Putnam:

> "I do not mean to flatter you when I say it is, indeed, a very excellent one. The manner in which you point out to Gov. Hunt [of New York and supporter of Bell] that his objections to the election of the Republican candidate apply with manifold force to the candidate he would elect instead, is truly admirable.
>
> "And now allow me to name one error. John Adams was not elected over Jefferson by the H.R.; but Jefferson was over Burr. Such is my recollection."

A few weeks later Putnam wrote,

> "That mistake in my Lockport speech as to John Adams, was a great blunder. After receiving your letter, a pamphlet edition of the speech was published & the error corrected."

Lincoln replied (9, 13):

> "You must not lay much stress on the blunder about Mr. Adams; for I made a more mischievous one, in the first printed speech of mine, on the Slavery question—Oct. 1854—I stated that the prohibition of slavery in the North West Territory was made a condition in the Virginia deed of cession— while, in fact, it was not. Like yourself, I have since done what I can to correct the error."

Self-Righting Mind

Enjoyment of self-respect and peace of mind depend upon being "right" in what a person believes and says and does and in being respectfully thought right by other people. Hence the importance of promptly correcting and accepting corrections from others of all wrongs and mistakes made. Being wrong in any way excites uneasiness and anxiety, for it invites critical attack.

Confucius is reported to have said, "he who does not correct an error, however small, commits a great one."

We find that throughout Lincoln's career he readily acknowledged his mistakes and immediately adopted suggested corrections.

When C. C. Nott edited the Cooper Institute speech for publication in book form he found that Lincoln's statement that Abraham Baldwin voted on the ordinance of '87 was wrong. He wrote to Lincoln that he would strike out his name in that place and change the number of times he was said to have voted from four to three (C. W., 4). Lincoln promptly accepted the correction and explained the error (9, 6, 1860):

> "I have looked over the sheets hastily, and herewith return them. You perceive I have touched them only very lightly. The notes you add I have not attempted to compare with originals, leaving that entirely to you. I think the notes are exceedingly valuable."

> On the Abraham Baldwin error he said (9, 22, 1860): "I could not find the Journal of the Confederation Congress for the session at which was passed the Ordinance of 1787—and . . . in stating Mr. Baldwin had voted for its passage, I had relied on the communication of Mr. Greeley, over his own signature, published in the New York *Weekly Tribune* of October 15, 1859. If you will turn to that paper, you will see that Mr. Greeley apparently copies from the Journal, and places the name of Mr. Baldwin among those of the men who voted for the measure."

Douglas versus Breckenridge Debate

We have found that since boyhood Lincoln delighted in writing amusing imaginary conversations between people in which he generally had them make, in great sobriety, ridiculous remarks to each other on a subject of public interest. He entertained himself with such dissertations and dialogues by professional humorists and we find both of these interests were consistent with his love of amusing stories on the frailties of human egotism.

"Louisville, Ky—Sep. 29, 1860

"Meeting & Dialogue of Douglas & Breckenridge—

DOUG—Well, you have succeeded in breaking up the Democratic party.
BRECK—Certainly, for the time being, the party is under a cloud, to say the least; but why you should say *I* did it, I do not comprehend.
DOUG—Perhaps I should change it to your *supporters,* rather than to *you.*
BRECK—The blame, as I conceive, is neither upon my friends or me.
DOUG—They insisted on having a plat-form, upon which *I* could not stand.
BRECK—Aye, and *you* insisted on having a platform upon which *they* could not stand.
DOUG—But *mine* was the true *Democratic* platform.
BRECK—That presents the exact point in dispute; my friends insist that theirs is the true Democratic platform.
DOUG—Let us argue it, then.
BRECK—I conceive that argument is exhausted; *you* certainly could advance nothing new, and *I* know not that I could. There is, however, a colatteral point, upon which I would like the exchange of a few words.
DOUG—What is it?

BRECK—It is this: We insisted on Congressional protection of Slave property in the national territories; and you broke with us professedly because
of this.

DOUG—Exactly so; I insisted upon non-intervention.

BRECK—And yet you are forming coalitions, wherever you can, with Bell,
who is for this very congressional protection of slavery—for the very
thing which you pretend, drove you from us—for Bell, with all his Know-
Nothingism, and anti-democracy of every sort.

DOUG—Bell is a good Union-man; and you, and your friends, are a set of
disunionists.

BRECK—Bah! You have known us long, and intimately; why did you never
denounce us as disunionists, till since our refusal to support *you* for
the Presidency? Why have you never warned the North against our disunion schemes, till since the Charleston and Baltimore sessions of the
National convention? Will you answer, Senator Douglas?

DOUG—The condition of my throat will not permit me to carry this conversation any further."

Urgent Demands for Expressions of Policy

In October it was generally conceded by the opposition that the
Republicans would elect the next President. Douglas had waged a terrific
campaign. Whereas Lincoln neither made a single political speech nor
committed himself to an appointment or arrangement, Douglas had addressed crowds in most of the important Southern as well as Northern
cities. He had tried to form working agreements with the Bell faction in
the North whenever it seemed feasible and had, in the South, tried to
compromise with Breckenridge. Better than any other Northern man,
Douglas knew the temper of the Southern people and the fatalistic meaning of their uncompromising determination to withdraw from the Union
and form their own Confederation of States if Lincoln was elected. To
save the Union he devoted the remainder of the time in Southern states,
pleading that if the Southern Democrats would unite with him they
could stop Lincoln and save the Union. But it was too late. The proud,
rejective attitudes of the radical Rhett and Yancey prejudice was set.
It had been agitated into an unreasoning, fighting pitch by tirades of the
most violent war propaganda in history, surpassed since only by the
paranoid fury of Hitler Nazi, and Stalin and Khrushchev Communist
accusations.

It was now clear that if Lincoln should be elected, the Southern
states would secede and form a confederacy and this would lead to
military efforts by the Federal government to preserve its own authority.
Business was sinking in confusion and depression, and the people were
appealing to Lincoln for a new statement of policy that would reassure
the conservative Northern as well as Southern people on the justice of
his administration toward the constitutional rights of the slave states.
Two private confidential letters written by him in the/last weeks preceding

the election show what he thought of his position in the dangerous confusion, but would not say for publication.

To J. E. Harvey, *editor of the North American and U. S. Gazette* (10, 2, 1860):

> "To comply with your request to furnish extracts from my tariff speeches is simply impossible, because none of those speeches were published. It was not fashionable here in those days to report one's public speeches. In 1844 I was on the Clay electoral ticket in this State (i.e., Illinois) and, to the best of my ability, sustained, together, the tariff of 1842 and the tariff plank of the Clay platform. This could be proven by hundreds—perhaps thousands—of living witnesses; still it is not in print, except by inference. The Whig papers of those years all show that I was upon the electoral ticket; even though I made speeches, among other things *about* the tariff, but they do not show *what* I said about it. The papers show that I was one of a committee which reported, among others, a resolution in these words.
>
> " 'That we are in favor of an adequate revenue on duties from imports levied so as to afford ample protection to American industry.'
>
> "But, after all, was it really any more than the tariff plank of our present platform? And does not my acceptance pledge me to that? And am I at liberty to do more, if I were inclined?"

W. S. Speer, of Shelbyville, Tenn., a publisher and an ardent Union man, appealed to Lincoln for a public statement, but Lincoln replied (10, 23, 1860):

> "I appreciate your motive when you suggest the propriety of my writing for the public something disclaiming all intention to interfere with slaves or slavery in the States; but in my judgment, it would do no good. I have already done this—many, many times; and it is in print, and open to all who will read. Those who will not read, or heed, what I have already publicly said, would not read, or heed, a repetition of it.
>
> " 'If they hear not Moses and the prophets, neither will they be persuaded through one rose from the dead.' "

"Many Chances to One This Is Hum-Bug"

Major David Hunter had written to Lincoln that he had received a report that a number of young Virginians had bound themselves under "solemn oath" to assassinate him if elected (C. W., 4). Lincoln's answer (10, 26, 1860) was marked private and confidential:

> "I have another letter from a writer unknown to me, saying the officers of the Army at Fort Kearney, have determined, in case of Republican success, at the approaching Presidential election, to take themselves, and the arms at that point, South, for the purpose of resistence to the government. While I think there are many chances to one that this is a hum-bug, it occurs to me that any real movement of this sort in the army would leak out and become known to you. In such case, if it would not be unpro-

fessional, or dishonorable (of which you are to be the judge) I shall be much obliged if you will apprize me of it."

Repitition Bears Appearance of Weakness

George T. M. Davis, an old friend of the bar and distinguished Mexican war veteran, and now a prominent New York business man, advised J. K. Dubois that New York and Southern business men were planning to create a money panic in the event of Lincoln's election. Dubois presented the letter to his chief, who thought it advisable to answer (10, 27, 1860):

> "What is it that I could say which would quiet alarm? Is it that no interference by the government, with slaves or slavery within the states, is intended? I have said this so often already, that a repetition of it is but mockery, bearing an appearance of weakness, and cowardice, which perhaps should be avoided. Why do not uneasy men *read* what I have already said? and what our *platform* says? If they will not read, or heed, then, would they read, or heed, a repetition of them? Of course the declaration that there is no intention to interfere with slaves or slavery, in the states, with all that is fairly implied in such declaration, is true; and I should have no objection to make, and repeat the declaration a thousand times, if there were no danger of encouraging bold bad men to believe they are dealing with one who can be scared into anything.
>
> "I have some reason to believe the Sub-National committee, at the Astor House, may be considering this question; and if their judgment should be different from mine, mine might be modified by theirs."

"Men Who Would Like to Frighten Me"

George D. Prentice, editor of the Louisville, Kentucky, *Journal* (Dem.), wrote frankly to Lincoln that although he was opposed to him he recognized that he would be elected, and wanted to suggest that he write a letter for publication that would express his "conservative views" and "assure the good citizens of the South" and "take from the disunionists every excuse or pretext for treason." (C. W., 4). It was the last such appeal answered by Lincoln (10, 29, 1860) before the election:

> "Your suggestion that I, in a certain event, shall write a letter, setting forth my conservative views and intentions, is certainly a very worthy one. But would it do any good? If I were to labor a month, I could not express my conservative views and intentions more clearly and strongly, than they are expressed in our plat-form, and in my many speeches already in print, and before the public. And yet even you, who do occasionally speak of me in terms of personal kindness, give no prominence to these oft-repeated expressions of conservative views and intentions; but busy yourself with appeals to all conservative men, to vote for Douglas—to vote any way which can possibly defeat me—thus impressing your readers that you think, I am the very worst man living. If what I have already said has failed to convince you, no repetition of it would convince you. The writing of your letter, now before me, gives assurance that you would publish such a letter from me as

you suggest; but, till now, what reason had I to suppose the Louisville Journal, even, would publish a *repe[ti]tion* of that which is already at it's command, and which it does not press upon the public attention?

"And, now my friend—for such I esteem you personally—do not misunderstand me. I have not decided that I will not do substantially what you suggest. I will not forbear doing so, merely on *punctilio* and pluck. If I do finally abstain, it will be because of apprehension that it would do harm. For the good men of the South—and I regard the majority of them as such—I have no objection to repeat seventy and seven times. But I have *bad* men also to deal with, both North and South—men who are eager for something new upon which to base new misrepresentations—men who would like to frighten me, or, at least, to fix upon me the character of timidity and cowardice. They would seize upon almost any letter I could write, as being an 'awful coming down.' I intend keeping my eye upon these gentlemen, and to not unnecessarily put any weapons in their hands."

On the back of the letter was written the following confession of doubt: "*Confidential.* The within letter was written on the day of it's date, and, on reflection, withheld till now. It expresses the views I still entertain."

Again Lincoln hesitated and reconsidered his best judgment and then reverted to it decisively, in the manner that conveyed to other minds an intuition that he was timid and weak, the very character that he knew "bad" men were trying to fix upon him.

Lincoln's characteristic inclination to add a variable negative to a reassuring positive statement tended to excite in other minds doubt of the strength of the latter. People are conditionally educated to arrive at conviction by considering only one side or the other of an issue. The cultural evaluation and consideration of both sides, as the doubtful way of science, leaves the question of the course of action incompletely determined, hence dependent on *proportion* of the values *for* and *against* as they may develop. We will see from now on that public demand for positive declarations of policy by the leader will increase in frequency and intensity, and Lincoln's cautiously doubtful ambivalent method of thinking and expressing himself will be so often insufficiently definitive and convincing that his own Cabinet and many Northern as well as Southern people will regard him as being too weak minded to solve the causes of the terrible conflict confronting the nation.

The Election

On election day, November 6, Lincoln remained in Springfield. Accompanied by Herndon he wandered about town to chat with friends, or to play handball for diversion. When it became certain in the evening that he would be the next President, the crowds in the streets of Springfield worked themselves into a frenzy of delight—all but Lincoln. While pleasure was evident in his face, he took the great turn of fortune and the acclamation of the people with no expression of happiness. He was too engrossed with the awful burden of responsibility that he felt now fate had decreed he must bear.

Mystifying Double Vision

Abraham Lincoln was a nervously tired, deeply impressed man when he went home after viewing the celebrations of Springfield's people in their pride and joy over his victory. When he entered his home he greeted proud Mrs. Lincoln with "Mary we are elected." Upon lying down on a couch in his bedroom to rest he had a mystifying experience with double vision. He later described it to different friends, including Noah Brooks and Ward Lamon, both of whom reported it as nearly as possible in Lincoln's own words. We give both accounts since there is some difference in the statements of Lincoln's reasoning about it.

Brooks version:

"It was just after my election in 1860, when the news had been coming in thick and fast all day and there had been a great 'hurrah boys,' so that I was well tired out and went home to rest, throwing myself down on a lounge in my chamber. Opposite where I lay was a bureau with a swinging glass upon it (and here he got up and placed furniture to illustrate the position), and looking in that glass, I saw myself reflected nearly at full length; but my face, I noticed, had *two* separate and distinct images, the tip of the nose of one being about three inches from the tip of the other. I was a little bothered, perhaps startled, and got up and looked in the glass, but the illusion vanished. On lying down again, I saw it a second time, plainer, if possible, than before; and then I noticed that one of the faces was a little paler—say, five shades—than the other. I got up, and the thing melted away, and I went off, and in the excitement of the hour forgot all about it—nearly, but not quite, for the thing would come up, and give me a little pang, as if something uncomfortable had happened. When I went home again that night, I told my wife about it, and a few days afterward I made the experiment again, when (with a laugh) sure enough! the thing came again; but I never succeeded in bringing the ghost back after that, though I once tried very industriously to show it to my wife, who was somewhat worried about it. She thought it was a 'sign' that I was to be elected to a second term of office, and that the paleness of one of the faces was an omen that I should not see life through the last term." (Tarbell, 1900, after Brooks.)

Lamon's version:

"As I [Lincoln] reclined, my eyes fell upon the glass, and I saw distinctly two images of myself, exactly alike, except that one was a little paler than the other. I arose and lay down with the same result. It made me feel quite uncomfortable for a few minutes, but, some friends coming in, the matter passed from my mind. The next day while walking the street, I was suddenly reminded of the circumstance, and the disagreeable sensation produced by it returned. I had never seen anything of the kind before, and did not know what to make of it. I determined to go home and place myself in the same position, and, if the same effect was produced, I would make up my mind that it was the natural result of some refraction or optics, which I did not understand, and dismiss it. I tried the experiment with the same result; and, as I had said to myself, accounted for it on some principle unknown to me, and it ceased to trouble me. But the God who works through the laws of

Nature might surely give a sign to me, if one of his chosen servants, even through the operation of a principle in optics." (Lamon, 1871.)

The accounts of Lincoln's mystifying double vision have been repeated or mentioned in nearly every biography of Lincoln as evidence of his clairvoyance by some and superstition and hallucination by others. It has had miraculous significance for millions of people. No one attempted to explain its actual nervous process until Kempf (1952) showed that it followed naturally from diplopia produced probably by the injury of his brain in childhood. Upon reclining on his back, when tired and relaxed, the divergence of the two eyes was increased, producing a double, more or less overlapping vision of his face when he happened to look into a mirror from that position. The one seen by the left eye was considerably weaker and seemed less real than the one seen by the right eye.

Lincoln probably had, since the cerebral injury, a tendency to have more or less dual overlapping vision, but like other people so afflicted when young, he had long past learned to disregard the shadowy image, and finally forgot about it. Now, under great fatigue, for "the first time," he said, he was surprised by seeing two images of his face, one paler than the other. The experience troubled him but he tried to pass it off as caused by some law of optics. Five years later, however, as President, when haunted by a premonitional dream of death, he discussed it with his old friend and personal bodyguard, Ward Lamon, as an occult "sign" of impending fate. After his election and during his presidency he intimated repeatedly that he anticipated a violent end to his life. He had, it seems, adopted the meaning given to it by his very superstitious wife.

It seems quite probable that Lincoln's firm conviction, held from boyhood all through his life, of being "chosen" by the Creator to perform a special work for the liberation of mankind from injustice, was reinforced by the "sign" of the double vision of his face. The involitional tendency of his left eye to look upward possibly influenced him unconsciously to develop a persistently firm self-controlling compensation that had profoundly self-assuring effects on his personal integrity so long as he thought his way through conflicting issues and administrative dilemmas conscientiously and rightfully. He must always avoid hasty thinking and radical or doubtful decisions lest his nervous controls break down in anxious self-doubt and confusion of visual imagery with nausea, dizziness and headache. The latter symptoms, being far more distressing, generally obscure the basic visual decoordination, hence no complaint is made of it until discovered by the physician.